SEEN BUT NOT SEEN

Influential Canadians and the First Nations from the 1840s to Today

Throughout the nineteenth and most of the twentieth centuries, the majority of Canadians argued that European "civilization" must replace Indigenous culture. The ultimate objective was assimilation into the dominant society.

Seen but Not Seen explores the history of Indigenous marginalization and why non-Indigenous Canadians failed to recognize Indigenous societies and cultures as worthy of respect. Approaching the issue biographically, Donald B. Smith presents the commentaries of sixteen influential Canadians – including John A. Macdonald, George Grant, and Emily Carr – who spoke extensively on Indigenous subjects. Supported by documentary records spanning over nearly two centuries, *Seen but Not Seen* covers fresh ground in the history of settler-Indigenous relations.

DONALD B. SMITH is a professor emeritus of history at the University of Calgary.

About the Cover Illustration

On 25 June 1969 the Liberal government of Pierre Trudeau tabled in the House of Commons the "Statement of the Government of Canada on Indian policy," popularly called "The White Paper" (in government, the term "white paper" is applied to policy proposals). If passed by Parliament, the new legislation would end the unique legal rights of status Indians. Reserves and the historic Indian treaties, as well as the Department of Indian Affairs and Northern Development itself, would disappear. Indigenous protest against the policy initiative arose immediately. Provincial and territorial First Nations political associations across Canada joined the National Indian Brotherhood (NIB; founded in 1968 and reorganized in 1982 as the Assembly of First Nations) to oppose it. Walter Deiter, a former chief of the Federation of Saskatchewan Indians and the NIB's founding president, led the fight against the attempt to end the special status of the First Nations.

On 4 June 1970 a phalanx of western chiefs, some dressed in traditional regalia, stood face to face with the prime minister and his full cabinet in the cavernous Railway Committee Room of the Parliament Buildings. Indian Association of Alberta (IAA) members Chiefs John Snow and Adam Soloway handed the position paper originally prepared by the IAA – entitled *Citizens Plus* but popularly known as "The Red Paper" – to the prime minister. Then Harold Cardinal, IAA President, spoke on the significance of treaty and Aboriginal rights. In response to strong First Nations' protests against the assimilationist White Paper, the federal government formally retracted it in 1971.

Rudy Platiel, a retired Toronto *Globe and Mail* reporter, witnessed the Red Paper's submission. Half a century later, he recalled: "In 1970 I was assigned by *The Globe and Mail* to travel for a year across Canada to write about the situation of Indigenous people – then called Indians. Despite the now continued existence of systemic racism, the march of Indigenous rights and their reality today is light years beyond anything I actually thought possible back then. This progress gives hope that despite our human flaws and occasional cruelty, as a nation we may one day yet reach a new dawn of acceptance and cooperation between two societies that at times seems so tantalizingly far beyond us today. There is indeed hope."

The image shows Prime Minister Trudeau and his Minister of Indian Affairs, Jean Chrétien, facing NIB President Walter Deiter.

SEEN
BUT
NOT SEEN

Influential Canadians and the First Nations
from the 1840s to Today

DONALD B. SMITH

UNIVERSITY OF TORONTO PRESS
Toronto Buffalo London

© University of Toronto Press 2021
Toronto Buffalo London
utorontopress.com
Printed in Canada

ISBN 978-1-4426-4998-9 (cloth)   ISBN 978-1-4426-2212-8 (ePUB)
ISBN 978-1-4426-2770-3 (paper)   ISBN 978-1-4426-2211-1 (PDF)

Library and Archives Canada Cataloguing in Publication

Title: Seen but not seen : influential Canadians and the First Nations from
   the 1840s to today / Donald B. Smith.
Names: Smith, Donald B., author.
Description: Includes bibliographical references and index.
Identifiers: Canadiana (print) 2020034644X | Canadiana (ebook)
   20200346539 | ISBN 9781442649989 (hardcover) | ISBN 9781442627703
   (softcover) | ISBN 9781442622128 (EPUB) | ISBN 9781442622111 (PDF)
Subjects: LCSH: Indigenous peoples – Canada – Public opinion. | LCSH:
   Canada – Ethnic relations. | LCSH: Canada – Race relations. | LCSH:
   Indigenous peoples – Canada – Social conditions.
Classification: LCC E98.P99 S65 2021 | DDC 305.897/071 – dc23

University of Toronto Press acknowledges the financial assistance to its
publishing program of the Canada Council for the Arts and the Ontario
Arts Council, an agency of the Government of Ontario.

Canada Council   Conseil des Arts
for the Arts   du Canada

Funded by the   Financé par le
Government   gouvernement
of Canada   du Canada

Canadä

ONTARIO ARTS COUNCIL
CONSEIL DES ARTS DE L'ONTARIO
an Ontario government agency
un organisme du gouvernement de l'Ontario

FSC
www.fsc.org

MIX
Paper from
responsible sources
FSC® C016245

Dedicated to the memory of John F. Leslie (1945–2017), historian, former manager of the Claims and Historical Research Centre at Indian and Northern Affairs Canada, and good friend for over thirty years.

Contents

viii   Contents

Illustrations

Maps

Prologue

Before reading a book it is desirable and quickens interest to know something with regard to the author.

A.C. Rutherford, foreword to *The Law Marches West* (1939)[1]

In the mid-1960s, as Canada approached its memorable Centennial year, most non-Indigenous Canadians harboured a long-established blindness to the Indigenous peoples in this country. I was one of them. Their history and contemporary living conditions remained unknown, a closed book. Yet, in these same years, the Indigenous peoples were on the verge of returning to the top of the public agenda for the first time since the North-West Resistance of 1885. Although I did not know it at the time, of course, two experiences in 1966 directed me towards a lifelong study of how non-Indigenous Canadians viewed Indians, as the First Nations used to be known. A January student conference at the University of Toronto, and a summer job on a railway gang in Western Canada, awakened me to Indigenous Canada. My journey visiting archives, reading constantly about Indigenous Canada, and travelling to First Nations communities seriously began half a century ago in my year at the Université Laval in Quebec City.

I was born in Toronto in 1946 and grew up in Oakville, located halfway between the cities of Hamilton and Toronto. During my boyhood I cannot recall a single reference in public or high school to the Mississauga First Nations, Ojibwe-speakers who call themselves, "Anishinabe" (meaning in English, "human being"), or in its plural form, "Anishinabeg."[2] I do not remember meeting anyone in Oakville who self-identified as "Indian." Indigenous people did not enter into the conversation. First Nations were not mentioned in the newspapers.

Cowboy movies and adventure films, such as those based on the American Davy Crockett, "King of the Wild Frontier," frequently appeared in our two local movie theatres. One film on a North American Indian theme made a lasting impression – because it portrayed the First Nations positively, without negative stereotyping. *The Light in the Forest* came out in 1958, the year before I entered high school. I read the 1953 historical novel by Conrad Richler, on which the film is based, some years later:[3] After a 1764 peace treaty between the Lenni Lenape (Delaware) and the British, the First Nations promised to return all the settlers' children taken in border skirmishes. A young man, adopted and renamed by the Delaware at the age of four, and raised by them for over a decade in the Ohio country, must now return against his will to his settler family in Pennsylvania, despite his wish to retain the language and rich culture of the Delaware that he now called his own.

At Central Public School we were not at all conscious of the Indigenous reality thousands of years old on our own schoolyard. For, as I have said, the First Nations were remote from public attention in the 1950s in our small southern Ontario town. A photo in the *Oakville Record-Star*, dated 5 July 1956, recreates the atmosphere of the last school day before the summer break: "Last Friday, photographer Charles Osland caught this happy group of youngsters running out of Central Public School as the school term ended."

Only decades later, when reading *Oakville and the Sixteen: History of an Ontario Port* (1953), did I learn about the Indigenous history of Oakville, in particular of our schoolyard's link with Aboriginal Canada. Local historian Hazel Mathews writes of the mid- and late nineteenth century, "A favourite pastime with several generations of children who attended the school was excavating in the playground, frequently with excellent results, for Indian bones and artifacts."[4]

Mention of North American Indians surfaced at the two southern Ontario summer camps I attended in those years: Camp Mazinaw east of Peterborough from 1954 to 1957 and Camp Kandalore in Haliburton from 1958 to 1962. Camp Mazinaw was situated close to Bon Echo, the Big Rock, whose granite face towers 100 metres above the waterline of Lake Mazinaw. In the mid-1950s we canoed regularly by the mysterious pictographs, or rock paintings located just above the water's edge, drawn in red ochre hundreds of years earlier. In 1959 this rock and the surrounding area became Bon Echo Provincial Park.

At the end of our several weeks at Camp Kandalore we had an Indian Council Ring. To the sound of beating drums, the campers entered into the lakeside circle. The evening began with the arrival by canoe of the camp director, in full chief's regalia, wearing a "Plains Indian" style

WHOOPEE! SCHOOL'S OUT FOR THE SUMMER

Last Friday, photographer Charles Osland caught this happy group of youngsters running out of Central school as the school term ended. It looks like they'll be going back to Central in the fall, as the School Board still hasn't come up with a replacement. The Central pupils have another reason to be happy. They have completed three years without an accident, and will receive their three-year Elmer award in September. Brantwood will get a first-year award, and Westwood will get a two-year award. This Friday, six Central school pupils will be among the nine Bicycle Roadeo winners getting a free trip to Toronto, which is sponsored by the Oakville Police Association and the Kiwanis.

0.1 The last day of school at Oakville's Central Public School in late June 1956, showing the author (*centre*), aged 10. Photographer: Charles Osland. Published in the *Oakville Record-Star*, 5 July 1956.

of headdress. Once the fire was lit, the dances and other "Indian" programming followed.[5] Camp leaders had some awareness of the rich First Nations heritage of the Great Lakes regions, but lacked understanding of what it involved. I do not remember meeting any Indigenous workers at either camp.

British Canada remains very much alive in the place names of Oakville and the surrounding area, first settled by Europeans in the early nineteenth century.[6] Our high school, Oakville Trafalgar, which is still there, takes the second half of its name from the township in which Oakville was located, just east of Nelson Township, named after England's most famous admiral, who in 1805 won his great naval victory over Napoleon at Trafalgar. The neighbouring community of Bronte honours Horatio Nelson's title, Duke of Bronte. Oakville's main street, now Lakeshore, was then known as "Colborne," named after a distinguished British Army officer at the 1815 Battle of Waterloo, who later became a governor of Upper Canada. Just to the east of Oakville was Peel County, recalling a mid-nineteenth century British prime minister.[7]

After a 1967 plebiscite to name the new community in south Peel County, the term "Mississauga" entered into Oakville's consciousness. The town (now city) of Mississauga was created on 1 January 1968.[8] The residents of south Peel submitted nearly nine hundred different names as suggestions,[9] with "Mississauga" consistently the frontrunner well ahead of alternatives like Malton, Sheridan, and Peel.[10] Voters chose "Mississauga" by nearly twelve thousand votes, a majority of nearly three to one over Sheridan, its rival in the final contest. Local historian Richard Collins suggests "Mississauga" appealed to young Canadians and new Canadians as it was "decidedly non-British and that fit well into the increasingly-colourful cultural quilt that Canada was becoming."[11]

My first known contact with North American Indians came in my second year at the University of Toronto at the "Trinity College Conference on the Canadian Indian," one of the first student-sponsored gatherings on Indigenous Canada.[12] The two-day meeting in January 1966 introduced participants to the concerns and aspirations of the Indigenous peoples. The Reverend John (Ian) MacKenzie, an Anglican minister who taught at Trinity College, was the moving force. MacKenzie was to become a member of the steering committee of the Indian Ecumenical Conference, which first met in 1970 in Montana and continued to do so annually at the Stoney Nakoda Reserve at Morley, Alberta, from 1971 to the 1990s. The conference played an important role in promoting the re-emergence of Native spiritual traditions. He later became the archdeacon of Caledonia in British Columbia, and was

0.2 John A. (Ian) MacKenzie (*standing fourth from left*) was one of the founding members of the Indian Ecumenical Conference and its steering committee, shown here at the 1971 gathering in Stoney Indian Park, Stoney Nakoda Reserve, Morley, Alberta. The first Conference took place In 1970 in Montana and continued at the Stoney Nakoda Reserve from 1971 to the 1990s, Reproduced with permission of the Centre for Indigenous Scholars, Sault Ste Marie, Ontario.

adopted by the Haida in 1975 and the Nisga'a in 1979.[13] The Encounter Club, the sponsoring undergraduate organization, made great efforts to bring Indigenous political leaders and students to the 1966 meeting at Trinity College.

In contrast with how things are today, the media and university scholars alike in the mid-1960s had little to say about Aboriginal Canada, really in those days an unknown topic. Peter Newman's popular study of Canada's political history from 1963 to 1968, *The Distemper of Our Times*, published in 1978, makes no reference to Indigenous issues. In 1966 the University League of Social Reform brought out an important volume, *Nationalism in Canada*,[14] which again, includes not a single article on Native concerns. The University of Toronto at that time offered no courses on the history of Indigenous Canada.

Over two days several hundred non-Indigenous and Indigenous participants met and exchanged views at Trinity College. The meeting received good coverage in the press, in all the major Toronto papers and the *Varsity*, the University of Toronto student newspaper. Arts events and films added a welcome addition to the talks, panel discussions, and seminars. The Indigenous delegates in attendance constituted a "Who's Who" of the Indigenous leadership of the day, including James Gladstone, the first First Nations Senator in Canada, and Gilbert Monture, the well-known Mohawk mining engineer and federal civil servant who was named that same year to the board of governors of the newly founded Trent University in Peterborough, Ontario. Also in attendance were members of the next generation of leadership, individuals that included the writer Basil Johnston; Stan McKay, a future moderator of the United Church of Canada; and youth leader Harold Cardinal, soon to become president of the Indian Association of Alberta. Unlike today, when approximately 30,000 First Nations students attend post-secondary institutions in Canada,[15] in 1965–6 only 131 status Indian students were enrolled full-time in Canadian universities.[16]

The following summer I learned more while working as a labourer with Indigenous people on a railway gang that maintained and repaired railway tracks in Manitoba. For the first half of my railway summer, the majority of workers were Cree and Métis from around The Pas and from Gillam, further north on the Hudson Bay railway line. The Indigenous workers spoke Cree among themselves. I didn't speak a word in their language, or know anything about their customs and traditions.

In the summer of 1967 I was a guide at the Ontario Pavilion at Expo '67 in Montreal and constantly worked to improve my spoken French. The Quebec-Canada relationship was the defining issue of the day. The Quiet Revolution contributed to a demand for additional powers for Quebec from Canada's federal government. The year before the Centennial, the newly elected Quebec government of Premier Daniel Johnson of the Union Nationale party stated its goal: "Equality or Independence." The new premier called for recognition of the two founding peoples – the French and the British – in a new constitution for Canada. President of France Charles de Gaulle, speaking from the balcony at Montreal's City Hall on 24 July 1967, declared: "Vive le Québec libre!" the slogan of the Quebec independence movement.[17]

Later that summer, René Lévesque, a popular political journalist and television commentator who had entered provincial politics in 1960 and served as minister of natural resources (1961–5), left the Quebec Liberal Party. In 1968 he founded the Parti Québécois – to work for Quebec's independence. If overshadowed by the constant drama of Quebec's possible separation from Canada, the Indians of Canada Pavilion at Expo '67 nonetheless attracted considerable attention.

The 225,000 status Indians constituted only about 1.5 per cent of Canada's total population of nearly twenty million, but the 1967 *Canada Year Book* reports they had "an annual increase rate of over three per cent, the greatest of any ethnic group in the country."[18] Financed by the federal government, but with substantial involvement from a nine-member Indian advisory council, the Indians of Canada Pavilion represented an Indigenous view of Canada.[19] Bluntly and uncompromisingly the exhibits expressed dissatisfaction with the status quo. The stylized steel and timber teepee, 30 metres tall, became one of the most popular visitors' stops at Expo.[20] As the Métis historian Olive Dickason later recalled, "The general public reacted with stunned disbelief that people in Canada were being treated in such a manner."[21] The Indians of Canada Pavilion displayed the work of distinguished Indigenous artists, who completed the large exterior works that decorated its outside walls; George Clutesi, Gerald Tailfeathers, Norval Morrisseau, and Alex Janvier were some of the artists in this group.[22]

After obtaining my Bachelor's degree in history at the University of Toronto, I began M.A. studies in Canadian history at the Université Laval in Quebec City in the fall of 1968. Intrigued by the relationship of the French with the First Nations in the sixteenth and seventeenth centuries, I studied the interpretations by French Canadian historians of what they termed, the "Heroic Period." I had begun in high school to cut out and file away interesting items on international affairs. Now I resumed the practice, but this time I narrowed my search to Indigenous Canada. Half a century of clipping and filing has resulted in a vast personal archive on the topic of what used to be called "Indian-White Relations."

Pierre Savard, my M.A. supervisor and a young member of Laval's Department of History, welcomed me. This Quebec historian counted among his ancestors a Huron (Wendat) grandmother,[23] but as his research focused on the European side of Canadian history, he arranged for me to take a private seminar with Jacques Rousseau, then teaching at Laval's Centre d'études nordiques. Rousseau was an eminent Quebec botanist and ethnologist. I had the privilege of being one of his last students, as he passed away in 1970. Thanks to the expert guidance of both of these scholars, in the fall of 1969 I defended my thesis, "French Canadian Historians' Images of the Indian in the 'Heroic Period' of New France, 1534–1663."

Research for my two histories of the nineteenth-century Mississauga (Ojibwe) on the north shore of Lake Ontario – *Sacred Feathers*, and its sequel, *Mississauga Portraits* – began at the University of Toronto in the early 1970s. My excellent supervisors in the doctoral program, J.M.S. Careless, the past chairman of the Department of History, and Ed Rogers, the ethnologist in chief at the Royal Ontario Museum, guided me. My Ojibwe language teachers in the early 1970s, Fred Wheatley and Basil Johnston, provided invaluable insights.

Awareness of everything relating to Indigenous Canada grew throughout Canadian society in the last decades of the twentieth century. Popular support for Indigenous issues increased substantially. Why did ignorance and apathy dominate to this point? In the 1990s I decided to write a study of non-Indigenous Canadians' perspectives of the First Nations, a work that now extends from the 1840s to 2020. This book was written principally over a period of four years (2016 to 2020). I thank my friend, the writer Katherine Govier, for the title – *Seen but Not Seen*. To keep the text to a manageable size, I discuss only the First Nations. Both the Métis and Inuit merit their own studies. After a discussion of John A. Macdonald, I review in more or less chronological order the viewpoints of fifteen other influential individuals, each of whom commented extensively on Indigenous subjects and has left behind a rich documentary record.

The text consists of this prologue, nine chapters, and an epilogue. Chapters one through five focus on a prime minister, a university president, a Christian missionary, a jurist, an Ottawa mandarin, and a female university professor. The five men demonstrated a variety of responses to the First Nations, but all five argued that European civilization must replace Indigenous cultures. The ultimate objective remained full citizenship and assimilation into mainstream society. The female professor showed a greater appreciation for cultural differences.

History is continually being reinterpreted, conditioned by the assumptions of the time and the place where it is written. New interpretations are advanced, and new facts uncovered. In *Seen but Not Seen*, I follow new developments and today's sensitivities, but I also try to understand people in their historical context, through the reconstruction of the atmosphere and mentality of their age to help reveal their outlooks and situations. I try to avoid, as much as I can, what historians call "presentism," the judgment of the past through the lens of the present.

Chapters six to nine deal with the twentieth century into the late 1960s. The choice of biographical subjects extends across Canada. I discuss nine male and female non-Indigenous observers: two anthropologists, a French Canadian Roman Catholic priest, a university professor, an artist, an Indigenous rights advocate, a high school teacher, an archivist-historian, a journalist, a botanist-ethnologist, and in the last chapter I include an outstanding First Nations leader. In an epilogue, I review the past half-century, a difficult topic for an historian, as we have neither all the necessary source materials, nor the needed time perspective. Throughout the text a number of prominent First Nations individuals make appearances, allowing for the introduction of Indigenous viewpoints towards non-Indigenous Canada.[24]

An important document that ushered in the modern era of Indigenous Canada's history provides a good starting point for the epilogue. In June 1969 the new Liberal government of Pierre Elliott Trudeau brought forward the "Statement of the Government of Canada on Indian Policy," popularly called the "White Paper," the term applied to government policy papers. The White Paper promoted the century-long goal of the Government of Canada of full integration of the First Nations into the dominant society, the end of Indian status, the reserves, and the historic Indian treaties.

Shortly before the White Paper, Walter Deiter, then the leader of the Federation of Saskatchewan Indians, and Dave Courchene, the president of the Manitoba Indian Brotherhood, had secured some badly needed federal funding for their cash-starved provincial organizations' work on reserves.[25] Funding opportunities greatly expanded with the White Paper, as the Liberal government now willingly supplied funds to Indian organizations to study the White Paper and present a formal response.[26] Until this transfer of funding Deiter, the first president of the National Indian Brotherhood, shored up the organization with personal loans.[27] The First Nations' response to the assimilationist document was a fiery rejection, the high point being the presentation of the "Red Paper" to the prime minister and the federal Cabinet in Ottawa on 4 June 1970. The image on the cover of this book conveys the tension of that moment. The Government of Canada formally retracted the White Paper in 1971.

Since the early 1970s writings on the Indigenous peoples and Indigenous peoples' issues has expanded incredibly. As the Canadian political scientist Alan C. Cairns states in his book *Citizens Plus*, published in 2000, "The literature – legal, historical, political, sociological, anthropological, feminist, and more – is now unmanageable."[28] The new communications platforms add to the challenge, with the entry of Facebook, Twitter, and YouTube. The epilogue to this book remains provisional, and most definitely, "a work in progress."

Unfortunately, documentary records by women are not abundant until the mid-twentieth century, and I recognize the imbalance. How Canadians of non-French and non-British origins viewed the First

Nations also merits fuller examination in a longer study. In terms of the multicultural Canada of today, another inequality arises. Canadians of British and French ancestry constituted the vast majority of Canada's population from the 1850s to the 1960s. Print sources are relatively abundant in French and English on many individuals of French and British origins. It is my hope that scholars familiar with the cultures and languages of Canadians of non-French and non-British origin will rectify this omission. I look forward to reading future work by others on this topic, and as a final introductory note, one day I hope to see a full study of the Indigenous populations' perceptions of non-Indigenous Canadians since the 1840s.

The text includes full documentation and bibliography, as well as fifty-three images and fifteen maps.

Throughout this manuscript written for a scholarly press I have heeded the advice the late Reverend Enos Montour (1899–1984), a retired United Church minister and a member of the Delaware community on the Six Nations Territory in Ontario, gave me forty-six years ago.[29] He kindly read and commented in 1974 on a draft of my Ph.D. thesis on the nineteenth-century Mississauga First Nations on the north shore of Lake Ontario. Generously, he said he liked what I had written but then calmly advised me that for readability I should "put more raisins in the dough." My hope is that *Seen but Not Seen* proves to be accessible to the general reader as well as probing and enlightening for the specialist.

Acknowledgments

The love, devotion and sacrifice of my wife, Nancy Townshend, over thirty-eight years of our marriage, and in particular the last five, have made this book possible.

Reaching back sixty years, I want to thank Bob Stevenson, my grade 10 social studies teacher at Oakville-Trafalgar High School in Oakville, Ontario, for encouraging me to keep clipping files on world affairs, which taught a discipline and a method of organizing material on a wide range of topics. From the time I started my graduate studies in Canadian history in 1968 I have kept files for half a century on a number of aspects of Canadian history; these files have been invaluable in the writing of *Seen but Not Seen*. These research notes are now in the University of Calgary Archives. Interested scholars and creative writers can gain access to this private archive on the history of Indigenous and non-Indigenous Canada since contact with Europeans.

Many individuals helped me with my research, formally and informally, in some cases over five decades. If I have omitted anyone in the following list I offer my deepest apologies: Kerry Abel, Tom Abler, Mark Abley, Michael Adams, George Anderson, Judy Aoki, Lisa Atkinson, Harold Averill, Agatha Barc, Ryan Barker, Jean Barman, Barb Barnes, Sally Barnes, James Bartleman, Peter Barton, David Bird, Alan Bowker, John A. (Sandy) Boyd, Kay Boyd, Gus Brannigan, Dave Brown, Jennifer S.H. Brown, Arni Brownstone, Karen Buckley, Doug Cass, Ted Chamberlain, Bailey Chui, Ella Monture Claus, James Cullingham, Doug Cuthand, Ed Dahl, Anita Damner, James Daschuk, François David, Marilyn Davidge, Malcolm Davidson, Hugh and Pauline Dempsey, Christine Dernoi, Corinne Desmettre, Jonathan Dewar, Mark DeWolf, Floyd Doctor, Edgar Dosman, Cynthia Downe, Patrice Dutil, Brendan Edwards, Art Einhorn, Suzanne Ell, Margery Fee, William Fenton,

Dennis Fisher, Tim Foran, Hamar Foster, Dan Francis, Doug Francis, Jim Frideres, Gerry Friesen, Alan Fry, Kim Fullerton, Kim Geraldi, Ian Getty, Andrea Gordon, Jean-Guy Goulet, Katharine Govier, David Grant, Manfred Grote, Patrice Groulx, Richard Gwyn, David Hall, Tony Hall, Laura Hallman, Louis-Edmond Hamelin, Michelle Hamilton, Carol Hanson, John Honderich, Peter Hutchins, Dean Jacobs, Kathleen James, David Jeffries, John Jennings, Keith Johnson, Sheila Johnston, Gwynneth Jones, Roma Kail, Alice Kehoe, Jennifer Keizer, Pat Kennedy, Nathalie Kermoal, Cecil and Cathy King, Sheldon Krasowski, Larry Krotz, Elizabeth Kundert-Cameron, Valérie Lacasse, Jonathan Lainey, James Lambert, Jeff Langlois, Sylvia Lassam, Paul Leatherdale, Laurie Leclair, Doug Leighton, John Leslie, Andrée Lévesque, Anne Lindsay, Jack Little, Richard Lueger, Harmut Lutz, Robert MacBain, Laurel MacDowell, Barry Mack, Colin McFarquhar, Ian MacKenzie, Brian MacLean, Hope MacLean, Rod Macleod, Bennett McCardle, Cathy McLay, David McLay, Heather Maki, Shawna Manchakowsky, Stuart Manson, Dennis Martel, Ged Martin, the Rt. Hon. Paul Martin, Courtney Mason, Elizabeth Mathew, Lea Meadows, Jim Miller, Meg Miner, Tom Molloy, Toby Morantz, Jean Morriset, Jim Morrison, Desmond Morton, John Moses, Lindsay Muir, Mary Murphy, Annie Murray, Barbara Nair, Keith Neuman, Kirk Niergarth, Karin Noble, Alison Norman, Andrew Nurse, John O'Connell, Rob Omura, Brian Osborne, Harold Otto, Carine Peltier-Caroff, Bill Perks, Marie-Louise Perron, Bill Peterson, Alison Pier, Rudy Platiel, Lori Podolsky, Will Pratt, Darren Préfontaine, Doug Rae, Trish Rae, Allisun Rana, Natalya Rattan, Kate Reed, Tim Reibetanz, Terry Reilly, Wendy Robbins, Roy Romanow, Jérôme Rousseau, Armand Ruffo, Peter Russell, Alan Sherwin, Hugh Shewell, Samatha Shields, Niigaanwewidam Sinclair, Brian Slattery, David Smith, Doug Smith, Ian Smith, Keith Smith, Nick Smith, Peter Smith, Bill Snow, Guy Spittal, Tim Stanley, Melvin Steinhauer, Darryl Stonefish, Molly Taylor, Christie Teterenko, Benoît Thériault, Jessica Todd, Scott Trevithick, Ken Tyler, Ron and Kip Veale, Jacqueline Vincent, Sylvie Vincent, Alison Wagner, Anthony F.C. Wallace, David Wallace, Wendy Wickwire, Shirley Wigmore, Jennifer Willard, Doug Williams, Glen Williams, Bernice Loft Winslow, Bonnie Woelk, Lana Wong, Sandra Woolfrey, Bill Wuttunee, Ji Zhao, Judy Zhao, Norman Zlotkin. Robin Poitras prepared all fourteen maps with the exception of map 3.2 by William Wonders. Mary Murphy took the author's photo in June 2018. I thank Dave Brown for the shooting and preparation of many of the images in the book. As Paul Wallace, the subject of the sixth chapter in *Seen but Not Seen* so appropriately wrote in the acknowledgments to one of his last books; "To all these the writer extends his warmest thanks. May their moccasins always be dry, their path free from logs and briars, and may the sun shine long in their lodges"[30]

I warmly thank all those at the University of Toronto Press (UTP) who helped with the production of *Seen but Not Seen*. I am most grateful to Len Husband, my editor at UTP, particularly for locating the striking image now on the book's cover. Kate Baltais has done incredible work in copyediting a complicated manuscript and in the process made important suggestions. Frances Mundy masterfully coordinated the production process until her retirement at the end of June 2020; it has been a real pleasure to work with Frances and Kate on both this and my previous book, *Mississauga Portraits* (2013), also published by UTP, and, as always, I am grateful for their patience and help. I warmly thank Robin Studniberg for her expert assistance with the final preparation of the book, and Breanna Muir and Anna Del Col for their help with the marketing. Mary Newberry of Mary Newberry Editorial Services has prepared excellent subject entries for the index, adding greatly to the volume. At an early stage I was most indebted to the anonymous reviewers for their valuable suggestions on the manuscript. I thank Peggy Stockdale and the UTP production team for managing the cover design process and transmission of the final text to the printer.

The final preparation of *Seen but Not Seen* has proceeded in most unusual times from the spring to fall of 2020. In the face of extraordinary challenges resulting from COVID-19, the University of Toronto Press has done an incredible job. I am most grateful to all of you!

Note on Terminology

The term "Indian" is used throughout the first nine chapters of *Seen but Not Seen* to reflect contemporary usage in Canada's first century, although sometimes I also use Indigenous and First Nations when speaking of these peoples at this time. From 1867 to the mid-1960s Indians and non-Indians alike used the word almost exclusively. The term is based on the confusion between the Americas and India, a misnomer from the start. The designation "Native peoples" was common in the 1970s, with "Aboriginal peoples" also gaining acceptance. Most recently the term "Aboriginal" is in the process of being replaced by the term "Indigenous," a term consistent with the United Nations Declaration on the Rights of Indigenous Peoples, adopted in 2007.[31] In the epilogue I favour "First Nations," particularly after the term came into widespread use in Canada in the 1980s. "First Nations" refers to those individuals who are officially known under the Indian Act as Indians, and it does not include Métis or Inuit peoples. First Nations is not used in the United States, where, "Native Americans" appears at present to be the preferred term.[32] Chelsea Vowel provides a helpful review of terminology in her *Indigenous Writes: A Guide to First Nations, Métis & Inuit Issues in Canada*, published in 2016.[33]

The terms used to designate the federal department with the constitutional responsibility for the First Nations have altered over time. From its creation in 1880 and until 1936 it was known as the Department of Indian Affairs. Downsized in 1936, it became the Indian Affairs Branch of the Department of Mines and Resources, and it was reassigned in 1949 to the Department of Citizenship and Immigration. In 1966 it re-emerged as a separate department, Indian Affairs and Northern Development, later briefly becoming Indian and Northern Affairs Canada. In 2011 a new title was assigned. Opposition to the word "Indian" led the government of Stephen Harper to alter the title of the department to

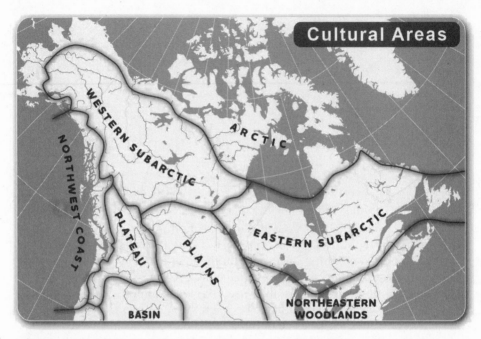

Map 0.1 Cultural Areas: the variety and diversity of cultural groups.

Map 0.2 Indigenous language groups within the boundaries of present-day Canada.

Aboriginal Affairs and Northern Development Canada. This designation, like its immediate predecessors, had a short life. The final report of the Truth and Reconciliation Commission in 2015 used "Indigenous" as a collective term to refer to the First Nations, Inuit, and Métis in Canada. The new government of Justin Trudeau changed the department's title again, to Indigenous and Northern Affairs Canada,[34] and in 2017 the responsibilities were split between two ministers, one for Crown-Indigenous Relations and the second for Indigenous Services.

There is a multiplicity and diversity of Indigenous peoples living on the land now known as Canada. They comprise many distinct societies with their own distinct cultures, languages, histories, and identities (see Map 0.1 and Map 0.2). As Kent Gooderham, the editor of the 1969 anthology, *I Am an Indian*, devoted to Indigenous writing, noted of the First Nations groups, "Separated by language, culture, and geography they are as different from one another as they are from the Europeans, Asians, and Africans who came to live among them."[35]

Some of the terminology, although appropriate at the time, is now dated. A number of First Nations communities have corrected their names in English. In contemporary studies it is important to recognize and respect the new names. In this historical study, however, with its emphasis especially on the years 1867 to 1967, the older nomenclature in English is by and large retained, for example, Blood, rather than Kainai; Ojibwe, instead of Anishinabe; Mohawk, rather than Kanyen'kehaha; Shuswap, in place of Secwepemc; Songhee, instead of Lekwungen; and Thompson, the name of the major river in their territory in British Columbia, rather than Nlaka'pamux. I include the Indigenous designation immediately after the first citation of the First Nation's identification in English. The usage of designations for First Nations groups is inconsistent, both through time and by various writers, whether Indigenous and not, so while I have attempted to be consistent, my usage may not always match that of others, especially with regard to pluralization. Thus, for example, while the Grand Council of the Crees (Eeyou Istchee) pluralizes Cree for itself, some Cree writers have not done (and do not do) so. In my writing in this book I have given the plural as Cree.

In this study the Métis include those individuals with joint Indigenous and non-Indigenous ancestry who identify as Métis, as distinct from First Nations, Inuit, or non-Indigenous people. I use "Métis" with an accent to refer to those Indigenous people descended from Scots, English, and other groups, as well as from French fur traders. The awkward and negative terms, "non-Aboriginal" and "non-Indigenous," are retained only for lack of something better. Occasionally I use the word "settler," and also "Euro-Canadian." In New Zealand they have the Maori word "Pakeha," which is used widely to refer to non-Maori, but we have no equivalent word in Canada.[36] Extremely useful for all aspects of contemporary usage is the style guide by Gregory Younging, *Elements of Indigenous Style: A Guide for Writing by and about Indigenous Peoples*, published in 2018.[37]

SEEN BUT NOT SEEN

Influential Canadians and the First Nations from the 1840s to Today

Chapter One

John A. Macdonald and the Indians

Recent assessments of Canada's first prime minister do not portray him in a good light. In the summer 2015 issue of the journal *Canadian Issues*, entitled "A-Historical Look at John A. Macdonald? Seeing Canada's First Prime Minister in the Context of His and Our Times," Thomas H.B. Symons identifies the dramatic shift in interpretation. Professor Symons, who was the founding president of Trent University and a former chairman of both the Ontario Human Rights Commission and the Historic Sites and Monuments Board of Canada, notes the replacement of a basically positive image by new values and attitudes. "What may be a little surprising," he writes, "is the extent and the vehemence of some of the negative assessments that are surfacing."[1] The more recent criticism focuses largely on Macdonald's policies towards Indians, as Indigenous peoples were then called. Today's critics have the benefit of knowing recent history, most particularly the horrific shortcomings of the Indian residential school system. James Daschuk, another contributor to the same summer edition of *Canadian Issues*, indicates just how far the new negativity has advanced when he states, "Recent serious and measured scholarship has begun to interpret the state-sponsored attack on indigenous communities as a form of genocide."[2]

John A. Macdonald's Indian policies deserve close examination, as he was by far and away the most important Canadian politician in the formation of Canadian Indian policy after Confederation. Throughout his administration, Macdonald sought to create a transcontinental nation out of the separate colonies and regions in British North America. He served as prime minister from 1867 to 1873 and again from 1878 to 1891. To begin on a positive note regarding the First Nations, Macdonald recognized the existence of Aboriginal rights in the soil, a right for which the Indian must be consulted and compensated. He recognized the importance of the Royal Proclamation of 1763. In December 1867

Canada acknowledged that Great Britain had already granted Canada ultimate title, but to obtain the right of full, unimpeded ownership of the land the new Dominion must consult and compensate the Indians for the loss of their right to live off the land in their traditional way.[3] The Government of Canada instigated the first treaties with the Plains Indians in the early 1870s, signing Treaty One in 1871, the same year as the United States, by statute, eliminated treaty making altogether. The Conservatives followed with treaties One to Three (1872–3) and the Liberals with treaties Four to Seven (1874–7).

On the other side of the ledger, as the attorney general of Upper Canada, or Canada West, Macdonald introduced the assimilationist Gradual Civilization Act of 1857 in the Assembly of the Canadas, the pre-Confederation union of the future Ontario and Quebec. Shortly after Confederation his government brought forward the Dominion's first coercive legislation relating to Indians, the Gradual Enfranchisement Act of 1869, an escalation of the 1857 Act. Both the Conservatives and the Liberals agreed on the need to absorb the First Nations into the dominant Euro-Canadian culture. Upon his return to the prime minister's office in 1878, Macdonald approved the Indian Act of 1876, which had been passed by the previous Liberal administration and is still in force today. The Indian Act classed the Indians as minors, hence, wards of the state. The prime minister himself chose to serve as the superintendent of Indian Affairs from 1878 to 1887. Macdonald created the Department of Indian Affairs in 1880, charged with the task of implementing the Indian Act across the country. The Canadian federal government's involvement with Indian residential schooling formally began in 1883, and Macdonald also oversaw implementation of the illegal "pass system" in the mid-1880s. Despite treaty promises, the Department of Indian Affairs required the First Nations to obtain a pass from the Indian agent if they wanted to leave their reserves, especially after 1885. The Liberal Opposition fully endorsed this regulation.

The story of Sir John A. Macdonald (1815–1891) is both very complex and very large. The contradictions of his Indian policy include his ruthless repressive measures immediately after the unrest of 1885, when his administration ruled the North-West Territories as a police state.[4] Deliberately his government withheld food rations to force uncooperative Plains First Nations to move onto reserves. In contrast, in 1885 Macdonald extended the federal franchise to adult male Indians in Central and Eastern Canada, if they met the property requirement – without obliging them to lose their Indian status. He wanted them to become involved and have some influence on the laws and policies that affected them.

What perceptions did John A. Macdonald have of North American Indians? What did he know about them? What motivated his policies towards the First Nations? To begin at the beginning, Ontario (then known as Upper Canada, and just before Confederation as Canada West) provides the best starting point.

John Alexander Macdonald and his parents moved to Kingston in 1820, when he was five years old. At the time, this was the largest urban centre in Upper Canada, with a population of approximately four thousand.[5] Only three of the five children born to Hugh and his wife, Helen Shaw Macdonald, lived to adulthood, John Alexander and his two sisters. The Macdonalds opened a store in Kingston. After their first two attempts ended in bankruptcy, the family tried again, this time in the countryside, at Hay Bay on the Bay of Quinte, about 50 kilometres to the west of Kingston. Eventually, his father achieved enough local prominence to be appointed a magistrate for the Midland District in 1829. Seeing John Alexander's promise in local schools, his parents sent him to Kingston for five years of rigorous schooling in the late 1820s.[6] Each summer he returned to the Bay of Quinte, and in 1830, at age 15, he began his articles in a Kingston law office, being called to the bar six years later. In the words of his biographer Donald Creighton, the ambitious young man knew "the law was a broad, well-trodden path to comfort, influence, even to power."[7]

The British had made treaties at the eastern end of Lake Ontario with the Mississauga, known in their Ojibwe language as Anishinabeg ("human beings"). John Graves Simcoe, the first lieutenant governor of Upper Canada (1791–6), recognized them as "the original proprietors of the Land."[8] The Royal Proclamation of 1763 had outlined the procedure to be followed when dealing with the First Nations of the Great Lakes. All private transactions involving land were now accordingly forbidden, and only after public purchase or a treaty with the Crown could settlers legally occupy First Nations lands.

The first Mississauga treaty in 1783, and the second in 1784, led to the displacement of Anishinabeg from the northeastern shoreline of Lake Ontario.[9] The one-time-only payment for the land included clothing, guns for those without them, powder and ammunition, and enough red cloth to make about a twelve coats and laced hats.[10] No official record of the two councils for these treaties survives, nor does a record of the payment for the second purchase.[11] No annuities, or annual payments, or reserves were provided. The British regarded these two treaties as land surrenders that extinguished all Mississauga claims forever.

The Anishinabeg's perception of the treaties differed from that of the British. The Anishinabeg received British trade goods in return for allowing the newcomers use of portions of their territory.[12] They regarded the treaties as agreements to live side by side and share the land. As Kahkewaquonaby ("Sacred Feathers"), known in English as Peter Jones, stated, "Each tribe or body of Indians has its own range of country, and sometimes each family has its own hunting grounds, marked out by certain natural divisions, such as rivers, lakes, mountains, or ridges; and all the game within these bounds is considered their property as much as the cattle and fowl owned by a farmer on his own land."[13] The land remained theirs, indeed they believed, as the Mississauga historian Doug Williams writes, "They could hunt along every shore, camp if need be on every shore in their territory and that the farmer would only stick to the fields."[14]

After the initial treaties, thousands of British North Americans who had supported the King in the Revolutionary War, came north as political refugees. Other non-Indigenous land seekers followed the Loyalists to what is now southern Ontario. In addition, more than 2,000 Iroquois (Haudenosaunee, or "People of the Longhouse," members of the Six Nations Confederacy) who had allied with the British Crown in the Revolutionary War arrived. Giving here their names in English first, the Six Nations comprised the Mohawk (Kanyen'kehaha, "People of the Flint"), Oneida (Onyota'a:ka, "People of the Standing Stone"), Onondaga (Ononda'gega', "People of the Hills"), Cayuga (Gayagohono, "People of the Marshy Area"), Seneca (Onondowaga, "People of the Great Hills"),[15] and Tuscarora (whose self-definition is traditionally interpreted as "Those of the Indian Hemp").[16] The largest nation in Canada was the Mohawk. The several hundred Mississauga at the eastern end of Lake Ontario had not anticipated the size of the migration. Nearly 4,000 British Loyalists settled in the Kingston area and around the Bay of Quinte in the mid-1780s,[17] as did approximately 120 Mohawk.[18] The British Canadian population around Kingston and the Bay of Quinte rose to about 17,000 by 1815.[19] When the Macdonald family arrived in Upper Canada, the Mississauga only numbered about 160 in the Bay of Quinte area, and approximately 100 around Kingston.[20]

The arrival of thousands of newcomers in the area around Belleville (located at the mouth of the Moira River and on the Bay of Quinte) and Kingston deprived the Anishinabeg of their land on the lakefront and of the inland resources they needed to support their way of life. The settlers occupied traditional fishing spots, logged their hunting grounds, and despoiled their gravesites. The newcomers had no understanding of the way of life of the Indigenous people. They occupied their territory, enriched themselves, and contrary to the treaties, fulfilled none of the oral promises the Anishnabeg remember as having solemnly been made by them.

Anxious to get along with the newcomers in their midst, the Bay of Quinte and Kingston area Mississauga in the mid-1820s converted to Christianity under the leadership of Indigenous Christian leaders. They pleaded for the use of a miniscule portion of lakefront, as they had no reserves. The new Christians and their British allies began a Methodist mission on the Bay of Quinte at one of the few locations in that area still free of Euro-Canadian settlement. Two hundred Anishinabeg were living on Grape Island by the end of 1828,[21] only some 10 or so acres (4 hectares) in extent,[22] which gave the mission an incredible density of approximately twenty people per acre.

In search of a proper land base for his community, John Sunday (or Shawundais), a veteran of the War of 1812 and later an ordained Methodist minister,[23] led the Grape Island Mission in the late 1830s, to relocate to Alderville, in the interior near Rice Lake. Here they settled on a still empty tract suitable for farming. Despite the government's initial treaty promises, and the Mississauga's loyal support in the War of 1812, the government had done very little to help them. Years later, in 1872, Chief Sunday reminded the member of Parliament from Kingston, and now the prime minister of Canada, that their old treaties in the Kingston and Belleville areas had not been respected. The agreements were "done in a most solemn manner, but now we see that one by one if not nearly all have been null and void."[24]

John A. Macdonald first met the Mohawk in the winter of 1832–3 after his employer sent his legal apprentice to set up a branch law office in the village of Napanee, 50 kilometres west of Kingston, close to the Mohawk of the Bay of Quinte. One of the young lawyer's earliest acquaintances was a Tyendinaga Mohawk named John Culbertson,[25] son of a Scottish fur trader and a daughter of John Deserontyon, the founder of the Iroquois settlement on the Bay of Quinte. John Culbertson's wife, Sarah Bowen, was non-Indigenous, the daughter of a British Loyalist family. In 1836 the entrepreneurial Culbertson, totally fluent in English, convinced the lieutenant governor of Upper Canada to give him approximately 800 acres of the Mohawk Tract, thus using his knowledge of his mother's culture and language for personal enrichment. Without paying a cent Culbertson obtained from the colonial authorities a huge portion of his people's land for personal speculation. He then proceeded to have village lots surveyed for sale at a village site for non-Indigenous settlers, naming it "Deseronto," after his grandfather.[26]

In 1839 Macdonald, then 24 years old, represented a Tyendinaga Mohawk named Brandt in a murder trial. John Culbertson acted as his

Mohawk interpreter. In his cross-examination in the Kingston court-room, the young lawyer cleverly extracted an important admission from the Crown's principal witness: the murder occurred in a darkened house when everyone was drunk, which made it impossible to be certain who held the knife used in the murder. The *Kingston Chronicle* described Macdonald's defence as "ingenious." Although the jury ruled manslaughter, the judge only imposed a six-month sentence on Brandt.[27]

Macdonald's first documented meeting with a Mississauga occurred a little over a year later, on 1 February 1841, when he chaired a Methodist Missionary Society meeting in Kingston, where the guest speaker was the celebrated Kahkewaquonaby (or Peter Jones), who was a Mississauga chief as well as an ordained Methodist minister.[28] Unlike many other Christian denominations at the time, the Methodist Church recognized Indigenous church leaders and put them in positions of leadership and authority in Indigenous churches. Under his leadership the Credit community adopted a written constitution and, while retaining some Indigenous governance practices, moved towards an elective system.[29]

In his remarks at this meeting, Chief Kahkewaquonaby – speaking in English – shared Anishinabeg perspectives with his Euro-Canadian audience. Three months later his article, "The Indian Nations," appeared in the *Monthly Review: Devoted to the Civil Government of Canada*. In this article, Jones recounts the story Elders told of first contact with the Europeans: "Our fathers held out to them the hand of friendship; they then asked for a small piece of land on which they might pitch their tents. By and by they begged for more, which was given them, and in this way they have continued ever since to ask, or take by force, what the Indians would not consent to give up."[30] Later, in his manuscript history, published in 1861, five years after his death,[31] Jones expanded on the period of initial contact in Upper Canada. When the British first arrived and made treaties with the Anishinabeg they treated them "as allies with the British nation, and not subjects; and they were so considered until the influx of emigration completely outnumbered the aborigines. From that time the Colonial Government assumed a parental authority over them, treating them in every respect as children."[32]

Kingstonians first heard of Peter Jones (1802–1856) after his 1833 marriage in New York City to Eliza Field, a wealthy and well-educated Englishwoman. In its editorial comment, the *Kingston Chronicle* showed its sense of racial superiority to Indians, even to Indian Christians, in stating, "Improper and revolting, we believe that the Creator of the Universe distinguished his creatures by different colours, that they might be kept separate from each other."[33] In contrast, John A. Macdonald accepted intermarriage between the First Nations and non-Aboriginals. He believed the First Nations could assimilate into the dominant Euro-Canadian society. By the standards of his day, the Kingston lawyer was a relatively tolerant individual in this regard.[34]

Macdonald knew of Indian-white racial mixing in early Upper Canada. Reverend William Macaulay Herchmer, an Anglican minister at St George's Church in Kingston, was his "school fellow and life long friend."[35] Herchmer's obituary, in the *Journal of Education for Upper Canada* in 1862, confirmed the story of an uncle of his who "engaged in the Indian trade, like many others similarly circumstanced, married a native woman." One of their Mississauga children became a Methodist minister, and the article continues, "On visiting Kingston in that capacity, Mr Herchmer readily claimed him as his kinsman, received him into his family, and subsequently showed him every attention."[36]

John A. Macdonald began his political career in 1843 as a city alderman. The next year, the by-then well-known lawyer handily won election as Kingston's member of Parliament. To finance his political career, Macdonald supplemented his legal income through the sale and rental of real estate.[37] Just two years earlier, the Act of Union had joined the two provinces of Lower and Upper Canada, naming them Canada East and Canada West, respectively. The capital alternated on a regular basis, as neither city would accept a permanent site for government in the other. First it was Kingston, then Montreal, and then in the 1850s and early 1860s the capital of the Province of Canada shifted between Toronto and Quebec City. Only the midway choice of Ottawa resolved the issue, in 1865. Macdonald was a member of the Legislative Assembly when in 1844 the Royal Commission of Inquiry into the Affairs of Indians in Canada, established in 1842 by Sir Charles Bagot, then governor general of the Province of Canada, submitted its report. The document, known to historians as the "Bagot Report," recommended "that the true and only practicable policy of the Government" was "to endeavor, gradually, to raise the Tribes within the British Territory to the level of their white neighbours; to protect them to undertake the offices and duties of citizens."[38]

By the middle of the nineteenth century, Toronto had become the largest city in Canada West, with a population three times that of Kingston.[39] A huge influx of Britons arrived in the mid-1820s, with even higher levels of British immigration in the 1830s and 1840s. Toronto's population grew at an astonishing rate, from roughly seventeen hundred in 1826, to over thirty thousand in 1850.[40] In the 1850s, Toronto had few Indigenous residents. Daniel Wilson (1816–1892) arrived from Scotland in

1853 to teach history and English literature at University College in the University of Toronto (see chapter four). Years later he recalled the absence of an Indigenous population, although "in the boyhood of the older generation of Toronto, hundreds of Indians, including those of the old Mississauga tribe, were to be seen about the streets."[41] The proximity of the Credit Mission, only 20 kilometres or so to the west, had meant a continuing North American Indian presence. Then, in 1847, the Mississauga left. Despite Peter Jones's determined efforts, the Anishinabeg failed to secure a title deed – or legal possession – to their remaining Credit River lands. Subsequently, they accepted an invitation from the Six Nations of the Grand River to establish a community beside them, which they called "New Credit."[42]

Indigenous Canada receded in Toronto's consciousness. A quick perusal of *Brown's Toronto General Directory 1856* reveals only one First Nations person from Canada can be said with certainty to have lived in the city that year,[43] and that person was Francis Assiginack, an Ottawa (Odawa) from Manitoulin Island, on the north shore of Lake Huron.[44] His father was a distinguished Odawa chief.[45] Francis Assiginack worked in the Indian Department on King Street, as well as in the department's satellite office in Cobourg, 100 kilometres to the east, as chief clerk and interpreter. A decade earlier, he had shown great promise as a student at Toronto's Upper Canada College. After he became seriously ill with consumption, he returned to Manitoulin, where he died in 1863 at Manitowaning.[46]

A number of individuals of mixed ancestry in mid-nineteenth-century Toronto went unnoticed as "Indians," as they did not self-identify as Indigenous.[47] In his book, *Prehistoric Man*, published in 1865, Daniel Wilson commented that as his "eye grew more familiar with its traces," he saw Aboriginal physical traits. "Nor are such traces confined to frontier settlements," he continued, in fact, he had seen "the semi-Indian features" at "Canadian Governor-General's receptions, in the halls of the Legislature, among the undergraduates of Canadian universities."[48] In the African Canadian community, William Peyton Hubbard, a future deputy mayor of Toronto in the early twentieth century, had both North American Indian and African heritage, but he did not self-identify as Indian.[49] In the eyes of those of European background, the known admixture of even minute quantities of African ancestry placed Hubbard in the African category.[50]

Only about fifteen thousand North American Indians were living in the Union of the Canadas in the early 1850s,[51] representing less than one per cent of the total population of approximately two million. The non-Indigenous populations outnumbered the self-identified Indigenous by over a hundred to one. Many British colonists expected the Indians to disappear in the near future. As the young Sandford Fleming, later to become known worldwide as the inventor of standard time, wrote in his diary in 1845, "They are dying away every year and it is supposed their race will soon be extinct."[52] The pressure on their remaining lands became intense. Lord Bury, who served as the superintendent general of Indian Affairs in 1855, noted how the British Canadian settlers "forcibly squat upon their lands and plunder their timber."[53]

In reality, the First Nations had no intention of disappearing into the dominant society. Many Indigenous people in Canada West realized that to hold onto the little parcels of land they did retain, their children must learn to speak, read, and write in English. Thirty leaders and about eighty community members met in 1846 with government officials at the Narrows (today's Orillia), where Lake Simcoe empties into Lake Couchiching, north of Toronto,[54] to discuss the establishment of residential or manual labour schools. The address from the Tyendinaga Mohawk Council stated their community sought boarding schools "to make our boys useful and industrious farmers and mechanics, and our girls good housekeepers."[55] With the understanding that Christian Indians themselves would soon control the boarding schools, most of the Ojibwe chiefs initially approved of the schools' goals and committed one-quarter of their communities' annuities or annual payments for the sale of their lands, for twenty to twenty-five years, to support them.[56] Many First Nations people came to regret their support of such institutions once they saw how non-Indigenous educators retained an iron fist control over the schools.[57] Many of their children returned strangers to their own land, culture, and community. The dominant society was, and remains – as current (2020) media coverage confirms – rife with racial prejudice.[58]

Named attorney general of Canada West in 1854, John A. Macdonald continued his political rise up the top rungs of the ladder of Canadian political power. As the First Nations comprised only a tiny proportion of the total population – and did not have the vote – Macdonald paid them little attention. This being said, in the spring of 1857 he did make one major intervention in Indian affairs. In mid-May, the member from Kingston rose in the Canadian Assembly to introduce one of the most important bills in the history of Canadian Indian policy, namely, the Act for the Gradual Civilization of the Indian Tribes in the Canadas. Neither Macdonald nor any other Cabinet member consulted any chiefs or Indian councils prior to the legislative debate.[59]

The Gradual Civilization Act, the precursor of the post-Confederation Indian Act of 1876,[60] established the procedures by which status Indians could become "enfranchised," or full citizens. The Act granted Indians the vote, the full rights of British subjects, and the ownership of 20 hectares (50 acres) of reserve land, the common size for a viable farm in Central Canada.[61] Any Indian adult male judged by a special board of examiners to be educated, free of debt, and of good moral character could apply. After a successful three-year trial period, the applicant gained full ownership of his 50 acres, which immediately ceased to be part of the reserve. It became theirs and could be sold to a non-Indian. As enfranchised Indians acquired individual portions of land or sold their land to other buyers, it was intended that the reserves would gradually disappear, as part of the normal flow of progress. Automatically, when an adult male enfranchised his wife and children also gained citizenship, and the government no longer recognized them as wards of the Crown, that is, as legal or status Indians. They gave up their Indians status, but in return gained the full rights of citizenship, including the right to vote, to own property, and to reside anywhere in Canada. The French word used in the "enfranchisement" legislation best captures the perception of what the word meant, to Canadian legislators: *émancipation*.[62]

The Gradual Civilization Act passed with only one dissenting voice, that of William Lyon Mackenzie.[63] All the major political parties and leaders endorsed it. In contrast, First Nations leaders denounced the Act,[64] as they correctly saw it as a negation of the treaties, an attempt to seize their remaining land base and to end any form of self-government they still retained. With the Gradual Civilization Act, the new central dynamic for Indian policy became assimilation. A huge protest meeting was held at Onondaga on the Six Nations Territory, but neither Macdonald nor any other Canadian politician paid any attention to this event, and the press ignored it entirely.[65]

In his early political career, Macdonald on at least one occasion worked for recognition of a First Nations treaty right.[66] Just a month and a half after the passage of the Gradual Civilization Act, as attorney general of Upper Canada, he gave his legal opinion of Treaty Twenty-Two, the British agreement of 1820 with the Mississauga for their three small reserves at Twelve Mile (Bronte) Creek, Sixteen Mile (Oakville) Creek, and the Credit River (the southern and northern sections of the Credit Reserve).[67] When consulted that summer, Macdonald stated that these lands were not an outright purchase, but instead a surrender in trust to the government, and consequently, "The profits of the land until sold, and the amount of money received on sale of any portion of it must be expended for the benefit of the Indians, according to the terms of the Trust, as specified in such deed."[68] He ruled that the Canadian government must fulfil its trust agreement to reimburse the

Mississauga of the Credit for land acquired by the Crown in Treaty Twenty-Two.

Indigenous issues occupied little of John A. Macdonald's attention after 1857 onward to the Confederation debates. The index to the printed volume of his letters for the years 1858 to 1861 includes only two references to Indians.[69] This suggests that politicians were convinced that the Indian question in the Canadas was over. The passage of the Gradual Civilization Act provided the solution, namely, the imminent assimilation of the First Nations.

An intervention in February 1870 in the House of Commons reveals Macdonald's outlook on Aboriginal land questions, before the numbered Western treaties from 1871 to 1877, when he stated that the Manitoulin Treaty of 1862 "was a good arrangement, and carried out with every fairness to those concerned."[70] Macdonald supported acquisition of the Great Manitoulin Island on the north shore of Lake Huron, even though in 1836 it clearly had been promised to the First Nations forever.[71] This was one of the very rare occasions that Macdonald agreed with the Toronto newspaper of George Brown, his great political rival. On 30 July 1863 the *Globe* declared, in reference to the Manitoulin First Nations, "They cannot be permitted to stand in the way of the advance of civilization on this continent."[72]

During the Confederation Debates at Charlottetown and Quebec in 1864, the politicians drafted a constitution – later called the British North America Act, 1867 – without consulting any of the First Nations. In the thousand pages of the 1864 *Confederation Debates in the Legislature of the Union of the Canadas*, only three references appear relating to Indians, and as the historical geographer John Warkentin summarizes, "Completely engrossed as they were with other matters, aboriginal peoples seemed not to exist."[73] The political scientist Peter Russell notes the climate of the times, when he states in his 2017 book, *Canada's Odyssey*, "In Canada at this time, there was not an ounce of respect in either the political or judicial branches of government for Indigenous peoples' right to govern themselves."[74] The Royal Proclamation of 1763 declares that Indians "should not be molested or disturbed" on their historic hunting grounds, yet the Fathers of Confederation ignored this ruling.[75] The British North America Act simply states, in Section 91(24), "Indians, and Lands reserved for Indians" are a federal responsibility.[76]

Immediately after Confederation pressures for assimilation increased. Hector Langevin, one of Macdonald's senior Cabinet ministers from Quebec, introduced in Parliament in 1869 the Government of Canada's first major piece of legislation relating to Indians, the Gradual Enfranchisement Act of 1869, built on the 1857 Gradual Civilization Act.[77] The

1869 Act endorsed the establishment in Eastern and Central Canada of elected band councils to replace hereditary chieftainships. The Gradual Enfranchisement Act also assumed the power to define who was an "Indian." The Act stipulated that when any status female Indian married a man without status both would lose their Indian rights, as would their descendants.[78] Another aspect of the Gradual Enfranchisement Act made non-Aboriginal women, if they married status Indian men, legal Indians. The "marrying-in" provision followed the convention of the time in the dominant society that a woman's identity derived from her father (if not married), or husband if married.[79] While gender discrimination received some support among the patrilineal Anishinabeg, many of the matrilineal Six Nations (or Iroquois), the Haudenosaunee, opposed it.[80]

Prime Minister Macdonald in 1871 held together a fragile country, scarcely four million strong, a country divided by deep regional and linguistic differences. Determined to prevent US economic expansion into Prairie lands north of the 49th parallel, Canada had expanded tenfold in just four years, from the Atlantic to the Pacific. It became one of the world's largest countries after the transfer of Rupert's Land and the North-Western Territory into the Dominion on 15 July 1870, followed by the entry of British Columbia into Confederation on 20 July 1871.[81] To entice British Columbia into the union, the new Dominion had promised to build a transcontinental railway to the new province. Macdonald saw the completion of the railway as the capstone of his work to build a strong British North American nation.

At the time of Confederation 175,000 Indians and Métis lived in what is known today as Western Canada.[82] Euro-Canadian settlement required the displacement of the Indigenous peoples on the Prairies. Both Conservatives and Liberals agreed on this. Although the Red River Métis under Louis Riel ably defended their own territory initially in 1869–70, in the long term they failed. The Métis province they had aspired to form in 1870 was soon transformed into a non-Indigenous one within less than a decade, due to the magnitude of the land rush from Ontario. The First Nations in the North West themselves soon faced the westward expansion of tens of thousands of Euro-Canadian settlers.

Macdonald and his political contemporaries believed that Canadian law applied before the signing of the treaties in Manitoba and the North-West Territories from July 1870.[83] The First Nations of the region, in fact, were already subjects of Canada and of Her Majesty's Canadian Government (the Crown) as were the Indians of Central and Eastern Canada whether or not treaties had been made with them.[84] The Government of Canada assumed its authority over the Plains and its peoples before any negotiations with them. The Dominion, for example, began in 1871 to send surveyors to divide 200 million acres of land into 1.25 million homestead-sized quarter sections,[85] before the western treaties were made. Those individuals who would build a homestead, and settle the land, obtained 160 acres of free land. The Canadian politicians saw the self-sufficient farmer and his family as the building block of western settlement.[86] The Dominion Lands Act of 1872 confirmed that the federal government had the right to impose it before the signing of the treaties. The establishment of the North-West Mounted Police (NWMP) by John A. Macdonald in 1873[87] and the creation of the Department of the Interior that same year provide two additional examples of the Dominion acting before obtaining prior agreements with the Prairie First Nations.[88] Furthermore, no mention was made to the passage of the Indian Act of 1876 at the signings of treaties Six in 1876 and Seven in 1877.

The treaties proved far more difficult for the Canadian government to secure than originally anticipated. The Government of Canada had not anticipated the pressure from the First Nations between Lake Superior and the Rocky Mountains. The First Nations endorsed the sharing of their land, but only if it was for mutual benefit. In his book, *No Surrender: The Land Remains Indigenous*, published in 2019, the historian Sheldon Krasowski describes in great detail how the Anishinabeg of the North-West Angle (northwestern Ontario) valued their hunting grounds, fisheries, and wild rice fields. The newcomers must recognize Indigenous Title and help them to adjust to a new way of life. The negotiations proved complex, and in fact, Canada had to try four times (from 1869 to 1873) to secure the North-West Angle, or Treaty Three.[89]

From 1867 to the year of his death in 1891, John A. Macdonald served as prime minister of Canada, with the exception of the four years of Liberal administration from 1874 to 1878. The Liberals under Alexander Mackenzie basically adopted Macdonald's Indian policy in the North West. The desirability and inevitability of assimilation was a shared belief of both political parties. The Conservatives and the Liberals alike worked to make treaties, place the First Nations on reserves, and abolish First Nations self-government.[90] In 1887 Macdonald made his often-cited declaration: "The great aim of our legislation has been to do away with the tribal system and assimilate the Indian people in all respects with the inhabitants of the Dominion, as speedily as they are fit for the change."[91] Macdonald maintained that Indians must be educated, Christianized, and transformed into self-reliant farmers. He believed this was possible. The First Nations

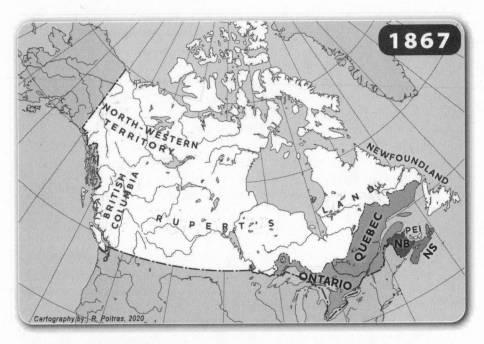

Map 1.1 Canada in 1867.

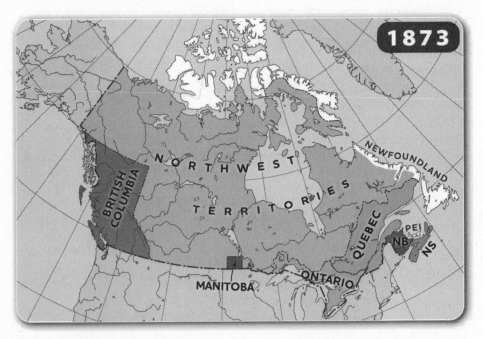

Map 1.2 Canada in 1873.

of southern Ontario became his model. Did not agriculture now provide the basic livelihood of the Mississauga at New Credit? Had not
the Six Nations on the Grand River adjusted well to Euro-Canadian
farming?[92]

Prime minister from 1874 to 1878, Alexander Mackenzie consolidated
the various laws relating to Indian Affairs. John A. Macdonald's comment on the Liberals' Indian Act of 1876 showed a deeper concern for
the First Nations than what is normally attributed to him. The leader of
the Opposition spoke against the suggestion that "every Indian, when
he becomes 21 years of age [gain] the right of absolute disposal of his
lands. I am afraid it would introduce into this country a system by
which land-sharks could get hold of their estates."[93] The Conservatives
accepted the Indian Act of 1876 upon their return to power two years
later. The Grand General Indian Council of Ontario in July 1876 initially
endorsed the revised Indian Act.[94] Throughout his final years in power,
Macdonald maintained a good relationship with the moderate Grand
Indian Council that represented a number of Anishinabeg communities
from throughout southern Ontario.[95] New Credit Head Chief Peter E.
Jones invited the prime minister in 1882 to attend the opening of New
Credit's new council house, the location of that year's meetings of the
Grand Council of Ontario.[96]

Back in office on a program of a "national policy" – higher tariffs to
protect Eastern Canadian industry, Western settlement, and a transcontinental railway – an enthusiastic Macdonald became his own minister of the interior, with responsibility for Indian Affairs. He also kept
the NWMP directly under his control.[97] Already he served as prime
minister, party leader, and minister of the interior at a time when the
Canadian Pacific Railway project demanded an enormous amount
of his time. He left Lawrence Vankoughnet, his deputy minister, in
what became the Department of Indian Affairs in 1880, in charge in
Ottawa. Edgar Dewdney was his Indian commissioner for the North-
West Territories from 1879 to 1888, where he enjoyed almost autocratic
powers.[98]

C.J. Brydges, a close Macdonald political confidant,[99] provides
insight into how the prime minister regarded the First Nations in 1879.
The Hudson's Bay Company's land commissioner notes that the prime
minister was "determined to do everything in his power to see that
the Indians are kept in a satisfied condition so as to avoid any of the
troubles which have arisen in the United States."[100] There was a potential military threat. Alexander Morris, lieutenant governor of Manitoba
and the North-West Territories, estimated in 1873 that the Plains First
Nations "could place 5,000 mounted warriors in the field."[101] Native

warfare was a major concern, as Canada's entire government budget in 1870 totaled only $19 million at a time when the United States spent $20 million annually on its Indian wars alone.[102]

Macdonald defended his government's Indian policies in the House of Commons. His spontaneous responses in Parliament reveal a great deal about his own mixed personal views of Indigenous people. The prime minister combined a romantic sentimentalism for North American Indians with a total disregard for their right to keep their ancestral cultures and religions. When he proposed the formation of a Department of Indian Affairs in 1880, Macdonald argued that it would advance "the interests of the Indians, civilizing them and putting them in the condition of white men." Then Macdonald added an historical reference: "We must remember that they are the original owners of the soil, of which they have been dispossessed by the covetousness or ambition of our ancestors. Perhaps, if Columbus had not discovered this continent – had left them alone – they would have worked out a tolerable civilization of their own. At all events, the Indians have been great sufferers by the discovery of America, and the transfer to it of a large white population."[103]

After the buffalo herds vanished on the Canadian side of the international border, Macdonald knew fully about the Indians' malnutrition, sickness, and death. He reported on southern Alberta in the *Annual Report of the Department of the Interior* in 1879, "The Indians were reduced to such extremities that they eat mice, their dogs and even their buffalo skins, and they greedily devoured meat raw when given to them."[104] He increased spending in the Department of Indian Affairs, but only initially.[105]

The voters came first. The First Nations did not have the franchise. In 1882 the Conservative government directed the little money they had in times of budgetary constraint for nation- and economy-building projects like canals, railways, and land surveys. The Canadian historian Robert Page notes, "The Macdonald Government lost its perspective on human priorities, such as the Métis land claims or starvation on the Indian reserves."[106] Beginning in the summer of 1882, Indian Affairs cut back the rations for Plains Indians by "between one-half to one-quarter."[107] Garrett Wilson, a distinguished Regina lawyer turned best-selling author, described in *Frontier Farewell*, his 2007 award-winning study of the 1870s and early 1880s in the Canadian West,[108] how the Macdonald government "made no attempt to disguise its policy of starvation." It used it first to force Sitting Bull and the Sioux (Dakota) refugees who had sought haven in Saskatchewan after the Battle of Little Big Horn back to the United States. Macdonald then turned the same strategy against the Treaty Indians. Unless they accepted life on the reservations, and learned the new and strange ways of Euro-Canadian farming, there would be no food. In Parliament, Wilson notes, "there was no criticism of this policy, only concern for the cost of feeding the multitude on the prairie. It was the temper of the times."[109] The Liberals, who in office had been even more devoted to government economy than Macdonald,[110] actually attacked him for making federal aid too generous.[111] In effect, they accused Macdonald of not starving the Indians enough.

The prime minister did worry about the quality of supplies provided to the Plains First Nations, those who followed government instructions. In a private letter to Indian Commissioner Dewdney, Macdonald insisted on 19 November 1883, "If there has been any connivance by any of our Agents or carelessness in securing inferior articles, they should be dismissed without mercy."[112] The great distances, and the lack of a proper transportation network before the completion of the CPR made the dispatch of provisions challenging. The shortage of equipment needed to mill grain into palatable food complicated the situation, as did the diminished fall 1883 harvest due to early frost. Mismanagement in the distribution of food added to the chronic malnutrition and hunger-related disease.[113]

Before 1886 neither Macdonald nor Vankoughnet had ever travelled west of southern Ontario.[114] The prime minister knew little about the Plains peoples, apart from the expenditures the Department of Indian Affairs made in the West. By the end of his administration approximately 95 per cent of the funds Parliament allocated to Indian Affairs went to Manitoba, the North-West Territories, and British Columbia.[115] The Plains Indian file was under Macdonald's watch, but he gave it little attention at the very time the amount of correspondence from the North West became a flood. The number of letters received at the Indian Affairs headquarters more than doubled between 1875 and 1880, and doubled again in the 1880s.[116]

In the early 1880s Macdonald approved the establishment of federally funded Indian technical schools. The prime minister explained in the House of Commons that he expected these industrial schools aimed at older students would contribute to the formation of "native teachers, and perhaps native clergymen and men who will not only be able to read and write, but who will learn trades."[117] The cooperation between the Christian churches and the federal government now became hand-in-glove as the cash poor government depended on the churches to run them.[118] The first of three "industrial schools," a large boarding school established on the Prairies away from the reserves, opened in 1883. All three soon were starved for funds. Within four years no money existed for improvements, as in Vankoughnet's words, this would "involve an expense to meet which the Department at the present time has not the means at its disposal."[119] Lack of proper oversight of the badly funded schools led to the mistreatment of students. The loss of their culture and language had enormous and grave long-term consequences. Only recently have the effects of trauma and inter-generational trauma become known.[120] In hindsight one asks, without the support of the children's parents themselves, could the schools have succeeded?

One aspect of his Indian Affairs career does separate Macdonald from other contemporaries: he believed in the importance of educating Indian girls as well as boys.[121] Macdonald made a gesture towards women's rights in the last months of his administration. On 31 January 1891, a Mohawk woman, Floretta Maracle, was appointed to an Indian Affairs clerkship. A decade earlier, Maracle had been one of the top students at the Mohawk Institute, the Anglican Indian residential school at Brantford, Ontario. In the 1880s nearly fifty male and female graduates became Indian schoolteachers.[122] Maracle had taught at a Six Nations day school for nearly ten years before she became the first status Indian female to receive a position in the Department of Indian Affairs.[123] She joined another former Mohawk Institute student, Joseph Delisle, who had been appointed as a clerk in 1880,[124] and David Osagee, a 21-year-old Ojibwe from Walpole Island,[125] who in 1889 had obtained a clerkship in the department's finance office.[126]

To those with little knowledge of Indigenous issues, Macdonald appeared well briefed on his Indian files. The Canadian journalist E.B. Biggar, one of the few members of the press to comment on the prime minister's views of the Indigenous peoples, wrote in his *Anecdotal Life of Sir John Macdonald*, published in 1891, "There could be nothing more instructive and entertaining than one of his conversational speeches on Indian affairs, of which department he was head for several years. No question would be asked but he had an answer for it and could give off-hand a history of each appointment, or a clear and instructive statement of every case of difficulty that had come up; while his knowledge of the character of the Indians was marvellous."[127] The reality was totally different from this.

As independent sovereign nations,[128] the Plains people felt totally betrayed. They looked on the treaties, in the words of the historians Walter Hildebrandt and Brian Hubner, to help them "benefit from the development of their lands in the same way the settlers and newcomers were to benefit."[129] Instead of the expected partnership based on mutual

1.1 Sir John A. Macdonald's study. Sir John's study at Earnscliffe, printed in *The Dominion Illustrated*, 20 June 1891, 581. The photo indicates the disorganization in his office at home in Ottawa, towards the end of his administration. C-011480. tif LAC.

respect and assistance, the First Nations soon found themselves subjugated and marginalized, and for those who openly resisted – starved. As the historian Hugh Dempsey writes, "The Indians believed they were being deliberately starved, so that the government could exterminate them."[130] Fortunately for Canada, despite the gross violation of the treaty promises, the vast majority of Plains Indian First Nations did not join the Métis resistance under Louis Riel in the spring of 1885.[131]

John A. Macdonald turned 70 years old in January 1885, and on account of his declining energy additional problems arose. His secretary, Joseph Pope, later admitted his many duties as prime minister had "left him little time for departmental administration."[132] After 1883 Macdonald developed the habit of putting aside some of his most challenging files to be looked at later. New incoming files soon buried these old ones.[133] In 1887 he surrendered the Department of Indian Affairs portfolio.

A contemporary First Nations assessment of Macdonald's performance in the West exists. Robert Steinhauer was a young Cree college student from Whitefish Lake, northeast of Edmonton. In 1886 Steinhauer sharply critiqued Macdonald's Indigenous policy. In his home community, Steinhauer's father, the Indigenous Methodist minister, Henry B. Steinhauer (or Shawahnekizhek), had taught the Cree how to farm and to overcome the disaster of the demise of the plains buffalo.[134] Then an undergraduate at Victoria College in Cobourg, Ontario, Robert Steinhauer wrote an article for *Acta Victoriana*, the college magazine. In "The Indian Question," he underlined the disappointments endured by the First Nations on the Prairies: "Ever since the treaties were signed, there has been much discontent, and complaints made by him [the Indian]. He asks those who have taken the ownership of his country to give him his rights, at least the fulfilment of the promises made to him." In the place of competent government intermediaries, they received Indian agents, selected "because they happen to be friends and right-hand supporters of the Government." In authority over them, Ottawa had placed "low and unprincipled characters."[135]

A serious challenge to the Government of Canada came on the Saskatchewan Plains in the spring of 1885. Worrying indicators surfaced in June 1884 after Louis Riel returned from the United States to help the Métis in Saskatchewan settle their claims of Indigenous Title. Unfortunately, at the same time, the financial problems of the Canadian Pacific Railway increased. Lack of cash threatened the completion of the CPR, the essential link in Macdonald's vision for the creation of a country stretching from east to west. Miraculously, the prime minister kept money flowing to the railway, but by applying most of his time and remaining energy to the CPR, he made huge additional mistakes in the vast area generally referred to as the "North West."[136]

One Euro-Canadian person living there advanced a visionary plan. William Henry Jackson (1861–1952) was Ontario-born and -raised and had attended University College at the University of Toronto, where he studied Classics from 1877 to 1880. His storekeeper father went bankrupt in late 1879. With his wife, he moved west, eventually to Prince Albert, very close to Batoche, the major Métis settlement in the South Saskatchewan River Valley. Will Jackson joined his parents in 1882. He forged a deep emotional link with the Métis. Romantically, Jackson saw the former buffalo hunters as the modern equivalent of the ancient Greeks, whom he idolized from his Classical studies. The young idealist came to see justice in the Métis cause, and volunteered in 1884 to become Louis Riel's English-language secretary. Jackson participated in the preparation of a petition that argued for Indigenous rights and for settler self-government. He opposed Central Canada's attempt to control its Prairie colony and imagined a society in which English and French, Indians and Métis would be equals.[137]

In Riel's camp, Jackson converted to Catholicism, and then – upon the outbreak of the resistance of 1885 – he accepted Riel as the prophet of a reformed Christian church. When the Canadians took Batoche on 12 May 1885, they seized Jackson, who had never advocated armed resistance or fought in any battle. Tried in Regina, the court judged the visionary insane, and committed Will Jackson to the first insane asylum established in Manitoba and the North West, at Lower Fort Garry, north of Winnipeg. During his stay in the asylum, Jackson wrote a letter to his family, with this assessment of Riel: "The oppression of the aboriginals has been the crying sin of the white race in America and they have at last found a voice." In the same letter, he asked for reading material, "for the monotony of this place is enough to drive a man crazy of itself." He requested the Bible, Horace's poems, Plato's *Republic*, and the American economist Henry George's *Progress and Poverty*.[138]

Will Jackson's residency at Lower Fort Garry proved brief. After only several months, he walked away from the light security institution, crossed the US border, and made his way to Chicago. He now self-identified as Métis, and later changed his name to the French-sounding Honoré Joseph Jaxon. At the turn of the century, Honoré Jaxon worked in the Chicago labour movement, in the Chicago Federation of Labor, and as an editorial writer at the *Union Labor Advocate*, its monthly publication. In the city, he gained the respect of Frank Lloyd Wright, the famous Chicago architect, who became a personal friend.[139]

During the troubles of 1885 the strain on the prime minister reached new heights. On 6 July, Macdonald lost control, and in Parliament he vigorously attacked the Indigenous peoples: "I have not hesitated to tell this House, again and again, that we could not always hope to maintain peace with the Indians; that the savage was still a savage, and that until he ceased to be savage, we were always in danger of a collision, in danger of war, in danger of an outbreak." Macdonald continued, "Look at the United States; along the whole frontier of the United States there has been war; millions have been expended there; their best and their bravest have fallen." Then, the prime minister made an extraordinary statement, one that awaits documentary confirmation: "I personally knew General Custer, and admired the gallant soldier, the American hero, yet he went, and he fell with his band, and not a man was left to tell the tale – they were all swept away."[140]

Alleged Indian involvement in the events of 1885 led the Conservatives to enact a number of draconian measures after the suppression of the troubles. The prime minister's greatest excess came with the Battleford trials of those Plains Indians accused of participation. The trials were conducted in English, a language none of the accused understood, and held without legal counsel. As the historian David Hall notes, "In effect Indians were tried in kangaroo courts that had little interest in the truth and were determined to produce convictions quickly and cheaply."[141] The eight First Nations men sentenced to death were publicly executed on 27 November 1885, on a massive gallows, even though Canadian law already banned such spectacles.[142] The prime minister held that the execution of these men, as well as Louis Riel, "ought to convince the Red Man that the White Man governs."[143] Before the mass executions, the federal government had tried and incarcerated Chief Poundmaker and Chief Big Bear, both of whom had, in fact, acted as peacemakers during the troubles.[144]

After the events of 1885 the federal government worked for the complete subjugation of the Plains Cree. The Department of Indian Affairs deposed chiefs and councilors of what it called "rebel" bands. Over a dozen bands held to be unfaithful to the Crown had their annuity payments specified in Treaty Six suspended from 1885 to 1888, without due process or any legal authority.[145] As the historians Blair Stonechild and Bill Waiser write, "The Canadian government chose to deliberately portray the Indians as willing accomplices of the Métis."[146] The authorities made the "pass system," already introduced in 1882, official in 1885, although it was totally illegal.[147]

In Central Canada, Macdonald's policy was an improvement on his abysmal performance on the Plains. He benefited in Ontario from personal connections with several middle-class Indigenous people well integrated into the settler society. As superintendent of Indian Affairs, for instance, he had gone out of his way to help Thomas Green, a bright Iroquois graduate of the Mohawk Institute, and later of Brantford High School.[148] Macdonald supported his efforts to complete his course in civil engineering at McGill University, which Green did in 1882. In turn, the young Mohawk assisted the prime minister in early 1886 with some very important advice. In 1885–6 Green worked as a surveyor in the North West. From Regina, Green wrote to Macdonald on 8 March 1886 to suggest that the dispatch of the army was not the way to win over the Plains Indians. Instead, he suggested, "a dozen, or so, of the principal chiefs of the different tribes of the N.W. Indians" should be taken to Ottawa to meet with the prime minister. "Good, honest and reliable interpreters," he added, should be hired to accompany them to see "the principal sights & cities of Ontario & Quebec" and "the most prosperous Indian reserves of these provinces." In short, Green wrote, "let them see how their Indian brethren are prospering in those provinces; let them understand that the Indian can subsist like the whiteman where there is no game; and let them understand that the government do not wish to exterminate them."[149]

Green's advice influenced Macdonald. Taking advantage of the newly completed CPR, the federal government in early fall 1886 sponsored two tours of what came to be called the "Loyal Chiefs" to Central Canada. These visits were a reward to the chiefs for their support during the troubles of 1885. They also were designed to show them the numerical and manufacturing strength of rapidly industrializing Central Canada. Numerically, the two provinces of Ontario and Quebec with a combined population of over three million people outnumbered two hundred to one the approximately fifteen thousand or so Plains Indians on reserves spread across the North West in the late nineteenth century.[150] At the same time, Macdonald wanted the "Loyal Chiefs" to attend the unveiling of a major monument in Brantford, Ontario, erected in honour of Joseph Brant, the great Iroquois leader who had sided with Britain in the American Revolution.[151] The prime minister held the Mohawk war chief in high regard, as he told the House of Commons in early May 1883, "An Indian, without a drop of white blood in his veins he was still a gentleman of culture."[152] Macdonald's plans for the Plains First Nations were modelled on the Six Nations and Mississauga communities in southern Ontario who had successfully adjusted to Euro-Canadian agriculture.

The two Blackfoot (Siksika) chiefs, Crowfoot and Three Bulls, left Alberta first in late September on a train to Regina, and then Winnipeg. In one hour they travelled across the Plains the same distance as on a day's journey on a horse.[153] The Prairie people had a name, "fire wagons," for the huge objects that travelled along like wagons breathing fire as they moved.[154] The two chiefs first visited Montreal, which at the time had a population of approximately two hundred thousand.[155] The majority in Canada's largest city were French Canadians. The Blackfoot to this day call the French, *nii?tsaapiikoan*, or "real White Men,"[156] as they were the first Europeans they met. The two Blackfoot next travelled to Quebec City and then to Ottawa, where the Blood (Kainai) chiefs Red Crow and One Spot, and the North Peigan (Piikuni) chief, North Axe, all Blackfoot speakers, joined them.[157] Surprise was constant for the chiefs – elevators, telephones, newspapers, and huge oceangoing steamships – but the trip did not convince them to become

1.2 Chief Crowfoot and children in 1884. The picture is incredibly tragic.
Two years later all nine children, several of whom were his own, had died of
tuberculosis. NA-1104-1 by Robert Goldthorpe Brook. Courtesy of Glenbow
Archives, Archives and Special Collections, University of Calgary.

Euro-Canadians. Upon their return, Father Léon Doucet, a Catholic
missionary to the Blackfoot-speaking peoples, recorded Crowfoot's and
Three Bulls' reaction to the buildings and the technology. The Catholic
priest commented, "They admired these marvels," but they returned as
proudly Indian as before.[158]

The prime minister invited the Alberta Blackfoot chiefs to visit Earnscliffe, his home, located on top of the limestone cliffs overlooking the
Ottawa River, with a fine view across the river to the Gatineau Hills.[159]
A group photo survives of Three Bulls, Crowfoot, Red Crow, North
Axe, and One Spot, with their interpreters, Father Albert Lacombe and
Jean L'Heureux, a shot that was taken on Earnscliffe's front lawn the
morning of Saturday, 9 October 1886.[160] Canada's first prime minister
and the celebrated Blackfoot (Siksika) chief spoke together in Earnscliffe's sitting room, where the Macdonalds received visitors, with

1.3 Five chiefs with their interpreters on the lawn in front of Earnscliffe on the morning of Saturday, 9 Oct. 1886. *L-R back row*: Father Albert Lacombe, Jean L'Heureux (interpreters). *L-R middle row*: Three Bulls (Blackfoot), Crowfoot (Blackfoot), Red Crow (Blood). *L-R front row*: North Axe (North Peigan), One Spot (Blood). NA-13-2, by John Woodruff, Department of the Interior. Courtesy of Glenbow Archives, Archives and Special Collections, University of Calgary.

1.4 Four Saskatchewan chiefs posed for a formal photograph in Brantford, 16 Oct. 1886. Ahtahkakoop (Cree) seated on the left, beside Kahkewistahaw (Cree). Mistawassis (Cree) is seated on the right. In the back row, Louis O'Soup (Saulteaux, Ojibwe) is on the left, and interpreter Peter Hourie is on the right. C-019258 LAC.

Father Lacombe acting as the interpreter.[161] In parting, Lady Macdonald presented a photo of her husband to Chief Crowfoot.[162] The prime minister gave each of the visitors $25, and promised, as the *Ottawa Evening Journal* reported, "to find a market for their surplus productions."[163]

Ten days later, in the early afternoon of 23 October, Macdonald again showed his interest in the Plains Indians who had been loyal in 1885. The prime minister welcomed the three Cree chiefs from Saskatchewan to Earnscliffe: Ahtahkakoop, Mistawasis, Kahkewistahaw ("Flying in a Circle"), and O'Soup, the Ojibwe (Saulteaux) member of the group.[164] They visited on their return from Brantford and the unveiling of the Brant monument. Both Mistawasis and Ahtahkakoop, unlike the visiting Blackfoot chiefs, were Christians. Ahtahkakoop greatly impressed Macdonald. The two men were approximately the same age, around 70. Through interpreter Peter Hourie, the prime minister asked if Ahtahkakoop would give a Cree name to his 17-year-old daughter. The Macdonalds were devoted to their daughter Mary, a victim of hydrocephalus, a debilitating disease leading to a great enlargement of the head. The semi-invalid had a major speech defect, was unable to walk, and had only limited use of her hands.[165] Every evening on his return from work, the devoted father spent an hour with his disabled daughter.[166] Ahtahkakoop consented, and gave Mary part of his name, which meant "Starblanket" in English. You will be called "Ahtahk," which means the "the Star."[167] Later that afternoon, the prime minister and his First Nations visitors met with the Privy Council, or Cabinet Secretariat, in the Parliament Buildings. After a short visit to Montreal, the Saskatchewan group departed for the West. Ahtahkakoop arrived back to his reserve in mid-November.[168]

By late 1886 Macdonald had accepted the reality that Canada's obligations to the Plains Indians, once envisaged as transitional and temporary, were actually permanent, obligatory, and costly.[169] The Ontario Liberal MP Malcolm Cameron, in April 1886, vigorously attacked in Parliament the Conservative government's incompetence in handling Indigenous issues on the Prairies, citing the government's own reports and those of several Protestant missionaries. The tired prime minister[170] never issued a rebuttal to Cameron, but instead directed Department of Indian Affairs officials in the North West to investigate the charges. As the Canadian historian Sarah Carter writes, "The inquest was scarcely independent and impartial; officials were asked to probe into accusations of their own wrongdoing."[171] Macdonald simply arranged for Indian Affairs to produce *The Facts Respecting Indian Administration in the North-West*. In late 1886, on the eve of a general election, he had

1.5 Sir John A. Macdonald, 1888, surrounded by papers and books on all sides. Photo taken in his study at Earnscliffe. LAC, online MIKAN 3218704.

the pamphlet printed and distributed across the country at public expense.[172] Having lost interest in the Indian Affairs portfolio, Macdonald relinquished it in 1887.[173]

Without question, Sir John A. Macdonald's record with the Indigenous peoples in the North West in 1885 was totally reprehensible, and his approval of the execution of Louis Riel a colossal error. Although repeatedly warned of the discontent in the early 1880s, the federal government had taken no real action to redress grievances. In the mid-1980s Canadian historians began to take a more critical perspective of Macdonald's administration of the Plains First Nations. John Tobias opened up the re-examination with his important 1983 article, "Canada's Subjugation of the Plains Cree, 1879–1885," published in the *Canadian Historical Review*,[174] and this was joined by Gerald Friesen's *The Canadian Prairies: A History*, one year later.[175] The Cree historian Blair Stonechild followed with his probing 1986 article using oral history testimony, "The Indian View of the 1885 Uprising."[176] Forty years later, James Daschuk, in *Clearing the Plains: Disease, Politics of Starvation, and the Loss of Aboriginal Life*, published in 2013,[177] underlined in the greatest detail the disastrous consequences of Canada's allegedly farsighted, generous, and supposedly honourable Plains Indian policy.

Sir John A. Macdonald appears in a more favourable light when his policies in Central Canada are compared with those on the Plains. In Ontario, a number of First Nations individuals recognized a positive contribution of the prime minister after the passage of his Electoral Franchise Act of 1885.[178] This Act gave the federal vote to all adult male Indians east of Manitoba who met the necessary property requirements. It recognized them as "persons," free to vote in federal elections. Contrary to a modern opinion, males who met the qualifications were not required to give up their Indian status.[179] In his own words, Macdonald found successful Indian farmers, for example, to be "steady, respectable, law abiding and God fearing people, and I do not see why they should not have the vote."[180] Macdonald wanted to bring educated male Indians who met the necessary property qualifications into the mainstream system. Only thirteen years later, in 1898, the Laurier government abolished the Electoral Franchise Act. Canada would wait until 1960 before registered First Nations people living on reserves gained the right to vote – without surrendering their Indian status.[181]

Peter E. Jones, MD (Queen's), the third son of Peter and Eliza Field Jones, his English wife, served in 1885 as chief of the Mississauga of New Credit. He congratulated the prime minister on the granting of the vote: "My Dear Sir John, – I should have written to you some time ago to thank you for making the Indian a 'person' in the Franchise Bill ... I now thank you on the part of the memory of my father and on the part of myself, as for many years we advocated and urged this step as the one most likely to elevate the aborigines to the position more approaching the independence of the whites."[182] The New Credit Mississauga placed the prime minister's portrait in their Council House.[183] Because he had protected their right to revenues from an 1820 trust agreement on their Credit lands in 1857, and later endorsed their claims for lost revenues from relinquishment of their Credit, Oakville, and Bronte lands,[184] John A. Macdonald had credibility among these Anishinabeg.

Support for the federal franchise came from other Anishinabeg communities in southern Ontario, too. A memorial from the Alderville Mississauga, the Ojibwe group who had relocated from Grape Island on the Bay of Quinte in the late 1830s, endorsed the extension of the franchise. The Alderville chief and council wrote the prime minister to say, "We shall always gratefully remember his goodness and Justice and the Honor and dignity he has conferred upon us."[185] Macdonald's support came from the Alderville elite, members of the community who had land and political roles.[186]

From the Georgina Island Ojibwe community on Lake Simcoe, north of Toronto, Chief Charles Big Canoe and band councillor James Ashquabe thanked the prime minister for his "earnest efforts to promote the welfare of the Indian people throughout the whole Dominion [...] we thank you most cordially for the gift of the franchise."[187] Big Canoe had taught himself to read and to write English. A farmer, he also kept cattle. At the time of a 1915 visit by a reporter from the *Toronto Star Weekly*, Keche Chemon (or Big Canoe) lived in a large frame house, painted white with green trimmings surrounded by a green lawn and flower gardens. Inside his parlour he had an attractive carpet on the floor, good upholstered chairs, and on the central table lay (beside the visitors' book) a book of hymns printed both in English and Ojibwe. On the exterior, Charles Big Canoe had adjusted very well to British Canada. But on no account did the respected Elder want to surrender his identity or his reserve. When the reporter stated, "The Government gave this island to the Indians, didn't they?" the chief drew himself up and corrected his visitor, "Oh no! We reserved this island when we sold our other property."[188]

Prime Minister Macdonald had two Six Nations acquaintances in Ontario, in addition to several middle-class Mississauga. He worked closely, for example, with Oronhyatekha (or Peter Martin), the prominent Mohawk doctor who later headed the fraternal organization, the Independent Order of Foresters.[189] After Oronhyatekha campaigned for Macdonald and the Conservatives in the 1872 election, he was named physician to the Tyendinaga Mohawk.[190] In 1884 Oronhyatekha spoke at the centennial of the arrival of the Mohawk to the Bay of Quinte. He is reported as stating that John A. Macdonald "had reason to be a friend to the Indians as he had got the idea of confederation from the confederacy of the Six Nations."[191] So great was the Mohawk doctor's admiration for Macdonald that he mentioned in a 1882 letter that he and his wife had decided to name their newborn son, "John Alexander." They planned to do this "so that in after years we could tell him after whom he was named and to instruct him to emulate his namesake in love and devotion to his country."[192] Although Oronhyatekha, like Dr Jones, strongly supported Macdonald's 1885 Electoral Franchise Act, he too kept his Indian status.[193]

Between 1857 and 1876 only one application for enfranchisement had been accepted. Resistance to enfranchisement remained intense. As the historian John Leslie has written, "Indian people simply wanted to remain as Indians. Culture, kin, and language were powerful bonds.[194]

Another contact of the prime minister was John Elliott, a young Mohawk leader at Six Nations[195] who sought to replace the hereditary council with an elected one. Those in favour of ending the rule of the traditional council had the support of one-fifth of the adult male population of the Six Nations community in 1890.[196] Elliott had been a student at the Mohawk Institute at the same time as Thomas Green.[197] Afterward he had studied at the Agricultural College at Guelph. A 1930 summary of former Mohawk Institute students recalled Elliott as a "great orator."[198] He worked first as a reporter for the Toronto *Mail*,[199] then in Ottawa as a clerk in the Department of Indian Affairs. He was a strong supporter of the prime minister and the Conservative Party. In a 10 January 1887 letter, Elliott recommended that Mohawk Fred O. Loft's letters to the department should go unanswered, as he "is a stiff & bigotted Grit, & desires to make a handle of everything which he elicits in the shape of information from 'Headquarters' against our party & Government."[200] John Elliott did not enfranchise.[201]

Through correspondence, Macdonald kept in touch with his First Nations contacts. The prime minister himself wrote Dr Peter E. Jones on 31 August 1886 to say that he hoped one day to see an Indian MP in the House: "The Franchise Act has now been in force for a year, and the Indians must see that their treaty rights have not been in the slightest degree affected since it became law [...] I hope to see some day the Indian race represented by one of themselves on the floor of the House of Commons."[202]

Dr Peter Jones had so fully integrated into mainstream Canadian society he was one of the few Indian leaders to accept the 1884 Indian Advancement Act, which provided for the annual election of councillors, limited power of taxation, responsibility for public health, and the enforcement of by-laws.[203] Macdonald proposed the bill to give the First Nations, "the opportunity of adapting themselves to the white system as much as possible."[204] The Mississauga of New Credit accepted becoming in effect a municipality, which freed them from the Indian Act's rules of wardship.[205] In 1886 the prime minister invited Dr Jones to make suggestions about changes to the Indian Act. He did. His recommendations that the Act's paternalist wording be removed and a greater degree of self-government be included were ignored.[206]

Peter Jones strongly supported the Conservative Party and its leader, yet he never applied to enfranchise. Macdonald understood the decision taken by Jones and other professionals who chose not to give up their Indian status. As the prime minister explained in the House of Commons on 4 May 1885, "They prefer to stick to the clan system, just as, until lately, in my own country, the Highlanders stuck to their clan system in the highland of Scotland. They desired not to be severed from their brethren."[207]

Sir John A. Macdonald knew a deep resentment existed in some communities against elected councils and municipal status, which were seen as measures designed to undermine directly First Nations sovereignty.[208] On 6 September 1886, just a month or so before the Western chiefs called at his home in Ottawa, Macdonald visited the Six Nations. A contemporary photo shows that a huge crowd met him at the Council House. The support appeared universal until the prime minister entered the building and gave his speech in English to the council, which was immediately interpreted into Mohawk. To his great disappointment, Macdonald learned that, in the most advanced and affluent Indian community in Canada, many feared assimilation. Chief William Smith, the Mohawk spokesperson for many of the hereditary chiefs, came out against both Macdonald's franchise bill of 1885 and the Indian Advancement Act of 1884.[209] Why should Indians participate in Canadian elections? Why should Indians adopt elected municipal governments? The Grand River Haudenosaunee emphasized their independence and sovereignty with their own political institutions. They were allies, not subjects of the British Crown.[210]

Macdonald chose not to pressure the Six Nations of the Grand River to adopt the elected system, as he did the Iroquois communities of Akwesasne in eastern Ontario and Kahnawake near Montreal.[211] At the Iroquois community of Tyendinaga, the Mohawk of the Bay of Quinte had elected their first Band Council in 1870. New Credit and Tyendinaga, well known to Macdonald since the late 1830s, stood among his most favoured First Nations communities. Among the "progressive" faction at Tyendinaga, the prime minister had the backing

1.6 Sir John A. Macdonald standing before the Six Nations of the Grand River Council House at Ohsweken, 6 Sept. 1886. The prime minister appears with a flower in his coat buttonhole before a large sign held by a First Nations man inscribed: "Sir John Our Great Chief." C-6134 LAC.

of Councillor Archibald Culbertson, the son of his acquaintance John Culbertson. Another ally was Chief Sampson Green, once a top student at the Mohawk Institute.[212] First elected chief in 1870, Green won in subsequent elections until 1888.[213] In Tyendinaga's memorial to Macdonald congratulating him on his 1878 election victory, Chief Green and Archie Culbertson's names head the list of five individuals who made this statement: "We cannot refrain from telling you the peculiar pleasure we experienced on hearing that you had become the *head* of the *Department of the Interior* and consequently Superintendent General of Indian Affairs as we have long been aware of the great interest you have always taken and shown for our people in this Dominion."[214] On Macdonald's visit to the community just before the federal election of

Map 1.3 Central Canada, late nineteenth century.

1887, Chief Green presented him with a fine cane.[215] Half a century later, Macdonald's appearance in the community was still remembered.[216]

In his interventions in the parliamentary debate in spring 1885 over the Electoral Franchise Act, evidence exists that John A. Macdonald endorsed biological racism. Although he accepted that adult male Indians in Eastern and Central Canada who met the property qualification deserved the federal vote – without losing their Indian status – he opposed Chinese enfranchisement.[217] Macdonald stated in the House of Commons in 1885 that the Chinese have "no British instincts or British feelings or aspirations, and therefore ought not to have a vote."[218]

British Columbian MPs had called for Chinese exclusion since 1878.[219] The prime minister apparently (no evidence at least has yet come to light) did not know any Canadians of Chinese background, which helps to explain the vehemence of his remarks. In early May 1885, he made an uncharacteristically vicious statement of unreasoning prejudice. Macdonald raised in the House of Commons the dangers of miscegenation: "The truth is, that all natural history, all ethnology, shows that, while the crosses of the Aryan races are successful – while a mixture of all those races which are known or believed to spring from a common origin is more or less successful – they will amalgamate. If you look around the world you will see that the Aryan races will not wholesomely amalgamate with the Africans or the Asiatics […] the cross of those races, like the cross of the dog and the fox, is not successful; it cannot be, and never will be."[220] Racist outbursts like this discomfited a number of Macdonald supporters in Parliament,[221] as well as outside, among them individuals like Principal George Monro Grant of Queen's University (see chapter three), who strongly defended Chinese immigrants in Canada.

Macdonald knew several middle-class individuals in the dominant society who had an Indigenous background. In French-speaking Canada, he had the full support of the powerful Bishop Louis-François Laflèche of Trois-Rivières, whose maternal grandmother was Métis from the North West and who had served as a missionary on the Plains in the late 1840s.[222] Other prominent individuals Macdonald knew with some North American Indian ancestry included Edward Clouston, general manager of the Bank of Montreal in 1890, whose mother was of British and Indigenous ancestry.[223] Isabella Sophia Hardisty, the wife of the Bank of Montreal's president, Donald Smith, Lord Strathcona, also had a British and Indigenous ancestry.[224] In politics, Macdonald knew Isabella Sophia Hardisty Smith's brother Richard Hardisty, the Hudson's Bay Company chief factor at Fort Edmonton, and he named him to the Canadian Senate in 1888.[225] Hardisty had married Eliza McDougall, sister of the well-known Methodist missionary John McDougall (see chapter two).[226]

The prime minister got on well with John Norquay, the Conservative premier of Manitoba (1878–87), who was of Cree and Orkney Island descent.[227] One of his Conservative Party contacts in Ontario in 1890 was Solomon White, mayor of Windsor, who had become the first Indian lawyer in Ontario; earlier this Wyandot (Huron) man had "enfranchised," one of the few status Indians to do so in the 1880s.[228]

The prime minister had a connection with Indigenous Canada in his own family. In 1887 his beloved 10-year-old granddaughter came to Ottawa from Winnipeg to attend boarding school. Every weekend,

Daisy Macdonald stayed with Sir John A. and Lady Macdonald at Earn-scliffe.[229] No doubt, grandfather heard a great deal about her school, "Miss Harmon's exclusive establishment for young ladies."[230] Daisy's headmistress, Abby Maria Harmon, was the daughter of fur trader Daniel Harmon and his wife, Lizette Laval Harmon, a woman of Cree and French Canadian descent. Former students later recalled Miss Harmon was "proud of her Cree blood and ancestry, and no less proud of her father's reputation as a fur trader and explorer."[231] Stewart Wallace, the Canadian historian, met her about 1900 and later wrote, "I well remember meeting her when I was a child; and she bore unmistakable signs of her Indian ancestry."[232]

The Canadian historian Bill Waiser defends Macdonald against charges of racism against the First Nations: "If Macdonald believed that Indians were a hopelessly doomed people, to be cast aside by the advance of civilization, then he would not have wasted time dealing with them."[233] Canada's first prime minister believed the First Nations were culturally, not biologically inferior, and that Christianity and a European education would eliminate the cultural inferiority. His political contemporaries shared his desire to see the First Nations enter the mainstream society, not to see them remain a separate people.

Depressing though it is from today's vantage point, the reality remains that in Canada in the 1870s, 1880s, and 1890s assimilation, or "civilization" at it was termed at the time, was the universally accepted approach. Macdonald and his non-Indigenous political contemporaries did not understand that the First Nations had different cultures that they were determined to retain. Their ancestors had lived in what is now Canada for five hundred or so generations at the moment of the Europeans' arrival, and despite the newcomers' intense pressures, the Indigenous peoples had no desire to disappear.

Chapter Two

John McDougall and the Stoney Nakoda

The Stoney Nakoda, or Stoney First Nations of southern Alberta, respected Reverend John Chantler McDougall (1842–1917) as a spiritual leader who emphasized the similarities between their own religious beliefs and Christianity. To quote the Stoney historian Chief John Snow, "There was simply not that much difference between what we already believed and what the missionaries preached to us. What differences there were did not seem very important."[1] John Laurie, a close friend of the Stoney Nakoda, noted in 1950 their continued "reverence and awe of John McDougall, who, until his death, was so closely linked with his Stoney friends."[2] The Methodist missionary lived with the Stoney at the Morley Mission[3] from its founding in 1873, until he and his family moved to Calgary in 1899.[4]

John McDougall spoke two foreign languages, Ojibwe and Cree, but he did not have fluency in Nakoda, the Stoney's Siouan language, one totally different from Ojibwe and Cree.[5] As the Stoney in Alberta, also called Mountain Stoney, were close allies with the Rocky Mountain or Woodland Cree,[6] many Stoney could converse in Cree,[7] as well as read the Methodist books that were printed in Cree syllabics.[8] McDougall himself had cooperated with Reverend E.B. Glass to compile a *Cree Hymn Book*, which was published in 1888 in syllabic characters.[9] Totally at ease in the language, McDougall talked to the Stoney Nakoda or Mountain Stoney in Cree.

In 1874 the Government of Canada gave Reverend John McDougall the task of notifying the Blackfoot-speaking nations (Niitsitapi) – the Blackfoot proper (Siksika), Blood (Kainai), and Peigan (Piikuni) – that a party of red-coated police, the North-West Mounted Police (NWMP), would soon be arriving. He explained to them in detail that in Central Canada treaties had been signed, lands set aside, and the government respected the rights of the First Nations.[10] Sweetgrass, a principal Plains

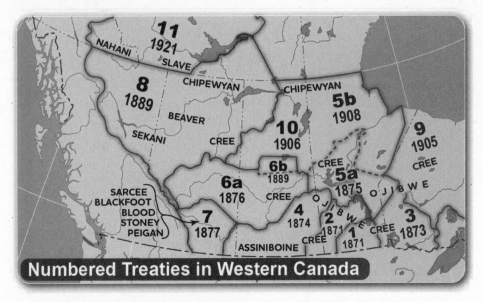

Map 2.1 The numbered treaties on the Plains.

Cree chief,[11] on McDougall's arrival to the Treaty Six meetings in 1876 introduced him in this fashion: "This young man speaks and understands just like ourselves. I have sent for him to tell us what the proposals of the treaty mean."[12] The Methodist missionary was an adviser to several First Nations at the signing of Treaty Six in central Alberta and Saskatchewan in 1876. The Canadian negotiators in the treaty process discussed the benefits of a treaty and stressed land sharing rather than land surrender.[13] McDougall played an important role at the signing of Treaty Seven in southern Alberta, an agreement that the Stoney Nakoda believed to be a peace treaty. During the negotiations, the chiefs' Stoney had to be translated into Cree to someone who spoke both Cree and English, and then the communication would finally be transferred to the Treaty Seven commissioners. In the words of Chief John Snow, "Given the difficulties in translation and the different cultural attitudes toward the use and ownership of land, our forefathers did not realize that they were ceding land to the white man for all time."[14]

The Government of Canada acted quickly in the mid-1870s, as it wanted to extinguish the Indian Title as soon as possible, before thousands of non-Indigenous ranchers and settlers arrived. Unfortunately, the farming potential of the Upper Bow River Valley remained unknown at the time of Treaty Seven. The hasty choice of a reserve on the advice of their missionary John McDougall and federal government officials proved disastrous. Over sixty years later, Reverend E.J. Staley, when he was the United Church minister at Morley, described the land as "nothing more than a rocky, hilly, gravel bed with only the thinnest smattering of soil covering it anywhere, except for a few hundred acres in its southeast corner."[15] A second major mistake occurred when Reverend McDougall recommended to the Treaty Seven commissioners that one, not three reserves, be established.[16] The Mountain Stoney had three main divisions, and required a reserve for each. The middle or Chiniquy band's hunting grounds extended along the Bow River and its tributaries. The territory of the southern, or Bearspaw band, reached down to Chief Mountain on the Montana border. The northern Goodstoney (later Wesley) band's territory included the land up to the Athabaska River.[17] On McDougall's recommendation, they only obtained one reserve, and that one was around the Methodist Mission at Morley.

The oldest Methodist mission in Alberta, the Cree Methodist Mission at Whitefish Lake, about 200 kilometres northeast of Fort Edmonton, was much more fortunate than Morley. Established in the late 1850s by Reverend Henry B. Steinhauer (or Shawahnekizhek), an Ojibwe Methodist missionary from Ontario, the area unlike that around Morley was acceptable for agriculture. At Whitefish, the Cree continued hunting, fishing, and gathering, and they also developed a core farming settlement, which the Stoney Nakoda never did. With crude homemade implements the Christianized Whitefish Indians broke the soil, and planted small gardens, built European-style houses, and raised domestic animals.[18] As a result, they were able to feed themselves after the demise of the buffalo herds on the Canadian side of the border with the United States in 1879.[19] They also had a good school, at least in the mid-1870s. Elizabeth Barrett, a trained Ontario schoolteacher, who taught at Whitefish for two years in the mid-1870s, prepared two of the Steinhauer sons, Egerton and Robert, for high school entrance in Ontario. Robert Steinhauer would eventually obtain his B.A. from Victoria College in 1887, the first status Indian in what is now Alberta to do so.[20]

Ranching proved possible at Morley, but even with the presence of a federal farm instructor some years later, farming never became viable there. Optimistically, John McDougall had at first believed that the three Stoney Nakoda or Mountain Stoney communities would adjust rapidly to gardening and raising livestock, supplemented by their traditional hunting and gathering. Once the reserve system was firmly in place, it was believed by the federal government that the Native self-supporting small-scale farmers would gradually discard their old ways and integrate fully into the neighbouring Euro-Canadian society. This did not happen, of course. Many Bearspaw community members continued to live south of Morley in the Foothills, and in the mid-1890s, a significant number of Goodstoney (later Wesley) band members established a settlement in the distant Kootenay Plains to the north.

McDougall later acknowledged his mistake. In the spring of 1909 he supported the petition of the northern Wesley band for a reserve of its own near the North Saskatchewan River.[21] In a letter to the deputy superintendent general of Indian Affairs the following year, McDougall explained that the Kootenay Plains were "the original home country of these people and they have always clung to it" and that only by "by force of circumstances over which these men had not [no] control" did they receive a reserve at Morley.[22] McDougall now unsuccessfully argued for reserve status for the Kootenay Plains. The interests of the Euro-Canadian settlers and developers in the area prevented this. Again, the newcomers came first, and the Stoney Nakoda request was denied.

In the late nineteenth century John McDougall had a prominent role in the settlers' world. In 1885 he served as guide, scout, and chaplain for the Alberta Field Force, organized by the Government of Canada to capture the Cree Chief Big Bear, whose community at Frog Lake, some 200 kilometres to the east of Edmonton, had joined Louis Riel in 1885. McDougall travelled with several Stoney scouts and the Cree Chief Samson from Battle River to reconnoitre the route to Edmonton for the advancing column of nearly a thousand troops.[23] A member of the Field Force recalled "the militant missionary" thirty years later, as a striking "figure of a man on a splendid horse, his rifle across his back, a black slouch hat on his head, his clothing either a buckskin coat or a dark semi-clerical double-breast."[24] The Cree-speaking Methodist missionary enjoyed respect among the First Nations, surprisingly even from Little Bear (or Imasees), a son of Chief Big Bear. Little Bear fled to Montana after the troubles of 1885. When he returned to Canada twelve years later, he sought out Reverend McDougall and asked that he accompany him to translate for him on his mission to Ottawa to meet with Prime Minister Wilfrid Laurier.[25] Big Bear's son kept to his ancestral religion, he had not converted to Christianity, but he trusted the Cree-speaking Methodist minister. McDougall travelled with Imasees to Ottawa from Alberta in 1897, and back again.[26]

In the Euro-Canadian Protestant world, John McDougall enjoyed respect as a role model, an evangelist who strictly practised the discipline of his faith. A devoted Methodist, he never consumed alcohol, smoked, or swore, and he faithfully accepted his church's strong prohibitions against theatre and card games. A great honour came to the veteran Prairie missionary in 1903 with the granting of an honorary Doctor of Divinity degree from the Methodists' Victoria College in the University of Toronto. Reverend Dr John C. McDougall was named president of the Methodist Conference in Canada in 1906.[27]

The Liberal government of Prime Minister Wilfrid Laurier recognized John McDougall's knowledge of Indigenous issues. From 1905 to 1910 he worked as a commissioner for the Department of Indian Affairs, at the same time that he held the position of Doukhobor commissioner.[28] As with other distinct communities, the federal government worked to "Canadianize" this Russian religious sect. It wanted them to abide by the Dominion Lands Act and end their communal ownership of land.[29] McDougall's more recent career included just one major "misstep." In the April 1913 provincial election, John McDougall ran as a Liberal in the riding of Calgary Centre with a platform that included the extension of the provincial vote to women, better treatment of the working class, and the advancement of economic development.[30] His program proved too progressive for Calgary at this time, when only males had the franchise, and McDougall lost to the Conservative candidate, although his party won the province.[31] Two years later, after the passage of a prohibition referendum in Alberta, the Liberal administration – fittingly in their partisans' opinion – appointed John McDougall to the post of Alberta's temperance commissioner.[32]

Gifted with a retentive mind and good powers of description, Reverend McDougall wrote prolifically: newspaper and magazine articles, reports, and a biography of his father,[33] as well as two novels.[34] Beginning in his mid-forties, he wrote half a dozen autobiographical volumes in which he recorded his early days on the Plains and in the Foothills of Western Canada from 1862 to 1876.[35] The accumulation of frustrating and demanding administrative work is the context in which he wrote his autobiographical volumes from the 1890s to 1910s. In his manuscripts, McDougall seems to have cheerfully escaped to memories of his action-packed adventuresome youth. His stories directly related to what he had seen or been told.

At the turn of the century, McDougall's books enjoyed great popularity in Protestant British Canada.[36] The *Canadian Baptist* commented on *Forest, Lake and Prairie*, which was published in 1895, "There are many graphic descriptions of scenes in that vast fertile region in those early years when travelling was difficult and dangerous."[37] The *Christian Guardian*, the Methodists' national newspaper, strongly endorsed McDougall's next volume, *Saddle, Sled and Snowshoe* (1896), stating, "He writes with the keenest enthusiasm: and this spirit possesses the reader of his thrilling pages."[38] The *Review of Historical Publications Relating to*

Canada, co-edited by George Wrong, professor of history at the University of Toronto, and H.J.H. Langton, librarian of the University of Toronto, commented positively on McDougall's 1903 book, *In the Days of the Red River Rebellion*. They noted, among other things, that the writer powerfully presented the impact of the smallpox epidemic in 1870: "Mr McDougall thinks that in it one half of the population of the country perished; the scenes he depicts remind us of the visitation of the Black Death in England in 1349."[39]

John Chantler McDougall was born 27 December 1842 in Owen Sound, then a tiny frontier village on the Georgian Bay of Lake Huron. His parents, George and Elizabeth McDougall, allowed their son full freedom to be with his Ojibwe friends,[40] and the boy grew up regarding Indigenous peoples as equals. "My mother says I spoke Indian before I spoke English," McDougall recalled in *Forest, Lake and Prairie*.[41] From the Anishinabeg he learned the life histories of the animals they hunted and their seasonal habits, about the edible plants, and how to catch fish at all times of the year. He loved his boyhood with the Anishinabeg. In his own words, "I grew up amongst them, ate corn-soup out of their wooden bowls, roasted green ears at their camp-fires, feasted with them on deer and bear's meat, went with them to set their nets and to spear fish at nights by the light of birch-bark flambeaux, and, later on, fat pine light-jack torches."[42] From the age of 10, John McDougall, already at ease in Ojibwe, interpreted for his father.[43] With an open and curious mind, he learned how the Ojibwe viewed and interacted with the world around them. When the thunder rumbled and the lightning flashed, the people knew the thunderbird, a huge white bird living in the clouds, was angry. When they heard "thunder bolts," they knew that the thunderbird was shooting through the air trying to kill the serpents, traditional enemies of the Ojibwe.[44] As they lived so close to nature they did not envisage any great division between themselves and the rest of creation. The non-Christian Ojibwe Elders, for instance, avoided cutting down living trees to save them from pain. As Kahkewaquonaby, or Peter Jones (1802–1856) noted in his *History of the Ojebway Indians* (1861), the Elders avoided cutting living trees. If they were cut, they said you could hear their wailing "when suffering under the operation of the hatchet or axe."[45]

Bilingual and bicultural, John McDougall referred to himself in the mid-1860s as "nine-tenths Indian."[46] Reverend John Maclean, a Methodist missionary among the Blood Indians in southern Alberta in the 1880s, confirms how indigenized McDougall had become. In his 1927 biography, *McDougall of Alberta*, Maclean noted that his missionary colleague knew Cree better than he knew English: "This was sometimes revealed in a hesitancy in his speech while addressing public audiences."[47] All his life John McDougall's English remained somewhat distinctive. The *Christian Guardian* commented in its obituary notice of 24 January 1917, "Lacking somewhat the graces of the polished orator, he more than made up for this by his clearness, directness, forcefulness and, above all, by the unique experience lying at back of it all."[48]

George and Elizabeth McDougall sent their son to mission schools at his father's successive postings,[49] although at age 12 he did attend the public school in Owen Sound for one winter. In school he learned of Canada's British heritage, of the great naval battles of Nelson and the land victories of the Duke of Wellington, certainly of Britain's economic dominance as the workshop of the world – leader in both steam engines and steel production. Two winters later (1857–8 and 1859–60), he studied in the preparatory department of the Methodist college in Cobourg, Ontario, named Victoria, after the great queen. Reverend John Burwash, later a prominent Methodist educator,[50] remembered McDougall at the college in 1857, fresh from Ojibwe country in the north: "McDougall could run faster and farther, jump farther and higher than any other Victoria student."[51]

The McDougall family moved to Norway House, the important fur-trading centre in northern Manitoba in 1860, and son John now learned Swampy Cree and became his father's Cree interpreter. The importance of the winter in the North West was evident from the variety of words for snow, or *kona* in Cree: for snowing they had the word *mispon*, for melting snow *sasken*, drifting snow *piwon*, and snowdrifts *papestin*.[52] McDougall taught at the mission school, which often had a daily attendance of eighty. In winter darkness in the early mornings, he drove a dog sled team, and he made extra money trapping. Later, in *Forest, Lake and Prairie*, McDougall wrote of his rigorous two years at Norway House: "Many a winter morning I rose at four o'clock, harnessed my dogs and drove miles back in visiting my traps, reaching home and having breakfast before daylight, as it was necessary, for a part of the winter, to begin school as soon as it was good daylight."[53]

John McDougall mastered well a second Cree dialect, Plains Cree, after his family moved onto the Prairies in 1862.[54] His initial meetings with Plains peoples greatly surprised him: "Here were plain hunters and buffalo Indians, and warriors. Some of these rode horses recently taken from the enemy. Some of them wore scalp-locks recently taken dangling from arm or leg, which not many moons since were the pride of the original owners, and on whose heads they had grown."[55] To protect their hunting grounds,[56] the Plains Cree roamed freely over the northern plains, often travelling nearly 1,000 kilometres in the course of a single summer.[57] On account of the declining buffalo herds retreating to the west, they ventured into Blackfoot country. The totally self-sufficient Plains Indians impressed McDougall. Take, for example, the Cree Ka-Kahe (or "The Hawk"): "The elasticity of his step, the flash of his eye, the ring of his voice – you *had* to notice him. To me he was a new type. He filled my ideal as a hunter and warrior."[58]

Farther to the west in the Foothills, McDougall respected the Mountain Stoney in what is now southern Alberta. His veteran Stoney Nakoda guide and interpreter, "the Tall One," known in English as James Dixon,[59] spoke correctly four distinct languages: Cree, Stoney, Blackfoot, and Kootenay (Kutenai). In his book, *Opening the Great West*, McDougall wrote of the Tall One, "All this country along the mountains from the Athabasca to the headwaters of the Missouri river was as familiar to him as his 160 acres is to a homesteader."[60] The Methodist missionary considered the Stoney Nakoda to be the epitome of fighting manhood. In 1891, in a letter to the editor of *Canadian Indian*, he wrote, "The Crees have been, and are to-day far more numerous than the Blackfeet; and as to fighting strength, the Stonies, though fewer in number, were more than their match!"[61]

With his First Nations friends John McDougall "engaged in all matters of athletics, foot races, horse races, anything for real fun and common brotherhood."[62] They freely shared with him stories about their way of life."[63] The Plains nations believed all things were alive and related to each other.[64] McDougall saw the First Nations as human beings and loved their stories of bravery, endurance, and remarkable journeys. He learned that the Plains peoples did not regard the taking of horses from enemy camps as theft. One warrior referred to it, as "bringing them in," and said, "Did you see that bunch of horses? He just now brought them home."[65] The Plains peoples held personal bravery in the highest esteem, and they shared almost everything. McDougall wrote in *Saddle, Sled and Snowshoe*: "What surprised me was that these men who went after buffalo and endured such physical hardship and nervous strain, did not receive any more than the rest in the partition of what buffalo might be brought into the pound. The man who owned the horse got the tongues, but those men who did the wonderful work of bringing them in had the glory."[66]

John's father, Reverend George McDougall, once wrote that the Indian woman was "the slave in all heathendom."[67] The statement was false, as his son discovered. A woman's day was "indeed, an extremely busy one,"[68] but in reality, women and men shared an equitable division of labour, one that compared well with the work burden of the pioneer farm wife. With his marriage to Abigail Steinhauer of Whitefish Lake in

March 1865,[69] John McDougall became further Indigenized. Abigail was the second eldest of nine children of Reverend Henry B. Steinhauer and Jessie Mamanuwartum, his Cree wife from Norway House.[70] The couple had known each other since John McDougall's first visit to Whitefish Lake in 1862. Cree became his language at home.[71]

Henry Steinhauer knew only too well the limitations of non-Indigenous church workers. As he wrote in the mid-1870s, "A foreigner, either as a Missionary or otherwise, will never take so well with the natives of this country, let him be ever so good and kind to them; there is always a distrust on the part of a native to the foreigner, from the fact that the native has been so long down-trodden by the white man."[72] John McDougall certainly knew this. As he wrote in 1878, many Plains First Nations believed "their missionaries were only agents of the Government in disguise, doing all they could to blind and bewilder the native, and thus aid in defrauding them of their country and freedom, and eventually their life."[73] Yet, despite widespread Indigenous concern about Euro-Canadians, the Steinhauers trusted John McDougall. Both families warmly welcomed the proposed marriage. George McDougall performed the wedding ceremony.[74] At the time, racial barriers in the non-Indigenous settlers' world were not rigid. A year later, John's sister, Eliza McDougall, married Richard Hardisty of the Hudson's Bay Company; this future chief factor of Fort Edmonton was of British and Indigenous ancestry.[75]

With her invaluable Indigenous knowledge, Abigail became John McDougall's great assistant in his mission work. As the oldest daughter, she helped her mother with the younger children. An experienced teacher, she taught at her father's school from the age of 13.[76] In McDougall's religious services, his wife Abigail "sang well," with the full sound and depth of her mother tongue. The Cree hymns were so important, as McDougall wrote, many of the "translations we used were full of the very pith of the gospel message."[77] McDougall admired his wife's resourcefulness and self-reliance, for Abigail a sixty-mile canter on the open plains was "a common experience."[78]

In quick succession, the McDougalls had three daughters, but tragically Abigail died in April 1871, at the beginning of their seventh year of marriage, shortly before she would have turned 23.[79] She left behind a baby, Augusta (or Gussie), and her two older sisters, Flora, aged four, and Ruth, two.[80] Now a widower, McDougall felt Abigail's loss deeply. The wife of his youth, he wrote, had "shared our mutual toils and triumphs when first we started out in the mission field."[81]

To help recover from the shock of his wife's passing, and the loss of three of his sisters several months earlier in the smallpox epidemic of 1870,[82] John McDougall left in summer 1872 for several months in Ontario.[83] On the way he attended in Winnipeg the first missionary Methodist conference in Western Canada. Preferring to "rough it," he camped on the prairie rather than stay as a guest in town.[84] In Ontario the mission worker spent most of his three-month leave near his childhood home on Georgian Bay, where the young widower fell in love. That autumn he returned to Alberta with his new bride, Elizabeth Boyd,[85] an Ontario cousin from Cape Rich just east of Owen Sound.[86] John and Elizabeth were married in September 1872. He was 30, and she 19.

Elizabeth, or Lizzie McDougall was an extraordinary woman, strong, self-reliant, and capable. Although raised on a comfortable Ontario farm, she adapted quickly to the Spartan existence of a Prairie missionary's wife. In her new home at Morley, she assumed responsibility, with her mother-in-law, of John and Abigail's three young daughters. John and Lizzie later had six children of their own, five boys and a girl.[87] Lizzie's capable managing of their large family allowed her husband full liberty to fulfil his missionary duties, which involved frequent long trips away from home.

Lizzie had no prior acquaintanceship with First Nations people. She had grown up in southern Ontario after the Ojibwe had become greatly outnumbered by Euro-Canadian settlers and pushed away from their hunting and fishing grounds. She mixed well with the Stoney, but she did not learn the Cree, or Stoney language.[88] At Morley, and after they moved to Calgary around 1900,[89] John McDougall continued to speak Cree, but never again as a first language at home. Lizzie and John named their Calgary house, "Nekenon," which meant "our home" in Cree,[90] and inscribed the word on the concrete sidewalk immediately before their doorstep.[91]

John McDougall encouraged his and Abigail's daughters to obtain the best Canadian education possible in preparation for their full entry into the newcomers' society. The patriotic Ontarian arranged for all three girls to attend boarding schools for four or five years in his home province.[92] Gussie McDougall remembers their young stepmother Lizzie treated all three "just like a sister."[93] All McDougall daughters married "white men," and their children, in the words of one of Ruth's granddaughters, "appear to have had little knowledge of their aboriginal heritage."[94] Flora married Magnus Begg, the Blackfoot Indian agent.[95] George Wheatley, Begg's successor as Blackfoot Indian agent, and Ruth wed shorty after them.[96] Gussie taught school at Morley, and looked after her grandmother, Elizabeth Chantler McDougall, until her death in 1903.[97] Later, Gussie married George Mathieson, a Scot, who farmed just west of Carstairs, to the north of Calgary.[98]

2.1 Couple in car in front of "Nekenon," 230 6th Ave. E, John and Lizzie McDougall's home in Calgary, ca. 1905. PB-707-3. Courtesy of Glenbow Archives, Archives and Special Collections, University of Calgary.

John McDougall knew the depth of anti-Indian sentiment on the Prairies. Unlike in the 1860s, when both he and his sister Eliza had married individuals of Indigenous backgrounds, that racial detail now became a liability, something to be hidden if not purged.[99] Fellow Methodist minister Reverend John Maclean commented in 1889, "In several of our western towns the hatred toward the Indians is great."[100] The Canadian historians R.C. Macleod and Heather Rollason Driscoll confirm that in the mid-1880s the *Calgary Herald* was "full of vitriolic descriptions of Native people."[101] Cecil Denny, an early NWMP officer,[102] wrote in his memoirs, "The white settler coming into the country to raise cattle or farm cared little what became of the poor Indian. If a cow was killed or a horse stolen, the Indians were to blame."[103]

A note in John McDougall's *Pathfinding on Plain and Prairie* indicates his sensitivity to racial slurs. He recalled the moment he introduced Abigail to his sister Eliza and his brother David, who had just returned from their studies in Ontario: "I was particularly pleased to note the manner of both my sister and brother towards my wife. The fact of her being a native did not in anywise affect the kindliness of their conduct toward her, for which I was very thankful."[104] McDougall detested the derogatory word, "squaw," which suggested disrespect and indolence. As he wrote in 1895, "In the name of decency and civilization, why call one person a woman and another a squaw?"[105] The veteran missionary always avoided, too, the harsh and inappropriate name, "half-breeds," and instead used the term, "mixed bloods."[106]

Just after the McDougalls moved to "Nekenon," John wrote *"Wa-pee Moos-tooch," or "White Buffalo," the hero of a hundred battles; a tale of life in Canada's great West during the early years of the last century*, that he self-published in 1908. As the *Calgary Herald* summarized, the novel "leads one through the life and trials and joys of a young Cree, from the time that he is a mere boy until such time as he becomes an honored chief among the chieftains of his race."[107] Skilfully, McDougall included stories he had heard and scenes he had witnessed of the Na-he-ya-wuk ("the Fit People").[108] References appear to both the Plains and the Woodland Cree indicating his familiarity with both ways of life. McDougall loved Cree place names.[109] Cree animal designations and place names he cherished appear in abundance in *"White Buffalo,"* for example, the huge *mis-ta-ya*, the grizzly; the tiny *peyao*, or prairie chicken; and *mistatim*, or big dog, their designation for horse.[110] Cree place names cited include ones for Maple Creek, Kahnemetaswayask-wazog, which means "where the timber runs out on to the plains"; for the Cypress Hills, Me-nah-tuh-gow, the beautiful forests; and for the land to the west of the Cypress Hills, the We-Kusk-wa-chee, or sweet grass buttes, or hills.[111]

The book *"White Buffalo"* conveys the atmosphere of the buffalo days full of physical challenges. Chasing buffalo on horseback took great discipline and stamina. Full of fire, the Northwest horse could outrun bison with ease.[112] As McDougall described, "Only those who have been there, who have taken part in this race, whose nostrils have been full of the dust of the great plains as this was raised by the rush and stampede and fierce gallop of the countless herds; only those whose blood has heated and whose nerves have tingled as they swept on over rough country, down hill and across valley, with countless badger holes on every hand, with danger to neck and limb omnipresent, with horse and man becoming as one in the rare excitement of the chase, only such can truly realize the exhilaration of the regular hunt on horseback over the great plains after these wild cattle."[113]

In the 1870s John McDougall witnessed many important events on the Plains: the smallpox epidemic of 1870, the coming of the North-West Mounted Police in 1874, and the signing of both Treaty Six in 1876 and Treaty Seven in 1877. His memoirs offer invaluable insights for Western Canadian historians. Although the veteran missionary, for example, had "the highest admiration"[114] for the NWMP, he saw nothing at all "heroic" about their 1874 Great March West. In McDougall's opinion, the several hundred Canadians consisted of "men, unused to this wilderness life, 'tenderfeet' for the most part."[115] He criticized their construction of a fort at the junction of the Bow and Elbow rivers, at present-day Calgary, two years before Treaty Seven was signed. The NWMP placed the fort directly in the buffalo's path. The Stoney feared this would entail hunger and possible starvation, and they asked their missionary, "What right had the white man at this time to establish centres without the government conferring first about it with the Indians?"[116] The great buffalo herds were gone on the Canadian side of the border with the United States in 1879. On a positive note, the Methodist missionary fully appreciated the NWMP's ending of the horrors of the whiskey trade. But others, he added, also deserved recognition for the peaceful occupation of the North West, namely, the Christian missionaries and, of course, the Plains peoples themselves: "The whole country was tired of tribal war and constant lawlessness, and was looking and longing of this change which was now brought about by the advent of the representatives of government and order."[117]

Because of his first-hand knowledge of both the Ojibwe (Saulteaux) and Cree languages, and his lifelong close contact with Indian people, one might well expect John McDougall's writings to be cherished historical sources, but they are not. The historian Ernest Nix explains, "His acknowledgement of his fitness is liberally sprinkled throughout his memoirs to the point that one must ask why this man who lived such a useful and notable life found it apparently so necessary to continually remind his readers of his own worth?"[118] John McDougall's boastfulness has deterred a number of university-based scholars from referencing his work.[119] As the Western Canadian literary historian Susan Jackel submits, "For many, then, it becomes less a question of giving John McDougall a second look than of giving him a first one."[120]

In McDougall's defence, Professor Jackel emphasizes the importance of his autobiographical books as valuable records of the turbulent years from 1860 to 1876. Others agree. In his pioneer study, *The North American Buffalo: A Critical Study of the Species in Its Wild State*, published in 1951, Frank Gilbert Roe underlines the contribution when he writes, "McDougall's writings are not professedly 'scientific': their unpretentious accuracy makes them so. As unconscious revelations of a long experience they are of unrivalled authority for daily life in their region."[121] The Alberta historian Hugh Dempsey concurs and recognizes the high degree of accuracy in the memoirs. Dempsey likes how McDougall reports events with little editorializing.[122] McDougall's contemporary, fur trader Isaac Cowie,[123] also praised his contribution: "By a combination rare, Dr McDougall was a man of action as well as an author whose books give intimate and accurate views of almost all phases of life and adventure in the wilds of the Saskatchewan."[124]

Explanations exist for John McDougall's excessive boasting. His lack of formal education caused personal insecurity. McDougall's ordination on 30 July 1872 was without any examination or trial sermon, being based solely on the merits of his twelve years of missionary service.[125] He had no formal theological training,[126] and he remained resentful that his schooling had been so limited. McDougall's first attempt to complete Victoria College ended at age 17 when his father in 1860 asked him to join him immediately at Norway House.[127] Twelve years later, the Church turned down his request to return to Victoria.[128] John McDougall recalled his conversation with Dr Morley Punshon, president of the conference of the Wesleyan Methodist Church in Canada: "In 1872, after twelve years of stirring life on the plains, I plead with Dr Punshon to let me go to college. I had the money. I hungered for the culture. 'No, my son,' said the President, 'The Lord is putting you through His own college; go back to your work'"[129]

With well-educated people John's boastfulness could surface. It certainly did in 1907 on the occasion of the summer visit of Robert Lowie, a graduate student from Columbia University in New York. The student of Franz Boas, the celebrated American anthropologist, arrived at Morley to undertake seven weeks of fieldwork. After he returned to New York, Lowie joined the staff of the American Museum of Natural History to work closely with Clark Wissler, a well-known student of the Plains peoples. From the 1920s to the 1940s Lowie taught at the University of California, Berkeley. When he retired in 1950 he enjoyed great renown as one of America's great anthropologists.[130]

The young anthropologist noticed favourably during his Morley visit that John McDougall "preached in very fluent Cree." Then Lowie commented on a negative characteristic, the missionary's well-known ego. Apparently, both the Methodist missionary and his brother David bragged constantly: "The two brothers would pooh-pooh the then world's marathon record as something they had often outdone in their youth." John, in particular, frequently enlarged "on his physical toughness – how of a freezing night he would make shift with a single blanket, wade across streams with hefty wives of less puissant fellow clerics in his arms, and so on. Later I hear it said that there were just three liars in Alberta: the trader was reckoned as one and his reverend brother as the other two."[131]

In terms of actual "wilderness" experience, the two men stood a galaxy apart. In his youth, John McDougall performed backbreaking labour, faced real physical danger in First Nations war zones, participated in buffalo hunts, experienced the full terror of a full-scale smallpox epidemic. In contrast, Robert Lowie could discuss German philosophy, European literature, the history and the methodology of science, and the most modern anthropological theories;[132] but at this stage in his career, the anthropologist disliked Stoney cuisine, could not handle horses well, and knew no North American languages.[133]

Peter Erasmus, a well-known Indigenous guide and interpreter, wrote of John McDougall, whom he had first met as a young man in the mid-1860s: "John worked like a trooper; it was all new work to him and he blistered his hands using the axe, but he persisted and did not complain. He was a likeable chap, always in good humour, who seemed to enjoy working."[134] As did others, Erasmus noted "his tendency to boast of his prowess," but he did not criticize him for it: "I did not attempt to discourage this tendency for I believed that a man who sets himself a high objective is quite likely to obtain some success in the matter."[135]

John McDougall's strong opinions could involve the man of the cloth in controversy. Somewhat impetuous, he favoured the direct attack over calm discussion. In 1895, for instance, he sent a thunderbolt against fellow Methodist missionary Reverend Egerton Ryerson Young[136] for the inclusion of alleged inaccuracies in his book, *Stories from Indian Wigwams and Northern Camp-fires*, published two years earlier.[137] Young felt some dramatic licence was permissible in his presentation of his eight years as a missionary in northern Manitoba. McDougall did not.[138] The intemperate exchanges between the two clergymen grew so heated and personal that in time the *Christian Guardian* refused to publish any more of them. Undeterred, McDougall then printed the letters privately: "The readers of Mr Young's review will have noticed that he speaks of me as childish, often mentioning me by name, if I was but a boy and he the veteran; while as to work and an understanding of the case in hands, our position is just the reverse – I am the veteran and he is the child."[139]

With great zeal, John McDougall waged an ongoing verbal battle with bureaucrats in the federal Department of Indian Affairs. Publicly, he expressed his low opinion of Indian agents in a letter sent to the *Calgary Tribune* in late December 1885.[140] He repeated the same charges three weeks later to the reporter George Ham of the *Toronto Daily Mail*. The Methodist missionary pointed out "the shameful and immoral lives" of a number of Indian Affairs employees in the North West, "a disgrace to the lowest barbarism, let alone civilization."[141] These comments reached the floor of the House of Commons, when on 15 April 1886 Malcolm Cameron, Liberal MP from Ontario (West Huron) an unrelenting critic of John A. Macdonald, quoted Ham's *Daily Mail* article several times.[142]

Deputy Superintendent General of Indian Affairs Lawrence Vankoughnet wrote the cleric a fiery reply.[143] McDougall stood his ground, and more than a quarter of a century later he repeated the charges he had made: "There were some fine exceptions in the service of the Indian Department but during the first years these were few and the Indian was most terribly disillusioned as to the character and lives of Government officials."[144] As McDougall had two Indian agent sons-in-law, he made sure to add in his condemnation of the poor quality of Indian agents, "There were some fine exceptions." Peter Grasse, the Stoney Nakoda farm instructor, served as the Methodist missionary's prime example of an incompetent Indian Affairs worker. In an 1897 communication, McDougall pronounced Grasse "a drunkard, and a gambler, and a blasphemer, and at times foul and brutish in his conduct."[145] Their bickering had begun in 1891 and continued to 1897. Apparently the farm instructor had greatly upset McDougall by criticizing the missionary's administration of the McDougall Orphanage, the mission's residential school. The dispute ended only when Grasse left the Morley Reserve, later in 1897.[146]

John McDougall focused his criticism of the Department Indian of Indian Affairs largely on the Indian Act and its numerous revisions.[147] The Indian Act of 1876 was not mentioned at the signing of Treaty Seven the following year. Imposed without any negotiation with the First Nations, the Indian Act transformed the Indigenous peoples, who had signed the treaty as equals, into dependants: "Paternalism has been carried to a criminal extreme."[148] The Government of Canada applied the Indian Act instead of observing the equality that was the basis of the treaty. The illegal pass system that began in full force after the troubles of 1885 proved another aggravation.[149] As McDougall wrote in 1905, "If he is a treaty Indian he cannot visit a friend on a neighbouring reserve without a permit. He cannot go to the nearest market town without a permit ... He cannot travel in peace without a permit. He cannot buy and sell without a permit. He may raise cattle, but he cannot sell them unless the Government official allows. He may cultivate the soil, but is not the owner of his produce."[150] As a ward of the Crown the Indian had no legal rights. In his autobiography, *Forty Years in Canada* (1915), the veteran Mountie Sam Steele confirms this. He wrote of his days in the force that the NWMP could arrest "an Indian at any time or place. They were wards and we were officers of the Crown, therefore there was no chance of a miscarriage of justice."[151]

In 1886 the Government of Canada sponsored two tours of what it termed "Loyal" First Nations chiefs to Central Canada: the first comprised five Alberta Blackfoot Confederacy chiefs[152] and the second, four Saskatchewan chiefs.[153] Because of John McDougall's vigorous attacks on the Department of Indian Affairs, the Indian Act, and the pass system, Deputy Superintendent General Vankoughnet refused any financial support for his plan to take three "Loyal" Methodist Chiefs to Central Canada.[154] McDougall now took another approach.[155] He wagered that collections taken at public meetings in the big (and small) Central Canadian churches could pay the bills. And so they did.[156] Methodism in the 1880s was the largest and most prosperous Protestant denomination in Ontario.[157]

McDougall selected three individuals of "quick eye and retentive mind" for the journey.[158] Chief Pakan of Whitefish Lake, known in English as James Seenum, was a fine-looking man, of "good physique, tall, straight, and strong,"[159] in his mid-forties.[160] Father Léon Doucet commented in his journal that in the buffalo days Pakan and his large hunting group from Whitefish Lake carried with them across the plains a large syllabic bible.[161] The respected leader spoke "in an easy conversational tone gesticulating in a natural fashion with a right hand like a trained orator."[162] As superintendent of Indian Affairs, John A. Macdonald had noted in his 1885 annual report, "Chief Pecan, alias Seenum, of Whitefish Lake" is "the most influential of the chiefs of that section of the country east of Victoria and west of Frog Lake, and has the most numerous band: which he managed to control, and they, led by their chief, successfully resisted an attempt made by a war party from Big Bear's band to pillage the store of the Hudson Bay Company at Whitefish Lake, one man having been killed in the encounter."[163]

Chief Pakan was a fighter and staunch defender of Indigenous peoples' interests. After the Department of Indian Affairs in 1884 denied the Whitefish community what the chief regarded as its proper land allotment as promised at Treaty Six, he travelled to meet the Indian commissioner in Regina. In Pakan's words, as later recalled by Peter Erasmus, "Promises by government people were like the clouds, always changing."[164] Nonetheless, his case was heard and, on this occasion, favourably. Pakan then negotiated for additional land for his community. Two years later, in Ottawa, he informed Vanknoughnet that their reserve "should be considered as the Private property of the Band," beyond the Indian agent's control; moreover, Whitefish Lake people must themselves control the sale of their hay and crops, and their cattle.[165] With John McDougall presumably as his interpreter, he made his plea, but this one went nowhere. Pakan, also without success, next urged the liberation of Chief Big Bear, who had been locked up in Stoney Mountain Penitentiary in Manitoba.[166] Chief Pakan explained that the Cree chief had sought to keep the peace, but had lost control of his community.

John McDougall saw first hand the physical cost of the Central Canadian journey on Chief Pakan. Lack of exercise and the strange diet took its toll. A Toronto *Globe* story on 2 September 1886 reported that Pakan, "who weighed 180 pounds when he first reached Toronto now weighs 205 – a clear gain of twenty-five pounds in one month."[167] The food they ate in Central Canada, complete with rich deserts such as pies, custards, and cakes, was far from their standard fare.[168] Two years earlier on a trip to Winnipeg, in 1884, the Blood Chief Red Crow had so enjoyed his first dish of ice cream he called the new delight "sweet snow."[169]

Chief Pakan noted the wealth of the towns and cities in southern Ontario. As John McDougall translated, the First Nations visitor said in Berlin (present-day Kitchener): "How many comforts and blessings you have – I am almost filled with envy – but I can see that it had taken long years to clear the forests and to pile up the stone, for I can see for myself that this has been a heavily timbered country and it has taken years of hard work for you to do what you have done."[170] The Cree chief's remarks after a tour of the Kingston penitentiary had a totally different tone: "If I ever should do anything which would bring me here, I will ask as a favour, to be killed at once, which would be better than this."[171] Repeatedly, Pakan stressed to his audiences his community's need for education. The examples of both Egerton and Robert Steinhauer had made a great impression. In Pakan's words, "My object in going east was to get more schools for my people. Schools are what we want, to educate our children, who are thirsting for knowledge."[172] From government officials, the Whitefish chief wanted for his people, good schools, economic development, secure title to their land, and the right to govern themselves.

John McDougall had known Chief Samson (or Kanatakasu)[173] of the Rocky Mountain Cree, then a man in his mid-fifties, for a quarter of a century. The Methodists had named him Samson after the strongest of the strong, the legendary Old Testament figure. After the death of the Methodist Cree Chief Maskepetoon, Samson had succeeded him.[174] McDougall warmly recalled their buffalo hunts together, "Those wild rides beside my friend when, with a peculiar whoop and cry, he would start a herd, and then, watching the wind and lay of country, continue to manoeuvre them homewards. What a voice he had, and such magnetism in the cry and yell he would give."[175] Another memory of the respected Cree warrior dated back to 1885: "I will never forget, in connection with the troubles of 1885, how bravely he sat his horse beside me, and with his hand on his revolver meant death to any man who should raise his gun against his friend John."[176]

The Loyal Methodist Chiefs made their first major stop in Toronto, "the largest city in English-speaking Canada,"[177] with a population at the time of approximately a hundred thousand. The visitors saw busy Yonge Street humming with street life, full of smells and sounds new to them, crammed with horse-drawn carriages and trolleys. The street lighting, which "seemed like the stars in heaven," entranced Chief Samson.[178] The height of the buildings amazed Chief Pakan.[179] The smells of the city were not as impressive. Only two years earlier the Ontario Board of Health termed Toronto Bay a disgrace, "little better than a cesspool."[180] On hot days in Toronto everyone in the city could smell the harbour.[181] The newspapers fascinated Samson. The Cree chief told a reporter in London, Ontario, with Reverend McDougall translating, "If anything happens in the great country over the water you have it in your paper; but the poor Cree knows nothing of the world or what is in it."[182] The telephone amazed them. On 20 August the *Hamilton Spectator* commented, "Two of them talked over the wires in the central offices in Toronto, and half the time they could not speak for laughing."

During the day the crowds greatly upset the visiting chiefs. The Euro-Canadian people came very close, as many had never before seen an Indigenous person. As Chief Samson told a reporter in London, he found the curious gazes annoying: "We like to see the great streets of our cities, and your factories, but what makes us hurry back to our hotel rooms is the way you people look at us. If we go along the street men and women stop to stare at us, and your children gather around and look into our faces and make remarks and laugh. We don't like that."[183]

McDougall had originally intended to take Bearspaw, an important Stoney Nakoda chief,[184] to accompany Pakan and Samson, but as he "could not reach him in time," at the last moment he selected Jonas Goodstoney, Chief Bearspaw's nephew,[185] a "young man who is fast adopting civilized habits and ideas."[186] Recently, Goodstoney had begun to farm and keep cattle and horses,[187] and he had just marketed some

2.2 The three "Loyal Methodist Chiefs" in Toronto, sometime between mid-Aug. and early Oct. 1886. *Left to right*: Rev. John McDougall, Chief Samson (Cree), Pakan or James Seenum (Cree), and Jonas Goodstoney (Stoney Nakoda), and Robert Steinhauer, standing behind Goodstoney. NA-4216-33 by J. Fraser Bryce, 107 King St., Toronto. Courtesy of Glenbow Archives, Archives and Special Collections, University of Calgary.

new potatoes.[188] The youngest of the three men[189] proved the most eager to adopt new ways. Goodstoney wore a dark tweed coat and vest and knickerbockers.[190] Chief Pakan joined him in wearing shoes in the cities, but Chief Samson kept to moccasins.[191] The Loyal Methodist Chiefs had an unforgiving schedule: "Nightly, and sometimes twice on Sunday, the Indians addressed thousands of their fellow citizens."[192] In McDougall's words, "We visited most of the cities and towns between Sarnia and Montreal" and attracted huge crowds in the metropolitan centres. McDougall continued his description in his 3 December letter to the editor of the *Calgary Herald*: "We examined the manufactories and beheld the crude material transformed into articles of use in every walk in life; saw iron cast into stoves, door locks, plows and car furnishings; saw wood made into paper covered with 'the news of the world'; looked at the wool as it came from the sheep and witnessed it turned into flannels and blankets; saw cotton as it grew made into prints; went to Eddy's Mills in Hull and saw the manufacture of pails, tubs, washboards, and matches for the millions."[193]

One of the most extraordinary encounters in the Methodist tour occurred in Toronto on the evening of 7 September. Prime Minister John A. Macdonald met Reverend McDougall and the Loyal Methodist Chiefs during a surprise visit to Metropolitan Church, then hosting the national Methodist General Conference. Macdonald arrived just as McDougall had begun to address the huge crowd of delegates. He had only been speaking for a few minutes, when a noisy disruption occurred as people recognized Macdonald. Immediately, the chairman of the session invited the prime minister to join the speakers, and McDougall told the crowd, "He was proud and, for his own part, delighted to have the honour of being on the same platform with John Macdonald, the Premier of our great Dominion."[194] Discreetly, of course, the Methodist minister omitted any reference to the Conservative government's refusal to pay a single cent for the Loyal Methodist Chiefs' tour.

Just before Pakan and Samson made short addresses, the Cree interpreter Robert Steinhauer and Chief Pakan sang the hymn, "Tell It Again," in Cree.[195] Yielding to the public clamour for him to speak, the prime minister now addressed the delegates by reviewing some highlights of his recent journey across Canada on the newly completed CPR. In his remarks, the consummate politician, angling for Methodist votes, even slipped in a word of praise for the McDougalls, saying, "I have been over a considerable portion of the country where Mr Macdougall has so long and so faithfully labored, as well as his revered father."[196]

The tour of the three Loyal Methodist Chiefs brought out large crowds. The expenses of the trip were covered, but in the end, the same longterm funding issues remained for John McDougall. As chairman of the Methodists' Saskatchewan District in the 1880s, McDougall oversaw an enormous district that extended roughly 1,000 kilometres north to south and more than 300 kilometres east to west. In addition, he administered the Morley Mission, with the added responsibility and expense of directing the McDougall Orphanage, the residential school on the north side of the Bow River just to the east of the reserve, opened in September 1883.[197] John McDougall adamantly opposed off reserve boarding schools. The pupils, he wrote, "came from fifty to seven hundred miles to these schools, and came from camps and homes from which there had not been any separation of the child from the parent in all their previous history. This new life demanded the immediate tearing asunder of these, the most holy and sacred of ties." McDougall preferred boarding schools on, or next to, the reserve, and with his characteristic optimism established one at Morley, the McDougall Orphanage.[198] Stoney children could remain in the community to learn how to farm and raise stock and be instructed on how to become citizens and to enter the larger society.

The Methodist missionary knew well the poor material conditions of the reserves. As McDougall wrote in 1905, "This civilization with its permanent home life and dwelling houses and fixed habitations and its multiple insanitation, has been cruel and full of disease-breeding to the Indian peoples. While their former life gave pure air and constant change of camp and scene, the steadily demanded need of a permanent residence on the reserve has thrust the Indian into crude cabins full of foul atmosphere and surcharged with the germs of terrible disease." In addition, the "change of diet from meat and fowl and fish to cereals and vegetables and salt and sugar and syrup" took the Plains people totally by surprise.[199] The McDougall Orphanage, or Indian Residential School at Morley became John McDougall's answer, but alas, it never met his ambitious goals. As long as he himself directed the institution, in the late nineteenth century, it survived, barely, but within a decade of McDougall's departure it closed.

Several challenges prevented the Orphanage's success, cultural factors in particular. The almost total control by Euro-Canadians, non-supportive of Indigenous culture, alienated the Stoney Nakoda. Interference in the students' lives was constant. In First Nations society interference is forbidden.[200] The McDougall Orphanage's physical discipline, in particular, was totally foreign and objectionable. Other obstacles the institution faced were chronic underfunding and staffing. It was difficult to attract and keep qualified teachers. North American Indian missions came

2.3 John McDougall (*centre, at the front*), with students and teachers at the McDougall Orphanage at Morley, Alberta, 1890s (?). NA-1677-1. Courtesy of Glenbow Archives, Archives and Special Collections, University of Calgary.

second in the late nineteenth century, as many Methodists directed their missionary interest to the exotic mission fields of China, India, and Japan. In Canada the Methodist Church sent the least qualified recruits to work with the First Nations and recent immigrants.[201] The federal government did little to shore up Native education. The Canadian economist Helen Buckley has tersely summarized how both Conservative and Liberal governments handled Indian education after the treaties: "The tragedy is the educational system they got, which in no way fitted them for Canadian society. It was a cheap and cheerless package judged good enough for an unimportant minority."[202]

Both his church and the Department of Indian Affairs left many expenses in John McDougall's own hands.[203] Occasionally he had to trade furs with the Stoney, just to keep his poorly funded mission solvent. Despite adverse criticism from his own church,[204] John and his merchant brother David continued trading. At one point, he tried to obtain a grazing lease on an unused section of the reserve,[205] but Indian Affairs refused the request.[206] Under extremely difficult financial conditions, the Methodist missionary persevered, unwilling to give up. The poorly paid, ill-trained, and overworked staff turned over constantly. Many children became ill at the underfunded institution as a result of its poor sanitation.[207] McDougall tried to establish a hospital on the Stoney Nakoda Reserve in conjunction with the residential school. At the turn of the century the Stoney hospital remained unoccupied for five years, as the Methodist missionary could not pay for a nurse or hospital furnishings.[208]

After John McDougall left Morley for Calgary in 1899, the residential school or Orphanage only lasted another ten years, until it closed for mismanagement.[209] Dr James Lafferty, in his 1907 study of students at five Indian boarding schools in Alberta, reported that 80 per cent of the students at the Indian Residential School at Morley had tuberculosis of the lungs.[210] The closing of the Orphanage in 1910 symbolized the failure of John McDougall's initiative, his two decades of intensive labour a failure. It is true that a small number of the pupils learned how to read, write, and do basic arithmetic, young men like Walking Buffalo (George McLean), the interpreter, and Dan Wildman, the blacksmith (see chapter nine). But these successful individuals were few in number.

In 1906 Frank Oliver, the new Liberal Interior minister and superintendent general of Indian Affairs, invited John McDougall to become an Indian commissioner for the western provinces, "inspecting, advising and helping the natives toward self-support and independence."[211] Alberta and Saskatchewan became provinces in 1905. Indian Affairs also instructed McDougall to work to reduce reserve size as soon as possible to free up more land for incoming settlers. As the historian Brian Titley has written, "Securing the surrender of Indian lands was a policy approved of by politicians of every persuasion."[212]

McDougall's acceptance of the job offer seems contradictory. His Indian sympathies were well known. Consistently, he publicly defended aspects of the Indians' old way of life, and yet, at the same time, the veteran Methodist missionary believed the small Indigenous communities must ultimately blend into the majority society. This was the conventional wisdom of the day, namely, that the First Nations societies were ultimately destined to disappear.

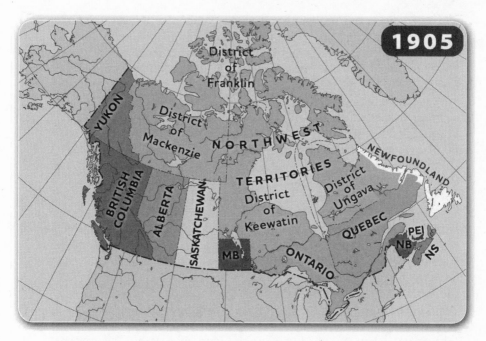

Map 2.2 Canada in 1905.

The First Nations population in Alberta continued to decline until into the 1920s.[213] Serious starvation and health issues predated Canada's acquisition of Rupert's Land in 1870. The historian James Daschuk has shown how from the 1730s onward, contagious diseases like smallpox, scarlet fever, measles, influenza, and tuberculosis ravaged the northern Plains.[214] In the 1870s and 1880s the population of the Treaty Seven area fell,[215] consumption (the term then used for tuberculosis) being the great killer.[216] According to federal government statistics, the Indian population in the Treaty Seven area dropped from almost 5,000 in 1896 to just over 3,000 in 1916. In short, Indigenous population numbers in twenty years had fallen by over one-third.[217] In contrast, Alberta's total population rose from 73,000 in 1901 to 375,000 just ten years later.[218] Within a generation, the First Nations had become only a very small proportion of the total population of Alberta.

John McDougall favoured the sale of what he called "surplus" land to ensure the survival of the First Nations who needed vast amounts of funding. Throughout the early twentieth century government social and health services were negligible or simply non-existent for both non-Indigenous and Indian peoples alike. Without a universal federal tax system, the Department of Indian Affairs used Indian annuities as well as revenues derived from Indian land sales to finance and support Treaty Indians. The Government of Canada relied on the charity of the Christian churches to run the schools, and parishioners often sent clothing to reserve Indians. The reliance on churches' badly financed Indian outreach meant poorly run schools and inadequate medical services.[219] Through the sale of land, McDougall believed, First Nations communities would be able to buy farm machinery to achieve economic self-sufficiency, and also pay for a first-class school system. In addition, he argued, some First Nations communities had surplus land, that is, land not needed for farming and raising livestock.

After his appointment as Oliver's special agent in negotiating land surrenders,[220] John McDougall initiated, or participated in, a number of negotiations from 1905 to 1910, including those regarding the Bobtail Reserve near Ponoka on the Calgary-Edmonton Trail,[221] Cote and Fishing Lake in Saskatchewan, and Swan Lake in Manitoba.[222] When McDougall approached the Tsuu T'ina (Sarcee) near Calgary to surrender a portion of their reserve southwest of Calgary, Chief Bull Head (Chula), a signatory of Treaty Seven,[223] bluntly told him, "My old friend John do not ask me while I live to let this land go. Ask the Government to refrain from pressing us on this subject. We say no."[224] Yet, there was some First Nations support for land sales. The proposal appealed, for example, to Chief Joseph Samson, son of the late Chief Samson,[225] John McDougall's excellent friend. At his reserve in central Alberta, Chief Samson had wanted his community to do more for themselves, but "they could do but little if they had no money to purchase horses and machinery."[226] In the end, Chief Samson reversed himself and voted against the proposed land sale. Showing good business acumen, he felt the community must hold out longer for the highest price they could obtain.[227]

In addition to travelling extensively across Prairie Canada in his official position, John McDougall spent the greater part of 1909 in British Columbia, visiting reserves in the Fraser Valley, the North and South Thompson valleys, Nicola, the Okanagan Valley, up the Skeena and the Babine country, and other areas in the interior of the province.[228] Frank Oliver asked him to investigate the size of the existing Indian reserves along the railway belt, a strip of land 20 miles wide on each side of the CPR in the interior of British Columbia, which had been given to the federal government as part of the 1871 agreement by which BC entered Confederation.[229] McDougall's report stated that the "vested right [of First Nations] to the ownership and long centuries of occupancy of the greater portion of the Province of British Columbia, has never been dealt with, by either the British or Canadian Governments."[230] This was true, but to the disappointment of Indigenous leaders in the south central BC interior, McDougall's report only recommended two additions to reserves in the Thompson (Nlaka'pamux) Territory, and listed reductions of several thousand acres in reserve size at Kamloops and in the Okanagan.[231]

John McDougall remained a prisoner of the thinking and the values of his times, a fervent advocate of "progress" and "development." As he had written just several years earlier, "He [God] made this big glorious country, it is His and we have felt that He will see to it that it is fully and successfully exploited."[232] McDougall constantly looked for good town sites and development opportunities. While the Methodist missionary rode across the Prairies, he confessed, "I was locating homes and selecting sites for village corners, and erecting schoolhouses and lifting church spires, and engineering railway routes, and hoping I might live to see some of this come to pass, for come it would."[233]

Pro-development he was, but, at the same time, almost alone among the Christian clergy of his day, John McDougall respected Native religion. He realized that their spiritual world was centred on the Creator, the Supreme Being who had established the world and all life. He preached tolerance at a time when most of his Euro-Canadian clerical contemporaries, in Brian Titley's words, "viewed indigenous religions with utter contempt."[234] In an important 1914 article, entitled "The Red Men of Canada's West Yesterday and To-day," John McDougall wrote, "These people were to a man most religious and intensely reverent."[235] He had publicly argued in 1908 that the Sun Dance should not be suppressed, for the Plains Indians were "just as much entitled to religious freedom as the white man."[236]

John McDougall repeatedly argued the Indian must be allowed to keep historic symbols of their old culture. The annual Banff Indian Days, for instance, should continue and thrive. They met a cultural need, allowing a people proud of their identity to celebrate their history and traditions. The *Calgary News Telegram* noted after McDougall's death, "Every summer at Banff when they have the Indian Pageant Dr McDougall rode in at their head."[237] He participated for the last time in 1916. McDougall helped to convince the superintendent general of Indian Affairs to allow the Plains peoples to participate in the first Calgary Stampede in 1912.[238] In the face of sport hunting groups that argued against Stoney Nakoda hunting outside and inside the national parks, the missionary unconditionally supported the Stoney's right to hunt game wherever they wanted to in their traditional hunting territory. McDougall added that they could fish at any time of year in all lakes, rivers, and streams.[239]

Yet, while Reverend McDougall held aspects of the old religion and culture in high esteem, overall he believed that Stoney Nakoda youth, the future generation, must eventually enter the mainstream society. In the Methodist missionary's words, Christianity provided the "clearer light."[240] Ultimately his objective, in the words of John Friesen of the Faculty of Education at the University of Calgary, and minister at the Morley United Church for many years, was "to take over and redesign Stoney values to fit a European anglo-Christian mould."[241] At their Methodist missionary's urging, for instance, the Stoney Council legislated against the making of drums until they were not allowed to keep them at all.[242]

Basically, what John McDougall wanted was equality. Shortly after the signing of the treaties, the Methodist missionary had called for the immediate observance of the treaty's terms.[243] No mention of the Indian Act had been made at treaties Six and Seven, both of which he witnessed. The Indian Act of 1876 described the Indians as wards of the Crown. Later amendments added additional paternalist features.[244] McDougall felt that the goal of the Canadian government should be the entry of the Indians as equals into Canadian society.

In mid-July 1916, several hundred Stoney Nakoda men, women, and children, close to half their total population, travelled by horse and wagon and on horseback to attend the Banff Indian Days, held that year on 14 and 15 July. They set up teepees on the spacious meadow at the base of the "mountain where the water falls," Cascade Mountain.[245] At their traditional camping area, they held their ceremonies, games, and socialized. For more than ten thousand years, North American Indians have lived and travelled thorough this region.[246] Here, at the 1916 Banff Indian Days, occurred the highlight of John McDougall's public life.[247] On late Saturday afternoon, 15 July, he interpreted at the induction of the Duke of Connaught, the governor general of Canada and Queen Victoria's only surviving son, as a Stoney Nakoda chief. The Duke of Connaught's godfather was the Iron Duke, the Duke of Wellington himself.

The ceremony occurred at the "Indian Village" just below Cascade Mountain.[248] A surviving ten-minute newsreel[249] confirms that McDougall did a splendid job. Later a note arrived from His Royal Highness, with an autographed photo of himself in Indian costume, with his interpreter in the foreground.[250] John McDougall died five months later, on 15 January 1917, at the age of 73. On 20 January the *Calgary Herald* ran on its front page a photo of him the previous July with the governor general, the Stoney Nakoda, and non-Indigenous dignitaries.

John McDougall truly lived in two worlds. He grew up with Ojibwe friends. His first wife was Cree. He was fluent in two Indigenous languages. In his writings, he emphasized positive aspects of Plains

2.4 The Duke of Connaught, governor general of Canada, on the extreme right, thanking the Stoney Nakoda for his induction as a Stoney Nakoda chief, 15 July 1916. John McDougall is shown in the centre of the photograph. NA-1571-1. Courtesy of Glenbow Archives, Archives and Special Collections, University of Calgary.

Indians way of life in the buffalo days. He championed the right of First Nations to participate in the Banff Indian Days and the Calgary Exhibition (and Stampede). He advocated for Stoney Nakoda hunting rights. Yet, ultimately John Chantler McDougall had the same blind spot as the others of his time. He worked for the cultural assimilation of the First Nations into Canadian society and did not see how the First Nations in the future could retain their culture and heritage. Like virtually everyone else of Anglo-Canadian background in Western Canada in his day, McDougall believed the First Nations, the French Canadians, and all immigrants must conform to the already fixed values and institutions of British Canada.[251] As the Canadian political scientist Alan Cairns has observed, "The possibility that separate self-governing Indian communities might persist indefinitely was not seriously considered in non-Aboriginal society until the mid-1960s in the Hawthorn Report."[252]

The Stoney Nakoda disagreed and sought to retain as much of their heritage as possible while adjusting to new ways of living in their ever-changing homeland.

Chapter Three

George Monro Grant: An English Canadian Public Intellectual and the Indians

George M. Grant (1835–1902), long-serving principal of Queen's University in Kingston, Ontario, stands out as one of the most open-minded Canadians of his era. In the late nineteenth century, an age in which few Anglo-Canadians, including Canada's first prime minister could speak French, he conversed easily in the language.[1] Grant believed in Canada as a British nation, but one of ethnic and religious diversity.[2] As early as 1881 the Presbyterian minister denounced restrictions on Asian immigration to Canada.[3] He contributed financially to the building of a synagogue in his hometown of Kingston,[4] and opened the door of the university to Roman Catholics.[5] Principal Grant admitted women to regular classes at Queen's in 1879, and endorsed the establishment of the Women's Medical College in 1883.[6] Grant made an impressive tribute to Robert Sutherland (c. 1830–1878), winner of fourteen academic prizes, first African Canadian graduate of Queen's University, first African Canadian lawyer in Upper Canada, and early benefactor of the university. Principal Grant placed a large granite tombstone in Toronto's newly established Mount Pleasant Cemetery to mark Robert Sutherland's connection with Queen's.[7] The university president spoke out publicly against the execution of Louis Riel in 1885.[8] He strongly supported the entry of North American Indians into mainstream Canadian society.

A high point of Queen's University's recognition of Indigenous Canada came at its 1886 spring Convocation when Reverend Silas Rand of Nova Scotia was bestowed with an honorary doctorate.[9] At the ceremony, Principal Grant officially presented the missionary to the Mi'kmaq to Chancellor Sandford Fleming. Grant had been in touch with Rand for nearly a decade, sometimes in Latin.[10] Rand's choice of Latin as their language of communication suited Principal Grant, who was quite at ease in the ancient tongue. When he toured Germany as a student in

1860, not knowing German, he had used Latin to communicate with German students.[11] In his introduction to Chancellor Fleming, Grant reviewed the Mi'kmaq missionary's career, lauding his extraordinary contribution to transform the Mi'kmaq into self-supporting Protestant farmers. Grant also praised Rand's outstanding contribution to scholarship on "the history, manners, customs, legends and language" of the Mi'kmaq and several other First Nations. Rand's major linguistic contribution was "a Micmac English Dictionary in which about thirty thousand words are collected and arranged."[12]

Grant explained Silas Rand's contribution to First Nations in the Maritime Provinces in these glowing terms: "When he began his work they were all in their primitive barbarism, with the vices of white men superadded; whereas, now many live in houses, own property and schools, have the gospel and other books in their own language, partake of our civilization and are inspired with our hope."[13]

Both Principal Grant and Reverend Rand shared a common outlook on North American Indians. Like many respected thinkers in late nineteenth-century North America, they believed in a cultural hierarchy, in which humanity moved from savagery, through barbarity to civilization. Just as the ancient Britons had progressed, so could the Mi'kmaq. Rand's 1850 pamphlet, *A Short Statement of Facts Relating to the History, Manners, Customs, Language and Literature of the Micmac Tribe of Indians, in Nova Scotia and P.E. Island*, compared the Indians of northeastern North America and the English: "The ancient inhabitants of England very much resembled the Indians of the western world. They lived in miserable cabins, in the midst of gloomy forests; they engaged in ferocious wars; they painted their bodies and dressed in skins."[14] Humanity's moral and social progress depended on changing the conditions under which they lived, through education and the alteration of the physical environment.[15]

Reverend Silas Rand received his honorary Doctor of Laws degree from Sandford Fleming, Queen's celebrity chancellor, who himself had never attended university. Canada's foremost railway surveyor and construction engineer, as well as an inventor and scientist,[16] had but two years earlier seen his 24-hour standard international time system win acceptance at the International Prime Meridian Conference in Washington, DC. Sandford Fleming's idea of a world map divided into twenty-four uniform time zones, with Greenwich, England, as the prime meridian, earned him the accolade, the "Father of Standard Time."

From his survey work throughout the Dominion of Canada, Fleming knew the First Nations well. In 1884 he estimated in his book, *England*

and Canada: A Summer Tour between Old and New Westminster, that of Canada's total population of about four million people, approximately 100,000, or roughly 2.5 per cent, were North American Indians. Their numbers were low in Central and Eastern Canada. "In Ontario they are seldom thought of," as they numbered only 18,000 individuals. In Quebec lived 12,000 Indians, and in the Maritime Provinces, only 4,000.[17] Their numbers were much greater, however, west of Ontario, with 36,500 in British Columbia, and in the North West "under the immediate care of the Government," 10,000. The population of Indians was 9,000 "in the more northern Hudson's Bay Territories, Labrador and the Arctic coast."[18]

Ironically, Silas Rand, who later did much to help rescue the Mi'kmaq language and folklore, was born in 1810 in Cornwallis, a village named after an individual aggressively hostile to the Mi'kmaq. In 1752 Edward Cornwallis, governor of Nova Scotia from 1749 to 1752, arrived in the area known to the Mi'kmaq as Chebooktook, meaning "great long harbour" or "biggest harbour." The British military officer came with approximately twenty-five hundred English settlers commissioned by George Montagu-Dunk, 2nd earl of Halifax, then president of the English Board of Trade and Plantations. Cornwallis established a naval and military base to counter the great French fortress of Louisbourg on Cape Breton Island. Upon arrival the English governor unilaterally expropriated Mi'kmaq land and renamed Chebooktook, "Halifax" – after his superior.[19] At no point did Cornwallis negotiate with the Mi'kmaq the terms by which the harbour might be transferred to the British.

The 1750s proved a brutal decade. The Mi'kmaq had fought for over half a century against the British to protect their homeland. Rather than seek compromise, Cornwallis opted for counter-violence, at one point offering rewards of 10 pounds (later raised to 50) for the scalp of any Indian brought into Halifax.[20] This was common practice for European colonial governments who encouraged Indian allies to kill and scalp enemy Indians.[21] The British also soon launched operations against the French-speaking Acadian setters, leading up to their eventual deportation. As the historian Caroline-Isabelle Caron writes, "Between the end of August 1755 and the fall of 1763, about eighteen hundred British soldiers systematically crisscrossed present-day Nova Scotia (starting with Grand-Pré), New Brunswick, and Prince Edward Island to capture Acadians, seize their lands and their livestock, and burn their houses."[22] Historians estimate that between 1755 and 1763 the British deported three-quarters of the Acadian population of approximately thirteen thousand. They expelled more than half that number in the first year alone.

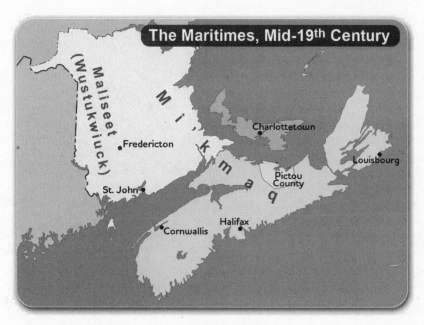

Map 3.1 The Maritimes, mid-nineteenth century.

The British North Americans who replaced the Acadians encroached on Indigenous hunting and fishing territories, helping themselves to Mi'kmaq land, fish, game, and timber. The British confiscated portions of their territories as Crown land without financial compensation. Quickly, they ignored their own peace and friendship treaties with the First Nations, made in 1726, and subsequently renewed in 1749, 1752, and 1760–1.[23] These treaties did not result in land surrenders or lead to the creation of reserves. In the Great Lakes area, the Royal Proclamation of 1763 protected First Nations land rights, but the British authorities ruled the document did not apply in the Maritime colonies.

The arrival of thirty thousand British Loyalist refugees in 1782–3 tripled Nova Scotia's non-Indigenous population to forty-two thousand.[24] The massive numbers of newcomers overwhelmed the Mi'kmaq, pushing them away from remaining fishing sites and hunting grounds, reducing them to poverty. By the 1850s Nova Scotia had set aside some reserves for the Mi'kmaq, but without proper legal descriptions and surveys settler encroachments continued. Immigrants could obtain title to land, but the Mi'kmaq could not, as they only received "licenses of occupation during pleasure,"[25] that is, a title without security of tenure.

3.1 Mi'kmaq wigwam, probably taken in Dartmouth, Nova Scotia, 1860. Photo no. 47728, National Anthropological Archives, Smithsonian Institution, Washington, DC.

Although Silas Rand's parents had little formal education, they respected learning. The Rands sent their eighth child, eighth in a family of twenty-two,[26] to school for four winters. At the age of 11, Silas left and worked as a farm labourer and then a brickmaker. His religious conversion at the age of 23 gave his life focus, and purpose. Ordained to the Baptist ministry in 1834, Silas Rand and his "excellent" wife, Jane McNutt,[27] whom he married in 1838, had a large family, eventually twelve children. Financially, it proved challenging after Rand left the regular ministry to evangelize among the Mi'kmaq, to reach out to those he called, "the rightful owners of the soil."[28] The missionary's amazing capacity for learning languages had allowed him already to master Latin, Greek, Hebrew, French, German, and Spanish; and now he added Mi'kmaq and the related Malecite or Maliseet (Wolastoqiyik or Wustukwiuck).[29] Rand loved Mi'kmaq, a language he described as "copious, flexible, and expressive."[30] Concerned that the Bible was not available to them in their own language, he began translating portions of it into Mi'kmaq.

Their language and mythology gave him many insights into Mi'kmaq culture.[31] He came to understand the people's feelings about their land from their vantage point: "The white man may pass from one end of Nova Scotia to the other, and travel all over the adjacent Islands, and see but little which reminds him, with any force, of those who once owned and occupied the soil; but the Indian can travel nowhere, and pitch his tent nowhere, without seeing that which forcibly reminds him of those who now have it in possession."[32] The gifted writer and speaker of their language also helped the Indians in the drafting of petitions to the colonial government.[33]

In November 1849 Silas Rand founded the Halifax-based Micmac Missionary Society, an overtly anti-Catholic organization. French Roman Catholic missionaries had gained influence over the Mi'kmaq in the seventeenth and eighteenth centuries and in the mid-nineteenth century with a spiritual approach that incorporated many Mi'kmaq old traditional beliefs and ceremonies.[34] Their attachment to their Roman Catholic faith made it impossible for Rand to make any headway, although the Mi'kmaq liked and respected him as an individual.[35] Despite his lack of converts,[36] Rand persevered with his Mi'kmaq studies.

Concerning Native land rights this friend of the Mi'kmaq was a true visionary. Rand called for the recognition of the Indigenous Title in Nova Scotia, and for compensation for lands lost.[37] In an 1854 address, Rand shouted from the platform: "Shame on us! We invade the territory of men made like ourselves, and fashioned in the image of God … we treat them as though they had no rights. We seize upon their country. We rob them of their lands. We drive them from their homes. We plunder them of all they hold dear and sacred; we deceive and defraud them – we violate the most solemn treaties made with them; we impoverish, degrade, despise and abuse them."[38] Information about Rand's advocacy of Indigenous land rights reached George Grant, now minister of Halifax's St Matthew's Church. The historian Barry Mack found among Grant's papers the draft of an extraordinary 1870 sermon, in which Grant poses this question, a revolutionary one for his Presbyterian congregation: "Who owned the lands of these Provinces originally? or in all of N[orth] A[merica]? If anyone, the Red Indians." Then he adds, "If a race superior to us came now to these shores, would they have the right to displace us in similar ways?"[39]

George Monro Grant was born on 22 December 1835 at Albion Mines (now Stellarton), next to present-day New Glasgow, in Nova Scotia's Pictou County.[40] In 1761 there were about 8,000 people of European descent living on mainland Nova Scotia, with the Mi'kmaq population numbering about half that number.[41] By the late 1830s about 200,000 people of European descent[42] lived in the colony, but only approximately 1,700 Mi'kmaq.[43] In Grant's home county, the 125 or so Mi'kmaq[44] had no official reserve. James Dawson reported on the Pictou Mi'kmaq: "At present they are driven from place to place, without a resting place for their feet – their game is gone – firewood is denied them, and the very sanctuaries of their dead, are in some instances desecrated and ploughed over."[45] In 1871 the population of Nova Scotia was 400,000,[46] and the Mi'kmaq numbered only about 2,000, that is, about half of one per cent of the province's population.

James and Mary Grant, George Monro's parents, had emigrated in the 1820s from Scotland to Pictou County. The arrival of the ship *Hector* in 1773, half a century earlier, marked the beginning of a more or less continuous Scottish immigration.[47] The evictions from the Highlands to make room for grazing sheep led thousands to migrate to North America across the North Atlantic. The 1871 census revealed the predominance of Scots in Pictou County. Fully 85 per cent of those in Pictou were of Scottish descent, and in terms of religious affiliation, over 80 per cent were Presbyterians.[48]

In Pictou County the Grants enjoyed little economic security, as James's attempts at farming, then teaching school, then legal work, and finally a commercial career all failed. The family's pillar of strength, Mary Monro Grant, raised the five children. Concerning her third child, George, she felt that "God had a purpose for him."[49] Anxious to gain a secure niche in their new society, George's parents did not teach him Gaelic, their ancestral language. To succeed he must have a complete mastery of spoken and written English. At age eight, George seriously injured his right hand, which ruled out heavy farm labour. His parents sent him to the well-respected Pictou Academy and later a Presbyterian seminary at West River, from which the excellent student was selected in 1853 to become one of the four beneficiaries of the established Church of Scotland's "Young Men's Scheme." The winners of the award could attend the University of Glasgow and enter its arts and theology course, to prepare in Scotland for the ministry.

Great achievement marked George Grant's seven years at the University of Glasgow. The capable and clever Nova Scotian took advantage of every opportunity to learn. The Canadian historian Carl Berger notes he "steeped himself in the writings of the romantics – Coleridge, Wordsworth, and Carlyle – and filled his notebooks with their epigrams."[50] An excellent student, Grant won numerous prizes in subjects as varied as Greek and chemistry, as well as an award for the oral translation from French to English of John Calvin's major theological work, *Institution de la religion chrétienne* (1541). With the award money for his essay on "The

Relations of Critical, Systematic and Historical Theology," he paid for a visit to Europe. Always an extrovert, he became captain of the football (soccer) team. Grant also served as president of the university's Conservative Club.[51] Away from the university, he volunteered in an inner-city mission in the Glasgow slums.[52] George Grant obtained his M.A. with great distinction.[53]

The newly ordained Presbyterian minister returned to Nova Scotia in the spring of 1861. Quickly he gained recognition as "a charismatic leader" with "a remarkable ability to kindle faith and extract work and money from others."[54] At the age of 27, Reverend George Monro Grant was appointed the minister of Halifax's St Matthew's Church, the largest and wealthiest Presbyterian congregation in the Maritimes, founded in 1750.[55] In the community, Grant helped to reorganize Dalhousie College, the provincial university. The public-spirited minister of St Matthews also participated in a host of organizations that included the direction of the School for the Blind, the Halifax Institution for the Deaf and Dumb, the Children's Home, the Halifax Industrial School, and the Young Men's Christian Association.[56] Grant regarded service to others as his Christian duty. In 1867, the year of Confederation, George Grant married Jesse Lawson, the eldest daughter of a prosperous merchant family that had lived in Halifax since its founding in 1749. Grant's "discovery" of North American Indians came about as a result of his travels in the North West in 1872.

The Presbyterian minister's visit to "Indian country" came through his close friendship with Sandford Fleming, at that time a member of his congregation. Having superintended the construction of the Intercolonial Railway from Quebec City to Halifax, Fleming was Prime Minister Macdonald's choice as the first engineer-in-chief of the railway to be built to the Pacific.[57] The speedy construction of a transcontinental railway became an important national political issue after Macdonald agreed, in 1871, to build it as the price of British Columbia's entry into Canada. In early 1872 Grant accepted Fleming's invitation to accompany the expedition as its secretary, historian, and chaplain. The skilled engineer and the gifted writer each brought a different range of knowledge and skills to the adventure. *Ocean to Ocean*, Grant's masterful travel narrative, chronicles their 8,000 kilometre journey by train, steamer, canoe, Red River cart, horse and stagecoach across British North America to Victoria on Vancouver Island.

George Grant left Halifax on 1 July 1872, Canada's fifth birthday, on a journey that lasted three and a half months. The party all met in Toronto, then set off by train to Collingwood on Georgian Bay to take a steamer to Thunder Bay. The section from Lake Superior to the Red

3.2 "At Toronto July 15th 1872 en route for the Pacific." They had gathered at the Queen's Hotel in Toronto before setting out on their journey to the Pacific Ocean. *Left to right*: James Robertson Ross, Dr Arthur Moren, Sandford Fleming, George Monro Grant (shown concealing his missing right hand), Frank Fleming (Sandford's son). V28 P-94.13, Queen's Picture Collection, Queen's University Archives.

River was by canoe, through Ojibwe (Anishinabe) territory. George Grant carefully wrote in his diary each evening. In the North West, Grant recognized the rights of First Nations to their land. At the outset of the canoe journey from Thunder Bay to Red River, he wrote, "In the name of justice, and of the sacred rights of property, is not the Indian entitled to liberal and, if possible, permanent compensation?"[58] Echoing the pronouncements of Silas Rand, he continued, that it was absolutely "incumbent on the Government of a Christian people to treat them not only justly but generously."[59] The Nova Scotian minister was sensitive to the reality of the North American Indians. Make fair treaties with them he urged, "on the principles of allotting to them reserves of land that no one can invade, and that they themselves cannot alienate, giving them an annual sum per family in the shape of useful articles, establishing schools among them and encouraging missionary efforts, and prohibiting the sale of intoxicating liquors to them."[60] Once the treaties or covenants were signed, the land became Canada's. The treaty was a single transaction, one which extinguished Aboriginal Title: "The ancient inhabitants of the land understand that they have no rights except what are expressly stipulated in solemn covenants, which covenants, too, are their most valued charters."[61]

In southwestern Manitoba, and later in the North Saskatchewan River Valley, George Grant discovered incredible future farmland with rich soil, flat land, without rocks or trees: "It is impossible to avoid the conclusion that we have a great and fertile North-west, a thousand miles long and from one to four hundred miles broad, capable of containing a population of millions."[62] In *Ocean to Ocean*, Grant announced a theme he unfailingly advanced from the publication of this book onward, namely, the necessity of Indigenous assimilation: "As the Indian has no chance of existence except by conforming to civilized ways, the sooner that the Government or the Christian people awake to the necessity of establishing schools among every tribe the better."[63]

Over the Prairie portion of the journey, veteran Methodist missionary Reverend George McDougall (father of John McDougall, see previous chapter), born and raised in Ontario, joined the party. No other single individual had such an influence on George Grant's perception of the Plains Indians. In Grant's words, "He was well known to us by reputation as a faithful minister and an intelligent observer of Indian character. He had been nine times over the plains and evidently knew the country better than our guides."[64] A later entry reads, "Mr McDougal [sic] in particular was invaluable. In every difficulty we called upon him and he never failed us. He would come up with his uniform sober pleasant look, take in the bearings of the whole case, and decide promptly what was to be done."[65]

George McDougall was born in 1820 in Kingston, Upper Canada, and grew up in the heavy bush country northwest of Barrie not far from Georgian Bay, where he farmed, hunted, and trapped to help support his family. The superb axe man[66] canoed and handled a pair of snowshoes like a Native.[67] Until the age of 18, the retired British sailor's son could neither read nor write, until he attended a tiny local school in the evenings. His conversion to Methodism the next year totally transformed his outlook, and led to a new life of service. His marriage to Elizabeth Chantler proved exceptionally blessed. This pious well-educated woman came from an English Quaker family, a religious community renowned for its concern for non-violence and social justice. Years later, Peter Erasmus, the Métis guide, and interpreter, recalled, "She was a very kindly woman. She hardly ever raised her voice to correct the children."[68]

The McDougalls lived on a farm in the Owen Sound area. George owned and sailed a vessel on Georgian Bay and worked locally as a Methodist preacher. In time, the church allowed him to obtain theological training at Victoria College in Cobourg, about 100 kilometres east of Toronto. After a year of study, he went to work at the Alderville Mission near Rice Lake, as the assistant of Reverend William Case. George McDougall helped the veteran Methodist missionary to the Ojibwe in southern Ontario run Alderville's boarding school. His farm background gave him, in the words of his biographer John Maclean, "a power in his hands which was well employed in teaching the Indians to become self-supporting."[69] William Case's dream became George McDougall's. At the 1846 Council of Ojibwe communities in southern Ontario, Case had called for the establishment of Indian boarding schools: "We see no reason why the Red man should not be as comfortable, respectable and happy as the white man." In time, he added, "You may, indeed live to see some of your sons doctors, attorneys and magistrates. This is a thing not at all improbable. You have already lived to see our warriors become Ministers of the Gospel, Interpreters, and Teachers of our Schools."[70]

After his Alderville posting, George McDougall went next to the Methodist mission near Sault Ste Marie and then to Rama north of Lake Simcoe.[71] Ordained as a Methodist minister in 1852,[72] he proved an energetic and successful missionary, at both postings. The Methodists next appointed him missionary superintendent for the North West, with headquarters at Norway House, at the north end of Lake Winnipeg, 2,000 kilometres to the west. Three years later, in 1863, George McDougall established his headquarters in a more central location for his huge district, 130 kilometres northeast of Fort Edmonton on the North Saskatchewan River. Without making too great a stretch of their imagination, the Methodists named their new mission settlement Victoria.

Great challenges followed for the McDougalls now located in a war zone between the Cree and the Blackfoot. The death of Maskepetoon (or Broken Arm), the Methodists' leading convert among the Cree proved a great loss. He was killed in 1869 on a peace mission to the Blackfoot. In late 1869–70 the worst catastrophe of all arrived, smallpox. The Blackfoot, McDougall wrote, "driven to desperation by the awful scourge which has cut off more than one-half of their tribe," stole "our horses and killed our cattle: articles of clothing and human hair, infected with the small-pox, have been left in our villages."[73] George McDougall lost two of his natural daughters, and an adopted Indian daughter in the epidemic. His son John, his missionary assistant, who almost died from the disease,[74] later wrote of the epidemic: "East and west and south, all over the land, the death role was fearful; fully fifty per cent of the people being carried away."[75] On top of these horrors that autumn, near the present-day site of Lethbridge in southern Alberta, the Cree with their Assiniboine allies attacked the Blackfoot nations greatly weakened by the smallpox. Armed with repeating rifles superior to the Cree and Assiniboine's inferior muzzleloaders, the Bloods and Peigans held their own and repelled the huge raiding party. Final estimates were that the attackers lost between two hundred and three hundred warriors, and the defenders about forty.[76]

The two Georges were absolute opposites. The well-schooled Presbyterian minister had an enviable command of English. His Methodist counterpart did not.[77] McDougall's reading centred on the Bible, and on Methodist church publications. Grant's had a wider compass. A major item, for example, in George McDougall's conversation was Roman Catholicism, "the blight of Christianity."[78] In an 1870 letter he lamented, "The man of sin is powerfully represented in this country. There are five Priests to one Protestant Missionary; they are anti-British in their national sympathies; and if we may judge the tree by its fruits, anti-Christian in their teachings."[79] George McDougall did not even bother to learn the proper identity of his Catholic opponents in what is now Alberta. He called them "Jesuits,"[80] while these priests actually belonged to the Oblate Order.[81] In contrast to his Methodist counterpart, George Grant had an unusual outlook for the times: he was tolerant towards Roman Catholics.

Peter Erasmus, George McDougall's talented Métis interpreter and guide in the early 1860s, found the Methodist missionary stiff and autocratic.[82] The need to spread the truth of Protestant Christianity alone commanded his attention. George Grant was much softer, and even had an appreciation of other faiths. The well-educated Presbyterian minister recognized the truths and accomplishments of other world religions.[83] McDougall so loathed "paganism" he approved the seizure and subsequent removal to Victoria of a First Nations sacred monument. Several hundred kilometres to the south stood the Manitou Stone, a meteorite that fell from space and landed intact on Earth.[84] The Blackfoot and the Cree included it in spiritual ceremonies, and left offerings. For many years, the site of the meteorite was a place of worship and reverence.[85] In 1866 the Methodists removed the Manitou Stone to the

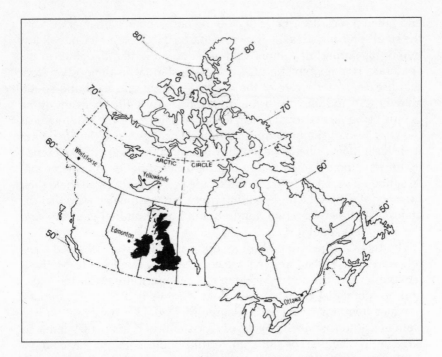

Map 3.2 "Relative Latitudinal Locations, Canada and the British Isles," courtesy of Dr William C. Wonders, University Professor Emeritus, Department of Geography, University of Alberta. "Ocean to Ocean," the immense size of Canada compared with the British Isles.

Victoria Mission,[86] and later sent it on its way to the museum at the Methodist Victoria College in Cobourg, Ontario.[87]

At Edmonton, George Grant said goodbye to George McDougall, after nearly a month together.[88] The Fleming expedition now travelled to the Rockies and made the arduous journey over "a sea of mountains" to the coast.[89] By foot and horseback they crossed over the Yellowhead Pass and down to the Pacific Ocean by the North Thompson and Fraser rivers, arriving at Burrard Inlet on 5 October, almost three months after setting out from Toronto on 15 July. In record speed Grant's book, *Ocean to Ocean*, came out in early 1873. It is remembered today as a classic in Western Canadian travel literature.[90]

George Grant's appointment as principal of Queen's University in 1877 marked his entry onto the national stage as a Canadian public figure. He helped to transform a small church college of ninety students in

Kingston, Ontario, into the university for eastern Ontario, with an enrolment of 850.[91] His commitment to Queen's is legendary. When someone once asked him why he sat up all night to save Pullman expenses, travelling second class on his repeated fundraising campaigns, he answered, "Because there is no third."[92] Right from the beginning of his appointment, George Grant proved an energetic, visionary university principal, loyal to his institution. When Premier Oliver Mowat invited him in 1883 to become minister for education for Ontario,[93] Grant declined the offer, and stayed to build Queen's. Its tall limestone clock tower and assembly and concert hall, Grant Hall, completed in 1905 and named posthumously in honour of George Monro Grant, remains Queen's best-known landmark.

In light of his new responsibilities as a college principal, Grant understandably wrote very little about Indigenous peoples, apart from a revealing reference in his travel book, *Picturesque Canada*. In his chapter on Manitoba, Grant wrote in the early 1880s, "The Indians of Manitoba are gradually disappearing before the stronger races."[94] Previously, the educator had stated, in *Ocean to Ocean*, his answer to the Native decline: "Little can be done with the old, and it may be two three or more generations before the old habits of a people are changed; but, by always taking hold of the young, the work can be done. A mission without schools is a mistake, almost a crime."[95]

Sandford Fleming invited George Grant to accompany him on a second western expedition in 1883. As a welcome break from his administrative duties, Grant accepted.[96] Two years earlier, the Canadian Pacific had changed the intended route for the transcontinental railway. Previously, it was assumed that the railway would travel along the North Saskatchewan River, from Winnipeg to Edmonton, and then through the mountains by way of the Yellowhead Pass. Suddenly, the CPR reversed itself and favoured a shorter route. It was decided that the railway should cross the southern Canadian Prairies and follow a more southern pass than the Yellowhead. The CPR now asked Sandford Fleming to report on the work of Colonel Rogers, then investigating the possibility of the Kicking Horse–Rogers Pass.

Fleming and Grant took a train to Calgary, arriving on 22 August 1883. The first CPR train had only reached the town ten days earlier. After just one day in Calgary, they left by wagon for Morley, where ten years earlier the McDougalls had moved their Methodist missionary headquarters from Victoria. They next entered the Rockies and advanced towards the Kicking Horse Pass down the Illecillewat, a challenging trip for two men now both well into middle age. On the evening of 23 August 1883, George Grant met John McDougall, "son of our old friend who had travelled with us eleven years ago from Fort Edmonton."[97] As John McDougall, now an ordained Methodist minister himself, explained, they had chosen to work with the Stoney as his father considered them, "Indians of the best type."[98] The McDougalls selected a traditional winter camping ground near the meeting of the Bow and Ghost rivers.[99] In Stoney Nakoda, the Bow Valley and Bow River were called Mînî Thnî Wapta, or Cold Water River.[100] In honour of Reverend Morley Punshon, then president of the Wesleyan Methodist Church Conference in Canada,[101] the Methodist mission site obtained the title of Morleyville, later shortened to Morley.

That evening John McDougall brought George Grant up to date on Western developments since the 1872 expedition. The two men stayed up long after midnight.[102] The next day, the principal of Queen's University commented in a letter to his wife, "I enjoyed my evening at Morley very much, & got a great deal of interesting information about the Indians ranching, shooting, fishing, farming, travelling & everything else pertaining to the North-West."[103] He heard the poignant story of John's father's death. Separated from John, George McDougall had perished in a severe blizzard in a January 1876 buffalo hunt near the newly constructed Fort Calgary. After his father's death, John McDougall had become the Stoney's main non-Indigenous contact. The Blackfoot even referred to the Morley Mission as "where John lives," or in Blackfoot, *tsawn-okoway*, the word *tsawn* being a Blackfoot adaptation of "John."[104]

The construction of the Canadian Pacific Railway had reached Morley. John McDougall described the impact of the several thousand men on grading and construction crews advancing across the Foothills. West of Morley the locating crew had commenced work in the Canmore Corridor. They passed Padmore (now Canmore) about the first of June.[105] The building of a railroad through the Upper Bow Valley was not anticipated in the 1870s; however, the switch to the southern route in 1881 ended the isolation of the Stoney Reserve.

Knowing that the CPR needed timber for railway ties and telegraph poles, John McDougall instructed the Stoney on the use of an axe and a whipsaw. He offered to help the CPR find a market and the railway indicated an interest, but once cutting began, the Department of Indian Affairs intervened. On 3 March 1883, William Pocklington, Indian Affairs sub-agent for Treaty Seven, presented McDougall with a formal notice to end the timber operation:[106] "Sir, – I have the honour to inform you that it has been reported to me that you have been trading with the Indians for timber cut by them on this reservation, contrary to the Indian Act."[107] The timber operation must end. Reluctantly John complied. He stopped the cut of timber and immediately reported the

3.3 A watercolour of the Stoney Indian Mission Buildings by the Rev. E.F. Wilson, 6 June 1887. NA-4094-3, Archives and Special Collections, University of Calgary.

incident to the CPR. While awaiting a reply, "the graders came along, and in doing their work, fires ran through the grass." A blaze reached the piling ground where McDougall had stored the ties already cut. In the Methodist missionary's words, "my kitchen and cook-house and five thousand ties" were all burned to ashes.[108] Three years later, McDougall bitterly recalled the injustice. He told George Ham, a visiting *Toronto Daily Mail* journalist, "Every movement to teach the Indian industry has been knocked on the head by the department."[109]

In the fall of 1886, John McDougall met George Grant again when the Methodist missionary brought the two Cree chiefs Samson and Pakan and the Stoney Nakoda Jonas Goodstoney to Ontario and Quebec. The trip was a thank you for their loyalty in 1885. After the "Loyal Chiefs" (see previous chapter) presentation at Kingston's City Hall on 24 August 1886, Principal Grant made a few remarks. As the *Kingston*

Whig-Standard reported, Grant welcomed the visitors and lauded the loyalty of the Christian chiefs in the 1885 rebellion and added, the "only way to make the Indians true men was to make Christians of them."

The high point in George Grant's interest in the First Nations came that same year, the year he proposed Reverend Silas Rand for an honorary doctorate in recognition of his linguistic work with the Mi'kmaq. The outspoken principal of Queen's University joined in the 1886 wave of protest against the Macdonald government's handling of the "Indian Question" on the Prairies. During the troubles of 1885 the Presbyterian community had proved remarkably sympathetic to the First Nations and the Métis. A number of them saw the injustice of Macdonald's iron-fisted administration of the North West. Reverend Daniel Miner Gordon had served as a chaplain with the Canadian military force that attacked Batoche, and he had written Grant to say that the Indigenous peoples were "very much worse off by reason of the advent of the whites ... It is a bitter mockery on the Christian name for us to apply it to ourselves as a people when we have treated the Indian in such a way as to make him partake of our worse vices and vilest diseases, and do nothing more than to help him than give him a bare pittance of food."[110] In a public lecture given in Halifax on 28 August 1885, Principal Grant called for clemency for Riel stating that to hang him "would be criminal on our part ... it would not only be a crime but a blunder ... Rather than hang him, I would open his prison doors and let him go free." George Grant predicted that Riel's execution would embitter the Métis "against us permanently."[111] At the 1886 Canadian Presbyterian General Assembly, Reverend William Caven, the principal of the Presbyterian Knox College, federated with the University of Toronto,[112] introduced a protest resolution: "That the General Assembly, whilst disclaiming all political party aims, feels bound to give expression to its convictions regarding the treatment of the Indians in the Northwest by the Dominion of Canada." Principal Grant supported the motion. After he emphasized the importance of the question, he proposed a standing vote. The Assembly agreed. By a standing vote the resolution carried.[113]

In 1886 George Grant also critically attacked the blatant disregard of Indigenous rights on the Pacific Coast. Fifteen years earlier, when British Columbia had joined Canada, it was anticipated that treaties would be signed with the resident First Nations. Despite the desire of both the Macdonald and the Mackenzie governments to make treaties following the protocol of the Royal Proclamation of 1763, the provincial government refused to cooperate. Grant vigorously defended the First Nations of Metlakatla in their fight for recognition of their land rights. He vigorously opposed the BC government's policy of refusing to make land treaties. In the late nineteenth century, Ottawa abandoned its initial attempt to exercise control over BC politicians, leaving the province in control of its own Indian policy (see chapter eight). Grant viewed treaties as essential in fair dealing with the Indians, and fully supported the efforts of the Anglican missionary William Duncan in the mid-1880s to secure provincial recognition of Indian land rights around the community of Metlakatla on the Pacific Coast in the northwestern corner of British Columbia.

Much of George Grant's continued esteem for the treaty process came from his friendship with Alexander Morris, federal commissioner for the Crown treaties Three, Four, Five, and Six, all signed between 1873 and 1876. These agreements included a great deal of what is now northwestern Ontario, Manitoba, Saskatchewan, and central Alberta. Since his youth, Morris had advocated for Canadian expansion westward, yet at the same time, he had always insisted that Indian rights be recognized well in advance of settlement.[114] Morris served as a trustee of Queen's University from 1858 onward; from 1883 to his death in 1889, he chaired its board of trustees.[115]

Grant greatly admired William Duncan, a former English elementary schoolteacher who became an Anglican missionary on the Pacific Coast. The two men corresponded in 1885 and 1886.[116] Grant was very impressed by Duncan's accomplishment in building a progressive village for the Tsimshian (Ts'msyen), an important First Nation on the Pacific Coast. Tsimshian remained the working language at Metlakatla, Duncan's model Christian settlement near present-day Prince Rupert.[117] The strong-willed Duncan developed a radical new economic system for a people who had relied on the salmon. The fishers now operated a sawmill, a store, and small cannery. Women spun wool; men constructed roads and houses and built a thousand-seat church. Metlakatla contained parallel rows of neat white houses with gardens and picket fences, a school, and street lamps, as well as the huge church.[118] The settlement had its own uniformed police force. The Christian Indians in the village learned new and different ideas concerning family life. The concept of discipline changed with flogging frequently resorted to, particularly for the young people.[119] Duncan's objective was to dismantle the institutional structure of Tsimshian society.[120] On the surface, at least, participation in secret societies, potlatching, winter ceremonies, and other practices from the old way of life vanished.[121]

As an individual of his times, as culture bound as any, George Grant endorsed William Duncan's total suppression of potlatch ceremonies. So did John A. Macdonald, who had strong feelings on the topic. At potlatches in British Columbia, the prime minister reported in April

1884, "They meet and carry on a sort of mystery; they remain for weeks and sometimes months, as long as they can get food, and carry on all kinds of orgies."[122] An amendment to the Indian Act passed later that month made the potlatch, the ceremonial giving away of wealth by the Pacific Coast peoples, a misdemeanour punishable by imprisonment. Macdonald argued, "Departmental officers and all clergymen unite in affirming that it is absolutely necessary to put this practice down."[123]

The principal of Queen's University knew nothing about the Pacific Coast peoples' variety of public gift-giving events that were accompanied by feasting and storytelling through song and dance. In the twentieth century, Indigenous individuals themselves and a number of anthropologists would make this information accessible to non-Indigenous Canadians. James Sewid (1913–1988), a Kwakiutl (Kwakwa̱ka'wakw) noted, for example, that the "whites" achieved their status positions through acquiring large amounts of money and other property, whereas the Pacific Coast peoples demonstrated the validity of their inherited status positions by giving away wealth.[124] George Grant, however, in *Ocean to Ocean*, wrote that potlatching "to the Anglo-Saxon mind borders on insanity," and he supported coercive action to eliminate it.[125] The virtues to inculcate in the Indians, Grant argued in the 1880s, were those of self-reliance and self-support, of industry and thrift.

Not everyone in his own church, or in the Canadian government shared Grant's enthusiasm about William Duncan. Macdonald, still the superintendent general of Indian Affairs until 1887, had his doubts about his contribution. He knew of Duncan's authoritarian, incredibly strict, management of the Metlakatla Mission. When the two men met for three hours in Ottawa in 1885,[126] Macdonald told Duncan to his face that he ruled like a dictator.[127] In light of his own policies on the Plains in the mid-1880s, the prime minister certainly knew how a dictator acted.

Grant paid no attention to charges against William Duncan, an individual he considered to be "among my most esteemed friends."[128] He championed the zealous assimilationist in several 1886 letters to the *Montreal Herald*.[129] Late that November Grant wrote, "Mr Duncan is the creator of the Metla-Kahtlaka as a Christian progressive community. They are no longer savages. They are not mere consumers, mere paupers dependent on Government rations. They are producers." Grant continued, "We are now spending more than a million annually on the poor remnants of the tribes of the plains, and there is not much to show for the million. Would it not be wise to learn a lesson from Metla-Kathla [Metla-Kahtlaka]"?[130]

Overall, George Grant paid more attention to the Indians at Metlakatla in BC than to the First Nations in the immediate vicinity of

Queen's University. Three years before he moved to Kingston in 1877, Grant wrote that districts in Ontario and Quebec included "self-supporting, moderately-civilised communities, round the churches and schools established on their reserves."[131] One of these, Tyendinaga, the Mohawk community of the Bay of Quinte, was located only 50 kilometres west of Kingston. Interestingly, in the 1880s, Tyendinaga made it clear they wanted to adjust to the dominant society, but they wished to maintain some of their ancient structures and practices. About twenty years earlier, Tyendinaga had transferred over to the elected system of governance, but in the late 1880s many in the community wanted to return to the traditional, hereditary system. In 1888 more than two hundred of nearly a thousand members of the community wrote to the governor general of Canada to inform him that they had revived their traditional council system. After twenty years under the elective system, they now appointed six hereditary clan chiefs to seats on the Bay of Quinte Mohawk Council.[132] When opposed by the Department of Indian Affairs, the opponents of the elected council system won council seats and then worked to re-establish the council of hereditary chiefs.[133]

Dr Peter Edmund Jones, the son of Kahkewaquonaby (or Peter Jones), the famous Mississauga chief and Methodist minister, would have been a good adviser for Principal Grant on Indigenous issues, but no evidence exists that Grant consulted him. Without a doubt, he is Queen's University's most prominent Indigenous graduate (M.D. 1866). He served from 1874 to 1877, and again from 1880 to 1886, as head chief, and later as the Indian agent for his community, known today as the Mississaugas of New Credit First Nation. By the late nineteenth century New Credit had become a successful farming community.[134] Peter Edmund Jones was a man of many interests. In 1886 he edited and published the *Indian*, the first Indigenous newspaper in Canada.

George Grant, by then a national figure, died in Kingston on 10 May 1902. Memorial tributes arrived at Queen's University from across the country. This great Canadian champion of the British Empire[135] had received a high honour less than a year earlier, with the announcement in London, England, that he was to be appointed a Companion of the Most Distinguished Order of Saint Michael and Saint George (CMG).[136] The Duke of Cornwall and York, the future King George V, then in Kingston on his Canadian tour, had intended to make the presentation at Queen's Fall Convocation, 15 October 1901. On hearing that Principal Grant was seriously ill, the duke went himself to his sick room in the Kingston General Hospital, "where his Royal Highness invested him with the insignia of the CMG, which dignity the King has recently conferred upon him."[137] In May 1902 fifteen thousand people came out to witness Principal Grant's funeral procession from the university to Catarqui Cemetery, a "stone's throw" away from the grave of Sir John A. Macdonald.

As an older man, Grant had distanced himself from Macdonald. The principal of Queen's University was a political independent and not a party man.[138] Although a Conservative, Grant did not always hold his local MP, and prime minister, in high regard. As he frequently told Queen's students, the ideal should be "pure, honest and economical government."[139] In his opinion, Canada's first prime minister had introduced many corrupt practices into Canadian politics, and he felt that the Conservatives' negligent administration of the North West caused the 1885 Rebellion. When once asked by the prime minister why he was not a steady friend, the principal of Queen's stated that he always supported the party when they were right. This answer did not impress Sir John A., who according to this legendary story that survives in several versions, replied, "Ah! But that is not the kind of a friend I mean – I mean a friend who would support me when he thinks I am wrong!"[140]

In the last fifteen years of his life, George Grant's interest in Indigenous Canada diminished greatly. Other national and international issues preoccupied him in the late 1880s and 1890s: the struggle to keep Canada out of an economic union with the United States, the urgency of strengthening Canada's ties with the British Empire, the need to build bridges between French- and English-speaking Canada, the plight of Armenians in Turkey, racist attitudes towards Oriental immigration, and combatting the mania for prohibition that swept over the Protestant churches. Like the politicians and the Canadian general public themselves, George Grant's interests turned away from Indigenous issues. As the populations of First Nations were small, and they continued to decline into the early twentieth century, their place in the public policy agenda became more and more marginal.

Looking back, George Monro Grant had no grasp of the Indigenous cultures. Like his contemporaries, he supported their replacement. Instead of the reinforcement of Indigenous cultures, Grant worked for their extinguishment. Such an individual, one so progressive and so full of good will towards his fellow human beings, nevertheless on the issue of Canada's First Nations peoples shared the same limited vision as most of his contemporaries.

Chapter Four

Chancellor John A. Boyd and Fellow Georgian Bay Cottager Kathleen Coburn

Canada divided sharply along ethnic lines a century and a half ago. Pierre Chauveau, the first premier of Quebec after Confederation, once likened Canada to the famous double spiral staircase of the Château de Chambord in France's Loire Valley, built to allow two persons to climb it without meeting, and to ascend without seeing each other, except at intervals: "English and French, we climb by a double flight of stairs toward the destinies reserved for us on this continent, without knowing each other, without meeting each other, except on the landing of politics."[1] While admitting the enormous distance between English- and French-speaking Canadians, this gap remained small when compared with the division that separated both groups from the First Nations. A century and a half ago Indigenous and non-Indigenous people in Central and Eastern Canada lived in virtual isolation from each other, complete strangers, not meeting even on "the landing of politics."

John Alexander Boyd (1837–1916) provides a perfect example of an urban Canadian who grew up with little familiarity with Indigenous peoples. The son of recent Scottish immigrants, he was born in Toronto (called York until 1834) on 23 April 1837. Two and a half decades earlier, the North American Indians had been important British military allies and an important reality in the Toronto area. They were allies again in the War of 1812. Thomas Ridout, of one of the early British families in York, wrote about them to a cousin in London, England, in early January 1813: "Here I am upon the north shore of Ontario, whose great surface is frozen as far as the eye can reach, & appears like an impenetrable forest of Pines ... [The] five Indian nations who have come down to the war are encamped on the skirts of the woods back of the Town. They keep us alive with their war dances & make the dark cedar woods echo with many savage yells."[2] In John Alexander Boyd's youth, the Indigenous people where he lived were small in number and quite remote from Torontonians' everyday concerns.

The Boyd family came to Canada from Lanark, Scotland, where James Boyd had worked as a wholesale trader. His son John attended the Ayr Academy, a secondary school in the town of Ayr on the southwestern Scottish coast, and then the University of Glasgow. Sir Daniel Sandford, the university's professor of Greek, noted the young man, "impressed me with a very favourable opinion of his abilities, diligence and general character."[3] John Boyd decided to become a teacher and seek his fortune overseas in British North America. After his arrival in Upper Canada in 1832 he founded the Bay Street Academy, on the west side of Bay Street, south of King, in what was then the fashionable west end of the city.[4] A decade later, the *British Colonist* described the "flourishing seminary," which had an enrolment of about 130 boys and girls, "children of substantial tradesmen and merchants, resident in Toronto."[5] In late 1842, John Strachan, the first Anglican bishop of Toronto, "examined with much care the different classes, and it was most satisfactory to the audience to witness the great proficiency of the scholars."[6] Several former Bay Street Academy students later achieved fame and fortune in the city, including John Macdonald, a wealthy Toronto merchant and philanthropist;[7] Sir Charles Moss, an important city lawyer and judge;[8] and William Henry Pearson, the general manager of the Consumers' Gas Company of Toronto.[9] At the Academy's annual awards ceremony in late 1843, the founder's precocious six-year-old son John Alexander carried off prizes in both English grammar and reading.[10]

Little is known about John Boyd's wife, Margaret McCallum, apart from the fact that in 1832 they had crossed the Atlantic aboard the same ship to North America: 32-year-old John Boyd alone, and Miss McCallum, 26 at the time, with members of her family. One suspects that the schoolteacher's eloquence captured Miss McCallum's attention, as his anonymous biographer notes that Boyd "had the poems of Burns at his tongue's end."[11] Romantic interest developed on the sea voyage of several weeks, as shortly after their arrival in York, John and Margaret were wed at St Andrew's Presbyterian Church. As a married woman Margaret, again using the words of her husband's anonymous biographer, "led a quiet and retired life, active in the kindly offices of home."[12] A God-fearing woman, she would read daily at home from her well-worn and well-marked Bible.[13] The Boyds lived in the same small frame two-storey building that housed the Bay Street Academy, with the northern doorway serving as the school entrance, and the southern as the entrance to the Boyds' home.[14] On Sundays the family attended St Andrew's. For reasons unknown, however, the Boyds in the early 1840s left the Presbyterians and joined the Baptist congregation that met in the chapel on neighbouring Bond Street.[15]

In 1845 the Bay Street Academy experienced financial difficulties.[16] A departure from the fashionable part of the city followed, with the Boyds relocating in reduced circumstances to the small Village of Eglinton, just north of Toronto. Here, on Yonge Street, John Boyd ran a small rural school for the next five years, while also working a 26-acre farm.[17] Focusing their attention on their only child, the Boyds prepared John Alexander for admittance to Upper Canada College, which was known to have a high academic standard. When Charles Dickens visited Toronto in 1842, the novelist made note that this male-only provincial grammar school offered "a sound education in every department of polite learning" and "at a very moderate expense."[18]

The young lad of 10, still just a "bairn," had a healthy commute to his new school, located about 8 kilometres to the south of where the Boyds were living, on King Street west of Yonge, at the corner of King and Simcoe. As classes started at 9 a.m.,[19] each school day he faced a hearty walk of 16 kilometres (10 miles), round-trip, "through rain and shine, snow and blow." With luck, some days the boy might get a "lift" on a farmer's wagon or, in winter, on a sleigh drawn by horses on a snow-covered Yonge Street.[20] His schoolteacher father had taught him well. The hardworking young scholar from Eglinton excelled at his studies, winning prizes in classics and general proficiency.[21]

John Alexander Boyd met several First Nations students at Upper Canada College. Samuel P. Jarvis, the chief superintendent for Indian Affairs for Upper Canada in the early 1840s, had placed them there, at the government's expense, "to have them trained like white boys of good family."[22] Two of the young men were just completing their final year during Boyd's first year, 1847–8.[23] They were Francis Assiginack, son of an important Odawa (Anishinabe) chief on Manitoulin Island, and Charles Keezhig, also from Manitoulin Island. As the 1844 *Report on the Affairs of the Indians in Canada* (the Bagot Report) notes, the experiment with the Indian students proved successful: "Most, if not all those who have received a good education, are equal, in every respect, to their white associates."[24] The school body also included at least one student of partial Indigenous background. Just five years before Boyd entered Upper Canada College, Norman Bethune, who later became a well-known Toronto physician, served as the College's head boy.[25] His father was Angus Bethune, a fur trader, and his Indigenous mother, Louisa Mackenzie. He was born at Moose Factory, on James Bay, headquarters post of the Southern Department of Rupert's Land, the vast fur trading empire of the Hudson's Bay Company.[26]

Fellow student James Macleod, son of a Scottish immigrant family from the Isle of Skye, and just a year older than Boyd,[27] came to know Charles Keezhig well. The accomplished athlete was legendary at Upper Canada College for the race he once ran against a British officer on a trotting horse down a kilometre (half-mile) stretch of University Avenue. The Indian runner reached Queen Street first.[28] James and his older brother Henry in 1847 invited Charles to spend the Christmas holidays with their family at their Yonge Street farm at Richmond Hill north of Toronto. James's father, Captain Martin Macleod had fought in Spain against Napoleon, in the War of 1812 in Canada, and had later served in the West Indies.[29] The retired British army officer admired the North American Indian, "a great chum of my boys,"[30] and "an interesting fine young youth [...] extremely gentle & mild in his manners." He did record one negative: "My only quarrel with him is that when we go out into the woods I seldom can manage to get a shot. Mr Keecheck is almost certain to be before me at the best runs" as he raced "through the most dense forest with the agility and precision of a Fox."[31]

John Alexander Boyd's decision to leave Upper Canada College in late July 1851[32] seems surprising. Again, parts of the puzzle are missing, but possibly his family's poor finances had a role. At age 14 he entered the business world, first in Toronto and later in Quebec City, the second largest urban centre in British North America, with a population at the time of approximately forty-five thousand, well ahead of Toronto's, at about thirty thousand, and behind Montreal's, with about sixty thousand.[33] In 1852 Quebec City served as the capital of the Province of Canada, and remained so until October 1855, when Toronto again became the seat of government. Quebec City's population was one-third English-speaking and two-thirds French-speaking, with a small North American Indian community nearby at Wendake.

It is most likely that John Alexander Boyd visited the "Huron village" when he lived in Quebec. All the standard guidebooks in the 1850s recommended it.[34] The Huron, or Wendat to use their own name for themselves, were one of the best-known Indian nations in North America. When the French first visited, the Wendat lived on a small peninsula between Georgian Bay and Lake Simcoe in southern Ontario. After the Iroquois from present-day New York State drove the Huron from their territory, in the early 1650s, several hundred Roman Catholic converts withdrew to the region around Quebec City. In 1697 the Wendat refugees moved to new homes and planted fields at Lorette, or Wendake, near the St Charles River, 15 kilometres north of Quebec City. In the century and a half to follow, the Wendat integrated closely with the dominant society around them. Most homes in the village resembled those of their French neighbours.[35] Due to their low population the Wendat community incorporated people from other Indigenous communities, captives from New England in the wars with the British, unwanted French children, and spouses from French Canadian society. Dedicated Catholics, many Wendat had lost their Huron language and spoke only French, but Wendake still remained a distinct separate Indigenous community.[36] Despite their parents' ethnicity or that of their spouses, the community identified as Wendat rather than as *canadien*.[37]

Quebec City in the cold bracing winter was oppressive especially because of the thousands of coal and wood fires pouring carbon into the air. In the Lower Town lived the "little people," *les gagne-petits*, who worked on the wharfs and in the timber trade, people dealing constantly with financial insecurity. No doubt Boyd, on a clerk's modest salary, lived frugally in the Lower Town, and by "1853 he is found ready to resume the round of studies as a college boy."[38] He returned to Toronto where again he excelled at his old school.[39] No longer did he need to make the long commute from north of the city, however, as now, once again, his family lived in Toronto.[40] Possibly his mother's poor health had necessitated his parents' move from Eglinton. Margaret Boyd died in Toronto in October 1854.[41] Her only child remained devoted to her memory. Nearly thirty years later, when George Theodore Berthon painted his portrait, the new chancellor of Ontario commissioned the artist to draw his beloved mother's portrait from a daguerreotype.[42]

The absence of surviving diaries and personal correspondence makes it difficult to probe into John Alexander's views at this time, but a surviving essay from his final year at Upper Canada College offers some insight. In 1855, aged 18, he wrote a prize-winning patriotic essay on "The Origins & Progress" of the Crimean War (1853–6), in which Britain, France, and Turkey fought against the Russian Empire. As did the English Canadian press, the high school student championed the justice of the war against despotic Russia.[43] Boyd ended with references to the victories "against the Muscovites,"[44] at Alma, Balaklava, and Inkerman with this triumphant statement: "My bosom swells with pride when I reflect that we too, Canadian though we be, participate in the glory of our mother-country and when I remember that a portion of that imperishable luster which surrounds the very name of Inkerman is reflected upon us!"[45]

Boyd entered the University of Toronto in the fall of 1856, just as construction began on what was to become the magnificent new University College, which opened two years later. As the number of full-time students remained small, just fifty-six in 1857,[46] the young scholar must certainly have known (or at least known of) James Ross from the Red

River Settlement in the North West. The son of an Okanagan woman and a Scottish fur trader father,[47] Ross was an outstanding student and in 1857, his final year, earned two university gold medals and a silver one.[48] Classes were small in the mid-1850s, in a typical year fewer than a dozen graduated with a Bachelor of Arts degree.[49] In his first year, no real surprise, the gifted John Alexander Boyd again won awards,[50] including a prize book, *The Historical and Other Works of William Robertson, D.D.*, duly signed by John McCaul, president of the university, and Daniel Wilson, one of his professors. Robertson, a widely read eighteenth-century Scottish historian, viewed the Natives in the Americas as "savages,"[51] apart from those in the Aztec and Inca empires.

About the time Boyd entered University College his father remarried. Eliza Lucinda McNally was an Irish Protestant schoolteacher from Dublin. Beginning in the mid-1840s Lucinda, with her three sisters, the Misses McNally, ran a well-known Toronto private school. The accomplished head mistress addressed her teachers of French, German, and Spanish in their own tongue.[52] No doubt, the skilled linguist helped her stepson in his studies by conversing with him in French and German. An advocate for racial justice, Eliza Lucinda had served on the executive of the Ladies Association of Toronto to help "Destitute Coloured Fugitives" – escaped American slaves – seeking refuge in Toronto.[53]

In his second year at University College, Boyd won three history books for heading all three of his classes in modern languages. All three volumes were by William Prescott. For English, Boyd received the noted American historian's *History of the Reign of Ferdinand and Isabella*; for French, his *History of the Conquest of Mexico*; and for German, his *History of the Conquest of Peru*.[54] Prescott was at the height of his fame in the 1850s.[55] The strength of his writing lay in his prolonged research, complemented by his excellent style and vivid presentation. The basic underlying assumption of his work and of the other giants of nineteenth-century American historical writing was the march of human progress.[56]

John Alexander Boyd studied under Daniel Wilson (1816–1892), the university's first professor of history and English literature, whose research background also included archaeology, anthropology, and art. The talented Scot in his youth had worked for two years as an engraver, and he had transferred to copperplate one of the works of J.M.W. Turner. He met the great English artist several times in London while completing the commission.[57] Daniel Wilson became a powerful intellectual force at the University of Toronto, and its second president.[58]

Not long after immigrating to Canada, Wilson published his major works, *Memorials of Edinburgh in the Olden Time* (1848) and *The*

Archaeology and Prehistoric Annals of Scotland (1851). His major anthropological work, *Prehistoric Man: Researches into the Origin of Civilisation in the Old and the New World*, written entirely in Canada, appeared in 1862.[59] For his generation, Wilson had advanced views.[60] This student of the Scottish Enlightenment believed that North American Indians had equal intelligence and ability to Europeans, and he welcomed them to continue to progress, and join the higher "civilization."[61] Wilson was in favour of racial intermarriage and the absorption of the Indians into the larger non-Indigenous society, writing, "It is the same process by which the world's old historic and unhistoric races were, in earlier centuries, blended into elements, out of which younger nations have sprung."[62]

Immediately after graduation in 1860 John Alexander Boyd apparently considered teaching. He soon wrote a school history textbook of about one hundred pages, entitled *Summary of Canadian History*, in which he presented Canada's story "from the time of Cartier's discovery to the present day."[63] Boyd's coverage of the Indigenous peoples was minimal, in fact, they only appear in regard to their relationship with the Europeans and receive no mention at all after the War of 1812. Yet, despite its brevity, the Scottish Canadian polymath Daniel Wilson saw promise in his former student's volume, and in a review published in the November 1860 issue of the *Canadian Journal*, Wilson called for a second book, "a full critical survey of the interesting story of Canadian discovery, settlement, and progress, through all the interesting events of its three historic centuries.[64] *A Summary of Canadian History* did well, selling eighteen thousand copies over five years,[65] serious sales even by today's standards.

Boyd's career plans changed and his enlarged study of Canada's past was never written. While he prepared his M.A. at University College[66] the young graduate student also articled in law.[67] After he completed his Master of Arts degree in 1861,[68] Boyd did not seek a teaching job, but introduced to the law, he now preferred the thrust and parry of courtroom debate to historical study and teaching. Two years later John Alexander Boyd, M.A., was called to the bar with honours.[69] His proud father and stepmother no longer lived in Toronto, as John Boyd had taken a clerkship position with the Post Office in Quebec City, capital of the Union of the Canadas. The American Civil War, now in its third year, overshadowed everything in August 1863. The previous month, the Battle of Gettysburg in Pennsylvania had ended with forty thousand casualties, almost the total population of Toronto at this time.[70] The war continued for another two years until the Union victory in 1865.

In the legal profession, John Alexander Boyd developed an admirable reputation in equity,[71] with a specialty in chancery, that part of the legal system that dealt with mortgages and estates.[72] The legal historian Peter Barton writes of Boyd, "Many of his decisions are still quoted and accepted as sound law."[73] In the 1870s Boyd worked for "Blakes," the elite Toronto firm founded by Edward and his brother Samuel Hume Blake.[74] The firm retained a high regard for him, indeed nearly a century later the firm's history mentioned John Alexander Boyd as "one of the most outstanding of the older partners in Blakes."[75] Boyd stayed at the firm until his appointment in 1881 as chancellor of Ontario, a position he held for the next thirty-five years.

The same year he was called to the bar, Boyd married Elizabeth Buchan, daughter of the bursar of the University of Toronto and its colleges, including Upper Canada College. In marrying one of the bursar's daughters, the young barrister became ever more closely tied to both Upper Canada College and the University of Toronto: all nine of their sons attended both institutions.[76] The three Boyd daughters did not attend university. Only in 1884–5 did women gain admittance to the University of Toronto, for the otherwise open-minded and erudite Daniel Wilson, now president of University College (and from 1889 to 1892 also president of the University of Toronto), opposed their entry. Although Wilson did believe in higher education for women, he felt that men and women should not be mixed in their most excitable years. As the Canadian historian Carl Berger writes, "He later admitted privately that lecturing on Shakespeare to young men in the presence of young women would be a trying ordeal because of the sexual allusions in some of the plays."[77]

John Alexander Boyd greatly respected his father-in-law David Buchan, who was born and raised in Glasgow, the son of a manufacturer and merchant. Buchan had practised law in Scotland until his involvement in the anti-slavery movement proved costly. Once he pronounced against slavery, his relatives who had West Indian ties and thus were "interested in the plantations and in the slave labor required to work them profitably,"[78] took their legal business elsewhere. David Buchan and his wife, Jane Griffith, decided to begin anew in Canada, emigrating in 1834. They came with capital. The Boyds' property in Eglinton was a modest 26 acres,[79] but the Buchans purchased a 250-acre farm near the Town of Paris, not far from Brantford, where in the 1830s and 1840s David and Jane raised their large family of eleven children.

A devoted Baptist, David Buchan helped to establish the first Baptist church in Brantford, and later that in Paris. He also tried, unsuccessfully, to help the small Six Nations Baptist community nearby. In 1844 he became the first signatory on a petition to start a school to be run by the English Baptist Missionary Society, which has "done much good work in East and West Indies."[80] About thirty Tuscarora names are listed on the petition. The Baptists in Canada and in neighbouring New York State, as did the Canadian Methodists, already had their own Indigenous ministry.[81] Like the Methodists, they publicly recognized Indigenous leaders and allowed them positions of leadership and authority. Many Tuscaroras in Canada and New York found the Baptist faith appealing, as the ordained ministers, licensed preachers, deacons, and other church officials were Haudenosaunee (Iroquois). The Indian church workers preached and ministered in Tuscarora as well as English. As with the Haudenosauee who followed the Longhouse faith, or Code of Handsome Lake, the Baptists prohibited alcohol and gambling for their members.[82] Nevertheless, in the end, the attempt to start a Baptist boarding school failed, as the Six Nations were already being served by the well-established Anglican-run Mohawk Institute.

A respected accountant and trained lawyer, Buchan became the bursar of the University of Toronto in 1853, where for many years he administered its finances "with great soundness and discretion."[83] Following his father-in-law's example, John Alexander Boyd devoted long hours to Yorkville (later Bloor Street) Baptist Church.[84] Three of his Buchan sisters-in-law created in 1876 the Women's Baptist Foreign Missionary Society of Ontario West, which sent female Baptist missionaries to India.[85] Boyd himself took on a considerable amount of charitable and community work, with the Home for Incurable Children on Bloor Street (a chronic-case hospital) and the Working Boys' Home (later Clifton House for Boys). For over a decade he also sat on the board of trustees of McMaster University,[86] and belonged as well to the University of Toronto senate. The public-spirited Torontonian served the musical community as president of the Toronto Conservatory of Music.

In 1881 the prime minister himself named John Alexander Boyd chancellor of Ontario, or head of the province's court of equity. The short congratulatory note that John A. Macdonald wrote to him reads: "My dear Mr Boyd, I have just received your note acknowledging your appt. as Chancellor of Ontario. I am happy to know that in selecting you I have chosen one who will do honour to the office and whose appt. merits the approval of the Bar and the public."[87] The *Canada Law Journal* welcomed the new chancellor, "known to all as a courteous gentleman and a favorite in the profession, a scholar of high attainment, an accomplished lawyer, gifted with an eminently judicial cast of mind."[88] Although several months later the Court of Chancery became part of the High Court of Justice for Ontario, with recourse beyond that body to the Ontario Court of Appeal, Boyd retained the title of chancellor throughout his legal career, and was indeed the last chancellor of Ontario.

In the early spring of 1885 Chancellor Boyd became the trial judge for the complex case, *Regina* v. *St Catharines Milling and Lumber Company*,[89] also known as the Indian Title, or the Ontario Lands case.[90] As the legal historian Sidney L. Harding has written, "Boyd was well schooled in the technical intricacies of the law, a conservative jurist who could be depended on to write nicely crafted opinions."[91] In an age when very few Canadians had university training, Boyd had both a B.A. and M.A. He had studied under Daniel Wilson, a scholar with an international reputation. At university he had won prizes in both modern languages and history. In addition, his fellow judges knew the well-respected Boyd was familiar with the Canadian Shield country, in which the Treaty Three area was located. The chancellor of Ontario loved the out of outdoors and always spent the annual three-month summer judicial recess on Lake Huron.[92]

For some years the Boyds had been spending their summers in Georgian Bay, on an isolated island 30 kilometres west of Parry Sound, adjacent to Parry Island, or Wasauksing, a First Nations community, far from Toronto's oppressive July and August heat and humidity. The Boyds belonged to the advance party of southern Ontarians in search of wild and rugged country with picturesque scenery.[93] These individuals of comfortable means sought to escape their congested city, whose population had more than doubled in a decade, from 85,000 in 1881 to over 180,000 in 1891.[94] Boyd and his three older sons, together with a Buchan brother-in-law, travelled by large square-stern rowboats through Georgian Bay during the summer of 1879. Two years later Boyd purchased Good Cheer, the home island, and three smaller ones. Until the railway reached the lumbering town of Parry Sound, every summer the Boyds made the arduous journey with all their supplies to Good Cheer Island by boat from Penetang Harbour, 80 kilometres to the south.

At Good Cheer the family initially lived in one or two cottages and numerous tents, but more elaborate structures followed in later years.[95] Pelham Edgar, professor first of French and then of English at Victoria College in the University of Toronto, once met the chancellor. A friend of the older Boyd brothers, he visited the main Boyd island in the 1890s, where he found "the sons all lived in tents adjacent to the paternal mansion."[96] With Edgar on the small schooner-rigged boat, "well equipped with provisions, both solid and liquid,"[97] travelled two Toronto friends: Gordon Laing, later general editor of the University of Chicago Press, and Stephen Leacock, soon to be recognized as one of Canada's most celebrated writers. Very quickly the discerning guests, all sharp observers of human character, realized that the chancellor, a strict teetotalling Baptist, suspected they might have brought liquor onto the island. Subsequently, in Pelham's words, "We had an uneasy feeling that our stay

4.1 A Georgian Bay Ojibwe, Isaiah Assance, and his family, ca. 1890. John Boyd would have seen but not seen individuals like this during holidays at his summer place. Probably photographed by D.F. Macdonald, Indian agent for Parry Island. S8236, Acc. 6287, Archives of Ontario.

might not be so prolonged as we had planned." Edgar Pelham recalled their abrupt departure in his memoir, *Across My Path*: "We had morning prayers before breakfast, and the Chancellor in a fluent improvisation was very courteous to us. He thanked our Creator for having brought us here so safely, and prayed that we might have as favorable winds for our departure. We left after breakfast."[98]

Boyd's legal qualifications and strong academic training constituted his great strengths for the St Catharines Milling case, his lack of contact with Indigenous people the weakness. Boyd knew next to nothing about contemporary Indian life and culture.[99] His experience paralleled that of seasonal residents then and now, as the historian Claire Elizabeth Campbell writes in her study of nature and history in Georgian

4.2 Chancellor Boyd with two of his sons and two of his grandchildren, Good Cheer Island, Georgian Bay, Ont., 1907. Photo courtesy of the late Kay Boyd.

Bay, entitled *Shaped by the West Wind*, "Two solitudes had developed between the reserves and the cottagers, for whom Georgian Bay meant the physical landscape. As far as the cottagers were concerned, Natives had faded into the background and into history."[100]

True, the chancellor encountered Parry Island (Wasauksing) people passingly on Georgian Bay, when out fishing or berry picking,[101] and a few Parry Islanders did speak some English.[102] Free from the city, Boyd loved to fish and to be out on the water.[103] Had he been more outgoing by nature, these interests might have served as a bridge with the Parry Islanders who knew some English. Yet, as the *Toronto Star* noted after his death, "Sir John, while courteous, considerate, and held in general regard, was not known as a 'mixer.' His application to his books precluded that phase of sociability."[104] Even with fellow lawyers, the *Canadian Law Times* wrote, Boyd seemed somewhat aloof: "It cannot be said that he encouraged intimacy – indeed he was somewhat reserved in manner."[105]

What makes the scholarly judge interesting, quite unconventional really, was the fact he kept an "Indian notebook" in the late nineteenth century, based on his extensive reading. He writes in an increasingly cryptic handwriting, in contrast to the bold clear script of his youth, a penalty of being obliged to write constant judgments, and taking notes in chamber. It reveals a deep interest and curiosity about North American history and language, with notes from the American ethnologist Henry Schoolcraft's volumes on the Ojibwe as well as one of the Ojibwe writer George Copway's books. Boyd examined closely Peter Jones's *History of the Ojebway Indians*. He recorded the Ojibwe names Jones provided for the seasons of the year, and many place names, such as Penetang, or "Pene-tanguishene," which translated into English was "Caving Sandbank."[106] Intrigued by the Algonquian word "Mississippi," Boyd broke it into its two components, "Missi" or "great" and "Sepe,"" river." The Indigenous past of southern Ontario intrigued him. From Peter Jones's *History*, Boyd discovered a reference to the victorious wars of the Ojibwe with the Iroquois, and in his notebook he recorded that before the arrival of the British the Ojibwe had pushed the Iroquois out of southern Ontario.[107]

Boyd loved to have his family around him and eagerly joined them in evenings of music and song.[108] Grandson Walter Boyd explains, "He himself had been an only child, his own mother had died when he was a comparatively young man and in addition his father's household seems to have been somewhat insecure at times due to financial ups and downs. Thus a settled life and a large family must have held tremendous appeal for him."[109] This being said, even with his family Boyd maintained an unbending sternness, especially on the Sabbath.[110] Was this a role he felt obliged to perform? On Sundays at Good Cheer, the eminent judge allowed his children no boating, no swimming for anything other than cleanliness, no reading of novels, no games of any kind – for reading he permitted only the Canadian Baptist newspaper and *Pilgrim's Progress*.[111] The Boyd family on Good Cheer Island in Georgian Bay lived in a totally different universe than the Anishinabeg of Parry Island. Indigenous rules of behaviour differed so radically. The chancellor's expectation of family obedience, for instance, was totally foreign to the late nineteenth-century Ojibwe, who encouraged children to be autonomous. The ethic of non-interference led parents to encourage their children to make their own decisions: "Children must learn on their own, by watching and by emulating what they see."[112]

The St Catharines Milling case arose from the long-standing dispute between Ontario and the Government of Canada over the proper location of the province's northwestern boundary. It originated in a dispute between the federal and provincial governments, and it had nothing to do directly with First Nations and the land. The origins of the Ontario-Manitoba conflict dated back to pre-Confederation days. The British had never established a precise boundary line between Rupert's Land and the colony of Upper Canada (Ontario). The original Hudson's Bay Company charter had provided a watershed definition of all the waters flowing into Hudson Bay. Article 6 of the British North America Act of 1867 assigned to the province the same territorial limits as the former Upper Canada (or Canada West), but the Act creating the Dominion of Canada did not specify the location of these boundaries. Ontario Premier Oliver Mowat argued that Ontario's western boundary should run due north from the source of the Mississippi River, from present-day Kenora, just north of Lake of the Woods. In contrast, Prime Minister John A. Macdonald and the federal Conservatives wanted the boundary drawn near the Lakehead on Lake Superior, roughly 400 kilometres east of the Lake of the Woods. Macdonald worked to restrict Ontario's area. He wanted a country in which Ontario would be only one of many provinces of moderate and balanced size, with the provincial units all subordinate to Ottawa.

The issue of the disputed territory – greater in area than all of England – remained unresolved into the early 1880s.[113] Legal chaos prevailed. Despite Ontario's protests, Macdonald in 1881 decided that the disputed territory belonged to Manitoba. As the Dominion of Canada controlled Manitoba's natural resources, this meant Ottawa collected the royalties from them. Ontario contested this. In 1884 the Judicial Committee of the Privy Council in London, the supreme court of the British Empire, upheld Ontario's position, fixing Ontario's western limits at the Lake of the Woods (the present boundary). Ontario had won, but the wily Sir John A. Macdonald refused to concede. Until ratified by legislation, the decision remained not binding, and despite Ontario's formal request, the federal government delayed implementing the Judicial Committee's advisory decision. Yes, Canada had received the ultimate title to the land from Great Britain, but Macdonald now argued, the Indians still enjoyed outright ownership, or a real estate interest in their ancestral territories. They had *fee simple* to use the phrase of English common law, subject to only one limitation: they could only sell or alienate their lands to the Crown.[114] This meant that outright control of the natural resources of the Treaty Three area passed to the federal government even if the land was within Ontario.

The official signing of Treaty Three in 1873 passed almost unnoticed in Central Canada.[115] Only the Toronto *Globe*, one of the country's two most widely read and influential English-language newspapers, paid

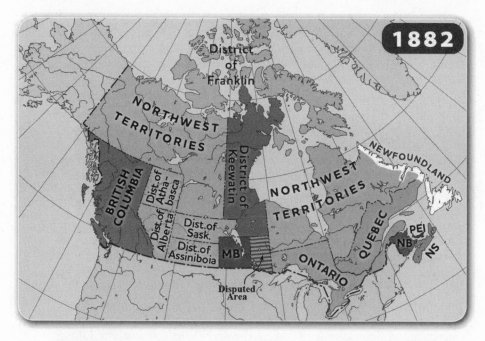

Map 4.1 Canada in 1882, showing the disputed territory between Ontario and Manitoba.

attention to it, but gave the story only one short paragraph.[116] The *Montreal Gazette*, the second of the most widely read and influential English-language newspapers of the day, made no reference to Treaty Three at all. Clearly, the signing of Treaty Three was not regarded as an important event, which, in hindsight, is extraordinary, as the Canadian interpretation of the treaty held that the Ojibwe had just turned over 55,000 square miles of their homeland to Canada.[117] The Central Canadian press failed to report how Anishinabeg negotiators had fought for a treaty based on a partnership of equals who shared the land and its resources. Only on its fourth attempt did the Government of Canada, by improving the terms, succeed in obtaining an agreement. The treaty commissioners emphasized treaty provisions that benefited the Anishinabeg, and apparently neglected to discuss the land cession clause.[118]

In 1884 Ontario directly challenged Ottawa's claim that the Indians had ownership of their lands. Oliver Mowat, premier of Ontario from 1872 to 1896, "the Christian politician" as he once termed himself,[119] argued, "The claim of the Indians is simply moral and no more."[120] The Royal Proclamation of 1763, on the basis of which the federal government had made treaties One to Three in the North West, had been, according to Mowat, "expressly repealed by the Quebec Act of 1774."[121] In contrast, Macdonald argued that the Crown indeed already owned the land, but he recognized that the Indians had an Aboriginal Title that constituted a legal burden on its sovereignty that must be purchased before the Crown could enjoy full possession of the land.[122]

Ontario launched a suit against the St Catherine's Milling and Lumber Company, a private corporation that in 1883 had been issued a federal timber licence.[123] In late 1884, Ontario filed suit in Chancery for the ejection of the Milling Company and for all damages incurred by its trespass. The Dominion of Canada now openly assisted the company to defend its claims. The case proceeded as a purely federal-provincial dispute without any consultation with the Anishinabeg residents of the territory. Oliver Mowat was Ontario's longest serving premier. During his premiership Ontario's frontier was pushed all the way to James Bay. In court cases, he helped secure for the province a resource-rich territory more than five times the size of Nova Scotia. Mowat's government passed significant legislation to protect industrial workers. Oliver Mowat is remembered for the creation of Algonquin Park in 1893 and as the premier who gave the province Queen's Park, its Parliament building, constructed from 1886 to 1892.[124] Once again, here is the discordant note regarding Indigenous rights: Whereas John A. Macdonald instigated the first treaties with the Plains Indians in the early 1870s, Oliver Mowat, in contrast, contended that First Nations had no legal title to their lands.[125]

Throughout the world, the late nineteenth and early twentieth centuries marked the high-water mark of European imperialism. From 15 November 1884 to 26 February 1885 the Berlin Conference decided the fate of Africa. The most powerful man on the continent, German Chancellor Otto von Bismarck, had invited all European powers to discuss problems arising out of the European penetration of Africa. Not one African participant was invited. Britain, France, Portugal, Belgium, and Germany obtained for themselves huge territories.

In North America the "Doctrine of Discovery," a legal concept used to justify European sovereignty over Indigenous lands, enjoyed great popularity.[126] Virtually the entire Euro-Canadian community – including Sir John Alexander Boyd – endorsed it. The silver-tongued Wilfrid Laurier popularly summarized the concept and its implications in 1886. That April the young French Canadian lawyer and MP from Quebec

City, who was to become the leader of the federal Liberal Party the following year, stated in the House of Commons:

> England, and all other Christian nations who planted colonies on this continent, always felt that it was not contrary to moral law to take possession, and even forcible possession, of territories which were roamed over rather than possessed by savage nations – territories which in their hands must forever have remained barren and unproductive, but which under civilised rule would afford homes and happiness to teeming millions. It has always been held as a doctrine of international law that when such territories were discovered, the discovering nations had paramount authority therein.[127]

As the Canadian legal historian Kent McNeil, writing in 2019, tersely summarizes, all the judges who sat from 1885 to 1888 on the St Catharines case "took it for granted that the Crown acquired sovereignty over Indigenous peoples in what is now Canada [...] without conquering or entering into treaty with them." McNeil adds in an endnote, "This assumption is still relied upon."[128]

Chancellor Boyd, as the trial judge, ruled on the nature of the rights the Indians had ceded in Treaty Three. The case was argued before him on 18 May 1885. Oliver Mowat, premier and attorney general of Ontario, himself presented the province's case. Boyd delivered his ruling on 10 June 1885, three weeks later. An examination of the chancellor's Circuit Books and reports of court proceedings reveals he had only eleven completely free days (excluding Sundays) in which to research and then write his decision.[129] For the depth and complexity of the legal issue of Indian Title, eleven years would have been more appropriate.

Boyd had but limited background on the legal status of Indians and Indian lands. In his judgment, he placed great weight on an American case ruled upon by Chief Justice John Marshall, that is, *Johnson* v. *McIntosh* (1823),[130] in which the court addressed the ownership of all "discovered" lands. The American legal historian Lindsay G. Robertson provides a description of the case in his 2005 book, *Conquest by Law: How the Discovery of America Dispossessed Indigenous Peoples of Their Lands*: "Discovery converted the indigenous owners of discovered lands into tenants on those lands. The underlying title belonging to the discovering sovereign. The indigenous occupants were free to sell their 'lease,' but only to the landlord, and they were subject to eviction at any time."[131] Boyd completely ignored, however, Marshall's later decision, that is, *Worcester* v. *Georgia* (1832), in which the US Supreme Court justice recognized the Cherokee's legal rights to their lands.[132]

Early that spring the "Riel Rebellion" had broken out in the North West. Chancellor Boyd had a personal connection to this. As soon as the news of Louis Riel's victory at Duck Lake (26 March) reached Toronto, his eldest son had volunteered for duty.[133] Alex Boyd left on 30 March, travelling with younger brother Len, who was so anxious to fight Riel he hid under a railway car seat until the volunteers were well out of Toronto.[134] While in transit to the North West, the Toronto soldiers learned that the Cree in Chief Big Bear's band at Frog Lake, about 150 kilometres to the northwest of Battleford, had taken up arms on 2 April, killing eight non-Indigenous Canadians and the part-Sioux Indian agent. Alex Boyd fought at Cut Knife Hill against Chief Poundmaker on 2 May 1885, in an unprovoked attack ordered by Colonel Otter of the Canadian forces.[135] Fortunately, the oldest Boyd son escaped injury in the unnecessary raid against a peaceful chief and his community that cost the Canadians eight killed and fourteen wounded. One of the chancellor's brothers-in-law, Major Lawrence Buchan, served as an adjutant on General Middleton's staff.[136] Although Batoche fell to Middleton on 12 May, and Riel surrendered himself on 15 May, chiefs Big Bear and Poundmaker remained at large when the St Catharines Milling case began, on 18 May.

Apart from the appearance of Alexander Morris, the lawyers in St Catharines Milling argued the case entirely on documents. As the Canadian historian Anthony J. Hall has written, "For the Victorians it was perfectly normal to legislate and to litigate questions of Indian right while taking absolutely no notice of the opinions and views of living Native people."[137] The court called only one witness: Alexander Morris, former lieutenant governor of Manitoba and the North-West Territories, and one of the commissioners who had negotiated Treaty Three. Morris later acted as commissioner for treaties Four, Five, and Six, as well as for the revision of treaties One and Two. At this time Morris was the deputy leader of the Conservative Opposition in the Ontario Legislature, and he simply confirmed that the commissioners had signed the treaty on the authority of the Canadian government.[138] He omitted to mention the Anishinabeg negotiators' position that the land was not surrendered or sold, but instead shared in peaceful coexistence between equals. Morris's nearly 500-page book, *The Treaties of Canada with the Indians of Manitoba and the North-West Territories*, published in 1880, was submitted as evidence.

Without a doubt, Alexander Morris was one of the most sympathetic and generous Canadians of his generation towards the First Nations,[139] but he too remained a prisoner of his times. At the end of his book, he describes the Indians in the North West as a "helpless population," who were "wards of Canada."[140] Morris fully endorsed assimilation, maintaining it would be good for them to adopt a superior way of life: "Let us have Christianity and civilization to leaven the mass of heathenism and paganism among the Indian tribes; let us have a wise and paternal Government faithfully carrying out the provisions of our treaties, and doing the utmost to help, and elevate the Indian population, who have been cast upon our care."[141]

The unrest in the North West greatly agitated Toronto, with a strong and ugly backlash in the city's sensationalist press. On 18 May, the very morning Chancellor Boyd heard the positions advanced in the St Catharines case, one of Toronto's biggest newspapers called for revenge. The Toronto *News*, which had a daily circulation of over twenty thousand copies, entitled its lead editorial, "What to Do with Them," and referred to the recently captured Louis Riel as "the cowardly half-breed dog." Regarding the "red devils" who participated in the troubles, the *News* continued, "It will be difficult to prove which Indians committed the murders, but it would be safe to hang every one of the bands engaged in the massacres. An Indian more or less, will hardly be worth haggling over. One thing is certain, no good Indian will be punished, for the simple reason that there are no good Indians."

Delivered on 10 June, Chancellor Boyd in his opinion fully accepted Ontario's position that the Indians did not own or possess their land, but merely occupied it, roamed over it, and supported themselves on it. The judge noted that the Ojibwe or Saulteaux (Anishinabeg) numbered only twenty-six to twenty-seven hundred in the Treaty Three area.[142] "As heathens and barbarians," he added, echoing the Doctrine of Discovery, "it was not thought that they had any proprietary right to the soil nor any such claim thereto as to interfere with the plantations and the general prosecution of colonization."[143] In short, the Indigenous peoples had no title to the territories they occupied. Legally, Europeans became the owners of the land simply by virtue of having arrived there. Ultimate title to British North America rested in the British Crown by right of discovery, occupation, and exploitation.[144] Writing in 2017, the Canadian political scientist Peter Russell summarizes the chancellor's judgment, as "indicative of the racism permeating Canadian relations with Aboriginal peoples at this time."[145]

After the chancellor's pronouncement in favour of Ontario, the case advanced to the Ontario Court of Appeal, which made its ruling in December 1885. The Supreme Court of Canada followed in November 1886. Both affirmed Ontario's possession of the disputed territory, although John Hagerty, Ontario chief justice and president of the Ontario Court of Appeal did not entirely agree with the chancellor.[146]

Like John A. Macdonald, Hagerty felt that British law recognized that the Indians had an Aboriginal right in the soil, and in Hagerty's words, "No surrender of Indian rights had been made, and, according to the settled practice of the United Provinces of Canada, evidenced and sanctioned by repeated statutes, no attempt appears to have been made to grant titles or encourage settlement so long as the Indian claim was unextinguished."[147]

The Judicial Committee of the Privy Council in England, Canada's highest court of appeal until 1949, in July 1888 again denied the Dominion's contention that the Indians had been the absolute owners of the land (in fee simple). At the same time the Judicial Committee ruled against Chancellor Boyd's opinion that the Royal Proclamation of 1763 no longer applied. Instead, it argued that through the Royal Proclamation the Indians had a property right to their land, a "usufruct" or a legal right to collect its produce. In short, the Indians had a usufructory right to use the land, but the ultimate title resided with the Crown.[148] *St Catherine's Milling and Lumber Co. v. the Queen* [1888] would prevail for nearly a century as the dominant "guide" for Indian Title, defining it as a usufructory right for Aboriginal people, one that existed and could be extinguished at the pleasure of the Crown.

Apart from their differing opinion about the Royal Proclamation of 1763, the Judicial Committee of the Privy Council said nothing about the chancellor's historical summary. None of the British Law Lords had ever visited Canada, or knew its history. The historical component of Chancellor Boyd's decision was to enjoy a long and respected life. In late 1885 Justice Hagerty had disagreed on the chancellor's interpretation of the Royal Proclamation of 1763, but at the same time, he had praised the "care and perspicacity" of his judgment.[149] Jurists continued to cite Boyd's historical summary into the late twentieth century.[150]

Chancellor Boyd's historical work was assumed to be scholarly and well based, but despite his best intentions, in fact, it was not. Boyd had neither the time to research the question fully, nor access to the necessary records. Well-organized Canadian archives remained far in the future. In writing his decision, Boyd relied heavily on the Bagot Report, prepared in the years 1842 to 1844, and published in 1845 and 1847. He summarized it as "an admirable *resumé* of what has been done in the earlier history of Canada."[151] It was not. The Bagot Commission, named after Sir Charles Bagot, then governor general of Canada, had not examined any documents from before 1827.[152]

Today, even the most cursory examination refutes Chancellor Boyd's assertion that the Royal Proclamation of 1763 no longer had the force of law after the passage of the Quebec Act in 1774. Four examples prove it did, the first being the statement on land rights made by Lieutenant Governor John Graves Simcoe to the Western Indians at Navy Hall, in Niagara, in 1793.[153] Second, one can cite the promise by Peter Russell, the administrator of Upper Canada in 1798, that the Mississaugas would never be forced to part with any of their land without their consent.[154] Third, William Claus, deputy superintendent-general of Indian Affairs in 1811, told the Anishinabeg of Lake Simcoe and Matchedash Bay that the King "never will take a foot of land from any of his Indian Children without their free consent."[155] Finally, in 1794, the Dorchester Instructions, issued by Guy Carleton, 1st Baron Dorchester, governor-in chief of British North America, expanded upon the Royal Proclamation's treaty-making principles: "All Purchases are to be made in public Council with great Solemnity and Ceremony according to the Ancient Usages and Customs of the Indians, the Principal Chiefs and leading Men of the Nation or Nations to whom the lands being first assembled."[156]

As did his mentor Daniel Wilson, John Alexander Boyd believed that humanity through history moved from savagery through barbarity to civilization. Chancellor Boyd wrote in his St Catharines Milling and Lumber Company decision that he hoped the North American Indians "may be led to settle down into the industrious and peaceful habits of a civilized people."[157] The Canadian historian George F.G. Stanley, writing in 1983, recreates the atmosphere of the late nineteenth century in this short summary that applies here: "The theory of empire, cultural and political, was one in which every white man believed, in those countries at least [Britain and France]; empire as an instrument for the betterment of mankind; empire as an instrument through which the more fortunate white man would assume the burden imposed on him by God; empire as an instrument not of oppression but of freedom, freedom from ignorance."[158]

Chancellor Boyd reached the apex of his career in 1901. Since 1887 he had served as president of the High Court for Ontario, the second-highest ranking justice in the province, with only the chief justice above him. Knighted in 1899,[159] in 1901, Chancellor John Alexander Boyd was named KCMG (Knight Commander of the Most Distinguished Order of Saint Michael and Saint George) by the Duke of Cornwall and York, the future King George V, while on his royal tour of Canada that year.[160]

Chancellor Boyd enjoyed the respect of his church, the legal profession, and his community. Highly esteemed by the University of Toronto, Boyd obtained the degree of Doctor of Laws (honoris causa) from his alma mater at the June 1889 commencement exercises; another distinguished recipient was Sir John A. Macdonald.[161] After years of service on the University of Toronto senate, Boyd was invited in 1900 to accept the chancellorship of the University of Toronto. Already serving as the president of the Toronto Conservatory of Music, one of the largest in the world, and the most important of the institutions affiliated with the university, he declined the honour.[162]

A terrible shock came a few days before Boyd turned sixty-five, on 23 April 1902. The chancellor learned that his eldest son Alex, a veteran of 1885, who had gone to fight for Britain in the South African or Anglo-Boer War, had died of typhoid or enteric fever in Pretoria. He had become an officer in the South African Constabulary, a semimilitary force. An outstanding athlete, Captain Alex Boyd had trained and then practised as a lawyer. The former captain of Toronto's Argonaut Rowing Club belonged to the crew of eight that competed in the Henley Royal Regatta in England in 1899.[163] Alex Boyd was buried in the Pretoria Cemetery, with a full military funeral. Colonel Sam Steele, the Canadian head of the South Africa Constabulary, served as the principal mourner.[164] About 15 or so metres from his grave lies that of Christian Victor, Prince of Schleswig Holstein, a grandson of Queen Victoria, who had died of enteric fever a year and a half earlier.

The chancellor carried on with his legal work fourteen more years, until his death at the age of 79 in late November 1916. On his deathbed, the dedicated judge endorsed his judgment of a case he had tried but a week earlier.[165] The University of Toronto senate passed a special resolution that noted the high estimation that Sir John Alexander Boyd enjoyed in the city of his birth, "his great attainments, his high character and his personal dignity mark him a model of what a British Judge should be."[166]

Like many other of his contemporaries in all walks of late nineteenth- and early twentieth-century Canadian society, Chancellor Boyd regarded his perspectives on the North American Indians as both fair and humane. He said in an arbitration case in 1895, "I have always advocated the rights of the Indians as far as I can, because I think, as a people, they have been hardly [badly] treated by the white incoming population."[167] With hindsight we now fully understand the catastrophic impact on Indigenous Title of his historical survey in the first St. Catharines Milling case.[168]

In the mid-twentieth century Kathleen Coburn, a Georgian Bay cottager a generation after Boyd, saw the First Nations in a refreshingly new perspective, largely thanks to her strong friendship with the Tabobandungs, a Parry Island (or Wasauksing) family. Kathleen Coburn came from a family with a deep sense of social justice. Her father, a Methodist minister, had taught his children "the Church was useless if it did not fight against social evils on every level."[169] At an early stage in her academic career, teaching English at Victoria University in the University of Toronto, the study of Samuel Taylor Coleridge drew her interest. The English romantic poet's concern for human rights attracted her: "He was excited by public affairs, and wrote powerfully as a journalist against slavery of all kinds – of children in the cotton factories, as well as slaves in the sugar plantations."[170] As did Coleridge, Coburn defended those removed from the centre of power and influence. Some years later, for example, she befriended Ethel Brant Monture, a Six Nations writer and public lecturer, and supported her work.[171] Although her Mohawk friend did not hold a university degree, Professor Coburn pointed out she had a world of far more experience and training "than many persons who have more paper certificates."[172]

Born in Stayner, Ontario, a small market town near Georgian Bay, Kathleen Coburn attended Harbord Collegiate in Toronto, after the family moved to the city from postings in rural churches in Ontario. In her last year at high school she served as the editor-in-chief of the *Harbord Review*. Louis Rasminsky, a future governor of the Bank of Canada, assisted as one of her two business managers.[173] Coburn entered Victoria, the chosen university for children of Methodist ministers, at the age of 19 in 1924. Seeing talent ready for recruitment, Pelham Edgar, chairman of the Department of English, invited her to enter Victoria's M.A. program in English and arranged for a readership with the responsibility of marking undergraduate essays.[174] She received both her B.A. (1928) and M.A. (1930) from Victoria, after which she studied at Oxford University, obtaining her B.Litt in 1932.

Upon returning to Toronto, Kathleen Coburn became an assistant to Norma Ford, Victoria's interim dean of women, with the responsibility of living as a don in Annesley Hall, the women's residence. The joy of her new position came not from her power at Annesley, "administering rules I did not believe in,"[175] but rather from her additional assignment, which was to teach one-third of her time in the English department. After Ethel Brant Monture discovered her long hours, her Mohawk friend sent her a card, with these words, "Around the college at midnight – how hard you are working! You are no better than I – drive yourself like a team of mules!"[176] All being said, as Coburn later wrote, "There were certain advantages in being a downtrodden female scholar with no permanent status for the first fourteen years of teaching."[177] Free from departmental administration, she could devote her summers to research and writing on Coleridge.

Gender discrimination on campus irritated the female academic. Coburn had grounds for her resentment, and I offer but one example that hints at the injustice. In September 1939, her Six Nations friend Ethel Brant Monture participated in the University of Toronto–Yale Conference on the North American Indian (see chapter seven). For breakfasts and dinners at the two-week gathering, the conference program outlined the daily schedule: "All meetings will be held in the Royal Ontario Museum where luncheon will be provided. Breakfast at 8.00 and dinner at 6.00 will be served to men in Hart House, five minutes walk from the Museum."[178] Women, however, could not dine there, as the original grant of the facility by the Massey family stipulated that Hart House was intended "for the exclusive use of the male members of the University." Only in 1972 did the University of Toronto admit women to Hart House on equal terms with men.[179] As Laurel Sefton MacDowell, an undergraduate history and political science student (1965–9) and a representative on the Students' Administrative Council at the time, recalls, "I think it's important for people to understand what Hart House was originally – essentially a men's club. And that had, I think, a profound effect on young men. They felt very privileged. They had a place to go to eat, and have discussions and to do their extra-curricular activities. And there wasn't an equivalent place for women."[180]

On the campus of Victoria College, and the larger University of Toronto campus, Kathleen Coburn encountered hostility from some male colleagues.[181] The journalist Christina McCall, a student there in the early 1950s, remembered Professor Coburn telling her seminar that women "are deemed inferior on sight, and it's up to us to refuse to be diminished by men and to affirm ourselves through excellence in one's work."[182] Determined to reach excellence, Kathleen Coburn achieved international recognition as a celebrated Coleridge scholar, obtaining honorary doctorates from a number of universities. Victoria University, in 2001, named its reading room in its E.J. Pratt Library after her.

Unlike Chancellor Boyd, Kathleen Coburn had close Indigenous friends in the Parry Island community.[183] Coburn and her friend Jessie Macpherson, Victoria's dean of women, bought a five-acre (about two-hectare) island off the southwestern shore of Parry Island in 1939. From all the local builders, she selected Johnson Tabobandung, an Ojibwe, to construct the cottage. As Coburn later recalled, "He built from an architect's blueprints, accurately and neatly, though his formal education consisted of one year or less at the reserve school." Kathleen and Jessie's decision to select him was unusual, defying as it did the conventional wisdom of Euro-Canadian Parry Sound. She later wrote, "The local prejudice against employing Indians in any capacity, let alone trusting them with responsibility, is general, deep-rooted, and often without the slightest basis in experience of them and their work."[184]

4.3 Kathleen Coburn at her cottage, on her island just west of Parry Island, Georgian Bay, mid-twentieth century. Kathleen Coburn Collection, Series 7, Box 73, file 8, Victoria University Library, University of Toronto. Reproduced with permission of the Victoria University Library.

From the Tabobandungs, Kathleen Coburn gleaned a central under-standing of the Ojibwe culture: the importance of reciprocity. She assisted them when asked, and even welcomed family members to stay at her Toronto home on their trips south. In return, the Ojibwe family helped to expand her worldview, and she came to see the resilience and value of their culture. Coburn wrote in her autobiography, entitled *In Pursuit of Coleridge*, "By the natural processes of friendship, inevi-tably slow in the first thirty years over a cultural divide, Johnson and Christina Tabobandung and their family, and others too, on the Parry Island Reserve, became a highly-valued part of our lives." The Tabo-bandungs annually opened and closed the cottage, installed the pump and repaired it, and endlessly cut and delivered and piled hundreds of cords of wood for the stove and fireplace.[185]

The 1930s proved a difficult decade for the First Nations. The Cana-dian social welfare historian Hugh Shewell notes, "The Depression generated little sympathy for the First Nations; in fact, it contributed to their even greater neglect."[186] The desperate economic circumstances led to more federal retrenchment in the face of what was now a numeri-cally growing population of status Indians. Already in 1927 the federal Department of Indian Affairs had outlawed the giving and raising of money for advancing a Native land claim, which made it almost impos-sible for Native bands to hire lawyers. [187] In 1933 the department went further and officially and explicitly imposed a ban on Indians travelling to Ottawa to discuss grievances and land claims.[188] Three years later, the newly elected Liberal government of William Lyon Mackenzie King, in 1936, demoted the Department of Indian Affairs into a massive minis-try called the Department of Mines and Resources. Dr Harold McGill replaced Duncan Campbell Scott (see chapter five) as deputy superin-tendent general of Indian Affairs from 1933 onward, and now headed the Indian Affairs Branch, on a lower level than a department. Shewell emphasizes that these administrative adjustments "reflected the low importance now attached to Indian matters, and marked the nadir of First Nations' status in Canada."[189]

Important information about the poor health conditions, unemploy-ment, and the shortcomings of the educational system for the Indig-enous peoples did surface and receive national attention during the Second World War, in the hearings of the House of Commons Special Committee on Reconstruction and Re-establishment. In 1944 business leaders, acknowledged experts in various disciplines, and government officials participated and shared their vision for an effective post-war social and economic transition.[190] One of the astonishing details that emerged was the fact that only two Indians were employed at the headquarters of the Indian Affairs Branch, which had a total administrative staff of five hundred.[191] By the mid-1940s Indigenous voices were beginning to be heard. Agitation for change came from emerging Indigenous political organizations from across Canada, including the recently reorganized Indian Association of Alberta. This is the atmosphere of concern in which Kathleen Coburn became involved in First Nations issues,[192] writing reviews of books on Indigenous peoples and sending letters on their behalf.

In her initial search for allies for the First Nations, early in 1943 Coburn contacted Aileen Ross, a sociologist recently arrived at the University of Toronto.[193] Did Professor Ross know any intellectuals in Canada possibly concerned about Aboriginal issues? Ross wrote to "Miss Coburn" on 5 February, saying that she had contacted a young McGill law professor who had a deep interest in human rights. John Humphrey's response at the time was understandable, considering the general ignorance of and indifference towards Indigenous issues at the time. In her letter Ross reported, "John is very interested in the Indian problem, but says he knows nothing about it."[194] Only five years later, Professor John Peters Humphrey, legal scholar, jurist, and human rights advocate, wrote the original draft of the United Nations Universal Declaration of Human Rights.[195]

In the 1940s Kathleen Coburn reviewed titles on Indigenous subjects for the progressive political and cultural magazine, *Canadian Forum*. Later, she prepared an early draft of an essay on "The Indian in Canadian Literature," but apparently she did not continue with it.[196] Her sensitivity for Indigenous issues mostly appears in her *Canadian Forum* book reviews. In the October 1942 issue, for example, she praises Richard Finnie's *Canada Moves North* (1942), a study of the North-West Territories, writing, "Mr Finnie's denunciation of our treatment of native populations, Indian and Eskimo, is scathing, unsentimental, and very constructive."[197] Her October 1944 review of *The North American Indian To-day*, the proceedings of the September 1939 University of Toronto–Yale Conference and published by the University of Toronto Press the previous year, was equally positive: "Ignorance of the conditions and problems of Canada's 120,000 Indians and the consequent indifference of most Canadians to the lot of this minority make a recent publication of the University of Toronto Press especially noteworthy."[198] Her warm friendship with the Tabobandung family of Parry Island introduced Kathleen Coburn to a new understanding of Indigenous Canada.

Chancellor John Alexander Boyd had an opportunity from the 1880s to 1910s to cross over the cultural barrier, but he did not take it. The existence of his "Indian notebook" establishes that the influential judge had a genuine interest in the Ojibwe language, the key to an understanding of the heritage and culture of the Anishinabeg. But all of Boyd's education, social, and professional life was in British Canada. Indigenous Canada was a closed book to him. He had no Indigenous friends. His personal reserve also helps explain why he made no attempt to reach out to and meet the Georgian Bay Ojibwe. In contrast, the Canadian anthropologist Diamond Jenness (1886–1969), for example, knew Parry Island well, having spent seven weeks there doing fieldwork in 1929 in the preparation of his monograph, *The Ojibwa Indians of Parry Island: Their Social and Religious Life* (1935).[199] Jenness had a wealth of experience travelling through Indigenous Canada, and had extensive reading, yet, in the end, he no more than Chancellor Boyd recognized Indigenous aspirations to survive as culturally distinct communities in their homelands.[200] In his important survey, *The Indians of Canada* (1932), Jenness openly stated, "Doubtless all the tribes will disappear. Some will endure only a few years longer."[201]

Chapter Five

Duncan Campbell Scott: Determined Assimilationist

Duncan Campbell Scott (1862–1947) enjoyed the support of six different ministers and of Parliament itself throughout his two decades as Canada's top civil servant in charge of Indian affairs from 1913 to 1932.[1] Shortly after taking up his position in the Department of Indian Affairs he declared, "The happiest future for the Indian race is absorption into the general population."[2] Scott's pride in his department's mission led him to insist upon meticulous record keeping. As the archivist Bill Russell has noted, "One must wonder whether as many of the records would have survived if the DIA [Department of Indian Affairs] records staff had not had this historical interest."[3] The abundant documentation allows for a full in-depth probe of this consummate career bureaucrat's relentless campaign to end the separation of First Nations from the dominant society. The fact that Parliament had little interest in the Indigenous peoples, and lacked any basic awareness and understanding of them, enabled the entrenched bureaucrat to be left alone and to do pretty much as he pleased.

Duncan Campbell Scott was born on 2 August 1862 in the Methodist parsonage at the corner of Metcalfe and Queen Streets in downtown Ottawa, located directly across from the Dominion Methodist Church where his father, who was born and raised in England, served as minister. Reverend William Scott began his ministry with the Ojibwe (Anishinabeg) in southwestern Ontario in the 1840s. Reverends Peter Jones and Scott approached Lord Elgin, the governor general of the Canadas in 1847 to help with the establishment of the Mount Elgin Indian Industrial, or Residential School at Muncey, 30 kilometres to the southwest of London, Ontario.[4] Shortly after this, Reverend Scott left the Indian mission work, and from the 1850s to 1870s he served with non-Indigenous Methodist congregations throughout eastern Ontario and western Quebec.

Following the death of his first wife, in 1859, the English minister married Canadian-born Isabella Campbell MacCallum, whose Gaelic-speaking parents had immigrated to Canada from Perthshire in the Scottish Highlands.[5] Young Duncan Campbell, their son, grew up in church manses in small towns and villages in rural Ontario and in Quebec. As he talked so little about his youth, little is known about it, apart from his early involvement in music. Introduced to the piano at age seven,[6] he developed a lifelong love passion for classical music. Years later, the career bureaucrat kept a piano with a silent keyboard in his office, allowing him to practise at intervals during his workday.[7] In high school, Duncan wanted to become a medical doctor, but his parents lacked the financial means to pay for his studies. After he left Stanstead Wesleyan College in the Eastern Townships, in 1879, he applied to the federal public service.

Thanks to his father's friendship with John A. Macdonald, 17-year-old Duncan Campbell Scott obtained a position as a junior copy clerk. When government offices came open, friends of the ruling party usually obtained them.[8] The prime minister acted on a letter from Conservative MP Charles Colby, a political ally in the Eastern Townships, who had written to him, saying, "You desired to be reminded after the Session of your intention and promise to provide a good permanent situation for Duncan Campbell Scott, son of your clerical and political friend and admirer Rev Wm Scott now of Durham Prov of Que."[9] In the interview that followed, the prime minister simply requested the young applicant to submit a specimen of his handwriting. It being found acceptable, he obtained a clerk's position in what became known the following year as the Department of Indian Affairs. As Scott remarked in an interview years later, "It was a very efficient system. You just had to be a friend of someone in the government."[10]

It can be said, with near certainty, that Duncan, a voracious reader, saw the article "In the North-West with 'Sitting Bull,'" in a summer 1880 issue of *Rose-Belford's Canadian Monthly and National Review,* written by Superintendent Edmund Dalrymple Clark of the NWMP on duty at Fort Walsh in the Cypress Hills.[11] Any story about Sitting Bull in Western Canada would have been "must reading" in the newly established Department of Indian Affairs in 1880. There was a personal link as well to the man who had hired him. Clark was one of the first NWMP officers commissioned in 1873, and John A. Macdonald's nephew by marriage. Horrible news arrived in the late fall 1880.[12] From the unsanitary water at Fort Walsh the highly regarded young officer contracted typhoid, and died.[13] Clark was a son of Major-General John Clark of the British Army, a brother of Isabella Clark Macdonald, John A.'s first wife, who died in 1857.[14] Life was perilous in the North West – encouragement for young Scott to keep his desk job in Ottawa.

Duncan Campbell Scott thrived in the Department of Indian Affairs, as it was very much his style, a "top-down" operation, firmly under the control of the deputy superintendent of Indian Affairs. In the early 1880s the "inside" staff at headquarters in Ottawa numbered, including part-time clerical workers, about forty people.[15] They had little specific training for their jobs.[16] The clerks copied by hand all correspondence into departmental letter books, and continued doing so until the introduction of typewriters some years later. By 1890 the department's operations across the country required the services of some 460 employees.[17] Most of these "outside service" employees worked for the department part-time during the busy seasons when payments were being disbursed. The most important "outside" employees were the Indian agents assigned to reserves across Canada and overseen by department-appointed regional superintendents. In the 1880s and early 1890s Scott trained under Lawrence Vankoughnet, Macdonald's loyal deputy superintendent of Indian Affairs, a model Victorian bureaucrat and a tyrant for economy and efficiency.

Intelligent and capable, Scott climbed the bureaucratic ladder from junior copy clerk to bookkeeper, to chief clerk, to accountant, to treaty co-commissioner (for Treaty Nine in northern Ontario), to superintendent of education. Any disagreements he had in the office, he kept within himself. His avoidance of conflict in the workplace, and his embracement of the status quo, aided greatly his steady career advancement.[18] In 1913 Scott achieved Ottawa mandarin status: he was appointed deputy minister, serving directly under Minister of the Interior William James Roche, who also acted as the superintendent general of Indian Affairs. Roche usually regarded Indian Affairs to be but a minor aspect of the portfolio, secondary to his first responsibility as minister of the interior[19] – this left his deputy as the effective decision maker. Scott did not encourage innovation. Well into the twentieth century, writes the historian Morris Zaslow, the department "was dominated by aging, conservative-minded administrators and antiquated policies and programs, and it underwent little change, notwithstanding the serious difficulties the native peoples faced."[20]

Scott was well paid. As the chief clerk of the Department of Indian Affairs, in 1905 he earned $2,500, eight times more than the $300 salary earned by teachers in many of the Indian residential schools.[21] His annual remuneration rose to $5,000 on becoming deputy minister.[22] In 1913 the 52-year-old career civil servant ran a department of approximately 725 individuals, with an inside service staff in Ottawa of 75 and an outside service staff across Canada of 650,[23] and he also ruled over approximately 100,000 registered, or status Indians.[24] Scott kept to a familiar routine at work, never allowing his day job to dominate. As his friend E.K. Brown, a professor and literary critic, commented after Scott's death, "The centre of his life was not in his office, where he seldom came early, and never stayed late."[25]

In the late nineteenth century the Government of Canada strengthened and intensified the already considerable powers of the Indian Act of 1876. Various amendments gave additional control to the local Indian agents. In the 1880s, for example, they acquired authority as justices of the peace. The agent thereby became the Indian Act's judge, jury, and enforcer. Section 3 was added in 1884 to ban dances and traditional ceremonies.[26] More important Indian Act amendments followed in the early twentieth century, including incentives in 1906 to encourage the sale of treaty land, and new provisions in 1911 for the expropriation of reserve land.[27] Scott endorsed the ironclad control so contrary to what the First Nations regarded as the spirit of the treaties. He stated in 1927, "There is no intention of changing the well-established policy of dealing with Indians and Indian affairs in this country."[28]

The senior civil servant lived in a fine three-storey brick house at 108 Lisgar Avenue, an easy walk to his workplace on Parliament Hill. This became his cherished sanctuary, his retreat, full of books and music. At home he welcomed literary friends and acquaintances to talk about cultural topics that interested him. His wide reading allowed him to make references to the great English writers of the previous centuries – Shakespeare, Donne, Keats, Milton, Wordsworth.[29] In 1906, Duncan selected his friend, Pelham Edgar, as commission secretary to the Treaty Nine Treaty Party.[30] Travelling though the rugged bush country of northern Ontario, Scott and Edgar, a professor of English at Victoria College in the University of Toronto, passed many happy hours together as canoe passengers, in complete detachment, reading the *Oxford Book of English Verse*. In Pelham Edgar's words, "D.C.S. and I sit side by side in the big bark canoe, and we gloat over things, cloud effects, peeps of vistas through the islands as they shift past us, and lights and shadows on the water."[31]

As well as books Scott had collected an extensive library of phonograph recordings of classical music.[32] Years later his friend Leonard Brockington, who served as the first chairman of the Canadian Broadcasting Corporation in the late 1930s, and later as the rector of Queen's University (1947–66) recalled, "If you pass by one summer evening and the window is open, you may hear strains of Bach, of Haydn, or of Mozart on the quiet air."[33] Scott also owned fine examples of Canadian art, with paintings by British Columbia's Emily Carr[34] and Quebec artist

5.1 Duncan Campbell Scott (*seated on extreme right*) and Belle Scott (*seated in the centre*) and two friends, with the English poet Rupert Brooke, Ottawa, July 1913. MS Coll. 13 (Duncan Campbell Scott Papers) Box 1B, Folder 8. Courtesy of the Thomas Fisher Rare Book Library, University of Toronto.

Clarence Gagnon.[35] Well into his retirement, he wrote an appreciative sketch of W.J. Phillips, the Canadian woodcutter and watercolourist.[36]

Duncan Campbell Scott enjoyed a great reputation for his interest in the arts in Ottawa and elsewhere in the Dominion. Elected a Fellow of the Royal Society of Canada in 1899, he became its president in 1921. The following year the University of Toronto awarded the accomplished poet, short story writer, and essayist, who had never attended university, an honorary doctorate.[37] A public-spirited individual, Scott helped with the founding of both the Ottawa Drama League and the Ottawa Little Theatre.[38]

A group photo taken in 1913 reveals the first Mrs Scott as a handsome woman of commanding presence. Dressed in black, she calmly dominates the scene.[39] Belle Botsford, a professional violinist from Boston, occupied a prominent social role in Ottawa, including playing the violin at the Ottawa Women's Morning Music Club.[40] The local papers reported on her tea and euchre parties. Proud of her social position, Mrs Scott cherished the souvenir cards she kept of the "at homes" of others, including those of the wives of six successive governors general. The well-dressed Ottawa socialite contrasted so with her reserved bookish husband, who wore "old-fashioned, small-lensed spectacles and conservative clothes."[41] In terms of their social life, Belle and Duncan had different preferences: she loved evening parties, he did not. Scott once confided to a friend that he did not "belong to the sort of people" who invited familiarity by using Christian names "at the first cocktail party."[42]

Belle and Duncan faced a horrifying personal crisis in 1907. In their marriage's thirteenth year, they lost their only child, 11-year-old Elizabeth, who died of scarlet fever while away at boarding school in France. After her death, Scott always kept several of her toys on the hearth of their music room.[43] The young English poet Rupert Brooke, who spent a week with the Scotts in July 1913, described his host in a letter to his mother: "He's about fifty & head of the Indian affairs in the civil service. They had one daughter who died six years ago, a child & it smashed them up rather. Also he leads rather a lonely life from the literary point of view, for there's hardly anybody he can talk to about such things."[44]

Shortly after Belle's death in 1929, Scott married again. He was 69 and surprisingly Elise Aylen, just 27, was young enough to be his granddaughter. They met at the Ottawa Poetry Club and married in 1931, on the eve of his retirement from Indian Affairs. Despite their forty-two-year age gap the union proved a happy one, from the date of their marriage to his death in 1947.[45] Scott became more relaxed and outgoing. The young woman proved to be a good influence on the elderly civil servant. Elise's later life establishes what a free spirit she truly was, a child of the global village. Shortly after her husband's death, she moved to Asia and lived in ashrams in India. For a decade the widow of Duncan Campbell Scott resided in the high Himalayas under the spiritual guidance of a guru, Swami Yogeshwarananananda.[46]

Duncan Campbell Scott had no close Indigenous friends.[47] Diamond Jenness, in fact, later recalled how the deputy superintendent general of Indian Affairs kept his distance from his "wards": "The head of the administration disliked them as a people, and gave a cool reception to the delegations that visited him in Ottawa."[48] At the turn of the century, Scott did know superficially, of course, the several First Nations people who worked as clerks in the "inside" service in Ottawa, a group that included Floretta Maracle from Tyendinaga (who in 1907 married Allan Johnson, a brother of Mohawk writer Pauline Johnson), and Joseph Delisle from Kahnewake.[49] The deputy minister knew best Charles Cooke, writer, translator, interpreter, and clerk, and a non-status Indian. Born in the Iroquois community at Oka, just outside of Montreal, Charles Cooke had moved as a young boy with his family to Muskoka.[50] Scott regarded Cooke, who worked with him in the department from 1893 to 1926, as "an intelligent young Mohawk,"[51] but even with this trusted employee he distanced himself. After Cooke proposed the establishment of a departmental collection of materials to include contributions about and originating from North American Indians, Scott cut back the proposal. He accepted the idea of a small departmental library, but later turned down the idea of an "Indian National Library," on the grounds of cost.[52]

What were Duncan Campbell Scott's inner thoughts of the First Nations? Some of Scott's poetry shows the influence of social Darwinism. Biological racism or social Darwinism was a pseudo-scientific way of thinking based on the application of Charles Darwin's theory of evolution in the animal kingdom to the human world. Even in academic circles, this theory dominated into the early decades of the twentieth century. The popular and purportedly scientific doctrine listed societies in a hierarchical order of "inferior" and "superior" races. Modern European nations, it was accordingly believed, were the highest and most developed human societies. Against them all other societies could be ranked. Duncan Campbell Scott's poem "Indian Place Names," for example, begins:

> The race has waned and left but tales of ghosts,
> That hover in the world like fading smoke
> About the lodges: gone are the dusky folk
> That once were cunning with the thong and bow;
> They lured the silver salmon from his lair,
> They drove the buffalo in trampling hosts,
> And gambled in the teepees until dawn,
> But now their vaunted prowess is all gone.
> Gone like a moose-track in the April snow.[53]

Another example of the doctrine's imprint appears in Scott's poem, "The Onondaga Madonna":

> She stands full-throated and with careless pose,
> This woman of a weird and waning race.[54]

5.2 E. Pauline Johnson, 1897. C-085125 LAC. Online MIKAN 319462 (item 1).

Yet, although Duncan Campbell Scott certainly believed in the hierarchical ranking of the "civilized" over the "primitive," only three times, by his biographer Stan Dragland's count, did he use in his writing the phrase "superior race."[55] In his defence, Canadian literature specialist Laura Groening argues that Scott was not a racist, after all he "urged inter-racial marriage and voting rights at a period in history when the most obvious social alternative was provided by his American neighbours who relegate their African-American population to a system of racial segregation."[56]

The deputy general superintendent of Indian Affairs knew fairly well only one Indigenous woman, and that was Pauline Johnson (1861–1913), known in Mohawk as Tekahionwake,[57] the foremost Canadian woman poet of the era.[58] They were almost exactly the same age. The Johnsons belonged to the Christian community, the majority religious group among the Six Nations of the Grand River. Her father was George H.M. Johnson, the government interpreter for the Six Nations Territory. To quote the description of his good friend, the ethnologist Horatio Hale, George H.M. Johnson "was both an Iroquois chief and an Anglo-Canadian gentleman, and in both capacities was highly respected."[59] Generally speaking, the Christian Iroquois promoted an adjustment to the larger society, through the adoption of European agriculture and education in English. In contrast, the Longhouse people championed the old ways of the Haudenosaunee. Roughly, a quarter of the Grand River community identified with the Longhouse faith.[60]

By Canadian law, Pauline was a status Indian, a ward of the federal government, as the Indian Act follows membership through the male line. In contrast, the Haudenosaunee traditionally traced clan membership through the female. Each person belonged to the nation of his or her mother.[61] This made Pauline's membership in the Six Nations problematic for some. Pauline's English mother, Emily Howells Johnson, was the sister-in-law of the wife of Reverend Adam Elliott, the Anglican missionary to the Six Nations. The Indigenous literature specialist Margery Fee comments in her 2015 book, Literary Land Claims, on the intricacies of Pauline's identity, asking, "Was she really Mohawk?" The professor of English at the University of British Columbia replies, "All her critics, myself included, obsess over her identity, however pathological this obsession may be. Her contemporaries' answers to the impossible question range from 'hardly at all' to 'absolutely.'"[62]

Pauline Johnson's family lived quite differently from most people in the Six Nations Territory. To please his English bride, George Johnson bought 200 acres (80 hectares) near the Anglican parsonage and built Chiefswood (now a National Historic Site), an impressive house that won him the Mohawk name of "Onwanonsyshon," "He Who Has the Great Mansion."[63] At home, the family always had servants, at least three: an Indian nursemaid, a non-Indigenous cook, and a stableman. Emily Johnson home schooled her children. She passed onto daughter Pauline her own love of music and literature. The favourites of her youth included Tennyson, Longfellow, Byron, and Keats.[64] Before Pauline Johnson attended Brantford Collegiate Institute, she only briefly attended a Six Nations school. She knew few Iroquois (Haudenosaunee) children,[65] and she did not have an in-depth knowledge of the Mohawk language.[66] Regardless of her distance from the other Six Nations children, Pauline Johnson identified herself completely with her father's people. Upon entering Brantford Collegiate in 1875, at the age of 14, she proudly proclaimed she was Mohawk.[67]

Duncan Campbell Scott knew of the violence in Pauline Johnson's childhood. "White ruffians," dealers in illicit whiskey and timber plundering, twice brutally assaulted her father George Johnson, who served as government interpreter and chief assistant to the non-Indigenous superintendent to the Six Nations Indians.[68] The first incident in 1865 left her father unconscious for five days. His attacker was imprisoned for five years. In a second incident, in 1873, George Johnson was shot and left for dead on the road by his home. His American friend Horatio Hale later wrote of the aftermath, "The malefactors were hunted down, and expiated their crime either in prison or by flight and self-banishment."[69] George Johnson died at the age of 67 in February 1884, his health having been seriously impaired by these two attacks.[70] Within less than a year, widow Emily Johnson and her two daughters left their beloved Chiefswood that they now let out for rental income, and settled in Brantford.[71]

In 1885 Pauline Johnson began to use "Tekahionwake,"[72] her great-grandfather's Mohawk name as her own, as well as Pauline Johnson, to sign the increasing number of poems and articles that she successfully submitted to Canadian magazines and newspapers. Dramatically, she would appear for the first half of her reading program in buckskins and the second in evening dress.[73] Her engagements multiplied. It is estimated that for the better part of two decades in Canada, the United States, and Great Britain, from 1892 to 1909, Pauline Johnson put on approximately two thousand performances.[74] Very early in her performance career Pauline Johnson's path crossed Duncan Campbell Scott's.[75] At a Canadian Literature Evening in Toronto on 16 January 1892, Scott heard Johnson's defiant rendition of "A Cry from an Indian Wife," about the North-West Rebellion of 1885, from an Indian woman's point of view. The three final lines defiantly proclaimed the Indians' ownership of the land, and challenged "the white's God":[76]

Go forth, nor bend to greed of white men's hands,
By right, by birth we Indians own these lands,
Though starved, crushed, plundered, lies our nation low ...
Perhaps the white man's God has willed it so.[77]

In 1895 the Scotts invited the visiting Pauline Johnson to dine with them in Ottawa at their home on Lisgar Avenue.[78] On stage, and even more so during her evening at the Scotts, Pauline Johnson had to be very careful not "to cross the line' and appear too critical of British Canada. In her presentations, the Mohawk writer praised both the National Policy of the ruling Conservative Party and the North-West Mounted Police.[79] Constantly, she avoided offending Scott, as he had enormous power in both the literary world and the Department of Indian Affairs. She certainly knew, for instance, the shortcomings of the Indian boarding schools, as her own brother Allen had run away from the Mohawk Institute. Indirectly, in her writing she inferred that the uprooting of children from their families was a mistake,[80] but she left it at that. As the literary critic Rick Monture writes, she could not afford to damage "her own tenuous career."[81]

Times proved extremely tough in the early 1890s with Canada losing population on a grand scale. From 1881 to 1891 Canadian emigration to the United States exceeded one million persons.[82] The country's total population in 1891 was just short of five million. Then at the end of the nineteenth century, Canada's economy recovered. As the Canadian historian Sarah Carter writes, "The Laurier Liberals were fortunate to win the election of 23 June 1896 just at the dawn of a new age of prosperity in Canada. Conditions favourable to the National Policy of industrialization, east-west railway traffic, and western settlement had at long last come into being."[83]

With the advent of more prosperous times, one might expect the Liberals to provide more generous support to the Department of Indian Affairs than the Conservatives had. False assumption. First, Clifford Sifton, Laurier's minister of the interior and superintendent general of Indian Affairs, now a Manitoban, imposed new financial restrictions on the department, cutting both personnel and salaries.[84] Second, he increased the pressure for the sale of reserve lands, to make more territory available for Euro-Canadian settlers.[85] In a 1897 letter, the Ontario-born and -raised Sifton wrote of the "Western" philosophy he had adopted as his own: "I have lived among western people nearly all my life, and know their way of looking at things; and one of the principal ideas western men have is that it is right to take anything in sight provided nobody else is in ahead of them."[86] Sifton had a low regard for Indigenous peoples: "I have no hesitation in saying – we may as well be frank – that the Indian cannot go out from school, making his own way and compete with the white man … He has not the physical, mental or moral get-up to enable him to compete. He cannot do it."[87]

In 1905 Frank Oliver from Alberta replaced Clifford Sifton as the minister of the interior and superintendent general of Indian Affairs, and he served in that position to 1911. As founding editor of the *Edmonton*

Bulletin, Oliver had written of Indian reserves, twenty-five years earlier, stating, "The land is needed by better men."[88] His administration was even more draconian than that of his predecessor. Under Sifton there were six Indian reserve surrenders in the Prairie West from 1896 to 1905. In the following five years, Oliver concluded eighteen.[89] The most controversial of Indian Act amendments, the Oliver Act, permitted the forced relocation of Indians from any reserves immediately adjacent to, or within towns of more than eight thousand inhabitants.[90]

Pressures for northern development increased across the country, but first the encumbrance or legal burden of the Indian Title had to be removed.[91] An 1894 federal law required provincial acceptance in any treaty negotiations. Three officials, two federal and one provincial, constituted the James Bay or Treaty Nine Commission to obtain an Indian treaty for northern Ontario. Due to his competence in handling money,[92] Frank Oliver approved the selection of Duncan Campbell Scott as one of the two federal commissioners. The Treaty Nine Commission made two summer expeditions across northern Ontario, the first in 1905, with the second the following year. At the numerous stops, such as that at Fort Hope in mid-July, the commissioners overlooked mentioning to the assembled Indians the new challenges the treaty would be bringing. In the words of James Morrison, legal and historical researcher, "They do not seem to have been told that they were giving up all of their own rights to their lands, except for certain small 'reserves'; nor that by agreeing to be good subjects of His Majesty, they were accepting governmental regulation of their traditional economy."[93] The treaty commissioners gave no consideration to helping the Indians share in the profits of the development of northern Ontario's mineral, hydro, and timber resources.[94] Together with the area added by the subsequent treaty adhesions in 1929–30, Treaty Nine, signed between Anishinabe (Ojibwe) and Omushkegowuk (Cree) communities and the Crown (both federal and provincial) in 1905–6, covers approximately two-thirds of the province of Ontario.[95]

From 1909 to 1913 Duncan Campbell Scott served as the superintendent of Indian education. He knew well the boarding schools' extraordinary mortality rate, writing in 1914, "Fifty per cent of the children who passed through these schools did not live to benefit from the education which they had received therein."[96] Defenders of the system pointed out that tuberculosis was also common on the reserves themselves, not just in the schools.[97] Dr Peter Bryce, the medical inspector to the Department of the Interior, with added Department of Indian Affairs responsibilities, refused to accept this. He sought to reform the residential school system from within, and insisted that the department do more to fight tuberculosis in the schools. A medical consensus now existed that tuberculosis, then usually called consumption or pulmonary phthisis, and the allied disease called scrofula (or glandular tuberculosis), were contagious.[98]

In his 1906 annual report Dr Bryce exposed the horrific state of Indian health in the boarding schools, due to overcrowding, lack of ventilation, and unsanitary conditions. The buildings were firetraps, as well as incubators of disease.[99] Most Indian agents in Western Canada confirmed the accuracy of the doctor's findings.[100] Bryce had the credentials to make his damaging critique. In 1882 he became the first secretary of the Board of Health of Ontario, a position in which he served to 1904. The public health pioneer became president of the American Public Health Association for the year 1900, the first Canadian to do so. He had come to Ottawa in 1904 as the chief medical officer of the Department of the Interior with responsibilities for both Immigration and Indian Affairs.[101] Dr Peter Bryce's assault unsettled Duncan Campbell Scott, not yet the top bureaucrat in the Department of Indian Affairs, but soon in 1909 to become superintendent of education, and in 1913 the deputy superintendent general himself. Over the years to follow, Bryce gave no ground and held that the government's record with respect to Indian health constituted "a national crime." Dr Bryce's charge resonates a century later.[102]

Frederick Ogilvie Loft (1861–1934), whose Mohawk name was Onondeyoh, was a provincial civil servant working in Toronto. Loft entered the debate about the boarding schools in 1908. Writing in the Toronto *Globe* of 8 February, the former Mohawk Institute student called for "better schools, which will provide education as taught in any public school in the Province." The following year, Loft elaborated in "The Indian and Education," a series of four articles for *Saturday Night*. Unlike fellow Mohawk Thomas Green, his experiences were negative. As Loft stated in his first essay, "The Indian child has been carried to school, at once alienating it from parental and home affection and ties." The meals were insufficient: "I recall the times when working in the fields I was actually too hungry to be able to walk, let alone work." Living conditions were substandard: "In winter the rooms and beds were so cold that it took half the night before I got warm enough to fall asleep."[103] Loft wanted day schools instead of boarding schools. Immediately, Deputy Superintendent General Duncan Campbell Scott made mental note of the troublemaker.

The final report of Canada's Truth and Reconciliation Commission, in fairness, notes that Scott's intervention in 1910 led to a residential school agreement that provided for a substantial increase in funding.[104]

Nevertheless, the poor living conditions at the schools endured, as after the outbreak of the First World War, all the money for improving school buildings vanished. Why was so little done? Scott's biographer Stan Dragland pointedly summarizes: "One has to keep reminding oneself that, for Scott and most of his contemporaries, the Indians *do not exist* as a people that must be reckoned with [...] powerless people *are* invisible. In any crunch they don't count."[105]

Three years later Scott himself became the deputy superintendent general of Indian Affairs, after the discovery that his predecessor Frank Pedley was profiteering from Indian land sales, the details of which circulated in the press.[106] To begin the urgent reform of the federal Indian administration, Scott issued a policy pamphlet to every Indian agent only two weeks after his appointment. It outlined specific instructions on "nearly every imaginable area of Indian life."[107] The highly skilled career bureaucrat cleaned up the administrative mess he had inherited, but the students in the poorly funded boarding schools continued to endure harsh conditions.

The First World War had a great impact on Duncan Campbell Scott. At the outset of the Great War, as it was then called, the department only reluctantly allowed Indians to enlist. But the mounting casualties overseas in 1915 and 1916, and especially in 1917 and 1918, transformed Scott into an enthusiastic promoter of Indian enlistments. By the end of the war, at least 4,000 status Indians out of a total population of approximately 100,000 had enlisted for active service in the Canadian Expeditionary Force. The strong status Indian participation paralleled the percentage of enlistments among non-Indigenous communities, roughly 620,000 Canadians in a total population of approximately 8 million.[108]

The reward for the valiant service of Indigenous men in the Great War proved slight, as the Indian Act remained firmly in place when the First Nations soldiers returned. Its draconian powers, in fact, were vigorously expanded. In 1918 the Department of Indian Affairs was given authority to spend band funds without band permission. The next year, the department gained the power to lease reserve surface rights for mining. School attendance at day or residential schools for all Indian children from 7 to 15 years of age became obligatory in 1920. It did not require that they attend residential school specifically, but frequently great pressure existed for many to do so.[109]

Enfranchisement, and with it the ending of Indian status, remained the department's cherished objective (see chapter one). On 28 September 1895, Scott visited Lorette or Wendake.[110] At the turn of the century, Léon Gérin, the pioneer French Canadian sociologist,[111] described the Huron community positively. During his visits to the community, Gérin had found the whitewashed wooden houses in the small and compact village immediately north of Quebec City to be as well kept up as those of the neighbouring French Canadian farmers and artisans. The four hundred or so Huron also had a reserve for hunting as well as a timber tract, but both were not adjacent to the village site.[112] Around 1900 some Wendat still practised hunting, trapping, and guiding, but the vast majority worked in the village itself, in manufacturing. The improved transportation system of the late nineteenth century allowed the Wendat to sell their moccasins and snowshoes throughout North America. In housing, dress, and religion, the Huron and the French Canadians surrounding Wendake appeared almost identical. The Wendat spoke exactly the same French as the French Canadians around them, with the identical accent and expressions.

Energetically, the Department of Indian Affairs encouraged the males in Wendake to give up voluntarily their Indian status. Regardless of the pressure, however, they showed little interest in forfeiting their national identity. They did not wish to own land individually. The Wendat resented the seizure of the lands they had once controlled in the Quebec City area. Antagonism also arose over the leasing of large tracts in their hunting grounds north of the village to sports clubs, followed by the province's creation, in 1895, of the Parc des Laurentides, a huge forest reserve and recreational area that the Wendat used for hunting, fishing, and harvesting. Gérin found that the Wendake Huron formed a culturally "separate group," who refused to abandon their First Nation status and Wendake[113] and unite to form a municipality with their non-Native neighbours.

Wendake became Duncan Campbell Scott's model community in favour of compulsory enfranchisement. Several years earlier the anthropologist Marius Barbeau (1883–1969) had undertaken extensive fieldwork in the community. Scott now commissioned Barbeau to write a follow-up study. Barbeau's report provided exactly the results wanted. The anthropologist argued, "There is little that distinguishes Lorette from the neighbouring Canadian villages, and comparatively few of its inhabitants have features that reveal an Indian ancestry."[114] Many Wendat looked like white persons.[115] In his assessment, Barbeau completely overlooked that the Wendat's culture was, like all cultures, dynamic and constantly changing, not static. In any event, the Huron's determined opposition led the federal government to reject Scott's recommendation to disestablish Wendake and make it into a municipality.

Well into the twentieth century Indian policy remained premised on the expectation that within several generations the First Nations would intermarry and blend totally into the dominant society. The assessment proved incorrect. At the end of the 1910s, the status Indian population in Canada had actually risen slightly.[116] How in terms of the new reality could the Government of Canada limit the number of people with Indian status, and diminish its financial responsibility? Duncan Campbell Scott brought forward plans in 1920 to implement the forced enfranchisement of selected status Indians. The proposed Bill 14 would allow the federal government to take away Indian status from any individual with, or without, that person's consent. In 1918, Fred Loft, the strong critic of the federal government's First Nations school policies, formed the League of Indians of Canada, the first pan-Indian political organization in the country. In Duncan Campbell Scott's mind, Fred Loft was an ideal candidate for forced enfranchisement.

Fred Ogilvie Loft was born on the Grand River Six Nations Territory in 1861. The Lofts, members of the Anglican Church, valued Euro-Canadian education.[117] Fred grew up on his parents' 200-acre (80-hectare) farm, and attended a nearby Indian primary school before spending an unhappy year in 1874 at the Mohawk Institute in Brantford. His older brother William attended the same school for three years,[118] and ran away three times.[119] After only one year there, younger brother Fred left forever. Even as a boy Fred showed great independence and determination. At the family farm, he loved to train horses that had never been ridden, and years later he recalled, "It is a wonder I am alive, for I've nearly been killed by my awful recklessness several times."[120]

To finish elementary school, Fred Loft walked from his parents' farm every day, a round trip of nearly 15 kilometres, to a school in neighbouring Caledonia, just east of the Six Nations Territory. Who inspired Fred Loft to make such a commitment to education? Who was his role model? Years later he told a Toronto newspaper reporter the following story: Without specifying his name, Onondeyoh mentioned that his childhood hero had been "an Indian graduate of McGill who was well dressed and prosperous, a perfect gentleman."[121] That individual was Dr George Bomberry, a Cayuga from the Six Nations Territory and a student at the Mohawk Institute in the 1860s. Bomberry obtained his medical degree from McGill University in 1875 and then practised among the Six Nations, until his death from tuberculosis in 1879.[122]

While attending high school in the town, Fred Loft did odd jobs working for his board and lodging. His success in high school instilled great self-confidence, and any prejudice he encountered did not discourage him. Discrimination was rife in non-Indigenous communities around the Six Nations Territory. As late as in the 1940s, George Beaver, a relative of the Lofts, recalls, "Native people were expected to be invisible. In stores, Natives could possibly work back in the stock-room but

5.3 Members of Fred Loft's family. His aunt Charlotte Smith appears second from the right, and apparently the woman second from the left is his mother, Ellen Loft. Ellen and Charlotte were sisters. Henri Loft, Fred and Affa's oldest daughter, gave a Toronto newspaper an interesting word picture of Charlotte: "One of my fondest childhood recollections is of great Aunt Charlotte. Captain [Joseph] Brant's great-granddaughter – a tall, friendly, fun-loving lady with jet black hair parted in the centre, a marvellous housekeeper and an immaculate, fastidious dresser – who sat for half an hour after each meal serenely and happily smoking her clay pipe. She was a wonderful person." The quote appears in the column, "A Mis-used Word," Toronto *Telegram*, 15 Oct. 1945. Photo courtesy of Bernice Loft Winslow.

never up front serving the public."[123] Fred Loft took any insults in his stride. Neophyte chiefs among the Six Nations were taught that they must develop a skin "seven thumbs thick" to endure disappointment and malicious comments.[124]

After the young Mohawk finished high school, he worked for several years in the forests of northern Michigan, rising from lumberjack to timber inspector, until ill health forced him to leave the bush. Upon his recovery, Fred Loft received a full scholarship to study at the Ontario

Business College in Belleville, Ontario.[125] On graduating, not finding work as a bookkeeper, he briefly worked as a journalist with the *Brantford Expositor*.[126] Fred Loft's staunch Liberal Party credentials and business background next helped him obtain a provincial civil service position. In 1887 the Liberal government in Toronto appointed him as an accountant in the bursar's office of the Asylum for the Insane, a position he held for the next three decades. The 37-year-old civil servant married in Chicago in 1898. He and his wife, Affa Northcote Geare, a Canadian of British descent, 11 years younger, had a family of three daughters, two of whom lived to adulthood.

A tall, physically impressive man, Fred Loft dressed conservatively in navy blue or dark grey suits. He sang, and as both he and his wife played the piano, they organized musical parties at their home. Loft had important connections in the city. A number of ministers, doctors, lawyers, and heads of organizations, counted the Lofts as friends. Fred Loft had met, for example, Sir Adam Beck, the father of Ontario Hydro, who gave him a photo of himself, which hung in the Loft home.[127] Through their shared interest in First Nations issues, he knew David Boyle, the curator of the Ontario Provincial Museum, who considered Loft "a highly intelligent gentleman, of good appearance, good address, and good common sense."[128] For some time, the Lofts lived on Jarvis Street near George T. Denison. Toronto's senior police magistrate described, in 1906, his Mohawk neighbour as "a respectable gentleman of fairly good education, and much better qualified for the franchise than 95 per cent of those who have it."[129]

The Lofts led a busy social life in Toronto. They had season's tickets to two theatres, and frequented the Orpen's racetrack. Affa participated in the American Women's Club, the United Empire Loyalists' Association of Canada (where her husband was occasionally a speaker[130]), and the Women's Art Association. The Lofts sent their daughters to the Model School, one of the most respected elementary schools in the city.[131] Fred Loft participated enthusiastically in the activities of his masonic lodge. Enjoying writing, the Mohawk civil servant contributed several articles on North American Indian topics to Toronto publications,[132] and he gave talks. Every Sunday, he attended church. Six Nations friends, such as the famous Iroquois runner Tom Longboat, were dinner and houseguests at the Lofts when passing through Toronto.[133]

Whenever possible, Fred Loft returned to the Six Nations to visit his elderly mother, a widow since his father's death in 1895. On Sundays he regularly attended neighbouring Christ Church in Cayuga. Well over two-thirds of a century later, Ella Monture Claus recalled Fred Loft at church service: he stood "so straight," and looked "so dignified." Fred

Loft, his wife, and their daughters wore beautiful clothes. "They were very elegant people."[134] Fred's niece, Bernice Loft Winslow, his brother William's daughter, remembered how her uncle loved to practise his Mohawk after the church service. The young girl noticed that he had lost some of his fluency living in the city. Occasionally, he put Mohawk words in the wrong places.[135]

Fred Loft's legal status under the Indian Act made him a ward of the Crown, on the same level as the residents of his place of work, the Hospital for the Insane. In 1906, Loft applied to enfranchise, to become a British citizen. After all, he had married a non-Indian, worked away from the Six Nations Territory, and he had lived for nearly two decades in Toronto. Yet, once he learned that the Six Nations Council wished him to remain a member, he withdrew his application.[136] With the council's encouragement, Loft now altered his career plans. On 28 January 1907, he wrote Prime Minister Wilfrid Laurier: "There is perhaps nothing I have desired in my life more than becoming if possible the Superintendent of the Six Nations of Brant; should it be considered by your Government that one of themselves would be capable of performing the duties of the office."[137] One week later, the Six Nations Council formally endorsed Fred Loft's application for the top civil service job in the Grand River community.[138]

Pauline Johnson intervened, and before the Six Nations Council's endorsement, she sent the prime minister a letter, on 18 January, surprisingly indicating her opposition to the selection of any Six Nations person to the post of superintendent. The poet and performer explained, "My people are a peculiar nation and one odd thing is their indifference to persons they know too well. An absolute outsider, an utter stranger, gains their allegiance and their confidence and loyalty to a far greater degree than those they know about the Reservation or its environments."[139] In respect to the nomination of Fred Loft, Pauline Johnson's opposition had deep roots. The animosity between the Johnson and Loft families extended back half a century. In 1859, George Johnson had unseated Peter Smith, Fred Loft's maternal grandfather, as the Six Nations interpreter, a coveted post that brought the officeholder, power, prestige, and a good salary.[140]

In any event, Pauline Johnson's fears that Fred Loft might be named the new Six Nations superintendent proved groundless. Duncan Campbell Scott had no desire whatsoever to see the Mohawk bookkeeper delve into the mismanagement of the finances – and lands – of the Six Nations. Loft had knowledge of the injustices.[141] A decade later, in early 1917, the Six Nations Council again attempted to have Fred Loft appointed their superintendent, and again their request was denied.[142]

Scott greatly feared status Indians with college and professional training. Just before the outbreak of the First World War, the Six Nations Council voted to pay for two young men to study law. They selected the well-respected Milton Martin, a Mohawk, and Jim Moses, a Six Nations Delaware, but the Department of Indian Affairs refused to sanction the expenditure. Scott told Martin on the occasion of a second request, made in Ottawa in person shortly after Milton returned after active service as a commissioned officer in the Canadian Infantry: "It's no use educating you Indians. You only go back to the Reserve anyway." Jim Moses did not accompany Martin. He had died in action while flying over Germany as an officer in the Royal Air Force.[143]

After war was declared in early August 1914, Fred Loft, the Six Nations volunteer with seven years active militia service, visited Indian reservations throughout Ontario to encourage First Nations recruitment. In order to qualify for overseas duty, he reduced his age on his enlistment form by eleven years, from 56 to 45.[144] Without any difficulty he passed his medical without suspicion of his real age. An impressive-looking man, Onondeyoh stood just over 5'11" and weighed a trim 170 pounds.[145] He received a commission as a lieutenant. On 7 August 1917, while he was overseas, the Six Nations Council conferred on Fred Loft a Pine Tree chieftainship, a rare honour given only to the most outstanding members of the Grand River Iroquois Confederacy.[146] A Pine Tree chief was neither an appointed war chief, nor a hereditary council member, but rather an individual recognized as a natural leader.

Although he went overseas with the 256th Railway Construction Battalion, Loft later transferred to the Canadian Forestry Corps in France. As a representative of the Six Nations Council, he had an audience with King George V at Buckingham Palace, on 21 February 1918, shortly before he left England to return to Canada.[147] The Mohawk officer told the king with great pride how his Indian foresters, in a crosscut-saw competition, cut through a log 15 inches in diameter in less than 20 seconds.[148] He was very proud of the Six Nations of the Grand River who made an enormous contribution to the war effort. Out of a total population of approximately forty-five hundred in 1914, nearly three hundred Grand River men volunteered for service overseas, and of these twenty-nine died in action, five died of wounds or illness, one became a prisoner of war, and one was reported missing in action.[149]

A month after the end of the war, in December 1918, Fred Loft founded the League of Indians of Canada,[150] with better education as its principal goal. Onondeyoh, to use his Mohawk name, wanted "schooling and training equal in standards as provided for the Canadian and foreign born children now in the country."[151] The league also worked to stop

5.4 Lieutenant Fred Loft of the Six Nations, with his company of men in the Forestry Corps, Canadian Expeditionary Force, Windsor Park, England, July 1917. Photo courtesy of his daughter, Affa Loft Matteson.

the seizure of Indian lands for returned soldiers (the Soldiers Settlement Scheme), the threat of forced enfranchisement, and the federal government's neglect of treaty rights.[152] To develop a self-supporting national Indian organization, each band was asked to pay annually a five-dollar fee, plus five cents for each band member.[153] The league held summer meetings at Sault Ste Marie, Ontario, in 1919; Elphinstone, Manitoba, in 1920; Thunderchild Reserve, Saskatchewan, in 1921 and 1922; and on the Samson Reserve at Hobbema in Alberta, in 1922. There was also a convention at Parry Sound on Georgian Bay on Lake Huron in June 1921.[154]

The progressive agenda of the League of Indians of Canada enjoyed wide appeal in Western Canada. This support immediately alarmed Duncan Campbell Scott, directly challenging his power. As well as Indigenous individuals, a number of Roman Catholic and Protestant clergy had come forward to assist the league's work.[155] According to one newspaper account, the summer convention at Hobbema in Alberta in 1922 attracted 1,500 Indians from Alberta and Saskatchewan.[156] Reverend Robert Steinhauer, an interpreter for the Loyal Methodist Chiefs in southern Ontario in 1886 (see previous chapter), and now an ordained Methodist minister for more than a quarter of a century, became the league's chief interpreter at Hobbema, translating from Cree to English and from English to Cree.[157] The Cree Anglican minister Edward Ahenakew agreed, in 1921, to found the Saskatchewan branch of the league and to serve as its vice-president.[158] Father Patrice Beaudry, of Edison, Alberta, a Métis Roman Catholic priest, served as the league's vice-president in Alberta.[159] Father Jean-Louis Le Vern, the principal of the Roman Catholic residential school for the Peigans (Piikuni) in southern Alberta,[160] forwarded donations to Loft made by Peigans in support of the league. Le Vern had become so close to the Peigans, whose language he spoke fluently, that he had a Blackfoot accent when he spoke his mother tongue, French.[161]

Pierre-Albert Picard of Wendake volunteered to be the league's liaison, from 1920 to 1922, with the French-speaking Indians in Quebec. Picard was a former grand chief and had worked as a draftsperson for the Quebec government.[162] A vivid picture of the League of Indians of Canada in its prime emerges from a close reading of the league president's surviving correspondence with Picard.[163] Fred Loft frankly shared his concerns about Duncan Campbell Scott after he met him in his office, during his visit to Ottawa to present his views on Bill 14, the proposal to introduce compulsory enfranchisement. The Mohawk found the austere bureaucrat free of even the most basic social graces: "He simply was mum as a post." His behaviour, he added, was "very unbecoming in view of his position."[164]

The president of the League of Indians of Canada had a realistic impression of the parliamentarians' lack of knowledge of Indigenous Canada. During the House of Commons committee hearings he attended in mid-April 1920, Fred Loft commented that perhaps not even 50 per cent of the MPs were familiar with the Indians' actual domestic and economic conditions. Support for this observation came from an unexpected quarter. Ernest Lapointe, a prominent Liberal francophone leader, revised Loft's estimate and suggested that "not ten per cent" did.[165] The 40-year-old Quebec MP's intervention was much appreciated by supporters of the League of Indians of Canada. Six feet tall with massive shoulders, the French Canadian politician towered over his colleagues, and he spoke his second language extremely well. Upon first being elected to the House of Commons fifteen years earlier, Lapointe immediately began to learn English, and he became very good at it. His

5.5 "Delegation of Indian Representatives who appeared before a House of Commons Parliamentary Committee to oppose the proposed bill of Enfranchisement [Bill 14]," April 1920. The BC Chiefs were also present (see chapter eight) to fight against Bill 13. At the time the photo was taken Fred Loft had returned to Toronto. In the first full row, second from the right, sits Duncan Campbell Scott, looking very ill at ease. He detested Indian rights delegations and here he finds himself among them. In the second full row standing at the extreme right is William Lyon Mackenzie King, Leader of the Opposition, who would become prime minister in 1922. In the middle of the same row, eighth from the left is Asa Hill from Six Nations. James Teit from British Columbia appears second from the left in the second full row; to his right is Pierre-Albert Picard from Wendake, Quebec. Third from the extreme right in the second full row is BC's Peter Kelly. BC's Andy Paull appears to be the individual in the third full row, fourth from the right.

LAC, online MIKAN 3362788-Indian Delegation photograph QMS 96161.

parliamentary speeches were a highlight "in the unending drone of the house."[166] Lapointe's interest in Indigenous affairs no doubt dated back to 1895, when he had served as a law clerk for François-Xavier Lemieux, famous as the defender of Louis Riel ten years earlier,[167] and his interest in Indigenous people continued throughout the 1920s and 1930s. After the Liberals came to power and he joined the federal Cabinet serving as Prime Minister William Lyon Mackenzie King's Quebec lieutenant, Lapointe appointed Aldéric Gros Louis, a Huron from Wendake as his chauffeur. The trusted employee later became his confidential messenger.[168]

As president of the League of Indians of Canada, Fred Loft's greatest ally was his typewriter, on which he kept up his voluminous correspondence. The *Toronto Mail* later recalled in his obituary: "Before and after he organized the League of Indians in Canada, he travelled for years almost continuously fixing up a trapper's dispute, appealing to officials at Ottawa for justice to his clients, after the war helping the Indian veterans who were entitled to pensions."[169] The newly created organization faced daunting challenges, as status Indians constituted only one per cent of the total Canadian population of approximately nine million. The First Nations themselves had strong regional and language differences, and they lacked the necessary financial resources to set up a strong organization. As president and secretary-treasurer, in short, as the holder of all executive offices himself, Fred Loft attempted to deal with every kind of complaint that reached his Toronto home from Indian communities across the country. Constantly, he sent letters to officials on behalf of individuals and bands, largely at his own expense.

Duncan Campbell Scott regarded the president of the League of Indians of Canada as a dangerous subversive. Early in 1921, negative remarks about the Department of Indian Affairs appeared in the *Toronto Star Weekly*, the weekend edition of the *Toronto Star*. The widely circulating newspaper quoted the Mohawk chief on 28 August 1920 as saying, "If anything is responsible for the backwardness of the Indians to-day, it is the domineering, dictating, vetoing method of the Indian Department. The position and treatment of the Indian to-day is as if he were an imbecile."[170] Scott ordered his agents to avoid all contact with Loft.[171] The deputy minister refused to allow the payment of delegates' travel expenses from band funds.[172] He put Loft under surveillance. Scott was appalled to learn in early 1922 that Father Le Vern had forwarded to the League of Indians of Canada donations from a number of Peigans. For this, Scott told Charles Stewart, the new superintendent general of Indian Affairs, that he intended "to report Father Lavern [*sic*] to the head of his Order."[173]

Scott worked energetically to have Fred Loft's Indian status removed, to "enfranchise" him. In early 1920 over thirty Indian spokespersons were invited to attend House of Commons hearings on Bill 14, the amendment to the Indian Act that proposed compulsory enfranchisement. The First Nations included half a dozen leaders from BC who also protested Bill 13, designed to confirm the removal of valuable reserve land in British Columbia. In his remarks in mid-April, Loft spoke against Bill 14. He accepted some form of integration as an ultimate goal, but he asked how could the federal government even consider such a policy, when the level of education in English was so low.[174] Despite vigorous Indian opposition to compulsory enfranchisement, Bill 14 passed on 25 June 1920, and compulsory enfranchisement became part of the Indian Act. Bill 13 also obtained parliamentary approval.

Early the following January, Duncan Campbell Scott instructed John D. McLean to compose a letter to "Mr F.O. Loft." Accordingly, the assistant deputy superintendent general wrote to Loft on 26 January, "Dear Sir: I have to inform you that the Department is considering the question of your enfranchisement under the recent amendments to the Indian Act. As you are doubtless aware, the amendments about referred to were intended to cover cases of Indians who, by educational qualifications, ability and responsibility, have become quite capable of taking their place in the community, on an equal footing with other citizens. It is considered that you possess these requirements in an eminent degree."[175]

A month later, Scott wrote Senator James Lougheed from Calgary, the new minister of the interior and superintendent general of Indian Affairs. In an attempt to discredit Loft, Scott termed him "a shallow, talkative individual." He continued his diatribe, writing, "He is one of the few Indians who are endeavouring to live off their brethren by organizing an Indian society, and collecting fees from them." Then came the final insult: "He volunteered for the war and looked very well in a uniform, but he was cunning enough to evade any active service."[176] This was quite erroneous. In reality, Fred Loft had signed up and gone overseas as an officer, but on account of his age, once it became known, was barred from active combat. Scott himself had not volunteered. In the end, Loft escaped enfranchisement as the Conservatives lost the federal election later that same year, and the new Liberal government of Mackenzie King adopted a more conciliatory stance and repealed compulsory enfranchisement.[177]

In 1921 Duncan Campbell Scott also faced Deskaheh, a new, truly radical Six Nations opponent. The moderate president of the League of Indians of Canada recognized that the Six Nations were "subjects" of His Majesty the King, "in no degree differing from the acknowledged and accepted status of other Indians of Canada."[178] In contrast to Fred

5.6 Deskaheh (Levi General) standing before the Palais de l'Athénée in Geneva with a group of Swiss supporters, 1923. The individual standing at the extreme left of the photo is holding the Friendship wampum belt, and the man standing in the front row at the right has the Two Row wampum belt. Bibliothèque de Genève.

Loft, the Cayuga chief, Deskaheh (or Levi General), sought international recognition of the Six Nations of the Grand River as a nation state. Deskaheh travelled to the League of Nations headquarters in Geneva, Switzerland,[179] where he embarrassed Scott and Canadian government officials by denouncing Canada's oppressive treatment of the "Red Man."[180]

Not everyone in the Six Nations community, however, supported Deskaheh and his followers. Some resented the anti-British nature of their campaign. In July 1922, Six Nations Council secretary Asa R. Hill[181] described the Cayuga chief as "an agitator of the worst type with no desire to come to any understanding. I am afraid that his actions will mean the breaking up of the confederacy."[182] Fred Loft also had personal doubts about the confrontational approach. In a December 1922 letter to recently elected Prime Minister Mackenzie King, Duncan Campbell Scott claimed that Chief Levi General (Deskaheh) had been acting as a "dictator," when in actual fact he occupied "no position superior to any other Chief of the Six Nations."[183] By 1923, however, Deskaheh and his backers controlled the Six Nations Council. Irritated by the Canadian government's actions, some of the moderates had joined Deskaheh's group, and the council now deposed Asa Hill at its secretary.

Although some countries in the League of Nations appeared willing to discuss the issue, British objections to review what it regarded as a domestic Canadian matter proved decisive. In 1923, Scott appointed Colonel Andrew Thompson, an Ottawa lawyer and former military officer, to head a special commission to investigate the affairs of the Six Nations of the Grand River. Deskaheh's supporters boycotted Thompson's hearings. In contrast, a number of Six Nations men who had fought overseas favoured the concept of "one person, one vote" in the selection of leaders of the Six Nations of the Grand Council and participated. Colonel Thompson's report recommended the establishment of an elected council. Without any consultation, the Government of Canada subsequently deposed the hereditary council and, although voter participation was slight, a new council was elected in October 1924 under the terms of the Indian Act.[184]

Disillusioned and in poor health, the Cayuga Chief Deskaheh left Geneva and returned to North America in early 1925. Deskaheh remained briefly with his American lawyer George Decker in Rochester, New York, and then stayed with his friend Chief Clinton Rickard on the Tuscarora Reservation in western New York, where he died on June 27 that same year. The major force behind the Six Nations of the Grand's independence movement was buried in the Upper Cayuga Longhouse cemetery at Six Nations. Two thousand people attended Deskaheh's funeral.[185]

Additional authoritarian measures marked Duncan Campbell Scott's years as deputy superintendent general of Indian Affairs. In 1884 the Macdonald government had prohibited the potlatch or gift-giving ceremony. Yet, on account of its poor legal definition of a potlatch, the amendment was not enforced. Scott now revised and strengthened the reference, making it easier for Indian agents to send potlatchers to jail. He sought the imprisonment of participants, the confiscation of their regalia, and the complete end of the potlatches and dances. The majority of potlatch prosecutions occurred between 1919 and 1922.[186] Participants found ways around the law, and small potlatches continued in secret throughout the 1920s and 1930s: the ceremony went underground.[187] Similarly, on the Plains, increased repression in the 1910s followed. In 1914 Scott secured an amendment to the Indian Act that prohibited Plains Indians from participating in dances away from their own reserves. With the cooperation of the Royal Canadian Mounted Police on both the Pacific Coast and on the Plains, the years 1921 and 1922 proved to be the peak years of prosecution. As Douglas Cole and Ira Chaikin write in their book, *An Iron Hand upon the People*, "Surprisingly, there were many more arrests and imprisonments on the prairies for dancing and giving away than in British Columbia."[188]

Paul Coze (1903–1972), an artist, anthropologist, and prominent member of the Scouting movement in France, visited Western Canada in the summer of 1928. This was the first of his four visits. Anxious to speak with Elders on Plains reserves, Coze soon found that they did not wish to meet him. At Lebret, Saskatchewan, it all became clear, when Father Joseph Poulet, the French Canadian principal of the neighbouring Indian Residential School at Lestock, learned of the problem. Everywhere Coze went he wore his Scout hat and uniform. Consequently, judging from his appearance, the First Nations naturally believed him to be a Mountie or member of the Canadian military, seeking to enlist them, then or later. Until Father Poulet explained who Coze really was, they wanted nothing to do with him.[189]

The Government of Canada's most devastating intervention against the First Nations came in the spring of 1927. Ten days before a Special Joint Committee of the Senate and House of Commons ruled unanimously that there was no Indian Title to British Columbia, a new amendment to the Indian Act became law:[190] Section 141 made it illegal to solicit funds from Indians for the pursuit of claims against the government, without the permission of the Department of Indian Affairs.[191] The offence was punishable by fine or imprisonment. This amendment had far-reaching consequences, and it remained in effect until the next general revision of the Indian Act, which would be in 1951.

Without question, Duncan Campbell Scott's unremitting opposition to the League of Indians of Canada hampered its growth in the mid-1920s. Apart from the branches in Alberta and Saskatchewan, the league's membership declined. Fred Loft's minimal resources, particularly after he retired from the Ontario civil service in 1926,[192] further accentuated its near demise. The fact that his wife's poor health in the late 1920s obliged the Lofts to move to Chicago for four years (1926–30) made it difficult for Chief Loft to maintain his contacts with league members. Loft also had lost the invaluable assistance in Quebec of Pierre-Albert Picard who, in the mid-1920s, became the Indian agent at Wendake.[193] Edward Ahenakew left after receiving a directive from his Anglican bishop to cease his activities with the league.[194]

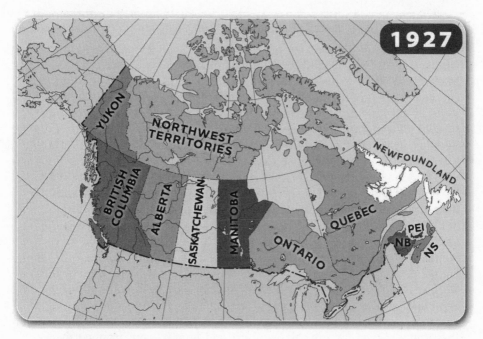

Map 5.1 Canada in 1927.

Only once did Fred Loft return to Saskatchewan. Several bands in the Prince Albert area had subscribed $100 to pay his expenses to attend a meeting at the James Smith Reserve on 6 and 7 June 1928,[195] where he emphasized the need to see the treaties observed, and spoke "very strongly" against the Indian boarding schools.[196] The Indian Department's W. Murison attended. The inspector of Indian agencies in Western Canada noted the Mohawk's moderation: "Chief Loft, in closing the meeting, said that the Indians were treated better in Canada than anywhere else, that they should be thankful to be under British rule. It was different in the United States."[197] According to the report by Corporal James Wood of the RCMP, who was also present, "He was most careful in not committing himself in stirring up trouble, simply promising to do his best to bring the Indians' grievances to the notice of the Government in a lawful and rational manner."[198]

After his return to Toronto in 1930, Onondeyoh attempted to resume the league's work in Ontario. He still had an undying faith in British justice. Now, on the eve of turning 70, he proposed to travel to London,

England, to appeal to the Privy Council, the supreme court of the British Empire, to secure recognition of the rights of Indians to hunt, trap, and fish without the restrictions of provincial game laws. He estimated the trip would cost $4,000, and through circulars requested contributions. Many chiefs ignored his appeal, some delivered his letter to the Indian agent, and only a tiny number sent anything.[199] Ironically, on this issue of hunting rights, Duncan Campbell Scott agreed, and he aggressively pushed the provinces in the early 1930s to relax their game laws.[200] His decision was based on economic, not humanitarian reasoning. Scott wanted the First Nations in isolated areas to continue their traditional livelihoods and not depend on expensive government relief for support.

Fred Loft had become Duncan Campbell Scott's perceived enemy, and despite the communality of interests on treaty hunting rights, this could not bring them together. Loft's independent voice must be silenced. As soliciting funds under Section 141, the 1927 amendment of the Indian Act, made the collection of funds for Indian claims illegal, Scott considered laying criminal charges against Loft for attempting to raise money for Indian Title issues.[201] He placed him under surveillance, but once Scott learned the cost of bringing witnesses from Western Canada, his enthusiasm for prosecution declined.[202] Second, once he learned in 1931 that Loft's appeal for financial support had failed, Scott dropped the idea of prosecuting him. By late 1932, the Mohawk leader's health had deteriorated greatly. Fred Loft died in Toronto in 1934.

Right to the end of his tenure as deputy superintendent general of Indian Affairs, Duncan Campbell Scott constantly reported his department's stellar service. In a paper that he prepared for the Fourth Bi-Annual Conference of the Institute of Pacific Relations, to be held at Hangchow, China, from 18 October to 3 November 1931, the veteran civil servant stressed that in Canada, all the Indians "have had their needs provided for and the Government has more than fulfilled the letter of its obligations."[203] The senior Indian Affairs bureaucrat retired in 1932. Throughout his career, Scott had believed fully in the Government of Canada's assimilationist model: "The great forces of intermarriage and education will finally overcome the lingering traces of Native culture and tradition."[204] This was the conventional wisdom, the "common sense" of the day. In hindsight, we know Duncan Campbell Scott and his generation made the wrong assessment. They miscalculated entirely the intensity with which First Nations people wished to retain their own Indigenous identity. To quote the Canadian historian Kerry Abel, in reference to the twentieth-century Dene in the North-West Territories, few outsiders appreciated the people's – legitimate – desire "to retain their sense of themselves in the face of what might appear to be overwhelming pressure."[205]

Chapter Six

Paul A.W. Wallace and *The White Roots of Peace*

In the November 1946 issue of the *Canadian Forum*, Kathleen Coburn commented favourably on *The White Roots of Peace*, by Paul A.W. Wallace, a Canadian then teaching English literature at a small liberal arts college in Pennsylvania. The professor of English at Victoria College found the volume to be "an interesting little book written with simplicity and directness." "The theme of Dr Wallace's idealistic essay," she added, "is the achievement by the Iroquois Indians of a united nations organization which has lasted five hundred years because of the soundness of the principles of order and justice on which it was founded."[1] The personal journey of Paul Wallace towards a positive understanding of Indigenous North America, so unusual for his day, began in Ontario.

Paul Anthony Wilson Wallace (1891–1967) was born in Cobourg, Ontario, but raised from the age two in Toronto. He belonged to a family with an exceptional Christian background. His mother, Joy Wilson Wallace, was the daughter of Reformed Episcopal Bishop Edward Wilson of Metuchen, New Jersey; and his father, Francis Huston Wallace, served as the dean of theology at Victoria College. The dean had graduated from the University of Toronto in 1873 where he won the gold medal in classics. He attended Drew Theological Seminary in New Jersey, one of the largest American Methodist colleges, and completed postgraduate studies in Germany at the University of Leipzig in 1876–7.[2] After several years in pastoral ministry, Francis Wallace joined the staff of Victoria College as the professor of New Testament exegesis and later as dean of theology. During his 1910–11 academic leave, the dedicated scholar returned to Germany and studied at the University of Berlin, where he enrolled in the course offered by Adolf von Harnack, the eminent theologian and radical church historian.[3]

In Toronto the Wallaces bought a comfortable semi-detached house at 95 Bedford Avenue, in an upper middle-class district, known as the

Annex, just north of Bloor Street,[4] and near the University of Toronto. Dean Wallace had but a short walk to Victoria College, which in 1892 had relocated from Cobourg. Paul Wallace grew up in "Toronto the Good,"[5] a city with a pronounced British orientation,[6] in fact, in the census of 1901, almost 92 per cent of the city's population of nearly 210,000 gave their ethnic origin as "British."[7] Torontonians at this time showed little interest in the city's or Canada's, for that matter, Indigenous past, let alone its present.[8] The year Paul Wallace was born, the Anglican bishop of Toronto commented that in the city, "not a man in a thousand is apt to give a spontaneous thought to the Indians all the year round."[9] That same year, Goldwin Smith, a former Regius Professor of Modern History at Oxford, now Toronto's leading "public intellectual," dismissed the North American Indian in two sentences: "The race, everyone says, is doomed ... Little will be lost by humanity."[10]

Paul Wallace attended Huron Street Public School, as had his older brother Edward and sister Muriel before him. He led a busy life, both at school and with his friends after hours. On 5 March 1906 he noted his school friend Greg Clark, a future celebrated Toronto journalist, had asked "if I'd be Scribe of the 'Council of the Red Triangle,' which is a secret society of his. I think that I'd like to be if I have time."[11] From a young age the records-conscious Torontonian kept a diary. At the end of 1902 he included a "memoranda" of the books he had read the previous year, an impressive list indeed for a precocious 11-year-old. His list included *Ivanhoe*, the Bible, *Pilgrim's Progress*, *Grimm's Fairy Tales*, *Gulliver's Travels*, and *Explorations and Adventures in Africa*.[12] The previous year, he had received three of the five novels in the Leather Stocking Tales series by popular American author James Fenimore Cooper: *The Last of the Mohicans* arrived for his birthday, 31 October 1901, followed by *The Pathfinder* and *The Deerslayer* that Christmas.[13] Fenimore Cooper's "noble savages" contrasted so with the "ignoble" variety omnipresent in his first high school history text. A sample passage on the North American Indian from W.H.P. Clement's *The History of the Dominion of Canada* (1895) reads: "Master of woodcraft, he was seen at his best when hunting. Upon the war-path he was cruel, tomahawking, scalping and torturing with fiendish ingenuity." Wallace made a drawing of a North American Indian in the frontispiece of his textbook.[14]

The Wallace family travelled every summer by train from Toronto to Penetanguishene on Georgian Bay, from where they proceeded by steamer to Go Home Bay, about 30 kilometres farther north. In the 1890s a group of University of Toronto professors established a summer colony there and named it the Madawaska Club.[15] Visually, the region became famous in Canada thanks to the intervention of Dr James

MacCallum, who had a professorial appointment at the University of Toronto. The wealthy Toronto eye doctor hosted many of the artists who from 1920 on would become known as the Group of Seven. At MacCallum's comfortable Go Home retreat, a number of Canadian iconic paintings such as Arthur Lismer's *September Gale* and Frederick Varley's *Stormy Weather, Georgian Bay*, were sketched. Group of Seven members J.E.H. Macdonald, Lawren Harris, Tom Thomson, and A.Y. Jackson also enjoyed Dr MacCallum's hospitality.[16]

The summer community was only accessible by boat,[17] and at Go Home Bay the Torontonians "roughed it." The Wallaces built their cottage in 1899.[18] Refinements came later. They cut wood for their stoves and carried their water themselves from the shoreline. After several years at Go Home Bay, the residents of the summer community screened in the front verandas of their cottages, thus ending the need for "smudges" to drive away the mosquitos.[19] The locality's name came from earlier lumbermen or hunters, who "plunged into the wilds" at this point and from here returned to "civilization." In consequence, they knew the bay as the Go-Home place.[20] Each winter the Madawaska Club employed Pete Laforge to fill the club's icehouse, which was quite an arduous task.[21] In the summers, Laforge supplied milk and some farm produce. From his many conversations with the colourful French Canadian farmer, Paul Wallace developed an interest in Quebec culture and folklore.

Paul Wallace had no contact with the neighbouring Mohawk, as they did not travel through the Go Home Bay area in summer. Immediately to the east at Gibson (Wahta) near Bala, there lived a group of about a hundred Iroquois, who in the early 1880s had left their home community of Oka, 50 kilometres northwest of Montreal. They became Methodists to protest the refusal of the Roman Catholic priests to recognize their land claim to their village and farms.[22] Paul Wallace did encounter Ojibwe from Christian Island, to the southwest, who camped at Go Home Bay every year during the blueberry season[23] and visited the cottages to sell their beautiful birch bark and porcupine quill baskets, canoe paddles, and blueberries. But, as the Anishinabeg spoke little English, the cottagers could not communicate with them.[24] Some of the summer residents opposed the Anishinabeg's visits and complained to the Department of Indian Affairs. In response, Duncan Campbell Scott obligingly issued a directive in 1915 ruling that the Ojibwe could not camp on Madawaska Club property, and with that the summer visits from Ojibwe ended.[25]

Summers at Go Home Bay consisted of long, lazy days of sunshine, mixed with days of lightning and summer storms.[26] Paul Wallace and his brother Edward, 11 years his senior, went on canoe trips together, paddling, portaging, and cooking their meals on stone fireplaces.[27]

Paul's "Indians" sprang forth directly from his vivid imagination, and his reading. A 1902 diary entry reads, "Monday May 26 [...] played Indian [...] played baseball."[28] He made his own Indian costume, and for several years he and his friends in Toronto organized "Indian" games and ceremonies. The "Mohawks" and the "Senecas" held their final feast on 6 March 1906. In his journal, the 14-year-old explained why the tribes decided to disband: "The paleface dogs are too many. They push us back, and back, and take our ground, and there aren't enough of us to stop them."[29] Years later Paul Wallace recalled, "I belong to a happy generation that nourished its youth on *The Leatherstocking Tales*. We used to spend our vacations playing Indian. We modeled ourselves on the Mohawks because they were the most fiendish of Cooper's Mingoes, and we acted out all the clichés. We roamed the forest with stealthy step, and of course we never let a twig snap."[30]

After six years at Huron Street Public School (1898–1904), Wallace attended Harbord Collegiate Institute for the next six (1904–10).[31] Large-scale Jewish and Italian immigration had made the neighbourhood around Harbord multicultural. The Italian neighbourhood formed a rectangle near the school, with the Jewish district around Spadina and the Kensington Market nearby. Throughout the school system of the day the emphasis was on British values and achievements. Many newcomers sought to assimilate as quickly as possible into the Canadian mainstream. To quote Rhoda Tepper, who wrote the entry "Ethnic Trends at Harbord," in the collegiate's centennial history, *The Happy Ghosts of Harbord*, assimilation was the shared objective of both the government and the Toronto Board of Education: "The response by immigrant children encouraged this goal. They were 'industrious, intelligent, respectful and obedient.'"[32] Paul Wallace did well at high school and, as Kathleen Coburn would roughly fifteen years later, he edited the school yearbook, the *Harbord Review*.[33] In his final year, Wallace won a university scholarship.[34] He lived at home and attended, of course, Victoria College.

Paul Wallace's older brother's distinguished career in the Methodist (later United) Church began while Paul was in high school. After graduating from Victoria's School of Divinity, Edward Wallace left for overseas mission work, one of the "Victoria Eight" who departed in the fall of 1906 as educational missionaries. In Sichuan Province (formerly spelled Szechwan) in Western China, the newly ordained Methodist minister acquired great renown for his work to standardize education there.[35] Within five years, he was appointed secretary of the Christian Educational Union of West China, entrusted to organize secondary and primary education for all Protestant missions in West China.[36] He introduced Chinese converts into leadership positions.[37] The distinguished administrator and educator was named in 1930 chancellor and president of Victoria University in the University of Toronto, and he held those two offices until his death in 1941. Edward and Paul's sister Muriel, six years older than Paul, began a teaching career in Ontario after obtaining her Bachelor of Arts degree at Victoria.

Dean Francis Wallace's sabbatical in Europe in 1910–11 allowed Paul, who had just graduated from Harbord, an opportunity to travel abroad. He and his sister Muriel accompanied their parents to Great Britain, France, Germany, Italy, and Switzerland. In Europe, Paul Wallace deepened an interest in other cultures and languages, perfecting both his German and French. In Switzerland the adventuresome 19-year-old discovered alpinism, and mountain climbing became the passion of his early twenties.[38] In September he entered first year at Victoria College.

As a member of the Alpine Club of Canada, Paul Wallace spent the summer of 1912 in the Canadian Rockies. He travelled west with his good university friend Harold Bennett.[39] A canoe trip at Go Home Bay just before departing for the Rockies put him in good physical shape for the mountains.[40] Formed only six years earlier, Canada's national alpine club had a membership of more than 650,[41] and it already organized annual summer camps for mountaineers of all skill levels. Veteran surveyor Arthur Wheeler served as the club's first president,[42] with Winnipeg journalist Elizabeth Parker as the club's honorary secretary.[43] In addition to Mrs Parker, who had done so much to establish the organization, many women participated.

The next summer Paul Wallace returned to the Rockies to work as the ACC's acting secretary-treasurer. Shortly after his arrival in Banff, he wrote and assured his concerned parents that the three Bibles they had mailed him sufficed, and he needed no more.[44] The Alpine Club of Canada made three attempts in the summer of 1913 to climb the risky and dangerous Mount Robson in British Columbia, the highest peak in the Canadian Rockies. Only one of the three succeeded. It was led by the 30-year-old Austrian guide Conrad Kain,[45] the most legendary of the "Swiss Guides."[46] The Canadian Pacific Railway had been importing professional mountain guides since 1899 from Switzerland and later Austria to teach safe guiding techniques.[47] That summer Paul translated from German into English Conrad Kain's stirring account of the "first ascent" of Mount Robson.[48] He had great admiration for this extraordinary Austrian alpinist: "I have known him climb down a mountain precipice which did not differ in any apparent essential way from the wall of the Empire State Building in New York – and go down it with something like the speed of an elevator."[49]

6.1 Paul Wallace took this photo summer of 1912, at Storm Mountain, BC, near the Vermilion Pass, Continental Divide on the border of Alberta and British Columbia. Mountaineering equipment was minimalist in those days. Blanche Hume is the spirited female climber shown in the photo. NA-4094-3 by Paul Wallace. Courtesy of Glenbow Archives, Archives and Special Collections, University of Calgary.

As recording secretary, Wallace took the minutes of the Alpine Club of Canada's two 1913 summer meetings: the first at the Alpine Meadows at Lake O'Hara in Yoho National Park and the second at the foot of the majestic Mount Robson. His summary appeared in the Banff *Crag and Canyon*.[50] A typed set of the meetings' minutes also survives in the ACC Collection in the Whyte Museum of the Canadian Rockies in Banff. An entry for the Mount Robson meeting speaks volumes about the ACC's lack of a meaningful relationship with the Stoney Nakoda at this time, for it reads:

> Re Nomenclature in Mt Robson Park, 4 August 1913. Resolved by the members of the Alpine Club of Canada assembled in camp at Robson Pass, that the Hon. W.R. Ross, Minister of Lands for British Columba, be hereby petitioned to use his influence to have the names given in the vicinity by the original explorer, Dr A.P. Coleman of the University of Toronto, our President, confirmed, and that such names given by him as have been changed by ruling of the Geographic Board of Canada may be reinstated and confirmed. Further that a large number of Stony Indian names recently proposed for topographical features in the said park, be not adopted as they have no meaning to one unacquainted with the language, and no history.[51]

"No history," indeed – quite an assessment for the six-year-old Alpine Club of Canada to make, since the Stoney Nakoda had been living in North America for at least the past ten millennia.

"No man is a hero to his valet," as the old expression goes. Initially kind and considerate, Arthur Wheeler in close quarters proved the total opposite, short-fused and authoritarian.[52] That fall the ACC president constantly asked Wallace to complete assignments that had nothing at all to do with the organization. In mid-November Paul finally rebelled: "I told him I couldn't do his personal work any more, because I needed all my time for the work I was paid for by the Alpine Club."[53] As Wheeler made no apology and refused to alter his behaviour, Wallace resigned as a matter of principle,[54] and returned to Toronto. The university administration allowed him to attempt to complete his third year work all in the second term, a formidable task. Wallace succeeded, and finished all the requirements successfully in late spring 1914.[55] On 19 March an extraordinary event had occurred just to the west of Victoria College: the opening of the Royal Ontario Museum, one of the most important structures built in Toronto in the twentieth century. The governor general, the Duke of Connaught, performed the ceremony before a thousand officials and friends of the museum on the top floor of the elegant and imposing building.[56]

When their parents left again for Europe, in the summer of 1914, Muriel and Paul joined them. War between France and Germany broke out while they were in Brittany. From France the 22-year-old Canadian wrote, "This quiet corner of the Breton coast has suddenly become sufficiently interesting through the approach of a great European war. I shall try to sketch a few of the things I have seen during the last few days, things which may appear perhaps more picturesque to a Canadian who has never before heard of war except in books and newspapers, than to the French people themselves who have been ready for the present mobilization."[57] On 4 August the British Empire joined France in its war against Germany and Austro-Hungary.

Paul Wallace graduated from Victoria College in spring 1915. Anxious to broaden his knowledge of Western Canada, he took a teaching position in Alberta. He had first enquired about one at Mount Royal College, a private primary and secondary school in Calgary with a Methodist affiliation, but it had no vacancies.[58] From late May to the end of December, Wallace taught a dozen children of various ages and grades at a tiny country school at Baraca,[59] a crossroads some 40 kilometres from Youngstown, in the east-central part of the province. Although part of Alberta's dry belt, in this year at least the district enjoyed abundant rainfall and heavy crops.[60] Settled only six years,[61] the country had been traversed by huge herds of buffalo just a generation before. On the Prairies, Wallace travelled everywhere on a small motorbike. A special treat was his day trip on horseback with a neighbour in early July, when they rode to Berry Creek and the Ribstone Hill. Wallace later wrote, "Ribstone Hill, over 100 feet high, affords an enchanting view of the cloud shadowed prairies where imagination replaces wheat fields with herds of buffalo, and homesteads with tepees."[62]

District School Inspector Frank Buchanan visited Paul Wallace's isolated school in early June,[63] and he liked what he saw, later commenting that the young Ontarian took unusual interest in his work and "used effective methods of instruction."[64] Inspector Buchanan mentioned to the promising young teacher in early September that, if he wanted, he could obtain a high school position, if he could wait a year.[65] But Wallace's ultimate career goal at this point was journalism, with teaching only as a backup. British Columbia and its mountains pulled him further westward.[66]

Paul Wallace moved to the City of Victoria early in January 1916, with the hope of finding a teaching position, but none was available,[67] apart from a position in a school in a very remote Indian coastal village. After the isolation of over half a year in Baraca, Wallace decided to stay in Victoria and spend the next few months "devoted to the pen."[68]

Through a correspondence course he studied creative writing, but it proved hard to place his completed work. Light-heartedly he wrote in a note on 19 March to Dorothy Clarke, a close friend who had returned home to England after a year's visit in Toronto, "I have no difficulty in getting rid of my stories. The MacDonalds with whom I am boarding have kindly offered me the use of their furnace."[69] Wallace persevered, and by late April he did place a few stories in several Canadian magazines but discovered how little they paid – and how slowly their editors made payments.[70]

Late that winter Wallace decided to enlist in the Canadian army after successfully writing in June the BC certification exam qualifying him for high school teaching.[71] He had no idea at this stage of the horrors of combat on the Western Front. Always the aspiring writer, he wanted to sign up, he said in a letter home, "to study soldiering from a writer's point of view."[72] His parents joined him for several weeks on the West Coast in June for a coastal voyage from Vancouver to the Alaskan Panhandle, and then they all returned to Toronto. According to plan, in early August [73] Paul Wallace enlisted with the Signal Corps of the Canadian Expeditionary Force, together with Victoria College friends Hal Bennett and Grant Robertson.[74]

After basic training in Canada, Wallace left for Britain on 11 November 1916.[75] The faithful correspondent kept his family informed of the surface aspects of army life. As his father would later recall, "Paul's letters were the excitement of every week; his stories of that vile hole, Crowborough Camp, and then of well organized Shorncliffe; his pictures, vivid and thrilling, of devastating air raids; his delight in his own success as a dispatch rider." The schoolteacher turned dispatch rider delivered urgent messages and orders between Canadian army camps in southeastern England on a cumbersome nearly 400 lb. motorbike, "distinctly awkward to restore to an upright position after a skid."[76] Wonderful news arrived in Toronto after Wallace visited Dorothy Clarke in Wales in February 1918: their engagement.[77] Then several weeks later the Wallaces received a horrific telegram from Ottawa, saying their son had suffered major head injuries in a serious motorcycle accident in England.[78]

Over the course of the weeks to follow, Paul Wallace's condition in hospital slowly improved, making his transfer to Canada possible in the early fall. The injured soldier returned to Toronto in October, with sadness, as his mother had passed away that summer.[79] Fortunately, in Canada his recovery accelerated. From January to June 1919 he attended the College of Education at the University of Toronto to obtain a specialist certificate in English and history to allow him to teach high school in Ontario.[80] He did so well that he received offers for several good positions in Ontario, and best of all, an offer of a lectureship in journalism from the Department of English at the University of Alberta.[81] He accepted the lectureship and returned in the summer to Britain to marry Dorothy. After their marriage in Wales, the newly-weds set off for Edmonton.

Paul Wallace, an alpinist in his university days, returned to Alberta, where he learned of a host of newly introduced names (in English) for hitherto unnamed mountains in the southern Canadian Rockies. At the end of the First World War, the Geographical Board of Canada (the federal naming authority) introduced a wave of designations after Allied military figures, and British ships and admirals involved in the Battle of Jutland. Just to cite one example, "Ubithka mâbi," the Stoney Nakoda name for a prominent peak west of Calgary in the Kananaskis country, that translates as "nesting of the eagle," now became known in English as Mount Indefatigable, named after the British battle cruiser that was the first ship sunk during the Battle of Jutland, 31 May 1916, which took 1,015 men to their deaths.[82]

Initially, the young couple enjoyed their new city, and the university, at which the first-year English course became Wallace's prime responsibility. The Writers Club he established in November 1919 proved very successful,[83] leading the university to endorse his proposal to introduce a course in journalism. Wallace wrote to his father on 28 March 1920, "All that I have ever done has been a preparation for this work." Immediately, he began to compile for his future students a "Deskbook for Journalists."[84]

Before he left Toronto for the University of Alberta, Wallace understood that he could prepare his M.A. on French Canadian folklore while teaching English and journalism as well. His interest in French Canadian traditional stories dated back to those early conversations with Pete Laforge, the local farmer at Go Home Bay.[85] Early in 1920 Wallace began to interview for his thesis old-timers in the Edmonton area, including Frank Oliver, resident there for nearly half a century and the first editor of the *Edmonton Bulletin*. The retired federal minister of the interior and superintendent general of Indian Affairs (1905–11), who had first arrived at Fort Edmonton in 1876 and been a spectator at Treaty Seven the following year, bluntly told the young lecturer his opinion of his thesis topic, namely, "there can be no legends here, because the old voyageurs married Indian wives and became quickly assimilated by the savages around them."[86]

At the university Paul Wallace formed a close lifelong friendship with a First Nations student, Edward Ahenakew. Through the Writers Club

6.2 League of Indians of Canada meeting at Thunderchild Reserve, 1922. At the front kneeling in the centre is Edward Ahenakew, and to the right, seated next to him, is Fred Loft. Several chiefs are shown wearing their treaty medals. R-A10196, Provincial Archives of Saskatchewan.

he chaired Wallace met the ordained Plains Cree Anglican minister, who at the time was studying medicine. Edward Ahenakew (1885–1961) was born at Sandy Lake about 100 kilometres west of Prince Albert on the reserve selected by Ahtahkakoop (or Starblanket), his grandfather's brother.[87] Through his two grandmothers, he was closely related to chiefs Mistawasis, Poundmaker, and Red Pheasant. After attending the Anglican mission school run by his uncle, Louis Ahenakew, Edward entered the Anglican boarding school at Prince Albert,[88] and there decided to become a Christian missionary. The promising student first attended Wycliffe College in the University of Toronto and finished his theological studies at Emmanuel College, which had just moved in 1909 from Prince Albert to Saskatoon to become affiliated with the new University of Saskatchewan. Edward Ahenakew graduated from Emmanuel

College in 1912, and after his ordination received his first posting at Onion Lake, a community that straddles the Alberta-Saskatchewan border north of Lloydminster.

The impact of the Spanish flu epidemic on the Plains in late 1918 and early 1919 convinced the Cree minister to apply to medical school, and he gained entry into the University of Alberta. During the first three months of the flu epidemic, in late 1918, nearly 4,000 Saskatchewan people died, and by the following April the total had risen by another thousand. The First Nations, in particular, suffered a very high mortality rate.[89] At the four Cree reserves at Hobbema, Alberta, located 100 kilometres south of Edmonton, 90 died out of a total population of 850.[90] Unfortunately, living alone in Edmonton, with limited means, and as a result of eating poorly, Edward Ahenakew so impaired his own health that he had to abandon his course of medical studies in his third year.[91] The strong bond established between the Indian minister and the university instructor lasted through the decades to follow, maintained through frequent correspondence.

Despite the optimism of Paul Wallace's first year at the University of Alberta, major problems arose in the second. Edmund Keeper Broadus, his M.A. thesis supervisor,[92] showed little interest in his topic. The frustration of working with an indifferent supervisor led Wallace to withdraw from the Master's program in late December 1920. Then a second serious crisis emerged: the university reversed its decision to introduce journalism as a full university program. Now there was no point for him to remain in Edmonton. Successfully, he applied to begin graduate work in English in the fall of 1922 at his alma mater, the University of Toronto.[93]

Unfortunately, neither Toronto nor any other university offered any courses in Canadian literature,[94] hence his first choice as a research field, Canada, was closed to him. Paul completed his M.A. thesis on "English Travel of the 17th Century in Europe,"[95] and then began his doctoral dissertation in English studies on Shakespeare's printers.[96] During his graduate program at the University of Toronto, Wallace worked as a sessional instructor in the Department of English, prepared his dissertation, and man of prodigious energy that he was, edited several early Canadian literary texts.[97] In 1923 he published *Selections from Sam Slick*, a volume of excerpts by mid-nineteenth Nova Scotia author Thomas Haliburton, as well as a new edition of *Winter Studies and Summer Rambles in Canada* by mid-nineteenth-century English writer Anna Jameson. That same year he also brought out his short story collection, *The Twist and Other Stories*, as well as *Baptiste Larocque: Legends of French Canada*, a translation of twenty-five French Canadian stories into English.[98] What a year! In April 1923, Paul and Dorothy's first son, Anthony Francis Clarke Wallace, was born in Toronto.

In 1923 and 1924 Wallace assisted his friend Edward Ahenakew both as an editor and a critic.[99] During his convalescence on the Thunderchild Reserve in Saskatchewan, the Cree minister wrote an unfinished manuscript that would not be published for half a century. It consisted of two parts. The first part was the memoirs of the elderly Chief Thunderchild, whom Ahenakew had interviewed in Cree at great length. As a young man, Thunderchild had been one of Big Bear's followers. As an eyewitness of events half a century earlier, he told gripping stories of buffalo hunts, raids against the Blackfoot, and hunger after the buffalo disappeared.[100] The second part included the fictional memoirs of a boarding school graduate, a description full of overwhelmingly negative observations, as the students left the schools belonging to neither Indigenous nor Euro-Canadian worlds. Ahenakew thought that perhaps in certain remote areas such institutions might make sense, but "for most Indian children, I hold that boarding schools are unnatural, that they are contrary to our whole way of life."[101] The opening line of the Cree minister's unpublished manuscript, completed in 1923, explained why he sought its publication: "The time has come in the life of my race when that which has been like a sealed book to the masses of our Canadian compatriots – namely the view that the Indians have of certain matters affecting their lives – should be known."[102]

In late winter 1922–3, Paul Wallace contacted Lorne Pierce, editor of the Ryerson Press, about his Cree friend's stories. Initially all looked promising. On 5 March 1923 he noted in his diary that Pierce "is very favourably disposed" to the manuscript, "but it will need to be edited carefully and cut down considerably."[103] Then, a disappointing letter arrived from the Ryerson Press editor: "He takes too much time walloping the Indian Dept., commencing with p. 16 and right thru. This would be all right once but it gets on ones nerves. We all agree with him." Pierce sought a traditional book: "We want the old civilization of the Indian in all its variety and beauty. Let him aim at 60,000 words and a $1.50 book." Pierce's concluding advice says volumes about the influential editor's avoidance of the unpleasant: "Give us the glamor of the past in all its purity and forget the present."[104] Ryerson Press faced a second challenge with the manuscript, namely, money to publish it. At the time Canada lacked cultural granting agencies. When approached, Duncan Campbell Scott refused Department of Indian Affairs funding, replying to Pierce on 16 October 1924, "I regret very much that we would have no funds to meet your suggestion with reference to Mr Ahenakew's manuscript, much as I would like to assist."[105] Edward

Ahenakew's book waited until 1973 for publication; he had died twelve years earlier, in 1961.[106]

Paul Wallace continued to encourage Edward Ahenakew with his writing, providing the Plains Cree with "an immediate audience, someone concrete to write to and to consult about writing."[107] Thanks to Ahenakew, Wallace learned a great deal about oral history and Indigenous traditions,[108] and this was very useful knowledge when, by an extraordinary set of circumstances years later, he came to write *The White Roots of Peace*. When the two men met in Toronto in mid-September 1924, they had an extremely frank exchange one evening at dinner in the Wallace home, and to use Paul's phrase, his "Indian education" had begun.[109]

Paul Wallace wrote a travel guide to Canada in 1924, "The Canadian Herodotus," inspired by the early Greek historian who, twenty-five hundred years earlier, had written accounts of the history and diverse cultures of the Middle East. Beginning on 29 October 1924, the *Christian Guardian*, the Methodist Church of Canada's weekly newspaper, ran excerpts of it for eighteen weeks, with entries on the cities and regions of Canada from the Atlantic to the Pacific. Wallace used material from his own travels across the country and from his extensive reading about both old and contemporary Canada. The well-written series ended on 1 March 1925, just two months before Paul Wallace's successful thesis defence on 4 May.[110] Wallace became the second candidate to obtain a Ph.D. in English from the University of Toronto, the first university in Canada to have a doctoral program in English.[111] Yet, despite his newly minted doctorate, his book on French Canadian legends, his editing work on early Canadian literary texts, and his historical travel book introducing Canadians to their country, Paul Wallace could not obtain a university position in Canada.

Fortunately, Wallace's close friend Harold Bennett, then teaching classics at Lebanon Valley College in Annville, Pennsylvania, stepped forward, and arranged for him to teach summer school there. The summer posting to the small liberal arts college in 1925 led to an offer to head its Department of English, an offer Wallace accepted.[112] The pay would be $4,200 a year, which was more than three times what he had earned from royalties from his books and articles (roughly $1,250) in the two-year period from 1923 to 1925.[113] The arrival of Paul and Dorothy's second son in late December 1926, David Harold Wallace (his second name was given in honour of Harold Bennett),[114] increased Wallace's financial responsibilities. Over the years he became more at ease in his new setting, and in 1940 he became an American citizen.[115]

Eager to get back to research and writing, the young college professor developed a new interest. Just 35 kilometres from Harrisburg, Annville stood in the heart of the "Pennsylvania-Dutch" country, where many people still spoke a German dialect. Wallace slowly transferred his interest in French Canadian to Pennsylvanian German folklore and history.[116] Professor Hiram Shenk, the Pennsylvania historian at Lebanon Valley College, introduced Wallace to the story of Conrad Weiser,[117] the early eighteenth-century Pennsylvanian Iroquois interpreter. Weiser's German immigrant parents had boarded him as a teenager with a Mohawk foster family for him to learn their language and their culture. The wealth of printed and manuscript sources, much of it in German, made the biography possible. Ever since his early travels in Europe, and his friendship with Conrad Kain, Wallace had been comfortable with the German language. Thus began Paul Wallace's historical study of North American Indians.

Wallace's new Weiser project took him back to Canada. Not content simply to read the surviving documents, he and his family visited descendants of the people that Conrad Weiser so admired for their honesty and democratic simplicity.[118] With his 9-year-old son David, Wallace travelled in early July 1936 to the Six Nations Territory on the Grand River. They stopped first at Smooth Town, the neighbourhood in which several hundred Delawares (or Lenni Lenape), "the Original People," resided.[119] The English named the Lenni Lenape, "Delawares," as they first encountered them seen on the river the English termed "Delaware" in honour of the Baron De La Warr, the first governor of Virginia.[120]

Frank Speck, an anthropologist at the University of Pennsylvania who had worked among the Six Nations Delaware, had recommended Wallace consult with the elderly Delaware Chief Joseph Montour, then in his mid-80s.[121] They met on a brutally hot summer day in July, when the thermometer registered 105 degrees Fahrenheit in the shade.[122] The patriarch of his people was the last hereditary officeholder among the Delaware, who now lived among the Six Nations.[123] The only schooling Chief Montour had received was his three years at the Mohawk Institute.[124] An advocate for the rights of First Nations, Montour had served as the first treasurer of the League of Indians of Canada, formed by Chief Fred Loft in December 1918 (see previous chapter).[125] Chief Montour enjoyed the respect of all three of the Lenni Lenape or Delaware communities in southern Ontario: Six Nations, Muncey near London, and Moraviantown near Chatham.[126]

Despite the heat, the elderly man stepped into Paul's car and guided the Wallaces to several of the Long Houses in the Grand River Territory.

6.3 Chief Joseph Montour and David Wallace, Six Nations, 1936. B/W15p, Paul A.W. Wallace Papers, American Philosophical Society, Philadelphia, Pa.

The Delaware orator, who for many years had been a preacher in the Methodist (now the United) Church, explained that followers of the Long House, "worship the same God we do." Chief Montour introduced the Wallaces to Jake Hess (or Chief Dehasedasgowa), a traditionalist leader could explain cultural issues fluently in English. As a younger man, Hess had assisted the late David Boyle, the curator-archaeologist for the Ontario Provincial Museum in Toronto (1896–1911) in his collection of a number of ethnographic objects.[127] After the two men met a second time, in 1937, Paul Wallace wrote his friend Joan Lyttleton, a New Zealand writer whom he had met in England during the war, "Dear old Chief Hess is as near to a saint as I can imagine. For hours we talked about religion and the other world. He preaches the religion of the Long House, as they call it, and lives the ethics of Christianity better than most Christians I know."[128]

Through Hess and Montour, Wallace, accompanied by his son David, first met Fred Loft's brother William. The Mohawk chief, then in his late seventies, with his daughter Bernice at his side, warmly welcomed them to their home.[129] Paul Wallace was most impressed by Bernice, and wrote to his anthropologist friend Marius Barbeau, "Miss Loft, as you no doubt know, is a highly intelligent young woman with a love of the ways of her people and at the same time with an understanding of scholarship and a grasp of English idiom."[130] Her parents had taught her to respect both Christian and Longhouse religious traditions. A skilled linguist, Bernice knew five Iroquoian languages: Mohawk, Oneida, Onondaga, Cayuga, and Seneca to speak; and could understand, but not herself speak the sixth, Tuscarora.[131] Wallace made two additional visits to the Six Nations in the late 1930s.[132] He came back briefly in October 1936, with both David and his older son Tony, then 13 years old, to visit Chief Montour. In August 1937 he made a third trip – this time alone to see the Lofts and Jake Hess.

In the 1930s most non-Indigenous Canadians knew absolutely nothing about the history and cultures of the Indigenous peoples of Canada. Three books published in the mid- and late 1930s underline this neglect and lack of curiosity. John Murray Gibbon's *Canadian Mosaic: The Making of a Northern Nation* (1938) popularized the concept of Canada as a nation of many peoples, but it did not include a single chapter on the Indigenous peoples.[133] A second influential volume, the League for Social Reconstruction's Research Committee's *Social Planning for Canada* (1935), also failed to mention the Indigenous peoples.[134] Later, the League for Social Reconstruction evolved into the intellectual brain trust that mapped out a good number of Canada's social welfare programs in the 1940s. In the late 1930s, however, it had a blind spot for the Indigenous peoples.

A third example, the historical survey entitled *The Canadians* (1939), written by the historian George Wrong, retired founder of the Department of History at the University of Toronto, made just one reference to the First Nations. Totally divorced from current realities, Wrong emphasized Canada's tolerant and fair treatment of its original inhabitants: "The native Indians, the oldest residents, are contented wards of the nation."[135] The anthropologist Diamond Jenness knew well the true state of the relationship. In 1954 Jenness recalled in a public address the 1920s, the decade in which he travelled to many Indigenous communities across Canada: "In every region I found a deep-rooted prejudice against them, a prejudice that was stronger in some places than in others but one which was noticeable everywhere from the Atlantic to the Pacific. It was strongest in western frontier settlements where the Indian population outnumbered the white and the latter was struggling to uphold its prestige. And it was least apparent in Quebec."[136] The actual situation was hushed up. When Jenness's monumental 400-page survey appeared in 1932, *The Indians of Canada*, it contained no references to treaties, the Indian Act, or residential schools – none. He had been instructed to leave aside any issue that might reflect on the Department of Indian Affairs policies.[137]

The most famous Indian of the day in Canada in the 1930s was the writer and lecturer Grey Owl. In memory no doubt of their early camping trips together at Go Home Bay, Edward Wallace in 1931 gave his younger brother Paul a copy of *The Men of the Last Frontier*, Grey Owl's first book, a collection of wilderness stories.[138] One passage in particular would speak directly to Paul A.W. Wallace, a Canadian army veteran. Here is how Grey Owl described the impact of the Europeans' arrival on the First Nations: "The passage of the paleface through his ancestral territories is, to the Indian, in effect, what the arrival of the German Army would have been to a conquered England. To them his progress is marked by a devastation comparable only with that left in the wake of a plague in a crowded metropolis."[139]

Grey Owl's four books, articles, and movies with the beaver made him a public figure on two continents in the mid-1930s. He became known as a champion of wildlife and of the great northern forests. The distinguished Canadian economic historian at the University of Toronto, Harold Innis, in 1935 termed Grey Owl "a famous conservationist."[140] The "publisher's note" in *The Men of the Last Frontier* explained that the author's father was a Scot and his mother "an Apache Indian of New Mexico."[141] Grey Owl spent roughly two decades in northern Ontario and Quebec, and he was now living in Saskatchewan. In late March 1938 the gifted Native lecturer addressed an audience of about three thousand in Toronto's Massey Hall, the largest concert hall in Canada at the time.[142] This triumphant talk came at the end of a seven-month lecture tour in Britain (his first was in 1935–6), Canada, and the United States on the importance of conservation. The Toronto *Globe and Mail* termed Grey Owl the "most famous of Canadian Indians."[143]

Grey Owl returned to his cabin in Prince Albert National Park in Saskatchewan totally exhausted. Taken immediately to hospital, he died in Prince Albert on 13 April 1938. In the days to follow came the incredible revelation that Grey Owl had an invented First Nations identity. The *Toronto Star* became one of the first papers to break the news in the story, "Grey Owl Really an Englishman, Old Friends Insist," written by Greg Clark, Paul Wallace's boyhood friend and schoolmate at Huron Street Public School and Harbord Collegiate Institute.[144] Now a leading *Star* reporter and columnist, Clark revealed his discovery that the Dominion of Canada's most famous "Indian" was really one Archie Belaney, born and raised in England, in the Channel town of Hastings. The English immigrant arrived in Canada in 1906, at the age of 17, and subsequently reinvented himself as an "Indian." Did Edward Wallace, who seven years earlier had given his brother Grey Owl's *The Men of the Last Frontier*, and who was now the president and chancellor of Victoria University in the University of Toronto, see the article and forward it on to his brother Paul in Pennsylvania?

Toronto finally heard authentic Indigenous voices in September 1939. T.F. McIlwraith of the University of Toronto, the first university appointment in anthropology in Canada,[145] organized with the assistance of Charles Loram of Yale University, a highly ambitious two-week gathering: the University of Toronto–Yale University Seminar Conference on "The North American Indian Today." By invitation, over seventy US and Canadian academics participated, as did twelve Indigenous delegates, one of whom was Ethel Brant Monture. For the first time in Canadian history, Indigenous people attended a Canadian scholarly meeting.[146]

From 4 to 16 September 1939 conference delegates heard from various non-Indigenous speakers about the cultures, reserve economics, health, and education of the North American Indians in both Canada and the United States. President Edward Wallace gave the valedictory address. Idealistically, the respected educational administrator predicted that "Christian motives" would resolve the problem of social and racial relations.[147] At the meetings, Canadian officials explained their long-standing goal of eventual assimilation. Earlier that year Thomas Crerar,

6.4 Delegates to the University of Toronto–Yale University Seminar Conference on "The North American Indian Today," 4–16 Sept. 1939. Photo taken at the back of the Royal Ontario Museum, Toronto, by Pringle & Booth. NA-3223-2, courtesy of Glenbow Archives, Archives and Special Collections, University of Calgary.

the federal minister responsible for the Indian Affairs Branch of the Department of Mines and Forests, had summarized the policy dating back to the Gradual Civilization Act of 1857, saying, "It was thought their reserves would become training schools in which they could learn to adapt themselves to modern conditions, and from which they would graduate as full citizens as soon as they were qualified."[148]

In contrast, US officials in the 1930s introduced a different approach. Instead of working to eradicate Native cultures and identities, they sought to strengthen them. John Collier, commissioner of the Bureau of Indian Affairs under President Franklin Delano Roosevelt, instituted an Indian "New Deal." Although he could not attend the Toronto meetings,[149] Collier's speech was read to the delegates. Two key lines summarized the new American strategy: "Indian administration in the United States has during the past decade reversed almost completely the policies which had governed Indian Affairs for over a century. These policies were motivated by the desire of the dominant race to acquire lands and resources held by the Indians."[150]

In the United States, the Indian Reorganization Act of 1934 ended the allotment system introduced by the Dawes Act of 1887. Since the passage of the Dawes, or General Allotment Act, more than 60 per cent of the remaining Indian land base had passed into non-Indigenous hands. With the appointment of John Collier as US commissioner of Indian affairs, the pendulum began to swing away from the unrelenting campaign to assimilate Native Americans. Collier made efforts to extend the Native Americans' land base, and worked to replace boarding schools with day schools. Small amounts of money became available for economic development. The Indian Reorganization Act gave Native American communities a measure of self-government.[151] Indigenous cultures were to be encouraged, not suppressed. This revolutionary approach was in total contrast to the inactivity on the Canadian side. J.C. McCaskill, one of Collier's key assistants, did attend the Toronto conference. Of Canadian officials, he wrote, "A more tight-lipped, defensive group I have never encountered. They had no problems, knew all the answers, and the Indians were doing beautifully."[152] In his 1947 book, *The Indians of the Americas*, Collier included his own impression of Canadian Indian policy: "Canada's Indian goal is to make Indians self-supporting and to Christianize them. She does not, officially, acknowledge that Indian heritage and Indian society have greatness in them."[153]

Unfortunately, the press paid little attention to the conference. Four days before it opened Hitler had invaded Poland. On 3 September 1939, the day before the conference opened, Great Britain declared war on Germany. Throughout the first two weeks of that September, the press focused on the rapid German advance deep into Poland. Midway through the sessions, Canada declared war on Germany, on 10 September. On the last day of the conference, 16 September, delegates met to pass resolutions urging greater attention to "the psychological, social, and economic maladjustments of the Indian populations of the United States and Canada."[154]

A committee was formed to collect and publish the conference papers and to exchange information. Then, the dramatic defection occurred. The Indigenous participants broke away from the main group and met separately to discuss their own resolutions. They did not need government officials, missionaries, "friends of the Indian," or Grey Owls, to speak for them. One of their resolutions stated, "We hereby go on record as hoping that the need of an All-Indian Conference on Indian Welfare will be felt by Indian tribes, the delegates to such a conference will be limited to the *bona fide* Indian leaders actually living among the Indian people of the reservations and reserves, and further, that such conference remain free of political, anthropological, missionary, administrative, or other domination."[155] Again, the Toronto media paid little attention. On 17 September Soviet armies crossed into eastern Poland and divided Poland with the invading Germans, which held until the temporary German-Soviet collaboration broke asunder with the launch of Operation Barbarossa, the German invasion of the Soviet Union, on Sunday, 22 June 1941.

Still wishing to keep up his Six Nation contacts, Paul Wallace returned to the Grand River on his fourth trip, in December 1942. At this point, only Chief William D. Loft (Dewaselakeh, meaning "Double Axe"), Fred's brother, was still living; both Joseph Montour and Jake Hess were gone.[156] Bernice Loft had married, and lived with her American husband, Arthur Winslow, in Galt, Ontario, away from the Grand River Territory.[157] Mrs Joe Longboat, a widow, was Chief Loft's housekeeper, and Wallace boarded with her during his stay of several days. "There is a couch in the kitchen which is to be mine," he wrote in his diary.[158] Thanks to Chief Loft, Wallace made the major research discovery of his four Grand River trips. As he later explained in a letter, "Chief Loft, who held the title of Sharenkhowane in the Six Nations Council in Canada, was a very fine gentleman and scholar. It was he who introduced me to the legend of Dekanawideh."[159]

On his last visit to see Chief William Loft in December 1942, Wallace found him, "sitting by the kitchen-living room stove, very feeble of body, but still amazingly keen of mind. He is just full of things I wanted to know about the League of Peace, Hiawatha, Deganawida."[160] They spent several days together, Wallace busily writing down in shorthand

6.5 Chief William Loft, on the right, shown chatting with a reporter from the *Brantford Expositor*. The photo appeared in the *Expositor* on his 80th birthday, 6 April 1938. Photo courtesy of Bernice Loft Winslow.

more stories of the Haudenosaunee, the People of the Longhouse. When his visitor finally stood up to leave, Chief Loft made the ultimate gesture: he gave him a Mohawk name, Ra-ri-wha-ro-rooks, "He Who Gathers Information,"[161] or simply "Gathering Information."[162] Chief William Loft died the following year. As Loft had first told him about the Peacemaker, the founder of the Iroquois Confederacy, Paul Wallace later dedicated his book, *The White Roots of Peace*, to him.[163]

Conrad Weiser, Paul Wallace's major academic contribution on the Iroquois, appeared in 1945, the year the Second World War finally ended. The narrative study of the life of Pennsylvania's Indian ambassador won the immediate praise of Carl Van Doren. The well-known American author and editor wrote in the New York *Herald Tribune*, on 13 January 1946, "Here the days of that old frontier came back in true and homely detail, twice as interesting as any historical novel I know dealing with their subject, and ten times as rich in essential materials." Paul

Wallace received a note from the anthropologist Frank Speck praising the book as "a grand big contribution, big in scope and significance."[164] The three scholars, Lyman H. Butterfield, the historian-editor of the landmark Adams Papers; Wilcomb E. Washburn, at the time a young American historian; and William N. Fenton already a distinguished American anthropologist, termed *Conrad Weiser* "one of the truly great source books on Six Nations history."[165]

In the early 1940s Paul Wallace decided to write a short account for the general reader on the history of the founding of the Iroquois Confederacy. Writing to William Fenton at the Smithsonian Institution in Washington, he explained his project "to make an attempt at interpreting some small part of the Iroquois mind by telling the story of the founding and preservation of the League."[166] Two versions of the foundation of the league existed in English, but both were unsatisfactory.[167] Fortunately, a composite account, a third translated text had just become available in English. In 1899 the anthropologist J.N.B. Hewitt had written down, in Onondaga, Chief John Arthur Gibson's account of the founding of the Iroquois League. William Fenton, working with Chief Gibson's son, Simeon Gibson, completed his English translation in late 1941,[168] and he now most generously made it available to Paul Wallace. In *The White Roots of Peace*, Wallace warmly thanks the American anthropologist, saying, "I should have been lost without the Gibson version, which tells a more coherent story than is found in the other versions, and which at the same time points the allegory with greater insight. I have in consequence leaned heavily on Dr Fenton's translation both for incident and for dialogue, and I have relied almost wholly on his scholarly interpretation of the triple message contained in the good News of Peace and Power."[169]

Published in 1946, *The White Roots of Peace* enjoyed wide acclaim,[170] quickly gaining recognition as "a classic of Iroquois literature."[171] Unlike *Conrad Weiser* it was a popular, not an academic book. *The White Roots of Peace* was inspired by Paul Wallace's global perspective, and interest in a world citizenship movement and the emerging United Nations.[172] In effect, it provided non-Indigenous North Americans with a short introduction to the history and culture of the Haudenosaunee. Nearly forty years after its initial publication, the Six Nations historian John Mohawk describes it as "brilliantly insightful in its rendition of elements of Haudenosaunee (or Iroquois) culture during the seventeenth century."[173]

Since its initial publication in 1946, *The White Roots of Peace* has never been out of print.[174] In its pages Dekanahwideh, the Peacemaker, emerges as an influential political thinker, one who brought the warring

6.6 Paul A.W. Wallace, ca. 1950. Photo courtesy of David H. Wallace.

Haudenosaunee nations into a complicated and sophisticated form of government. In *The White Roots of Peace*, Paul Wallace reveals the genius of the Five (later Six) Nations political federation. In July 1949 several Mohawk from the Akwesasne Reserve on the New York State side of the Canada–US border adopted Paul Wallace into the Turtle clan.[175] Ray Fadden (Aren Akweks), the schoolteacher son of an Irish father and a Mohawk mother, suggested the adoption. In the 1930s and 1940s Fadden had helped to organize the Akwesasne Mohawk Counsellor Organization, somewhat modelled on the Boy Scouts. Many Iroquois youth on both sides of the American and Canadian border learned Six Nations and other North American Indian songs, dances, stories, crafts, and Indigenous survival skills. Paul Wallace's writings on the Haudenosaunee greatly impressed Ray Fadden.[176]

The White Roots of Peace acted as a counter-balance to the contemporary image of the North American Indians as bloodthirsty "primitives." In Ontario, for instance, Stewart W. Wallace's *A First Book of Canadian History* (1928) dominated the elementary school textbook market for more than two decades. It sold over half a million copies in sixteen editions between 1928 and 1944.[177] In the 1930s and 1940s it was the only authorized Canadian history text in Ontario public schools,[178] and it contained an extremely negative portrayal of North American Indians. Milton Martin was a Six Nations veteran of the First World War, after which he became a Toronto schoolteacher and then principal, a brigadier general in the Second World War, and after that war, a respected provincial magistrate in Ontario.[179] In 1929, the year after it came out, Martin protested against passages in the first edition of *A First Book of Canadian History* that referred to his ancestors as "great thieves," "barbarians," and "people of a very primitive order." Yet, the author, University of Toronto Professor Stewart W. Wallace, head of the university library, consented to change one line only. "On the whole, it is clear that the original inhabitants of Canada were savages of a very low order," now became "On the whole, it is clear that the original inhabitants of Canada were of a somewhat primitive type."[180]

After the publication of *Conrad Weiser* and *The White Roots of Peace*, Paul Wallace continued to teach at Lebanon Valley College. He had a reputation as a superb lecturer. Upon his retirement from teaching, in 1949, his writing of narrative history gained momentum. Shortly after leaving the college, he became editor of *Pennsylvania History*, serving in that position from 1951 to 1957. Then, in his late sixties and early seventies, he worked for eight years (1957–65), as associate historian for the Pennsylvania Historical and Museum Commission, and he now published almost exclusively on Pennsylvania themes.[181] Wallace kept the mastery of his craft to the end. The historian Francis Jennings described Wallace's second to last book, *The Indian Paths of Pennsylvania*, as a "model of clarity."[182] Loyal to the institution that had made his career in university teaching possible, Wallace ended his writing career with the 1966 publication, *Centennial History of Lebanon Valley College*.

Paul Wallace had known George Brown, the founding general editor of the *Dictionary of Canadian Biography*, for half a century. With Wallace's best friend Harold Bennett as his partner, Brown had won the University of Toronto tennis doubles championship in 1913.[183] For the first volume of the *DCB*, covering those who died between the years 1001 and 1700, the author of *The White Roots of Peace* wrote a sketch of Dekanahwideh, introducing Canadians to the founder of the Iroquois Confederacy.[184] André Vachon, the assistant director of the French language edition of the dictionary, the *Dictionnaire biographique du Canada*, judged it, "excellent."[185] In the *American Anthropologist*, William N. Fenton, the distinguished American student of the Six Nations, termed it a "splendid picture of Dekanahwideh."[186]

The new awareness in the late twentieth century of the history of Indigenous Canada owes much to the *Dictionary of Canadian Biography / Dictionnaire Biographique du Canada*. From early 1959 until his death in 1963, George W. Brown served as the first general editor of "the largest sustained historical research project ever undertaken in Canada."[187] The University of Toronto professor knew more than most academics about how to reach a large audience from his writing of textbooks for high school students. Probably the best-selling book of all time by any Toronto academic is George Brown's *Building the Canadian Nation*, which sold more than six hundred thousand copies.[188] Early in the life of the biographical dictionary project, it was decided to have both an English and French language version of the texts, a collaboration of both the University of Toronto Press and Les Presses de l' Université Laval. For our understanding of our past, every Canadian owes a great debt to this incredible series of fifteen volumes, available in English and French, and now accessible on the World Wide Web with additional volumes as they are produced. Volume 1, *1000–1700*, of the *Dictionary of Canadian Biography / Dictionnaire Biographique du Canada* appeared in 1966.

This visionary statement by Jacques Rousseau and George Brown in their joint essay, "The Indians of Northeastern North America," announced the inclusion of the Indigenous peoples: "THIS VOLUME of the Dictionary contains the biographies of 65 Indians. In many ways they are a group apart. For almost all of them the information is fragmentary. Like fireflies they glimmer for a moment before disappearing again into the dark forest of unrecorded history."[189] Paul Wallace immediately recognized the fine work of the essay's principal author, the French Canadian scholar, Jacques Rousseau. After he read an early draft, he wrote to George Brown, saying, "I have taken very great pleasure in going over Rousseau's article, which I find brilliant and illuminating."[190]

Of the sixty-five sketches in the first volume, Paul Wallace commented as an "outside reader" on fifty-five of them.[191] His remarks reveal his insight as both a popular writer and a skillful editor. Enthusiastically, he responded to the call to help with, "I'll tackle the job with infinite pleasure and do my best. Working with Indians and for the better relations of French and English in Canada is like an old dream come true."[192] Wallace's commentary on the sketch of Membertou, the important Mi'kmaq chief, reveals his ideal in a biographical sketch, when he wrote, "This is a brilliant piece of work: meaty, well-organized, illuminating. It not only tells the facts and introduces the problems, but at the same time brings the character alive."[193] In contrast, he wrote frankly of one contributor who had simply missed the target, saying, "Materials have been collected, but they have yet to be given background and interpretation."[194]

The friendship between Paul Wallace and Edward Ahenakew continued throughout their lives. In a 1948 letter, Ahenakew thanked Wallace for his interest in Plains Cree folklore, history, and culture, pointing out, "Apart from yourself no one ever showed any interest in such things."[195] In a 1961 letter to his friend, Wallace explained why he wanted to know more about Native history, "I think the best way to encourage interracial understanding is through history-learning to know the magnificent contributions to human advancement that each people, each race, has made. The stories you used to tell me touched me deeply, and introduced me to a whole range of ideas to which I had been a stranger."[196] Paul A.W. Wallace – "this kind, cheerful, and scholarly gentleman," as his obituary in *Pennsylvania History* so aptly described him[197] – died at age 75 in March 1967.

Chapter Seven

Quebec Viewpoints: From Lionel Groulx to Jacques Rousseau

The first French settlers located their community at the confluence of the Ottawa and the St Lawrence, the two great rivers of the fur trade. In the early 1660s the French colony remained only a shadow along the shoreline between Ville Marie, later renamed Montreal, and the outpost of Tadoussac, located downstream from Quebec.[1] In the 1650s and early 1660s the young colony of New France suffered greatly and nearly collapsed from attacks by the Iroquois. Ville Marie stood as the advance guard of the French settlements of Trois-Rivières and Quebec itself. The worst years for casualties were 1660 and 1661, during which time fifty-eight colonists of New France were killed and another fifty-nine captured.[2] The colony consisted in 1663 of only about three thousand French settlers with between eight hundred and nine hundred at Quebec, and no more than two hundred each in both Trois-Rivières and Ville Marie.

Pierre Boucher was the governor of Trois-Rivières when he wrote in 1663, "We cannot go to hunt or fish without danger of being killed or taken prisoner by those rascals; and we cannot even plough our fields, much less make hay, without continual risk: They lie in ambush on all sides."[3] The French relied on militia units, erected stockades, and adopted their enemy's guerrilla warfare tactics. Every individual capable of bearing arms had to be prepared at all times to fight for their lives. When the settlers departed for their fields, they carried sickles in their hands and slung firearms across their backs.

There used to be a small marble plaque in southeast Montreal that recalled a 1662 clash and those perilous days. The historic marker was put up on a wall of a building at the northwest corner of La Gauchetière and rue St André. The *Chatelaine* magazine journalist Catherine Breslin noticed and mentioned the small historical sign in her 1969 article, "The Other Trudeaus: In 1659 a young Frenchman, Etienne Truteau, landed in Quebec to father a long line of hardy farmers that continued right down to Joseph, grandfather of Canada's Prime Minister." Just change the reference to "great-grandfather of Canada's prime minister" and the sentence applies today to Prime Minister Justin Trudeau. The plaque, demolished with the building sometime in the 1970s, commemorated a furious skirmish of three French colonists against the Haudenosaunee. The text on it read, "Ici Truteau, Roulier & Langevin-Lacroix resistèrent à 50 Iroquois 6 mai 1662 (Here Truteau, Roulier & Langevin-Lacroix resisted 50 Iroquois, 6 May 1662)."[4]

The events of the "Heroic Period" of New France (1534–1663) remained in the collective memory of French Canadians in the St Lawrence Valley into the late nineteenth century. The French Canadian historian Benjamin Sulte[5] emphasizes the heroics of the conflict with the Iroquois in New France in his eight-volume *Histoire des Canadiens français 1608–1880*, published between 1882 and 1884. Sulte writes, "Chacun de nous compte un ancêtre enlevé, brûlé, mangé par les Iroquois (Each of us has an ancestor seized, burned, eaten by Iroquois)."[6] In the words of Marcel Trudel, a distinguished Quebec historian of New France from the mid-1630s to the mid-1660s, the colony lived "through the most painful hours of its history."[7] When Jacques Rousseau (1905–1970) was born, little attention was being paid to the Indigenous population of the St Lawrence Valley. The First Nations by then represented but a tiny portion of the population of Quebec, less than one per cent.[8] This figure might well be underestimated, however, since because of racial prejudice, many Québécois felt no incentive to emphasize their Indigenous ancestry. Part of the French Canadians' lack of enthusiasm for the First Nations in the mid- and late nineteenth century came from the Natives' resistance to giving up their separate national identities.

The testimony of a contemporary Roman Catholic missionary suggests the First Nations enduring pride and desire to remain Indian. Abbé Joseph-Pierre-Anselme Maurault (1819–1871) captures this in his 1866 work, *Histoire des Abénakis depuis 1605 jusqu'à nos jours*.[9] Maurault lived among the Abenki at their village of Odanak, on the banks of the St François River, just east of Montreal. Odanak, meaning "at the village," was one of the four major Roman Catholic mission stations that also included Wendake (Huron) at Quebec, and Kahnawake (Iroquois) and Kanestake or Oka (Iroquois and Algonquin) near Montreal. The missionary had spent twenty-five years with the Abenaki,[10] and by the time he compiled his history, spoke their language fluently. At one point in his account, Maurault describes their self-image. The Abenaki considered themselves, the Indian race, "la plus parfait (the most perfect)."[11] In the past, Maurault reports, the Abenaki's admiration for

Europeans was high, but only if they could live as they did, as people who could travel though the forest without a guide, and tolerate hunger, thirst, and fatigue. To any "white man" who approached their standard, the Abenakis gave the greatest compliment, and said they were "presqu'aussi habile qu'un savage (almost as skillful as an Indian)."[12] Maurault adds that many Abenaki spoke English or French so well that visitors believed they were French or English themselves,[13] but the Abenaki showed no interest in the idea of assimilating.

In the mid- and late nineteenth century, various opinions circulated in French Quebec about the First Nations in the St Lawrence Valley. Joseph-Charles Taché (1820–1894) was a medical doctor, politician, writer, and civil servant with a deep interest in the First Nations. As a young man, Taché was termed "one of the cleverest men that the province has produced."[14] He was a descendant of Pierre Boucher, the early governor of Trois-Rivières, and also related to Louis Hébert, New France's first farmer, and to Louis Jolliet, the explorer who had travelled in the early days of New France from Quebec to the Mississippi River.[15] One of his brothers was Archbishop Alexandre-Antonin Taché of St Boniface in Manitoba. In his youth, several of Jean-Charles Taché's friends called him "the Iroquois," because of his love of wilderness travelling. He searched in the late 1840s and early 1850s for Indian encampments at the mouths of the major rivers that flowed into the lower St Lawrence near his home at Rimouski. He wanted to learn oral traditions and traditional stories to use in his writings.[16] Taché believed that the First Nations undeniably had a land claim to the St Lawrence Valley, but he added only a small payment was in order, as the Natives had received already generous recompense: they had received the gift of Catholicism, "le don de la Foi (the gift of their Faith)."[17]

Philippe Baby Casgrain (1826–1917) was a Quebec lawyer and long-time parliamentarian with strong opinions on the topic of North American Indians, and he voiced them. Casgrain, at the time a Quebec Liberal MP, showed his "erudition" in the House of Commons. He introduced biologically determinist arguments in parliamentary debate in 1885, arguing that the Indians were simply "not capable of being civilized." They were inherently and hopelessly inferior, and Casgrain added, "Everybody would prefer the vote of one white man to the votes of five Indians." All being said, Casgrain echoed the prevailing belief that Indians were a vanishing people. Their numbers had plummetted, and they were "gradually disappearing from the country."[18]

In Jacques Rousseau's boyhood, another consideration arose to curb enthusiasm for the First Nations: contemporary racial thinking. As the French journalist André Siegfried comments on the national feeling of

Anglo-Canadians in the English translation of his 1906 study, *The Race Question in Canada*, "Their patriotism is made up in large measure of haughty belief in British superiority, asserted sometimes offensively, at the expense of the impliedly inferior French."[19] The aspersion that large numbers of French Canadians had intermingled with the Indigenous population greatly reduced their "standing." The French would be viewed as an inferior people if they had mixed with a "backward race."[20] Georges Vattier, a French professor teaching at the Royal Military College in Kingston, Ontario, from 1918 to 1925[21] notes in his book, *Essai sur la mentalité canadienne-française*, that Anglo-Canadians often said of the French Canadians, "la plupart sont des métis (the majority are Métis)." This made them inferior people.[22]

Eugène Rouillard (1851–1926) was a leading Quebec geographer of the day. Rouillard objected to the abundance of North American Indian place names in Quebec, and in 1908, as secretary of the Commission de Géographie de Québec, he began a campaign to remove Indian names from places in Quebec. The urgency arose from Rouillard's fear that outside of the province the idea would grow that Quebec, which was an "essentially French province," actually had deep Indigenous ties. Starting in 1912 the Commission de Géographie de Québec eliminated thousands of Indian names from maps of Quebec.[23] Lionel Groulx (1878–1967), the leading French Canadian historian, thundered against all those who suggested that *métissage* had been extensive in the French Regime in the St Lawrence Valley. He stated this in the first edition of his *La naissance d'une race* (1919).[24] In later editions, Groulx greatly toned down the passage, and in the second (1930) and third (1938) editions, even added an explanatory footnote to explain why he had included it. Groulx wanted to refute the claim of métissage by critics anxious to prove French Canadians belonged to an inferior "race."[25]

Early in the twentieth century negative attitudes towards the First Nations dominated in both French and English Canadian historical writing. Basically for these authors, the story of Canada began with the arrival of Europeans. Historians, both popular and academic, remained ill informed about Indigenous history. A prime example is McGill University Professor Stephen Leacock (1869–1944). By the outbreak of the Second World War, Leacock's long and successful writing career reached back over half a century, as a political scientist and a popular historian, and most surprising for a university professor, as a humorist. At one time, in fact, Leacock was the best-selling humorist in the English language, with books of his translated into more than seventeen languages. Leacock had become an English Canadian cultural icon with manifold honours and accolades, including seven honorary doctorates for literary excellence.[26]

Wearing his historian's hat,[27] in 1941 Stephen Leacock wrote *Canada: The Foundations of Its Future*, under commission from Sam Bronfman, of Seagram Distilleries. The enthusiastic whiskey merchant, anxious to help Canada's war effort, paid to send the popular history of Canada, free of charge, to schools, libraries, and prominent persons in North America and Great Britain. Bronfman had 160,000 copies printed,[28] and Seagram's even mailed a copy to Joseph Stalin, warmly inscribed –

> To Marshal Joseph Stalin,
> mighty leader, of mighty peoples, in war
> so vigorous as in peace far-seeing,
> whose hammer pounds Fascism, and
> whose scythe reaps freedom, this
> history of his ally and neighbour is
> respectfully inscribed.[29]

Bronfman wanted the beautifully illustrated English-language volume to be an uplifting contribution to the national cause in the Second World War, during which from mid-1941 we had been Allies of the Soviet Union against the Axis powers. He paid for a superb example of the bookmaker's art with nine outstanding Canadian artists commissioned to contribute thirty-one full-page illustrations, and small decorative sketches throughout the volume.[30] Initially, Leacock's completed draft contained several imperfections from the viewpoint of the Seagram committee that examined it. The swipes that Leacock took at immigrants, French Canadians, Roman Catholic priests, Americans, and the Irish, had to go. Reluctantly, the author revised his text, all the while complaining that this meant the loss of "some of the virility of the book."[31] Leacock left the anti-Indian approach unaltered in *Canada: The Foundations of Its Future*. His initial pages in the first chapter, "The Empty Continent," summarize his belief that Indigenous history was so thin, it did not merit telling: "We think of prehistoric North America as inhabited by the Indians, and have based on this a sort of recognition of ownership on their part. But this attitude is hardly warranted. The Indians were too few to count. Their use of the resources of the continent was scarcely more than that by crows and wolves, their development of it nothing."[32]

Stephen Leacock, who in the summers lived away from Montreal at his nineteen-room county home at old Brewery Bay near Orillia on Lake Couchiching, should have known better. An Indigenous example of advanced fishing technology stood several kilometres from the loft of his boathouse where he loved to write each morning: Mnjikaning, or the Fish Weirs, is one of the oldest human developments in North America. For some five thousand years Indigenous peoples, at what is now known as the Atherley Narrows, used a complex system of underwater fences to harvest fish. As an example of an extremely efficient food-gathering technology, Mnjikaning Fish Weirs is now a National Historic Site of Canada.[33]

In Montreal, it is hard to imagine an individual more opposite to Stephen Leacock than Abbé (later in 1943 Chanoine, or Canon) Lionel Groulx. Within the same city, the two men lived in totally separate universes. Sherry Simon, in her study, *Translating Montreal: Episodes in the Life of a Divided City*, makes reference to another early twentieth-century city in which the two major groups as in Montreal also mingled on the city's streets, but lived culturally separate lives. She cites Sir Cecil Clementi, British governor of Hong Kong from 1925 to 1930, who observed the British and Chinese saw each other every day and yet, "move in different worlds," and had no real understanding of the mode of life, or ways of thought of the other.[34] The anglophones and the francophones in early twentieth-century Montreal lived in similarly different worlds. Leacock favoured the closest ties possible for Canada with the British Empire. Groulx, in contrast, dreamed for the greatest independence from this Empire. Yet, despite their fundamental ideological differences, the two men did share similar views with regard to North American Indians.

Into the mid-twentieth century, Abbé Lionel Groulx was French Canada's most famous historian.[35] Born in 1878 into a rural Quebec family at Vaudreuil near Montreal, young Lionel attended village schools and then classical college. The intense religious atmosphere of his school years led him to enter the Church as a priest and teacher. His two great passions included the education of young French Canadians and the study of history, a discipline in which he actually had had little formal training. A strong French Canadian nationalist, Groulx believed that French Canadians' pride in their past would give them confidence in their future. The priest-historian urged a rejection of urban mores and championed the province's rural values.

Groulx's early historical work was triumphant and inspiring. In vigorous prose, he emphasized the Catholic foundations of New France, and the colony's incredible strength in its conflicts with the First Nations and later the English. The gifted teacher was able to study for three years in Europe, including theological studies in Rome and literary studies in Fribourg, Switzerland. In 1915 Lionel Groulx became the first full-time university professor of Quebec history by obtaining a posi-tion at the Montreal branch of the Université Laval, soon to become the Université de Montréal, where he taught until 1949. Groulx explained his philosophy of history in a 1925 lecture in which he insisted that "in history there are always two great actors: man and God."[36] The priest's intense interest in history led him to found, in 1946, l'Institut d'histoire de l'Amérique française, and this was followed in 1947 by his creation of the *Revue d'histoire de l'Amérique française*, a new professional histori-cal quarterly. Since its founding in 1920, the *Canadian Historical Review*, published in Toronto, had antagonized French Canadians by refusing to publish articles in French, a policy it altered only in the 1960s.[37] At the time of Lionel Groulx's death in 1967, the *Revue d'histoire de l'Amérique française* was outselling the *Canadian Historical Review*.[38]

Early in his career, the self-taught chronicler of his nation's, that is, French Canada's past chose the seventeenth-century soldier Adam Dol-lard des Ormeaux (1635–1660) as the model of what all French Canadi-ans should strive to become. With a party of sixteen Frenchmen and a small number of Huron and Algonquin allies, Dollard died at the age of 25 defending an improvised fort at the Long Sault on the Ottawa River. Groulx saw him as the soldier-saint who gave his life to save Montreal. The priest-historian advanced this position in *Si Dollard revient* (1919), repeated in it in *Le Dossier de Dollard* (1932), and finally, reintroduced it again in *Dollard, est-il un mythe?* (1960). Groulx held firmly to his belief that Dollard and his group left Montreal in the full knowledge that they would not likely return. By the 1930s, however, there was consider-able evidence that Dollard and his party had had no suicidal intent. Actually, they had left on a mission to locate an Iroquois war party and claim the furs that the Haudenosaunee themselves had seized from the Algonquins. Lionel Groulx, however, did not accept this view.[39] He also maintained his opinion that the heroic skirmish took place on the north side of the Ottawa River in what is now Quebec, even though by the late 1950s ample historical and archaeological data indicated the engage-ment occurred on the south, or Ontario side of the river.[40]

In 1950 Lionel Groulx published the first of four volumes of his life's work, the *Histoire du Canada français depuis la découverte*, an expansion of history lectures he had originally given on the radio, in roughly a hundred 15-minute radio broadcasts.[41] Three subsequent editions of the *Histoire* followed. The author felt a human tie to the Iroquois wars in the French Regime, particularly because in 1690 his direct ancestor Jean Grou, together with three companions, had been killed by Iroquois commandos on their farm at Pointe-aux-Trembles.[42] In his treatment of Indigenous Canada, Groulx maintained his familiar negative tone, full

7.1 Abbé Lionel Groulx, 1960, shown holding a copy of his book, *Dollard, est-il un mythe?* (Dollard, is he a myth?), published in that same year. C-016657 LAC.

of unfavourable stereotypes and misinformation. He termed the Indian "primitive," a people who had spent thousands of years "dans le même état de vie, dans les mêmes routines dégradantes (in the same state of existence, with the same disgusting habits)." To the priest-historian, the Indigenous peoples' faith consisted of a "paganism têtu, moeurs privée et publiques aussi déplorables[43] (stubborn paganism, private and public customs as deplorable)."

Interest in Indigenous issues in both French and English Canada approached zero in the 1930s and 1940s. Canadians lacked any appreciation and background knowledge of Indigenous history and cultures. In English Canada four major texts in Canadian political science appeared between 1944 and 1947, and in all four the commentary on Indigenous Canada remained minuscule to non-existent.[44] Admittedly, there were a few Canadian university scholars who did undertake research in English-speaking Canada on Indigenous history. In 1936 George F.G. Stanley published *The Birth of Western Canada: A History of the Riel Rebellions*, in England, but the book had a very small circulation in Canada.[45] It would have no circulation at all for two decades, after a German air attack in late December 1940 destroyed the premises of his English publisher, Longmans Green. Finally, in 1961, the University of Toronto Press brought out a second edition.[46] The New Brunswick Museum published in 1937 an important study by the anthropologist A.G. Bailey, entitled *The Conflict of European and Eastern Algonkian Cultures, 1504–1700: A Study of Canadian Civilization*, which reviewed the first two centuries of contact between the First Nations and Europeans in the Maritimes. The anthropologist and archaeologist Bruce Trigger has identified Bailey's book as "the first recognizable work of ethnohistory published anywhere in North America."[47] But the Museum gave it only a small print run, and within a few short years it "became virtually exhausted."[48] As Trigger writes, "It was not until a new generation of Canadian anthropologists and historians turned to the study of Native history that Bailey's pioneering work was appreciated for its true worth."[49] As did other Canadian academics of the day, Bailey believed that assimilation was the ultimate outcome of social change.[50]

Anglo-Canadian historians' indifference towards Indigenous Canada is confirmed by the fact few Canadian academics had participated in the 1939 Toronto–Yale Conference on the North American Indian Today. As George Stanley later recalled, "Indian Department officials and missionaries turned out in good numbers, but Canadian university professors were conspicuous by their absence. I am not exaggerating when I say that only three professors of the University of Toronto were in attendance, two anthropologists and one economist." Two other professors participated in the conference, both from New Brunswick: George Stanley, historian, and A.G. Bailey, anthropologist.[51] Not a single French Canadian historian attended.

The indifference of English-speaking Canadian historians to Indigenous history continued for decades more. Textbook authors, at best, confined the Indians to an introductory chapter. In spring 1944 the historian Donald G. Creighton published his book entitled *Dominion of the North: A History*, which quickly became a classic work by a master stylist and went through numerous editions and reprintings. *Dominion of the North* avoided a description of North American Indian society, and instead, the first full chapter, covered "The Founding of New France, 1500–1663."[52] Diamond Jenness's book, *The Indians of Canada*, had come out in 1932. In that work, Jenness outlines how the original peoples of the Americas had first crossed the Bering Strait between fifteen and twenty thousand years before the arrival of Europeans, and subsequently migrated throughout the Americas. Regardless, Creighton's focus was uniquely on the achievements of the Europeans.[53] The well-known Canadian historian Arthur Lower completed his history of Canada, *Colony to Nation*, in 1946; it went through five editions. The preface to the first edition, also included in the last (in 1977), contained his interpretation of the relationship between Natives and newcomers, as a "clash between backward and advanced cultures."[54]

In the mid-1940s Edgar McInnis, another professional Canadian historian, worked away diligently on his one-volume study,[55] *Canada: A Political and Social History*. It had an even longer life than Creighton's *Dominion of the North*. University instructors adopted McInnis's book as a course text in Canadian history classes into the 1980s. From 1947 to 1969 it sold more than two hundred thousand copies.[56] McInnis refers at greater length to North American Indians than Creighton, but with an equal lack of awareness. One sentence encapsulates McInnis's point of view: "The aborigines made no major contribution to the culture that developed in the settled communities of Canada."[57] McInnis avoids mentioning improvements in transportation, winter survival skills, military support, invaluable participation in the fur trade, or herbal cures. Lionel Groulx, who in his four-volume *Histoire du Canada français* (1950–2) cited English-language Canadian historians such as Lower, Creighton, and McInnis,[58] learned no new approaches to the history of Indigenous Canada from their work.

Regarding student interests, William John Eccles taught Canadian history at the University of Manitoba in the years 1953 to 1957, afterwards at the University of Alberta for six years, and finally, at the University of Toronto from 1963 until his retirement in 1983.[59] Looking back in 1987 to his early teaching career in the 1950s, Eccles recalled how difficult it had been to discuss the role of Indians in Canadian history. When he introduced the First Nations, "the pencils went down, heads began to turn, and the chatter began." By the mid-1980s, however, the reaction was totally different: "No essays topics are more popular than those dealing with the Indian; on every examination paper, at least one question on them has to appear. A few lectures do not suffice; new courses on the Indian peoples are required."[60]

An historical breakthrough came in 1960 from the periphery of the Canadian historical profession.[61] That year Stanley Ryerson, a Canadian Marxist historian, published his popularly written book, *The Founding of Canada: Beginnings to 1815*.[62] Ryerson recognizes the significance of the Indigenous peoples and shows a remarkable sensitivity to them. In the opening pages of his book, he notes, "The written record of our country's history covers less than five centuries. Before that there were more than two hundred centuries of human habitation, struggle and achievements."[63] Ryerson reviews each of the major cultural groups of the "first dwellers in our land," the hunters, foodgatherers, and agriculturalists. From the outset, the Marxist writer kept a sharp eye on economic developments, and followed the European traders, noting, "It was on the labour of the native peoples they built their fortunes."[64] Ryerson underlines the Europeans' dependence on the Indians from the very moment of first contact. He submits, "What to the Europeans was 'discovery' was, in some respects, at least, rather in the nature of a conducted tour: everywhere Indians guided them, paddled them, taught them woodcraft."[65] As the Canadian historian Robert Sweeny later commented, "In 1960 Ryerson wrote the first history of Canada to reject the founding myth of Cabot, Cartier, and Champlain in favour of a recognition of the historical significance and agency of indigenous peoples."[66] *The Founding of Canada* sold very well in its four editions (1960, 1963, 1972, and 1975), for a total of twelve thousand copies.[67]

The first full-time university professor of Quebec history remained unimpressed. In his 1961 review of Stanley Ryerson's book, Lionel Groulx attacked the author for his presentation of the Indians and the settlers: "En d'autres pages où il aborde les rapports entre Indiens et colonisateurs, il reserve toute sa pitié pour ces faibles, ces misérables victimes du mercantilisme européen[68] (On other pages where he discusses the relations between the Indians and the settlers he reserves all his pity for the weak ones, these miserable victims of European mercantilism)." The French translation, *Les origines du Canada*, came out in 1997.[69]

The Quebec botanist and ethnohistorian Jacques Rousseau challenged old attitudes towards the First Nations in Quebec, and also in the rest of Canada. From an early age Rousseau had a great curiosity about the natural and human worlds around him. He was at ease in other cultures: in the mid-1940s he taught for one month in Haiti, followed by several months in Mexico.[70] Truly multidisciplinary, this world-class botanist became competent in other disciplines, including ethnobotany, anthropology, linguistics, geography, ethnohistory, and the history of science (particularly botany).[71] Jacques Rousseau made a major contribution to the study of Indigenous Canada.[72] His writing has a timeless quality for its originality and Rousseau's unusual ability to write for non-Indigenous readers about his experiences within a subarctic hunting and gathering society. He also had the tremendous advantage of knowing not just the documents, but also the land and the challenges of travel in the wilderness.

In the early 1960s Rousseau's experience as a twentieth-century *coureur des bois*, and his own honesty, cost him his friendship with Lionel Groulx. The split came over the site on the Ottawa River where Dollard des Ormeaux met his martyrdom, undoubtedly about 80 kilometres north of Montreal. Groulx argued for the north bank of the Ottawa near Carillon by the Long Sault rapids, but an archaeologist, Thomas Lee, demonstrated through his archaeological excavations and from the description by the fur trader Pierre-Esprit Radisson that it had happened on the old Ross Farm on the south bank. Alas, the issue had a major political dimension: Carillon was in Quebec and the old Ross Farm was in Ontario. In the mid-1950s, to get a first-hand view for himself, Rousseau hired a local canoeist to run the Long Sault rapids. He returned convinced that the south bank on the Ontario side best fit the surviving physical description of the site of the skirmish.[73] Others had declined to contradict the best-known historian of French Canada of the day, but the dedicated scientist was not so deterred.[74]

From the 1940s to 1960s Jacques Rousseau wrote a number of full articles on the First Nations of Quebec, published mainly in *Les Cahiers des Dix*,[75] and he contributed other important historical essays to the *Revue d'histoire de l'Amérique française*. One of his major essays was written in collaboration with his wife, Madeleine Aquin Rousseau.[76] He also completed well over a hundred newspaper articles on the First Nations, with the great majority of them appearing in *La Patrie*, a mass circulation Montreal newspaper. Although short, these descriptive articles contain excellent ethnographical detail. They describe Rousseau's rich personal experiences while travelling alone with First Nations hunters and trappers. He reports all aspects of their lives, including food, clothing, travel,

7.2 Jacques Rousseau. Photo by Denis Plain, *Perspectives*, 23 May 1970. A painting
by the Ojibwe artist Norval Morrisseau is in the background.

shelter, and technology. In 1966 Jacques Rousseau gave a thirteen-part
television series on "L'Indien et notre milieu."[77] His 1966 essay, "The
Indians of Northeastern North America," written with George Brown
and published in the first volume of the *Dictionary of Canadian Biography / Dictionnaire Biographique du Canada,* has by now reached a wide
audience. Rousseau was the principal writer. Two scholars, Camille
Laverdière and Nicole Carette have produced a valuable bibliography
of Rousseau's work, with extensive biographical information.[78]

   Louis-Edmond Hamelin was one of Quebec's most distinguished
geographers, founder of the Centre d'études Nordiques at Université
Laval, and an expert on the study of northern Quebec. Hamelin describes

Jacques Rousseau as "un grand personage presque sans equivalence au Québec (a distinguished personality almost without an equivalent in Quebec)," adding that from the 1940s to 1960s, he was "le scientifique le plus connu au Québec et l'un des plus connus â l'étranger (the best known scientist in Quebec and one of the best known abroad)" From this distinguished scholar, Hamelin learned a tremendous amount: "Je fais partie des gens qui ont beaucoup appris de lui. Il était en avance sur son temps; il était un encyclopédie vivante sur un très grand nombre de sujets[79] (I was among those that learned a great deal from him. He was ahead of his times, he was a living encyclopedia on a very large number of subjects)."

Jacques Rousseau was born in St Lambert, now a suburb of Montreal, in 1905. He belonged to a large family of twelve boys and two girls. His father was an electrical engineer and industrial contractor, at first in Montreal and then in Montmagny, Quebec. His maternal grandfather was a medical doctor and founder of the chemistry department of the Université Laval at Montreal.[80] As a young man, Rousseau encountered serious health problems, and for two years he was taught by two private tutors, one being his eldest brother Georges. Very bright and curious about all that was around him, Rousseau had a deep early interest in the natural world.

Before he completed his B.A., awarded by the Université de Montréal (now separated from Université Laval) in 1926, Jacques Rousseau was a voluntary assistant to Brother Marie-Victorin (1885–1944), a pioneer of botany in Quebec. The well-known scientist had recently founded the Institut botanique at the new Université de Montréal. In 1935 he completed La Flore Laurentienne, a comprehensive botany of Quebec, which remains today an indispensable reference for Quebec botanists and naturalists. Under the supervision of Brother Marie-Victorin, Rousseau competed his Ph.D. dissertation in 1934. Shortly after the granting of his degree, he married his fiancée, Madeleine Aquin, with whom he had a most happy marriage, until his death in 1970. They had three children, Lise, François, and Jérôme.

Throughout the 1930s the young instructor at the Université de Montréal aided Brother Marie-Victorin in his campaign to establish a world-class botanical garden in Montreal, a goal achieved with the establishment of the Jardin Botanique in 1938. In effect, Jacques Rousseau was the co-founder of the Jardin. After Marie-Victorin's untimely death in an auto accident in 1944, Rousseau was selected as the second director of the Montreal Botanical Garden, where he worked from 1944 to 1956. For sixteen years in the 1930s and early 1940s, Rousseau also served as the secretary general of the new Association canadienne-française

7.3 Jacques Rousseau (*fourth from the right, standing*) with his parents, Lacasse and Gabrielle Fafard Rousseau (*sitting in the centre*) and his eleven brothers and two sisters. Courtesy of François Rousseau and Jérôme Rousseau.

pour l'avancement des sciences, which vigorously promoted science in French Canadian society.[81]

A prolific writer and conference presenter, Jacques Rousseau gained an international reputation. His biological fieldwork described 130 botanical species. Eight botanical entities were named after him.[82] Elected a Fellow of the Royal Society of Canada in 1942, member of the Société des Dix in 1951, and member of the Order of Canada in 1969, he earned many honours. From 1956 to 1959 he was head of the History Branch of the National Museum of Man in Ottawa. After teaching for three years at the Sorbonne in Paris, Rousseau returned to Canada in 1962, to teach at the Université Laval in Quebec City. Monseigneur Vachon, then the rector, had recruited the eminent scientist as a professor and research director.

Throughout his career Jacques Rousseau organized botanical expeditions to all the regions of Quebec, in particular, to the High North. His interest in subarctic peoples arose out of his knowledge of northern flora, and how the First Nations made use of them. Gradually, his interest in ethnography grew, and his study of North American Indian lifestyles expanded. In 1943 Rousseau visited Manouane, an Attikamek community in the upper St Maurice watershed, 200 kilometres north of Joliette. He had distant links with this First Nation, as one of his ancestors in the early period of New France was an Attikamek woman,[83] daughter of Étienne Pigarouich, a seventeenth-century Indigenous spiritual leader.

Based on the 120 official marriages contracted between First Nations and non-Aboriginals during the French Regime, demographers contacted by Jacques Rousseau calculated that in 1970 over 40 per cent of French Canadians had at least one North American Indian ancestor in their family trees.[84] In 1945 Rousseau noted his connection with Pigarouich in his popular study of human genetics, L'Hérédité et l'homme. In his chapter, "Sommes-nous parents avec tous nos ancêtres," he mentions his ancestor Marguerite Pigarouich, who was baptized in 1647. She was the daughter of Étienne Pigarouich, "célèbre sorcier des Trois-Rivières."[85] The degree of Amerindian ancestry was admittedly very slight, dating back to the time of early New France;[86] nevertheless, Jacques Rousseau was very proud of his link with Pigarouich. This was an extraordinary assertion to make in 1945, as few individuals in mainstream society at that time wanted to claim even the slightest Indigenous background.[87] The Indigenous peoples still had a truly negative image.

Outdated viewpoints about the First Nations remained entrenched in the work of many mid-twentieth-century Canadian historians. For thirty years the most popular Canadian history text at the senior level in French-language Quebec secondary schools remained the Histoire du Canada by Father Paul-Émile Farley and Father Gustave Lamarche,[88] in which are echoed the same old negative sentiments. Farley and Lamarche describe the First Nations as "orgueilleux, vindicatif, sensuel et manquant totalement de caractère"[89] (proud, vindictive, sensual, and totally lacking in character)." Their religion consisted of "superstitions puériles et souvent grossières (childish and often vulgar superstitions).[90] The Indians could not be trusted in treaty making, for with them, "la mauvaise foi régnait habituellement dans la négociation des traits" (bad faith usually dominated in the negotiation of treaties)."

At first the young ethnobotanist shared the same stereotypes about northern Indians' cruel nature, as did others without having had any real contact with them. One of Jacques Rousseau's best popular articles appeared in a 1954 issue of *L'Action universitaire*, entitled "Du bon sau-vage de la littérature à celui de la réalité (From the good savage of lit-erature to that of reality)." Here Rousseau explains his own intellectual journey: "J'ai déjà affirmé dans de doctes écrits que les Indiens primitifs de la forêt étaient cruels. A cette époque je n'avais jamais vu d'Indiens et les connaissais comme tout le monde à travers les livres [...] Une meilleure connaissance de la forêt et de ses hommes m'a obligé depuis à nuancer mon jugement [...] Bien plus, je suis maintenant convaincu que le chasseur de la forêt boréale doit être essentiellement pacifique[91] (I once stated in scholarly writing that the primitive Indians of the for-est were cruel. At the time I had never seen Indians and I knew them as everyone else from books ... A better awareness of the forest and its inhabitants led me to nuance my assessment ... In addition, I am now convinced that the hunter of the northern forest is essentially peaceful)."

For three decades Jacques Rousseau pointed out injustices committed against the Indigenous peoples, and he contributed greatly to correcting non-Aboriginals' ethnocentric and racist views, for example, he con-tested the stereotyping of the First Nations as constantly at war. True, warfare existed, but it was only a minor aspect of their culture: "Il leur arrivait, comme aux Blancs, de guerroyer, mais leur culture reposait d'abord sur la paix et le travail[92] (It did happen, as among the Whites, to make war, but their culture was based first and foremost on peace and work)." In fairness, he added, critics must first compare the First Nations in war with the terror exercised in the European pogroms, and the concentration camps of the Second World War.[93] Jacques Rousseau had first-hand knowledge of the horrors of that war, which had taken a heavy toll on the Rousseau family. Two of his brothers, Philippe, age 23, and Maurice, 25, both lieutenants in the 1st Canadian Parachute Bat-talion, died in France. Philippe died on D-Day, 6 June 1944, and Maurice lost his life behind German lines in France three months later.[94]

As Rousseau wrote in an English-language article in 1969, "Speaking as a White man – forgetting my small proportion of Indian blood – we came here two or three centuries ago, often un-welcomed; we took, usually without compensation or agreement, ground belonging to the Amerindian bands, and disturbed the Aboriginal population in its ways of living."[95] Correcting false images was one of Rousseau's major objectives in his articles on Amerindians. He made a special point, for example, of explaining the equality of women and men in the world of the subarctic Indigenous peoples.

With his customary skill in explaining complex issues for a general audience, Jacques Rousseau touched upon the diversity of Indigenous peoples' cultures and languages. The First Nations varied greatly in size, social organization, and economic activities. This one sentence illustrates Rousseau's ability to communicate to a general audience: "S'il n'existe pas de caractère stéréotypé pour tous les cheminots d'Amérique ni pour les pêcheurs gaspésiens ou les colons d'une paroisse abitibienne, les Indiens chasseurs d'une même peuplade ne sont pas non plus identiques[96] (If there is no stereotypical character for all the railway workers of America, or fishers of the Gaspé, or settlers in a parish in Abitibi, the Indian hunters of the same small tribe also are not all the same)." Just two years before Jacques Rousseau's death in 1970, Marcel Trudel, the well-known Quebec historian of New France, acknowledged his contribution in his historical survey, *Initiation à la Nouvelle-France: Histoire et institutions*, giving special thanks to Jacques Rousseau for "bien des éclaircissements (clearing up many questions)."[97] Trudel recommended to readers the essay, "Les Premiers Canadiens," which had appeared in the 1960 issue of *Cahiers des Dix*; and Rousseau's 1966 essay with George Brown, "The Indians of Northeastern North America," in the first volume one of *Dictionary of Canadian Biography / Dictionnaire Biographique du Canada*.

Thanks to his botanical, linguistic, and historical background, Jacques Rousseau resolved one of the great mysteries of Canadian history. In the winter of 1535–6, twenty-five members of Jacques Cartier's expedition died from scurvy at Stadacona (the present-day site of Quebec City), a disease caused by insufficient vitamin C in the diet. To their good fortune, Domagaya, son of Stadacona Chief Donnacona, informed them of the remedy. A tea made from the bark of the evergreen Anneda ("tree of life") saved the other eighty-five or so remaining party members, who suddenly recovered. For more than four centuries the origin of the remedy remained unknown. In 1945 Rousseau identified the Anneda as the white cedar or arborvitae (*Thuja occidentalis* L.).[98] To use the description provided by Marc-Adélard Tremblay and Josée Thivierge of Jacques Rousseau's scholarship in general, "One gains from his work almost a feeling that a police enquiry is in progress from the way in which everything is turned over systematically and nothing left to chance. Each fact is systematically compared, classified and analyzed down to the last detail."[99]

Jacques Rousseau conducted major botanical and ethnological fieldwork in the mid-1940s in the district around Lake Mistassini (meaning "Big Rock," a reference to a large glacial erratic along its northeastern shore).[100] The Mistassini Cree still maintained much of their fur trade economy at this time. Lake Mistassini is located about 600 kilometres north of Montreal, in the black spruce forests of Northern Quebec.[101] From this starting point the Indigenous people could travel down the rivers on either side of the Height of Land, to James Bay to the north or the Saguenay River to the east. Between Mistassini and James Bay there were fifty portages.[102] This was on the major trading route from James Bay to Lac St Jean. From the east side of the Lake Mistassini the waters flowed to Lac St Jean and entered the St Lawrence at Tadoussac.[103] In June 1947 the linguist Jean-Paul Vinay of the Université de Montréal joined Jacques Rousseau on a trip to the Mistassini. The language of the Mistassini people interested him greatly. Vinay recorded the name of several portages in the immediate area, an easy one, the *natohkamishishioukapotagan* ("the portage that goes towards the small pond") and the famous two- to three-mile ordeal, the *kapochepouchekochitechininaneouchoukapotagan* ("the portage from which you get foot blisters in travelling by snowshoes").[104]

Several of Rousseau's most interesting popular articles appeared in the 1950–1 series, "Les Indiens," in Montreal's *La Patrie*. He included much of the best of his *La Patrie* material in his later articles in *Cahiers des Dix*. In contrast, the well-known anthropologist Marius Barbeau had little impact in the French-language press, as he wrote usually in English and not for newspapers. Barbeau had little impact on the popular perception of the First Nations in Quebec, whereas Jacques Rousseau assuredly did.[105] As Claude Gélinas writes of Rousseau, "sans contredit, l'intellectuel de son époque qui a le plus contribué à faire la promotion de la connaissance des populations autochtones du Québec[106] ("without question, the intellectual of his day who contributed the most to promote awareness of the Indigenous population of Quebec)."

The Mistassini, called "Cree" in English, had a unique culture, as Jacques Rousseau's articles made clear. In the 1940s the community remained well isolated; neither the federal nor the provincial government paid much attention to it. For most of the year the population lived in small, scattered hunting groups, with the winter hunting and trapping culture still autonomous. Few Europeans were interested in settling in the subarctic until after the Second World War, when the search for northern minerals and forest resources accelerated. The Mistassini controlled their territory until the second half of the twentieth century, when the Quebec government showed an interest in northern Quebec, and began in the 1960s asserting its presence.[107] They called it "Nouveau Quebec," quite an understatement, as the anthropologist Toby Morantz points out, since "it was 'new' to the Quebec people, not the Crees and Inuit who had occupied it for millennia."[108]

Hunters and their families in the mid-1940s spent summers at the Mistassini Hudson's Bay Company post at the southeastern end of Lake Mistassini, or in the fishing or berry-picking camps in the surrounding area.[109] Then they moved onto their isolated hunting territories in the bush. As the journalist Boyce Richardson wrote in in his 1975 book, *Strangers Devour the Land,* in the early twentieth century the 250 or so Indians at Mistassini "spent most of the year spread out over the huge territory of their hunting grounds, an area as large as Britain."[110] It was estimated in 1952 that the Mistassini population of 646 exploited a combined area of some 42,500 square miles. The density average of the Mistassini territory was one person to every 66 square miles.[111]

In his travels with First Nations people in remote parts of Quebec, Jacques Rousseau lived as they did, canoeing, portaging, travelling in winter on snowshoes, and helping with the setting up of camp. He learned to speak some Montagnais (Innu),[112] and tried to act within the norms of their culture. His articles reveal his admiration for the ingeniousness and adaptability of the Indigenous peoples.[113] In his words, "pour pénétrer le processus mental d'autrui on doit faire table rase de sa propre dialetique et adopter celle de l'interlocuteur[114] (to enter into the thought processes of another person one must efface one's own way of reasoning and adopt that of one's interlocutor)." Rousseau believed in the participant observation approach. There is a spontaneity to his writing, such as the lead he used for his survey of Innu gastronomy, "Astam Mitchoun!" which appeared in the 1957 issue of *Cahiers des Dix*: "Lorsque je parcourais la forêt ou la toundra avec des indigènes, en quête de données biologiques et ethnologiques, j'entendais toujours avec plaisir cet appel: 'Astam mitchoun!' – 'Vite, venez manger!' (When I travelled through the forest or the tundra with Indigenous people in search of biological or ethnological information, I always heard with pleasure the call 'Astam mitchoun! Come let's eat!')."[115] With Jacques Rousseau, we enter into the camps of the First Nations and join them in canoe journeys not as intruders but as participants. He catches the colour and sounds of the Mistassini camps.

The Quebec scientist's openness allowed him a privileged view of the life of the Mistassini on the land. He witnessed religious ceremonies few non-Aboriginals had seen. He was one of the very few ethnographers to see the Shaking Tent ceremony.[116] After several long stays in the mid-1940s, Rousseau became aware of the coexistence among the Mistassini of two religious systems, one traditional and the other Christian, within the same individual. The Mistassini kept both their ancestral and Christian religious traditions, simultaneously. The Mistassini were a deeply spiritual people. Totally sincere, they behaved as Anglicans in their short summer visits at Mistassini Post, but while in the bush in their solitary camps, they held to their Indigenous rites and rituals. Jacques Rousseau identified this religious dualism.[117]

Jacques Rousseau explained his overall philosophy in the guide to his 1966 televised course, "*L'Indien et notre milieu.*" It was not necessary for all citizens, all peoples, to be made over on the same model – "façonnés sur le même modèle." For, "en s'intégrant dans notre société, les indigènes apporteront quelque chose de valable, s'ils restent eux-mêmes. Leur culture est menacée de disparaître quand elle pourrait nous fournir un apport si précieux[118] (in integrating into our society, Indigenous people will bring something valuable, if they remain themselves. Their culture is threatened with disappearing when it might furnish us with such a precious contribution)."

Unfortunately, the approach Rousseau recommended was not followed. By the 1950s the shortcomings of sending children away to federal Indian residential schools became increasingly obvious. As Toby Morantz writes, "Undoubtedly the education system was one of the most destructive southern institutions imposed upon the Cree. It tore the children away from the cultural context in which their parents had been raised, provoking what must have been a heart-breaking generation gap."[119] That being said, she adds, for a small group of former students, the experience had some benefits. They now met southern society on its own terms, and at the schools made contacts with other Cree and formed networks that enabled them to fight the Quebec government's unilateral decision in the early 1970s to build a massive hydroelectric dam on Cree territory.[120]

Through talks, guest lectures, and publications in the 1950s and 1960s, until his death in 1970, Jacques Rousseau continued to share his knowledge of Indigenous Quebec. As a young Quebec university student, Andrée Lévesque, recalls, "Before doing history, I was in geography at Université de Montréal and Laval in the late 50s. I remember that it was taken for granted that Aboriginal people were declining in number and getting assimilated, and that it was too late to do anything. Jacques Rousseau was invited to give some lectures one year and we loved him."[121]

Unfortunately, the new knowledge of Indigenous peoples did not really enter the Quebec school system until the turn of the millennium. Mid-twentieth-century school texts did little to convey an understanding of Indigenous history and culture. Two ethnologists, Sylvie Vincent and Bernard Arcand have made a thorough examination of the textbooks approved by the Quebec Ministry of Education for usage in 1976–7. In their study, *L'image de l'Amérindien dans les manuels scolaires du Québec*, published in 1979,[122] Vincent and Arcand found the history books, especially those dealing with the French Regime (1534–1760), inadvertently led students towards racism and discrimination against the First Nations. In an English-language summary, the two writers note,

"To sum up, the Amerindians are simply accused of having hindered the economic development of the colony and the enrichment of Europeans. In laying stress on the supposedly bellicose and cruel nature of the Indians, historians also throw into relief the heroism of the first Quebecers."[123] A further reference notes, "In their superficial descriptions, the authors of history textbooks maintain that Amerindians languages and technologies are poor, and that their economies, their religions and their social and political organisations are inferior."[124]

Yet, there were undercurrents of change. An undergraduate's paper, "La contribution de l'indienne à notre histoire," in the December 1964 issue of the student journal, *Lettres et ecritures, Revue des étudiants de la Faculté des lettres de l'Université Laval*, provides an excellent example of a new mind towards the First Nations. The undergraduate essay contained more wisdom about the reality of the French Regime than did the textbooks used in Quebec's elementary and secondary schools. Denys Delâge, a student in the Faculté des lettres, pointed out the misconception that Europeans were the first to travel interior trade routes, not so, for "non seulement chaque tribu indienne connaissait à merveille son territoire de chasse, mais il existait avant la venue des Blancs un commerce international en Amérique du Nord (not only did each Indian tribe know well its hunting territory well, but there also existed in North America before the arrival of the Whites an international commerce)."[125]

Historians at the university level ignored the Native topic. In a 1966 volume on the social and economic history of Quebec from 1760 to 1850, the Indigenous people receive only five references.[126] The subsequent volume on the economic history of Quebec from 1851 to 1896, published five years later, only contains one mention of the Aboriginal peoples.[127] The founding of the academic journal, *Recherches amérindiennes au Québec*, in 1971[128] would help enormously to improve the awareness of Indigenous Quebec. A breakthrough in university and college textbooks came in 1976 with the publication of *Histoire du Québec*, a collaborative work under the direction of the Laval historian, Jean Hamelin. The work devoted, for the first time, two entire chapters to the First Nations.[129]

First Nations writers in Quebec began to publish poems, short stories, novels, histories, and biographies in the 1970s, introducing francophone readers to new Indigenous viewpoints.[130] An Antane Kapesh, the first published Innu woman writer in Quebec,[131] is the author of *Je suis une maudite Sauvagesse / Eukuan nin matsshimanitu innu-iskueu*, which came out in 1976. She summarizes eloquently in her own language, Montagnais (Innu), translated into French, what her people had undergone, and were still undergoing. She presents her vision of the

7.4 "Histoire du Canada. Les Autochtones. Doucement! A la file indienne." *Le Devoir*, 18 March 1983, p. 6, an editorial cartoon from an important Montreal newspaper on the entry of Indigenous peoples into Canadian history books. The newspaper cartoon was kindly forwarded to me in 1983 by my former M.A. thesis adviser at Université Laval, Pierre Savard.

Innu's dispossession. No longer would this strong self-reliant woman tolerate inequality and discrimination:[132] "Quand le Blanc a voulu que les Indiens vivent comme des Blancs, il ne leur a pas demandé leur avis et il ne leur a rien fait signer disant qu'ils acceptaient de renoncer à leur culture pour le reste de leurs jours[133] (When the White man wished that the Indians lived like Whites, he did not ask for their advice, and nothing to sign that accepted the renouncement of their culture for the rest of their lives)."

The Indigenous peoples in the rugged Laurentian Shield and farther north remained unknown to southern Quebecers well into the 1970s. Most of the northern area was officially labelled as unmapped.[134] When Quebec's young Premier Robert Bourassa announced the gigantic James Bay hydro project in 1970, to quote Roy MacGregor in his biography of James Cree leader Billy Diamond, "No one in his entire government had even considered for a moment that there was an obligation – even if only out of politeness – to let the Crees know what the government had in mind for their land and rivers."[135] Equally appropriate is the comment by the journalist Dominique Clift in the *Montreal Star*, 5 May 1971: "One had the impression that here was the greatest public works project since the Pyramids; that James Bay was the answer to every political and economic problem which is facing Québec today, such as unemployment nationalism, terrorism, agitation and so on."[136] The non-Indigenous population of Quebec was unprepared for the response that came from the First Nations. Toby Morantz summaries the situation well when she writes, "When school textbooks or historical documentaries aired on television fail to mention that the land on which the Quebecois are living has not yet been ceded by the Indians, can one expect the larger population to react any differently?"[137]

Jacques Rousseau acted as a bridge when there were few bridges between Quebec francophones and the Indigenous peoples. Shortly after Rousseau's death, Aurélien Gill, a future chief of the Montagnais (Innu) community of Pointe Bleu (known now by its Innu name of Mashteuiatsh) in the Saguenay region, recalled what Jacques Rousseau had once said to him. The First Nations leader, who later would serve for ten years (1998–2008) in the Canadian Senate, remembered very clearly the visionary's words: "Si seulement tous les Indiens pouvaient retrouver la fierté d'être Indien ils seraient tellement puissants, intellectuellement parlant, qu'ils imposeraient au monde actuel la culture la plus humaine et la plus libre qui soit par cette philosophie de l'acceptation de 'l'être tel qu'il est,' le monde européen en serait gêné, lui qui tente constamment de changer les autres peuples[138] ("If only all the Indians could find again the pride of being Indian, they would be so powerful, intellectually speaking, that they would impose on today's world the most humane and free culture that could be by this philosophy of acceptance of 'being what one is,' the European world would be ashamed to try constantly to change other peoples)."

Chapter Eight

Attitudes on the Pacific Coast: Franz Boas, Emily Carr, and Maisie Hurley

Franz Boas (1858–1942) stands out as one the most influential North American anthropologists of the twentieth century.[1] His extensive contact with Canada began in 1883–1884 with his participation in a German expedition to Baffin Island. This year in the Arctic, just three years after Britain had transferred the Arctic Islands to Canada, introduced Boas to intensive ethnological fieldwork among the Inuit and to specimen collecting. After that his focus became British Columbia, where he made eight visits between 1886 and 1931. From Columbia University in New York he kept in close touch with his two resident "assistants": the Indigenous George Hunt on the Pacific Coast and the Scottish Canadian James Alexander Teit in the BC interior. Most of Boas's knowledge of the plateau peoples in interior BC came from his twenty-eight-year collaboration with Teit. The seasoned ethnographer, translator, and backwoods guide provided the eminent anthropologist Boas with invaluable field data. Teit collected his ethnological data, in the words of his biographer, the historian Wendy Wickwire, through "years of field research, often on horseback, in some of the remotest regions of the province."[2]

Born and educated in Germany, Franz Boas was the son of liberal Jewish parents and raised in an educated upper middle-class family fully assimilated into German society and culture.[3] Originally a physicist, Boas's interest later turned to the study of people and their environment, and he developed a competence in all the four fields of anthropology: ethnology, linguistics, physical anthropology, and archaeology.[4] On his return to Berlin from his Baffin Island fieldwork, Boas obtained a temporary assistantship at the Royal Ethnological Museum of Berlin, at the time when nine Bella Coola (Nuxalk) from British Columbia were visiting the German capital. With his facility with languages, Boas soon conversed directly with them. In late 1886 he decided on a three-month field research trip to British Columbia, travelling to the Pacific Coast on

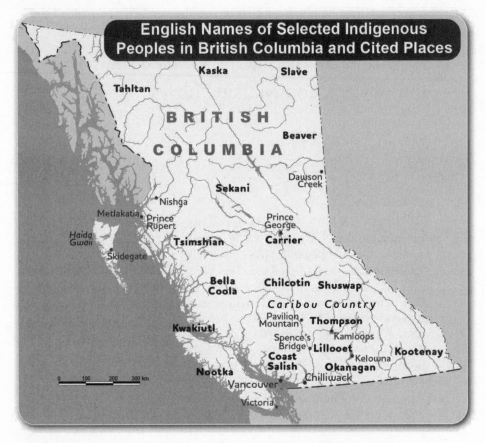

Map 8.1 English names of selected Indigenous peoples in British Columbia.

the newly completed Canadian Pacific Railway. By the time he left BC he had collected over a hundred traditional stories.[5] Feeling his Jewish birth and liberal politics would hold back his academic career in Germany, and drawn to his romantic interest, his fiancée Marie Krakowizer who then lived in New York City, Boas decided his real career opportunities were in the United States. Upon reaching New York City on his return from British Columbia, he married Marie and within two years had committed himself to a North American career.[6]

Franz Boas returned to the Pacific Coast in May 1888, this time under the auspices, and with the financial support of the North-Western Tribes of Canada Committee of the British Association for the Advancement of

Map 8.2 Selected Indigenous peoples in British Columbia.

Science. Fortunately, the German scientist had met Horatio Hale (1817–1896) at the 1886 meeting of the American Association for the Advancement of Science in Buffalo, New York.[7] The distinguished American/Canadian ethnologist from Clinton, Ontario, who also had a long North American career in law and business, headed the ethnological survey of the northwest tribes of Canada funded by the British association and the Canadian government.[8] Boas accepted Hale's' invitation to return to do ethnographic fieldwork in British Columbia,[9] under his (i.e., Hale's) direction.

During his first week in Vancouver in the spring of 1888, Boas learned of the Indian Land Title question, the inescapable reality of relations regarding Indigenous and non-Indigenous people in British Columbia. In a conversation with Chief Joseph near Vancouver on the north shore of Burrard Inlet, the elderly chief told Boas about the seizure of his people's land, even though "God gave this land to my ancestors."[10] Franz Boas's sympathies for the four decades to follow remained solidly with the First Nations, who had inhabited the area for millennia. From Fort Rupert on Vancouver Island, he wrote his son Ernst forty years later, "I had a council with the Indians, who are really suffering because of the stupid persecution of their customs by the government."[11] Yet, at the same time, Boas had to keep on good terms with Canadian authorities and not antagonize his host government.

Through their correspondence, Hale supported Boas's conviction that anthropologists must avoid judging foreign cultures by the standards of their own culture. The two men shared a common outlook on what became known as "cultural relativism," and both rejected the earlier belief in a hierarchy of societies and their evolution from one stage of development to another. Boas's "distaste for racism and of any kind of prejudice"[12] made him a constant critic of European cultural superiority. His students at Columbia University, a group that would include A.L. Kroeber, Ruth Benedict, Margaret Mead, Edward Sapir, Clark Wissler, Paul Radin, Frank Speck, and Robert Lowie,[13] expanded the distribution of his anti-racist message across a continent, indeed, across the world.

Horatio Hale had conducted extensive ethnographic and linguistic research for four years in Polynesia and on the Pacific Coast before Franz Boas was born. After graduation from Harvard, where he had been in the same 1837 class as Henry David Thoreau,[14] Hale joined the Wilkes Pacific Expedition of 1837–1842, an American government scientific mission to the Pacific Ocean. Later he studied law, the profession of his father and brothers, and moved to Chicago. After his Canadian wife inherited land in Huron County, at Clinton near London, Ontario, Hale became involved in local real estate development and the management of her property. As the volunteer chairman of the Clinton High School Board, the progressive thinker gained admittance for girls as well as boys to the school, a privilege previously denied them. In the 1870s Hale returned in retirement to his early linguistic and ethnological studies. He regularly visited the nearby Six Nations Territory on the Grand River, corresponded widely, and travelled occasionally to consult libraries and attend meetings of academic societies. In 1884 Hale became the research director of the Committee on the North-Western Tribes of Canada, established at the Montreal meeting of the British Association for the Advancement of Science.

The Hales and the Six Nations interpreter George Martin Johnson and his family became close friends. On at least one occasion, Johnson's daughter Pauline stayed with the Hale family in Clinton.[15] George's father, John Smoke Johnson, a veteran of the War of 1812, served as Hale's principal informant for his classic work, *The Iroquois Book of Rites*, published in 1883. From his many visits to the Six Nations the ethnologist and linguist had an opportunity to see Haudenosaunee society from the inside. He found the people "most kindly and generous," individuals who showed "constant good humour, unfailing courtesy, ready sympathy with distress, and a truly lavish liberality."[16] On one major aspect of Indigenous research, Horatio Hale stood leagues ahead of many non-Indigenous scholars in Canada: he put aside his pen and paper and went among the people he studied to learn from them. He urged historians to consult Indigenous people about their past, stating, "Our students of history have been too frequently a book-worshipping race, unwilling to accept any testimony with regard to ancient events which is not found in some contemporary page, either written or printed."[17]

The fiercely independently minded Franz Boas did not take well the older scholar's close supervision, his tight control.[18] Hale reacted, and wrote Boas on 13 July 1889, "I cannot understand why you should persist in causing me an immense amount of useless trouble, as well as much annoyance, by objecting to my instructions, which you are expressly engaged to carry out."[19] In a letter to his wife, Marie, two weeks later, Boas gave his side of the story: "You cannot imagine how angry I am with Hale's instructions. Apparently he is not familiar with the existing literature on the coastal tribes, otherwise he would not state that the tribes of the west coast are the least known. The opposite is the fact."[20]

Franz Boas's professorship in anthropology at Columbia University from 1899 to 1936 allowed him to mentor a number of graduate students. Before obtaining his appointment at Columbia, he had taught at Clark University in Massachusetts, where his first graduate student was Alexander Chamberlain, a Canadian who like Chancellor John Alexander Boyd studied modern languages and history with Daniel Wilson. Under Boas's guidance, the young scholar obtained the first doctorate ever given in anthropology in North America, with his dissertation on the Mississauga or Anishinabeg on the north shore of Lake Ontario.[21] In 1891 Chamberlain undertook fieldwork among the Kootenay (Kutenai or Ktunaxa) in the southeastern corner of British Columbia. Very gifted with languages, Chamberlain spoke French, German, and Italian,[22] and he learned enough Kootenay for limited conversations during the half-year he spent with them. His popularly written essay, "The Human Side of the Indian," based on his visits to the Kootenay reveals their humanity, and his. While among them, Chamberlain explains, he had first to convince them that "his advent is not connected with the attempts of white men to steal or ill use their women – these are the two chief sins laid to the charge of the 'superior' race."[23]

John Swanton was a young American anthropologist who completed his Ph.D. at Harvard but had studied linguistics under Franz Boas at Columbia. Swanton, like Boas, championed the retention of the old culture. Boas arranged for his former student to work with the Haida on Haida Gwaii (Queen Charlotte Islands) in 1900–1, recording their stories. Swanton's comment to Boas about the local Christian missionaries certainly questioned the usefulness of their mission. He criticized them for suppressing all the old dances, and having all the old houses destroyed. The missionaries, Swanton concluded, had ruined "everything ... that makes life worth living."[24]

Indigenous reactions to the theft of their land, and to the imposition of the Indian Act, became more vocal in Vancouver around 1920. The First Nations lived on the small Tsliel Waututh (formerly Burrard) Territory, the Squamish reserve at Ustlawn on the north shore of Burrard Inlet opposite Vancouver, the Musqueam reserve on the north arm of the Fraser River to the south, as well as in other communities as one moved up the Fraser Valley. Greater Vancouver's population at this time was approximately 220,000.[25] Throughout BC Indians at this time comprised less than 5 per cent of the total population.[26] Chief Joe Capilano (c. 1854–1910), a high-profile Squamish leader in the Vancouver area, led a First Nations delegation to London in 1906 to present a petition about their claims of Indigenous Title and Sovereignty to King Edward VII.[27] Capilano's name was well known in the city, as he had recounted Squamish legends to Pauline Johnson, who had chosen to retire in Vancouver after her performing career ended. The Iroquois writer recorded many of Capilano's stories in her last book, *Legends of Vancouver*. Pauline Johnson herself had acted as mistress of ceremonies at the chief's home after his funeral in March 1910. A very large crowd of Indians and non-Natives gathered to pay their final respects to the man known as "Hi-Ash Joe," "Hi-Ash" or "Hyas," meaning in Chinook, the language of trade in the late nineteenth-century Pacific Northwest (with its simplified grammar and a vocabulary drawn from several Indigenous languages and French and English), "Big or Huge."[28] Chief Capilano was so politically active during his lifetime that the BC Indian Affairs superintendent had considered arresting him. At the time, the Criminal Code ruled it an offence to incite or "stir up" Indians to disorderly behaviour (see chapter five).[29]

In the 1910s a new generation of Indigenous leaders had come forward, arriving from an unlikely source: the Indian residential schools. After Chief Capilano's death, Andy Paull (1892–1959) became Vancouver's best-known Indigenous political leader. The short, powerfully built man had attended his reserve's Catholic school for seven years, where he had a positive experience.[30] He fought hard to prevent his school's closing in the 1950s.[31] As a member of one of the prestigious families at the North Vancouver Mission Reserve, Paull had influence in his community.[32] Moreover, Andy Paull had legal training. The community Elders at Ustlawn years earlier had selected this young Squamish man to become their future spokesperson. He first received special training in the history, culture, and traditions of the Squamish, then worked in a downtown Vancouver law office after leaving residential school.[33] During these years, Paull "memorized large sections of statutes, laws, and documents relating to Indian affairs, especially Indian land."[34] Had he consented to give up his Indian status, he could have written the BC bar examination, but Andy Paull refused to enfranchise. As he could not vote, he could not enter the BC bar.[35]

During his four years in a Vancouver law office, Andy Paull acquired an in-depth knowledge of Canadian law and of legal procedures regarding Indians, particularly in respect to land rights. Many years later he won praise for his presentation of "interesting and well-argued legal briefs on many questions."[36] In the early 1850s the colony of Vancouver Island made fourteen small treaties, but then the process of treaty making completely broke down. In the late 1850s the Fraser River Gold Rush on the mainland brought a huge influx of non-Indigenous people to the area. No further treaties followed on Vancouver Island or in the new colony, British Columbia, founded on the mainland in 1858.

The refusal to acknowledge the legitimacy of Indigenous land claims dated back to 1864, upon the retirement of James Douglas, governor of both colonies. After the two colonies merged in 1866, the new united colony of British Columbia continued to take Indian lands and then assign small tracts to the respective communities as reserves.[37] Douglas's departure introduced a new harshness to BC Indian policy. Reserves previously laid out were reduced in size, or even taken away. On the established reserves, families obtained a maximum of 10 acres (4 hectares). As the historian Jean Barman notes, "By comparison, British subjects by birth or naturalization, a simple process for whites, could pre-empt 160 acres (65 hectares) and then purchase up to 480 (195 hectares) more."[38] The First Nations were prohibited from pre-emptying or buying lands outside their reserves. The political scientist Paul Tennant writes of the First Nations, "Confined to their small reserves, they could nurture a deepening sense of injustice as they witnessed the takeover of their surrounding traditional lands without regard to aboriginal title."[39]

When British Columbia entered Confederation, in 1871, the terms of union gave jurisdiction over Indian matters to the federal government, as Ottawa promised "a policy as liberal as that hitherto pursued by the British Columbia Government shall be continued by the Dominion Government after the Union." This statement was total hypocrisy. For one thing, BC's Indian policy in the 1860s was the complete opposite of liberal.[40] Paul Tennant summarizes the situation in the late 1880s, when provincial politicians unanimously "believed the white myth that Indians had been primitive peoples without land ownership, and they accepted the white doctrine that extension of British sovereignty had transformed an empty land into unencumbered crown land."[41]

The Government of Canada, with its constitutional responsibility for Indians, did little to champion the interests of the First Nations, especially in the face of intense provincial political opposition. Treaty Eight included the northeastern corner of BC east of the Rocky Mountains, and when signed in 1899, it became the only section of mainland British Columbia under treaty.[42] Communities of First Nations elsewhere in the province continued to call for the recognition of their Indigenous Title. A number of Christian missionaries, such as William Duncan, provided initial support for the First Nations, and argued that their territory must be purchased before settlement proceeded. John A. Macdonald himself told Parliament in 1881 that he was "strongly of the opinion that if the Government raised the question of the Indian title [in BC], the Courts of this country and the Courts of England, at all events, would maintain the right of the Indians and their title to the occupation of the soil until the right whatever it might amount to was extinguished."[43] British Columbia refused to discuss the question of Indigenous Title. Macdonald and the federal government had little manoeuvrability on this issue, as the province had control over all public lands. Ottawa had no land to give to the Indigenous peoples in British Columbia.

The BC government's policy of allocating small reserves, and later diminishing them in size, continued into the early twentieth century. The crisis point arrived when the small reserves could not sustain their traditional economies.[44] Finally, in the early 1910s, the province agreed to address the reserve-allotment question with Ottawa – without any discussion of the vital question of Indigenous Title to British Columbia – just the reserve boundaries.[45] Had the title question been left on the agenda, there would have been no McKenna-McBride Royal Commission. Headed by a federal Indian Affairs commissioner and the BC premier, the commission held hearings from 1913 to 1916 concerning the

8.1 Sir John A. Macdonald and Lady Macdonald at the Stave River, a tributary of the Fraser, just east of the future City of Vancouver, 24 July 1886. NA-4967-132 by O.B. Buell. Courtesy of Glenbow Archives, Archives and Special Collections, University of Calgary.

size of existing reserves in British Columbia. As all five commissioners were non-Indigenous,[46] understandably First Nations distrust arose. Andy Paull had left his job as a longshoreman to act as a commission interpreter in Salish-speaking areas.[47] The commissioners created some new reserves and added area to others, but they also eliminated from reserve status valuable land long coveted by Euro-Canadian settlers and land speculators. These tracts became known as the "cut-off lands."

In response to the McKenna-McBride process, the Allied Indian Tribes of British Columbia was formed in 1916.[48] Andy Paull, together with Haida Peter Kelly,[49] another former Indian residential school student, led the new organization that included Indigenous groups from across BC, with Kelly as the chairman and Paull as secretary. The Allied Tribes fought back, demanding that acknowledgment of their Indigenous Title must precede the boundary adjustments of reserves. Extinguishment of Native Title must come first. With the assistance of Arthur O'Meara, an Anglican minister and a non-Native lawyer who acted as their legal counsel,[50] and the invaluable help of James Teit, whose first wife was Indigenous,[51] the Allied Tribes prepared their case.

For three years, the two governments kept the Royal Commission's 1916 report with its recommendation on the "cut-off lands" secret. Throughout the hearings, the commissioners had assured the Indigenous communities they visited that no land would be taken without the consent of the Indian bands themselves. In the end, this was another broken promise. With the strong support of Duncan Campbell Scott, Department of Indian Affairs officials accepted the McKenna-McBride Report – without consent from the First Nations.[52] A section in the Indian Act, one based on the Royal Proclamation of 1763, required band consent for the removal of Indian land; therefore, federal legislation was required to do so. Accordingly, Bill 13 was introduced to adopt the McKenna-McBride Report and its final recommendations. The Allied Tribes of British Columbia held a meeting in June 1919 at Spences Bridge, a village at the confluence of the Thompson and Nicola rivers in south-central BC. Peter Kelly was confirmed as chairman of their executive committee, Andy Paull as "recording secretary," and the appointment of James Teit as their secretary was renewed.[53] Representatives of the Allied Tribes spent several months in Ottawa in 1920 unsuccessfully challenging Bill 13.[54] "The solution," in the words of the historical geographer Cole Harris, "was imposed on Native peoples, who had consistently opposed the assumptions on which the report rested, the procedures it followed, and the recommendations it offered."[55]

Peter Reginald Kelly (1885–1966) was born at Skidegate on Haida Gwaii in 1885. Shortly before his birth his father and mother had converted to Methodism. Although committed Christians, his parents had no desire to assimilate. They wanted their son to have a dual training. Over and over they told him the history of his clan as well as the traditions of the Haida people. At the age of 80, Peter Kelly could still recount the history and the stories.[56] In addition to learning Indigenous ways, Kelly became familiar with the newcomers' world. He attended the Methodist mission school at Skidegate, where he learned to speak, read, and write English and to keep sums. As was the case in many First Nations day schools, attendance was erratic, as families left regularly for their camps to gather food, catch and dry salmon. In all, he had a little more than one year of continuous schooling from age six to 12.[57]

Peter Kelly's mother and stepfather (his father had died several years earlier) decided to send their son to the Coqualeetza Industrial Institute, the Methodist Indian residential school for Indigenous students, near Chilliwack in the Lower Fraser Valley, about 100 kilometres to the east of Vancouver. In 1900, 15-year-old Peter Kelly and another young Haida became the first two students from Haida Gwaii at Coqualeetza. Health conditions at the school were not always good,[58] and students attempted to run away on a regular basis,[59] but Kelly made a good transition. He enjoyed his half-day of work in the fields and taking care of animals, sang in the choir, and actively participated in school sports. His teachers soon recognized his exceptional ability in academic studies, and before long they allowed him to work the full day on his academic subjects. Three years later, Peter Kelly became one of the first two Coqualeetza students to write and pass the BC high school entrance examinations.[60]

Peter Kelly returned home to Haida Gwaii in 1904, where he became the first Indian teacher at the Skidegate day school.[61] Wishing to obtain a full secondary school education, he studied high school subjects at night, as well as theology and the law, as it applied to Indigenous peoples.[62] In 1906 he married one of his students, Gertrude Russ, a daughter of Amos (Gedanst) Russ, a renowned Haida Methodist evangelist,[63] and his wife, Agnes Hubbs.[64] He spent five years as a teacher at Skidegate and then three years as a lay preacher in the First Nations community of Hartley Bay on the northern mainland coast.

While teaching at Skidegate, Kelly had represented the Haida during discussions with the provincial government about Indigenous Title. He was the youngest of all the First Nations delegates to attend a 1911 conference with the provincial government. In Victoria he excelled, as he could explain to others the meaning and substance of provincial laws and edicts. He became known as *Klee-Als*, "the Orator."[65] Kelly left Hartley Bay in 1913 and registered as a theology student at Columbia College in New Westminister, BC. Upon graduation three years later the newly ordained Methodist minister was posted to Nanaimo on Vancouver Island, where from 1916 to 1930 he ministered to both Native and non-Native congregations.

In the late 1910s and 1920s Peter Kelly and Andy Paull were two of the most prominent leaders of the Allied Indian Tribes of British Columbia. Devoted principally to recognition of Indigenous Title, the other major concerns of the Allied Tribes included improved medical care and better education. The organization's executive worked closely with a remarkable non-Indigenous ally, James Alexander Teit (1864–1922), who lived at Spences Bridge on the western shore of the Thompson River, and had helped Franz Boas with his research on the Indians of the BC interior. Born and raised in Lerwick, the principal town of the Shetland Islands, Teit came at age 19 to the interior of British Columbia, where he supported himself by doing farm work, hunting, and guiding. Quickly, this self-reliant young man settled into his new life and became close to Indigenous people. In a marvellous word portrait, Judy Thompson, the museum curator who has written on ethnographic material collected by James Teit, recreates his initial journey into the Indigenous world: "People who knew him spoke of his quiet, unassuming manner, his friendly personality and his ability to get along well with people from diverse backgrounds, all qualities which would have eased his way into the Native community."[66]

All of this would not have been enough for his acceptance. Falling in love with Lucy Antko, a Thompson (Nlaka'pamux, roughly pronounced "In-kla-KAP-muh")[67] woman, in time turned James Teit from outsider into insider. His relationship with Lucy led to marriage in 1892. Marriage to a non-Indian had great consequences for Lucy, as under the Indian Act she now lost her Indian status and the right to live on her reserve.[68] Teit continued to immerse himself in learning about the history and culture of his wife's people. He learned of the serious reverses the Indigenous peoples in the interior of BC had experienced in the previous generation: "In the early sixties many tribes were reduced one-half by an epidemic of smallpox, and some bands were practically exterminated. Since then other epidemics, venereal diseases and intoxicants introduced by the whites have gradually diminished their numbers."[69]

In British Columbia, James Teit always wore moccasins and a fringed buckskin jacket.[70] The Scot from the Shetland Islands did not believe in assimilation, but held that the First Nations had much to teach the newcomers. He saw the peoples of BC's interior, in the words of his biographer Wendy Wickwire, as "fully functioning members of an ongoing *living* culture that was under assault by settler colonialism."[71] From 1908 to his death Teit took on political advocacy, acting as a translator, secretary, and lobbyist.[72] He juggled his paid ethnographic work for Franz Boas with his unpaid activist work for the First Nations leaders involved in the assertion of First Nations Title.[73] As early as 1913 the Department of Indian Affairs had gathered a thick dossier on James Teit's activities on behalf of Indigenous rights.[74]

Teit made several political lobbying trips to Ottawa with delegations of chiefs. Aware of "white" discrimination against Indians, he wrote Edward Sapir at the Victoria Memorial Museum in Ottawa, before

8.2 James Teit and his first wife, Susanna Lucy Antko. Photograph by Harlan I. Smith, 1897. Photo 11686, American Museum of Natural History, New York, NY.

his first trip, in 1912. "As every hotel will not admit Indian chiefs," he asked if Sapir could "locate a suitable stopping place for us." Lodgings were arranged at the Grand Union Hotel and Sapir went further, offering the BC chiefs his workplace, the Victoria Memorial Museum, as a "daytime refuge" for them.[75] Another visit was the one in early 1920, with Peter Kelly and Andy Paull and other BC First Nations leaders, when they went to present their case against Bill 13, which was designed to reduce BC reserve size without Indian consent, and its companion piece, Bill 14, which sought the compulsory ending of Indian status (see chapter five).

James Teit was a beloved individual in Indigenous British Columbia. The friend and advocate of the First Nations could converse without hesitation in three southern interior languages.[76] He impressed even Native speakers, who said that in a darkened room he spoke the language so fluently and his accent was so good, "you couldn't tell him from an Indian speaking."[77] James Teit died in late 1922. Peter Kelly warmly remembered him: "He was not just a friend, he was a brother of the Indians in this Province. He had their utmost confidence. He had their implicit trust; he was looked to, not as white man, not as a sojourner among the Indians in this Province, but one of them; one who could present their views perhaps better than any other man of the present generation."[78] James Teit's story merits greater attention, as do the lives of William Henry Jackson (Honoré Jaxon), Horatio Hale, and a small number of others – true non-Indigenous friends of the Indigenous peoples.

Until the publication of Judy Thompson's beautifully illustrated volume on James Teit's collecting work among the Tahltan people of northwestern BC and Wendy Wickwire's remarkable biography, Teit had remained in the shadows, his enormous contribution to the Indigenous peoples in BC left essentially unrecognized. In contrast, the artistic and literary contributions of Emily Carr (1871–1945) are, justifiably, well known. The celebrated artist remains today one of the best-known non-Indigenous observers of the First Nations in British Columbia. Born and raised in the province, the Victoria painter, in the words of her biographer Gerta Moray, sought "to change the settler community's racist views of the Native population in British Columbia."[79] During her travels and sketching trips to northern villages early in the twentieth century, Carr developed a fascination for the people and their ways and worked to change prejudices against them.[80] Emily Carr's interest in the First Nations was apolitical.[81] Surprisingly, she had great empathy with the First Nations, but appears to have had little awareness of the Indigenous rights movement, in particular the fight to obtain recognition of Indigenous Title. Carr is "virtually silent" about relations between Indigenous people and the federal and provincial governments.[82]

The fifth child in a family of five girls and one boy, Emily Carr was born in Victoria in 1871, the year that British Columbia became a province of the Dominion of Canada. Victoria itself was less than thirty years old. Emily's father Richard Carr was a well-to-do wholesale merchant who had built his family a fine home near the foot of Beacon Hill. Born and raised in England, he was stern and domineering in contrast to his warm and uncomplaining English wife, also named Emily. The youngest Carr daughter showed her independence of her father in reacting against the family routine that, in her words, "ran with mechanical precision,"[83] starting daily with a cold bath, followed by morning prayers.[84] She refused restraints. Later as she grew older she was at last allowed to range the surrounding fields and woods by herself.[85] From an early age, Emily Carr "gave evidence of unusual interest and talent in drawing."[86]

After the death of her mother when she was 14, and her father two years later, Emily was left in the care of Edith, a dictatorial eldest sister, called "Dede" (pronounced Dee-dee"). As biographer Paula Blanchard points out, Emily Carr's six autobiographical books are highly crafted. The oppression, for example, allegedly inflicted by Dede might well have been exaggerated: "Often it has been possible to check her memories by comparing one version with another, and then the distortions come to light fairly easily."[87] As her friend and sketching partner Edythe Hembroff-Schleider writes, Emily Carr was "a story-teller rather than a precise recorder of facts."[88]

In Victoria, Carr regularly saw the Lekwungen people, now legally known as the Songhee and Esquimalt nations. The Songhee spoke a Straits Salish language (Lekwungen) and at the time lived in an area that is now the city's urban core.[89] Victoria grew and the First Nations village on the harbour became the most valuable commercial property in the city.[90] With an extraordinarily high death rate due primarily to disease, the Songhee continued to decline in numbers into the early twentieth century.[91] In 1911 they were relocated to a new reserve across the harbour at Esquimalt, but in the late nineteenth century their canoes were a familiar sight at the wharves. Natives sold fish and berries door to door. Forbidden to cross over to the reserve, Carr would sit on the Customs House Wharf and watch the canoes and individuals moving in front of the plank-sided community houses.[92] Her early notebooks contain a number of tiny sketches of Indian canoes. The art curator Doris Shadbolt notes the attraction the famous painter felt to them: "The native's plight as outcasts from conventional society only

8.3 Emily Carr and her sisters, ca. 1888. *Left to right*: Edith, Elizabeth, Clara, Alice, and Emily. A-02037. Courtesy of the Royal BC Museum and Archives, Victoria, BC.

made them potentially more appealing to Carr since she felt herself to be something of a social misfit."[93]

Emily Carr attended Victoria High School for just one year, then dropped out and refused to go back.[94] Drawing remained her passion, but Victoria lacked proper facilities for the study of art. She wanted to leave the island, not just to study painting, but also to escape from the hovering presence of her sister's constant Bible study, good works, and church attendance. When an opportunity arose for her to attend the California School of Design in San Francisco, Carr took it, and spent three years at the school, returning home in late 1893. Ambitious to learn more about more modern trends in painting, she resolved to go further afield, to Europe. For the next five years, she taught drawing and painting to Victoria children, in order to save money for a future European trip. In the summer of 1899 Carr left for London and the Westminster School of Art.

A year before her departure for England, Emily Carr was introduced to what later became her life's work, and upon which much of her reputation rests. Carr completed her first notably Indian drawings and watercolours on a spring 1899 visit to Ucluelet,[95] a remote Nootka (Nuu-chah-nulth) village on the west coast of Vancouver Island.[96] The villagers liked her, and they gave her the Nootka name, *Klee Wyck* (Laughing One).[97] The choice of her subject for the watercolour, *Cedar Canim's House, Itedsu*, shows the 28-year-old artist's interest in Indian village scenes. Indian and coastal rain forest themes became the subjects of her greatest art.

Overall, Emily Carr's four and a half years in England proved unhappy ones. After the vastness of British Columbia, she found England confining. Lonely, ill, and homesick, she suffered a mental breakdown that necessitated a stay of over a year in a sanatorium. By late 1904 she was back in Victoria. Offered a teaching job in Vancouver she settled there, where she happily taught for several years.[98] Through an exchange of baskets for old clothes, she met Sophie Frank, a Salish woman from Andy Paull's reserve in North Vancouver, who became a lifelong friend, until Sophie's death in 1939.[99] Carr visited Frank in her community, which a century ago was quite poor. Simon Baker, a future Squamish chief, later recalled, "We lived in shacks with outside toilets. We used coal oil lamps and wood stoves. Most of our clothes were homemade from old clothes given to us by white people."[100] As the reserve was so small, the name of the colourful and prominent Andy Paull must have arisen many times, but as she was not interested in political issues, Carr apparently made no attempt to meet him.

Although Emily Carr frequently sketched Indigenous people in North Vancouver, or in Victoria, she herself dated her conscious commitment

8.4 Emily Carr, *Ada and Louisa outside Cedar Canim's House, Itedsu*, 1899.
Watercolour, 17.9 × 26.5 cm. PDP 2158. Courtesy of the Royal BC Museum and
Archives, Victoria, BC.

to Indian subjects back to 1907, when she and her sister Alice made a
summer trip to Sitka, Alaska.[101] Carr was 36 years old. As they passed
many Indian villages along the coast, their cedar ceremonial poles
touched Carr greatly. In her own words, "By the time I reached home
my mind was made up. I was going to picture totem poles in their own
village settings, as complete a collection of them as I could."[102] The next
summer she travelled to Kwakiutl (Kwakwa̱ka'wakw) villages at Alert
Bay and Campbell River, and she returned the next year as well. Carr
also travelled inland to paint the Indians at Lytton and the mountains
near Hope and Howe Sound north of Vancouver. Carr found her travels
and her project of making a visual record of the poles rewarding. Emily
Carr now had a mission, in the words of biographer Maria Tippett, to
"salvage the dying heritage of the British Columbia Indians."[103] Yet, at
the same time, she realistically knew she needed further art training,

and a year or so in Paris provided exposure to post-impressionism, a style of painting Carr found far more exciting, imaginative, and complex than what she had studied in England.

In 1912, the summer after her return from France, Emily Carr set out on her first major sketching trip, along the coast of Vancouver Island to the Skeena Valley and then to Haida Gwaii. At the time, the 41-year-old artist made this journey, many of the villages, even in the most isolated areas, had been greatly depopulated and some entirely deserted. In summer, many people worked at seasonal jobs in the canneries.[104] Intrepid Emily Carr sought out ceremonial poles in abandoned and overgrown locations that outsiders found difficult to reach. Funding was a major problem, as she had no financial backers, no government position. On occasion, she stayed with missionaries[105] and relied on the assistance of Indian agents and cannery managers.[106] One of her contacts became William Halliday (1866–1957), the Indian agent to the Kwakiutl at Alert Bay and one of the most determined opponents of the potlatch on Vancouver Island.[107]

Beginning in 1912 Emily Carr, now a Paris-trained modern artist,[108] began developing her new Indian sketches into canvases.[109] As the art historian Gerta Moray writes, these paintings showed First Nations villages on a grand scale, "revealing the cultural vigour of which the monumental totem poles were a testimony."[110] Carr's paintings gave "extensive and positive testimony to Native cultural identity."[111] In *Klee Wyck*, her collection of Indian stories, published in 1941, Carr objected to the missionaries' contempt for traditional culture.[112] The schools had a pronounced negative impact on the children and their families, in weakening relationships, and in associating First Nations languages and customs with shame and stigma.[113]

Peter Kelly's family and his wife's relatives resided on Haida Gwaii. William Russ, Kelly's brother-in-law, and his wife, Clara, lived at Skidegate, where they welcomed Emily Carr in 1912. Kelly was not living on Haida Gwaii that summer. William and Clara Russ took the young Victoria artist in their gasoline-powered boat to deserted Haida village sites, fed her local fish, and helped set up her camp.[114]

Clara and Will later appear as "Louisa and Jimmie" in *Klee Wyck*, Carr's delightful book of sketches.[115] In 1928 Carr stayed with the Russes at their comfortable home in Skidegate. She completed portraits of both of them.[116] As Peter Kelly was a close relative, and easily Skidegate's "most prominent citizen,"[117] the Russes must have mentioned him to Carr, and his advocacy for Indigenous Title. In the story "Friends," Carr relates that "Louisa," pseudonym for Clara Russ, once asked her whether or not she should send one of her two sons to a residential school: "If he

8.5 Emily Carr, *Indian House Interior with Totems*, 1912–13. Oil on canvas, 89.6 × 130.6 cm. One of Emily Carr's two large 1912 Kwakiutl (Kwakwaka'wakw) canvases. Emily Carr Trust, VAG 42.3.8. Photo: Ian Lefebvre. Vancouver Art Gallery.

was your boy Em'ly, would you send him away to school?" She replied, "NO."[118] In contrast, at no point does Carr comment on the question of Indigenous Title. She was, indeed, once again, totally apolitical. In her 1954 foreword to Carol Williams Pearson's *Emily Carr as I Knew Her*, Kathleen Coburn, of the English department at Victoria College at the University of Toronto, provided this summary of Emily as introduced in her close friend's memoir. In a sentence, Carr emerges as "a lonely, fiercely gentle woman, fond of children, Indians, animals and all outcasts, proud, hurt, impatient, blunt, amusing, difficult and Klee Wyck, the Laughing One – this is a person we know."[119]

From 1913 to 1927 Emily Carr drew back from her Indian painting, and came close to abandoning it.[120] The response to her April 1913

8.6 Emily Carr, centre, taken at Ts'aa7ahl'Illnagaay/Caatl, Haida Gwaii, in 1912, with her Haida guide Clara Russ, and "chaperone" Edna Leary. William Russ, Clara's husband, took the picture. F-07756. Courtesy of the Royal BC Museum and Archives.

week-long exhibit of her Indigenous work in Vancouver was painful. And she never mentioned that week in her own writings.[121] The exhibition included nearly two hundred paintings, drawings, and sketches, a number of which dated back to 1899. The public, Paula Blanchard writes, did not buy her work. It was fine to see Native art in an exhibition, "but one didn't hang it on one's walls."[122] A subsequent June showing in Carr's recently constructed studio apartment in Victoria resulted in only a few sales. Her attempts to convince the provincial government to acquire the collection as a pictorial record of First Nations villages proved unsuccessful. Unable to live from her painting, Carr became bitter and disillusioned. Her work had apparently done little to change non-Indigenous British Columbians' attitudes to the First Nations population. As Gerta Moray writes, "Her empathy with First Nations cultures struck no answering cords."[123]

Abandoning her career as a full-time artist, Emily Carr now did little painting. She had no salary, no kind patron paying her travel expenses, no one buying art supplies for her. She spent the next fourteen years running a boarding house in Victoria, raising dogs, hooking rugs, and making pottery. In her new life as a landlady, an occupation she 'loathed,"[124] Carr did not have the time or the money to go north.[125] Her reputation for eccentricity grew, as at various times between 1913 and 1927 she filled her household with a bizarre assortment of animals, including her dogs, a monkey, a cage full of chipmunks, several cats, raccoons, and a white rat.[126] This decade and a half of struggle and discouragement constitute Emily Carr's "lost years" as an artist.

At no time in this period, or after, it did Emily Carr lose her friendly attitude towards the First Nations, fellow outsiders like herself. In Victoria she always protested whenever she saw Indigenous people being treated discourteously.[127] Bruce Hutchison (1901–1992), the celebrated BC journalist, who lived most of his life in Victoria, remembered her in his autobiographical memoir, *The Far Side of the Street*, "as a dowdy, dumpy woman with many pet animals, and a monkey riding on her shoulder. The world of art remembers her as Victoria's only true genius and perhaps the only painter of any nation who could understand and paint the Pacific rain forest."[128] The turning point in Emily Carr's professional career began when she was in her mid-50s.

An invitation to join a 1927 exhibition of West Coast Indian art at the Victoria Museum in Ottawa totally changed Emily Carr's life, at age 56. Reinforced by the warm reception and admiration of her work in Toronto by the Canadian group of artists known as the Group of Seven, she returned to painting "Indian" subjects. The anthropologist Marius Barbeau also befriended her. Carr abandoned her tenants in Victoria, and the next year made another trip north, up the Nass and Skeena rivers and once again to Haida Gwaii. Emily Carr's most mature work dates from this time.[129] Full of new confidence, and a sense of purpose, the artist entered the most productive period of her life. Group of Seven member Lawren Harris (1885–1970) became a great influence, so much so that she dedicated her autobiography to him. After Harris told her to look within herself, Carr's vision became bolder.

The year 1927 was a very important one for the First Nations in British Columbia. Although the Allied Indian Tribes of British Columbia had obtained no redress on the "cut-off lands" question, they did obtain, at last, an opportunity to speak about the Indian Title question in Ottawa. The Allied Tribes viewed this as their first stop before their presentation of their case in London before the Judicial Committee of the Privy Council. Peter Kelly and Andy Paull helped draft their petition to be presented to the 1927 Special Joint Committee of the Senate and House of Commons formed to examine BC land claims. They repeated once again that Indigenous Title had not been extinguished. Unknown to the Allied Tribes, however, Duncan Campbell Scott had already pronounced upon the issue during the Special Joint Committee's initial closed hearing. In his lengthy statement, Scott accepted that treaty making was usually a political necessity, but then stated that, in the case of British Columbia, the granting of reserves, and the spending of federal money on Indian health, welfare, and education constituted adequate compensation. No further settlement was necessary.[130] Although both Kelly and Paull spoke eloquently, the legislators rejected the Allied Tribes claim. As during the McKenna-McBride Commission process, the Special Committee members had had their minds already made up before the first Indigenous witnesses even spoke.[131]

While the committee turned down the Allied Tribes petition, it did establish an annual grant of $100,000 for Indians in British Columbia in place of treaty annuities (the so-called BC Special). The Allied Tribes wanted their Indigenous Title recognized.[132] The catastrophic blow to the First Nations of British Columbia had come ten days earlier when royal assent had been given to an amendment to the Indian Act (Section 141) that prohibited Indians from raising funds for land claims, without the approval of the Department of Indian Affairs.[133] The Allied Tribes ceased to exist. In the 1920s, to quote Paul Tennant, "land claims were successively investigated, denied, and outlawed."[134]

No evidence exists that the apolitical Emily Carr directly followed either the "cut-off lands" or Indian Title controversies. As Greta Moray writes, "She was aware that they were experiencing rapid cultural adaptation, were appropriating aspects of white values and technology, and that in this sense they were a 'passing race.'"[135] In the early twentieth century, "expert" opinion endorsed the idea of a "passing race." Pierre Duchaussois, author of *Aux Glaces Polaires*, his 1921 popular survey of Roman Catholic missions in northern Canada, predicted that as a result of epidemics and negligent government policies the decrease in Indigenous population numbers would culminate in their *"extinction définitive."* [136] Ten years later, the highly respected Canadian anthropologist Marius Barbeau wrote, "At present the indications point convincingly to the extinction of the race."[137] In his general text, *The Indians of Canada*, published in 1932, Diamond Jenness concurred. English-speaking Canada's foremost anthropologist in the early twentieth century[138] agreed.[139]

According to federal government statistics, the Indian population reached its lowest point in 1929, when only 22,600 Indians were reported as living in British Columbia.[140] But Barbeau and Jenness overdramatized the situation with their verdict that the Indians had entered into a state of total collapse. The prediction that the First Nations would disappear was just a forecast – and it was wrong. Improved nutrition and hygiene, as well as continued progress in the prevention and treatment of infectious disease, contributed throughout the mid-twentieth century to a gradual increase in the First Nation population, from the 1930s. By 1939 the status Indian population was estimated to be growing at the rate of one per cent per annum.[141] This put greater pressure on reserves across Canada, as they were not meant to provide for an increasing Indian population.

Like all cultures, Indigenous culture was ever changing, and ever evolving. Emily Carr's 1928 oil painting *Skidegate* caught this. It signalled "the continuity of a hybridized Native culture."[142] Old practices combined with new, and this meant the culture survived, not disappeared. Gerta Moray summarizes this well: "The modern houses of the village spread up the slope from the beach onto a hillside already cleared of its ancient forest, while the figure of Raven, the Haida culture hero, creator of the first people and bringer of light to humans, watches over the village."[143]

During Emily Carr's 1927 visit to Ottawa, she enjoyed the Barbeaus' hospitality for two weeks in their cultured home. There were evenings at the Barbeaus when Marius, in Emily's words, "beat a great Indian drum and sang some Indian songs that were very touching and real."[144] Barbeau visited Carr in 1929 in Victoria. During a 1930 trip to Ottawa, Carr returned again to the Barbeaus' as a houseguest.[145] She was most impressed by his extensive fieldwork in northwestern BC.[146] It is unknown if the anthropologist made reference to Peter Kelly to Emily Carr,[147] but in 1927 Barbeau mentioned the Haida in a lecture, entitled "The Native Races of Canada," presented to the Royal Society of Canada. Again, Barbeau advanced his central theme that North American Indian society had collapsed, and their traditional practices were disappearing. He inferred that the survivors were racially mixed: "Nations, thirty thousand strong, as the Haidas of the Queen Charlotte Islands, in two generations, dwindled to a mere remnant of six hundred half-breeds."[148]

What was Marius Barbeau's position on land claims in 1927? As the art historian Leslie Dawn has written, "He had already implied publicly on many occasions that if such claims had once existed, this was no longer the case since all traditional culture had disappeared."[149] The anthropologist strongly valued aspects of Indigenous culture, and recognized the injustices of Europeans towards them, but he did not believe the First Nations or their culture had a future. This influenced Carr, and possibly held her back from activism in championing Indigenous land rights. Political talk barely touched her consciousness.

8.7 Emily Carr, *Skidegate*, 1928. Oil on canvas, 91.7 × 132.2 cm. Gift to the Art Gallery of Ontario from the J.S. McLean Collection, by Canada Packers Inc., 1990. 89/781. Image © Art Gallery of Ontario.

In the summer of 1928 Emily Carr set out for the Skeena and Nass valleys. This time she was more prepared than on earlier trips to live among the Indians. She now chose to sleep in their villages and avoided the mission houses.[150] Her knowledge of anti-Indian sentiments grew. Racial prejudice was even mentioned in the annual reports of the Department of Indian Affairs. The department's report of 1912, for example, states, "When applying for work outside of the reserve he [the Indian] is often refused because white men are as a rule unwilling to work alongside of Indians."[151] In the northwestern portion of BC, in the Skeena Valley, which Carr visited in 1928, relations were atrocious. Diamond Jenness reported in the 1920s that in Hazelton, which had a population of approximately three hundred white inhabitants to perhaps four hundred Indians, "No Indian might walk beside a white man or woman, or sit on the same side in the village church."[152]

Alan Fry, an Indian agent for fifteen years in rural British Columbia in the 1950s and 1960s,[153] observed the consequences of the all-prevalent racism. The First Nations have endured, he wrote in 1994, the "pain of having been belittled, communally and individually, for generations by an insensitive and dominant society. To have it forced upon you, irrespective of any truth, that you are inferior, that your people are inferior, to be reduced to beggary in your own land, to be stripped not only of power but of dignity as well – these are beyond the imagination of those of us who take for granted the accidents of birth which give us a place at the larger table."[154]

Emily Carr made her last sketching trip to the North Coast in August 1930.[155] Poor health made travel increasingly difficult,[156] and Indian subjects ceased to be her major preoccupation. After she left the Indigenous themes, Carr turned to the lush colours of the coastal rain forest, to her own vision of the wilderness.[157] The artist said she was painting "her own vision now, thinking of no one else's approach, trying to express her own reactions."[158] Carr still remained emotionally attached to the Indigenous peoples. Her memories of her visits to Indian country remained strong when she wrote her book of sketches and stories – her well-written tales of her travels along the coast won *Klee Wyck* the Governor General's Award for the best book published in Canada in 1941.

George Clutesi (1905–1988), a young Nookta (Nuu-chah-nulth) artist and later writer, visited Emily Carr several times shortly before her death. Clutesi cherished her memory, as she had helped to give him a sense of confidence in his own goals: "She made it so very simple for me to see how important it was to remain myself, and to not change my style despite what might become." And, "It was largely because of her counseling that [....] I paint the way I feel."[159] With regard to Emily Carr's art and writing on the Pacific Coast Indigenous peoples, Maria Tippett offers this balanced assessment: "Through her paintings and short stories, she created an awareness of First Nations culture among an initially unsympathetic, non-native audience."[160] Emily Carr died in Victoria in 1945 at the age of 74. She willed her paints, brushes, and unused canvases in her studio to her young artist friend George Clutesi.[161]

The Second World War drew a line between two different periods of non-Indigenous perceptions of the First Nations. The Canadian public's attitude towards the First Nations improved, both during and immediately after the war. The impressive Aboriginal participation in the Canadian armed forces, as well as the expansion of the resource frontier in northern areas where the Indigenous peoples still dominated, led to a greater awareness of Indigenous Canada. All of this being said, the

Canadian historian Scott Sheffield notes, "The essential nature of the relationship between Canadians and the First Nations remained intact, the deeply rooted assumption that English Canada's race, society, and way of life were superior to those of the 'Indian.'"[162]

In the midst of the war, the BC journalist Bruce Hutchison's well-composed and engaging book, *Canada: The Unknown Country*, won the Governor General's 1942 Literary Award for Creative Non-Fiction.[163] First published in the United States, this book was written, as the author mentions in his foreword, "to give the stranger a general glimpse of the surface of Canada and something of the substance, the people, the problems, the history, and the future beneath the surface."[164] Reprinted in Canada the following year and several times afterwards, the last occasion being in 2010, the historian Jack Little has called it "perhaps the most popular of the books describing the country in the twentieth century."[165] Yet, in hindsight, its lack of attention to the Indigenous peoples indicates Hutchison's lack of perception of their importance. This blind spot towards the First Nations is a true record of the times. Just one substantial reference to the BC Indigenous peoples appears in *The Unknown Country*, a reference to Hazelton and the surrounding area.[166] The First Nations remained unnoticed by a man who had grown up in BC and had travelled through the Fraser River Valley,[167] the Cariboo, the Chilcotin, the North Thompson country, the Kootenays, the Okanagan, the rain forest of Vancouver Island, and many other regions of his beloved province.[168]

Bruce Hutchison and his wife, Dorothy, particularly liked the Cariboo country, the rolling inland plateau of BC where Ernie Carson, the local MLA and a Cabinet minister, had invited them repeatedly in the 1930s to his huge ranch at Pavilion Mountain. Hutchison's father had arrived during the Cariboo Gold Rush and amassed a ranch of over 5,000 acres.[169] Perfectly legal, all had been handled according to the law of the day. From the 1860s to at least 1910, writes the historian Keith Smith, "There was scarcely a public figure in British Columbia who did not acquire large holdings of agricultural, pastoral, or mineral lands."[170] The impact of the settlers' acquisition of vast tracts of unceded land in the Cariboo became better known with the publication, in 1989, of Joanne Drake-Terry's book, *The Same as Yesterday: The Lillooet Chronicle the Theft of Their Land and Resources*. Drake-Terry notes, "As a consequence Indian people soon found that their chances to hunt, gather food, trap wild animals, graze their cattle and till arable land were being curtailed. One settler in Upper Lillooet territory, Robert Carson, claimed 4,000 acres at Pavilion Mountain in the centre of the Lillooets' favourite hunting area."[171]

In the 1930s and 1940s the First Nations in British Columbia faced many challenges. After the collapse of the Allied Indian Tribes of British Columbia, the challenges posed by the expanding industrial fishery led First Nations fishers in northwestern BC to establish a new political association. The coastal fishing industry was the only economic sector in the province in which Indigenous people gained a good income and had financial independence.[172] Alfred Adams was a commercial Haida fisherman, a graduate of the Anglican residential school at Metlakatla, and an Anglican lay minister.[173] He called the meeting in 1931 that led to the formation of the Native Brotherhood of British Columbia, inspired by the Alaska Native Brotherhood. The organization's core strength came from well-known Protestant families on the north and central coast. "Onward Christian Soldiers" became the new organization's official song. The major executive function of the Brotherhood was bargaining on behalf of its fishing membership.[174] The Native Brotherhood also concerned itself with equality, the advancement of day over residential schools, the franchise, welfare matters, and an end to discrimination, with but very few references to the potlatch.[175] Because of the prohibition of such activity in the Indian Act, as revised in 1927, the Brotherhood avoided the term "aboriginal rights," but silently they remained an objective. Soon the multipurpose organization grew into what became the most influential Indigenous organization in British Columbia.[176] In view of the province's vast geographical, language, cultural, and spiritual differences, this was an enormous accomplishment.[177]

Maisie Campbell-Johnston, later Maisie Armytage-Moore, but best known as Maisie Hurley (1887–1964), in 1944 became the first woman admitted to the Native Brotherhood of British Columbia, as an associate life member. She had grown up in small interior settlements where her father's work as a mining engineer took him. Her response to the First Nations resurgence in the 1940s contrasted greatly with that of Emily Carr half a century earlier. For this non-Indigenous woman, the political struggle became her mission. Following Maisie's birth in Swansea, Wales, in 1887, and their several years in India the family relocated to British Columbia in 1891. At Aspen Grove, a hamlet in the BC interior, near Spences Bridge, Maisie became a popular playmate of local Indigenous children.[178] An adventurous young woman, she loved riding and roping and also breaking in wild horses, bareback.[179]

Her early life proved a continual alteration of good and bad fortune. Shortly after her brief unhappy marriage to the sedentary Reginald Armytage-Moore in 1909, Maisie left him to travel in Washington and Oregon states with Martin Murphy, an Irish immigrant, labourer, part-time boxer, and heavy drinker. Murphy and Maisie had five children.

To quote Eric Jamieson, Maisie's biographer, Murphy was not "every woman's dream, but he was smart, self-taught and well-read, and he represented two of the things that were missing in Maisie's life: risk and adventure."[180] Trying to support a large family on an itinerant labourer's wage eventually took its toll. Maisie returned to Vancouver in 1924, and in the city she drew ever closer to the Indigenous peoples of British Columbia, with her new life's partner, Tom Hurley, a renowned Vancouver criminal lawyer. Maisie joined his law practice as his secretary and law clerk. In the days before Legal Aid, Tom Hurley defended many of his Indigenous clients free of charge.[181]

By chance one day in Vancouver in 1944 Maisie Hurley met her Haida friend Alfred Adams on the street, on his way to see his doctor. Adams knew his cancer was terminal and that he had not much longer to live, in fact, one year later he was gone. Knowing Maisie's great strengths and her love of the Indian, the Haida Elder that day made a request: "I want you to give your life to my people by telling the white people about them." The First Nations, Adams added, needed a strong spokesperson to tell others in print about their work, their grievances, and their desire to educate their children.[182] Maisie accepted the challenge, and in December 1946 she launched the *Native Voice*, a monthly newspaper established first to advocate for Indigenous people, and second, to inform non-Natives about the Indigenous reality. The *Native Voice* became the official organ of the Native Brotherhood of British Columbia. As Maisie later wrote Hugh Dempsey, a young journalist in Edmonton at the time who contributed articles to her paper in the early 1950s, "I have worked with the Indians and then the Native Brotherhood for many years," and seeing the need, "I founded this paper on a shoestring (my own) in 1946 and it is growing in spite of many setbacks – run purely to help the Indian cause."[183] The staff were all Indigenous, with the exception of publisher Maisie Hurley herself, and the advertising manager. The first editor was Tsimshian (Ts'msyen) Jack Benyon, a First World War veteran.[184] The second editor was Coast Salish Ruth Smith, a graduate of the Coqualeetza Residential School, a Vancouver secretary, and the mother of two young children.[185] Within two years, the monthly paper had three thousand subscribers.[186]

In its editorials and news stories the *Native Voice* championed justice for the First Nations. After the Second World War, social security programs were gradually provided to Canadians, but initially, Indian peoples did not receive the same social security benefits as non-Indians. The *Native Voice* fought for the full extension of social security benefits to Indians as well as non-Indians.[187] British Columbia argued that Indians, at least reserve Indians, were a federal responsibility.[188] At all levels, the *Native Voice* reported on the struggle for equality. It noted, for example, in its August 1954 issue, "Discriminatory Signs Removed at Brotherhood Request," that apparently discriminatory signs had been in place for years in the cannery at Namu, a small fishing port on BC's central coast. The signs on the doors of two adjoining women's rest rooms read "NATIVES" only and "WHITES ONLY." "This decision to remove the signs is trivial," the paper commented, "but as a reflection of attitudes of people nowadays, it becomes very important because it shows people as having more of an understanding of each other than was the case in the past."

One of the *Native Voice's* greatest campaigns in 1960 was its protest against the BC government's confiscation of reserve land for a highway at Kitwanga, near Hazelton. In a fiery editorial, the publisher Maisie Hurley wrote, "[Social Credit Minister of Highways P.A. Gaglardi] has trespassed on and bulldozed a piece of land four miles long and 200 feet wide – Crown granted Indian Reserve land of Kitwanga held in trust for the British Columbia non-Treaty Indians by the Federal government."[189] On a non-political note, the paper paid attention to cultural events devoting, for example, its entire July 1961 issue to the Haudenosaunee writer Pauline Johnson, to mark the centenary of her birth.[190]

The *Native Voice* reprinted articles from other newspapers, such as a piece by G.M. Mortimore that had appeared in the *Victoria Daily Colonist*, entitled "Indian Artist Makes Eloquent Plea," in the *Voice's* December 1949 issue.[191] It described how the Indian artist George Clutesi had hitchhiked from Port Alberni to Victoria to address a two-day sitting in the Legislature Building of the Royal Commission on National Development in the Arts, Letters and Sciences, chaired by Vincent Massey (the Massey Commission). Clutesi held the commissioners' concentrated attention with his plea for racial equality, educational changes, and the revival of Indigenous arts. Indians needed to maintain their traditions and their pride in their ancestors' achievements, for "without that feeling we are going to be a lost race for the rest of our lives."[192]

The *Native Voice* reported Native Brotherhood of BC news in detail, particularly from its conventions.[193] It covered important conferences on Indian affairs, such as that at the University of British Columbia in the early spring of 1948.[194] First Nations leaders like Andy Paull, Frank Assu, Guy Williams, and George Clutesi stated their views on education, health, and arts and handicrafts. Clutesi eloquently explained, "Take a small child away from his parents, brothers and sisters and home environment and the shock is too great. Often the initiative is killed, and without initiative a child cannot learn. Education is not just book-learning; it includes the love imparted when the child sits on his

8.8 Maisie Hurley (on the right) at the Salish canoe races in North Vancouver, May 1962. Photo by Stanley Triggs. VPL 85804, Vancouver Public Library.

mother's or father's knee and learns of traditions, history and the difference between right and wrong."[195]

The *Native Voice* reported vicious racism, a reality for Indigenous peoples. Editor Ruth Smith reported a very alarming story in the April 1948 issue. The account entitled "The Stone Wall" reads, "Recently on a steamer going up the coast, three young Indian girls were travelling, quartered in the steerage room below. Terrifying screams kept most of the passengers awake one night and nothing seemed to be done until nearly morning. On inquiry by a passenger, it was found the youngest, 13 years of age, was subjected to rape, and only through the interference of a logger was anything done – *and only by the logger*" (the last five words are printed in bold face).[196] An equally upsetting detail followed. It read, "The deep concern of a young white woman was ridiculed by this remark made by an elder woman: 'I wouldn't worry myself too much if I were you. If she isn't a prostitute now, she soon will be, like the rest of them!'"

For a presence in Central Canada, Maisie Hurley appointed in 1947 the Delaware Indian, Jasper Hill (Big White Owl), to become the paper's eastern editor.[197] Born in 1902 at Moraviantown, near Chatham, Ontario, Hill grew up on the Delaware Indian Reserve until 1920, when his father enfranchised,[198] and the family had to leave the registered membership list. His schooling ended at grade 9 in the public school in Chatham. For many years Jasper Hill wandered across Canada working as woodcutter, farm labourer, factory worker, hunter, and trapper. He travelled with the Wallace Brothers Shows of Canada every summer for fourteen years, which gave him an opportunity to meet Indigenous people all across the country. Throughout he remained proud of his heritage and ancestry. Upon retiring from "Show Business," as he called the circus, Hill worked for the Canadian Red Cross Society in Toronto as the supervisor of shipping and receiving, for more than a quarter of a century.[199] For many years Hill contributed to newspapers and magazines articles and letters about Indians under his pen name of Big White Owl.[200] Maisie Hurley later praised Big White Owl as the *Native Voice*'s "most stalwart pillar."[201] His contributions favoured historical and cultural aspects,[202] but touched upon political questions on occasion. Very active in the Toronto Indigenous community the Delaware became the first president of the Toronto (later the North American) Indian Club of Canada, in 1952.[203]

In the early 1960s Big White Owl strongly opposed the pressure from the Government of Canada to move Indians, often ill-prepared into urban areas: "This nasty business of integrating the North American Indian people into slum communities of the big cities is shameful, unfair and utterly disastrous. It is a plan of extermination by assimilation. It is plain legalized genocide."[204] He continued, "Indian people who migrate to the cities, minus a skilled trade or good education are doomed to slowly rot away on welfare handouts, and drift into the lowest sector of white and Negro peoples, where alcoholism, crime and social disease are rampant."[205] This is one of the first times the word "genocide" appears in print to describe Canada's Indian policy.[206]

The Native Brotherhood of British Columbia and the *Native Voice* scored a great victory when, in 1949, BC extended the provincial vote to status Indians, without requiring them to give up their status. Another advance came that same year when Frank Calder, a Nishga'a graduate of Coqualeetza Residential School, and later the first status Indian in BC to graduate from university,[207] was elected to the provincial legislature, as MLA from Atlin in the province's northwestern region. The *Native Voice* now set its sights on the gaining of the federal franchise without the renouncement of Indian status. To the paper's great joy this was obtained in 1960. Peter Kelly, active in the Native Brotherhood until his death in 1966, made an enormous contribution to the goal of working for the federal franchise and the recognition of First Nations land rights in British Columbia. Guy Williams, also a Coqualeetza graduate, the Brotherhood's president in 1966, and later a member of Canada's Senate,[208] noted immediately after Peter Kelly's death his enormous contribution: "For over fifty years the Reverend Peter R. Kelly laboured for his people and fought for equality, making over thirty trips to Ottawa for Indian rights and claims."[209]

In the early 1960s the old question of Indigenous Title to land in British Columbia again came to the fore, and the issue is well covered in the *Native Voice*. When Tom Hurley became ill, the task of presenting his legal arguments in court fell to Thomas Berger, a young lawyer with whom the Hurleys had worked for a number of years and on several cases.[210] Berger now entered into Indigenous law. From Maisie Hurley, Tom Berger had learned something he had not been taught at law school, namely, the concept of Aboriginal Title and the legitimacy of Indian land rights. Gradually, he had become convinced from both an historical perspective and a legal one that Maisie was right.[211] Shortly after her husband's death, Maisie visited Berger's office, and in her commanding voice she told him, "Now Tommy, *you* will have to defend the Indians." This is exactly what the young lawyer proceeded to do for more than a half century, to become "a lifelong defender of Aboriginal causes."[212]

On 4 April 1964, the *Weekend Magazine*, a Saturday supplement carried in the *Vancouver Sun* and other newspapers across the country, published a full feature article about the founder and publisher of the *Native Voice*. The title of Patrick Nagle's piece reads, "Maisie Says B.C. Still Belongs to the Indians." In three lines Maisie summarized her viewpoint, "All the Indians want is what is theirs. They don't want to assimilate. They are a wonderful people with magnificent traditions of their own."[213] Maisie Hurley died on 3 October 1964, after an incredible life during which she had accomplished so much to bring forward a positive appreciation of the Indigenous peoples of Canada.

Chapter Nine

Alberta Perspectives: Long Lance, John Laurie, Hugh Dempsey, and Harold Cardinal

In the 1920s Chief Buffalo Child Long Lance (1890–1932) presented a welcome positive image of the First Nations in Western Canada. After service overseas in England and France, the Canadian army veteran took his discharge and went to work for the *Calgary Herald*. After three years at the *Herald*, he left the Prairie city in search of opportunities to write about the Indigenous peoples in British Columbia, and then Saskatchewan and Manitoba. He explained the urgency of his task in a piece that appeared in the *Winnipeg Tribune* of 10 February 1923, "While historical societies are daily springing into existence all over the west in a concerted endeavor to preserve the early history of this broad country before all of the old-timers have passed away, the aboriginal history of the Canadian west is silently passing into oblivion, unnoticed by the hurrying crowds who are yet but pioneers in this territory."

The handsome, well-dressed stranger called at the offices of the *Vancouver Sun* in late April 1922.[1] The newspaper took him on and in introducing him to its readership provided a short biographical summary of this extraordinary visitor. Included among the impressive details listed on his resume[2] was a reference to his three years at the famous Carlisle Indian School in Pennsylvania, established to bring Native Americans from across the United States into the mainstream society. Jim Thorpe, one of the greatest all-round athletes in the early twentieth century, and a 1912 Olympic Gold Medalist, had also attended Carlisle Indian School. In 1879 Captain Richard Henry Pratt had established the flagship Indian boarding school gifting it with its school motto: "To civilize the Indian, get him into civilization. To keep him civilized, let him stay."[3] Pratt left Carlisle in 1904, but the school's "civilization" mission lived on. Long Lance epitomized what the school's founder had worked so hard to achieve and became a well-groomed, well-spoken

North American Indian, totally at ease and fully integrated into the dominant society.

Long Lance's record in the First World War made a lasting impression in Vancouver. According to the *Sun* of 7 May 1922, the Canadian Army veteran had won the Croix de Guerre.[4] A quarter of a century later, another Vancouver newspaper, Maisie Hurley's *Native Voice*, recalled in a 1947 editorial, "When war broke out, Long Lance went overseas as a private in the Canadian infantry and retired as a captain after three years' service during which he was wounded at Vimy Ridge and Lens."[5]

Every Sunday in the late spring and summer, Long Lance wrote a weekly article for the *Vancouver Sun* on Indigenous British Columbia. The final such contribution appeared on 27 August 1922, entitled "Chief Long Lance Takes His Readers across Broad Plains." He ended his series with a farewell to the Pacific Coast: "With the assurances that my previous articles on the Indians of British Columbia have been the cause of a measure of enlightenment and pleasure to a large group of *Sun* readers, I shall now take them on a brief trip through my own country, the Plains. And in doing so, I shall begin with my fellow tribesmen the Blood Indians of Alberta." The Blood (Kainai), with the Blackfoot (Siksika), and the Peigan (Piikuni), were the three Blackfoot-speaking nations in the Blackfoot Confederacy. Then Long Lance returned to the Plains.

In the early winter Long Lance published the first of his Plains First Nations stories in the Regina *Leader*, under the title "Red Men of the West – Yesterday and Today." He indicated his theme of cultural persistence in the second article, which appeared on 16 December. The old Indian did not fear change, but worried that his son might be "made into a 'white man,' and that he might be lost to his home and people." After his *Leader* series ended, Long Lance secured a new assignment, writing feature articles for the *Winnipeg Tribune* on the Indians of Manitoba. The *Tribune* liked his approach, and prefaced his article of 3 March 1923 with "Chief Buffalo Child Long Lance emphasizes the important part Red Men have played in building up our present civilization."

At a Canadian Authors Association event in mid-January 1923, in Winnipeg, Long Lance met a clergyman who knew his home community well, a "former missionary of Blood reserve."[6] Reverend John Maclean lived in the city at that time and worked as the librarian at the Methodists' Wesley College (now the University of Winnipeg).[7] Long Lance mentioned that he belonged to the "Blood tribe of Indians," but that "his mother was of the Cherokee tribe."[8] Casually, he introduced this interesting detail about his mother belonging to the Cherokee Nation to explain his lack of fluency in Blackfoot.

MacLean's Magazine, February 1, 1929

The Last Stand of Almighty Voice

A thrilling description of one of the most, poignantly dramatic episodes in the history of the Canadian Northwest

By CHIEF BUFFALO CHILD LONG LANCE

the Indian of that day, Almighty Voice had become famed throughout the region as a runner, a hunter, and a man of indomitable courage and independence. Altogether, he was a dauntless, resourceful, physically powerful, and enduring young warrior, who could well justify the alarm which his reappearance had now aroused throughout the white settlements of that vast open territory.

It was in the afternoon when Corporal Dickson told Almighty Voice that "he was going to be hanged." That night in the little mounted-police guard-house, which still stands at Duck Lake, Saskatchewan, the mounted police chained Almighty Voice to a heavy iron ball and left him to roll up in his Indian blanket and go to sleep on the floor of the guardroom. Corporal Dickson was on duty to guard him until midnight; then he was to be relieved by another "mountie" who was sleeping upstairs.

Shortly before eleven that night Corporal Dickson decided that he wanted to go off duty a little early, so he got up from the dimly-lighted table at which he was sitting in the guardroom and took the butt of his rifle and banged the ceiling with it to awake his relief man.

"Come on down!" he shouted up. "I want to go a little early to-night. Want to get over to Mac's before he closes."

"All right," answered the other Mountie. But instead

to the table. Stopping just behind the sleeping Mountie, he reached over his shoulders and picked up the bunch of keys lying beside his hands, and stooped forward and unlocked the heavy manacle around his ankle. With short, quick steps he made for the door.

Once outside of that door, he knew that he was safe; for no one, white or red, had ever beaten him in a foot-race.

He sprang across the back yard of the guard-house, and with a mighty leap cleared the high fence without touching it. He sped like a doe toward the Saskatchewan River. Six miles of incredible running brought him to the western bank of this broad, swift-flowing stream. Without stopping to get his breath, he broke off several heavy saplings and lashed them into a three-cornered raft. He stripped and threw his blanket and clothing on to this raft, and pushing it ahead of him, he swam a half-mile to the other side of the river. He resumed his long, fourteen-mile run, and before it was yet daybreak he arrived panting and sweating at the door of his mother's lodge.

His mother, Spotted Calf, is also my adopted mother, and that is why I am able to record the inside story of this famous man-hunt, which to-day is so simply dealt with in history and is all books on the Northwest Mounted Police. Spotted Calf and her husband

Chief Buffalo Child Long Lance, author of this article, and adopted son of Spotted Calf, the mother of Almighty Voice.

Editor's note: This thrilling description of the last stand of Almighty Voice is a chapter from Chief Long Lance's own life story. As the narrative opens Long Lance's tribe

9.1 The title page of Long Lance's article, "The Last Stand of Almighty Voice," *MacLean's* magazine, 1 Feb. 1929.

After several years as a full-time writer in Western Canada, Chief Buffalo Child Long Lance had developed an engaging popular style. Major North American newspapers and magazines in the mid-1920s purchased his articles for their amazing human interest. With his 1924 account of the "last stand" of the Plains Cree Almighty Voice (or Kitchi-manito-waya, c. 1875–1897) in central Saskatchewan, he hit a "home run." Arrested for butchering a government steer, as Long Lance recounts the story, Almighty Voice escaped the tiny prison in Duck Lake, but killed a North-West Mounted Police officer in pursuit. Immediately, he became the most sought-after man in the Canadian North West, successfully evading police for nearly two years, until surrounded in 1897 on a bluff near his reserve. Almighty Voice and two of his relatives dug themselves in, awaiting the assault. For three days, the three Cree men held off a posse of a hundred police and volunteers, killing three of their attackers. At the end of the third day, the Canadians bombarded the bluff with heavy gunfire, killing all three Indigenous defenders. The last evening Almighty Voice's mother dramatically stood on a hill nearby singing her son's death song.

Long Lance sold his imaginative story, full of embellishments, to the *Winnipeg Tribune*, the Montreal *Family Herald*, and *MacLean's* magazine in Toronto.[9] The travelling journalist continued to search out important stories, a number of them about injustices committed against the First Nations. He discovered in his interviews that Canada's federal government had not always handled Indian issues in the generous spirit that Canadians assumed it had. In a 3 March 1923 article in the *Winnipeg Tribune*, he reviewed the 1907 land sale at St Peter's, at Selkirk, north of Winnipeg. "As a result of a series of cloudy transactions," and "considerable crooked work," the First Nations "sold" their good agricultural lands at St Peters and moved to their present location, an isolated spot with inferior soil at Fisher River northwest of Winnipeg: "Here they live today, harboring considerable discontent over the manner in which they were treated in this deal."[10]

The Cree of Beardy's Reserve near Duck Lake, Saskatchewan, heard Long Lance was in the area, and contacted him in late May 1923. White Owl, "a fine old warrior of 70 winters" approached the journalist, saying, "When you visited this Reserve last year we were away, hunting in the north. We heard yesterday that you were on One Arrow's Reserve, visiting the camp of Almighty Voice's father. We know the work you are doing – writing the history of the Indians. So we invited you here today to tell you what we did in the Rebellion, and to have you join us in our annual feast."[11] They had a major grievance. The Beardy's First Nation claimed compensation for their treaty annuities illegally withheld for three years after the 1885 Resistance. It would take them over eighty more years to obtain the annuities owed.[12]

Long Lance wrote a number of Alberta Indian stories in the mid-1920s. One of the best accounts described his two weeks in 1923 with the Stoney Nakoda. At the Calgary Stampede in early July that year, the Stoney invited him to their Sun Dance at Morley on 20 July, to be followed by their annual stampede the next day. At its conclusion the visiting journalist travelled with the Stoney from Morley to Banff Indian Days, 25–6 July,[13] a journey of 65 kilometres, with a stop to camp at Canmore, the halfway point.[14] It was a treat for the Stoney Nakoda to enter the national park, in which they were forbidden to hunt. They could camp in the Banff Park during Indian Days, but just for their duration, two days.[15] In the words of an annual participant, Walking Buffalo (or George McLean), "When we go to Banff every summer, it is like a medicine for us. Our chests bulge out to the air of the mountains. When we get back to the reserve, we feel better."[16]

Among the Stoney Nakoda, Long Lance conversed at length with Calf Child, also known as White Head, whose English name was Hector Crawler.[17] The noted spiritual leader and healer often attended services at the Morley Methodist Mission Church, and as he explained to Long Lance, "That is the way we should all work in religion – one religion help the other. Every Sunday I go to church to show my people how to do it; and then when I come home from church I come to this chair (his little throne) and I pray again in my own way."[18] Already, Long Lance knew from Reverend John Maclean's book, *Canadian Savage Folk: The Native Tribes of Canada*,[19] published in 1896, that many Stoney found comfort in Christianity. As Maclean wrote, "The hymns taught the people in those early years are still remembered, but the tunes have undergone a change, a peculiar Indian turn having been given to them, so that they have become essentially Indian tunes, founded upon their English predecessors."[20] Chief Hector personally respected Christianity, but he kept to his ancient faith. His son-in-law, Walking Buffalo, had far greater exposure to "whites" than did most Stoney.

Walking Buffalo attended the McDougall Orphanage in the mid-1880s,[21] and then the Methodist Indian Residential School at Red Deer to the north. Later, he worked for a short period in Calgary as a blacksmith and a police scout.[22] His equivalent of a grade 4 schooling[23] made him one of best English-speakers in the community. He had received his English name, George McLean, following a visit in early 1884 to the McDougall Orphanage by Reverend John Maclean. The little Indian boy was brought into the schoolroom to join the dozen or so boys and girls, "clean, neatly dressed, and happy." Over the next two hours, "he passed through all the initiation ceremonies of hair-cutting, washing, and donning a suit of clothes."[24] The young boy received his clothes for school from church parcels from Central Canada, but his English last name came from the minister.[25] Like Hector Crawler, his father-in-law, Walking Buffalo successfully combined both faiths, for him Christian values strengthened his Indigenous spirituality. When he married Flora, Chief Hector's daughter, he followed both Methodist and Stoney marriage customs. The young man negotiated with his future father-in-law, paid the agreed number of horses, then escorted Flora to the reserve church to have the Methodist minister pronounce them man and wife.[26]

From his visits to a number of Plains Indian communities, as well as from his extensive reading, Long Lance gained enough information to convey "authenticity" to non-Indigenous readers. His writings, particularly his 1928 autobiography, entitled *Long Lance*, favourably impressed feature writer Wilfrid Eggleston (1901–1986) who interviewed him for the *Toronto Star Weekly* in the spring of 1929.[27] After six years in Western Canada, Long Lance had moved to New York City in late 1927 where his autobiography appeared the following year. Although the journalist initially submitted his manuscript as children's fiction, his New York publisher suggested that to keep book sales and circulation mounting, the volume should be advertised as his own life story.[28] Anxious to see his book have the greatest impact possible, Long Lance agreed. In 1928 the Cosmopolitan Book Corporation published *Long Lance*, a study of the last days of the buffalo and the era of intense Plains Indian warfare. Critics loved his saga of his Blackfoot people. Paul Radin, a well-known American anthropologist, endorsed the book in the New York *Herald Tribune* of 14 October 1928 as "authentic" and an "unusually faithful account of childhood and early manhood."[29] In its review, Britain's *New Statesman* wrote, "This book rings true; no outsider could explain so clearly how the Indians felt."[30]

Long Lance's literary success led to an invitation in 1929 to take a leading role in *The Silent Enemy*, a film about Indians in northern Canada before the arrival of the Europeans. Buffalo Child Long Lance played a brave northern hunter who saved his people from "the silent enemy": starvation! On Long Lance's return from the filming location in Temagami, Ontario, Eggleston interviewed him in his Toronto hotel room. The *Toronto Star Weekly* writer himself came from Alberta. In the mid-1910s the Egglestons homesteaded near the hamlet of Orion, just west of Manyberries, in the southeastern corner of Alberta near the Montana border, 80 kilometres south of Medicine Hat. Just across the US border on the southern horizon rose the Sweetgrass Hills of Montana. Initially, the rains fell annually on the short-grass prairie and the Egglestons homesteaded on. Then came the drought. The Egglestons had settled in one of the most arid parts of the Canadian Prairies. A decade trying to farm in this dry and unforgiving land eventually defeated his parents. Eggleston left Orion as a young man, worked hard in banks in Saskatchewan and Alberta to save money to pay for his higher education, and eventually, in 1928, obtained his B.A. from Queen's University. He had a most successful career as a writer in Ontario, and after the Second World War founded Carleton University's School of Journalism in Ottawa.[31]

In retirement Wilfrid Eggleston wrote a memoir of Canadian writers he had known, entitled *Literary Friends*. In his reference to Long Lance, he recalled how impressed, and at the same time, puzzled he was by his masterly English style, "It was difficult enough for a boy raised in an English home and attending an English school to acquire such skills – but an Indian boy on the range speaking his own native tongue and never making contact with English language and literature? Amazing!"[32] Long Lance had mentioned to Eggleston that he had been born somewhere near the Alberta-Montana border, as the *Toronto Star Weekly* writer phrased it, a "Blood Indian born on the border country around Alberta and raised in the tribe."[33] But something seemed to be, well, not quite right.

Non-Indigenous North Americans knew little about the First Nations, which offered the self-declared "Blood/Cherokee" considerable personal privacy. Long Lance also protected himself from personal investigation by providing few details about his boyhood. Just to play it safe, he had dedicated *Long Lance*, "to a friend of the Indian: Hon. Duncan Campbell Scott, Deputy Superintendent-General of Indian Affairs." Warm words they were, intended no doubt to deter the master controller of the Department of Indian Affairs from directing his staff to make a thorough inquiry into Chief Buffalo Child's Indian background.

While non-Indigenous North Americans might know little about North American Indians, Plains Indians knew who they were. To the Blackfoot and Blood Indians, Long Lance talked and behaved like a "white man." He did not know how to dress, sing, or dance, like a traditional Plains Indian. Chauncey Yellow Robe, one of the Native Americans involved in the filming of *The Silent Enemy* raised his suspicions about Long Lance's true identity to the film's producers. After Long Lance's death in Los Angeles in early 1932, most likely a suicide, the story of his true origins in the southern United States came to light.

Chief Buffalo Child Long Lance was neither Blackfoot nor Blood Indian from the Plains of Montana and Alberta, but rather a man of mixed heritage: European, Native, and African American. He was born Sylvester Clark Long, and he was raised in the factory town of Winston-Salem, North Carolina, where the state classified his family as "colored." As he looked "Indian," he had learned some Cherokee, and as he had obtained several endorsements that he was Indian, he gained entrance to Carlisle Indian School, where he changed his last name, from "Long" to "Long Lance." Upon his enlistment in the Canadian army in 1916, he continued to self-identify as an Indian. After his 1922 adoption by the Bloods as an honorary chief, "Buffalo Child," from then on he became "Chief Buffalo Child Long Lance." Cynics assert that most autobiographies contain a fair portion of fiction, but Long Lance's was unique in that, in his case, his life story was fiction from beginning to end. The Canadian novelist Katherine Govier included Long Lance in her recent Alberta novel, *The Three Sisters Bar & Hotel*. In admiration, she writes, "Long Lance could hardly be improved upon; he was a self-created work of fiction."[34]

His invented Plains Indian identity notwithstanding, Chief Buffalo Child Long Lance made a positive contribution to non-Indigenous Canadians' perceptions of the First Nations of Canada. As the Alberta historian and museum curator Hugh A. Dempsey has noted, he conducted "valuable field work at a time when few ethnologists, and even fewer journalists, were concerned about the history of the Indian."[35] In the twentieth century, Long Lance, Hugh Dempsey himself, and a third individual, Calgary high school teacher John Laurie, all helped to make Indigenous history better known to non-Indigenous Canadians, and especially Albertans.

By his own account, John Laurie (1899–1959), a schoolteacher originally from Ontario, first visited the Stoney Nakoda Reserve on 30 June 1926. While out riding west of Jumping Pound Creek, near the Morley Station, his saddle horse cast a shoe and urgently he needed a blacksmith. Several inquiries led him to Dan Wildman, official interpreter, stockman, and reserve blacksmith. Wildman had been a good student at the McDougall Orphanage School, years ago, before it closed.[36] He had survived the regimentation, strict discipline, and strange food. He had learned English, and at the same time, kept his first language. Wildman shoed the horse, and invited Laurie to stay overnight. On that occasion, John Laurie also met Jacob Swampy and George McLean (Walking Buffalo).[37]

John Laurie heard the well-known story on the reserve of how Walking Buffalo, and others like Dan Wildman, had won concessions from Calgary Power over land encroachments just a decade earlier. He learned how tenacious the Stoney could be when fighting for their treaty rights. With its population increasing tenfold, from forty-four hundred in 1901 to nearly forty-four thousand in 1911,[38] neighbouring Calgary needed a major power supply. The Stoney reached their first waterpower agreement with Calgary Power just before the outbreak of the First World War. After they opened their hydroelectric generating facilities on the reserve at Horseshoe Falls, the company then proposed a larger second dam and power station at neighbouring Kananaskis Falls. Without any prior notification, Calgary Power began construction work on the second reservoir before having secured a settlement, a clear trespass on the property of the Stoney Nakoda. The Stoney immediately threatened an armed attack on Calgary Power's Kananaskis Falls development, if the company failed to provide what they considered adequate compensation. Walking Buffalo, Dan Wildman, and Jonas Benjamin took their case to Ottawa in early 1914,[39] and won. The Stoney obtained their price, $16,500 (or $25 per person) and a yearly rental of $1,500 for the water rights.[40]

9.2 Canadian National Railways poster: "It's Mine! Canada – The Right Land for the Right Man." Probably 1920s. The settlers' view of the Canadian Plains. Glenbow Poster-18. Courtesy of Glenbow Archives.

In 1927 John Laurie returned to Morley to help with the construction of the historic cairn in honour of the missionaries George and John McDougall (see chapter two), which was to be placed in front of the old McDougall Church. The Calgary high school teacher had been living in Alberta at this point for about six years. On this visit, Laurie first met Reverend E.J. Staley,[41] who had become the United Church minister to the Stoney the previous year and who went on to serve at Morley for the next twenty-six years.[42] Staley and Laurie became good friends.

John Laurie fully explained his personal background to Reverend Staley, just as he did to all those he met in Calgary. He stated that he received his early education in Britain. His official personnel file at the Calgary Board of Education contains the "Statutory Declaration" with the key details. Completed on 1 April 1933, it states, "I was born on the 23rd day of October, 1899, at London, England." His "Teacher's Permanent Record" confirms he received his elementary education and some of his high school in Great Britain.[43] When he received an honorary doctorate from the University of Alberta in 1956, Dr H.T. Coutts included additional details apparently obtained from Laurie himself. The dean of Education reported: "Born in Scotland in 1899 John Laurie spent his early childhood in Ontario. After ten years of basic education in England, he returned Ontario and graduated from the Galt Collegiate in 1916."[44] Shortly before his death, in 1959, John Laurie also talked of his English background in the short manuscript autobiography he dictated to Marjorie Bond, a former student. He mentioned that he had spent eight years in England as a young boy with his wealthy grandmother at her home near Oxford where he was "subjected to a series of exasperated governors and tutors."[45]

Fortunately, in the mid-1980s, I was able to contact Marion Laurie Corman, John Laurie's sister, at her home in Ontario.[46] She explained that John's story of his British birth and years of residence in England were fictional and, in fact, her brother had received all of his education in Ontario. Also, the claim, which he advanced in the 1940s and 1950s, that he had some Indian ancestry was fictional.[47] Laurie Meijer Drees, the historian of the Indian Association of Alberta writes, "John Laurie plainly wanted others to believe that he was directly connected to Indian peoples, perhaps in order to explain his interest in Indian issues to bolster his credibility as an expert on Indian affairs."[48]

To follow both the documentary record and his sister's account, John Lee Laurie was born in Blenheim Township in Oxford County, Ontario, on 23 October 1899.[49] The family farm was located only a few kilometres from Ayr, a small Scottish community west of Galt (now Cambridge). John helped at home doing all the farm chores with his father.[50] He was a typical farm boy, with what appears from his later autobiographical musings, a very strong imagination. John really grew up as an only child as his only sibling Marion was nine years younger. As a boy, he loved horses and enjoyed reading. Years later he recounted playing with children from the Six Nations of the Grand River near Brantford, but in reality, Marion points out, this community is miles away and the information false.[51] In his boyhood, John Laurie, like Archie Belaney, in Hastings, England (the future Grey Owl), identified closely with North American Indians, without having met any.

John Laurie's family fully supported his education, first at the neighbouring one-room rural school, then the Ayr Continuation School, and then the Collegiate Institute in Galt.[52] He attended Trinity College at the University of Toronto, where he studied English and history and languages. A century ago Trinity College had the reputation of holding particularly close to its British heritage. Its founder, Anglican Bishop John Stachan, established the college in 1852 to be "a place of sound learning and religious education in accordance with the principles and usages of the Church of England in Canada."[53] Trinity's atmosphere no doubt served to put an extra gloss on Laurie's desire to connect his boyhood to England. A college friend recalls him as "rather reserved," but nevertheless "an extremely pleasant companion and everyone in our year liked him," with interests more scholarly than athletic.[54] Laurie spent several months in 1918 as a cadet pilot in the Royal Air Force (the Royal Canadian Air Force would only be established after the Great War). He never served overseas. His certificate of service contains a full physical description: "Height: 5'5"; Colour of hair: light brown; Eyes: blue; Complexion: fair."[55]

After his demobilization in January 1919, John Laurie returned to complete his second year at Trinity. The college was small, only about 150 students (roughly 90 male, and 60 female), and it was just preparing to move from its Queen Street West campus to the University of Toronto's main campus.[56] Financial reasons perhaps explain why Laurie left the college to teach school in Western Canada the following year, first in a small town in southwestern Manitoba and then in two small hamlets between Rocky Mountain House and Red Deer in central Alberta. By correspondence he finished his final year, obtaining his B.A. degree in 1923. John Laurie then taught for three years at Western Canada College, a private school for boys in Calgary modelled on the traditions of Upper Canada College in Toronto and English public schools.[57] He taught Latin, history, and English, until 1927, when the college closed because of constant financial troubles, climaxed by the embezzlement of the school's operating funds by the college's secretary-treasurer.[58] Momentarily without a job, Laurie was fortunately able to obtain a teaching position at Crescent Heights High School, where he taught English and drama for the next thirty years until his retirement in 1956. Fellow teacher Douglas Harkness remembered him as well read and a "good conversationalist." At Crescent Heights, John Laurie helped as staff adviser for the school yearbook, and produced the annual school play.[59] His best friend at the school, the politically minded Aylmer Liesmer, who taught geography and mathematics, introduced him to the Co-operative Commonwealth Federation,[60] the new progressive political party that worked for social justice and the protection of civil liberties.

A 1939 invitation to a music festival at Morley from Reverend Staley totally redirected John Laurie's life. The United Church minister knew that the Calgary schoolteacher loved music and asked him to adjudicate at a school concert, where Laurie heard Ed Hunter, a 15-year-old Stoney, play a violin solo. Immediately recognizing his talent, Laurie, at his own expense, arranged for Hunter to take lessons with a Calgary music teacher. Later, the English teacher obtained permission for the young Stoney to attend Crescent Heights High School. Ed Hunter became the first Stoney ever to attend a city high school, and he later attended the Southern Alberta Institute of Technology,[61] boarding at John Laurie's home. Other First Nations students followed, including Allan[62] and Gerald Tailfeathers[63] of the Bloods, and Gordon Crowchild of the Tsuu T'ina (Sarcee). Bill McLean, Walking Buffalo's son, stayed at John Laurie's for two years. In 1939–40 Bill went to Crescent Heights High School, and the following year to the Southern Alberta Institute of Technology.[64] The men lived in Laurie's basement. He made all the meals, and paid for the groceries out of his own salary.[65]

Ed Hunter's parents regularly welcomed the Calgary high school teacher to their home. Because of Laurie's kindness, the Hunters rejoiced that their son Ed could escape the Morley residential school, which Chief Enos had once described as "jail more or less" where the children "only received half a day's education."[66] In 1940 Chief Enos Hunter and his wife, Margaret, adopted the Calgary teacher as their own son with the name of "White Cloud."[67] Chief John Snow remembered John Laurie's visits to the Hunters and to the reserve: "He used to eat bannock, lard, and dried meat, and drink tea with us in our humble cabins. That was the best we could offer him at the time. There was no indoor plumbing or central heating in our homes, but he was always welcome and happy to come."[68] In winter, Laurie accompanied the Hunter family with their team of horses and sleigh into the forest to cut firewood. A farmboy himself, he was not afraid of hard physical work. Eager to learn, John Laurie mastered enough Stoney to follow conversations.[69] Respecting their dual religious heritage, he joined the Hunter family at the United

Church Sunday services at the Morley Church on the Morley townsite[70] and attended with them the annual Sundance, the Stoney sacred religious ceremony.[71]

In view of John Laurie's close contact with the Stoney, the Indian Association of Alberta in 1944 invited him to become its secretary. The association's foundations dated back to Fred Loft's League of Indians of Canada. Stan Cuthand has written of the league, "As such, it was the first expression of political unity by the Indian people of Western Canada, who began the fight for better services and for a better future."[72] The league's early work in Western Canada contributed to the creation of both the Indian Association of Alberta in 1939 and the Federation of Saskatchewan Indians in 1944. On the positive side, the fact that residential schooling had made English a common second language for the young helped make possible the formation of a modern Indigenous political organization in Alberta. The automobile also eventually opened up many rural Indian communities to political organization.

John Laurie thought the Indian Association of Alberta could help the First Nations integrate into non-Indian society, his ultimate goal for them.[73] In an article in the Crescent Heights student newspaper, *The Crescent Clipper*, he noted, "Indians wish to have their reserves for many years to come; they like to speak their own languages and keep up their own customs."[74] All this being said, the high school teacher believed assimilation remained the best goal.[75] Laurie ends his manuscript history of the IAA with: "Actually the Indian at present represents about one per cent of the population of the country; therefore, he must be prepared to accept in full the mode of life of the remaining ninety-nine percent."[76] In a 1950 article in the *Canadian Cattlemen*, John Laurie best summarizes his integrationist outlook: "What the Indian needs is equal education and vocational opportunities for a few generations and a slow development of responsibility within the reserves with all present rights guaranteed for ever – as they were promised at the first Treaty – until the average Indian owns his own farm machinery, buys and sells his own grain and cattle and learns to plan the future."[77]

Prepared to fight injustice, the new secretary of the Indian Association of Alberta wanted to learn as much as possible about Indian living conditions throughout the province. Every weekend and all summer, Laurie held meetings with First Nations leaders from Lesser Slave Lake in the north to those on the Blackfoot Confederacy reserves in the south. He wrote extensively on Indian subjects for Western Canadian newspapers and magazines.[78] As a bachelor now entering his early forties, with no family in the province, assisting the Indian Association became the central focus of his life. Years later Gordon Crowchild recalled that the

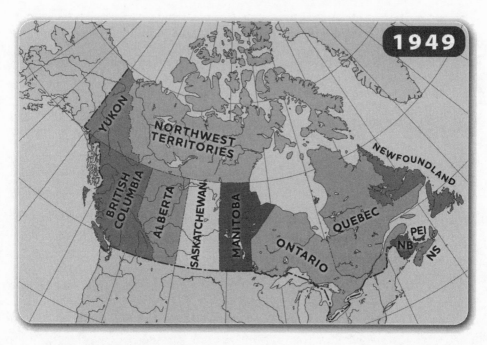

Map 9.1 Canada in 1949.

chain-smoking Laurie often worked well into the night in his main floor room, typing up association correspondence.[79]

In March 1943 the federal government, in the midst of the Second World War, established the House of Commons Special Committee on Reconstruction and Re-establishment to look into the prospective economic, social, and political conditions in post-war Canadian society. The advent of the welfare state in the 1940s, marked by the introduction of unemployment insurance in 1940, followed by the family allowance five years later, necessitated an assessment of existing policies and programs. John Laurie knew about the increase in the population of status Indians that was occurring at the same time that living conditions on the reserves were deteriorating. At the request of the Indian Association of Alberta, he sent the Reconstruction and Re-establishment Committee a strong brief in 1944, calling for improved educational facilities, enhanced vocational training, and greater access for Indians who lives on reserves to health and welfare services as well as social security benefits. Treaty rights must be respected.[80] At the conclusion of its hearings, the Special Committee advised a thorough review of the Indian Act and called for a complete parliamentary inquiry into Indian administration in Canada.[81]

Alberta Indian Tribes Will Demand New Deal

Revision of Educational System, No Alienation of Treaty Rights and Improvements at Morley Requested by Conference

The Alberta council of Indian tribes. . . Left to right, back row, Chief John Crane, Sam Minde, Peter Burnstick, John Laurie, Dan Wildman, J. F. Dion. Front row, left to right, Chief Enos Hunter, John Rabbitt, Alberta Lightning, John Calihoo, Malcolm Norris, Chief Reuben Bull.

9.3 "Alberta Indian Tribes Will Demand New Deal," *Calgary Herald*, 3 July 1945. *Left to right, back row*: Chief John Crane, Sam Minde, Peter Burnstick, John Laurie, Dan Wildman, J.F. Dion. *Left to right, front row*: Chief Enos Hunter, John Rabbit, Albert Lightning, John Calihoo, Malcolm Norris, Chief Rueben Bull. Kathleen Coburn saved the article, by Fred Kennedy, in her file, with other Indian clippings. Kathleen Coburn Fonds, Box 061 (04), Victoria University Archives in the University of Toronto.

John Laurie served on the executive of the Indian Association of Alberta for almost twelve years,[82] helping to draw up petitions and the annual IAA memorials, and travelling to Ottawa on Indian business at his own expense five times (1944, 1946, 1947, 1951, and 1953). He did not try to run the meetings, but just stayed at his table and took the notes. The IAA memorials dispatched to the federal government helped Treaty Indians obtain old age pensions, family allowances, and improved health care. The Stoney Nakoda also received additional lands at Morley, and small reserves at Eden Valley to the south and on the Kootenay Plains (Bighorn) near Nordegg to the north.[83]

John Laurie, the high school teacher, learned a great deal from the First Nations. As he told a reporter in February 1948, "I am pleased to stay in their camps and in their homes and I receive them in mine. I like to travel with them, attend their sundances and powwows. In addition to Indian lore, they have taught me tolerance, patience and persistence."[84] Constantly, he encouraged members of the Indian Association of Alberta to seek reform within existing governmental channels.[85] Through his involvement with the Co-operative Commonwealth Federation, Laurie learned about the political process. He called on the assistance of fellow teacher Douglas Harkness, who was elected to Parliament after the war, and became a prominent member of the federal Conservative Party. In his maiden speech to the House of Commons in 1945, Colonel Harkness moved that "the government take steps necessary to include under the Old Age Pensions Act all Indians who might be eligible."[86] As a CCF member of the Alberta Legislature from 1944 to 1952, Laurie's good friend Aylmer Liesmer helped with provincial contacts.[87]

Hugh Dempsey (b. 1929) succeeded John Laurie as secretary of the Indian Association of Alberta and served in that position from Laurie's death to 1965.[88] In 1986 Dempsey wrote, "There can be no question that the association would have failed had it not been for Laurie."[89] Those contacted by John Laurie sent letters of support for the Indian Association to the Indian Affairs Branch of the Department of Mines and Forests in Ottawa. Groups who sent such letters of support included the Optimist Club of Calgary, the University Women's Club of Calgary, the Canadian Authors Association, and the Calgary Council of Home and School Associations.[90] John Laurie's strong organizational skills proved invaluable, and to quote Hugh Dempsey again, "Laurie's genius and persistence turned a well-meaning group of Indians into a viable political force."[91]

Ruth Gorman (1914–2002) proved a great asset to the Indian Association of Alberta after John Laurie convinced her to serve as the

9.4 John Laurie shown with Chief Frank Cardinal and his wife, Agnes (Cunningham) Cardinal, Driftpile, Alberta, 1951, parents of Harold Cardinal, future Alberta First Nations leader, then six years old. Frank Cardinal appears in his chief's coat furnished by the government. In a *Toronto Star* article, "Ottawa Supplies Clothing to Heads of Indian Tribes," 3 Mar. 1930, writer Wilfrid Eggleston explains the coats were made up "by the inmates of the Kingston penitentiary." NA-4212-29. Courtesy of Glenbow Archives, Archives and Special Collections, University of Calgary.

9.5 John Laurie's induction as an honorary Stoney Nakoda chief, Banff, 17 July 1948. NA-1241-346. Courtesy of Glenbow Archives, Archives and Special Collections, University of Calgary.

association's unpaid legal counsel. He won her support by reminding her of the extraordinary contribution her lawyer father Mark Bennett Peacock had made in the early 1930s by defending the Stoney in an important hunting and fishing case. The prominent Calgary barrister himself had absorbed the total cost of litigation.[92] In the following years and on many occasions, without any payment whatsoever, Ruth Gorman explained the Indian Act to members of the Indian Association of Alberta, in workshops and at meetings.[93] The Calgary lawyer made her greatest contribution leading the successful IAA-sponsored 1957 legal battle that allowed over a hundred individuals on the Samson Reserve to retain their Indian status.[94]

John Laurie also recruited Anne Downe, who brought the issue of Indian education before the national Home and School Association. As president of the Crescent Heights Home and School Association, Downe also volunteered to assist Laurie with his considerable IAA administrative duties. In the 1940s she organized adult education classes for members of the Indian Association at Paget Hall, the Anglican Cathedral's meeting place in downtown Calgary. The classes focused on how to conduct meetings, achieve success in job interviews, and write business letters.[95] In Edmonton, the Committee of Friends of the Indian (after 1951 known as the Friends of the Indians Society), led by Reta Rowan, also became a valuable ally of the Indian Association of Alberta.[96]

In 1946 the federal government established a Special Joint Committee of the Senate and the House of Commons on the Indian Act. The committee sat from 1946 to 1948 through three sessions of Parliament. Its major focus was the renovation of the Indian Act, which brought the Indian Affairs Branch under public scrutiny – a rare development. After it had heard evidence on administrative matters from Indian Branch officials, the committee welcomed Indians to participate. This invitation marked the first time policy-makers had sat down with the Indian leadership on a formal basis and consulted with them about their views of existing policy.[97] Representatives of First Nations and Native rights associations testified in 1946 and 1947, with their contributions being recorded in the committee's proceedings. The Special Joint Committee delivered its final report on revision of the Indian Act in June 1948.[98]

Diamond Jenness made a dramatic intervention before the Joint Committee on 25 March 1947, when he elaborated on his plan to "liquidate" the "Indian problem" in twenty-five years.[99] Jenness wanted to see the Indians become full participants in modern Canadian life, by "merging them into the rest of the population on an equal footing."[100] He sought, his biographer Barnett Richling notes, "to dismantle the state-sanctioned system of segregation."[101] His proposal to terminate special status and bring about the "liquidation" of the reserve proved popular, as many members of the Joint Committee endorsed the eventual elimination of the reserve system.[102] As Alan Cairns points out, Jenness "spoke for his generation of anthropologists. His policy proposals for Canadian Indians in 1947 and later for Inuit were basically arguments for crash programs in assimilation."[103] After three years of public hearings, the Special Joint Committee produced its final report, with the goal of the First Nations full entry into mainstream society endorsed – but with the term "assimilation" now replaced by the more politically correct, "integration."[104]

In 1956 a heart condition forced John Laurie to officially resign as secretary of the Indian Association of Alberta,[105] as well as to resign from
teaching. That year Calgary's Junior Chamber of Commerce named him
the city's outstanding citizen of the year, and the University of Alberta
awarded him the honorary degree of doctor of laws.[106] John Laurie spent
the last three years of his life documenting Stoney Nakoda culture for
the Glenbow Foundation, and working with Eddie Hunter on a Stoney
Nakoda dictionary and grammar.[107] John Laurie Boulevard, a major
east-west expressway in northwest Calgary is named in his honour.

John Laurie died on 6 April 1959 at the age of 59, beloved by the First
Nations in Alberta. The Tsuu T'ina (Sarcee) held a memorial on their
reserve. Chief David Crowchild had been one of Laurie's closest friends
and had adopted him as his brother.[108] John Laurie's former students,
First Nations friends, teaching and personal friends filled Calgary's
Anglican cathedral for the funeral. After the service at the Cathedral
Church of the Redeemer, some forty cars drove west along the old Banff
road to Morley. The McDougall Memorial Church was filled to capacity.
As Walking Buffalo said, "Thanks to this friend we have got nearer to
God."[109] An Indian choir sang hymns in the Stoney language. Alberta's
great crusader for Indigenous rights was buried in the Wesley cemetery
just north of the McDougall Memorial Church, opposite the grave of
Enos Hunter, his adopted father.[110]

Hugh Dempsey, the first archivist of the newly formed Glenbow-
Alberta Institute, served as secretary of the Indian Association of
Alberta from 1959 to 1965. He has made an enormous contribution to
bettering non-Indigenous understanding of the First Nations. As an
archivist, museum administrator, writer, and educator, Dempsey has
collected historical manuscripts and photos and recorded the oral memories of First Nations people, as well as those of non-Indigenous Albertans. For over sixty years, he has edited a major historical quarterly,
Alberta History (formerly the *Alberta Historical Review*), and he has written twenty-three full-length books[111] and edited another seventeen, in
addition to writing several hundred articles, thus reaching a large audience. Through numerous public lectures and membership on various
historical and commemorative committees, Hugh Dempsey has made
additional invaluable contributions to the advancement of Alberta's
heritage, Indigenous and non-Indigenous.

Hugh Dempsey's mother, Lily Louise Sharp, was an English war
bride who came from Folkestone on the English Channel. In his autobiography, *Always an Adventure*, Dempsey recalls how she taught him
"to be independent and encouraged him to be creative."[112] In 1916 she
married Canadian soldier Otto Lionel Dempsey and became a farmer's

wife. After the Great War the Dempseys first farmed in central Alberta, at Edgerton near Wainwright, where Hugh, the youngest of their four sons, was born on 7 November 1929. After the Depression and the drought of the early 1930s forced the Dempseys off their farm, the family moved to Edmonton when Hugh was five. Extremely poor, Dempsey recalled that he usually went barefoot in summer and in winter wore moccasins with rubbers pulled over them and sealer rings to keep them from falling off.[113] Now that they were in the city, the Dempsey family had electricity, running water, and close neighbours.

Entering elementary school in 1935 Hugh Dempsey found he enjoyed it, particularly art, his best subject. In his autobiography, Dempsey's mother clearly emerges as the major influence in his childhood. He loved reading, particularly the bundles of English children's magazines his grandmother Sharp forwarded each Christmas. With his mother's approval, Dempsey entered the workforce early. He obtained his first summer job when he was eight years old, as a delivery boy on a milk wagon, with pay of 5 cents and, if he was lucky, a bottle of milk. Other part-time jobs followed, such as snow shovelling, collecting bottles, and later gardening and working as a handyman.[114]

Hugh Dempsey left high school in 1947 after completing grade 11. Fortunately, after a few false starts, he obtained a job as a copy boy with the Edmonton *Bulletin*. After only a few days there, he realized that he really wanted to be a writer. Already he had developed work habits of long hours, marked by efficient use of time, and he advanced quickly at the paper. He rose within two years to junior then senior reporter, and at the tender age of 21, became the provincial editor. As a reporter for the *Bulletin*, Hugh Dempsey attended a convention of the Indian Association of Alberta in early 1950, where a chance meeting with Pauline Gladstone, the attractive daughter of President James Gladstone, changed his life. They began dating and discovered they had a great deal in common. They felt at home together wherever they went. Hugh's mother became a lifelong friend of Pauline's, and Pauline's father came to regard Hugh as a son.[115]

The *Bulletin* folded in 1951 and Hugh Dempsey, now an experienced journalist, became an Alberta government publicity writer for the next five years. He and Pauline married in August 1953. As Hugh Dempsey later wrote in *The Gentle Persuader*, his biography of James Gladstone, "I had become part of a close-knit extended family of brothers, sisters, aunts, uncles, cousins, and people whose exact relationship was uncertain. That is a wonderful thing about Indian families – blood lines are less important than a mutual acceptance of someone as 'family.'"[116]

9.6 Wedding photo of Pauline and Hugh Dempsey, 31 Aug. 1953. Courtesy of Hugh and Pauline Dempsey.

Hugh and Pauline's wedding led to an interesting legal situation, caused by the federal Indian Act. As Dempsey explained in a 1961 interview, "When my wife married me, she legally became no longer an Indian. At the same time, her brother married a white girl, and the girl legally became an Indian. This gives us a situation where my wife, who was raised on the Blood Reserve and speaks the language fluently, is not an Indian; but her sister-in-law, who was raised in a white community and does not speak the language, is legally an Indian."[117] Bill C-31, an amendment to the Indian Act finally changed this regulation in 1985. In terms of Hugh Dempsey's entry into a First Nations family, his marriage also brought him into the ranching world. In the acknowledgments in his 1995 book, *The Golden Age of the Canadian Cowboy*, Hugh Dempsey paid this tribute to Pauline: "I'm proud to say that my wife comes from a ranching and rodeo family, so I have been privileged over the years to absorb something of the ethics and ethos of a cowboy life. Perhaps that's why I'm so much of an admirer."[118]

Shortly before his marriage, Dempsey began to assist Reverend W. Everard Edmonds with the *Alberta Historical Review*, the Historical Society of Alberta's new quarterly journal. In his spare time the skilled journalist helped the retired Alberta high school teacher on the editorial, production, and sales side of the enterprise. When the 83-year-old Edmonds retired in 1958, his young assistant succeeded him.[119] Hugh Dempsey, the second editor of the *Alberta Historical Review*, which in 1975 became *Alberta History*, remained at the helm of the Western Canadian history magazine for almost two-thirds of a century (to late 2020).

The *Alberta Historical Review* used the photo of a mural by H.G. Glyde as the cover image for its spring 1953 issue. It also included a full-page piece about this remarkable mural painted directly on the wall over the main interior entrance to the large reading room, located on the second floor in the University of Alberta's new Rutherford Library.[120] The Glyde mural, entitled *Alberta's History*, stands over 20 feet long by 8 feet high and is set 15 feet above the floor. Henry George Glyde (1906–1998) was the English-born and -trained founder and head of the university's Department of Fine Arts. Arriving in Alberta in 1935, he had immersed himself in the artistic life of his new home. As pointed out by his biographer Patricia Ainslie, Glyde had "a major role in the development of art in the province."[121] As a gift in gratitude for the opportunities Alberta had provided him, the artist worked for four months with several student assistants on his ambitious project.[122] He generously donated it to the university, at the opening of its new library on 15 May 1951.[123]

Alberta History, in its selection of characters and events, represents a composite of how many Western Canadian writers then presented the province's history from "roughly 1850 to 1880."[124] Famous Roman Catholic missionary Albert Lacombe, and his Protestant (Methodist) counterpart John McDougall, appear as heroic figures in the midst of their Indigenous converts and followers. One of the original Mounties who founded Fort Macleod in 1874 is shown, "symbolical of law and order."[125] Crowfoot, the famous Blackfoot (Siksika) chief, is seen standing with his head bowed. Most of the faces of the Indigenous people are hidden. The buildings shown include Lacombe's mission at St Albert, the historic McDougall Church at Morley, and the Big House at Fort Edmonton that was built by John Rowand, the colourful chief factor with the Hudson's Bay Company, with some teepees in the background.[126] In the mural, the "white" males appear as the main actors.

James G. MacGregor (1905–1989), president of the Historical Society of Alberta several times in the 1950s, completed and published his book, *History of Alberta*, in 1972.[127] Several of his chapter titles reveal similar themes as in the Glyde Mural, including "Alberta's Earliest White Men," "John Rowand's Regime, 1830–1854," and "White Progress to 1881." But, at the same time, MacGregor innovates and includes full sketches of the Indigenous peoples. The titles of two of his early chapters, for instance, read, "The First Albertans" and "The End of the Plains Indians' Freedom, 1874–1881." The explanation for his new approach surfaces in the author's acknowledgments: "I must single out one for help in an aspect of our history about which all too little has been written. That individual is Hugh Dempsey, archivist of the Glenbow-Alberta Institute, whose kindness in letting me study the manuscript of his forthcoming book on Chief Crowfoot made possible what little insight I have gained into the way of life of our fascinating prairie predecessors."[128]

Hugh Dempsey joined the Glenbow Foundation in Calgary in 1956 as archivist, and then he served as curator-director from 1967 to his retirement in 1991. Through Pauline and her family, Dempsey gained an entry into the world of the First Nations and became interested in the history and culture of each of the Indigenous communities in what is now Alberta. Dempsey's six years as secretary of the Indian Association of Alberta gave him additional contacts with First Nations peoples throughout the province. Pauline fully supported him in his many Glenbow, Indian Association of Alberta, and community commitments. James Gladstone, her father, also became an invaluable ally. Hugh Dempsey became a bridge between two worlds, communicating invaluable information about the Indigenous world to non-Indigenous Albertans.

9.7 *Alberta History*, 1951, by Henry George Glyde (b. 1906–d. 1998). University of Alberta Museums Art Collection (1965.34). University of Alberta Museums. Image © 2005 University of Alberta. Reproduced with permission of the Estate of H.G. Glyde.

Precious information for Dempsey's writing on the Blackfoot and Blood came through James Gladstone, the Blood rancher and a former president of the Indian Association of Alberta who, in 1958, became the first status Indian named to the Canadian Senate. In *Always an Adventure*, Hugh Dempsey describes his father-in-law's skill as an interpreter, "In speaking to me, he gave me everything that was said, including the conversations. That was one thing I noticed about Blackfoot storytelling. Even though an incident might have occurred two or three generations earlier, the informant would speak as though he had been there, complete with conversations."[129] Speaking with Gladstone in Blackfoot, the old people told of buffalo hunts, battles, the supernatural, and the accomplishments of great chiefs.[130]

Oral history is not an easy matter. It involves much more than a simple conversation with an Elder. The written as well as the oral records must be reviewed in depth, and the fact always remembered that some Elders have better memories than others. Hugh Dempsey conducted his interviews in the mid-1950s with Blackfoot Confederacy members – some of them, unilingual speakers – accompanied by James Gladstone acting as his interpreter. The elderly individuals he met were grounded in a Blackfoot-speaking world. Dempsey summarizes in his memoirs, "Over a period of time, I developed a couple of methods for determining the accuracy of elders. For example, I would pick out nine or ten statements of fact from an elder and compare them with different sources, such as statements of other elders, fur trade records and government documents. If I could find comparative data for even half of them and they checked out, then I knew the elder was reliable."[131]Central to Hugh Dempsey's writing about Indigenous history in southern Alberta is Treaty Seven. On 22 September 1877, the four nations of the Blackfoot Confederacy (Blackfoot, Blood, Peigan, and Tsuu T'ina) and the Stoney Nakoda signed this vitally important agreement with the Government of Canada. Each side came to the negotiations in early fall 1877 with their own agenda. The Blackfoot had wanted the Cree, Métis, and other outsiders from the north and east expelled from their hunting grounds, as well as protection provided for the remaining buffalo herds. The Government of Canada sought title to lands belonging to the First Nations. In his recent book, *The Great Blackfoot Treaties*, published in 2015, Hugh Dempsey writes, "In the end, the Blackfoot got neither and the government got all." But he points out one benefit for the First Nations: "Without realizing it, the Blackfoot and Stoneys established a relationship with the government that would ultimately save many lives when the buffalo were destroyed, and in the end – although this was perhaps not understood at the time – the reserves became havens for a dispossessed people."[132] Totally unforeseen, the buffalo disappeared on the Canadian side of the 49th parallel in 1879, and on the American in 1883.

Hugh Dempsey began to write his first book, an in-depth biography of Chief Crowfoot, in the late 1950s. The young writer-archivist could not find a publisher for his manuscript on the man who had been the most important spokesperson for the Blackfoot Confederacy at Treaty Seven. Although in 1958 Dempsey had produced a solidly researched and well-written text, only in 1972 did the biography appear in print. The publishers he first approached had told him no market existed for Canadian history. The closest he came to an offer to publish was from Macmillan of Canada, who told him they would bring it out if he cut it by two-thirds and rewrote it as a children's book.[133] Finally, an American company, the University of Oklahoma Press,[134] brought it out and Hurtig Publishers in Edmonton distributed it in Canada.

Crowfoot did well in both sales and reviews. In June 1974 the Calgary and Edmonton school boards presented copies of the book at a national education conference at Banff to the superintendents or directors of education of all the larger cities across Canada.[135] Dempsey was 41 years old, and now on his way to becoming a highly successful author. After *Crowfoot*, he published a new book almost every year for the next twenty years. What is his secret? He told George Melnyk, in a 1995 interview for the second volume of his *Literary History of Alberta*, that he saw himself as "a writer who has entered the field of history. I tried not to be an academic writer. When you write something you should try to communicate to your audience, whoever that audience happens to be."[136]

Hugh Dempsey has received many municipal, provincial, and national honours over the course of his long career, from an honorary doctorate from the University of Calgary, to the Order of Canada, to Alberta's prestigious Sir Frederick Haultain Award. When he took early retirement from the Glenbow in 1990, becoming chief curator emeritus, the museum named the reading room at the library and archives after him. One of what he regards as the greatest honours of his career was his adoption as an honorary chief of Bloods in 1967. At this ceremony, Hugh Dempsey received the Blackfoot name of Potaina (or "Flying Chief"), Pauline Dempsey's grandfather.[137]

The 1960s proved an important decade for Indigenous Prairie Canada. Roughly four decades earlier, the prolific journalist Chief Buffalo Child Long Lance could write in an article "Where Are Western Canada's Indians?" (*Vancouver Sun*, 7 June 1924), "One may live in any of the western cities for years without laying eyes on an original inhabitant of the country." The Indian reserves and Métis settlements were most frequently found in Western Canada in more remote areas, away from the main centres of development.[138] In the 1960s many Indigenous people had migrated to urban centres in search of jobs, housing, and schools for their children.[139] They now constituted a large and visible part of the population in cities such as Winnipeg, Regina, and Edmonton.[140]

In October 1966 the federally appointed Hawthorn Commission produced the first of two volumes of *A Survey of the Contemporary Indians of Canada: Economic, Political, Educational Needs and Policies.*[141] No discussion had occurred when the commission, chaired by the anthropologist Harry B. Hawthorn, was appointed that it must include an "Indian" component in the senior research team. At the time there were few Indigenous university graduates, and even fewer with graduate degrees.[142] Despite the absence of a single Indigenous person on the senior research team, the commission took a very pro-Indigenous position, although it surprisingly made no reference to treaties.[143] The Hawthorn Report, for the first time suggested that separate self-governing Indian communities might persist indefinitely.[144] The Report accepted the idea that "Indians" could be distinct peoples within the Canadian state, that is, they could be "Citizens Plus."

The growing awareness of Indigenous Canada had led to the formation of the Indian-Eskimo Association of Canada, which had its origins in the Canadian Association for Adult Education, in the mid-1950s.[145] The anthropologist Sally Weaver describes the IEA as a citizens' organization with both Indigenous and non-Indigenous members, but "largely a white liberal group whose aims were to raise public consciousness about the substandard conditions in Indian communities and to advocate changes in government priorities and policies."[146] The organization also addressed the non-Indigenous public's ignorance of, and apathy to, Indigenous issues. In the words of the historian Joan Sangster, "Rather than endorse demonstrations, it often provided background information."[147] Formally established in 1960, the Indian-Eskimo Association of Canada organized workshops to discuss, for example, Indigenous housing, community and economic development, and hunting and trapping rights. In 1966 the association brought forward an extensive study on the legal aspects of Indian rights and treaties. This led to the IEA's publication four years later of *Native Rights in Canada*, the first synthesis of Canadian Indian law, written by Douglas Sanders and later revised by Peter Cumming and Neil Mickenberg (1972).[148]

As Canadian society became more conscious of human rights, the limitations of federal Indian policy administered by an authoritarian, highly centralized and underfunded branch of government gained attention. Many non-Indigenous friends of the Indigenous peoples wanted to accelerate Indian integration and work to end Indian poverty and alienation. The emphasis of governments was on economic and social development. By the 1970s Indigenous people constituted about one-third of the membership of the Indian-Eskimo Association.[149] A discussion took place at the IEA's annual meeting held in Calgary in the early fall of 1967, one that set the stage for the non-Indigenous/ Indigenous dialogue that would continue for decades to follow. Over a hundred delegates came to the stately Palliser Hotel from Ontario and Western Canada, the majority of them non-Indigenous, but with a number of Indigenous people in attendance, as well.

The discovery of oil at Leduc, south of Edmonton, in February 1947 had launched Calgary into a new era of opulence and expansion, as it became the headquarters of the thriving post-Leduc oil and gas industry. Thousands of newcomers moved to the city. The veteran journalist James Gray recalls late 1940s and early 1950s Calgary in his memoir, *Troublemaker!* (1978), "On a five-minute walk from the Palliser Hotel, you would encounter accents ranging from Louisiana Patois to Texas drawl, New England twang, and upper-crust English."[150] The new petroleum-based boom saw Calgary spread out, annexing the surrounding suburbs.[151] The construction of the University of Alberta in Calgary in the early 1960s led to the establishment in 1966 of the independent University of Calgary.[152] All of this phenomenal development occurred within the lifespan of one individual. On 26 May 1966 the revered Stoney Nakoda Elder Tatanga Mani (or Walking Buffalo, or George McLean, then in his mid-90s), attended the University of Calgary's first convocation. Born in the early 1870s, he had seen the last buffalo herds in the area before their disappearance in 1879. As the Alberta historian Grant MacEwan wrote in his biography, *Tatanga Mani: Walking Buffalo of the Stonies*, published in 1969, "Buffalo herds disappeared before Walking Buffalo was old enough to pursue them in the role of hunter, but he accompanied the older hunters as a child and could recall the slaughter, the hours spent in skinning, and the odour of meat drying in the sun."[153]

The construction of new office buildings for banks and oil company offices put pressure on the older buildings of the city's core. Launched in 1966, Urban Renewal caused entire blocks to be replaced by modern buildings.[154] During Calgary's frenzy for urban renewal, the downtown CPR station was razed, and for a while the iconic Palliser Hotel itself was in danger.[155] Nekenon, John McDougall's beloved residence on 6th Ave SW, went down among the early casualties. Here Reverend McDougall had written his last two published books, *In the Days of the Red River Rebellion: Life and Adventure in the Far West of Canada* (1903) and *On Western Trails in the Early Seventies: Frontier Life in the Canadian North-West* (1911). He left unfinished his manuscript on the years 1875–6, published in 1970 as *Opening the Great West*.[156]

9.8 Daisy and David Crowchild, Howard and Mabel Beebe, President Herb Armstrong, Tatanga Mani (Walking Buffalo) and Ruth Gorman, honorary degree recipient at the University of Calgary's first convocation in 1966. Photo by Neil Crichton. University of Calgary Archives.

At the end of September 1967, Calgary hosted the Indian-Eskimo Association's important national meeting with over 125 participants arriving from all across the country. Summer was now over. The air had turned crisp, and the leaves yellow. Martin O'Connell, the newly elected IEA president entitled his presidential address, "Talk with Us by the Fires of the Days to Come." He took as his theme the message at the exit of the Indian Pavilion at Expo '67. As they left that pavilion Canadians, celebrating their Centenary, received an invitation:

Walk in our moccasins the trail from our past.
Live with us in the here and now.
Talk with us by the fires of the days to come.[157]

Over a year earlier, the Toronto journalist Wendie Kerr had written an in-depth article on the dedicated O'Connell, "A White Man Fights for the Indians: As an economist and a Canadian he cannot tolerate the inequality under which the Indian citizen is forced to live." The story ran in the *Mirror*, published in Scarborough, Ontario, on 12 October 1966. Kerr explains that this concerned citizen's interest in Native issues began when teaching on Vancouver Island in the early 1940s. On Sundays, he played the organ in a little church with an almost entirely Indian congregation: "Gradually I got to know the people visiting their potlatch ceremonies and so on." He came to know a number of the Cowichan: "They were virtually integrated – earning good money – in the lumber mills, logging camps and on the coastal ships as longshoreman. Most were fine, intelligent people ready for integration."

Martin O'Connell, a senior accountant who had just turned 50, made an outstanding presidential speech. Half a century later, the historian John Leslie read the printed version of the talk. The lifelong student of Canadian Indian policy commented, "It's certainly the best and most comprehensive assertion of the views of the IEA. I found his analysis of Indigenous poverty most insightful and disturbing. He could be describing reserve conditions today. What an indictment of our Indigenous policy!"[158] O'Connell emphasized economic and social development to reduce poverty and empower Indigenous communities rather than advancing in his remarks specific legal and political issues.

Harold Cardinal was just 22 years old when he attended the Calgary meeting in 1967, as president of the Canadian Indian Youth Council. Born in High Prairie, Alberta, and raised in the Sucker Creek Reserve, Cardinal attended Indian residential school in Joussard and St Francis Xavier High School in Edmonton before studying sociology at St Patrick's College, which later became part of Carleton University, in Ottawa. With his excellent command of English, Cardinal had acted from age 16 as his father's interpreter,[159] and attended meetings of the Indian Association of Alberta with him. In 1966, the Canadian Union of Students appointed Harold Cardinal their associate secretary of Indian affairs, and later that same year he was elected president of the Canadian Indian Youth Council,[160] founded in 1964, "to fight for the interests of Indian youth."[161]

More than twenty years later, Harold Cardinal eloquently summarized in one sentence his understanding of the relationship between the First Nations and the newcomers. The quote sums up so well his life-long outlook as a political leader: "When treaties were signed between Indian First Nations and representatives of the Crown, the Indian First Nations viewed themselves as independent sovereign nations entering

9.9 Harold Cardinal, ca. 1970. Photo J285, Provincial Archives of Alberta. Courtesy of the *Edmonton Journal*, a Division of Postmedia Network and the Provincial Archives of Alberta.

into formal treaty agreements and relationships with another sovereign nation."[162] The young Cree wanted full recognition of First Nations distinct legal rights acknowledged in the treaties. At the 1967 meeting of the Indian-Eskimo Association in Calgary, Cardinal spoke out after hearing President O'Connell's speech and the other presentations, saying, "When we want advice we'll ask for it, but we are tired of free advice when we don't need it. Unless the Indian people can become 'masters of our house,' we shall never be on equal footing with our fellow citizens. We do not want to become brown white men."[163]

Harold Cardinal represented a whole new generation of young Indigenous people who spoke English and/or French well, who had travelled and read widely, and who were prepared to speak out on issues of concern. These young leaders wanted to see the First Nations take control of their own lives. In the words of George Manuel, a veteran political leader from British Columbia, Harold Cardinal "successfully combined a traditional knowledge with higher academic learning, and the strength and vigour of youth."[164] The Indian-Eskimo Association, as well as the larger non-Indigenous society, John Leslie notes, had totally underestimated "how strong the Indians' desire to remain as Indians with their rights, cultures and languages was."[165] On the first page of *The Unjust Society*, Harold Cardinal wrote in 1969, "Now, at a time when our fellow Canadians consider the promise of the Just Society, once more the Indians of Canada are betrayed by a programme which offers nothing better than cultural genocide." Again, the term "genocide."

In 1985 John Webster Grant commented on how, fifteen years earlier, "after centuries of exhortation by white mentors the Indians began to speak up vocally for themselves." The well-respected church historian continued, "Soon angry Indians began to rewrite Canadian history with the roles of heroes and villains reversed. Harold Cardinal's *The Unjust Society*, which appeared in 1969 was one of the first and for this reason perhaps the most shocking." Looking back, Grant added, "White Canadians, accustomed to thinking themselves as benefactors struggling at considerable cost to help the Indians achieve a new and higher life, suddenly found themselves portrayed as destroyers of culture they had never taken pains to appreciate."[166]

Epilogue: The First Nations and Canada's Conscience

From the 1840s onward Canadian Indian policy sought the First Nations' abandonment of their land, traditional activities, communal values, and ancient rights in exchange for the privileges and opportunities of British, later Canadian citizenship.[1] The dominant society failed to listen to the Indigenous peoples who called, for instance, for schooling – not for aggressive assimilation. They did not want, as the Canadian historian J.R. Miller has written, "a barrage of Christian, Euro-Canadian teachings that denigrated Native ways."[2] The integrationist perspective continued into the late 1960s, culminating with a proposal to end Indian status, reserves, and the historic Indian treaties. Alan Cairns has written in reference to the earlier attempt to give the federal government authority to enact the compulsory enfranchisement of Indians, "The 1969 White Paper proposed applying the 1920 policy – abandoned in 1951 – to the entire status Indian population."[3]

The White Paper gave new life to First Nations political organizations. Indigenous protest against the policy initiative arose immediately, as the First Nations had been bypassed and not included in the final deliberations that produced the document.[4] In addition, the policy denied them the special rights the government-sponsored Hawthorn Report of just two years earlier had recognized and recommended.[5] First Nations from coast to coast stepped forward to denounce the document. As the anthropologist Sally Weaver notes, "The White Paper became the single most powerful catalyst of the Indian nationalist movement, launching it into a determined force for nativism – a reaffirmation of a unique cultural heritage and identity."[6] The National Indian Brotherhood, founded in 1968 and reorganized in 1982 as the Assembly of First Nations, described the White Paper as a document designed to bring about "the destruction of a Nation of People by legislation and cultural genocide."[7]

Implementation of per capita grants to Indian political organizations in 1968 encouraged these associations and facilitated their expansion. The federal government recognized that the First Nations could not effectively present their position without funding. After 1969 government financial support reached a new unprecedented level.[8] With core funding, it became possible to have salaried political leaders,[9] which allowed Indigenous organizations to expand, and to better serve their constituents. The increased financial resources allowed them to lobby government, research Indigenous Title, and develop educational curriculum.[10] It was in Ottawa's interest to provide financial support, as the existence of strong First Nations political organizations in Canada helped to keep out radical United States Indian groups like the American Indian Movement.[11] The increasing use of modern technology enabled the resurgent Indigenous leadership in Canada to communicate easily in a new common language, English, and in parts of Quebec, in French.

First Nations political groups had been relatively weak until the White Paper was proposed and before they started receiving funding from the federal government. According to the 1966 Hawthorn Report, entitled *Survey of Contemporary Indians of Canada*, "As a group Indians are a special segment of the disadvantaged poor who are usually unskilled in the arts of applying pressure, possess few organizational means of effectively doing so, and who, until recently were deprived of the franchise."[12] For persons with registered Indian status a new political era began in Canada in 1969. In less than two years their political organizations successfully waged a campaign that led to the official retraction in March 1971 of the White Paper by the Government of Canada.[13] Public awareness of the Indigenous peoples was growing. Edgar Dosman, a Canadian political scientist, most perceptively identified this significant change in *Indians: The Urban Dilemma*. Dosman's 1972 book begins with this arresting line: "Tolerant, prosperous and smug Canada has awakened to a racial problem and is painfully adjusting to a historical sin."[14]

Over the past half-century the values, attitudes, and assumptions of many non-Indigenous Canadians towards the First Nations have undergone radical and extraordinary change. Indigenous issues in Canada have become increasingly important on the public agenda. No longer is it assumed that the Indigenous peoples should, and will be absorbed into mainstream culture. High rates of natural increase, new legal definitions of "Indian," and the growth in the numbers of individuals self-identifying as Indigenous have contributed to a perception of the demographic importance of the Indigenous peoples.[15] A quick summary follows of significant developments that have contributed to this shift in perceptions and awareness. This overview looks first at a number of social and cultural developments since the Second World War, and then focuses, in point form, on a selection of major legal and historical events over the past fifty years and up to the present time (summer 2020).

The aftermath of the Second World War contributed greatly to new attitudes among the non-Indigenous population of Canada. The Canadian historian E. Palmer Patterson, in his 1972 book, *The Canadian Indian: A History Since 1500*, identified one major explanation for this, namely, "the recession of European self-confidence."[16] The Western European powers Britain, France, the Netherlands, Belgium, Portugal, and Spain had all dismantled their colonial empires. The discrediting of race theory during and after the war fostered to a new awareness and tolerance of cultural differences. At the same time, the impressive Indigenous participation in the Canadian armed forces in the military struggle awakened many Canadians to the urgency of improving Indigenous social and economic conditions. After the Second World War Canadians wanted to create a country to match the values and principles for which they had fought.[17]

A major revision of the Indian Act in 1951 removed a number of its negative features, including the prohibition of pursuing Indigenous Title and the banning of dances and ceremonies, including potlatches. The chiefs and councils obtained additional powers to act as municipal governments. The word now used to describe the policy, "integration," remained the goal of education, the churches, and federal Indian policy in general. In the 1950s and 1960s several factors converged that made it impossible for Canadians to return to the pre–Second World War indifference to the Indigenous peoples. The post-war expansion of the resource frontier into areas where the First Nations numerically dominated made a better understanding of their history and cultures essential. In the United States the rise of the civil rights movement raised Canadian consciousness, too, of civil rights abuses towards the Indigenous peoples in Canada. A number of liberal-minded non-Indigenous Canadians, in fact, looked upon the Indian struggle in Canada as an equivalent of the African American struggle,[18] although in reality it was quite different. The expanding Indigenous population from the 1950s onward, at a much greater rate than the non-Indigenous population and continuing so to this day, as well as migration in increasing numbers into urban areas made the Indigenous peoples, especially in Western Canada, much more visible.[19]

Several Christian denominations have stepped forward to promote a new awareness of Indigenous people. The United Church of Canada, in 1986, made the first apology for its former assimilationist outlook, admitting, "We tried to make you be like us and in so doing we helped to destroy the vision that made you what you were."[20] As the 1991 Apology to the First Nations of Canada made by the Oblate Conference of Canada, a Roman Catholic missionary order, summarizes, "Anthropological and sociological insights of the late 20th century have shown how deep, unchallenged, and damaging was the naïve cultural, ethnic, linguistic, and religious superiority complex of Christian Europe when its Peoples met and interrelated with the aboriginal Peoples of North America."[21] In 1998 Minister of Indian Affairs and Northern Development Jane Stewart made the first formal apology on behalf of the Government of Canada, saying, "Our purpose is not to rewrite history but, rather, to learn from our past and to find ways to deal with the negative impacts that certain historical decisions continue to have in our society today."[22]

The number of First Nations students in high school has increased over the past twenty years. Today (2020) the secondary school graduation rate is now about 40 per cent, a great improvement, but still only one half of the graduation rate for non–First Nations students that stands at 80 per cent.[23] A welcome development is the growing number of First Nations men and women who now have some postsecondary education.[24] Non-Indigenous Canadians' awareness of the Indigenous peoples has grown as both groups meet in education, health, the civil service and the trades. An Indigenous middle class is growing, as well-trained secondary and postsecondary graduates are securing positions in the private sector and in government.[25] The First Nations writer Tomson Highway summarized the new situation in 1989, explaining, "We now have chiefs with degrees in the arts and in the sciences, we have Indian lawyers, we have Indian businessmen and businesswomen who can negotiate the complexities of the modern corporation and of free enterprise, and we have artists – writers not least among them – who are just now beginning to make their presence felt in the national and international arenas."[26]

Previously, the Indian Act had made no provision for education of status Indians beyond the age of 16.[27] Only in the late 1950s did the federal government provide informal assistance for a small number of status Indians to attend universities. In the 1970s the formalization of a post-secondary assistance program led to a rapid increase in the number of First Nations students graduating from universities and colleges and Native-run educational institutions.[28] Indigenous graduates entered graduate schools in increasing number in the 1990s and the years to follow, some later taking up teaching positions. These scholars have contributed to a renaissance in Aboriginal research and knowledge at the post-secondary level.[29]

Indigenous scholars have made important contributions both in historical and legal writing. Dr Olive Dickason became a Canadian historian after a distinguished career in journalism. The Métis scholar made Indigenous history her life's work from her fifties right up until her death in 2011.[30] Dickason's important contributions include her first major book,

The Myth of the Savage and the Beginnings of French Colonialism in the Americas, published in 1984,[31] where with these words she describes so well the French and European outlook whereby, "The duty of Christians, as the children of God, was clear: legally to claim non-Christian territory in order to implant the faith and to lead the inhabitants into civilization."[32] Perhaps of greatest value to the general public has been Olive Dickason's popular historical survey, *Canada's First Nations: A History of Founding Peoples from Earliest Times*, published in 1992 and followed by several subsequent editions.[33] Similarly, in the world of legal scholarship, the Ojibwe scholar John Borrows has played a major role. He explores traditional Indigenous worldviews, providing new insights, in his *Recovering Canada: The Resurgence of Indigenous Law*,[34] a collection of his published work from 1996 to 2001, and in his 2011 book, *Canada's Indigenous Constitution*.[35] Today, a growing number of Indigenous legal scholars have gained academic positions in Canadian colleges and universities. By the mid-1990s more First Nations students were graduating in law than in any other professional category.[36] Greg Poelzer and Ken S. Coates report in their 2015 study, *From Treaty Peoples to Treaty Nation* that, in 2015, "the percentage of Indigenous lawyers is higher than the percentage of Aboriginal people in the Canadian population.[37]

Non-Indigenous scholars have introduced new perspectives on the First Nations from anthropology, archaeology, geography, law, linguistics, sociology, and other disciplines. In the important field of the history of Indigenous Canada, a new critical approach has added to public understanding. The Department of Indian Affairs contributed greatly to the challenging of widespread assumptions by making Department of Indian Affairs records more accessible to researchers on microfilm and by providing basic reference works like *The Historical Development of the Indian Act from Colonial Days to 1951*.[38] The historian Andrew Nurse has noted a most welcome development. He writes, "Increasingly, historians have come to realize that First Nations' traditions provide valuable historical information, affording an alternative window into Canada's past, compensating for the biases inherent in non-Native primary documents."[39]

The mainstream society has new opportunities to learn about contemporary Indigenous Canada through the arts. Exposure to Indigenous novels, short stories, plays and poetry, art and dance have greatly contributed to making Canadians better informed of Indigenous realities, and to breaking deeply entrenched stereotypes. Until the 1970s Indigenous literature remained on the margins of literary Canada and, in the eyes of the general public, virtually non-existent.[40] After the introduction of the White Paper more and more writers stepped forward to tell their stories. Best-selling non-fiction books appeared, including Harold

Cardinal's *The Unjust Society* (1969),[41] and the autobiography of Métis writer and educator Maria Campbell, entitled *Halfbreed* (1973).[42] Cardinal wrote his powerful book "to bring to the Canadian public, perhaps for the first time, a voice that was ours, a voice that reflected First Nation thoughts and reactions to the situation facing us."[43] The Cree leader underlined the First Nations concerns about the Canadian government discussing "'the two founding peoples' without giving recognition to the role played by the Indian even before the founding of the nation-state known as Canada."[44] Maria Campbell in *Halfbreed* movingly describes her experiences as an Indigenous woman in Canada from the 1940s to 1970s. Both books inform non-Indigenous readers of the deep racism, intolerance, and injustice that many Indigenous people experience.

During the 1980s and 1990s contemporary Indigenous literature made considerable inroads into Canada's literary consciousness. Indigenous writers began to use fiction to document their lives and those of fellow Indigenous people.[45] Writer James Bartleman, a retired Canadian diplomat and Ontario's first Indigenous lieutenant governor, notes that fiction has several great advantages over non-fiction, namely, "A novel takes the reader inside the heads of its characters, and when a character laughs the reader laughs, when a character suffers the reader suffers, when a character rages against injustices of humankind and divine providence the reader does likewise and so on."[46] To select but one example, in his best-selling semi-autobiographical novel, *Keeper 'n Me* (1994), the late First Nations novelist Richard Wagamese describes his growing up in foster homes from age 9 to 16, and his never-ending search for his Anishinabe identity. The Ojibwe writer published fourteen books in his lifetime, including his breakthrough novel, *Indian Horse* (2012), about a talented Indigenous hockey phenomenon who never escaped the legacy of the Indian residential school he had attended.[47] The successful film adaptation of the novel premiered at the 2017 Toronto International Film Festival and obtained general theatrical release across Canada in 2018.[48]

Thomas King, a Native American (Cherokee) from the United States who came to Canada in 1980 to teach Native American Studies at the University of Lethbridge has done a great deal to make Indigenous literature known to Canadian readers. His first novel, *Medicine River* (1990),[49] was later adapted as a television movie, and shown nationally. His best-selling second novel, *Green Grass Running Water*,[50] became a finalist for the 1993 Governor General's Award. Since then Thomas King has produced numerous publications, including *The Truth about Stories*, a compilation of talks for his CBC Massey Lectures in 2003.[51] In 2014 he became the first Indigenous writer to win the Governor-General's Literary Award for English-Language Fiction for his novel,

The Back of the Turtle.[52] His 2012 popular history and personal memoir, *The Inconvenient Indian: A Curious Account of Native People in North America*, became a national bestseller in Canada, and a volume used as a text in university and college courses.[53]

Contemporary Indigenous drama and poetry in Canada owes much to the success of Thomson Highway, specifically in his two early plays, *The Rez Sisters* (1986) and its companion piece, *Dry Lips Oughta Move to Kapuskasing* (1989). These plays tied the oral roots of Indigenous creative writing to contemporary political issues. Through the rapid development of Indigenous theatre, audiences across Canada learned of the barriers of injustice and prejudice Indigenous people face, as well as the strength of their oral traditions.[54] In addition to drama, poetry has flourished in recent years, with a number of Indigenous poets winning important literary awards. This poetry has addressed, in the words of the Ojibwe scholar Armand Ruffo, "the theme of counteracting the erasure of identity and culture."[55] In 2013 the Métis writer Katherena Vermette became the first Indigenous poet to win the Governor General's Literary Award for English-Language Poetry. She won it for *North End Love Songs*, an ode in praise of her Winnipeg neighbourhood.[56] In 2016 the Anishinabe poet Liz Howard won the Griffin Poetry Prize for *Infinite Citizen of the Shaking Tent*, becoming the first Indigenous poet to do so.[57]

Indigenous art has helped Canadians learn about the Aboriginal peoples and their history and cultures. A growing number of First Nations artists have achieved international reputations, individuals such as Norval Morrisseau,[58] Daphne Odjig,[59] and Bill Reid,[60] who have used their art to strengthen and affirm their Indigenous identity. In the field of architecture, Douglas Cardinal[61] has won international awards for his work, which includes the Canadian Museum of Civilization (now the Museum of Canadian History) in Gatineau, across the Ottawa River from the Canadian Parliament Buildings; and the National Museum of the American Indian in Washington, DC. Indigenous filmmakers have contributed to a greater awareness of Indigenous realities. The Abenaki singer, writer, and filmmaker Alanis Obomsawin is best known for her documentary films.[62] She has produced many films for the National Film Board of Canada, one of the best known concerns the Oka Crisis, entitled *Kahnesatake: 270 Years of Resistance* (1993). A 2001 film directed by Inuit filmmaker Zacharias Kunak, entitled *Atanarjuat: The Fast Runner*, was the first feature film written, directed, and acted entirely in the Inuktitut language. It enjoyed great commercial and critical success.[63]

Indigenous issues are present everywhere in Canada. In a halting fashion, many non-Indigenous Canadians have changed direction, leaving indifference and ignorance behind, and they are now attempting to establish an

Map 10.1 Canada in 2020.

equitable and mutually beneficial relationship with the First Nations, to achieve reconciliation. The final report in the Environics Institute's *Canadian Public Opinion on Aboriginal Peoples* in 2016 suggests that the values, attitudes, and assumptions of many non-Indigenous Canadians towards the First Nations have improved: "Over the past few decades, there has been notable progress in the appreciation of Aboriginal history and culture, in the clarification of Aboriginal and treaty rights, and in the acknowledgement of mistreatment and abuse by institutions and other parts of society."[64] Today, a growing number of Canadians realize Indigenous peoples "experience considerable disparities with the rest of the population in such areas as income, education and health outcomes. Aboriginal peoples are vastly over-represented in the country's prisons and in foster care."[65]

The public acknowledgment today of the traditional lands on which public meetings and events occur has now become a common practice across Canada, an expected protocol.[66] The First Nations have long included such statements in their community gatherings. Land acknowledgment statements appear to have begun in non-Indigenous Canada around 2003, when Martha Piper of the University of British Columbia publicly recognized that the educational institution of which she was president at the time was on traditional Musqueam territory.[67] This non-Indigenous tribute to the First Nations stewardship of the land would have been almost unimaginable a decade earlier,[68] and utterly inconceivable at the moment of the introduction of the White Paper in 1969. It is but a tiny gesture, but a beginning – much much more must be done.

Without any doubt Canada has treated the Aboriginal peoples badly and continues to do so today. Writing as historians, we must record this. I hope that a dedicated scholar will write a full companion volume on non-Indigenous Canadians' attitude towards the Indigenous Peoples over the past half century. My focus in *Seen but Not Seen* is on a more distant past. A 1968 quote by Walter Deiter, the first president of the National Indian Brotherhood, whose photo appears on the cover of this book, best summarizes the situation from the 1840s to the late 1960s: "We don't really understand one another."[69] The lesson I take from all of this? We should always keep in mind that in judging the past those responsible were individuals of their times, and the times were not ours. For me the good news is, over the course of my three-quarters of a century in this country, I now see a growing political, regional, and public awareness of Indigenous Canada – Seen and Now Seen.

Over the past half century the First Nations emerged as political forces because of their initiatives to safeguard their Indigenous rights. Important political and legal developments have led many non-Indigenous Canadians to alter their perspectives of the First Nations over this period. A new awareness of the importance of human rights from the 1950s onward has transformed Canada. By the early 1970s every province had human rights codes. In 1982 Canada placed the Charter of Rights and Freedoms into its Constitution.[70] The following short chronology introduces in point form a selection of potential legal and political topics and events that might be examined in a future scholarly study of the most recent period of Canadian history with a focus on Influential Canadians and the First Nations / Influential First Nations and Non-Indigenous Canadians, beginning with the 1970 Red Paper and ending with the blockades in early 2020 – just a few short weeks before the novel coronavirus pandemic changed everything everywhere.

- **June 4 1970.** Prime Minister Pierre Elliott Trudeau and his full Cabinet met with First Nations leaders in Ottawa. Alberta chiefs, Adam Soloway (of the Blackfoot, or Siksika) and John Snow (of the Stoney Nakoda), handed the prime minister their "Red Paper," a response to the government's 1969 "White Paper," and based on the Indian Association of Alberta's position paper, "Citizens Plus." In response to the Red Paper, the federal government in March 1971 formally retracted the White Paper.[71]

10.1 Harold Cardinal, President of the Indian Association of Alberta, addressing Prime Minister Pierre Elliott Trudeau at the presentation of the Red Paper in Ottawa, 4 June 1970. He spoke to the significance of treaty and Aboriginal rights. Canapress Photo Service.

10.2 Minister of Indian Affairs Jean Chrétien speaking to First Nations delegates at the presentation of the Red Paper in Ottawa, 4 June 1970. Duncan Campbell. PA-170161, LAC.

- **1973**. The Supreme Court of Canada issued a decision in the Nisga'a or Calder case.[72] Although the Nisga'a from northwestern BC lost their case 4:3 on a technicality, they gained on another front. Six of the Court's seven judges recognized, for the first time, the existence of "Aboriginal title to land" in Canadian law.[73] This eventually led to the Nisga'a Treaty in 2001.
- **1973**. The Native Law Centre at the University of Saskatchewan was founded. It has contributed greatly to a new awareness of Indigenous legal rights. National in scope, the NLC was designed to help registered Indians, Inuit, non-registered Indians, and Métis from across Canada become successful law students. In 2018 the NLC added a Cree name, and it is now called the Wiyasiwewin Mikiwahp Native Law Centre. Today, Indigenous law graduates who are alumni of the NLC Summer Program number over 1,700.[74]

- **1974**. The Office of Native Claims opened in Ottawa.[75] The federal government invited First Nations groups to file what it calls "comprehensive claims" for areas not already under treaty and "specific claims" for grievances over lands already included in treaty, lost reserve lands, and the management of trust money. Comprehensive settlements have become modern treaties.
- **1975**. The James Bay and Northern Quebec Agreement was signed, making it the first modern treaty contracted with Indigenous peoples. Through this negotiated agreement the Cree gained additional control over their government, education, and health services. The Cree and Inuit in Quebec retained ownership of lands in and around their communities, as well as exclusive hunting, fishing, and trapping rights over a larger area.[76]
- **1977**. The Mackenzie Valley Pipeline Inquiry or Berger Commission issued its Final Report. Justice Thomas Berger led the Inquiry to investigate the social, economic, and environmental impact of a proposed natural gas corridor that would run though the Mackenzie River Valley and the Yukon. The Report made the vital point that the North was the Indigenous peoples' homeland, not simply a resource frontier for southern Canada.[77] The accessible (i.e., readable) and well-illustrated report established a new model for a Royal Commission. It changed the way northern development was done.[78]
- **1982**. Section 35(1) of Canada's new constitution, the Constitution Act, 1982, "recognizes and affirms existing Aboriginal and treaty rights." Prior to this, the courts had held that Aboriginal treaties could be amended or overridden by federal statute without the Aboriginal parties' agreement.
- **28 June 1985**. Bill C-3l was passed, removing enfranchisement from the Indian Act. It restored Indian status to all those women who had married non-Indians and thereby lost their status under the Indian Act, and gave status to the immediate descendants of these women. By 2012, because of Bill C-31, nearly 150,000 women and their children had regained their Indian status.[79]
- **1987**. Several First Nation groups returned as visible First Nation communities with Indian status. In response to pressure from Euro-Canadian settlers, the Malecite or Maliseet (Wolasioqiyik or Wustukwiuck) of Viger, at Cacouna, near Rivière-du-Loup in Quebec, had sold their reserve in 1869.[80] By the 1950s the community, while still recognized as a First Nation by the federal government, had almost vanished, with no band council and no community organization. Numbers swelled after the passage of Bill C-31, leading to their recognition as a nation by Quebec's National Assembly, and

with the federal government's approval, the Malecites of Viger again established their community organization.[81]

- **June 1990.** The Meech Lake Accord was designed to bring Quebec into Canada's constitutional family, following amendments to the Constitutional Act, 1982. This was in response to Quebec's desire for constitutional recognition as a "distinct society." The Meech Lake Accord did not, however, address Indigenous and other groups' concerns, and it was not ratified. In the spring of 1990, Elijah Harper, an Indigenous MLA in the Manitoba Legislature, withheld his vote on a technical point long enough to delay Manitoba's ratification of the accord until after the deadline for doing so had passed. On 22 June the Meech Lake Accord died.[82] The lasting lesson of the experience for Elijah Harper was, in his own words, "We need many more aboriginal people elected across this country."[83]

- **July 1990.** The outbreak of the Oka crisis followed the failure of the Meech Lake Accord by just a month.[84] In July the Mohawk of Kanesatake resisted attempts by the Town of Oka, 50 kilometres to the northwest of Montreal, to expand a golf course on disputed lands that included a Mohawk cemetery. The 78-day armed stand-off that followed between the Mohawk and the federal and Quebec governments proved the catalyst for Ottawa to create the Royal Commission on Aboriginal Peoples.

- **1992.** The Charlottetown Accord promised to recognize the Indigenous peoples as founding peoples. The Accord accepted the inherent Aboriginal right of self-determination within Canada by recognizing Aboriginal governments as one of Canada's three orders of government. For some Canadians, it promised too much; for others, too little. The Charlottetown Accord failed to win majority support in several provinces in a national referendum held in 1992. Even First Nations communities opposed it.[85]

- **1993.** The Yukon Umbrella Final Agreement was signed, leading to individual treaties with Yukon First Nations.[86]

- **1995.** Ojibwe (Chippewa) protestors occupied Ipperwash Provincial Park in southwestern Ontario with the intent to reclaim disputed Indigenous land expropriated from them during the Second World War. Ontario Provincial Police stormed the barricades, leaving one First Nations defender, Dudley George, dead. The 2007 *Report of the Ipperwash Inquiry*, headed by Justice Sidney B. Linden, revealed "intolerant racial and cultural attitudes towards First Nations people."[87]

- **1996.** The first volume of the report by the Royal Commission on Aboriginal Peoples (1991–6) was published. Following Oka, Prime

Minister Brian Mulroney appointed this commission to investigate the "evolution of the relationship of aboriginal peoples (Indian, Inuit, and Métis), the Canadian government, and Canadian society as a whole."[88] The findings provide a benchmark description of the situation at the end of the twentieth century. As the Report's first volume states, "Within a span of 25 years, Aboriginal peoples and their rights have emerged from the shadows, to the sidelines, to occupy centre-stage."[89]

- **21 June 1996**. The first National Aboriginal Day was held to celebrate Indigenous achievements. In 2017 the name was changed to National Indigenous Peoples Day.[90]
- **11 December 1997**. The Supreme Court of Canada ruled on the Delgamuukw case, thereby recognizing the existence of unextinguished Aboriginal Title in BC.[91] Among the most significant aspects of the case, the Court recognized oral histories as legitimate evidence, alongside written records. Delgamuukw has greatly broadened Indigenous Title claims.
- **7 January 1998**. Minister of Indian Affairs and Northern Development Jane Stewart, speaking on behalf of the Government of Canada, expressed in a *Statement of Reconciliation* "profound regret" for the establishment of the Indian residential school system. The federal government in *Gathering Strength: Canada's Aboriginal Action Plan*, which Minister Stewart introduced in this same address, agreed to establish the Aboriginal Healing Fund, with $350 million to support community-based healing initiatives.[92]
- **26 April 1999**. The Nisga'a Final Agreement (Bill 51) was granted Royal Assent. This was the first comprehensive claim to be settled south of the Yukon and Northwest Territories since the James Bay Agreement in 1975. BC's first modern treaty[93] lifted the Nisga'a from under the Indian Act. The lawyer and historian Garrett Wilson has commented on the complexity of The Nisga'a Treaty. It consists of more than 1,500 pages of sophisticated provisions, in contrast to Treaty Seven in 1877 whose text is only twenty paragraphs easily printed on four pages.[94]
- **17 September 1999**. The Supreme Court of Canada decided the case of *R. v. Marshall* regarding fishing rights and thereby confirmed the growing legal and political recognition of Aboriginal rights in Atlantic Canada. The Court concluded that the peace and friendship treaties made in 1760–1 between the Mi'kmaq and the Maliseet (Wolastoqiyik) and the British gave the former a treaty right to earn "a modest income" in the Atlantic commercial fishery. The Marshall decision reinstated the legal authority of the eighteenth-century treaties.[95]

- **1 April 1999.** The Territory of Nunavut in the eastern and central Arctic came into existence after years of negotiation, beginning with the signing seven years earlier of a land claims agreement.[96] Nunavut, in which the Inuit constitute 85 per cent of the total population, has three official languages: Inuktitut, English, and French.
- **1992–2003.** Three of the five Dene groups in the Northwest Territories (Gwich'in, Sahtu Dene, and Tlicho, or Dogrib) signed agreements with the Government of Canada. Indigenous self-determination became a reality in these regions.
- **2002.** The Government of Quebec and the Grand Council of the Crees (Eeyou Istchee), made the "Paix des Braves," which takes its name from the phrase that means in French that only the most courageous can make peace with their adversaries. This essentially economic agreement provides for revenue sharing derived from mining, hydroelectric developments, and forestry carried out on the Cree's traditional lands.[97]
- **November 2005.** The Kelowna Accord was concluded by Prime Minister Paul Martin, the provincial and territorial governments, and five national Indigenous organizations. It involved a federal commitment of $5 billion over the first five years of a ten-year initiative to improve Indigenous peoples' education, health care, housing, economic development, and social services. Upon their election to office early the next year, the Conservatives under Stephen Harper rescinded the Accord.[98]
- **2006.** The Residential School Settlements Agreement was concluded by the Government of Canada and the churches involved in the Indian residential schools with the vast majority of the schools' former students. The historian J.R. Miller hailed the achievement of this difficult multimillion-dollar out-of-court settlement, "a near miracle."[99] Implementation began in 2007.
- **11 June 2008.** Prime Minister Stephen Harper issued a full apology for the Government of Canada's support of Indian residential schools, which states, "The government now recognizes that the consequences of the Indian residential schools policy were profoundly negative and that this policy has had a lasting and damaging impact on aboriginal culture, heritage and language."[100]
- **2009.** The Government of Canada renamed the Queen Charlotte Islands, originally so designated after a late eighteenth-century vessel named for the wife of King George III. Haida Gwaii means "islands of the people" in the Haida language. The name change recognizes the importance of cultural names to the First Nations.[101]

- **2010**. During the opening ceremonies of the Vancouver Winter Olympics, the organizers gave head-of-state status to the chiefs of the four First Nations on whose lands the games took place.[102]
- **Winter 2012–13**. The Idle No More movement emerged. It was a response to the deeply felt frustration of many Indigenous people with the federal government, and their own Indigenous political leadership. Rallies occurred in dozens of cities. There were block-ades of major highways, drumming flash mobs in malls, and round dance rallies. The organizers used Facebook, YouTube, and Twitter for the extremely simply message: "Stand up, be heard and let the country know that Aboriginal peoples, communities, and cultures are alive."[103]
- **26 June 2014**. The Supreme Court of Canada ruled on *Tsilhqot'in Nation v. British Columbia* and with that ruling recognized Aborigi-nal Title on the land of traditional Chilcotin (Tsilhqot'in) territory in central BC, amounting to some 1,750 square kilometres in extent. The Court had held in its 1997 Delgamuukw decision that Aborigi-nal Title had not been extinguished in either pre- or post-Confedera-tion legislation in British Columbia. For this decision the Court also relied heavily on its 1973 Calder (Nisga'a) decision.[104]
- **2015**. The Truth and Reconciliation Commission was established as part of the Indian Residential Schools Settlement Agreement. Almost overnight, the phrase "cultural genocide" jumped from relative obscurity (although it had been used earlier) into official Canadian language, especially after Supreme Court Chief Justice Beverley McLachlin used it in a speech in May 2015 to describe Canadian policy towards the Indigenous peoples. Several days later the TRC used the phrase as the central organizing theme in its interim final report. The federal government accepted all of the TRC's 94 Calls to Action, which apply to every major agency and institution in Canada, including governments, churches, the legal system, schools, and universities, as well as museums and archives.[105]
- **November 2015**. A dramatic development in the history of the relationship between the Indigenous peoples and Canada's legal system occurred, with the appointment of Liberal MP Jody Wilson-Raybould, a First Nations woman, as Canada's minister of justice and attorney general.[106] She served for over three years. Wilson-Raybould is a member of the We Wai Kai Nation (also known as the Cape Mudge First Nation) of Vancouver Island, a lawyer, and former regional chief of the BC Assembly of First Nations. At pres-ent she is an independent MP in the House of Commons.

- **2016.** The implications of the *Daniels* v. *Canada* case before the Supreme Court of Canada are not entirely clear at this point. The Court ruled that Métis and non-status Indians are "Indians" under Section 91(24) of the Constitution Act, 1867, originally known as the British North America Act. As the Daniels decision did not give the Métis or non-status Indians, Indian status under the Indian Act, Métis are not becoming status Indians.

- **August 2016.** The National Inquiry into Missing and Murdered Indigenous Women and Girls began its work.[107] Established as a key government initiative to address the disproportionally high levels of violence faced by Indigenous women and girls, the Inquiry was also the Government of Canada's response to the TRC's Call to Action no. 41.

- **October 2017.** Minister of Crown-Indigenous Relations Carolyn Bennett announced a proposed settlement with First Nations and Inuit Sixties Scoop survivors. The "Sixties Scoop" describes the practice of provincial child welfare agencies, from the late 1950s into the 1980s, of removing Indigenous children from their families and placing them in foster homes or with non-Indigenous adoptive parents.[108] This has caused great harm.[109]

- **3 June 2019.** The National Inquiry into Missing and Murdered Indigenous Women and Girls had issued an interim report in November 2017. It now delivered its Final Report with recommendations. The Report runs over 1,200 pages and concludes that these thousands of murders and disappearances constitute a "Canadian genocide."[110]

- **February 2020.** The RCMP arrested protestors in northwestern British Columbia opposed to the construction of a Coastal Gas Link pipeline across unceded Wet'suwet'en. Territory. Supporters across Canada shut down rail service to back the Wet'suwet'en hereditary chiefs. Most of the elected chiefs in the area, elected under the Indian Act, support the building of the pipeline. The blockades are down, negotiations continue.

- **March to June 2020.** The COVID-19 epidemic took the world by surprise. Dr Theresa Tam, Canada's chief public health officer, raised in early May the high risk of "severe outcomes" for the Indigenous Peoples from the disease, given heath care inequities, higher rates of underlying medical conditions, and challenges of remote and fly-in communities. Indigenous communities are indeed vulnerable in times of pandemic. In May 2020 the federal government announced it was committing $285 million to support public health responses to COVID-19 in Indigenous communities.[111]

Notes

Prologue

1 Hon. A.C. Rutherford, first premier of Alberta, foreword in Sir Cecil E. Denny, *The Law Marches West*, edited and arranged by W.B. Cameron, 2nd ed. [1939] (Toronto: J.M. Dent, 1972).

2 The term is also spelled "Anishinaabe" and "Anishinaabeg." Donald B. Smith, *Mississauga Portraits: Ojibwe Voices from Nineteenth-Century Canada* (Toronto: University of Toronto Press, 2013), xvi and 289n9.

3 For a good academic review of the children's book, *The Light in the Forest*, see Maurice D. Schmaier and Conrad Richter, *Ethnohistory*, 7/4 (1960): 327–98.

4 John A. Williams, "Reminiscences," in possession of Mrs Sydney Williams, Eberts, Ont., referenced in Hazel Mathews, *Oakville and the Sixteen: The History of an Ontario Port* (Toronto: University of Toronto Press, 1953; reprinted with corrections in 1971 and 1994), 109. For background on the identity of possible First Nations groups using this site through time, see Frank A. Dieterman, ed., *The First 10,000 Mississauga Years* (Toronto: Published by Eastendbooks for the Mississauga Heritage Foundation, 2002). For an overview of the history of the First Nations in southern Ontario, see Edward S. Rogers and Donald B. Smith, eds., *Aboriginal Ontario: Historical Perspectives on the First Nations* (Toronto: Dundurn, 1994). The natural history of the Oakville area is reviewed in the *Sixteen Mile Creek 1958 Conservation Report* (Toronto: Ontario Department of Planning and Development, 1958).

5 Beverley Haun, *Becoming Kirk Wipper: The Story of the Museum's Founder* (Peterborough, Ont.: Canadian Canoe Museum, 2013), 102–6.

6 An interesting study of English-speaking Canada in this period is C.P. Champion, *The Strange Demise of British Canada: The Liberals and*

Canadian Nationalism, 1964–1968 (Montreal and Kingston: McGill-Queen's University Press, 2010).

7 Alan Rayburn, *Place Names of Ontario* (Toronto: University of Toronto Press, 1997), 266.

8 Richard Collins, "How Mississauga Got Its Name. Part 8 of 8: Democracy Rules, Finally," *Heritage News*, 24/4 (Fall 2011): 6, 14.

9 Ibid., "Part 6 of 8: The Name Game," *Heritage News*, 24/2 (Spring 2011): 6.

10 Ibid., "Part 7 of 8: Anything but 'Mississauga,'" *Heritage News*, 24/3 (Summer 2011): 6.

11 Ibid., "Part 5 of 8," *Heritage News*, 24/1 (Winter 2010): 6.

12 Don Smith, "Don Smith '68 Recalls the 1966 Trinity Conference on the Canadian Indian," *Trinity Alumni Magazine*, (Spring 1999): 4–6.

13 John Perry, "A Life Ministering to First Nations," *Tidings: The University of King's College Alumni Magazine*, (Winter 2004): 22.

14 Peter Russell, ed., *Nationalism in Canada* (Toronto: McGraw-Hill, for the University League for Social Reform, 1966).

15 James S. Frideres and René R. Gadacz, *Aboriginal Peoples in Canada*, 9th ed. (Toronto: Pearson, 2012), 116–18.

16 Typed list, "Indian Students Attending University, 1965–66," in University of Toronto, Trinity College Archives, Encounter Club Papers, F2012, file 985-0075/001 (04).

17 Alas, due to a linguistic misunderstanding, I missed hearing Charles de Gaulle speak on 24 July 1967, after which Prime Minister Lester Pearson immediately cancelled de Gaulle's invitation to visit Ottawa. I had gone to the French Pavilion a day or so before to ask where de Gaulle would be speaking on his Montreal visit. I was told the "Hôtel de Ville." As I did not know the location of this particular hotel, no doubt a small one, I dropped the idea of attending. Later I discovered that "hôtel de ville" is, of course, "city hall" in French!

18 R.F. Battle, "Indians in Transition," in *Canada One Hundred, 1867–1967*. Prepared in the Canada Year Book Handbook and Library Division, Dominion Bureau of Statistics. Published under the authority of the Hon. Robert J.H. Winters, minister of Trade and Commerce (Ottawa: Queen's Printer, 1967), 64.

19 Myra Rutherdale and Jim Miller, "'It's Our Country': First Nations' Participation in the Indian Pavilion at Expo '67," *Journal of the Canadian Historical Association*, 17/2 (2006): 148–73.

20 John Lownsbrough, *The Best Place to Be: Expo 67 and Its Time* (Toronto: Allen Lane, 2012), 204.

21 Olive Patricia Dickason, *Canada's First Nations: A History of Founding Peoples from Earliest Times*, 3rd ed. (Toronto: Oxford University Press, 2002), 375).

22 Rutherdale and Miller, "Indian Pavilion," 159.

23 Conversation with Pierre Savard, 12 June 1994.

24 These "appearances" are in no way complete, but just fleeting introductions by a documentary non-Indigenous historian. Full biographical sketches await a scholar with expertise in Indigenous oral histories. The Indigenous Studies professor Dr Winona Wheeler, a member of the Fisher River Cree First Nation in Manitoba, points out challenges in her essay, "Cree Intellectual Traditions in History," in Alvin Finkel, Sarah Carter, and Peter Fortna, eds., *The Wests and Beyond: New Perspectives on an Imagined Region* (Edmonton: AU Press, 2010), 47–61.

25 Harold Cardinal, *The Rebirth of Canada's Indians* (Edmonton: Hurtig, 1977), 170–1.

26 Laurie Meijer Dress "White Paper: Aboriginal Contributions to Canadian Politics and Government," in Cora J. Voyageur, David R. Newhouse, and Dan Beavon, eds., *Hidden in Plain Sight* , vol. 2 (Toronto: University of Toronto Press, 2011), 287.

27 J. Rick Ponting and Roger Gibbins, *Out of Irrelevance* (Toronto: Butterworths, 1980), 199.

28 Alan C. Cairns, *Citizens Plus: Aboriginal Peoples and the Canadian State* (Vancouver: UBC Press, 2000), 6.

29 Rev. Enos Montour is the author of *The Feathered U.E.L.'s* (Toronto: Division of Communication, United Church of Canada, 1973). He also wrote a semi-fictional account of an Indian boarding school based on his four years at Mount Elgin Residential School in Ontario, from age 11 to 15. It appeared in mimeograph form the year after his death, as "Brown Tom's Schooldays" (Waterloo, Ont.: Elizabeth Graham, 1985).

30 Paul A.W. Wallace, "Acknowledgements," in *Indian Paths of Pennsylvania* (Harrisburg, Pa.: Pennsylvania Historical and Museum Commission, 1965), iii.

31 Environics Institute for Survey Research, *Canadian Public Opinion on Aboriginal Peoples* (Toronto: Author, 2016), 3.

32 Thomas King, *The Inconvenient Indian: A Curious Account of Native People in North America* (Toronto: Doubleday, 2012), xiii.

33 Chelsea Vowel, *Indigenous Writes: A Guide to First Nations, Métis and Inuit Issues in Canada* (Winnipeg: HighWater Press, 2016), 8–36.

34 J.R. Miller, *Residential Schools and Reconciliation: Canada Confronts Its History* (Toronto: University of Toronto Press, 2017), xiii.

35 Kent Gooderham, *I Am an Indian* (Toronto: Dent, 1969), x.

36 Paul Tennant, *Aboriginal Peoples and Politics: The Indian Land Question in British Columbia, 1849–1989* (Vancouver: UBC Press, 1990), xii.

37 Gregory Younging, *Elements of Indigenous Style: A Guide for Writing by and about Indigenous Peoples* (Edmonton: Brush Education, 2018).

1. John A. Macdonald and the Indians

1 Thomas H.B. Symons, "John A. Macdonald: A Founder and Builder," *Canadian Issues*, (Summer 2015): 6.

2 James Daschuk, "Acknowledging Patriarch's Failures Will Help Canada Mature as a Nation," *Canadian Issues*, (Summer 2015): 45. In his endnote Daschuk cited Alex Woolford, Jeff Benvenuto, and Alexander Laban Hinton, eds., *Colonial Genocide in Indigenous North America* (Durham: Duke University Press, 2014).

3 D.J. Hall, *From Treaties to Reserves: The Federal Government and Native Peoples in Territorial Alberta, 1870–1905* (Montreal and Kingston: McGill-Queen's University Press, 2015), 42–3, 10.

4 Donald Swainson, "Canada Annexes the West: Colonial Status Confirmed," in Bruce Hodgins, Don Wright, and Welf Heick, eds., *Federalism in Canada and Australia: The Early Years* (Waterloo, Ont.: Wilfrid Laurier University Press, 1978), 137–57.

5 Ged Martin, *Favourite Son? John A. Macdonald and the Voters of Kingston, 1841–1891* (Kingston: Kingston Historical Society, 2010), 3.

6 J.K. Johnson and P.B. Waite, "Sir John Alexander Macdonald," *Dictionary of Canadian Biography (DCB)*, vol. 12, *1891–1900* (Toronto: University of Toronto Press, 1990), 591–2.

7 Donald Creighton, *John A. Macdonald: The Young Politician* (Toronto: Macmillan, 1952), 19.

8 John Graves Simcoe to Henry Dundas, dated York, Upper Canada, 20 Sept. 1793, in *The Correspondence of Lieut. Governor John Graves Simcoe*, vol. 2, *1793–1794*, edited by E.A. Cruikshank (Toronto: Ontario Historical Society, 1924), 61. For full details on the early Mississauga treaties, see Donald B. Smith, *Mississauga Portraits: Ojibwe Voices from Nineteenth-Century Canada* (Toronto: University of Toronto Press, 2013), 44–51, 216–20.

9 Donald B. Smith, "The Dispossession of the Mississauga Indians: A Missing Chapter in the Early History of Upper Canada," *Ontario History*, 73/2 (June 1981): 72.

10 Ibid. 74.

11 Extract of a letter from W. Crawford, Esq., to Sir John Johnson, Bart., dated at Cataraqui, 14 Aug. 1784, in Canada, Legislative Assembly, "Report of the Special Commissioners Appointed on the 8th of September, 1856, to Investigate Indian Affairs in Canada," Sessional Papers, 1858, appendix 21. This report is not paginated.

12 Donald B. Smith, *Sacred Feathers: The Reverend Peter Jones (Kahkewaquonaby) and the Mississauga Indians* (Toronto: University of Toronto Press, 1987), 22–31. Helpful for understanding their viewpoint is George S.

Snyderman, "Concepts of Land Ownership among the Iroquois and Their Neighbours," in William N. Fenton, ed., *Symposium on Local Diversity in Iroquois Culture*, Smithsonian Institution, Bureau of American Ethnology, Bulletin 149 (Washington, DC: US Government Printing Office, 1951), 15–34, esp. 28.

13 Peter Jones, *History of the Ojebway Indians: With Especial Reference to Their Conversion to Christianity* (London: A.W. Bennett, 1861), 71. This work appeared posthumously, five years after Jones's death in 1856.

14 Doug Williams, *(Godigaa Migizi), Michi Saagig Nishnaabeg: This Is Our Territory* (Winnipeg: ARP Books, 2018), 65.

15 Susan M. Hill, *The Clay We Are Made Of: Haudenosaunee Land Tenure on the Grand River* (Winnipeg: University of Manitoba Press, 2017), 5.

16 David Landy, "Tuscarora among the Iroquois," in Bruce G. Trigger, ed., *Handbook of American Indians*, vol. 15, *Northeast* (Washington, DC: Smithsonian Institution, 1978), 524.

17 Brian S. Osborne, "Frontier Settlement in Eastern Ontario in the Nineteenth Century: A Study in Changing Perceptions of Land and Opportunity," in David Harry Miller and Jerome O. Steffen, eds., *The Frontier: Comparative Studies* (Norman: University of Oklahoma Press, 1977), 208.

18 Charles Hamori-Torok, "The Iroquois of Akwesasne (St Regis), Mohawks of the Bay of Quinte (Tyendinata), Onyota'a:ka (the Oneida of the Thames), and Wahta Mohawk (Gibson), 1750–1945," in Edward S. Rogers and Donald B. Smith, eds., *Aboriginal Ontario: Historical Perspectives on the First Nations* (Toronto: Dundurn, 1994), 262. The majority of the Six Nations settled in the Grand River Valley west of Lake Ontario.

19 Osborne, "Frontier Settlement," 211.

20 R.W. Shaw, "The Treaty Made with the Indians at Kingston, May 31, 1819, for the Surrender of Lands," *Ontario Historical Society: Papers and Records*, 27 (1931): 540–2. Canada, *Indian Treaties and Surrenders from 1680 to 1900 – In Two Volumes* (Ottawa: Printed by Brown Chamberlin, Printer to the Queen's Most Excellent Majesty, 1891), 1: 62–3.

21 William Case to Robert Alder, dated Alderville, 16 Mar. 1843, United Church Archives, Toronto, Wesleyan Methodist Missionary Society Papers, Box 27, file 185. Peter Jones, *Life and Journals of Kah-ke-wa-quo-na-by Rev. Peter Jones, Wesleyan Misionary*, published under the direction of the Missionary Committee, Canada Conference (Toronto: Anson Green, at the Wesleyan Printing Establishment, 1860) 261, entry of 1 Oct. 1829.

22 For the lease for Grape Island, see George F. Playter, *The History of Methodism in Canada: With an Account of the Rise and Progress of the Work of God among the Canadian Indian Tribes* (Toronto: Published for the Author by Anson Green, 1862), 292–3. For a short summary of the Grape Island

experiment, see Richard Boehme, *Mission on Grape Island* (Bloomfield, Ont.: 7th Town Historical Society, 1987).

23 See "Warrior Preacher: John Sunday, or Shawundais (ca. 1795–1875)," in Smith, *Mississauga Portraits*, 212–44. Today, the Methodists are part of the United Church of Canada, since church union with the Congregationalists and the majority of Presbyterians in 1925.

24 Chief John Sunday to Sir John A. Macdonald, 1 Nov. 1872, Library and Archives Canada (LAC), Indian Affairs Record Group (RG10), vol. 1159, mfm T-1472. I thank Jim Morrison for this reference.

25 Macdonald's reference to the Culbertson family was made in the House of Commons on 4 May 1885. See Canada, *House of Commons Debates* (1885), 1575. The prime minister mentioned Chief Culbertson and his father without giving their first names. The full names appear in Canada, *Indian Treaties and Surrenders*; Chief Archibald Culbertson is mentioned in 2:143 and his father, John Culbertson, in 1:101, 123, 136.

26 Gerald E. Boyce, *Historic Hastings* (Belleville, Ont.: Hastings County Council, 1967), 274. I thank Trish Rae for additional background information about John Culbertson.

27 Richard Gwyn, *John A., the Man Who Made Us: The Life and Times of John A. Macdonald*, vol. 1, *1815–1867* (Toronto: Random House, 2007), 53–4. My thanks to Trish Rae for further details in a notation by Rev. Saltern Givins in the Tyendinaga Parish Church Records, Burials, 11 July 1839. I also thank Trish Rae for a copy of "Trial of Brandt Brandt, a Mohawk Indian, for Murder," *Chronicle & Gazette and Kingston Commercial Advertiser*, 2 Oct. 1839. A full account appears in William R. Teatero, "'A Dead and Alive Way Never Does': The Pre-Political Professional World of John A. Macdonald" (M.A. thesis, Queen's University, 1978), 200–6.

28 Missionary anniversary for Kingston, *Upper Canada Herald*, 9 Feb. 1841, reprinted in the *Christian Guardian*, 17 Feb. 1841.

29 Heidi Bodaker, "Anishinaabe Toodaims: Contexts for Politics, Kinship, and Identity in the Eastern Great Lakes," in Carolyn Podruchny and Laura Peers, eds., *Gathering Places: Aboriginal and Fur Trade Histories* (Vancouver: UBC Press, 2010), 97–8.

30 Kahkewaquonaby, "A short account of the Customs and manners of the North American Indians, particularly of the Chippeway Nation," *Monthly Review: Devoted to the Civil Government of Canada*, 1/5 (May 1841): 313.

31 Jones, *History of the Ojebway Indians*.

32 Ibid., 217.

33 *Kingston Chronicle and Gazette*, 21 Sept. 1833.

34 *Affectionately Yours: The Letters of Sir John A. Macdonald and His Family*, edited by J.K. Johnson (Toronto: Macmillan, 1969), 160.

35 Sir John A. Macdonald to L.W. Herchmer, 22 July 1872, LAC, Sir John A. Macdonald Fonds, Political Papers, MG26-A, R14424-0-3-F, cited in Rod Macleod, *Sam Steele: A Biography* (Edmonton: University of Alberta Press, 2018), 339n24.

36 "Rev. William Macaulay Herchmer, M.A.," *Journal of Education for Upper Canada*, (Apr. 1862): 59. Also see Donald B. Smith, "The Herchmers' Secret," *Beaver*, outfit 310/4 (Spring 1980): 52–8.

37 Johnson and Waite, "Macdonald," 592.

38 "Report on the Affairs of the Indians in Canada," Appendix T, "Journals of the Legislative Assembly of Canada, 1847." The appendices are not paginated. The quote appears on the first page of "Section III." The Bagot Report was submitted in 1844, and published in two parts in 1845 and 1847.

39 Brian S. Osborne and Donald Swainson, *Kingston: Building on the Past* (Westport, Ont.: Butternut Press, 1988), 166.

40 Frederick H. Armstrong, *City in the Making: Progress, People and Perils in Victorian Toronto* (Toronto: Dundurn, 1988), 16. "Table IV. Population Growth in Central Canadian Cities, 1851–1921," in J.M.S. Careless, *Toronto to 1918: An Illustrated History* (Toronto: Lorimer, 1984), 200.

41 Daniel Wilson, "The Present State and Future Prospects of the Indians of British North America," in *Proceedings, Royal Colonial Institute*, vol. 5 (1874), 234. I thank Bennett McCardle for this reference.

42 The tract of land was formally confirmed as the Mississaugas of the New Credit Reserve in 1903. Margaret Sault, *The History of the Mississaugas of the New Credit First Nation* (Hagersville, Ont.: Lands, Research and Membership of the New Credit First Nation, n.d.), 12.

43 *Brown's Toronto General Directory 1856* (Toronto: Maclear & Co, 1856), 320.

44 H.G. Tucker, "A Warrior of the Odahwahs," *Ontario Historical Society: Papers and Records*, 18 (1920): 32.

45 Cecil King has written his biography, *Balancing Two Worlds: Jean-Baptise Assiginack and the Odawa Nation, 1768–1866* (Saskatoon: Saskatoon Fastprint, 2013).

46 See the biographical note in the *Canadian Journal*, new series (n.s.) 3 (1858): 115; and Douglas Leighton, "Francis Assikinack," *DCB 9, 1861–1870* (1976), 10–11.

47 David Faux, "Documenting Six Nations Indian Ancestry," *Families*, 20/1 (1980): 14.

48 Daniel Wilson, *Prehistoric Man* (London: Macmillan, 1865), 524.

49 Catherine Slaney, *Family Secrets: Crossing the Colour Line* (Toronto: Natural Heritage Books, 2003), 114–18. Stephen L. Hubbard, *Against All Odds: The Story of William Peyton Hubbard, Black Leader and Municipal Reformer* (Toronto: Dundurn, 1987), 12.

50 Robin W. Winks, *The Blacks in Canada: A History* (Montreal and Kingston: McGill-Queen's University Press, 1971), 480.

51 Smith, *Sacred Feathers*, 224, 329.

52 Sandford Fleming, diary entry for 28 June 1845, LAC, Sir Sandford Fleming Fonds, Diaries 1843–1852, MG29-B1, R7666-12-4-E, Diary 1843/45. I thank Martha Kidd of Peterborough, Ont., for this reference. Other contemporary forecasts of the extinction of the North American Indian in Upper Canada or Canada West include the following: John Richardson, "A Trip to Walpole Island and Port Sarnia," *Literary Garland* (Montreal), Jan. 1849, reprinted in A.H.U. Colquhoun, ed. *Tecumseh and Richardson* (Toronto: Ontario Book Co, 1924), 70–1; Samuel Strickland, *Twenty-Seven Years in Canada West*, 2 vols. (London, 1853; facsimile edition published in 1970 in Edmontron by Hurtig), 2:68.

53 Viscount Bury to Sir Edmund Head, governor general of Canada, dated Indian Department, Toronto, 5 Dec. 1855, enclosure no. 2, in Correspondence relating to Alterations in the Organization of the Indian Department 1856 (247), vol. XLIV, in *Irish University Press Series of British Parliamentary Papers, Correspondence and Papers Relating to Canada 1854–58, Colonies Canada 21* (Shannon: Irish University Press, 1970), 18. On Bury, see Donald B. Smith, "Lord Bury and the First Nations: A Year in the Canadas," in Myra Rutherdale, Kerry Abel, and P. Whitney Lackenbauer, eds., *Roots of Entanglement: Essays in the History of Native-Newcomer Relations* (Toronto: University of Toronto Press, 2017), 49–93.

54 *Minutes of the General Council of Indian Chiefs and Principal Men, held at Orillia, Lake Simcoe Narrows, On Thursday, the 30th, and Friday, the 31st July, 1846 on the Proposed Removal of the Smaller Communities, and the Establishment of Manual Labour Schools* (Montreal: Printed at the Canada Gazette Office, 1846).

55 Ibid., 11.

56 *The Final Report of the Truth and Reconciliation Commission*, vol. 1, *Canada's Residential Schools: The History, Part 1, Origins to 1939* (Montreal and Kingston: Published for the Truth and Reconciliation Commission by McGill-Queen's University Press, 2015), 75–7. *Minutes*, 6.

57 Eileen M. Antone, "The Educational History of the Onyota'a:ka Nation of the Thames," *Ontario History*, 85/4 (Dec. 1993): 313.

58 As one specific example, a century later former residential school student Eleanor Brass, a sister of Walter Deiter, the founding president of the National Indian Brotherhood (1968–70), found that off reserve she faced a colour line almost impossible to breach. Eleanor Brass, *I Walk in Two Worlds* (Calgary: Glenbow Museum, 1987), 28–9, 33, 38, 44–5.

59 "Civilization of the Indians," Legislative Assembly, 15 May 1857, *Globe* (Toronto), 16 May 1857. Also see the account in "House of Assembly: Toronto, 15 May 1857," *Daily Colonist*, 16 May 1857.

60 Peter H. Russell, *Canada's Odyssey: A Country Based on Incomplete Conquests* (Toronto: University of Toronto Press, 2017), 89.

61 Hall, *Treaties*, 340n57.

62 Claude Gélinas, *Les Autochtones dans le Québec post-Confédéral, 1867–1960* (Sillery, Que.: Éditions du Septentrion, 2007), 40.

63 Lillian F. Gates, *After the Rebellion: The Later Years of William Lyon Mackenzie* (Toronto: Dundurn, 1988), 277. The member for Haldimand did so, Gates writes, "because he believed the bill would injure settlers in the counties of Brant and Haldimand who were eager to have Indian land bought on the market," *Journal of the Legislative Assembly of [United] Canada*, (22 May 1857): 473–4."Grand River Settlement," *Toronto Weekly Messenger*, 5 June 1857, 2.

64 John S. Milloy, "The Early Indian Acts: Developmental Strategy and Constitutional Change," in Ian A.L. Getty and Antoine S. Lussier, eds., *As Long as the Sun Shines and Water Flows: A Reader in Canadian Native Studies* (Vancouver: UBC Press, 1983), 59.

65 "David Thorburn, Transmits Minutes of a Great Council […] with the Six Nations & a deputation of Chiefs from 15 different Bands from the 20th to 29th Sept. 1858," LAC, RG10, vol. 245A, Docket 11,486–11500. "Council of Indian Chiefs," *The Grand River Sachem*, 6 Oct. 1858; I thank Anne Unyi, curator of the Heritage and Culture Division, Edinburgh Square Heritage and Cultural Centre, Caledonia, Ont., for bringing this article to my attention The *Globe* only allotted the story fewer than 100 words on 14 Oct. 1858, and that article stated the Council was held "last week," but it had actually ended two and a half weeks earlier.

66 John Leslie, "The Indian Act: An Historical Perspective," *Canadian Parliamentary Review*, (Summer 2002): 24.

67 Canada, *Indian Treaties and Surrenders*, 1:50–3.

68 John A. McDonald [Macdonald] to R.J. Pennefather, Supt. Gen. I[ndian] Affairs (copy) dated 2 July 1857, LAC, RG10, 2242, file 47,080, mfm reel C-11186. Treaty 22 & Treaty 23 Reserve Claim, 28 May 2018, Mississaugas of the New Credit First Nation, submitted to the Government of Canada and to the Government of Ontario, 41.

69 *Letters of Sir John A. Macdonald*, 593–626.

70 John A. Macdonald, 24 Feb. 1870, in Canada, *House of Commons Debates* (1870), 173.

71 David Shanahan, "The Manitoulin Treaties, 1836 and 1862: The Indian Department and Indian Destiny," *Ontario History*, 86/1 (Mar. 1994): 26–7.

72 "The Troubles on the Manitoulin," *Globe*, 30 July 1863.

73 John Warkentin, "Geography of Confederation," Department of Geography Discussion Paper No. 57, York University, Toronto, Oct. 2004, 16–17.

74 Russell, *Canada's Odyssey*, 189.

75 Gwyn, *John A.*, 416.

76 "The British North America Act. VI. Distribution of Legislative Powers," reprinted in R. Douglas Francis and Donald B. Smith, eds., *Readings in Canadian History Pre-Confederation* (Toronto: Holt, Rinehart and Winston, 1982), 527. Macdonald himself probably inserted this reference to Indians. As J.K. Johnston, a Macdonald biographer writes, "He drafted almost all of what was to be Canada's constitution," in Johnson, ed., *Affectionally Yours*, 85.

77 Russell, *Canada's Odyssey*, 188.

78 J.R. Miller, "Macdonald as Minister of Indian Affairs: The Shaping of Canadian Indian Policy," in Patrice Dutil and Roger Hall, eds., *Macdonald at 200: New Reflections and Legacies* (Toronto: Dundurn, 2014), 323. This clause appears to have been inserted to protect Indian lands; it worked to prevent non-Indian men from becoming members of reserves by marrying women who lived there.

79 Hall, *Treaties*, 340n59.

80 Ted Binnema, "Protecting Indian Lands by Defining *Indian*, 1850–76," *Journal of Canadian Studies*, 48/2 (Spring 2014): 23–5.

81 Morris Zaslow, *The Opening of the Canadian North, 1870–1914* (Toronto: McClelland and Stewart, 1971), 1.

82 R. Cole Harris, "Peopling," in Paul Robert Magocsi, ed., *Encyclopedia of Canada's Peoples* (Toronto: University of Toronto Press, 1999), 1049.

83 Hall, *Treaties*, 39. In chapter four, Hall mentions the St Catharines Milling and Lumber Company case. The Judicial Committee of the Privy Council, then the supreme court of the British Empire, ruled in July 1888 that title to the soil rested with the Crown even before the treaties. See Zaslow, *Opening*, 150.

84 Hall, *Treaties*, 21. The historian John Leonard Taylor comments: "The land cession treaties made between the Crown and various groups of Indians in Canada implied the recognition of an aboriginal title to the territory occupied by the Indians concerned. Although Indian title was undefined, it was clearly regarded by the Government as something less than ownership. The basic purpose of the land cession treaty was to 'extinguish' Indian title to a specified area in order to clear any obstructions to the Crown's title." John Leonard Taylor, *Treaty Research Report: Treaty Six (1876)* (Ottawa: Treaties and Historical Research Centre, Indian and Northern Affairs Canada, 1985), 2.

85 Beth LaDow, *The Medicine Line: Life and Death on a North American Borderland* (New York: Routledge. 2001), 18–19.

86 Bettina Liverant, "Patterns on the Land: Themes of Order and Wilderness in Planning, Calgary 1869 to 1966" (M.A. thesis, University of Calgary, 1998), 39.

87 Renamed in 1904 the Royal North-West Mounted Police (RNWMP) and, in 1920, the Royal Canadian Mounted Police (RCMP).

88 Hall, *Treaties*, 28–9.

89 Sheldon Krasowski *No Surrender: The Land Remains Indigenous* (Regina: University of Regina Press, 2019), 87–127.

90 Milloy, "Indian Acts," 62–3.

91 John A. Macdonald, "Return to an Order of the House of Commons, dated 2 May," Canada, Sessional Papers (no. 20b) 1887, 37, cited in J.R. Miller, *Skyscrapers Hide the Heavens: A History of Native-Newcomer Relations in Canada*, 4th ed. (Toronto: University of Toronto Press, 2018), 207.

92 Smith, *Sacred Feathers*, 244.

93 John A. Macdonald, 21 Mar. 1876, in Canada, *House of Commons Debates* (1876), cited in Mary-Ellen Kelm and Keith D. Smith, *Talking Back to the Indian Act: Critical Readings in Settler Colonial Histories* (Toronto: University of Toronto Press, 2018), 42.

94 Allan Sherwin, *Bridging Two Peoples: Chief Peter Edmund Jones, 1843–1909* (Waterloo, Ont.: Wilfrid Laurier University Press, 2012), 77–8. Norman E. Shields, "Anishinabek Political Alliance in the Post-Confederation Period: The Grand General Indian Council of Ontario, 1870–1936" (M.A. thesis, Queen's University, 2001), 58.

95 Shields, "Council," 99.

96 Peter E. Jones to John A. Macdonald, dated Hagersville, 28 Aug. 1882, LAC, Macdonald Papers, MG26-A, vol. 387, 182861–2, mfm reel C-1758. Darin P. Wybenga, *A Celebration of Versatility: Mississaugas of the New Credit Historical Council House* (Brantford, Ont.: Paramount Printers, 2015). Macdonald did not attend the opening.

97 Except for the four years in which he was in Opposition (1873–78) the NWMP remained Macdonald's direct responsibility until his death in 1891. S.W. Horrall, *The Pictorial History of the Royal Canadian Mounted Police* (Toronto: MGraw-Hill, 1973), 12.

98 Douglas Leighton, "A Victorian Civil Servant at Work: Lawrence Vankoughnet and the Canadian Indian Department, 1874–1893," in Getty and Lussier, *As Long as the Sun Shines*, 104–19. Brian Titley, *The Frontier World of Edgar Dewdney* (Vancouver: UBC Press, 1999), viii, 49.

99 Alan Wilson, introduction in *The Letters of Charles John Brydges 1879–1882: Hudson's Bay Company Land Commissioner 1878–1882*, edited by Hartwell Bowsfield (Winnipeg: Hudson's Bay Record Society, 1977), xxii.

100 Brydges, *Letters*, 39.
101 Robert J. Talbot, *Negotiating the Numbered Treaties: An Intellectual and Political Biography of Alexander Morris* (Saskatoon: Purich, 2009), 80.
102 J.R. Miller, *Compact, Contract, Covenant: Aboriginal Treaty-Making in Canada* (Toronto: University of Toronto Press, 2007), 156.
103 John A. Macdonald, 5 May 1880, in Canada, *House of Commons Debates* (1880).
104 Canada, *Annual Report of the Department of the Interior*, 1879, 12, cited in Isaac Kholisile Mabindisa, "The Praying Man: The Life and Times of Henry Bird Steinhauer" (Ph.D. dissertation, University of Alberta, 1984), 427.
105 Patrice Dutil, *Prime Ministerial Power in Canada: Its Origins under Macdonald, Laurier, and Borden* (Vancouver: UBC Press, 2017), 73.
106 Robert Page, "The Railway Analogy," in Martin O'Malley, *The Past and Future Land: An Account of the Berger Inquiry into the Mackenzie Valley Pipeline* (Toronto: Peter Martin, 1976), 68. His testimony was given at the formal hearing of the Berger Inquiry in Yellowknife, 27 Apr. 1976.
107 Arthur J. Ray, *The Canadian Fur Trade in the Industrial Age* (Toronto: University of Toronto Press, 1990), 41.
108 "Obituary. Garrett Wilson," *Regina Leader-Post*, 24 Aug. 2017. *Frontier Farewell*, won the 2007 Saskatchewan Book Award for Scholarly Writing.
109 Garrett Wilson, *Frontier Farewell: The 1870s and the End of the Old West* [2007] (Regina: University of Regina Press, 2014).
110 Macleod, *Sam Steele*, 33.
111 James Daschuk, *Clearing the Plains: Disease, Politics of Starvation, and the Loss of Aboriginal Life* (Regina: University of Regina Press, 2013), 133.
112 John A. Macdonald to "My dear Dewdney," "Private," dated Earnscliffe, Ottawa, 19 Nov. 1883, Edgar Dewdney fonds, M-320-1, Glenbow Archives, Archives and Special Collections, University of Calgary.
113 Daschuk, *Clearing the Plains*, 133–6.
114 Joyce Katharine Sowby, "Macdonald the Administrator: Department of the Interior and Indian Affairs, 1878–1887" (M.A. thesis, Queen's University, 1984), 24, 401. Ken Cruikshank, "David Lewis Macpherson," *DCB* 12, *1891–1900* (1990), 687.
115 Miller, "Macdonald," 324.
116 Bill Russell, "The White Man's Paper Burden: Aspects of Record Keeping in the Department of Indian Affairs, 1860–1914," *Archivaria*, 19 (1984–85): 59, 61.
117 John A. Macdonald, Canada, House of Commons *Debates*, 9 May 1883, 1108.
118 The federal government ran on a very small budget, and revenue was overwhelmingly raised from customs and excise taxes.

119 Lawrence Vankoughnet to John A. Macdonald, 26 Aug. 1887, LAC, RG10, vol. 6001, file 1-1-1, pt. 1, cited in *Final Report of the Truth and Reconciliation Commission*, vol. 1, 205.

120 James S, Frideres, *Indigenous Peoples in the Twenty-First Century*, 3rd ed. (Don Mills, Ont.: Oxford University Press, 2020), 83.

121 Miller, "Macdonald," 326.

122 Elizabeth Graham, compiler, *The Mush Hole: Life at Two Indian Residential Schools* (Waterloo, Ont.: Heffle, 1997), 9.

123 Ibid., 87, 220. "Miss Florence Maracle," *Our Forest Children*, 3/11 (Feb. 1890): 141. This short article states, "This is the first instance on record in which an Indian *lady* has secured an appointment in the departmental buildings in the history of the Government." "Return A (1) of Officers and Employees of the Department of Indian Affairs, for the year ended 30th June, 1891," *Annual Report of the Department of Indian Affairs for the Year Ended 31st December 1891* (Ottawa: Queen's Printer, 1892), 3, original emphasis.

124 Graham, *Mush Hole*, 219. "Return A (1)," ibid.

125 David W. Osahgee, Walpole Island, Personal Records of the First World War, Regimental no. 845067, enlisted 28 Feb. 1916, LAC Website, "Personal Records of the First World War." His birth date appears as 22 June 1868. Also, see my files on both Floretta Maracle (013.04) and David Osahgee (013.16) in Donald B. Smith, Research notes for *Seen but Not Seen*, Accession no. 2016.42, Archives and Special Collections, University of Calgary (cited henceforth as the Smith fonds).

126 "Return A (1)," *Annual Report of the Department of Indian Affairs 1891*, 3. "An Indian in Office," *Our Forest Children*, 3/4 (July 1889).

127 E.B. Biggar, *Anecdotal Life of Sir John Macdonald* (Montreal: John Lovell, 1891), 175.

128 Harold Cardinal, "Indian Nations and Constitutional Change," in J. Anthony Long and Menno Boldt, in association with Leroy Little Bear, eds., *Governments in Conflict? Provinces and Indian Nations in Canada* (Toronto: University of Toronto Press, 1988), 84.

129 Walter Hildebrandt and Brian Hubner, *The Cypress Hills: An Island by Itself* (Saskatoon: Purich, 2007), 122.

130 Hugh Dempsey, *Big Bear: The End of Freedom* (Vancouver: Douglas & McIntyre, 1984), 202. In a fascinating comment in her *Medicine that Walks: Disease, Medicine, and Canadian Plains People, 1840–1940* (Toronto: University of Toronto Press, 2001), Maureen Lux notes that, with regard to the rations supplied, "Chemicals added to the meat and flour may have been an attempt to preserve the rations, or this may have been an attempt to salvage already spoiled food. In any case, it is clear from the elders' testimony that the people understood that they had been poisoned" (60).

131 Miller, *Skyscrapers*, 185.

132 Joseph Pope, quoted in Dutil, *Power*, 77.

133 Richard Gwyn, *Nation Maker, Sir John A Macdonald: His Life, Our Times*, vol. 2, *1867–1891* (Toronto: Random House, 2011). Gywn comments, "His administrative practices became slapdash," 387.

134 Melvin D. Steinhauer, *Shawahnekizhek–Henry Bird Steinhauer: Child of Two Cultures* (Edmonton: Priority Printing, 2015), 99.

135 R.B. Steinhauer, "The Indian Question," *Acta Victoriana*, 9/6 (Mar. 1886): 5–6.

136 Gywn, *Nation Maker*, 417.

137 I thank Magnus Isacsson for his help with this summary, email to me, 26 Mar. 2010.

138 William H. Jackson to "my dear Family," dated Lower Fort Garry, 19 Sept. 1885, Archives of Manitoba, cited in Donald B. Smith, *Honoré Jaxon: Prairie Visionary* (Regina: Coteau Books, 2007), 6, 205–6.

139 Smith, *Jaxon*, 141–3, 145, 156, 172, 204.

140 John A. Macdonald, 6 July 1885, in Canada, *House of Commons Debates* (1885), 3119. It would be fascinating to learn when and where John A. Macdonald met General George Armstrong Custer.

141 Hall, *Treaties*, 150.

142 Gwyn, *Nation Maker*, 475.

143 J.A. Macdonald to E. Dewdney, 20 Nov. 1885, Glenbow Archives, Dewdney Papers, Box 2, file 38, 587–8, quoted in Blair Stonechild and Bill Waiser, *Loyal till Death: Indians and the North-West Rebellion* (Calgary: Fifth House, 1997), 221.

144 Gloria Galloway, "Ottawa moving to exonerate First Nations Chief convicted of treason," *Globe and Mail*, 10 Jan. 2018. Poundmaker was convicted of treason in 1885 and exonerated by the federal Government of Canada in 2019. See "Trudeau exonerates Chief Poundmaker of 134-year-old treason conviction," *National Post*, 24 May 2019.

145 Laura Stone, "Saskatchewan First Nation wins $4.5-million from Ottawa: A Saskatchewan group has been awarded treaty payments over a century in the making," *Globe and Mail*, 28 Dec. 2016.

146 Stonechild and Waiser, *Loyal till Death*, 239.

147 John Jennings, *The Cowboy Legend: Owen Wister's Virginian and the Canadian-American Ranching Frontier* (Calgary: University of Calgary Press, 2015), 3, 250–1.

148 Graham, *Mush Hole*. 219. Donald B. Smith and Floyd Doctor, "Thomas Daniel Green," *Dictionary of Canadian Biography*, completed 2020 and soon to be made available on the World Wide Web. "Thomas Daniel Green," *Annual Report 1936, Association of Ontario Land Surveyors*, 124.

149 T.D. Green to the Rt. Hon. Sir John A. Macdonald, dated Indian Office, Regina, 8 Mar. 1886, LAC, Macdonald Papers, MG26-A, vol. 424, 206289, mfm C-1775.

150 Dashuk, *Clearing the Plains*, 172.

151 Hugh A. Dempsey, *Red Crow: Warrior Chief* (Saskatoon: Western Producer Prairie Books, 1980), 164, 168–9.

152 John A. Macdonald, quoted in Canada, House of Commons *Debates*, 9 May 1883, 1100.

153 D'Arcy Jenish, *Indian Fall: The Last Great Days of the Plains Cree and the Blackfoot Confederacy* (Toronto: Penguin, 2000), 293. John C. Ewers writes, "A normal day's march was about ten to fifteen miles," in his *The Blackfeet: Raiders on the Northwestern Plains* (Norman: University of Oklahoma Press, 1958), 94.

154 Hugh A. Dempsey, "The Fearsome Fire Wagon," in Hugh A. Dempsey, ed., *The CPR West: The Iron Road and the Making of a Nation* (Vancouver: Douglas & McIntyre, 1984), 60.

155 Robert Prévost, *Montreal: A History*, translated by Elizabeth Mueller and Robert Chodos (Toronto: McClelland and Stewart, 1993), 311. According to the 1891 census, Montreal had a population of roughly 215,000, compared with Quebec City's 63,000 and Toronto's 180,000.

156 Allan R. Taylor, "Note Concerning Lakota Sioux Terms for White and Negro," *Plains Anthropologist*, 21/71 (1976): 64.

157 For a full account of the visits in 1886 of twelve Plains Indian chiefs to Central Canada, see Donald B. Smith, "Worlds Apart," *Canada's History*, (Oct./Nov. 2017): 30–7; a longer fully documented version of this paper, entitled "Chiefs Journey," is available at https://www.canadashistory.ca /explore/first-nations-inuit-metis/chiefs-journey, accessed 5 June 2020.

158 Entry for "1886. Visit of Crowfoot and Other Chiefs to the East," in Father Léon Doucet, *Mon Journal: The Journal and Memoir of Father Léon Doucet o.m.i., 1868 to 1890*, transcribed and translated by Bronwyn Evans, edited by Mario Giguère and Bronwyn Evans (Calgary: Historical Society of Alberta, 2018), 163. The original French text reads, "Ils admirèrent ces merveilles … Ils revinrent aussi Sauvage qu'avant," 326.

159 A good overview of Earnscliffe appears in Norman Reddaway, *Earnscliffe: Home of Canada's First Prime Minister and since 1930 Residence of High Commissioners for the United Kingdom in Canada* (London: Commonwealth Relations Office, 1955).

160 Glenbow Archives, NA-13-2; also LAC, PA 45666. Photograph by John Woodruff, Department of the Interior.

161 "A peaceful pow-wow: The Indian chiefs visit the Premier and Lady Macdonald – Crowfoot's speech," *Montreal Daily Herald*, 11 Oct. 1886. This clipping and others relating to the tour of the Alberta chiefs to Central Canada is included in the collection of newspaper accounts of the 1886 Blackfoot tour, compiled by Hugh Dempsey and now in the Glenbow Archives, M1833.

162 "Our Indian visitors: The great Blackfoot chief and his first lieutenant," *Ottawa Free Press*, 9 Oct. 1886.

163 "The chiefs: Crowfoot and his companions visit Sir John," *Ottawa Evening Journal*, 9 Oct. 1886.

164 "Indian chiefs: They interview Sir John Macdonald and the other ministers," *Ottawa Free Press*, 23 Oct. 1886.

165 Cyril Greenland and John D. Griffin, "The Honourable Mary Macdonald: A Lesson in Attitude," *Canadian Medical Association Journal*, vol. 125 (1 Aug. 1981): 306. I thank Allan Sherwin for bringing this article to my attention.

166 Reddaway, *Earnscliffe*, 21.

167 Edward Ahenakew, "The Story of the Ahenakews," edited by by Ruth Matheson Buck, *Saskatchewan History*, 27/1 (Winter 1964): 17.

168 Deanna Christenson, *Ahtahkakoop: The Epic Account of a Plains Cree Head Chief, His People, and Their Struggle for Survival, 1816–1896* (Shell Lake, Sask.: Ahtahkakoop Publishing, 2000), 580.

169 Hall, *Treaties*, 9, 122.

170 Carmen Miller, "Sir John Joseph Caldwell Abbott," *DCB* 12, *1891–1900* (1990), 8.

171 Sarah Carter, *Lost Harvests: Prairie Indian Reserve Farmers and Government Policy* (Montreal and Kingston: McGill-Queen's University Press, 1990), 132.

172 Malcolm Cameron, 20 June 1891, in Canada, *House of Commons Debates*, 5th Parliament, 1st Session, vol. 1 (1891), 1484–5. I thank Rob Omura for this reference.

173 The fact that Macdonald left behind an enormous mass of papers, official and unofficial, and private, makes the fullest examination possible. Once combined with the rich records of the Department of Indian Affairs that he headed for a decade, an in-depth review of his Plains Indian administration can be made.

174 John L. Tobias, "Canada's Subjugation of the Plains Cree, 1879–1885," *Canadian Historical Review*, 64 (1983): 333–49.

175 Gerald Friesen, *The Canadian Prairies: A History* (Toronto: University of Toronto Press, 1984). Both Tobias's and Friesen's contributions on this question are recognized in Arthur J. Ray, Jim Miller, and Frank J. Tough, *Bounty and Benevolence: A History of Saskatchewan Treaties* (Montreal and Kingston: McGill-Queen's University Press, 2000), 208.

176 A. Blair Stonechild, "The Indian View of the 1885 Uprising," in F. Laurie Barron and James B. Waldram, eds., *1885 and After: Native Society in Transition* (Regina: Canadian Plains Research Center, 1986), 155–70. This article was later followed by the full book-length account, Stonechild and Waiser, *Loyal till Death*.

177 Daschuk, *Clearing the Plains*.

178 Good overviews of the Act are provided by Malcolm Montgomery, "The
     Six Nations Indians and the Macdonald Franchise," *Ontario History*, 57
     (1965): 13–25; and by J.I. Little, "Courting the First Nations Vote: Ontario's
     Grand River Reserve and the *Electoral Franchise Act* of 1885," *Journal of
     Canadian Studies*, 52/2 (Spring 2018): 538–69.

179 A misunderstanding holds that Macdonald, like his successors Laurier
     and Mackenzie King, only favoured Indians having the federal vote
     "on condition that we stopped being Indian." See George Manuel and
     Michael Posluns, *The Fourth World: An Indian Reality* (Don Mills, Ont.:
     Collier Macmillan, 1974), 124. Macdonald's Electoral Franchise Act of
     1885 actually allowed those males who met the qualifications to keep
     their Indian status.

180 John A. Macdonald, May 1885, in Canada, *House of Commons Debates*
     (1885), 1576.

181 Little, "First Nations Vote," 538–9, 558.

182 Kahkewaquonaby, MD, chief, to Sir John A. Macdonald, read out in the
     House of Commons Debates (1885), 8 June 1885. Allan Sherwin examines
     in depth Dr Peter E. Jones's connection with John A. Macdonald in his
     Bridging Two Peoples.

183 "The Missassaugua Indians: An important meeting of the Tribe
     yesterday," *Hamilton Spectator*, 21 Nov. 1894.

184 Sherwin, *Bridging*, 89–92.

185 Memorial of Mitchell Chubb, Chief; Peter Crowe, councillor; Joshua
     Blaker, councillor; Allan Salt, councillor; E. Comego, councillor; George
     Blaker, secretary, LAC, Macdonald Papers, MG26A, vol. 335A, 15133.

186 Those signing were the chief and councilors, the "haves" who held the
     largest amount of land and livestock in the community. See Art Beaver,
     "Dancing the Rice: Aboriginal Self-Government Is the Community
     Reclaiming Traditional Cultural Values / Mnoomini-Gaawin: Nishinaabe
     Gimaawin na Dani-Daapinaawaa Nishinaabe oodenoo" (M.A. thesis,
     Canadian Heritage and Development Studies, Trent University, 2000), 64.

187 Charles Big Canoe, chief, and James Ashquabe, councillor, to the Rt. Hon.
     Sir John Macdonald, Superintendent General of Indian Affairs, not dated,
     LAC, Macdonald Papers, MG26A vol. 335A, 151507.

188 La Cerise, "Ojibway Indians of Georgina Island in Lake Simcoe: A happy
     and contented colony of 130 members – Old Chief Big Canoe one of
     nature's gentlemen, who lives in a well-furnished modern house and
     idolizes his grandchildren, just like any white grandfather would do,"
     Toronto Star Weekly, 1 Oct. 1915, 17. Charles Big Canoe knew his Ojibwa
     culture intimately. He wrote, e.g., this in the preface to Rev. Egerton
     Ryerson Young's collection of Ojibwa stories, *Algonquin Indian Tales* (New
     York: Abingdon Press, 1903): "Dear Friend: Your book of stories gathered

from among my tribe has very much pleased me. The reading of them brings up the days of long time ago when I was a boy and heard our old people tell these tales in the wigwams and at the camp fire" (3).

189 There are 10 letters from Oronhyatekha to John A. Macdonald in the Macdonald Papers in LAC. Oronhyatekha to Macdonald, 5 Jan. 1882, LAC, Macdonald Papers, MG26a, vol. 390, 185208.

190 Keith Jamieson and Michelle A. Hamilton, *Dr Oronhyatekha: Security, Justice, and Equality* (Toronto: Dundurn, 2016), 123.

191 Dr Oronhyatekha, quoted in "Tyendinaga Reserve, Mohawk Centennial," *Tribune* (Kingston, Ont.?), undated clipping, reporting on 100th anniversary of their landing at Tyendinaga, 4 Sept. 1884, Rev. R.S. Forneri Scrapbook, Diocese of Ontario Archives, Kingston, Ont. I thank Norman Knowles for this reference.

192 Oronhyatekha to Macdonald, 5 Jan. 1882. Jamieson and Hamilton, *Oronhyatekha*, 156. Unfortunately, the little boy died at the age of two, in 1884.

193 Jamieson and Hamilton, *Oronhyatekha*, 145, 159; Little, "First Nations Vote," 552n40.

194 Milloy, "Indian Acts," 61. Status Indians who obtained a university degree were not automatically "enfranchised," as stated, e.g., by Thomas King, *The Inconvenient Indian: A Curious Account of Native People in North America* (Toronto: Doubleday, 2012), 71. James R. Miller confirms this in his article, "Research and Outcomes at the Truth and Reconciliation Commission," *Canadian Historical Review*, 100/2 (June 2019): 174–5. The late John Leslie sent this email to me on 10 Dec. 2012: "The provision enfranchising automatically doctors, lawyers, ministers/missionaries, and university graduates ['ipso facto'] first appeared in the 1876 Indian Act in Section 86(1) [...] In practical application, the 1876 initiative was inoperable. In 1880, Section 99(1) replaced Section 86(1). Section 99(1) contained a new clause '... upon petition to the Superintendent General, ipso facto become and be enfranchised ...' He then became eligible for an allotment of reserve land. But, again, few, if any, 'educated' Indians applied. My research has turned up no examples. Indeed, very few Indians enfranchised at all until D.C. Scott's amendments in 1919–1920. It seems to me the barriers I cited for failure in 1876 account for a similar lack of results after 1880. Indian people simply wanted to remain as Indians. Culture, kin, and language were powerful bonds."

195 There are a dozen letters from John W.M. Elliott to John A. Macdonald in the Macdonald Papers, most notably, J.W.N.[M.] Elliott to John A. Macdonald, dated Ottawa, 25 June 1890, "private," LAC, Macdonald Papers, MG26-A, 243042. On John Elliott, see "Noted Chief of Six Nations is buried in East," *Calgary Herald*, 31 May 1921. His father was not

Indigenous; see Smith, *Mississauga Portraits*, 86. As a young man, Elliott had attended the Mohawk Institute at Brantford; see Graham, *Mush Hole*, 219. Later he attended the Agricultural College at Guelph, Ontario, in the late 1870s; see Elliott to Macdonald, dated Toronto, 24 Nov. 1886, LAC, Macdonald Papers, MG26-A, 212175. Elliott was a grandson of John Smoke Johnson, the speaker of the Six Nations Council for nearly half a century, hence by the European system of recognizing kinship, a first cousin of Pauline Johnson; see "Ohsweken," *Brantford Weekly Expositor*, 9 Apr. 1914, 2. The Smith fonds contains three files on Elliott (012.16, 012.17, and 047.17).

196 Weaver, "Six Nations," 532. Weaver wrote of the members of the reform movement of 1890: "Few could claim hereditary chieftainship titles and most felt that education should be a requisite for council office. In 1890 they drafted a petition signed by some 20 percent of the male adults in the community, urging the government to apply the elected system to the reserve, but their activities in subsequent years went unheeded by the federal government."

197 Capt. J.W.M. Elliott to the Rt. Hon. Sir John A. Macdonald, dated Six Nations Reserve of the Grand River, 29 Oct. 1886, "private," LAC, Macdonald Papers, MG26-A, vol. 430, 211406.

198 Graham, *Mush Hole*, 219

199 "Noted Chief of Six Nations is buried in East."

200 Capt. J.W.M. Elliott to the Rt. Hon. Sir John A. Macdonald, dated Six Nations Reserve of the Grand River, Onondaga, Ont., 10 Jan. 1887, "private," LAC, Macdonald Papers, MG26A, vol. 430, 213303. All my notes on J.W.M. Elliott are in my file 012.17, "J.W. M. Elliott," in the Donald B. Smith fonds, Acc. 2016.42, Archives and Special Collections, University of Calgary (hereafter, Smith Fonds).

201 Elliott served as Mohawk chief in the Six Nations Confederacy. He appears standing at the back in the photo, "The Last Hereditary Council on the Six Nations' Reserve," in A. Leon Hatzan, *The True Story of Hiawatha and History of the Six Nation Indians* (Toronto: McClelland and Stewart, 1925), 156.

202 John A. Macdonald to Dr Peter E. Jones, 31 Aug. 1886, LAC, Macdonald Papers, MG26-A, Letterbook 24, 8.

203 Olive Patricia Dickason, *Canada's First Nations: A History of Founding Peoples from Earliest Times*, 3rd ed. (Don Mills: Oxford University Press, 2002), 266–7.

204 John A. Macdonald, House of Commons *Debates*, 1884, vol. 1, 540.

205 Sherwin, *Bridging Two Peoples*, 84.

206 Ibid. 85–8, 152. Dr Jones's recommendations that the Act's paternalist wording be removed, and a greater degree of self-government be included, were ignored.

207 John A. Macdonald, 4 May 1885, in Canada, *House of Commons Debates* (1885), 1574.

208 Kelm and Smith, *Talking Back*, 64–5.

209 John W.M. Elliott to John A. Macdonald, dated Onondaga, Ontario, [1886] LAC, Macdonald Papers, MG26A, vol. 430, 211401. Also see "Sir John's Visit," *Weekly Expositor* (Brantford), 10 Sept. 1886, 4. I thank Denise Kirk, Local History Librarian, Brantford Public Library, for this and other references to Macdonald's visit to the Grand River Six Nations Territory on 6 Sept. 1886.

210 Sally M. Weaver, "Six Nations of the Grand River, Ontario," in Bruce G. Trigger, ed., *Handbook of North American Indians*, vol. 15, *Northeast* (Washington, DC: Smithsonian Institution, 1978), 531.

211 David Blanchard, *Seven Generations: A History of the Kanienkehaka* (Kahnawake: Kahnawake Survival School, 1980), 362–7. Thomas Stone, "Legal Mobilization and Legal Penetration: The Department of Indian Affairs and the Canadian Party at St Regis, 1876–1918," *Ethnohistory*, 22/4 (Autumn 1975): 375–408.

212 Graham, *Mush Hole*, 87.

213 I am greatly indebted to Trish Rae for background information on both Archie Culbertson and Sampson Green.

214 LAC, Macdonald Papers, MG26A, vol. 304, 138675–6, original emphasis.

215 Samuel Barton Burdett, MP, 31 Mar. 1890, in Canada, *House of Commons Debates* (1890), 2730.

216 "Hepburn is first premier to visit Indians since Sir John A. Macdonald," *Toronto Daily Star*, 4 Dec. 1936.

217 Timothy J. Stanley, "'The Aryan Character of the Future of British North America': Macdonald, Chinese Exclusion, and the Invention of Canadian White Supremacy," in Dutil and Hall, *Macdonald at 200*, 115.

218 John A. Macdonald in Canada, *House of Commons Debates* (1885), 1582, cited in Peter Ward, *White Canada Forever: Popular Attitudes and Public Policy Toward Orientals in British Columbia* [1978], 2nd ed. (Montreal and Kingston: McGill-Queen's University Press, 1990), 41.

219 Ibid., 119.

220 John A. Macdonald in the House of Commons, 4 May 1885, reproduced in Sarah Katherine Gibson and Arthur Milnes, eds., *Canada Transformed: The Speeches of Sir John A. Macdonald* (Toronto: McClelland and Stewart, 2014), 407–8. Despite this vicious racial statement about African Canadians, Macdonald believed that those of African origin who lived in Canada, and who qualified, deserved the franchise.

221 Timothy J. Stanley, "John A. Macdonald, 'the Chinese' and Racist State Formation in Canada," *Journal of Critical Race Inquiry*, 3/1 (2016): 23.

222 Nive Voisine, "Louis-François Laflèche," *DCB* 12, *1891–1900* (1990), 506. Timothy P. Foran, *Defining Métis: Catholic Missionaries and the Idea of Civilization in Northwestern Saskatchewan, 1845–1898* (Winnipeg:

University of Manitoba Press, 2017), 18–21, 141. Father Albert Lacombe, the veteran Quebec-born priest on the Canadian Plains claimed his maternal grandmother was Métis, but no documentary evidence survives to support this claim. Soeur de la Providence, *Le Père Lacombe: "L'homme au bon coeur" d'après ses mémoires et souvenirs* (Montreal: Le Devoir, 1916), 3.

223 Shirlee Anne Smith, Hudson's Bay Company Archives, to Donald B Smith, 30 Dec. 1988. Carman Miller, "Sir Edward Seaborne Clouston," *DCB* 14, *1911–1920* (1998), 219–22.

224 J.G. MacGregor, *Senator Hardisty's Prairies (1849–1889)* (Saskatoon: Western Producer Prairie books, 1978), 3–5.

225 Ibid.

226 Shirlee Anne Smith, "Richard Charles Hardisty," *DCB* 11, *1881–1890* (1982), 383.

227 Gerald Friesen, "John Norquay," ibid., 642–3.

228 "Solomon White," *Commemorative Biographical Record of the County of Essex, Ontario* (Toronto: J.H. Beers, 1905), 64; Peter E. Paul Dembski, "Solomon White," *DCB* 14, *1911–1920* (1998), 1053–4. "Solomon White dies in Cobalt," *Windsor Evening Record*, 13 Nov. 1911.

229 John A. Macdonald to Louisa Macdonald, 14 Oct. 1887, and Mary Macdonald to Louisa Macdonald, 10 Dec. 1887, in Johnson, *Affectionately Yours*, 172–3.

230 Madge Macbeth, *Over My Shoulder* (Toronto: Ryerson Press, 1953), 85.

231 John Spargo, *Two Bennington-Born Explorers and Makers of Modern Canada* (n.p.p.: n.p. 1950), 70.

232 W. Stewart Wallace, "The Wives of the Nor'westers," in his *Pedlars from Quebec and Other Papers on the Nor'Westers* (Toronto: Ryerson Press, 1954), 68.

233 Bill Waiser, *A World We Have Lost: Saskatchewan Before 1905* (Markham, Ont.: Fifth House, 2016), 503. On a positive note the Canadian historian Maureen Lux writes in *Medicine that Walk: Disease, Medicine and Canadian Plains Native Peoples, 1880–1940* (Toronto: University of Toronto Press, 2001), that, in 1879, he showed great concern about smallpox and the First Nations. After an outbreak in Manitoba his administration began "vaccinating as many Native people as possible every spring." This program continued well into the twentieth century (page 139).

2. John McDougall and the Stoney Nakoda

1 Chief John Snow, *These Mountains Are Our Sacred Places: The Story of the Stoney People* (Toronto: Samuel Stevens, 1977), 17.

2 John Laurie, "Home on the Kootenay Plains," *Canadian Cattlemen*, (Aug. 1950): 22–3.

3 John McDougall called Morley his "strategic centre," in *On Western Trails in the Early Seventies: Frontier Life in the Canadian North-west* (Toronto: William Briggs, 1911), 26.

4 *Missionary Outlook*, (Dec. 1899): 267.

5 Rev. Thomas Woolsey mentions, "He speaks the Cree language remarkably well, [and] is gradually acquiring a knowledge of the Stone Indian." Thomas Woolsey to Enoch Wood, dated Edmonton House, 1 Jan. 1864, in Hugh A. Dempsey, ed., *Heaven Is Near the Rocky Mountains: The Journals and Letters of Thomas Woolsey, 1855–1869* (Calgary: Glenbow Museum, 1989), 148.

6 Hugh A. Dempsey, *Maskepetoon: Leader, Warrior, Peacemaker* (Victoria, BC: Heritage House, 2010), 116.

7 Robert H. Lowie, "The Assiniboine," *American Museum of Natural History*, vol. 4 (1909): 7.

8 John Maclean, *Canadian Savage Folk: The Native Tribes of Canada* (Toronto: William Briggs, 1896), 28.

9 That same year, again with Rev. Glass, John McDougall also brought out a *Primer and Language Lessons* in Cree and English. John Maclean, *McDougall of Alberta: A Life of Rev. John McDougall, D.D., Pathfinder of Empire and Prophet of the Plains* (Toronto: Ryerson Press, 1927), 261.

10 Hugh A. Dempsey, *Crowfoot: Chief of the Blackfeet* (Edmonton: Hurtig, 1972), 82.

11 Sheldon Krasowski, *No Surrender: The Land Remains Indigenous* (Regina: University of Regina Press, 2019), 189.

12 Sweetgrass's words recalled in John McDougall, *Opening the Great West: Experiences of a Missionary in 1875–76*, with an introduction by J. Ernest Nix (Calgary: Glenbow-Alberta Institute, 1970), 58.

13 Krasowski, *No Surrender*. 2, 73, 120, 158, 212, 272.

14 Snow, *These Mountains*, 28–9.

15 E.J. Staley, "The Stoney Indians at Morley, Alberta," *Canadian Cattlemen*, (Mar. 1941): 531.

16 James Ernest Nix, "John Chantler McDougall," *Dictionary of Canadian Biography* (*DCB*), vol. 14, *1911–1920* (Toronto: University of Toronto Press, 1998), 696.

17 Ian A.L. Getty, "Chiniquay," *DCB* 13, *1900–1910* (1994), 195.

18 Melvin D. Steinhauer, *Shawahnekizhek–Henry Bird Steinhauer: Child of Two Cultures* (Edmonton: Priority Printing, 2015), 52, 54, 99.

19 Donald B. Smith, "A Missionary Family: Henry Steinhauer, or Shahwahnegezhik (ca. 1817–1884) and Sons Egerton Ryerson Steinhauer (1858–1932) and Robert Steinhauer (1861–1941)," in *Mississauga Portraits: Ojibwe Voices from Nineteenth-Century Canada* (Toronto: University of Toronto Press, 2013), 245–76.

20 Donald B. Smith, "Elizabeth Barrett," *Alberta History* 46/4 (1998): 19–27. Smith, *Mississauga Portraits*, 261–4.

21 Snow, *These Mountains*, 69.
22 John McDougall to the Deputy Superintendent General of Indian Affairs, 10 Nov. 1910, LAC, RG10, file 339151, cited in Snow, *These Mountains*, 73.
23 Jack Dunn, *The Alberta Field Force of 1885* (Calgary: Author, 1994), 79.
24 Clarence Grahame, quoted in "Pioneer Methodist Missionary of West goes to his rest, *Calgary Herald*, 16 Jan. 1917.
25 *Manitoba Free Press*, 1, 5, 9, 22 Feb. 1886. Maclean, *McDougall*, 229–31.
26 James Dempsey, "Little Bear's Band: Canadian or American Indians?" *Alberta History*, (Autumn 1993): 5. *Edmonton Bulletin*, 1 Mar. 1897. John McDougall to Sir Wilfrid Laurier, 11 Sept. 1905, LAC, Sir Wilfrid Laurier Fonds, Laurier Papers, MG26-G, R10811-5-9-E, 161073–4.
27 Sarah Carter, "The Missionaries' Indian: The Publications of John McDougall, John Maclean and Egerton Ryerson Young," *Prairie Forum*, 9/1 (1984): 29. Nix, "McDougall," 696.
28 Frank Oliver, 13 Dec. 1907, in Canada, *House of Commons Debates*, 10th Parliament, 4th Session, vol. 1 (1907), 688. Maclean, *McDougall*, 241.
29 Nix, "McDougall," 696. George Woodcock and Ivan Avakumovic, *The Doukhobors* (Toronto: Oxford University Press, 1968), 220–2.
30 Nix, "McDougall," 696.
31 The Legislative Assembly Office and the Office of the Chief Electoral Officer, *A Century of Democracy: Elections of the Legislative Assembly of Alberta, 1905–2005* (Edmonton: Legislative Assembly of Alberta, 2006), 55.
32 John Maclean, *Vanguards of Canada* (Toronto: Missionary Society of the Methodist Church, 1918), 208.
33 John McDougall, *George Millward McDougall, the Pioneer, Patriot and Missionary* (Toronto: William Briggs, 1888).
34 John McDougall, *"Wa-pee-moostooch," or "White Buffalo," the hero of a hundred battles; a tale of life in Canada's Great West during the early years of the last century* (Calgary: Printed for the Author by the Herald Job Printing Co, 1908). The second novel was *Katrine, the Belle of the North*, a short work of six chapters published in *Onward*, a Methodist publication, mentioned in Maclean, *McDougall*, 266.
35 This is a list of his published autobiographical works, in chronological order, all the titles were published by William Briggs in Toronto: *Forest, Lake and Prairie: Twenty Years of Frontier Life in Western Canada, 1842–62* (1895); *Saddle, Sled and Snowshoe: Pioneering on the Saskatchewan in the Sixties* (1896); *Pathfinding on Plain and Prairie: Stirring Scenes of Life in the Canadian Northwest* (1898); *In the Days of the Red River Rebellion: Life and Adventure in the Far West of Canada* (1903); *On Western Trails in the Early Seventies: Frontier Life in the Canadian North-west* (1911). A sixth volume, *Opening the Great West: Experiences of a Missionary in 1875–76*, was left unpublished at the time of his death; the Glenbow-Alberta Institute in Calgary brought it out in 1970.

36 Susan Jackel, "Images of the Canadian West, 1872–1911" (Ph.D dissertation, University of Alberta, 1977), 181.
37 The *Canadian Baptist's* review of *Forest, Lake and Prairie*, reprinted on the last page of McDougall, *Saddle, Sled and Snowshoe*.
38 The review in the *Christian Guardian* of *Saddle, Sled and Snowshoe*, reprinted on the second last page of *Pathfinding on Plain and Prairie*.
39 Review of *In the Days of the River Rebellion*, in the *Review of Historical Publications Relating to Canada*, vol. 8, *Publications of the Year 1903*, 141.
40 Maclean, *McDougall*, 6–8, 13.
41 McDougall, *Forest, Lake and Prairie*, 12.
42 Ibid.
43 Maclean, *McDougall*, 261.
44 Emerson Coatsworth (Wah-sah-wah-gurh), Upper Canada College, Ontario, "The Ojibway of Rama (Ontario)," *World Youth*, (8 Apr. 1939): 19.
45 Jones, *History*, 104.
46 McDougall, *Pathfinding*, 61.
47 Maclean, *McDougall*, 241. The Western Canadian literary scholar Susan Jackel has suggested that McDougall's knowledge of North American Indian languages had an impact on his writing in English. In her opinion, his prose style sometimes suggests he is writing English as a second-language. Jackel admits how difficult it is for a non-linguist, "not conversant with the vocabulary and syntax of Cree" to elaborate on this; but, she adds, a study in comparative linguistics might tell us a great deal about McDougall's "personal experiment in multi-culturalism." See, Jackel, "Images," 292, also 289–302, 327–30.
48 "The late John McDougall," *Christian Guardian*, 24 Jan. 1917.
49 Susan Jackel, introduction to John McDougall, *In the Days of the Red River Rebellion* (Edmonton: University of Alberta Press, 1983), xix. Maclean, *McDougall*, 13.
50 "Rev. John Burwash, M.A., D.Sc., LL.D," *Minutes of the Toronto Methodist Conference 1914*, 21–2. I thank Neil Semple for this reference. His brother was the well-known Methodist educator, Nathanael Burwash. See Marguerite Van Die, "Nathanael Burwash," *DCB* 14, *1911–1920* (1998), 161–4.
51 The quote is taken from the obituary of Rev. John McDougall in the *Vancouver Daily News*, 21 Jan. 1917. The clipping is in the United Church Archives, Toronto, Rev. John McLean Collection. Also see comments on his first winter at Victoria, in McDougall, *Forest, Lake and Prairie*, 43–9.
52 Joseph F. Dion, *My Tribe, the Crees* (Calgary: Glenbow Museum, 1979), 2.
53 McDougall, *Forest, Lake and Prairie*, 82.
54 Maclean, *McDougall*, 261.
55 McDougall, *Forest, Lake and Prairie*, 187.

56 Dempsey, *Maskepetoon* 47.

57 Deanna Christenson, *Ahtahkakoop: The Epic Account of a Plains Cree Head Chief, His People, and Their Struggle for Survival, 1816–1896* (Shell Lake, Sask.: Ahtahkakoop Publishing, 2000), 124.

58 McDougall, *Forest, Lake and Prairie*, 154–5, original emphasis.

59 John W. Niddrie, "Memories of Morley," edited by J.W. Chalmers, *Alberta History*, (Summer 1992): 12. The sketch of James Dixon also appears in John W. Niddrie, *Niddrie of the Northwest: Memoirs of a Pioneer Canadian Missionary*, edited by John W. Chalmers and John J. Chalmers (Edmonton: University of Alberta Press, 2000), 60.

60 McDougall, *Opening the Great West*, 27. On James Dixon, see Nix, *Buffalo*, 98n1.

61 John McDougall to the editor, *Canadian Indian*, 1/5 (Mar. 1891): 173.

62 McDougall, *In the Days of the Red River Rebellion*, 25.

63 McDougall, *Saddle, Sled and Snowshoe*, 280–1.

64 The Indigenous journalist Dianne Meili spent a year and half in the late 1980s interviewing Elders on reserves throughout Alberta who were born in the early 1900s. She reported her findings in *Those Who Know: Profiles of Alberta's Native Elders* (Edmonton: NeWest Press, 1991), ix–x.

65 McDougall, *"Wa-Pee-Moostooch,"* 9. See also Sarah Carter, "Man's Mission of Subjugation: The Publications of John Maclean, John McDougall and Egerton R. Young, Nineteenth-Century Methodist Missionaries in Western Canada" (M.A. thesis, University of Saskatchewan, 1981), 96.

66 McDougall, *Saddle, Sled and Snowshoe*, 280–1.

67 George McDougall, second letter, dated Blackfeet Country, 2 Sept. 1862, *Christian Guardian*, 11 Mar. 1863.

68 McDougall, *Pathfinding on Plain and Prairie*, 12–13. See also Kristin Burnett, "Aboriginal and White Women in the Publications of John Maclean, Egerton Ryerson Young, and John McDougall," in Sarah Carter, Lesley Erickson, Patricia Roome, and Char Smith, eds., *Unsettled Pasts: Reconceiving the West through Women's History* (Calgary: University of Calgary Press, 2005), 109.

69 John McDougall Family Register, McDougall Family fonds, M-729-13, Glenbow Archives, Archives and Special Collections, University of Calgary. I thank Jim Bowman for this reference.

70 On the Steinhauer family, "A Missionary Family," in Smith, *Mississauga Portraits*, 245–76. On Abigail, the unpublished report by Sally Swenson, written in Nov. 1996, *"Who Is Abigail? An Adopted Woman's Late Discovery of Her Rich Heritage Illuminated by the Life of Abigail Steinhauer McDougall, 1848–1871* (Ottawa: n. p.p., 1996), photostat 26 pp., is very valuable. A copy is in my file 020.13, "Abigail Steinhauer McDougall," in the Smith Fonds.

71 Jackel, "Images," 289.

72 Henry B. Steinhauer, quoted in *Missionary Society Report*, (1874–75): xx.
73 John McDougall, dated Morley, 1 June 1878, *Missionary Notes of the Methodist Church of Canada*, (Aug. 1878): 315.
74 McDougall, *Pathfinding*, 38.
75 Shirlee Anne Smith, "Richard Charles Hardisty," *DCB* 11, *1881–1890* (1982): 383.
76 Henry B. Steinhauer, "White Fish Lake," *Missionary Society Report*, (1860–61): xxvii. Abigail was the second oldest child in the Steinhauer family, and the oldest girl.
77 McDougall, *Pathfinding*, 169.
78 Ibid., 96. For an estimate of distances covered on horseback on the open plains, see Eric Ross, *Beyond the River and the Bay* (Toronto: University of Toronto Press, 1970), 73. Ross, a historical geographer, writes that on some occasions, the First Nations "ride as far as 70 miles in 12 hours, but 40 or 45 miles is a more common day's ride."
79 Abigail was born in June 1848. See Smith, *Mississauga Portraits*, 397n101.
80 Nix, *Buffalo*, 71. John McDougall Family Register, Glenbow Archives, Archives and Special Collections, University of Calgary. I thank Jim Bowman for this reference.
81 John McDougall, letter dated Morleyville, 1 Feb. 1877, *Methodist Missionary Notices*, (June 1877): 206.
82 Nix, "McDougall," 65. His two sisters Flora and Georgiana died, as well as his adopted Indian sister, Anna.
83 Maclean, *McDougall*, 71.
84 Nix, *Buffalo*, 74.
85 Ibid., 79.
86 Edna Kells, "Those Wonderful McDougall Women. Elizabeth McDougall and her Daughters. Pioneer Women on the Alberta Frontier," edited by W. Everard Edmonds, 1967, chapter 5, Elizabeth Boyd McDougall (Mrs. John McDougall), 2. Lizzie's mother was a sister of Rev. George McDougall, John's father. Elizabeth Boyd's family name of Lizzie is used in the manuscript. A copy is now held in the Edmonton City Archives, Edna Kells Collection.
87 Kells, "McDougall Women," chapter 5, 37.
88 Ibid., chapter 5, 35.
89 *Gronlund's Directory of the City and District of Calgary 1902*, 75.
90 Kells, "McDougall Women," chapter 5, 38.
91 Trudy Soby, *Be It Ever So Humble* (Calgary: Century Calgary, 1975), photos 85, 86, 87.
92 Linda Bruce, "Pioneering almost fun, early residents recall," *Calgary Herald*, 8 July 1950, 4. All three girls applied for, and received Métis script files. Will Pratt kindly located and showed me copies of the files at LAC, Department of Interior, RG15, D-II-1, vol. 577, file 179576 (Flora

McDougall); RG15m, D-II-1, vol. 187, file HB 2483 (Ruth McDougall); RG10, D-II-1, vol. 536, file 156141 (Augusta McDougall). The three files include references to their schooling in Ontario. Flora and Gussie were away for five years, and Ruth for four.

93 Audiotape of interview with Gussie McDougall Mathieson, 10 Sept. 1957, Provincial Archives of Alberta, Accession no. 67.189 reel II, 65 minutes in length.

94 Swenson, "Who Is Abigail?" 21.

95 Methodist Church Mission Morleyville, North-West Territories, Marriage Register, Glenbow Archives, Archives and Special Collections, University of Calgary, McDougall Family Papers, M732, folder 13. The marriage took place on 18 Dec. 1886. John McDougall was the minister.

96 Ibid. The marriage took place on 14 Dec. 1887. John McDougall was the minister. John Julius Martin, "George H. Wheatly," *The Prairie Hub* (Strathmore, Alta.: Strathmore Standard, 1967).

97 Audiotape with Gussie McDougall Mathieson, 10 Sept. 1957. "In memory of Mrs McDougall, wife of Rev. George McDougall," *Missionary Outlook*, (Oct. 1903): 235.

98 "I Remember, Mrs Augusta Mathieson," *Calgary Herald*, 2 Dec. 1958.

99 Bill Waiser, *A World We Have Lost: Saskatchewan Before 1905* (Markham, Ont.: Fifth House, 2016), 569.

100 John McLean [Maclean], *The Indians, Their Manners and Customs* (Toronto: William Briggs, 1889), 284.

101 R.C. Macleod and Heather Rollason Driscoll, "Natives, Newspapers and Crime Rates in the North-West Territories, 1878–1885," in Theodore Binnema, Gerhard J. Ens, and R.C. Macleod, eds., *From Rupert's Land to Canada* (Edmonton: University of Alberta Press, 2001), 250.

102 Alan B. McCullough, "Sir Cecil Edward Denny," *DCB* 15, *1921–1930* (2005), 274–6.

103 Sir Cecil E. Denny, *The Law Marches West* [1939], edited and arranged by W.B. Cameron (Toronto: J.M. Dent, 1972), 202–3.

104 McDougall, *Pathfinding*, 98.

105 John McDougall, *"Indian Wigwams and Northern Camp-fires": A Criticism* (Toronto: Printed for the Author by William Briggs, 1895), 12–13. Muriel Stanley Venne, "The 'S' Word: Reclaiming 'Esquao' for Aboriginal Women," in Carter et al., *Unsettled Pasts*, 123–7.

106 Maclean, *McDougall*, 170.

107 "An Indian's story. Rev. Dr. McDougall gives life history of a Cree, Wa-Pee-Moostooch, his joys and trials – all phases of life contained in interesting work," *Calgary Herald*, 13 Oct. 1908.

108 McDougall, *"White Buffalo,"* 1.

109 John McDougall, quoted in Maclean, *McDougall*, 180.

110 McDougall, "White Buffalo," 4, 14, 9, 164.

111 Ibid., 114, 11.

112 Ross, *Beyond the River and the Bay*, 84.

113 McDougall, "White Buffalo," 219–20.

114 Maclean, *McDougall*, 232.

115 McDougall, *On Western Trails*, 215–16.

116 McDougall, *Opening the Great West*, 17.

117 McDougall, *On Western Trails*, 216.

118 J. Ernest Nix, introduction to McDougall *Opening the Great West*, 10.

119 Jackel, introduction, xv–xvi. Carter, "The Missionaries' Indian," 27.
     R. Douglas Francis, "Review Article Alberta Historic Sites," *Journal of
     Canadian Studies*, 16/2 (Summer 1981): 130.

120 Jackel, "Images," xvi.

121 Published by the University of Toronto, the quotation appears on p. 909.

122 Hugh Dempsey, personal communication, 16 Jan. 2012, 11 Dec. 2015,
     9 June 2016. Dempsey, *Maskepetoon*, relies heavily on several of John
     McDougall's books; see bibliography, 247.

123 For background on Cowie, see David Reed Miller, introduction to the
     Bison Book Edition, in Isaac Cowie, *The Company of Adventurers: A
     Narrative of Seven Years in the Service of the Hudson's Bay Company during
     1867–1874 on the Great Buffalo Plains* (Lincoln: University of Nebraska
     Press, 1993; originally published in 1913 in Toronto by William Briggs),
     9–21.

124 Isaac Cowie, "Four peacemakers and pioneers who witnessed and took
     part in the transformation of the great lone land," *Manitoba Free Press*, 27
     Jan. 1917, 13.

125 Nix, *Buffalo*, 76.

126 One assessment of an early sermon of John McDougall's survives.
     In April 1875 Richard Nevitt, the NWMP assistant surgeon, a recent
     graduate of Toronto's Trinity Medical School, heard a sermon of
     McDougall's at Fort Macleod. He noted in a letter, "It was a very ordinary
     affair, good because earnest but nothing striking about it." R.B. Nevitt, *A
     Winter at Fort Macleod*, edited by Hugh A. Dempsey (Toronto: McClelland
     and Stewart, 1974), 85.

127 Maclean, *McDougall*, 14.

128 Nix, *Buffalo*, 79.

129 John McDougall, dated Morley, Nov. 1892, in "Along the Line: The Indian
     Work, Saskatchewan District," *Missionary Outlook*, (Apr. 1893): 52.

130 Paul Radin, "Robert H Lowie 1883–1957," *American Anthropologist*, n.s.
     60/2 (Apr.1958): 358–75.

131 Robert Lowie, *Robert H. Lowie Ethnologist: A Personal Record* (Berkeley:
     University of California Press, 1959), 96–7. In the *The Diaries of Edmund*

Montague Morris: Western Journeys 1907–1910, transcribed by Mary Fitz-
Gibbon (Toronto: Royal Ontario Museum, 1985), Morris records the same
story, but with the twist that John McDougall is one of the three liars and
his brother David the other two (46, entry for 1907).

132 Radin, "Lowie," 359.
133 Lowie, *Ethnologist,* 10, 18–19, 93, 95. John McDougall had been dead over
forty years at the time his visitor's autobiography appeared. He would
have been upset to learn that the distinguished academic, with all his
erudition, occasionally used the pejorative term "squaw" to designate a
Native woman, and "squaw man" for a non-Indigenous man married to a
North American Indian woman; see 10, 94, 95, 104.
134 Erasmus, *Buffalo Days and Nights* (Calgary: Fifth House, 1999), 165.
135 Ibid., 166.
136 Another good example is his treatment of the general secretary of the
Canadian Methodist Conference, Rev. Lachlan Taylor, who toured the
western missions in 1873. See Jackel, "Images," 213–15.
137 Published by Charles H. Kelly in London, England.
138 Jennifer S.H. Brown, "Egerton Ryerson Young," *DCB* 13, *1901–1910*
(1994), 1122. Tanya Middlebro, in "The Life and Thought of the Reverend
Egerton R. Young (1840–1909)" (M.A. thesis, Carleton University, 2003),
presents Young's side of the debate, 162–5.
139 McDougall, *"Indian Wigwams and Northern Camp-fires,"* 27.
140 "The Indian Question." Letter to the Editor, dated Morley, 30 Dec.,
Calgary Tribune, 9 Jan. 1886.
141 G.H.H. [George H. Ham], article dated Macleod, N.W.T., 18 Jan. 1886,
"Among the Bloods. Rev. John Macdougall on the Indians and their
grievances. He arraigns the government officials," published in the
Toronto *Daily Mail,* 30 Jan. 1886. John McDougall's exact description
of the agents first appeared in his 30 Dec. 1885 letter to the *Calgary
Tribune.*
142 Malcolm Cameron, 15 Apr. 1886, in *House of Commons Debates,* 5th
Parliament, 4th Session, vol. 1 (1886), 720–1, 725, 729. Peter A. Russell,
"Malcolm Colin Cameron," *DCB* 12, *1891–1900* (1990), 147–9.
143 Lawrence Vankoughnet to John McDougall dated Ottawa, 5 Feb. 1886,
McDougall Family fonds, M729, file 41, Glenbow Archives, Archives
and Special Collections, University of Calgary. Ham's Toronto *Daily
Mail* article of 30 Jan. 1886, citing John McDougall's charges is included
in LAC, Macdonald Papers, MG26-A, vol. 113, 35799–801. On 2 Feb.
1886, three days later, Vankoughnet wrote to Macdonald, ibid., 433239.
In a subsequent letter to the prime minister, 25 Feb. 1886, Vankoughnet
termed John's brother, David McDougall, "a great scoundrel," ibid.,
vol. 291, 133279. I thank Will Pratt for these references.

144 John McDougall, "The Red Men of Canada's West Yesterday and To-day," *The Albertan, Calgary, The 100,000 manufacturing, building and wholesale book editions of the Morning Albertan*, 1914, 146.

145 (Copy) John McDougall to Rev. A. Sutherland, dated Morley, 28 Jan. 1897, LAC, RG10, vol. 3966, file 151384, 9. For Peter Grasse's side of the controversy, see his letter to Hayter Reed, Indian Commissioner, Regina, 31 May 1892, ibid., vol. 3881, file 94262; and his letter to the Indian Commissioner, Regina, dated Morley, 21 Dec. 1896, ibid., vol. 3966, file 151384, 9. I thank Will Pratt for pointing out this correspondence.

146 Glenbow Archives, Gilbert and Luella Goddard Fonds Inventory.

147 For a short summary see, John F. Leslie, "The Indian Act: An Historical Perspective," *Canadian Parliamentary Review*, (Summer 2002): 23–7.

148 John McDougall,"The Future of the Indians of Canada," a paper read before the Missionary Convention at Edmonton, *Canadian Methodist Magazine*, 61 (1905): 246.

149 Sarah Carter, "Controlling Indian Movement: The Pass System," *NeWest Review*, (May 1985): 8–9. F. Laurie Barron, "The Indian Pass System in the Canadian West, 1882–1935," *Prairie Forum*, 13/1 (Spring 1988): 25–42.

150 McDougall, "Future of the Indians," 246.

151 Colonel S.B. Steele, *Forty Years in Canada: Reminiscences of the Great North-West with Some Account of his Service in South Africa* (New York: Dodd, Mead & Co., 1915), 265. For background on the famous Sam Steele, see Rod Macleod's excellent *Sam Steele: A Biography* (Edmonton: University of Alberta Press, 2018).

152 Dempsey, *Crowfoot*, 201–6. Hugh A. Dempsey, *Red Crow: Warrior Chief* (Saskatoon: Western Producer Prairie Books, 1980), 157–72.

153 Christensen, *Ahtahkakoop*, 547–86.

154 For a full account of the visits in 1886 of 12 Plains Indian chiefs to Central Canada, see "Worlds Apart," *Canada's History*, (Oct.–Nov. 2017): 30–7. a longer fully documented version of this paper is available at CanadasHistory/WorldsApart.

155 "Town Topics," *Sarnia Observer*, 8 Oct. 1886. Lawrence Vanknoughnet to Sir John A. Macdonald, 27 Dec. 1886, LAC, RG10, Deputy Superintendent General's Letterbooks, vol. 1091, 363, mfm C-7219.

156 "Pakan and Samson:.Enthusiastic reception at Elm Street Church," *Toronto Mail*, 18 Aug. 1886. "Visit of Indian Chiefs," *Berlin Daily News* (Kitchener), 11 Sept. 1886. "The Indian Braves," *Port Hope Weekly Guide*, 24 Sept. 1886. "Loyal Indian Chiefs," *Daily Review* (Peterborough, Ont.), 24 Sept. 1886.

157 Neil Semple, "Ontario's Religious Hegemony: The Creation of the National Methodist Church," *Ontario History*, 77/1 (Mar. 1985): 19.

158 John McDougall, Letter to the Editor, dated Morley, 27 Nov. 1886, *Calgary Tribune*, 3 Dec. 1886. I thank Hugh Dempsey for this reference.

159 O. German, "Pukan," *Missionary Outlook*, 6/7 (July 1886): 90.

160 "Three Western Indians," *Globe*, 8 Aug. 1886.

161 Doucet, *Journal*, 53, 221.

162 Maclean, *McDougall*, 162.

163 John A. Macdonald, Superintendent of Indian Affairs, in Canada, Department of Indian Affairs, *Annual Report, 1885* (Ottawa: Maclean Roger and Co. 1886), ix–xiv; reprinted in Keith D. Smith, ed., *Strange Visitors: Documents in Indigenous-Settler Relations in Canada from 1876* (Toronto: University of Toronto Press, 2014), 61.

164 Peter Erasmus, *Buffalo Days and Nights*, 270.

165 Memorandum, 7 Jan. 1887, LAC, RG10, Deputy Superintendent General's Letterbooks, vol. 1092, 453, mfm C-7219. "Our loyal Indians: Interviewing Deputy Minister of Indian Affairs this afternoon," *Ottawa Free Press*, 29 Sept. 1886.

166 "Departmental and other notes," *Ottawa Citizen*, 30 Sept. 1886. "News of the Day," *Globe*, 1 Oct. 1886.

167 "Local News," *Globe*, 2 Sept. 1886.

168 Dempsey, *Red Crow*, 169.

169 George H. Ham, *Reminiscences of a Raconteur*, 116, quoted in Dempsey, ibid., 142.

170 John McDougall translating Pakan's remarks, "Visit of Indian Chiefs," *Berlin Daily News*, 11 Sept. 1886.

171 John McDougall, citing Pakan, "Rev. John McDougall," *Calgary Tribune*, 3 Dec. 1886.

172 Pakan's remarks, translated by John McDougall, "Missionary Meeting," *Regina Leader*, 19 Oct. 1886.

173 "Kanatakasu. (Samson) Historical Chronology." I thank Doug Rae for showing me this summary. A copy is in my file 023.18, "Samson, 19th century to late 20th century, in the Smith Fonds.

174 Nix, *Mission*, 35–6.

175 McDougall, *In the Days of the Red River Rebellion*, 94.

176 John McDougall, dated Morley, Nov. 1892, in "Along the Line," 5.

177 C. Pelham Mulvany, *Toronto Past and Present: A Handbook of the City* (Toronto: W.E. Caiger, Publisher, 1884), 1,

178 Samson, quoted (translated by John McDougall) in "Three Western Indians."

179 "Surprised Indians," *Toronto Evening Telegram*, 11 Aug. 1886.

180 Ontario Board of Health, *Annual Report, 1884*, 98, quoted in Gregory A. Kealey, *Hogtown: Working Class Toronto at the Turn of the Century* (Toronto: New Hogtown Press, 1974), 24.

181 Desmond Morton, "The Crusading Mayor Howland," *Horizon Canada*, 2/23 (1985): 550.

182 Samson, translated by John McDougall, "The Poor Cree," *London Daily Free Press*, 6 Sept. 1886.

183 Ibid.
184 Hugh A. Dempsey, "Crowfoot, Bearspaw, Deerfoot and Crowchild: Indians Behind the Place-Names," in Max Foran and Sheilagh S. Jameson, eds., *Citymakers: Calgarians After the Frontier* (Calgary: Historical Society of Alberta, Chinook Country Chapter, 1987), 50–2.
185 Maclean, *McDougall*, 162.
186 John McDougall, Letter to the Editor, dated Morley, 27 Nov. 1886, *Calgary Tribune*, 3 Dec. 1886. I thank Hugh Dempsey for this reference.
187 "Our Indian Visitors," Toronto *Daily Mail*, 19 Aug. 1886.
188 Maclean, *McDougall*, 164.
189 "Welcome to the Loyal Chiefs," *Orillia Packet*, 3 Sept. 1886. He is sometimes referred to as Jonas Goodstoney; see Maclean, *McDougall*, 272.
190 "A Council of Braves," *British Whig* (Kingston), 25 Aug. 1886. "Three Loyal Chiefs," *Belleville Intelligencer*, 2 Sept. 1886.
191 "From the Northwest," *Hamilton Spectator*, 20 Aug. 1886.
192 McDougall, Letter to the Editor, *Calgary Tribune*, 3 Dec. 1886.
193 Ibid.
194 "Missionary Meeting," Toronto *Daily Mail*, 8 Sept. 1886.
195 Ibid.
196 John A. Macdonald, quoted in ibid.
197 James Ernest Nix, "John Maclean's Mission to the Blood Indians 1880–1889" (M.A. thesis, McGill University, 1977), 222–3.
198 John McDougall, "'The Future of the Indians of Canada,' a paper read before the Missionary Convention at Edmonton," *Canadian Methodist Magazine*, 61 (1905), 246.
199 Ibid., 245.
200 Jean-Guy A. Goulet, *Ways of Knowing: Experience, Knowledge, and Power among the Dene Tha* (Vancouver: UBC Press, 1998), 47.
201 Rosemary R. Gagan, *A Sensitive Independence: Canadian Methodist Women Missionaries in Canada and the Orient, 1881–1925* (Montreal and Kingston: McGill-Queen's University Press, 1992), 5.
202 Helen Buckley, *From Wooden Ploughs to Welfare: Why Indian Policy Failed in the Prairie Provinces* (Montreal and Kingston: McGill-Queen's University Press, 1992), 51.
203 Nix, "McDougall," 696.
204 J. Shaw to John McDougall, dated the Methodist Church Missionary Department, Toronto, dated 11 Oct. 1887, McDougall Family fonds, M 729, file 44, Glenbow Archives, Archives and Special Collections, University of Calgary.
205 Treaty 7 Elders and Tribal Council with Walter Hildebrandt, Dorothy First Rider, and Sarah Carter, *The True Spirit and Original Intent of Treaty 7* (Montreal and Kingston: McGill-Queen's University Press, 1996), 268.
206 Nix, "McDougall," 696.

207 Rev. Marchmont Ing, the missionary at Morley from 1903 to 1911, stated, "The children at the Institute were dying off in larger number than those left on the reserve." See "The Memoirs of Rev. Marchmont Ing. Excerpted by Debbie Marshall," *Journal Alberta & Northwest Conference, United Church of Canada Historical Society*, (May 2013): 41. The entire document is available at the Provincial Archives of Alberta, "Memoirs of Rev. Marchmont Ing (1870–1947)," 37 pp., accession no. 2008.0353 SE.

208 Maureen K. Lux, *Medicine That Walks: Disease, Medicine, and Canadian Plains Native People, 1880–1940* (Toronto: University of Toronto Press, 2001), 116.

209 Jean L. Johnson, "The McDougall Orphanage," in his *Big Hill Country: Cochrane and Area* (Cochrane, Ont.: Cochrane and Area Historical Society, 1977), 91.

210 *The Final Report of the Truth and Reconciliation Commission*, vol. 1, *Canada's Residential Schools: The History, Part 1, Origins to 1939* (Montreal and Kingston: Published for the Truth and Reconciliation Commission by McGill-Queen's University Press, 2015), 407.

211 Maclean, *McDougall*, 244.

212 E. Brian Titley, *A Narrow Vision: Duncan Campbell Scott and the Administration of Indian Affairs in Canada* (Vancouver: UBC Press, 1986), 22.

213 Hugh A. Dempsey, "The Role of Native Cultures in Western History: An Alberta Focus," in John W. Friesen, ed., *The Cultural Maze: Complex Questions on Native Destiny in Western Canada* (Calgary: Detselig, 1991), 43.

214 James Daschuk, *Clearing the Plains: Disease, Politics of Starvation, and the Loss of Aboriginal Life* (Regina: University of Regina Press, 2013), 22, 37, 41, 55, 67, 77, 80.

215 Rev. John McLean [Maclean] M.A., Blood Reserve Alberta Canada, "The Blackfoot Indian Confederacy" (Ph.D. dissertation, Illinois Wesleyan University, Bloomington, Illinois, 1888), iii, RG 13-3/2: Non-Resident Theses, Tate Archives & Special Collections, The Ames Library, Illinois Wesleyan University, Bloomington, Illinois. I thank Meg Miner, university archivist and special collections librarian, for her invaluable assistance in sending me a scan of the thesis.

216 G. Graham-Cumming, "Health of the Original Canadians, 1867–1967," *Medical Services Journal of Canada*, 23/2 (1967): 118.

217 Keith D. Smith, *Liberalism, Surveillance, and Resistance: Indigenous Communities in Western Canada, 1877–1927* (Edmonton: AU Press, 2009), 96.

218 M.C. Urquhart and K.A.H. Buckley, eds., *Historical Statistics of Canada* (Toronto: Macmillan, 1965), 14. See Series A2-14, Population of Canada, by province, census dates, 1851 to 1961.

219 Pamela White, "Restructuring the Domestic Sphere – Prairie Women on Reserves: Image, Ideology and State Policy 1880–1930" (Ph.D. dissertation, McGill University, 1987), 62–3.

220 Peggy Martin-McGuire, "First Nation Land Surrenders on the Prairies 1896–1911," prepared for the Indian Claims Commission, Ottawa, Sept. 1998, 208. Keith D. Smith, "'Certain Doubtful Transactions' in the Treaty 7 Region After 1877," in his *Liberalism, Surveillance, and Resistance*, touches on McDougall's involvement, 197–222, 280–7.

221 David Lupul, "The Bobtail Land Surrender," *Alberta History*, 26/1 (Winter 1978): 29–39.

222 Martin-McGuire, "Land Surrenders," 281, 290, 435–6, 488. He also made a report for Frank Oliver on the St Peter's Reserve in which, to quote the *Manitoba Free Press*, "Visiting Indians. Rev. John McDougall returns from St Peter's Reserve," 1 Nov. 1910, "Interested people ... secured possession of valuable tracts for comparatively small sums." The most complete account is "The Report Prepared for The T.A.R.R. Centre of Manitoba, Inc." by Tyler, Wright & Daniel Ltd, 1979 and 1983, entitled "The Illegal Surrender of St Peter's Reserve." John McDougall's involvement is discussed on pp. 482–92. McDougall's report was tabled in the House of Commons on 11 Jan. 1911; see "New Reserve is well situated: Rev. John McDougall makes report to federal dovernment," *Manitoba Free Press*, 12 Jan. 1911.

223 Hugh A. Dempsey, "Chula," *DCB* 14, *1911–1920* (1998), 213–15.

224 Chief Bull Head, quoted in a letter from John McDougall to Frank Pedley, 5 Feb. 1906, LAC, RG10, vol. 7543, file 29, 120-1, pt. 1, cited in Patricia K. Wood, "Pressured from All Aides: The February 1913 Surrender of the Northeast Corner of the Tsuu T'ina Nation," *Journal of Historical Geography*, 30 (2004): 121.

225 Joseph Pope, *The Tour of Their Royal Highnesses, the Duke and Duchess of Cornwall and York through the Dominion of Canada in the year 1901* (Ottawa: S.D. Dawson, 1903), 80. "One of last hereditary Indian Chiefs, Joe Samson, 76, Hobbema leader, dead," *Edmonton Journal*, 10 Feb. 1942.

226 Chief Joseph Samson's remarks reported by W.S. Grant to David Laird, 18 July 1905, LAC, RG10, vol. 3563, file 82-25, quoted in Lupul, "Bobtail Land Surrender," 31–2.

227 Lupul, "Bobtail Land Surrender," 34.

228 Maclean, *McDougall*, 244–5.

229 Wendy Wickwire, *At the Bridge: James Teit and an Anthropology of Belonging* (Vancouver: UBC Press, 2019), 200–1.

230 John McDougall to Frank Oliver, Minister of the Interior, 23 Sept. 1910, quoted in Maclean, *McDougall*, 246.

231 Wickwire, *At the Bridge*, 200–1.

232 John McDougall, "Through the Foothills," *Calgary Herald*, 26 June 1902, reprinted in *Alberta History*, 23/2 (1975): 1.

233 McDougall, *Pathfinding on Plain and Prairie*, 265.

234 Titley, *Narrow Vision*, 171.

235 McDougall, "The Red Men," 146.

236 Rev. John McDougall, cited in the *Manitoba Free Press*, 19 Oct. 1908, LAC, RG10, vol. 3825, file 60, 511–12; cited in Katherine Pettipas, *Severing the Ties That Bind, Government Repression of Indigenous Religious Ceremonies on the Prairies* (Winnipeg: University of Manitoba Press, 1994), 141.

237 "Empire builder and missionary, Rev. Dr. John McDougall, has passed away," *Calgary News Telegram*, 16 Jan. 1917. The microfilm copy of the newspaper at the Glenbow Library contains the first half of the article. The full version appeared in another edition of this same issue. The only known copy of the full article is contained in the biographical file for Rev. John McDougall, United Church Archives, Toronto. It is marked, John Maclean Collection Obituary (duplicate). Rev. John Maclean misidentified it as from the *Calgary Herald*.

238 Hugh Dempsey, "Native Peoples and Calgary," in Donald B. Smith, ed., *Centennial City* (Calgary: University of Calgary, 1994), 31.

239 Donald B. Smith, "Rev. John McDougall and the Duke of Connaught," *Alberta History*, 65/1 (Winter 2017): 10.

240 John McDougall, *Pathfinding on Plain and Prairie* (Toronto, 1898), 80, cited in Emma LaRocque, *When the Other Is Me: Native Resistance Discourse, 1850–1990* (Winnipeg: Unversity of Manitoba Press, 2010), 42.

241 John W. Friesen, *Aboriginal Spirituality and Biblical Theology: Closer than You Think* (Calgary: Detselig, 2000), 152.

242 Maclean, *McDougall*, 260. "The Western Indians," *Brandon Sun*, 10 June 1886: "The Stoney Indians, under his ministration legislated in their councils against even the making of drums, and now they are not permitted to be kept or brought on their reserves."

243 John McDougall, letter dated Morley, 10 June 1878, published in the *Christian Guardian*, 31 July 1878.

244 John McDougall, "The Red Men of Canada's West Yesterday and To-day," *The Albertan, Calgary. The 100,000 manufacturing, building and wholesale book editions of the Morning Albertan*, 1914, page 146.

245 E.J. Hart, *The Place of Bows: Exploring the Heritage of the Banff-Bow Valley: Part I, to 1930* (Banff: EJH Literary Enterprises, 1999), 61.

246 Ibid., 9.

247 Ian Getty, "Stoney-Nakoda," *Canadian Encyclopedia* at http://www.thecanadianencyclopedia.ca/en/article/stoney-nakoda/.

248 Maclean, *McDougall*, 259.

249 The Archives of the Whyte Museum of the Canadian Rockies in Banff has a video copy.

250 Maclean, *McDougall*, 259.

251 Howard Palmer, *Patterns of Prejudice: A History of Nativism in Alberta* (Toronto: McClelland and Stewart, 1982), 179.
252 Alan C. Cairns, *Citizens Plus: Aboriginal Peoples and the Canadian State* (Vancouver: UBC Press, 2000). 54. The Hawthorn Report is briefly introduced in chapter nine.

3. George Monro Grant

1 D.B. Mack, "George Monro Grant," *Dictionary of Canadian Biography (DCB)*, vol. 13, *1901–1910* (1994), 407.
2 W.E. McNeill, "The Story of Queen's," in Robert C. Wallace, ed., *Queen's University: A Centenary Volume, 1841–1941* (Toronto: Ryerson Press, 1941), 18–19.
3 Mack, "Grant," 407.
4 Barry Mack, "George Monro Grant: Evangelical Prophet" (Ph.D. dissertation, Queen's University 1992), 357n28. In his *Exiles from Nowhere: The Jews and the Canadian Elite* (Montreal: Robin Brass Studio, 2008), Alan Mendelson suggests that Grant was not entirely favourable to the Jewish population in Canada (93–111).
5 Graham Carr, "Book Review of *True Patriot Love: Four Generations in Search of Canada*," *Canadian Historical Review*, 91/2 (June 2010): 340.
6 Mack, "Grant," 406.
7 "Naming pays last tribute to Robert Sutherland, 'Canada's first black university graduate,'" *Queen's Gazette*, 4 Oct. 2009.
8 Ibid., 298.
9 "Convocation," *Queen's College Journal*, 13/12 (14 May 1886): 157, 168.
10 One of the letters in Latin in LAC, G.M. Grant Papers, MG30, vol. 2, 510–15, is dated 7 Apr. 1878, 512. Other letters are undated; see vol.1, 21–31; vol. 2, 516–20; vol. 6, 2180–2180A. I thank Egmont Lee for translating them for me.
11 Mack, "Evangelical Prophet," 128.
12 George Grant, quoted in "Convocation," 157, 168.
13 Ibid. 168.
14 Silas T. Rand, *A Short Statement of Facts Relating to the History, Manners, Customs, Language and Literature of the Micmac Tribe of Indians, in Nova Scotia and P.E. Island. Being the Substance of Two Lectures Delivered in Halifax, in November 1849, at Public Meeting held for the purpose of instituting a mission to that Tribe* (Halifax: James Bowes and Sons, 1850), 6. On the same page, Rand includes this wonderful reference; "The well-known advice of Cicero's friend, not to purchase his slaves from among the British captives, as they were too stupid to learn anything, occurs immediately to one's thoughts while reflecting on the possibility

of elevating the Indian from his present degradation, to the rank of a man."

15 Robert E. Bieder, *Science Encounters the Indian, 1820–1880: The Early Years of American Ethnology* (Norman: University of Oklahoma Press, 1986), 9.

16 Lorne Green, *Chief Engineer: Life of a Nation Builder, Sandford Fleming* (Toronto: Dundurn, 1993), 166–8.

17 Sandford Fleming, *England and Canada: A Summer Tour between Old and New Westminster* (Montreal: Dawson Brothers, 1884), 382.

18 Ibid.

19 David Wills, "Halifax – toponymic tidbits," *Canoma*, 25/2 (Dec. 1999): 11.

20 Judith Fingard, Janet Guildford, and David Sutherland, *Halifax: The First 250 Years* (Halifax, NS: Formac, 1999), 14. In 2018 Cornwallis's statue was removed from the Halifax site on which it had stood for 85 years. See Aly Thomson, "Halifax's Cornwallis statue removed," *Calgary Herald*, 1 Feb. 2018.

21 James Axtell, *The European and the Indian: Essays in the Ethnohistory of Colonial North America* (Oxford: Oxford University Press, 1981), 16–35, 207–41.

22 Caroline-Isabelle Caron, *The Acadians*, Canadian Historical Association Immigration and Ethnicity in Canada Series, Booklet 33 (Ottawa: Canadian Historical Association, 2015), 10.

23 See William C. Wicken, *Mi'kmaq Treaties on Trial: History, Land, and Donald Marshall Junior* (Toronto: University of Toronto Press, 2002).

24 L.F.S. Upton, *Micmacs and Colonists: Indian-White Relations in the Maritimes, 1713–1867* (Vancouver: UBC Press, 1979), 78.

25 Harald E.L. Prins, *The Mi'kmaq: Resistance, Accommodation, and Cultural Survival* (Fort Worth, Tx.: Harcourt Brace, 1996), 168.

26 Dorothy May Lovesay, *To Be a Pilgrim: A Biography of Silas Tertius Rand, 1810–1889, Nineteenth Century Protestant Missionary to the Micmac* (Hantsport, NS: Lancelot Press, 1992), 7.

27 Ibid., 23.

28 Rand, quoted in ibid., 41.

29 Lovesay, *Rand*, 11, 218. Judith Fingard, "Silas Tertius Rand," *DCB* 11, *1881–1890* (1982), 722.

30 Rand, *Short Statement*, 18.

31 Thomas S. Abler, "A Mi'kmaq Missionary among the Mohawks: Silas T. Rand and His Attitudes toward Race and 'Progress,'" in Celia Haig-Brown and David A. Nock, eds., *With Good Intentions: Euro-Canadian and Aboriginal Relations in Colonial Canada* (Vancouver: UBC Press, 2006), 72, 74.

32 Rand, *Short Statement*, 6–7.

33 Lovesay, *Rand*, 107–11.

34 Janet Elizabeth Chute, "Ceremony Social Revitalization and Change: Micmac Leadership and the Annual Festival of St Anne," *Papers of the Twenty-Third Algonquian Conference* (Ottawa: Carleton University, 1992), 45–62.

35 Virginia P. Miller, "Silas T. Rand, Nineteenth-Century Anthropologist Among the Micmac," *Anthropologica*, 22/2 (1980): 236, 242.

36 Upton, *Micmacs and Colonists*, 169. He made just one convert.

37 Abler, "Rand," 74.

38 *Christian Messenger* (Halifax), 15 Mar. 1855, cited in D.G. Bell, "Was Amerindian Dispossession Lawful? The Response of 19th-Century Maritime Intellectuals," *Dalhousie Law Journal*, 23 (2000): 179.

39 LAC, G.M. Grant Papers, vol. 20, sermon on Gal. 6: 2–5, quoted in Mack, "Evangelical Prophet," 180.

40 Biographical details on George Grant are from Mack, "Grant," 403–9, and from his invaluable, Ph.D. dissertation, "George Monro Grant: Evangelical Prophet" (1992).

41 Wicken, *Mi'kmaq Treaties*, 7–8.

42 Rosemary E. Ommer, "The 1830s," in Phillip A. Buckner and John G. Reid, eds., *The Atlantic Region to Confederation: A History* (Toronto: University of Toronto Press, 1994), 285.

43 J. Bernard Gilpin, "Indians of Nova Scotia," *Nova Scotian Institute of Science Proceedings and Transactions*, 4 (1875–1878), in H.F. McGee, *The Native Peoples of Atlantic Canada: A Reader in Regional Ethnic Relations* (Toronto: McClelland and Stewart, 1974), 111.

44 Gilpin, "Indians of Nova Scotia," 111.

45 James Dawson, quoted in Joseph Howe, "Report on Indian Affairs," in the *Journal of the Legislative Assembly for Nova Scotia*, (1844), Appendix 50, reprinted in McGee, *Atlantic Canada*, 92.

46 Phillip A. Buckner, "The 1860s," in Buckner and Reid, *Atlantic Region*, 363.

47 Mack, "Evangelical Prophet," 22–3.

48 Jean Barman, *Sojourning Sisters: The Lives and Letters of Jessie and Annie McQueen* (Toronto: University of Toronto Press, 2003), 14–15.

49 William Lawson Grant and Frederick Hamilton, *Principal Grant* (Toronto: Morang & Co, 1904), 11.

50 Carl Berger, *The Sense of Power: Studies in the Ideas of Canadian Imperialism 1867–1914* (Toronto: University of Toronto Press, 1970), 24.

51 Mack, "Grant," 404.

52 Ibid., 69, 72.

53 Mack, "Evangelical Prophet," 66n1.

54 Ibid., 141.

55 Grant and Hamilton, *Principal Grant*, 58.

56 Mack, "Evangelical Prophet," 184; Mack, "Grant," 405.

57 Green, *Chief Engineer*, 69.
58 George M. Grant, *Ocean to Ocean: Sandford Fleming's Expedition through Canada in 1872. Enlarged and Revised Edition* [1873] (Toronto: Bedford Brothers, 1877; facsimile edition published in 1967 in Rutland, Vt., by Charles E. Tuttle), 61.
59 Ibid., 62.
60 Ibid., 104.
61 Rev. George M. Grant, "The Great West. Part III," *Good Words*, 15 (June 1874): 410.
62 Grant, *Ocean to Ocean*, 190.
63 Ibid., 178–9.
64 Ibid., 88.
65 Ibid., 167.
66 Freda Graham Bundy, "Alberta's Pioneer White Settler," *Alberta Folklore*, 2/1 (Mar. 1946): 29. William Gladstone, a former fur trade employee and early settler knew George McDougall in what is now Alberta in the 1860s and1870s. For a sketch of "Old Glad," as he was known, see Hugh A. Dempsey, *The Gentle Persuader: A Biography of James Gladstone, Indian Senator* (Saskatoon: Western Producer Prairie Books, 1986): 4-10.
67 John McDougall, *George Millward McDougall: The Pioneer, Patriot and Missionary* (Toronto: William Briggs, 1888), 11.
68 Peter Erasmus, as told to Henry Thompson, *Buffalo Days and Nights* (Calgary: Fifth House, 1999), 167.
69 John McLean (Maclean), *The Hero of the Saskatchewan: Life Among the Ojibway and Cree Indians in Canada* (Barrie, Ont.: Barrie Examiner Printing and Publishing House, 1891), 5.
70 *Minutes of the General Council of Indian Chiefs and Principal Men, held at Orillia, Lake Simcoe Narrows, on Thursday, the 30th and Friday, the 31st July, 1846, on the proposed removal of the smaller communities and the Establishment of the Manual Labour Schools, From notes taken in Shorthand and otherwise, by Henry Baldwin, of Peterborough, Barrister at Law, Secretary to the Chiefs in Council* (Montreal: Printed at the Canada Gazette Office, 1846), 9–10.
71 McDougall, *Pioneer, Patriot and Missionary*, 25.
72 Ibid., 61.
73 George McDougall, dated Victoria, 16 Aug.1870, *Wesleyan Missionary Notices, Canada Conference*, n.s., vol. 9 (Nov. 1870): 143.
74 McDougall, *Pioneer, Patriot and Missionary*, 155.
75 Ibid., 167.
76 Hugh A. Dempsey, *Red Crow: Warrior Chief* (Saskatoon: Western Producer Prairie Books, 1980), 72.
77 Susan Jackel, "Images of the Canadian West, 1872–1911" (Ph.D. dissertation, University of Alberta, 1977), 129.

78 Rev. G. McDougall, letter from Garden River, Upper Canada, dated
    28 Jan. 1857, in *Wesleyan Missionary Notices, Canada Conference*, vol. 13
    (1 Aug. 1857): 207.
79 Rev. G. McDougall, letter dated Victoria, 9 Jan. 1870, *Wesleyan Missionary
    Notices, Canada Conference*, n.s., vol. 7 (May 1870): 101. This quote is
    reprinted in McDougall, *Pioneer, Patriot and Missionary*, 146–7.
80 Rev. G. McDougall, second letter, dated Blackfeet Country, 2 Sept. 1862,
    Christian Guardian, 11 Mar. 1863.
81 For the Oblate outreach in Western Canada, see Raymond J.A. Huel,
    Proclaiming the Gospel to the Indians and the Métis (Edmonton: University of
    Alberta Press, 1996).
82 Peter Erasmus, as told to Henry Thompson, in *Buffalo Days and Nights*,
    158, 178–9.
83 Mack, "Evangelical Prophet," 256–7.
84 A very good popular summary of the meteorite is contained in the
    Manitou Stone information guide, *Manitou Asiniy: The Manitou Stone*
    (Edmonton: Royal Alberta Museum, n.d.). I thank Marilyn Davidge for
    showing me this publication. The Manitou Stone is now on display in a
    stand-alone space in the new Royal Alberta Museum. See Clare Clancy,
    "The Future of Alberta's Past," *Calgary Herald*, 4 Oct. 2018, A8.
85 Doug Cuthand, *Askiwina: A Cree World* (Regina: Coteau Books, 2007), 15.
86 The best overview of the Manitou Stone is that by Howard Plotkin,
    "The Iron Creek Meteorite: The Curious History of the Manitou Stone
    and the Claim for Its Repatriation," *Earth Sciences History*, 33/1 (2014):
    120–75. In 1870 the meteorite was at the Victoria Mission. The British
    army officer William Butler saw it there and wrote: "In the farmyard of
    the mission-house there lay a curious block of metal of immense weight;
    it was rugged, deeply indented, and polished on the outer edges of the
    indentations by the wear and friction of many years. Its history was a
    curious one. Longer than any man could say, it had lain on the summit
    of a hill far out in the southern prairies. It had been a medicine-stone of
    surpassing virtue among the Indians over a vast territory. No tribe or
    portion of a tribe would pass in the vicinity without paying a visit to this
    great medicine." William Francis Butler, *The Great Lone Land: A Narrative
    of Travel and Adventure in the North-West of America* (Edmonton: Hurtig,
    1968; originally published in 1872 in London, England, by Sampson Low,
    Marston, Low & Searle), 304.
87 George McDougall, dated Edmonton, 20 July 1874, *Wesleyan Missionary
    Notices, Canada Conference*, n.s., 25 (Nov. 1874): 398. Perhaps McDougall
    took the meteorite with him to Edmonton when he moved there in 1871.
    It was shipped to Victoria College in Ontario in 1874. First it travelled to
    the college's original location in Cobourg, and then in the early 1890s to

the new Victoria College building on the University of Toronto campus. For years the original meteorite, and later a replica stood on a pedestal directly in front of the chapel in the Old Vic building. Paul A.W. Wallace, "The Canadian Herodotus, Chapter XIII – The Open Prairie," *Christian Guardian,* 28 Jan. 1925, 7. Dr Kingsley Joblin, Vic '32, confirmed the location of the iron meteorite in the late 1920s and early 1930s. Interview by telephone, Toronto, 25 June 1993. It remained there, before the chapel, in the 1940s, as David Knight, a Victoria undergraduate at the time, informed me in a telephone interview, 24 June 1993.

88 Mack, "Evangelical Prophet," 157.
89 Ibid., 299.
90 Grant and Hamilton, *Grant*, 138.
91 Mack, "Grant," 406.
92 McNeill, "The Story of Queen's," 19.
93 Hilda Neatby, Frederick W. Gibson, and Roger Graham, eds., *Queen's University*, vol. 1, *1841–1917* (Montreal and Kingston: McGill-Queen's University Press, 1978), 160.
94 Principal Grant, D.D., "The North-West: Manitoba," in George Monro Grant, ed., *Picturesque Canada: The Country As It Was and Is*, 2 vols. (Toronto: Beldon Bros. 1882), 1:301.
95 Grant, *Ocean to Ocean*, 178–9.
96 Peter Waite has edited Grant's account of the 1883 trip in a series of three articles: "Across the Rockies and the Selkirks with G.M. Grant in 1883," *Canada: An Historical Magazine*, 1/1 (Autumn 1973): 32–51; 1/2 (Winter 1973): 57–69; 1/3 (Spring 1974): 43–54. In early 1884, Grant reported on the trip in a Toronto publication, *The Week*. Waite's edited text is based on these articles, in consultation with Grant's original notes in LAC, G.M. Grant Papers, Diaries, 1882–90, MG29, D38, vol. 9.
97 George M. Grant, "The C.P.R. by the Kicking Horse Pass and the Selkirks. III. The Mission at Morley," *The Week*, 10 Jan. 1884, 85. Waite's edited account does not include Grant's conversation with John McDougall at Morley; for this, see this cited article in *The Week*, as well as Grant's original notes in LAC, G.M. Grant Papers, Diaries, 1882–90, MG29, D38, vol. 9, 1–11. The Morley section in the diary is contained in the brown notebook entitled "Case of Revd John McDougall, Morleyville & his Stoney Indians, versus Govt of Cdn, rep[resented] by Mt. Police, proprietors Coc[hrane] ranche & others."
98 Grant, "C.P.R. by the Kicking Horse Pass," 85.
99 From 1873 to 1875 the mission was located about 3 km north of the Bow River on a small lake, but it was moved to its present-day site two years later. See Nix, *Mission*, 89.

100 Roland Rollinmud and Ian A.L. Getty, foreword in Courtney W. Mason, *Spirits of the Rockies: Reasserting an Indigenous Presence in Banff National Park* (Toronto: University of Toronto Press, 2014), xi.

101 William Westfall, "William Morley Punshon," *DCB* 11, *1881–1890* (1982), 719–20.

102 Grant, "C.P.R. by the Kicking Horse Pass," 85.

103 George Grant to "Dearest Mother" [his wife], dated between Padmore & Aylmer Park, Friday afternoon [24 Aug. 1883]. Letters sent by G.M. Grant to his wife, 11 Apr. 1882 to 18 June 1885, LAC, G.M. Grant Papers, Correspondence, MG29 D38, vol. 34.

104 Hugh A. Dempsey, *Indian Names for Alberta Communities* (Calgary: Glenbow-Alberta Institute, 1969), 15.

105 John D.R. Holmes, "The Canmore Corridor, 1880–1914: A Case Study of the Selection and Development of a Pass Site," in L.A. Rosenvall and S.M. Evans, eds., *Essays on the Historical Geography of the Canadian West* (Calgary: Department of Geography, University of Calgary, 1987), 36.

106 The exact date of the notice appears in Grant's original notes in LAC, G.M. Grant Papers, Diaries, 1882–90, MG29, D38, vol. 9, 8. The notes are a good supplement to the summary provided in Grant's article, in *The Week*, 10 Jan. 1884, 85–6.

107 W. Pocklington, Sub-Agent, Notice, quoted in Grant, "C.P.R. by the Kicking Horse Pass," 86. The Indian Agent for Treaty Seven, Cecil Denny, reported on John McDougall's activities in a letter to the Indian Commissioner Edgar Dewdney, dated Fort Macleod, 15 Mar. 1883, LAC, RG10, vol. 3627, file 6230. I thank Will Pratt for this reference.

108 John McDougall, quoted by Grant in "C.P.R. by the Kicking Horse Pass," 86.

109 John McDougall, quoted by G.H.H. [George Ham]. "Among the Bloods. Rev. John Macdougall on the Indians and their grievances," Toronto *Daily Mail*, 30 Jan. 1886.

110 Daniel Miner Gordon, quoted in D.B. Mack, "Daniel Miner Gordon," *DCB* 15, *1921–1930* (2005), 414.

111 *Halifax Morning Herald*, 29 Aug. 1885, cited in George F.G. Stanley, "New Brunswick and Nova Scotia and the North-West Rebellion, 1885," in John E. Foster, ed., *The Developing West: Essays on Canadian History in Honor of Lewis H. Thomas* (Edmonton: University of Alberta Press, 1983), 87.

112 Brian J. Fraser, "William Caven," *DCB* 13, *1901–1910* (1994), 181–4.

113 "The Assemblies, the Indians," *Presbyterian Record*, 11/7 (July 1886): 192. I thank Barry Mack for this reference.

114 Alexander Morris, *Nova Britannia; or, Our New Canadian Dominion Foreshadowed, being a Series of Lectures, Speeches and Addresses, edited with notes and an introduction by a member of the Canadian Press* (Toronto: Hunter

Rose & Co, 1884), 88. Jean Friesen, "Alexander Morris," *DBC* 11, *1881–1890* (1982), 612.

115 Friesen, "Morris," 609, 614.

116 See the letters of William Duncan to Grant in LAC, G.M. Grant Papers, MG30, vol. 5, 1980a–d (31 Aug. 1885), and vol. 6, 2033–42 (16 Apr. 1886). I thank Barry Mack for bringing this correspondence to my attention.

117 Jean Usher, *William Duncan of Metlakatla: A Victorian Missionary in British Columbia* (Ottawa: National Museum of Man, 1974), 94.

118 Ibid., 1, 69. Daniel Raunet, *Without Surrender, Without Consent: A History of the Nishga Land Claims* (Vancouver: Douglas & McIntyre, 1984), 45.

119 Usher, *William Duncan*, 82–3.

120 Ibid., 64.

121 Ibid., 1, 49.

122 John A. Macdonald, 7 Apr. 1884, in Canada, *House of Commons Debates* (1884), 1399.

123 John A. Macdonald, quoted in Forrest E. LaViolette, *The Struggle for Survival: Indian Cultures and the Protestant Ethic in British Columbia* (Toronto: University of Toronto Press, 1961), 43.

124 James P. Spradley, "James Sewid's Adaptation to Culture Conflict," in James P. Spradley, ed., *Guests Never Leave Hungry: The Autobiography of James Sewid, a Kwakiutl Indian* (Montreal and Kingston: McGill-Queen's University Press, 1972),

125 Grant, *Ocean to Ocean*, 323.

126 Usher, *William Duncan*, 130.

127 Duncan to Grant, 31 Aug. 1885.

128 G.M. Grant letter dated Queen's University, Kingston, 17 Nov. 1886, published in the *Montreal Herald*, 20 Nov. 1886.

129 The letters appeared in the *Montreal Herald* on 20, 25, and 29 Nov. 1886.

130 G.M. Grant, letter dated Queen's University, Kingston, 26 [?] Nov. 1886, published in the *Montreal Herald*, 29 Nov. 1886.

131 Rev. George M. Grant, "The Great West. Part III," *Good Words*, 15 (June 1874): 408.

132 Gerald F. Reid, "'To Renew Our Fire': Political Activism, Nationalism, and Identity in Three Rotinonhsionni Communities," in Brian Hosmer and Larry Nesper, eds., *Tribal Worlds: Critical Studies in American Indian Nation Building* (Albany, NY: State University of New Press, 2013), 37. I thank Trish Rae for bringing this article to my attention.

133 Ibid., 43–4.

134 Allan Sherwin, *Bridging Two Peoples: Chief Peter E. Jones, 1843–1909* (Waterloo, Ont.: Wilfred Laurier University Press, 2012), 132–3. This book is the best source for all details about Dr Jones's life and the history of the Mississaugas of New Credit First Nation in the later nineteenth century.

No evidence exists that Principal Grant and Dr Jones, Queen's best-known Aboriginal alumnus, communicated with each another.

135 Grant's imperialism was really one variety of Canadian nationalism. See Carl Berger's chapter on Grant in *The Sense of Power*, 9. Grant once said, in 1898, "We are Canadian, and in order to be Canadian we must be British." The quote appears in Norman Penlington, *Canada and Imperialism 1896–1899* (Toronto: University of Toronto Press, 1965), 66.

136 Chancery of the Order of Saint Michael and Saint George, Downing Street, 9 Oct. 1901, *London Gazette*, 11 Oct. 1901, 6641.

137 Joseph Pope, *The Tour of Their Royal Highnesses, The Duke and Duchess of Cornwall and York through the Dominion of Canada in the Year 1901* (Ottawa: King's Printer, 1903), 128. Ken Cuthbertson, "Archives makes a serendipitous discovery," *Queen's Gazette*, 27 Oct. 2008, 1–2. I thank Heather Home for her help in locating this article.

138 Mack, "Evangelical Prophet," 5.

139 Ibid., 334.

140 R.J. Manion, *Life Is an Adventure* (Toronto: Ryerson Press, 1936), 236. A slightly different version appears in T.R. Glover and D.D. Calvin, *A Corner of Empire: The Old Ontario Strand* (Cambridge: Cambridge University Press, 1937), 165–6. I thank Barry Mack for this reference.

4. Chancellor John A. Boyd and Kathleen Coburn

1 Pierre J. O. Chauvreau, *L'Instruction publique au Canada* (Quebec, 1876), 355, quoted in Mason Wade, *The French-Canadian Outlook* (Toronto: McClelland and Stewart, 1964), 1–2.

2 Thomas Gibbs Ridout to Elizabeth Ward, 5 Jan. 1813, in Edith G. Firth, ed., *The Town of York, 1793–1815: A Collection of Documents of Early Toronto* (Toronto: Champlain Society, 1962), 287.

3 "John Boyd," *Commemorative Biographical Record of the County of York, Ontario* (Toronto: J.H. Beers & Co, 1907), 540. Walter H.C. Boyd, *The Last Chancellor* (Hamilton: McMaster Media Production Services, 1995), 1.

4 D.R. Keys, "In Memoriam. Sir John Boyd," *University [of Toronto] Monthly*, 17 (1916–17): 134.

5 "Bay Street Academy, Toronto," *British Colonist*, 29 Dec. 1841.

6 Ibid., 4 Jan. 1843.

7 Michael Bliss, "John Macdonald," *Dictionary of Canadian Biography* (*DCB*) 11, *1881–1890* (Toronto: University of Toronto Press, 1982), 551.

8 Alexander Reford, "Sir Charles Moss," *DCB* 14, *1911–1920* (1998), 771.

9 W.H. Pearson, *Recollections and Records of Toronto of Old* (Toronto: William Briggs, 1914), 231. W. Stewart Wallace, *The Macmillan Dictionary of Canadian Biography*, 3rd ed. (Toronto: Macmillan, 1963), 586.

10 "Bay Street Academy, Toronto," *British Colonist*, 27 Dec. 1844.

11 "John Boyd," *Commemorative Biographical Record*, 540.

12 Ibid. Boyd, *Last Chancellor*, 4.

13 "John Boyd," *Commemorative Biographical Record*, 541.

14 J. Ross Robertson, *Robertson's Landmarks of Toronto*, vol. 1 (Toronto: Author, 1894), 241. Boyd, *Last Chancellor*, 4.

15 "John Boyd," *Commemorative Biographical Record*, 541.

16 John Boyd, "Bay Street Commercial and Classical Academy," *British Colonist*, 1 Aug. 1845.

17 W.H.C. Boyd, "The Last Chancellor," *Law Society of Upper Canada Gazette*, 15/1 (Dec. 1981): 357. The location of the farm and school was on the east side of Yonge St, just south of what is now Blythewood Road. Boyd, *Chancellor*, 8.

18 Charles Dickens, *American Notes*, cited in the *College Times*, (Summer 1910): 30, quoted in Richard Howard, *Upper Canada College, 1829–1979: Colborne's Legacy* (Toronto: Macmillan, 1979), 44.

19 Howard, *Upper Canada College*, 71. Today the Royal Alexandra Theatre is located on a portion of the college's old athletic field. Robert Brockhouse, *The Royal Alexandra Theatre: A Celebration of 100 Years* (Toronto: McArthur & Co, 2007),

20 "John Boyd," *Commemorative Biographical Record*, 542. Boyd, *Chancellor*, 8.

21 "John Boyd," *Commemorative Biographical Record*, 542.

22 A.H. Young, ed., *The Roll of Pupils of Upper Canada College* (Kingston: Crozier and Edgar, 1917), 15.

23 Upper Canada College first Quarter ending 20th Dec. 1847, University of Toronto Archives, Upper Canada College Cumulative List of Pupils, A74-0018/037(02).

24 The Report of what is generally called the Bagot Commission. The report is unpaginated, but the quote can be found on p. 2, of sec. 3. See *Report on the Affairs of the Indians in Canada*, App. T, *Journals of the Legislative Assembly of Canada*, 1847.

25 George Dickson and G. Mercer Adam, com. and ed., *A History of Upper Canada College, 1829–1892* (Toronto: Russell & Hutchison, 1893), 279.

26 Mary Larratt Smith, *Prologue to Norman: The Canadian Bethunes* (Oakville, Ont.: Mosaic Press / Valley Editions, 1976), 65–6. Heather McDougall, "Norman Bethune," *DCB* 12, *1891–1900* (1990), 106. His grandson was the famous-twentieth century Dr Norman Bethune, renowned for his medical work in the Spanish Civil War and, later, China. Eric Arthur, Howard Chapman, and Hart Massey, *Moose Factory 1673 to 1973* (Toronto: University of Toronto Press 1949), 1, 7.

27 Young, *The Roll*, 128, 394. R.C. Macleod, "James Farquharson Macleod," *DCB* 12, *1891–1900* (1990), 672–5. Three decades later, in 1877, James

Macleod would serve as one of the two government commissioners for Treaty Seven with the First Nations of southern Alberta.

28 Howard, *Upper Canada College*, 76. James Cleland Hamilton, "Famous Algonquins: Algic Legends (Read 28 Nov. 1898)," *The Canadian Institute Semi-Centennial Volume*, vol. 6 (Toronto: Murray Printing Co, 1899), 302.

29 Edward Marion Chadwick, "Macleod," *Ontarian Families: Genealogies of United Empire Loyalist and Other Pioneer Families of Upper Canada* [1894] (Lambertville, NJ: Hunterdon House, 1970), 49.

30 Henry Macleod, four years older than James, was also a student at the school in 1847. Upper Canada College Cumulative List of Pupils. Henry's date of birth appears in Chadwick, "Macleod," 49.

31 Martin Macleod to Mrs Mary Ferguson, dated Drynock, 22 Dec. 1847, Toronto Reference Library, Baldwin Room, Martin Macleod Letter Books, vol. 1.

32 Boyd, *Chancellor*, 9.

33 John Hare, Marc Lafrance, and David-Thiery Ruddel, "Tableau 10. La population de Québec, 1608–1871," *Histoire de la Ville de Québec 1608–1871* (Montreal: Boréal, 1987), 324. Paul-André Linteau, *The History of Montréal: The Story of a Great North American City*, translated by Peter McCambridge (Montreal: Baraka Books, 2013), 72.

34 Ruth B. Phillips, *Trading Identities: The Souvenir in Native North American Art from the Northeast, 1700–1900* (Montreal and Kingston: McGill-Queen's University Press, 1998), 130–1.

35 Thomas Peace, "Maintaining Connections: Lorette during the Eighteenth Century," in Thomas Peace and Kathryn Magee Labelle, eds., *From Huronia to Wendakes: Adversity, Migrations, and Resilience, 1650–1900* (Norman: University of Oklahoma Press, 2016), 77, 82–3.

36 Ibid., 76.

37 Ibid., 96–7.

38 "John Boyd," *Commemorative Biographical Record*, 542.

39 Ibid.

40 Boyd, *Chancellor*, 9

41 "John Boyd," *Commemorative Biographical Record*, 541.

42 Boyd, "Last Chancellor," 366.

43 A.W. Rasporich, "Imperial Sentiment in the Province of Canada during the Crimean War 1854–1856," in W.L. Morton, ed., *The Shield of Achilles: Aspects of Canada in the Victorian Age* (Toronto: McClelland and Stewart, 1968), 156, 163–4.

44 J.A. Boyd, "The Origins & Progress of the Present War," Upper Canada College Prize Essay for 1855," 12. Copy deposited in the University of Toronto Archives.

45 Boyd, "Origins," 16.

46 Martin L. Friedland, *The University of Toronto: A History*, 2nd ed. (Toronto: University of Toronto Press, 2013), 36.

47 Sylvia Van Kirk, "'What if Mama Is an Indian?' The Cultural Ambivalence of the Alexander Ross Family," in Jacqueline Peterson and Jennifer S.H. Brown, eds., *The New Peoples: Being and Becomjng Métis in North America* (Winnipeg: University of Manitoba Press, 1985), 208.

48 W.D. Smith, "James Ross," *DCB* 10, *1871–1880* (1972), 629.

49 Douglas Richardson, *A Not Unsightly Building: University College and Its History* (Toronto: Mosaic, 1990), 72.

50 University of Toronto Commencement, 26 June 1857 and 15 June 1858, University of Toronto Archives, P87.0046. Dickson and Adam, *History of Upper Canada College*, 285.

51 Robert F. Berkhofer, Jr, *The White Man's Indian: Images of the American Indian from Columbus to the Present* [1978] (Toronto: Random House, 1979), 48.

52 Robertson, *Landmarks of Toronto*, vol. 3, 241.

53 The Toronto *Globe*, 31 May 1853. Eliza had two sisters, who taught in her school. As the most outgoing, I am assuming the Miss McNally who is referenced was Eliza. I thank Colin McFarquhar for this item.

54 Each of the prize books has bookplates indicating the award: William Prescott's *History of the Reign of Ferdinand and Isabella* (London: George Routledge & Co, 1854); *History of the Conquest of Mexico* (London: Routledge, 1857); and *History of the Conquest of Peru* (London: Routledge, 1858).

55 Samuel Eliot Morison, "Prescott the American Thucydides," in Emily Morison Beck, ed., *Sailor Historian: The Best of Samuel Eliot Morison* (Boston: Houghton Mifflin, 1977), 344.

56 David Levin, *History as Romantic Art: Bancroft, Prescott, Motley, and Parkman* [1959] (New York: Harcourt, Brace & World, 1963), vii, 27.

57 Marinell Ash, "Daniel Wilson: The Early Years," in Marinell Ash and colleagues, *Thinking with Both Hands: Sir Daniel Wilson in the Old World and the New*, edited by Elizabeth Hulse (Toronto: University of Toronto Press, 1999), 20–2.

58 Friedland, *University of Toronto*, 43–4.

59 Bruce G. Trigger, "Sir Daniel Wilson: Canada's First Anthropologist," *Anthropologica*, 8 (1966): 22.

60 Alice Beck Kehoe, *The Land of Prehistory: A Critical History of American Archaeology* (New York: Routledge, 1998), 37.

61 Douglas Cole, "The Origins of Canadian Anthropology, 1850–1910," *Journal of Canadian Studies*, 8/1 (Feb. 1973): 35.

62 Daniel Wilson, "The Present State and Future Prospects of the Indians of British North America," *Proceedings, Royal Colonial Institute*, vol. 5 (1874), 244. I thank Bennett McCardle for pointing out this article to me.

63 J.A. Boyd, "Preface dated Toronto, August, 1860," in *A Summary of Canadian History, from the time of Cartier's Discovery to the present day* (Toronto: Adam Miller, 1869).

64 D.W. [Daniel Wilson], "Review of *A Summary of Canadian History, from the time of Cartier's Discovery to the present day*. By J.A. Boyd, B.A. (Toronto: James Campbell, 1860)," *Canadian Journal*, n.s., 30 (Nov. 1860): 538.

65 The cover jacket states "Eighteenth thousand," *A Summary of Canadian History, from the time of Cartier's Discovery to the present day*. By J.A. Boyd, B.A. (Toronto: James Campbell, 1865). There were additional printings in 1866, 1867, and 1871.

66 *University College Calendar 1861–62*, 58.

67 Boyd, *Chancellor*, 12. In the summer of 1860, he was entered on the books of the Law Society of Upper Canada as an articled student.

68 *University College Calendar 1861–62*, 58.

69 Prof. J.L. Gilmour, "The Late Sir John A. Boyd, K.C.M.G.," *Canadian Baptist*, (28 Dec. 1916).

70 D.C. Masters, *The Rise of Toronto 1850–1890* (Toronto: University of Toronto Press, 1947), 73. The population of Toronto in 1860–61 was 45,000.

71 Peter G. Barton, "Sir John Alexander Boyd," *DCB* 14, *1911–1920* (1998), 126.

72 Patrick Brode, *Death in the Queen City: Clara Ford on Trial, 1895* (Toronto: Natural Heritage Books, 2005), 78–9.

73 Barton, "Boyd," 126.

74 "John Boyd," *Commemorative Biographical Record*, 541.

75 Allan Graydon, QC, "Some Reminiscences of Blakes," photostat, dated 7 Feb. 1970, 15. Copy given to me by the late Robert M. Brown of Blake, Cassels and Graydon, and now deposited with my research notes in my file "Blake Cassels," 026.18, in the Donald B. Smith fonds, Acc. 2016.42, Archives and Special Collections, University of Calgary (hereafter, Smith Fonds).

76 Keys, "In Memoriam. Sir John Boyd," 135.

77 Carl Berger, "Sir Daniel Wilson," *DCB* 12, *1891–1900* (1990), 1113.

78 John A. Boyd. "David Buchan," *McMaster University Monthly*, (Feb. 1897): 196.

79 Boyd, Chancellor, 8.

80 Petition of certain Tuscarora Indians recd 12 Apr. 1844; in the file, "Application of an Allotment of Indian Land for the purpose of an Educational Institution proposed to be established by the Baptist Society, Tuscarora 8/12 Apr. 1844," LAC, RG7 G20, vol. 30/31, Governor General's Civil Secretary's Correspondence, no. 3410, mfm reel H-1356.

81 David R. Elliott, "Canadian Baptists and Native Ministry in the Nineteenth Century," *Historical Papers 2000: Canadian Society of Church History*, (2001): 153–4.

82 Anthony F.C. Wallace, *Tuscarora: A History* (Albany: State University of New York Press, 2012), 93–5.

83 W. Stewart Wallace, *A History of the University of Toronto, 1827–1927* (Toronto: University of Toronto Press, 1927), 67.

84 Gilmour, "Boyd."

85 Paul R. Dekar, "Jane Buchan," *DCB* 13, *1901–1910* (1994), 121–2.

86 Barton, "Boyd," 127.

87 John A. Macdonald to John Alexander Boyd, dated Stadacona Hall, Ottawa, 7 May 1881, Law Society of Upper Canada Archives, CA ON00311, PF163-2000070-001. I thank Paul Leatherdale for this reference.

88 *Canada Law Journal*, 1 (1881): 353, cited in Boyd, *Last Chancellor*, 45.

89 S. Barry Cottam explains the spelling of the company's name in, "Indian Title as a 'Celestial Institution': David Mills and the St Catherine's Milling Case," in Kerry Abel and Jean Friesen, eds., *Aboriginal Resource Use in Canada: Historical and Legal Aspects* (Winnipeg: University of Manitoba Press, 1991), 262. The company spelled its name "St Catherine's" but all three Canadian Courts, or lower courts, used "St Catharines." The Privy Council, the highest court, followed the company's spelling. Here the spelling of the Canadian Court Reports is used, "St Catharines," as our focus is on Chancellor Boyd's ruling in June 1885.

90 Anthony J. Hall, "The St Catherine's Milling and Lumber Company versus the Queen: Indian Land Rights as a Factor in Federal-Provincial Relations in Nineteenth-Century Canada," in Abel and Friesen, *Aboriginal Resource Use*, 268.

91 Sidney L. Harring, *White Man's Law: Native People in Nineteenth-Century Canadian Jurisprudence* (Toronto: University of Toronto Press, 1998), 134.

92 Boyd, *Chancellor*, 53.

93 Patricia Jasen, "Native People and the Tourist Industry in Nineteenth-Century Ontario," *Journal of Canadian Studies*, 28/4 (Winter 1993–94): 5.

94 "Table IV. Population Growth in Central Canadian Cities, 1851–1921," in J.M.S. Careless, *Toronto to 1918: An Illustrated City* (Toronto: James Lorimer, 1984), 200.

95 Boyd, *Chancellor*, 51–2.

96 Pelham Edgar, *Across My Path*, edited by by Northrop Frye (Toronto: Ryerson Press, 1952), 96. Leacock's biography places the 2-week Georgian Bay trip in the 1890s. See Ralph L. Curry, *Stephen Leacock: Humorist and Humanist* (Garden City, NY: Doubleday, 1959), 59.

97 Edgar, *Across My Path*, 95.

98 Ibid., 96.

99 The chancellor apparently did not know, e.g., the Georgian Bay Anishinabeg's (Ojibwe's) understanding of what had been said at the Robinson Huron Treaty of 1850. Although the written text of the treaty specifically refers to "The Islands" opposite the northern and eastern shores of Lake Huron, from Sault Ste Marie to Penetanguishene, the Georgian Bay Ojibwe maintain that they only ceded "aki," the Anishinabe (Ojibwe) word for land or soil, not the "minis," their word for island. Instead of reserving the Thirty Thousand Islands for the Anishinabeg (the plural form of Anishinabe), they argue, the government unilaterally granted the timber cutting rights. In time it began selling the islands themselves to cottagers. See Peter H. Russell, "Native Roots," *Wind, Water Rock and Sky* (N.p.p.: Cognashene Book, 1997), 22, 85; and also Robin Jarvis Brownlie, *A Fatherly Eye: Indian Agents, Government Power, and Aboriginal Resistance in Ontario, 1918–1939* (Don Mills, Ont.: Oxford University Press, 2003), 13–14, 67, 71.

100 Claire Elizabeth Campbell, *Shaped by the West Wind: Nature and History in Georgian Bay* (Vancouver: UBC Press, 2005), 104.

101 Good sources on Parry Island in the nineteenth century include the following: E.S. Rogers and Flora Tobobondung, "Parry Island Farmers: A Period of Change in the Way of Life of the Algonkians of Southern Ontario," in David Brez Carlisle, ed., *Contributions to Canadian Ethnology* (Ottawa: National Museums of Canada, 1975), 247–359; Diamond Jenness, *The Ojibwa Indians of Parry Island, Their Social and Religious Life* (Ottawa: King's Printer, 1935); Franz M. Koennecke, *Wasoksing: The History of Parry Island, an Anishnabwe Community in the Georgian Bay 1850 to 1920* (M.A. thesis, University of Waterloo, 1984).

102 Information from Fred Wheatley, Toronto, 3 Jan. 1972. I took Ojibwe language lessons from Fred Wheatley from Wasoksing, at the Toronto Native Friendship Centre, during the winters of 1971–72, and 1972–73.

103 Boyd, *Chancellor*, 52–3.

104 "Chancellor Sir John A. Boyd is dead after short illness," *Toronto Star*, 23 Nov. 1916.

105 "The Last Chancellor of Ontario," *Canadian Law Times*, 36/12 (Dec. 1916): 912.

106 Peter Jones, *History of the Ojebway Indians: With Especial Reference to Their Conversion to Christianity* (London: A.W. Bennett, 1861), 164.

107 John Alexander Boyd, "Indian Notebook," 21. Peter Barton showed me in 1996 a copy of the notebook. A photocopy is in my file 028.16, "Indian Notebook circa 1880s–early 20th century" in the Smith fonds.

108 Boyd, *Last Chancellor*, 110.

109 Boyd, "Last Chancellor," 360.

110 Edgar, *Across My Path*, 96.

111 Elizabeth Boyd Andras, *A Little Bit of Good Cheer* (Toronto: Privately printed, 1972), not paginated, but the information appears on p. 13.

112 Rupert Ross, *Dancing with a Ghost: Exploring Aboriginal Reality* [1992] (Toronto: Penguin, 2006), 18.

113 Two good overviews of this complicated issue are Morris Zaslow, "The Ontario Boundary Question," in his edited work, *Profiles of a Province* (Toronto: Ontario Historical Society, 1967), 107–17; and Christopher Armstrong, "Remoulding the Constitution," in *The Politics of Federalism: Ontario's Relations with the Federal Government, 1867–1942* (Toronto: University of Toronto Press, 1981), 8–32. A short popular summary appears in Joseph Schull, *Ontario Since 1867* (Toronto: McClelland and Stewart, 1978), 95–101.

114 Hall, "St Catherine's Milling," 273.

115 In the early 1870s, before the Anishinabeg in the future Treaty Three area accepted the idea of a treaty in 1873, there had been greater media interest. See Sheldon Krasowski, "Treaty Three: The North-West Angle Treaty," in *No Surrender: The Land Remains Indigenous* (Regina: University of Regina Press, 2019), 87–128.

116 Mark Cronlund Anderson and Carmen L. Robertson, *Seeing Red: A History of Natives in Canadian Newspapers* (Winnipeg: University of Manitoba Press, 2011), 41.

117 "The North-West Angle Treaty, Number Three," in Alexander Morris, *The Treaties of Canada with the Indians of Manitoba and the North-West Territories* (Toronto: Belfords, Clarke & Co, 1880), 320–9. By the terms of Treaty Three the Ojibwe (Anishinabeg) each obtained a gift of $12 and an annuity to each of $5. Each chief and headman received $25 and $15, respectively, every year. The federal government also promised $1,500 annually for twine for fishnets and ammunition, gifts of tools and supplies, and the promise of schools. Apart from areas retained as Indian reserves, established on the basis of 640 acres for a family of five, in accordance with Treaty Three the Ojibwe turned over 55,000 square miles of their homeland.

118 Krasowski, *No Surrender*, 87, 101.

119 Norah Storey, "Oliver Mowat," in Gerald Hallowell, ed., *The Oxford Companion to Canadian History and Literature* (Toronto: Oxford University Press, 1967), 174, mentions the premier's description of himself as "the Christian Politician."

120 Oliver Mowat in *R* v. *St Catharines Milling and Lumber Company* (1885), 10 O.R. 196 (Chancery) 199.

121 Ibid., 201.

122 Hall, *Treaties*, 10, 15, 24, 27.

123 S. Barry Cottam explains the spelling of the company's name, in "Indian Title as a 'Celestial Institution': David Mills and the St Catherine's Milling Case," in Kerry Abel and Jean Friesen, eds., *Aboriginal Resource Use in Canada: Historical and Legal Aspects* (Winnipeg: University of Manitoba Press, 1991), 262.

124 Donald Swainson, "Ontario on the Rise," *Horizon Canada*, 6/66 (June 1986): 1561–7. Paul Romney, "Sir Oliver Mowat," *DCB* 13, *1901–1910* (1994), 724–42.

125 Mowat in *R* v. *St Catharines Milling*, 199.

126 For a discussion of the "Doctrine of Discovery," see *The Final Report of the Truth and Reconciliation Commission*, vol. 1, *Canada's Residential Schools: The History, Part 1, Origins to 1939* (Montreal and Kingston: Published for the Truth and Reconciliation Commission by McGill-Queen's University Press, 2015), 15–20.

127 Wilfrid Laurier, 20 Apr. 1886, in Canada, *House of Commons Debates* (1886), 809–10, cited in Glen Williams, *Blood Must Tell: Debating Race and Identity in the Canadian House of Commons, 1880–1925* (Ottawa: Willow BX Press, 2014), 60.

128 Kent McNeil, *Flawed Precedent: The St Catherine's Case and Aboriginal Title* (Vancouver: UBC Press, 2019), 7, 194n15.

129 Boyd, *Last Chancellor*, 127n14.

130 McNeil, *Flawed Precedent*, 52, 54, 63. Chancellor Boyd termed *Johnson* v. *McIntosh* (1823) "a classical judgement," in *R* v. *St Catharines Milling and Lumber Company* (1885), 10 O.R. 196 (Ch) 209. For an in-depth review of the chancellor's handling of the trial, see "Chancellor Boyd's Trial Decision," in *Flawed Precedent*, 44–77.

131 Lindsay G. Robertson, *Conquest by Law: How the Discovery of America Dispossessed Indigenous Peoples of Their Lands* (Oxford: Oxford University Press, 2005), x.

132 Harring, *White Man's Law*, 137.

133 "Alexander James Boyd," *Commemorative Biographical Record*, 5.

134 "Northwest veteran John L. Boyd passes," *Toronto Star*, 31 May 1935. The reference to Len appears in the article, "Rebellion of 1885 is recalled. Rev. Principal Lloyd at St George's gives an interesting lecture on his personal experience in the stirring days of the Riel Rebellion," *Saskatoon Daily Phoenix*, 9 Oct. 1909.

135 Chief Poundmaker, who was erroneously regarded as a member of the Métis resistance of 1885, was exonerated by the Canadian government in spring 2019. Stephanie Taylor, "Trudeau exonerates Chief Poundmaker of 134-year-old treason conviction," *National Post*, 24 May 2019.

136 Charles Pelham Mulvaney, *The History of the North-West Rebellion of 1885* (Toronto: A.H. Hovey & Co, 1885), 66.

137 Hall, "St Catherine's Milling," 281."

138 Alexander Morris, quoted in evidence taken at the trial held in Toronto before Chancellor Boyd, 18 May 1885, *In the Court of Appeal* (Toronto: Dudley & Burns, Printers, 1885), 10–12. A copy is in my file 027.26, "St. Catharine's Mill Case, Appeal Case Fall 1885," in the Smith fonds.

139 Robert J. Talbot, *Negotiating the Numbered Treaties: An Intellectual and Political Biography of Alexander Morris* (Saskatoon: Purich, 2009), 143, 158, 175.

140 Alexander Morris, *The Treaties of Canada with the Indians of Manitoba and the North-West Territories* (Toronto: Belfords, Clarke & Co, 1880), 295–6.

141 Ibid., 296–7.

142 *R v. St Catharines Milling and Lumber Company* (1885), 10 O.R. 196 (Ch), 228.

143 Ibid., 206.

144 A useful discussion of late nineteenth-century thought on treaties appears in D.J. Hall, *From Treaties to Reserves: The Federal Government and Native Peoples in Territorial Alberta, 1870–1905* (Montreal and Kingston: McGill-Queen's University Press, 2015), 42–3.

145 Peter H. Russell, *Canada's Odyssey: A Country Based on Incomplete Conquests* (Toronto: University of Toronto Press, 2017), 203.

146 Harring, *White Man's Law*, 139.

147 Chief Justice John Hagerty, cited in Archer Martin, *The Hudson's Bay Company's Land Tenures* (London: William Clowes and Sons, 1898), 97.

148 Harring, "Liberal Treatment," 342.

149 John Hagarty, Chief Justice of Ontario, quoted in *R v. The St Catharines Milling and Lumber Company*, *Ontario Practice Reports* (1886), 13 O.A.R. (Ontario Court of Appeal Reports) 148. For biographical information on Hagerty, see Graham Parker, "Sir John Hawkins Hagarty," *DCB* 12, *1891–1900* (1990), 399–400.

150 5 O.R. (26) 620. The most recent example would be the 1985 Bear Island decision, *Attorney-General for Ontario v. Bear Island Foundation et al.* (1985), *Ontario Reports*, second series, vol. 49, part 7 (1985), 382. I have a whole file on this in the University of Calgary Archives, file 027.23, "St Catharines Mill: Citing of Chancellor Boyd 1885," in the Smith fonds.

151 *R v. The St Catharines Milling and Lumber Company* (1885), 10 O.R. 196 (Ch) 211.

152 "Report on the Affairs of the Indians in Canada," in Legislative Assembly, *Journals*, Session 1844–5, vol. 4, Appendix EEE, 5: "The Commissioners have not had an opportunity, and they did not consider it necessary, to examine the official correspondence prior to the year 1827." I thank Jim Morrison for this insight. The "Bagot Commission" actually was headed by British civil servant Rawson W. Rawson and following the custom

of naming Royal Commissions after the head commissioner, should be named the Rawson Report after him, not the governor general, Charles Bagot. Despite this convention, it is universally known as the Bagot Report. Communication with Douglas Leighton, June 2018.

153 Speech of Colonel Simcoe to the Western Indians, Navy Hall, 22 June 1793, published in *The Correspondence of Lieutenant-Governor John Graves Simcoe*, edited by E.A. Cruikshank, 5 vols. (Toronto: Ontario Historical Society, 1923–31), 1: 364.

154 Peter Russell to Robert Prescott, 3 July 1798, published in *The Correspondence of the Honourable Peter Russell*, edited by E.A. Cruikshank, 3 vols. (Toronto: Ontario Historical Society, 1932–36), 2:199.

155 Proceedings of a Meeting with the Chippewa Indians of Matchedash and Lake Simcoe at Gwillembury, 8–9 June 1811, Archives of Ontario, CO 42, 351, 132, on microfilm.

156 *John Graves Simcoe, Correspondence*, 3:240–2. The quotation by Lord Dorchester is cited in John S. Long, *Far Northern Ontario in 1905* (Montreal and Kingston: McGill-Queen's University Press, 2010), 24.

157 *R v. The St Catharines Milling and Lumber Company* (1885), 10 O.R. 196 (Ch) 228.

158 George F.G. Stanley, "As Long as the Sun Shines and Water Flows: An Historical Comment," in Ian A.L. Getty and Antoine S. Lussier, eds., *As Long As the Sun Shines and Water Flows* (Vancouver: UBC Press, 1983), 13.

159 Barton, "Boyd," 126–7.

160 Chancery of the Order of Saint Michael and Saint George, Downing Street, 9 Oct. 1901, *London Gazette*, 1 Oct. 1901, 6641.

161 Boyd, *Last Chancellor*, 75.

162 Keys, "In Memoriam. Sir John Boyd," 136.

163 "Alexander James Boyd," *Commemorative Biographical Record*, 544.

164 "Military Funeral," *Transvaal Advertiser*, 23 Apr. 1902. I thank Chris Saunders for this reference. I also thank Rod Macleod, Sam Steele's biographer, for sending me a transcript of Steele's letter to his wife about Boyd's funeral, dated Pretoria, 23 Apr. 1902: Major General Baden Powell "stayed over for the funeral with A.D.C. He is to write Sir John. I wrote him two letters of condolence when it happened and also describing the funeral." I thank Sean Morrow for taking me when in Pretoria in April 2016 to see Alex Boyd's grave. Some years earlier, Nico van der Walt and Phil Minnaar helped me to learn its location. See Rod Macleod's well-written *Sam Steele: A Biography* (Edmonton: University of Alberta Press, 2018).

165 Boyd, *Last Chancellor*, 113.

166 A memorial entitled, "Meeting of the Senate of the University of Toronto 9th Mar. 1917." The memorial is signed by W.R. Meredith, chancellor

of the University of Toronto and chief justice of Ontario, and by Robert Falconer, president of the University. Chancellor Boyd died 23 Nov. 1916.

167 "Chancellor Boyd in Unsettled Accounts Arbitration, *The Mississagua Indian*," copy in the Archives of Ontario, F1027; Arbitration Proceedings 63, transcript for 13 Nov. 1895, Quebec City.

168 Barton, "Boyd," 127.

169 Kathleen Coburn, *In Pursuit of Coleridge* (Toronto: Clarke, Irwin, 1977), 10. I warmly thank Ted Chamberlin for giving me a copy of this excellent book. Kathleen Coburn was a valued friend.

170 Coburn, *In Pursuit*, 12.

171 For background on Ethel Brant Monture, see Cecilia Morgan, "Performing for 'Imperial Eyes': Bernice Loft and Ethel Brant Monture, Ontario, 1930s–60s," in Katie Pickles and Myra Rutherdale, eds., *Contact Zones: Aboriginal and Settler Women in Canada's Colonial Past* (Toronto: UBC Press, 2005), 67–89. Kathleen Coburn's correspondence with Ethel Brant Monture is in University of Toronto, Victoria University Library (VUL), Kathleen Coburn Collection, Box 007 (03).

172 Kathleen Coburn, quoted in Angela Burke, "Ethel Brant Monture, champion of her people," *Toronto Star Weekly*, 3 Oct. 1953, 4.

173 *The Harbord Review*, Harbord Collegiate Institute, May 1924 masthead page, VUL, Kathleen Coburn Collection, Box 35, file 20. Julius Molinaro, "Louis Rasminsky," *The Happy Ghosts of Harbord: A History of Harbord Collegiate Institute 1892–1992*, and in *Harborite no. 30, Centennial Number, Spring 1992*, 131–2.

174 Donald Urquhart, "Kathleen Coburn," *Acta Victoriana*, 74 (1949/50): 41.

175 Coburn, *In Pursuit*, 40.

176 Ethel Brant Monture to Kathleen Coburn, card sent sometime in June 1953, VUL, Kathleen Coburn Collection, Box 007 (03). A happy story, in 1953, Coburn finally was appointed professor of English at Victoria. Victoria University in the University of Toronto, E.J. Pratt Library, Special Collections (VUL), Fonds 35, Kathleen Coburn Collection.

177 Coburn, *In Pursuit*, 59.

178 A copy of the program can be found in LAC, RG10, vol. 3186, file 464, 314.

179 Robert Craig Brown, *Arts and Science at Toronto: A History, 1827–1990* (Toronto: University of Toronto Press, 2013), 222. See also Friedland, *University of Toronto*, 272–4, 393.

180 Laurel Sefton MacDowell, quoted in interview in "Not Behaving Like Ladies," available at http://harthouse.ca/about-us/laurel-macdowell/.

181 "Interview: Kathleen Coburn," *Acta Victoriana*, 108/2 (Spring 1984): 20–4. It was Pelham Edgar who appointed her to the Victoria English department. See Lorne Macdonald, "An Inquiring Personality: Interview with Kathleen Coburn," *University of Toronto Review*, 4 (Spring 1980): 17.

182 Christina McCall, *My Life as a Dame: The Personal and the Political in the Writings of Christina McCall*, edited by Stephen Clarkson (Toronto: House of Anansi, 2008), 29.
183 Here I am following the spelling of the family name in English, "Tabobandung," as used in Coburn, *In Pursuit*, 65–6, 163–5, 168.
184 Kathleen Coburn, "The Case of Mr Ojibway," *Canadian Forum*, (Oct. 1942): 215.
185 Coburn, *In Pursuit*, 66. For her correspondence with the Tabobandung family, see VUL, Kathleen Coburn Collection, Box 007 (02), Tabobandung (1946–56).
186 Hugh Shewell, *"Enough to Keep Them Alive": Indian Welfare in Canada, 1873–1965* (Toronto: University of Toronto Press, 2004), 116.
187 Miller, *Skyscraper*, 228.
188 John F. Leslie, "Assimilation, Integration or Termination? The Development of Canadian Indian Policy, 1943–1963" (Ph.D. dissertation, Department of History, Carleton University, 1999), 67.
189 Shewell, *"Enough to Keep Them Alive,"* 121.
190 John F. Leslie, "A Historical Survey of Indian-Government Relations, 1940–1970," Ottawa: Paper prepared for Royal Commission Liaison Office, Dec. 1993, 3.
191 Session 1944, House of Commons, *Special Committee on Reconstruction and Re-Establishment, Minutes of Proceedings and Evidence No.9, Wednesday, May 24, 1944* (Ottawa: King's Printer, 1944), 294.
192 Allen Mills, *Fool for Christ: The Political Thought of J.S. Woodsworth* (Toronto: University of Toronto Press, 1991), 16.
193 Aileen Ross spent three years at the University of Toronto as a lecturer in sociology, 1942–45. Years later she recorded how dull she had found the university. The Montrealer fled back to McGill to teach in their sociology department. Her comments add to an understanding of life for women faculty at the University of Toronto in the mid-twentieth century: "Perhaps because it was wartime there was very little social mixing amongst the staff. And, women were not allowed into Hart House at the time, where presumably the male staff cavorted in their off-hours." McGill University Archives, Aileen Ross Papers, Aileen Dansken Ross, Autobiography, MG 4134, 90-081, file 1. I warmly thank Lori Podolsky, McGill University Archives, for her help with my research on Aileen Ross's papers at McGill.
194 Aileen Ross to "Miss Coburn," dated 5 Feb. 1943, VUL, Kathleen Coburn Collection, Box 062 (04).
195 "Obituary. John Peter Humphrey. Wrote Human Rights Declaration," *Globe and Mail*, 16 Mar. 1995.

196 Kathleen Coburn, "The Indian in Canadian Literature," dated Victoria College, 11 Feb. 1948, VUL, Kathleen Coburn Collection, Box 061 (04).

197 Kathleen Coburn, "Review of *Canada Moves North* by Richard Finnie," *Canadian Forum*, (Oct. 1942): 221.

198 Kathleen Coburn, "The Red Man's Burden. Review of *The North American Indian To-day*, ed. C.T. Loran (*obit.*) T.F. McIlwraith, "University of Toronto Press. 1943," *Canadian Forum*, (Oct. 1944): 153.

199 Diamond Jenness, *The Ojibwa Indians of Parry Island: Their Social and Religious Life* (Ottawa: King's Printer, 1935).

200 Barnett Richling, *In Twilight and in Dawn: A Biography of Diamond Jenness* (Montreal and Kingston: McGill-Queen's University Press, 2012), 291.

201 The book was published in 1932 by the King's Printer in the National Museum of Canada, Bulletin 65 Anthropological Series No. 15. The quote appears on p. 264.

5. Duncan Campbell Scott

1 *The Final Report of the Truth and Reconciliation Commission*, vol. 1, *Canada's Residential Schools: The History, Part 1, Origins to 1939* (Montreal and Kingston: Published for the Truth and Reconciliation Commission by McGill-Queen's University Press, 2015), 276.

2 Duncan Campbell Scott, "Indian Affairs, 1867–1912," in Adam Short and Arthur G. Doughty, eds., *Canada and Its Provinces*, vol. 7, Section 4, "The Dominion" (Toronto: Glasgow, Brook & Co, 1914), 623.

3 Bill Russell, "The White Man's Paper Burden: Aspects of Record Keeping in the Department of Indian Affairs, 1860–1914," *Archivaria*, 15 (Winter 1984–85): 70.

4 "Industrial Schools at Alderville and Mount Elgin," in *Report of the Special Commissioners Appointed on the 8th of September, 1856, to Investigate Indian Affairs in Canada* (Toronto: Queen's Printer, 1858), not paginated.

5 The memoir by E.K. Brown, "Duncan Campbell Scott: A Memoir," David Staines, ed., *E.K. Brown – Responses and Evaluations: Essays on Canada* (Toronto: McClelland and Stewart, 1977), is the best source on Scott's background and youth.

6 Ibid., 113.

7 Madge Macbeth, *Over My Shoulder* (Toronto: Ryerson Press, 1953), 143. Arthur S. Bourinot, ed., *More Letters of Duncan Campbell Scott* (Ottawa: Published by the Editor, 1960), 2.

8 John English, "Patronage," in Gerald Hallowell, ed., *The Oxford Companion to Canadian History* (Don Mills, Ont.: Oxford University Press, 2004), 477.

9 C.C. Colby to Sir John A. Macdonald, dated Stanstead, Que., 16 June 1879, LAC, Sir John A. Macdonald Fonds, MG26-A, R14424-0-3-F, Political Papers, vol. 206.

10 Duncan Campbell Scott quoted in the *Ottawa Citizen*, 4 Aug. 1945, quoted in E. Brian Titley, *A Narrow Vision: Duncan Campbell Scott and the Administration of Indian Affairs in Canada* (Vancouver: UBC Press, 1986), 24.

11 The article appeared in an 1880 issue, on pp. 66–73, and was excerpted in the *Manitoba Free Press*, 24 July 1880. Jack Dunn helped me enormously with the NWMP background of Supertintendent Clark.

12 John Peter Turner, "Death of a Fine Officer," in *The North-West Mounted Police, 1873–1893*, vol. 1 (Ottawa: King's Printer, 1950), 538–9.

13 Jack F. Dunn, *NWMP: The North-West Mounted Police, 1873–1885* (Calgary: Author, 2017), 185, 545, 550.

14 See John A. Macdonald, *Affectionately Yours: The Letters of Sir John A. Macdonald and His Family*, edited by J.K. Johnson (Toronto: Macmillan, 1969), 33.

15 Brian Hubner, "'An Administered People': A Contextual Approach to the Study of Bureaucracy, Records-Keeping and Records in the Canadian Department of Indian Affairs, 1755–1950" (M.A. thesis, Archival Studies, University of Manitoba, 2000), 49.

16 Robin Jarvis Brownlie, *A Fatherly Eye: Indian Agents, Government Power, and Aboriginal Resistance in Ontario. 1918–1939* (Don Mills, Ont.: Oxford University Press, 2003), 32.

17 Titley, *Narrow Vision*, 13.

18 Macbeth, *Over My Shoulder*, 136.

19 Titley, *Narrow Vision*, 13.

20 Morris Zaslow, *The Northward Expansion of Canada, 1914–1967* (Toronto: McClelland and Stewart, 1988), 161.

21 Mark Abley, *Conversations with a Dead Man: The Legacy of Duncan Campbell Scott* (Madeira Park, BC: Douglas & McIntyre, 2013), 38. In the city, female teachers obtained half the salary of a male. In 1884 the average salaries of public school teachers in Toronto were $720 for males and $324 for females. C. Pelham Mulvany, *Toronto Past and Present: A Handbook of the City* (Toronto: W.E. Caiger, 1884), 80.

22 "Frank Pedley has resigned his lucrative Ottawa post, succeeded by Duncan Scott," *Toronto World*, 15 Oct. 1913. I thank Bill Loft for this reference.

23 Hubner, "Administered People," 55–6.

24 Hugh Shewell, *"Enough to Keep Them Alive": Indian Welfare in Canada, 1873–1965* (Toronto: University of Toronto Press, 2004), 24, 109.

25 Brown, "Duncan Campbell Scott," 112.

26 John F. Leslie, "The Indian Act: An Historical Perspective," *Canadian Parliamentary Review*, (Summer 2002): 25.

27 *Canada's Residential Schools: The History, Part 1, Origins to 1939*, 289.

28 Duncan Campbell Scott, cited in John Leonard Taylor, *Canadian Indian Policy during the Inter-War Years, 1918-1939* (Ottawa: Department of Indian Affairs and Northern Development, 1984), 5.

29 Jonathan F. Vance, *A History of Canadian Culture* (Don Mills, Ont.: Oxford University Press, 2009), 246.

30 Sandra Campbell, "A Fortunate Friendship: Duncan Campbell Scott and Pelham Edgar," in K.P. Stich, ed., *The Duncan Campbell Scott Symposium* (Ottawa: University of Ottawa Press, 1980), 113–26.

31 Professor Pelham Edgar, "Twelve Hundred Miles by Canoe, Among the Indians in Northern Waters," *Canada*, (5 Jan. 1907): 510.

32 Macbeth, *Over My Shoulder*, 142.

33 Leonard W. Brockington, "The Other Page: Duncan Campbell Scott's Eightieth Birthday," *Saturday Night*, (1 Aug. 1942): 25.

34 Ibid., 141.

35 Titley, *Narrow Vision*, 28.

36 Duncan Campbell Scott, *W.J. Phillips* (Toronto: Ryerson Press, 1947).

37 George Wicken, "Duncan Campbell Scott," in William Toye, ed., *The Oxford Companion to Canadian Literature* (Toronto: Oxford University Press, 1983), 740.

38 Robert L. McDougall, introduction in *The Poet and the Critic: A Literary Correspondence between D.C. Scott and E.K. Brown*, edited by Robert L. McDougall (Ottawa: Carleton University Press, 1983), 1.

39 Sandra Gwyn, *The Private Capital: Ambition and Love in the Age of Macdonald and Laurier* (Toronto: McClelland and Stewart, 1984), 455.

40 Stan Dragland, *Floating Voice: Duncan Campbell Scott and the Literature of Treaty 9* (Toronto: House of Anansi Press, 1994), 79–82.

41 Macbeth, *Over My Shoulder*, 146.

42 Duncan Campbell Scott to E.K. Brown, 18 Oct. 1942, in *The Poet and the Critic*, 30.

43 Dragland, *Floating Voice*, 255.

44 Rupert Brooke to his mother, dated Ottawa, July 1913, cited in Sandra Martin and Roger Hall, eds., *Rupert Brooke in Canada* (Toronto: Peter Martin, 1978), 45.

45 Gwyn, *Private Capital*, 466–7.

46 Ibid., 470.

47 Brendan Frederick R. Edwards, *Paper Talk: A History of Libraries, Print Culture, and Aboriginal Peoples in Canada before 1960* (Lanham, Md.: Scarecrow Press, 2005), 94–5. Scott did approve the establishment of a much-scaled down departmental library, rejecting Charles Cooke's full proposal.

48 Diamond Jenness, "Canada's Indians Yesterday. What of Today?" *Canadian Journal of Economics and Political Science*, 20 (1954): 98. Shortly before he retired in 1932 Scott wrote his literary friend William Deacon on 2 August 1931 that he would soon be "released from my fifty years' imprisonment with the Savages," quoted in Clara Thomas and John Lennox, *William Arthur Deacon. A Canadian Literary Life* (Toronto: University of Toronto Press, 1982), 145.

49 "Mohawk Paper," *Sudbury Journal*, 30 May 1901.

50 Brendan F.R. Edwards, "'A most industrious and far-seeing Mohawk scholar:' Charles A. Cooke (Thawennensere), Civil Servant, Amateur Anthropologist, Performer, and Writer," *Ontario History*, 102/1 (Spring 2010): 83–103. See p. 84 for the explanation why Cooke was raised Mohawk but was never recognized under the Indian Act as a member of any band. This is truly extraordinary, as his contribution to the Iroquoian peoples is immense, thanks, in particular, to his recording over several decades of more than 6,000 Iroquoian personal names. See Charles A. Cooke, "Iroquois Personal Names – Their Classification," *Proceedings of the American Philosophical Society*, 96/4 (Aug. 1952): 427–38. Anthropologist Marius Barbeau terms Cooke's work on names a "monumental accomplishment." Marius Barbeau, "Charles A. Cooke, Mohawk Scholar," ibid., 424.

51 Duncan Campbell Scott, quoted in 1904, in Edwards, "Mohawk," 91.

52 Edwards, *Paper Talk*, 94–5.

53 Duncan Campbell Scott, "Indian Place-Names," in *The Poems of Duncan Campbell Scott* (Toronto: McClelland and Stewart, 1926), 22.

54 Ibid., 230.

55 Dragland, *Floating Voice*, 123. Interestingly, Scott's predecessor as deputy superintendent general of Indian Affairs embraced the phrase, "survival of the fittest," and used it in a 1906 letter to Frank Oliver, minister of the Interior. See Sessional Paper No. 27 (6–7 Edward VII, 1906–07), Annual Report of the Deputy Supt.-Gen. Pedley to Oliver, Nov. 1906, xxix; cited in John Leslie and Ron Macguire, eds., *The Historical Development of the Indian Act*, 2nd ed. (Ottawa: Treaties and Historical Research Centre, Research Branch, Corporate Policy, Department of Indian and Northern Affairs Canada, 1979), 105. Pedley asks "whether or not the time has arrived for leaving ... [the Indians] to the operation of the natural law which tends towards the survival of the fittest."

56 Laura Groening, "Duncan Campbell Scott: An Annotated Bibliograpy,' in Robert Lecker and Jack David, eds., *The Annotated Bibliography of Canada's Major Authors*, vol. 8 (Toronto: ECW Press, 1994), 476.

57 The secondary literature on Pauline Johnson (Tekahionwake) is extensive. Two well-written and most enjoyable biographies are Charlotte Gray, *Flint & Feather: The Life and Times of E. Pauline Johnson,*

Tekahionwake (Toronto: HarperCollins, 2002), and the older work by Betty Keller, *Pauline: A Biography of Pauline Johnson* (Vancouver: Douglas & McIntyre, 1981). A valuable academic treatment is Veronica Strong-Boag and Carole Gerson, *Paddling Her Own Canoe: The Times and Texts of E. Pauline Johnson (Tekahionwake)* (Toronto: University of Toronto Press, 2000). Rick Monture provides the viewpoint of a Six Nations academic, in *We Share Our Matters: Two Centuries of Writing and Resistance at Six Nations of the Grand River* (Winnipeg: University of Manitoba Press, 2014). Sheila M.F. Johnston, *Buckskin & Broadcloth: A Celebration of E. Pauline Johnson – Tekahionwake, 1861–1913* (Toronto: Natural Heritage / Natural History Inc, 1997) contains interesting excerpts from her writing and commentary about her, as well the richest collection of images.

58 Strong-Boag and Gerson, *Paddling Her Own Canoe*, 120.

59 Horatio Hale, "An Iroquois Condoling Council," *Proceedings and Transactions of the Royal Society of Canada*, 2nd series, vol. 1, sec. II (1895): 46; reprinted in Horatio Hale, *The Iroquois Book of Rites and Hale on the Iroquois* (Ohsweken, Ont.: Iroqrafts, 1989), 340.

60 Sally M. Weaver, "Chapter 10. The Iroquois: The Grand River Reserve in the Late Nineteenth and Early Twentieth Centuries, 1875-1945," in Edward S. Roger and Donald B. Smith, eds., *Aboriginal Ontario: Historical Perspectives on the First Nations* (Toronto: Dundurn, 1994): 182–212. For the size of the religious groups at Six Nations, see Table 10.1, on 219.

61 A. LaVonne Brown Ruoff, introduction in E. Pauline Johnson, *The Moccasin Maker* (Tucson: University of Arizona Press, 1987), 1–2. On the membership issue, see Anthony F.C. Wallace, *Tuscarora: A History* (Albany: State University of New York Press, 2012), 164–6.

62 Margery Fee, *Literary Land Claims: The "Indian Land Question" from Pontiac's War to Attawapiskat* (Waterloo, Ont.: Wilfrid Laurier University Press, 2015), 119.

63 Horatio Hale, "Chief George H.M. Johnson, Onwanonsyshon: His Life and Work Among the Six Nations," *Magazine of American History*, 13 (Jan.–July 1885): 140.

64 Gray, *Flint & Feather*, 78.

65 Keller, *Pauline*, 25, 29.

66 Strong-Boag and Gerson, *Paddling Her Own Canoe*, 175. Gray, *Flint & Feather*, 47.

67 Keller, *Pauline*, 35.

68 Hale, "George H.M. Johnson," 138.

69 Ibid., 139.

70 Ibid., 142.

71 Gray, *Flint & Feather*, 84.

72 Keller, *Pauline*, 46.

73 Strong-Boag and Gerson, *Paddling Her Own Canoe*, 98, 109, 113.

74 Fee, *Literary Land Claims*, 121.

75 Strong-Boag and Gerson, *Paddling Her Own Canoe*, 120.

76 Ibid., 150.

77 "A Cry from an Indian Wife," quoted in Gray, *Flint & Feather*, 144.

78 Gray, *Flint & Feather*, 222. Strong-Boag and Gerson, *Paddling Her Own Canoe*, 120–1.

79 Daniel Francis, *The Imaginary Indian: The Image of the Indian in Canadian Culture* (Vancouver: Arsenal Pulp Press, 1992), 122.

80 Gray, *Flint & Feather*, 267.

81 Monture, *We Share Our Matters*, 109.

82 Marcus Lee Hansen, *The Mingling of the Canadian and American Peoples* (New Haven: Yale University Press, 1940), 183.

83 Sarah Carter, *Lost Harvests: Prairie Indian Reserve Farmers and Government Policy* (Montreal and Kingston: McGill-Queen's University Press, 1990), 237.

84 D.J. Hall, "Clifford Sifton and Canadian Indian Administration 1896–1905," *Prairie Forum*, 2/2 (1977); reprinted in Ian A.L. Getty and Antoine S. Lussier, eds., *As Long as the Sun Shines and Water Flows: A Reader in Canadian Native Studies* (Vancouver: UBC, 1983), 122, 124.

85 Peter A. Russell, *How Agriculture Made Canada: Farming in the Nineteenth Century* (Montreal: McGill-Queen's University Press, 2012) 225, 228.

86 Clifford Sifton, quoted in John W. Dafoe, *Clifford Sifton in Relation to His Times* (Toronto: Macmillan, 1931), 153.

87 Hall, "Sifton," 126.

88 *Edmonton Bulletin*, 17 Jan. 1881, quoted in Stewart Raby, "Indian Land Surrenders in Southern Saskatchewan," *Canadian Geographer*, 17 (1973): 39, and cited in David Lupul, "The Bobtail Land Surrender," *Alberta History*, 26/1 (Winter 1978): 29.

89 David J. Hall, "Frank Oliver," *Dictionary of Canadian Biography*, at http://www.biographi.ca/en/bio/oliver_frank_16E.html.

90 Carter, *Lost Harvests*, 245. J.R. Miller, *Skyscrapers Hide the Heavens: A History of Indian-White Relations in Canada*, 3rd ed. (Toronto: University of Toronto Press, 2000), 275.

91 John S. Long, *Treaty No. 9: Making the Agreement to Share the Land in Far Northern Ontario in 1905* (Montreal and Kingston: McGill-Queen's University Press, 2010), 3–4, 31.

92 Dragland, *Floating Voice*, 94.

93 James Morrison, "The Poet and the Indians," *Beaver*, (Aug.–Sept. 1988): 14. For the meeting at Fort Hope (Eabametoong), see Long, *Treaty 9*, 174–87, 381.

94 Titley, *Narrow Vision*, 74.

95 James Morrison, foreword in his *Treaty Research Report – Treaty Nine (1905–06): The James Bay Treaty* (Ottawa: Treaties and Historical Research Centre, Indian and Northern Affairs Canada, 1986). John Leslie, "Treaty Nine," in *The Canadian Encyclopedia*, at https://thecanadianencyclopedia.ca/en/article/treaty-9.

96 Scott, "Indian Affairs, 1867–1912," 615.

97 D.J. Hall, *From Treaties to Reserves: The Federal Government and Native Peoples in Territorial Alberta, 1870–1905* (Montreal and Kingston: McGill-Queen's University Press, 2015), 270–5. Frank Oliver, in Canada, *House of Commons Debates*, 10th Parliament, 4th Session, vol. 1, 624.

98 Hall, *Treaties*, 263. Only in 1944 was a recognized medical cure developed. See Katherine McCuaig, *The Weariness, the Fever, and the Fret: The Campaign against Tuberculosis in Canada, 1900–1950* (Montreal and Kingston: McGill-Queen's University Press, 1999), 4.

99 Canada, *Annual Report of the Department of Indian Affairs, 1906*, 274–5, referenced in *Honouring the Truth, Reconciling for the Future: Summary of the Final Report of the Truth and Reconciliation Commission of Canada* (Ottawa: Truth and Reconciliation Commission of Canada, 2015), 97.

100 Megan Sproule-Jones, "Crusading for the Forgotten: Dr Peter Bryce, Public Health, and Prairie Native Residential Schools," *Canadian Bulletin of Medical Health*, 13 (1966): 212.

101 Henry James Morgan, ed., *The Canadian Men and Women of the Time: A Hand-book of Canadian Biography of Living Characters*, 2nd ed. (Toronto: William Briggs, 1912), 164. Adam J. Green, "Humanitarian, M.D.: Dr Peter H. Bryce's Contributions to Canadian Federal Native and Immigration Policy, 1904–1921" (M.A. thesis, Queen's University, 1999), 20–1, 29.

102 The title of the historian John S. Milloy's best-selling study of the development and impact of the Indian residential schools is based on Bryce's phrase, "a national crime." See John S. Milloy, *A National Crime: The Canadian Government and the Residential School System, 1879 to 1986* (Winnipeg: University of Manitoba Press, 1999).

103 F. Onondeyoh Loft, "The Indian and Education," *Saturday Night*, (12 June 1909). I thank Fred Loft's grandson, Lee Waldron, for bringing this article, and the series, to my attention. On his year at the Mohawk Institute, also see Fred Loft, quoted by W. Murison, Inspector of Indian Agencies, to W.M. Graham, dated Regina, 26 July 1928, LAC, RG10, vol. 3211, file 527787, pt. 1. I thank Richard Lueger for this reference.

104 *Canada's Residential Schools: The History, Part 1, Origins to 1939*, 277.

105 Dragland, *Floating Voice*, 111, original emphasis.

106 A helpful review is Theodore Binnema, "'Entirely and Highly to Their Benefit': A Glimpse of Corruption in the Canadian Indian Affairs Department in the Laurier Era," prepared for presentation at the

Canadian Historical Association, and the Canadian Indigenous / Native Studies Association Conference, Edmonton, Alta., 29 May 2000.

107 Shewell, *"Enough to Keep Them Alive,"* 96.

108 D.C. Scott, "The Indians and the Great War," Dominion of Canada, *Annual Report of the Department of Indian Affairs for the Year ended March 31, 1919* (Ottawa: King's Printer, 1920), reprinted in in P. Whitney Lackenbauer and Craig Leslie Mantle, eds., *Aboriginal Peoples and the Canadian Military: Historical Perspectives* (Kingston: Canadian Defence Academy Press, 2007), 73. Scott adds that there were also "undoubtedly cases of Indian enlistment which were not reported to the department." Timothy C. Winegard, *For King and Kanata: Canadian Indians and the First World War* (Winnipeg: University of Manitoba Press, 2012), 6.

109 Leslie, *Historical Development of the Indian Act*, 1:105–6. A 1920 Indian Act amendment compelled parents to send their school-aged children to a residential or a day school, either type of school. See *Canada's Residential Schools: The History, Part 1, Origins, to 1939*, 278–80, and 280–8. There were always more eligible young people outside the boarding schools than in them. See James R. Miller, "Research and Outcomes at the Truth and Reconciliation Commission," *Canadian Historical Review*, 100/2 (June 2019), 174. Fierce interdenominational rivalries and a shortage of day schools led many into residential schools.

110 "Religious Services Stopped," *Quebec Saturday Budget*, (5 Oct. 1895). I thank Jonathan Lainey for this reference.

111 His name is celebrated today in the title of one of the Quebec government's most prestigious awards, *Le Prix Léon-Gérin*, given annually to a leading Quebec scholar in one of the social sciences. For a good short review of his life see the essay by Jean-Charles Falardeau, "Léon Gérin, His Life and Work," in Laurier L. LaPierre, ed., *Four O'Clock Lectures: French-Canadian Thinkers of the Nineteenth and Twentieth Centuries* (Montreal: McGill University Press, 1966), 59–75. The only current full biography is that by Hervé Carrier, sj, *Le sociologue canadien Léon Gérin 1863–1951: Sa vie, son oeuvre, ses methods de recherche* (Montreal: Éditions Bellarmin, 1960).

112 A short summary of his work in English appears in the essay, "The Hurons of Lorette," from the *Transactions of the Ottawa Literary and Scientific Society*, read 26 June 1900. Full treatments of Wendake at the turn of the century appear in the two articles by Léon Gérin: "Le Huron de Lorette," *La Science sociale*, 16/22 (1901): 334–60, and *La Science sociale*, 17/13 (1902): 319–42. The two French language articles are reproduced in Denis Vaugeois, ed., *Les Hurons de Lorette* (Sillery, Que.: Éditions du Septentrion, 1996), 21–60.

113 Gérin, "Le Huron de Lorette," 340–2.

114 C.M. Barbeau, "The Indian Reserve of Lorette (Quebec), a report concerning its proposed disestablishment," LAC, RG10, vol. 6810, file 470-2-3, pt. 7, 2.
115 Andrew Nurse, "'But Now Things Have Changed': Marius Barbeau and the Politics of Amerindian Identity," *Ethnohistory*, 48/3 (Summer 2001): 452. I have relied on this article heavily for its description of Marius Barbeau's relationship with the twentieth-century Wendat. See also Barbeau, "The Indian Reserve of Lorette (Quebec)," 21 pp.
116 Departmental Annual Report, 1917, Report of the Deputy Superintendent General, 9; quoted in John Leonard Taylor, *Canadian Indian Policy during the Inter-War Years, 1918–1939* (Ottawa: Indian Affairs and Northern Development, 1983), 211.
117 The term "educated" is used here to indicate a Western European education, as North American Indian children were educated by their communities.
118 "Chief So-ren-ho-wa-neh marks his 80th birthday," *Brantford Expositor*, 6 Apr. 1938.
119 Interview with William Loft's daughter Bernice Loft Winslow (1902–1997), Whitman, Mass., 9 Jan. 1993.
120 "Uncle Deyoh" [Fred Loft] to "Dorothy," dated France, 2 Dec. 1917. The letter was shown to me by his daughter Affa Loft Matteson.
121 Mildred Cory, "Delay Indian enfranchisement – until Aborigines are educated," *Toronto World*, 6 June l920. A copy is in LAC, RG10, vol. 3211, file 527787.
122 Allan Sherwin, *Bridging Two Peoples: Chief Peter E. Jones, 1843–1909* (Waterloo, Ont.: Wildrid Laurier University Press, 2012), 76, 78, 130–1. Elizabeth Graham, compiler, *The Mush Hole: Life at Two Indian Residential Schools* (Waterloo, Ont.: Heffle, 1997), 217.
123 George Beaver, preface in Bernice Loft Winslow, *Iroquois Fires: The Six Nations Lyrics and Lore of Dawendine (Bernice Loft Winslow)*, with introductory and afterword material by George Beaver, Bryan Winslow Colwell, Donald Smith, and Robert Stacey (Ottawa: Penumbra, 1995), 9.
124 Anthony F.C. Wallace, *The Death and Rebirth of the Seneca* [1969] (New York: Vintage, 1971), 73.
125 Fred Loft entered the Ontario Business College on 1 Mar. 1886, student no. 4430, Registration Records, Ontario Business College, Belleville, Ontario. I thank Gerry Boyce of Belleville for obtaining this information for me.
126 [Fred Loft] "Notes," was the author, no doubt, of the article, "On the Reserve," which appeared in the *Brantford Expositor* on 1 Sept. 1886. All Eastern Canadian male status Indians who met the property qualification

had just received the federal franchise, and they would retain it until the Liberals withdrew the right in 1898.

127 Henrietta Geare McGuigan to Richard Lueger, 21 Sept. 1977. A copy of this letter was sent to me by Richard Lueger.

128 David Boyle, quoted in "The influence of an Indian with Indians," *Toronto Star*, 11 Feb. 1907, 9. For background on Boyle, see Gerald Killan, *David Boyle: From Artisan to Archaeologist* (Toronto: University of Toronto Press, 1984).

129 George T. Denison to the superintendent general of Indian Affairs, dated Toronto, 29 May 1906, LAC, RG10, vol. 7241, file 8032-67. On the Denison family, see David Gagan, *The Denison Family of Toronto, 1792–1925* (Toronto: University of Toronto Press, 1973).

130 About 1907 he gave an address on "Captain Joseph Brant – Thayendanega," published in the United Empire Loyalists' Association of Canada, *Transactions*, (1904–13), 57–61; and he spoke again some years later on "Iroquoian Loyalists," *Transactions*, (1914–16), 68–79.

131 Affa Loft Matteson, the Lofts' younger daughter, helped me in the early 1990s with this summary. I also thank Richard Lueger, the author of the extremely useful M.A. thesis in Canadian Studies at Carleton University, "A History of Indian Associations in Canada (1870–1970)." In the summer of 1973, he interviewed by telephone Henrietta Loft McGuigan, Fred and Affa Geare Loft's older daughter. He shared his notes with me in a letter of 8 July 1992; he also forwarded Henrietta McGuigan's response to the references to Fred Loft in his thesis (see 146–7 in particular). Mrs McGuigan wrote her letter to Richard Lueger on 21 Sept. 1977.

132 Several of Fred Loft's longer articles include "The Indian and Education," which appeared in *Saturday Night*, 12 and 19 June and 3 and 17 July 1909; "Indian Reminiscences of 1812," *Saturday Night*, 11 Sept. 1909; and "The Snow-Snake and the Indian Game of Snow-Snaking," *Annual Archaeological Report 1912, Being Part of Appendix to the Report of the Minister of Education, Ontario* (Toronto: King's Printer, 1912), 69–71. An early letter to the editor appeared in 1896: F.O. Loft (Ononhdiyoh), Toronto, 15 Oct., "Indians and the Franchise," *Globe*, 7 Nov. 1896. I thank Hugh Dempsey for this reference.

133 Lueger, "Indian Associations," 146.

134 Interview with Ella Monture Claus, at her home at Tyendinaga, 5 Nov. 1994.

135 Telephone interview with Bernice Loft Winslow, Whitman, Mass., 17 Apr. 1993.

136 Odom 2406, 16 Jan. 1907: Six Nations Council declined to endorse enfranchisement of F.O. Loft. I thank Anne Scott, records manager, Six Nations Council, for this information.

137 Loft to Laurier, 28 Jan.1907, LAC, Sir Wilfrid Laurier Fonds, MG26-G, Laurier Papers, 118777.

138 Odem 2755, 5 Feb. 1907: Six Nations Council endorses application of Frederick O. Loft as Superintendent of the Six Nations. "The Six Nations want an Indian as Superintendent," *Toronto Daily Star*, 8 Feb. 1907.

139 Pauline Johnson to Sir Wilfrid Laurier, dated Halifax, 18 Jan. 1907, LAC, Laurier Papers, 118439, C-842, image 740. Keller, *Pauline*, 112.

140 Six Nations Council Minutes, 1859, 3–11, cited in Sally M. Weaver, "Iroquois Politics, 1847–1940" (1975), unpublished ms. on deposit at the Woodland Cultural Centre, Brantford, Ont., 334.

141 F. Onondeyoh Loft to F. Pedley, Dept. Supt. Indian Affairs, dated 256 Jarvis St, Toronto, 15, 19, and 27 May and 14 Aug. 1908 and 16 Mar. 1910, LAC, RG10, vol. 2179, file 36539-3, pt. 2, 328077, 332147, 328469, 326539, mfm reel C-11174.

142 Odem 9l, 92, 3 Jan. 1917, Six Nations Council recommends that F.O. Loft be made Superintendent.

143 Forrest E. LaViolette, *The Strugge for Survival: Indian Cultures and the Protestant Ethic in British Columbia* (Toronto: University of Toronto Press, 1961), 164–7; and the very important manuscript (typed copy), Milton Martin, "Dictatorship in Canada –The Indians of Canada," in the Milton Martin file, Woodland Cultural Centre, Brantford, Ont., no date, p. 17.

144 See his military service record, Lieutenant Frederick Ogilvie Loft, LAC, Government Records Branch, particularly the "Officers' Declaration Paper."The details of his military service in the First World War presented in this section are taken from this file. A copy is in my file 047.10, "Fred Loft, Military Record 1917–1918," in the Smith fonds.

145 Ibid., Medical History Sheet, Military Service Record, dated Camp Borden, Ont., 15 June 1917.

146 Odem Six Nations Council, 7 Aug. 1917, F.O. Loft made honorary chief.

147 King George V's diary for 21 Feb. 1918 contains reference to the audience: "Saw Sir Alfrd Mond, Genl. Trenchard (Flying Corps), Genl. Ashmore, who is in command of anti-air defences in London, Adml. Brock, who was at Scapa, & Lt. Lost, in Canadian Forestry Corps, he is Chief of the Six Nations Tribe in Ontario." Fred Loft's name is spelt "Lost" in the entry – this is a mistake. The audience is also mentioned in the printed *Court Circular*. I thank Pamela Clark, deputy registrar, Royal Archives, Windsor Castle, Berkshire, England, for forwarding this information to me, 18 Dec. 1992.

148 "Six Nations Chief quits Civil Service," *Brantford Expositor*, 2 Feb. 1926. I thank Denise Kirk for this article.

149 John Moses, "The Return of the Native: Six Nations Veterans and Political Change at the Grand River Reserve, 1917–1924," in Lackenbauer and Mantle, *Aboriginal Peoples and the Canadian Military*, 121.
150 "Indian Tribes form League: Six Nations and Ojibways band together to claim their rights," *Brantford Expositor*, 21 Dec. 1918. I thank Denise Kirk for this reference.
151 Chief (Lieut.) F.O. Loft, "The Indian Problem," *Woman's Century*, (Nov. 1921): 6.
152 F.G.G. [Frederick G. Griffin], "Indians want equal chance with their white brothers, Original inhabitants of Canada not getting same opportunities as immigrants," *Toronto Star Weekly*, 28 Aug. 1920. Griffin was one of Canada's most celebrated reporters and magazine writers in the 1920s and 1930s for the *Toronto Star* and the *Toronto Star Weekly*. See Ross Harkness, *J.E. Atkinson of the Star* (Toronto: University of Toronto Press, 1963), 181.

"The League of Indians of Canada Constitution, By-Laws and Regulations," in F.O. Loft, 75 Madison Ave, Toronto, dated 15 Apr. 1920, to W.A. Boys, Chairman Indian Committee, House of Commons, Ottawa, Exhibit No. 37, LAC, Special House of Commons Committee, Apr. 1920, Part One: Exhibits (No. 1-53), mfm reel T-14571. Cory, "Delay Indian Enfranchisement." "Indian Chief states views on condition of his race," *Globe*, 2 Mar. 1921. Loft, "Indian Problem," 6.
153 Peter Kulchyski, "'Considerable Unrest': F.O. Loft and the League of Indians," *Native Studies Review*, 4/1–2 (1988): 104.
154 F.O. Loft, "League of Indians of Canada. Annual Report for 1921," dated 16 Dec. 1921, Bibliothèque et Archives nationales du Québec (BANQ), Fonds Famille Picard (P882-P883). The rich archival source, the papers of the Picard family at Wendake, are described in Jonathan Lainey, "Le fonds Famille Picard: Un patrimoine documentaire d'exception," *Revue de Bibliothèque et Archives nationales du Québec*, no. 2 (2010): 94–105.
155 F.O. Loft, "League of Indians of Canada. Annual Report for 1921."
156 "1,500 Braves attend Pow Wow, Edmonton," *Regina Leader*, 30 June 1922.
157 Ibid.
158 F.O. Loft, "League of Indians of Canada. Annual Report for 1921."
159 "Big meeting of Indians is held near Edmonton," *Calgary Albertan*, 26 June 1922. Patrice Beaudry became the Alberta vice president. On Beaudry, see Gaston Carrière, "Patrick Beaudry," in *Dictionnaire biographique des Oblats de Marie-Immaculée au Canada*, 2 vols. (Ottawa: University of Ottawa Press, 1976), 1:59–61.
160 Gaston Carrière, "Jean-Louis Le Vern," *Dictionnaire biographique des Oblats*, 2:325–6.

161 Paul Coze, *Cinq Scouts chez les Peaux-Rouges* (Paris: Librairie des Camps-Elysées, 1932), 143. Coze (1903–1974) was a French artist, anthropologist, and writer who visited Western Canada three times in the late 1920s and 1930s. He writes of Le Vern whom he met at the Catholic Mission on the Peigan Reserve in southern Alberta: "Il parle française avec un accent pied noir pronounce et ses yeux brillent quand il raconte la vie de son people. Il l'aime. (He speaks French with a Blackfoot accent and his eyes shine when he speaks about the life of his people. He loves them)." The same year that his account of his 1930 travels in Western Canada appeared, Diamond Jenness used Coze's painting of "A Sioux Indian," as the frontispiece of his *The Indians of Canada*, published in 1932, with numerous subsequent editions.

162 Patrick Brunelle, "Les Hurons et l'émancipation: Le maintien d'une identité distincte à Lorette au début du XXe siècle," *Recherches amérindiennes au Québec*, 30/3 (2000): 79. Thomas Peace and Kathryn Magee Labelle, eds., *From Huronia to Wendakes: Adversity, Migrations, and Resilience, 1650–1900* (Norman: University of Oklahoma Press, 2016), 156–7, 176n84.

163 F.O. Loft to P.A. Picard, dated 75 Madison Ave, Toronto, 9 Sept. 1920, BANQ, Fonds Famille Picard (P882-P883). P.A.P. [Picard] to Lieut. F.O. Loft, dated Huron Village of Lorette, 29 Mar. 1922, ibid. I thank Jonathan Lainey for bringing this correspondence to my attention.

164 F.O. Loft to "My dear brother Picard," dated 75 Madison Ave, Toronto, 25 Feb. 1920, ibid. Apparently Scott was also antagonistic to Loft because he had worked to secure funding for his daughter, Henri Loft, to attend the University of Toronto for one year. On 31 December 1919 Scott wrote J.P. Wright, the Indian agent at Fort Frances, Ontario: "I took a particular interest in this fellow's daughter and we strained ourselves to give the girl advantages at Toronto University and this is the sort of thanks one gets for it." Duncan Campbell Scott to J. P. Wright, 31 Dec. 1919, LAC, RG 10, vol. 3211, file 527,787, cited in Keith D. Smith, ed., *Strange Visitors: Documents in Indigenous–Settler Relations in Canada from 1876* (Toronto: University of Toronto Press, 2014), 133. The University of Toronto Archives confirms that she attended for one year at the end of the First World War.

165 Ernest Lapointe, quoted 14 Apr. 1920, before the Special Committee of the House of Commons, appointed to consider Bill 14, to amend the Indian Act (Appendix 3, *Journals of the House of Commons*, 1920), LAC, RG 14, vol. 666, 280, mfm T-14571.

166 Lita-Rose Betcherman, *Ernest Lapointe: Mackenzie King's Great Quebec Lieutenant* (Toronto: University of Toronto Press, 2002), 36.

167 Ibid., 4.

168 Klaus Neumann, "Backstage with Uncle Louis: The faithful Indian confidential messenger who works for St Laurent," *Maclean's*, (Sept. 1957): 3.

169 "Famous Indian Chief passes: A benefactor of his people. Frederick Ogilvie Loft was known throughout entire Dominion," *Toronto Mail*, 7 July 1934.

170 F.G.G., "Indians Want Equal Chance."

171 Titley, *Narrow Vision*, 104–6.

172 Lueger, "Indian Associations," 140.

173 Duncan Campbell Scott to Charles Stewart, dated Ottawa, 3 Feb. 1922, LAC, RG10, vol. 3211, file 527787, pt. 1. Raymond J.A. Huel, *Proclaiming the Gospel to the Indians and the Métis* (Edmonton: University of Alberta Press, 1996), 219–20.

174 Fred Loft, 14 Apr. 1920, before the Special Committee of the House of Commons, appointed to consider Bill 14, to amend the Indian Act (Appendix 3, *Journals of the House of Commons*, 1920), LAC, RG14, vol. 666, 277, 273–4, mfm T-14571. Loft repeated this charge in his article, "The Indian Problem" 6: "Within the last two years, in the process of organizing the league of Indians of Canada, which is designed to unite all the tribes and nations of this Dominion, to see what can be done by Indians to raise themselves above themselves, it has been discovered that scarcely five per cent of the adult population of a vast majority of reservations in Canada is competent to write a coherent intelligible letter." By the department's own statistics in 1914 only 31% of Indians in Manitoba spoke English, 22% in Saskatchewan, and 15% in Alberta. Office of Census and Statistics, *The Canada Yearbook 1914*, 640, cited in Winegard, *For King*, 72, 186.

175 J.D. McLean, Asst. Deputy Superintendent General, Office of the Deputy Superintendent General, Department of Indian Affairs to Mr F.O. Loft, 75 Madison Ave, Toronto, Ont., 26 Jan. 1921, LAC, RG10, vol. 7421, file 8032-67.

176 Duncan Campbell Scott to Sir James Lougheed, dated Ottawa, 21 Feb. 1921, LAC, RG10, vol. 3211, file 527787.

177 David J. Hall and Donald B. Smith, "James Alexander Lougheed," *Dictionary of Canadian Biogrpahy* (*DCB*), vol. 15, *1921–1930* (Toronto: University of Toronto Press, 2005), 609–10. Morris Zaslow, *The Opening of the Canadian North, 1870–1914* (Toronto: McClelland and Stewart, 1971), 163.

178 F.O. Loft to Rt. Hon. W.L.M. King, Premier of Canada, dated 75 Madison Ave, Toronto, 18 Dec. 1922, LAC, RG10, vol. 2285, file 57169-1B, pt. 3, mfm reel C-11195. My thanks to Scott Trevithick for bringing this

letter to my attention. For the political context of this period, see Scott Trevithick, "Conflicting Outlooks: The Background to the 1924 Deposing of the Six Nations Hereditary Council" (M.A. thesis, University of Calgary, 1998).

179 Fred Loft's stance on the question of an elected council for the Six Nations of the Grand River is unknown. The only statement of his that survives on the question appears in a story in the *Brantford Expositor*, 19 Sept. 1923, entitled "Investigation in full swing regarding Six Nations Indians." The writer reports Loft as saying "that the Six Nations reserve was the only one in Canada where the old custom was adhered to. Other reserves had the elective system and both systems had their faults though in many cases it would be found that the big fault lay not with the system, but with the people that were administering it."

180 Joelle Rostkowski has written two summaries of Levi General in Europe: "The Redman's Appeal for Justice: Deskaheh and the League of Nations," in Christian Feest, ed., *Indians and Europe: An Interdisciplinary Collection of Essays* (Aachen: Ed. Herodot, Rader-Verl., 1987), 435–53; and "Deskaheh's Shadow: Indians on the International Scene," *Native American Studies*, 9/2 (1995): 1–4. Also see Laurence M. Hauptman, "The Idealist and the Realist: Chief Deskaheh, Attorney George Decker, and the Six Nations' Struggle to Get to the World Court, 1921–1925," in his *Seven Generations of Iroquois Leadership: The Six Nations since 1800* (Syracuse: Syracuse University Press, 2008), 124–42, 247–52.

181 Asa R. Hill, "The Historical Position of the Six Nations," *Ontario Historical Society, Papers and Records*, 19 (1922): 103. Also see Trevithick, "Conflicting Outlooks," 66n42.

182 A.R. Hill to A.G. Chisholm, 6 July 1922, LAC, RG10, vol. 2285, file 57169-1B, pt. 3, mfm reel C-11195, cited in Trevithick, "Conflicting Outlooks," 95.

183 Loft to King, , 18 Dec. 1922.

184 Moses, "Return of the Native," 126–7. Titley, *Narrow Vision*, 124–6.

185 Hauptman, "Chief Deskaheh," 142. The funeral cortege from the Sour Spring Longhouse to the cemetery was one mile long.

186 Christopher Bracken, *The Potlatch Papers: A Colonial Case History* (Chicago: University of Chicago Press, 1997), 209.

187 Douglas Cole and Ira Chaikin, *An Iron Hand upon the People: The Law against the Potlatch on the North West Coast* (Vancouver: Douglas & McIntyre, 1990), 138–9, 165.

188 Ibid., 176.

189 Coze's story about the First Nations in the Lebret area appears in Paul Coze, *Wakanda* (Paris: Alexis Redier Editeur, 1929), 94. Biographical

information about Father Poulet appears in Gaston Carrière, *Dictionnaire biographique des Oblats de Marie-Immaculee au Canada*, vol. 3 (Ottawa: Editions de 'Universite d'Ottawa, 1979), 98–9. For background on Paul Coze, see the catalogue prepared by Daniel Dubois, *Paul Coze: Wakanda* (Paris: Drouot, 2015). I am most endebted to Corinne Desmettre, archivist of the Scouts Guides de France for background on Paul Coze. Diamond Jenness used four of Paul Coze's First Nations portraits in *The Indians of Canada*: the frontispiece and opposite p. 326 (portraits of Sioux), opposite p. 336 (Tsimshian), and opposite p. 384 (Chipewyan).

190 Hamar Foster, "Letting Go the Bone: The Idea of Indian Title in British Columbia, 1849–1927," in Hamar Foster and John McLaren, eds., *Essays in the History of Canadian Law*, vol. 6, *British Columbia and the Yukon* (Toronto: University of Toronto Press, 1995), 29–31.

191 *The Final Report of the Truth and Reconciliation Commission*, vol. 1, *Canada's Residential Schools: The History, Part 1, Origins to 1939* (Montreal and Kingston: Published for the Truth and Reconciliation Commission by McGill-Queen's University Press, 2015), 289–90.

192 "Chief of Six Nations retires from Ontario Civil Service," *Globe*, 2 Feb. 1926.

193 Patrick Brunelle, "Un cas de colonialisme canadien: Les Hurons de Lorette entre la fin du XIXe siècle et le début du XXe siècle" (Mémoire de maîtrise, Université Laval, 1998).

194 David R. Miller, "Edward Ahenakew's Tutelage by Paul Wallace: Reluctant Scholarship, Inadvertent Preservation," in Carolyn Podruchny and Laura Peers, eds., *Gathering Places: Aboriginal and Fur Trade Histories* (Vancouver: UBC Press, 2010), 251.

195 C.F. Schmidt, Indian Agent, to D.C. Scott, dated Duck Lake, Sask., 19 June 1928, LAC, RG10, vol. 3211, file 527787, pt. 1.

196 W. Murison, Inspector of Indian Agencies, attended the meeting at the James Smith Reserve. He reported to William Graham, Indian Commissioner in Regina that, in response to Fred Loft's comments, Chiefs Isaiah Badger of Red Earth, Andrew Lafond of Petquakey's, Albert Stagg of Moose Lake, and Robert Bear of John Smith's spoke strongly in favour of boarding schools. Murison includes comments by these supporters of the schools. He claimed, e.g., that "Chief Albert Stagg, of Moose Lake, said that they had a Day School which was of very little use to them, as they have to make their living by hunting and trapping, and as they have no place to leave their children they had to take them along with them. He says they would be very thankful if they could have a Boarding School." "Rev. H.V. Bird" was present at the meeting. His presence possibly had an impact on the testimonies. John Milloy has references to "Rev. E. Bird," Principal of the Anglican MacKay School in

The Pas, Manitoba, in *A National Crime*, 134, 147–8, 151; possibly this is the same individual. W. Murison, Inspector of Indian Agencies, to W.M. Graham, Indian Commissioner, 26 July 1928, LAC, RG10, vol. 3211, file 527787, pt. 1.

197 Murison to Graham, 26 July 1928.

198 Jas. S. Wood, D/Corpl. Reg. no. 5569, "Report re 'Convention of Indians' James Smith Reserve," I.R. no. 100, Sask., 9 July 1928, LAC, RG10, vol. 3211, file 527787, pt. 1.

199 Lueger, "Indian Associations," 137.

200 David Calverley, *Who Controls the Hunt? First Nations, Treaty Rights, and Wildlife Conservation in Ontario, 1783–1939* (Vancouver: UBC Press, 2018), 73, 87.

201 The clash between Duncan Campbell Scott and Fred Loft is covered well in Titley, *Narrow Vision*, 102–9; Kulchyski, "'Considerable Unrest'"; and Taylor, *Canadian Indian Policy*, 167–78, 183.

202 Taylor, *Canadian Indian Policy*, 182.

203 Duncan Campbell Scott, *The Administration of Indian Affairs in Canada* (Toronto: Canadian Institute of International Affairs, 1931), 2.

204 Scott, "Indian Affairs, 1867–1912," 623.

205 Kerry Abel, *Drum Songs: Glimpses of Dene History* (Montreal and Kingston: McGill-Queen's University Press, 1993), 269.

6. Paul A.W. Wallace

1 Kathleen Coburn, "Review of *The White Roots of Peace* by Paul A.W. Wallace," *Canadian Forum*, (Nov. 1946): 18.

2 "Dean Wallace resigns chair, will abandon all work at Victoria University next August," *Globe*, 22 Mar. 1920. I thank David H. Wallace for additional biographical details on his grandfather sent in an email to me, 24 Aug. 2017.

3 Goldwin S. French, "Francis Huston Wallace," *Dictionary of Canadian Biography (DCB)*, vol. 15, *1921–1930* (Toronto: University of Toronto Press, 2005), 1052.

4 Jock Carroll, *The Life & Times of Greg Clark, Canada's Favorite Storyteller* (Toronto: Doubleday, 1981), 64.

5 C.S. Clark's *Of Toronto the Good: A Social Study – The Queen City of Canada as it is* (Montreal: Toronto Publishing Co, 1898; facsimile edition published in 1970 in Toronto by Coles) provides a full overview of the city in the 1890s.

6 Randall White, *Too Good to Be True: Toronto in the 1920s* (Toronto: Dundurn, 1993), 181.

7 J.M.S. Careless, *Toronto to 1918: An Illustrated History* (Toronto: Lorimer, 1984), 202.

8 The indifference extended into the mid-twentieth century. Eric Arthur, *Toronto: No Mean City* (Toronto: University of Toronto Press, 1964), xvi–xvii.

9 Edward F. Wilson, "The Canadian Indian Research and Aid Society," a statement outlining the decision to cease publication of the *Canadian Indian*, with the final issue, Sept. 1891, included at the beginning of the mfm copy of the *Canadian Indian* (1890–91).

10 Goldwin Smith, quoted in Carl Berger's introduction to Goldwin Smith, *Canada and the Canadian Question* (Toronto: University of Toronto Press, 1971), xi. He repeats this theme in his "Review of Francis Parkman's Works," *Review of Historical Publications Relating to Canada*, vol 3, *Publications of the year 1898* (Toronto: University of Toronto; published by the Librarian, 1899), 24.

11 Paul A.W. Wallace, "Diary 1906," University of Toronto, Victoria University Archives, Fonds 2187–Wallace Family Fonds, Records of Paul Anthony Wilson Wallace (hereafter, VUA, Wallace Records), entry for 5 Mar. 1906, 2018.07V10-3. For Clark's biography, see Carroll, *The Life & Times of Greg Clark*.

12 Paul A.W. Wallace, "Diary #2 [1902]," VUA, Wallace Records, 2018.07V10-2.

13 Paul A.W. Wallace, "Diary 1903," ibid.

14 W.H.P. Clement, *The History of the Dominion of Canada* (Toronto: Copp, Clark, 1898), 12–13. Tony Wallace showed me his father's textbook at his home in Aston, Pa., 8 May 1993. Inside the volume is the inscription: "Paul Wallace 95 Bedford Road Toronto Sept. 15th 1904" Paul also made a drawing of a North American Indian in the frontispiece. W.H.P. Clement later became a member of the BC Supreme Court. See Daniel Francis, *The Imaginary Indian: The Image of the Indian in Canadian Culture* (Vancouver: Arsenal Pulp Press, 1992), 159–60.

15 Percy J. Robinson, convenor; George R. Anderson, David R. Keys, the historical committee, *The Madawaska Club Go-Home Bay, 1898–1923* (N.p.p.: N.p., 1923?), 9.

16 Douglas Cole, "Artists, Patrons and Public: An Enquiry into the Success of the Group of Seven," *Journal of Canadian Studies*, 13/2 (Summer 1978): 70. Roger Burford Mason, "Dr James MacCallum: Patron and Friend of Canada's Group of Seven," *Canadian Medical Association Journal*, 155/9 (1 Nov. 1996): 1333–4.

17 *Madawaska Club*, 10. The cottagers travelled to Go Home Bay by steamer from Penetang Harbour.

18 Ibid., 23

19 Robinson, *Robinson*, 32–3.

20 *Madawaska Club*, 11.

21 Gilbert de B. Robinson, *Percy James Robinson 1873–1953: Classicist, Artist, Teacher, Historian* (Toronto: University of Toronto Press, 1981), 32. Reference is made to Pete Laforge in W.J. Loudon, *Studies of Student Life*, vol. 8, *Pioneers, Being a short history of the founding of the Madawaska Club, and of its early settlement on Georgian Bay during the years 1898–1903* (N.p.p.: n. p., n.d.), 164–9. A number of references to Pete Laforge appear in Paul A.W. Wallace Diary for 1922–25, e.g., the entries for 21 June, and 1, 7, 26, and 29 July 1922, VUA, Wallace Records, 2018.07V12-1.

22 Paul only learned about them in the early 1920s. Paul A.W. Wallace, Diary for 1922–25, entry for 14 July 1922, at Go Home Bay; and also the entries for 15 July and 29 July 1924, ibid.

23 *Madawaska Club*, 27.

24 Robinson, *Percy James Robinson*, 32.

25 *Madawaska Club*, 28.

26 Carroll, *Greg Clark*, 63.

27 Paul A.W. Wallace, "The House Not Made with Hands," 3 vols., ms., 1:12. Shown to me by A.F.C. Wallace, 8 May 1993. A copy is now in VUA, Wallace Records, 2018.07V19-2.

28 Paul A.W. Wallace, "Diary #2 [1902]," ibid., 2018.07V10-2.

29 Paul Wallace, "Delivered at the Disbanding of the Iroquois," in "Scribbling Book, 1905–06," ibid., 2018.07V10-3.

30 Paul A.W. Wallace, "The Five Nations of New York and Pennsylvania," *New-York Historical Society Quarterly*, 37/1 (July 1953): 228. I thank David Wallace for bringing this article to my attention.

31 Paul A.W. Wallace, Curriculum Vitae, ca. 1965, sent to me by David Wallace.

32 Rhonda Tepper, "Ethnic Trends at Harbord," in Julius Molinaro, *The Happy Ghosts of Harbord: A History of Harbord Collegiate Institute 1892–1992*, in *Harborite*, no. 30, Centennial no., (Spring 1992), 27.

33 He edited the school year book in 1908. Molinaro, *Happy Ghosts*, 107.

34 Ibid., 47.

35 Robert Wright, *A World Mission: Canadian Protestantism and the Quest for a New International Order, 1918–1939* (Montreal and Kingston: McGill-Queen's University Press, 1991), 166.

36 Francis Huston Wallace, "Memories: A Family Record," 268. The entire manuscript was transcribed by his grandson David H. Wallace and is now included in VUA, Fond 2186, Francis Huston Wallace, 2018.07V2-8–10.

37 Alvyn Austin, "Wallace of West China: Edward Wilson Wallace and the Canadian Educational Systems of China, 1906–1927," in Alvyn J. Austin and Jamie S. Scott, eds., *Canadian Missionaries, Indigenous*

Peoples: Representing Religion at Home and Abroad (Toronto: University of Toronto Press, 2005), 122.

38 Wallace, "Memories," 240.

39 Paul Wallace to "Dear Mother," dated Vermilion Pass Camp, 4 Aug. 1912, Paul A.W. Wallace fonds, Correspondence M1277, Glenbow Archives, Archives and Special Collections, University of Calgary (henceforth cited as Wallace, GLENBOW, UofC).

40 Ibid.

41 PearlAnn Reichwein, *Climber's Paradise: Making Canada's Mountain Parks, 1906–1974* (Edmonton: University of Alberta Press, 2014), 34.

42 PearlAnn Reichwein, "Arthur Oliver Wheeler (1860–1945)," ibid., 17–19.

43 Ibid., 22–4.

44 Paul A. Wallace, Glenbow Archives, Wallace Papers, AW193, file 1, 2, cited in Leslie Bella, *Parks for Profit* (Montreal: Harvest House, 1987), 43.

45 Bella reviews Paul Wallace's term as the Alpine Club's secretary-treasurer in his *Parks*, 43–5. For Wallace's account of the Alpine Club of Canada's camp in 1913, see Paul A.W. Wallace, "The Canadian Herodotus. Chapter XV–The Rocky Mountains," *Christian Guardian*, 11 Feb. 1925, 7–8.

46 Zac Robinson, "Storming the Heights: Canadian Frontier Nationalism and the Making of Manhood in the Conquest of Mount Robson, 1906–1913," *International Journal of the History of Sport*, 22/3 (May 2005): 425.

47 Ibid., 418.

48 Conrad Kain, translated by P.A.W. Wallace, "Mount Robson Reprise," originally from the 1914 *Canadian Alpine Journal*, reprinted in Brian Patton, ed., *Tales from the Canadian Rockies* (Edmonton: Hurtig, 1984), 180–5, and later in David Stouck and Myler Wilkinson, eds.,*Genius of Place: Writing About British Columbia* (Vancouver: Polestar Book Publishers, 2000), 114–22.

49 Wallace, "The House Not Made with Hands," 1:153.

50 "Climbing the Big Peaks: An Account of Alpine Climbing 1913, by A.O. Wheeler's Camp Secretary, Paul A.W. Wallace," *Crag and Canyon* (Banff), 30 Aug. 1913. Carlton McNaught, "In the Mountains with the Alpine Club of Canada," *Saturday Night*, (23 Aug. 1913).

51 [Paul A.W. Wallace], "Notes by the Camp Fire, O'Hara Camp, 16 July 1913" and "Re: Nomenclatures in Mt. Robson Park, 4 Aug. 1913," Whyte Museum of the Canadian Rockies, Banff, Alpine Club of Canada Fonds, M200/AC 27 15A. In a letter home to his mother in Toronto, Paul writes, "The Secretary of the Smithsonian Institute was camped near by. He has been casting lustre on his nation by trying to change all the names Dr Coleman gave in the region." Paul Wallace to "Dear Mother," dated Banff, 20 Aug. 1913, Wallace, GLENBOW, UofC.

52 Bella, *Parks*, 43–5.

53 Paul Wallace to "Dear Mother," dated Sidney, BC, 15 Nov. 1913, Wallace, GLENBOW, UofC.

54 Paul Wallace to "Dear Father," dated Sidney, BC, 25 Nov. 1913, Wallace, GLENBOW, UofC.

55 Francis Huston Wallace, "Memories: A Family Record," 269. The entire manuscript was transcribed by David H. Wallace, and kindly made available to me.

56 Donald Jones, "The Royal Opening of a 'Royal Museum,'" in *Fifty Tales of Toronto* (Toronto: University of Toronto Press, 1992), 7–11. Lovat Dickson, *The Museum Makers: The Story of the Royal Ontario Museum* (Toronto: Royal Ontario Museum, 1986), 33–9.

57 Paul A.W. Wallace, "Composition book, account of experiences in France in August 1914, story sketches," VUA, Wallace Records, 2018.07V11-2.

58 Letter to Rev. G.W. Kerby, D.D., Mount Royal College, 23 Apr. 1915, 95 Bedford Rd, Toronto, Whyte Museum, Alpine Club of Canada Fonds, M22 AC 27 16.

59 Wallace, "Memories," 280.

60 Jean Burnet, *Next-Year Country: A Study of Rural Social Organization in Alberta* (Toronto: University of Toronto Press. 1951).

61 Paul Wallace to "Dear Mother," dated Baraca, Alta., 12 Oct. 1915, Wallace, GLENBOW, UofC.

62 Paul Wallace to "Dear Father," dated Baraca, Alta., 4 July 1915, Wallace, GLENBOW, UofC.

63 Paul Wallace to "Dear Mother," dated Baraca, Alta., 11 June 1915, Wallace, GLENBOW, UofC.

64 F.G. Buchanan to Paul Wallace, telegram dated Hanna, Alta., 9 Dec. 1918, VUA, Wallace Records, 2018.07V14-30.

65 Paul Wallace to "Dear Mother," dated Baraca, Alta., 10 Sept. 1915, Wallace, GLENBOW, UofC.

66 Paul Wallace to "Dear Mother," dated Baraca, Alta., 6 Dec. 1915, and his earlier letter to her, dated Baraca, Alta., 20 Nov. 1915, Wallace, GLENBOW, UofC.

67 Paul Wallace to "Dear Mother, and family," dated Victoria 4 Jan. 1916, Wallace, GLENBOW, UofC.

68 Paul Wallace, to "Dear Mother," dated Victoria, 25 Jan. 1916, Wallace, GLENBOW, UofC.

69 Paul Wallace to Dorothy Clarke, dated Victoria, 19 Mar. 1916, Wallace, GLENBOW, UofC.

70 Paul Wallace to "Dear Folks," dated Victoria, 30 Apr. 1916, Wallace, GLENBOW, UofC.

71 Paul Wallace to "Dad," dated Victoria, 27 Feb. 1916, Wallace, GLENBOW, UofC.

72 Paul Wallace to "Mother," dated Victoria, 8 Mar. 1916, Wallace, GLENBOW, UofC.
73 The date of his enlistment appears at the outset of "The Diary of Sapper Paul A.W. Wallace," VUA, Wallace Records, 2018.07V11-5.
74 Wallace, "Memories," 284.
75 Wallace, "Diary of Sapper," 11 Nov. 1916.
76 Paul Wallace to Dorothy Clarke, dated Shorncliffe, 28 Mar. 1917, VUA, Wallace Records, 2018.07V19-1.
77 Paul Wallace to Muriel Wallace, dated Shorncliffe, 17 Feb. 1918, ibid.
78 Wallace, "Memories," 285.
79 Ibid., 287.
80 Wallace, CV, ca. 1965.
81 Wallace, "Memories," 288.
82 Donald B. Smith, "The Great Wars in the Rockies. Towering Monuments," *The Beaver*, 70/1 (Feb./Mar. 1990): 46–7; and William L. Putnam, Glen W. Boles, and Roger W. Laurilla, *Place Names of the Canadian Alps* (Revelstoke, BC: Footprint Publishing, 1990), 147. For the Stoney name for Mount Indefatigable, see *Ozade–Mnotha Wapta Mâkochî: Stoney Place Names*, prepared by the Chiniki Research Team: Marcella Crawler, Casey Labelle, Duane Mark, Wilfred Mark, and Karen Wyllie (Morley, Alberta: Chiniki Band Council, 1987), 37.
83 Paul Wallace to "Dearest Father," dated Edmonton, 2 Feb. 1920, Wallace, GLENBOW, UofC. "Writers' Club," *Gateway* (1920), 74.
84 I thank David H. Wallace, son of Paul Wallace, for sending me a photocopy of the "Deskbook for Journalists."
85 Interview with David Wallace, Baltimore, Md., 9 May 1993.
86 Frank Oliver, "The Blackfeet Indian Treaty," *MacLean's*, 15 Mar. 1931, 8–9. 28, 32, 56. Paul Wallace to Dean Kerr, chairman, Committee on Graduate Studies, University of Alberta, dated 23 Dec. 1920, American Philosophical Society Library (APSL), Philadelphia, Pa., Paul A.W. Wallace Papers.
87 One of best histories of a First Nations community is Deanna Christensen's *Ahtahkakoop: The Epic Account of a Plains Cree Head Chief, His People and Their Struggle for Survival 1816–1896* (Shell Lake, Sask.: Ahtahkakoop Publishing, 2000).
88 Edward Ahenakew, "The Story of the Ahenakews," edited by Ruth Matheson Buck, *Saskatchewan History*, 27/1 (Winter 1964): 12.
89 Eileen Pettigrew, *The Silent Enemy: Canada and the Deadly Flu of 1918* (Saskatoon, Sask.: Western Producer Prairie Books, 1983), 7, 63, 78–83.
90 P.E. Breton, o.m.i., *Hobbema: Une florissante misson indienne de l'Ouest* (Edmnton: Editions de l'Ermitage, 1962), 35.
91 Ruth M. Buck, "Canon Ahenakew Dead: A Churchman and Warrior," *Native Voice*, (Sept. 1961): 3. Stan Cuthand, introduction to Ruth M. Buck,

ed., *Voices of the Plains Cree* [1973] (Regina: Canadian Plains Research Center, 1995), xii.

92 Ernest George Mardon and Austin Mardon in collaboration with Elizabeth Hulse, "Edmund Kemper Broadus," *Dictionary of Canadian Biography* at http://www.biographi.ca/en/bio/broadus_edmund_kemper_16E.html.

93 Paul A.W. Wallace to "Dear Father," on University of Alberta letterhead, 29 Dec. 1921, Wallace, GLENBOW, UofC.

94 Laura Smyth Groening, *E.K. Brown: A Study in Conflict* (Toronto: University of Toronto Press, 1993), 4, 6.

95 Paul A.W. Wallace, "English Travel of the 17th Century in Europe" (M.A. thesis, University of Toronto, 1923).

96 Paul A.W. Wallace, "Shakespeare and His Printers" (Ph.D. dissertation, University of Toronto, 1925). A copy is in the University of Toronto Archives, UTA T79-0011 (74).

97 Greg Gatenby, *Toronto: A Literary Guide* (Toronto: McArthur, 1999), 320, 397.

98 Paul A.W. Wallace published four books in 1923: *Baptiste Larocque: Legends of French Canada* (Toronto: Musson, 1923); *Selections from Sam Slick*, edited vol. (Toronto: Ryerson, 1923); Anna Jameson's *Winter Studies and Summer Rambles in Canada*, edited vol. (Toronto: McClelland and Stewart, 1923); and his collection of short stories, *The Twist and Other Stories* (Toronto: Ryerson, 1923).

99 David Miller, "Edward Ahenakew's Tutelage by Paul Wallace: Reluctant Scholarship, Inadvertent Preservation," in Carolyn Podruchny and Laura Peers, eds., *Gathering Places: Aboriginal and Fur Trade Histories* (Vancouver: UBC Press, 2010): 255.

100 Alan B. McCullough, "Peyasiw-Awasis (Thunderchild also known as Kapitkow)," *DCB* 15, *1921–1930* (2005), 830–1.

101 Edward Ahenakew, *Voices of the Plains Cree*, edited by Ruth M. Buck (Regina: Canadian Plains Research Center, 1995), 134. The passage is reprinted in the *The Final Report of the Truth and Reconciliation Commission*, vol. 1, *Canada's Residential Schools: The History, Part 1, Origins to 1939* (Montreal and Kingston: Published for the Truth and Reconciliation Commission by McGill-Queen's University Press, 2015), 180.

102 Ahenakew, "*Voices of the Plains Cree*, 9.

103 Paul A.W. Wallace Diary for 1922–25, entry for 5 Mar. 1923, VUA, Wallace Records, 2018.07V12-1.

104 Lorne Pierce to P.A.W. Wallace, dated the Ryerson Press, "Tuesday night" [Spring 1923], ibid.

105 Duncan C, Scott to "Doctor Pierce," dated Ottawa 16 Oct. 1924, Queen's University Archives, Kingston, Ont., Lorne Pierce Fonds, Location 2001, Box 1, file 11. I thank Brendan Edwards for bringing this letter to my attention.

106 Edward Ahenakew's book, with which Paul Wallace had provided much encouragement and help, was finally published in 1973 in Toronto by McClelland and Stewart and reissued again in 1995 by the Canadian Plains Research Center in Regina.

107 Cuthand, introduction, xx.

108 Winona Wheeler, "Cree Intellectual Traditions in History," in Alvin Finkel, Sarah Carter, and Peter Fortna, eds., *The West and Beyond: New Perspectives on an Imagined Region* (Edmonton: AU Press, 2010), 47–61.

109 (Copy) Paul Wallace to M.D. Deardorff, dated 13 Oct. 1945, APSL, Wallace Papers.

110 Wallace, "Shakespeare and His Printers."

111 Robin Harris, *English Studies at Toronto: A History* (Toronto: University of Toronto Press, 1988), 63.

112 Interview with David Wallace, Baltimore, Md., 9 May 1996.

113 For his advances and royalties, see the last page of the notebook entitled, "Paul A.W. Wallace, University of Alberta." He made approximately $500 on *Baptiste Larocque*; $150 for his book of short stories, *The Twist*; $150 for the excerpts from the "Sam Slick" stories; $50 for Anna Jameson's writings on Upper Canada; and $350 for "The Canadian Herodotus." His salary at Lebanon Valley College ($4,200) appears in the document, "Application for State Employment," ca. 1956. Both documents are in the possession of David Wallace.

114 Interview with David Wallace, Washington, DC, 19 Nov. 2016.

115 Certificate of Citizenship, no. 4623145, 24 June 1940, in the possession of David Wallace.

116 Anthony F.C. Wallace and David H. Wallace, "Paul A.W. Wallace Remembered (1891–1967)," in Paul A.W. Wallace, *Conrad Weiser, 1696–1760: Friend of Colonist and Mohawk* (Philadelphia: University of Pennsylvania Press, 1945; reprinted in in 1996 in Lewisburg, Pa. by Wennawoods, 1996), iii–iv. Both of Paul Wallace's sons followed him in research careers, Tony as an anthropologist/ historian and David as a historian/museum curator. Both provided invaluable assistance with this biographical sketch of their father.

117 Wallace, *Weiser*, 572.

118 Paul A.W. Wallace,"People of the Long House," *American Heritage*, 6/2 (Feb. 1955): 26.

119 Frank G. Speck, in collaboration with Jesse Moses, *The Celestial Bear Comes Down to Earth* (Reading, Pa.: Reading Public Museum and Art Gallery, 1945), 14.

120 Paul A.W. Wallace, *Indians in Pennsylvania* (Harrisburg, Pa.: Pennsylvania Historical and Museum Commission, 1975), 16.

121 Paul A.W. Wallace to Frank Speck, dated 11 Sept. 1945, APSL, Wallace Papers.

122 Paul A.W. Wallace, "An Indian Preacher," 3, ibid.. This is the shorter version of the paper (5 pp.); the longer version, "Chief Joseph Montour: An Old-time Methodist Preacher Among the Delawares," is 9 pp. Also in APSL, Wallace Papers, there is a third version (5 pp.) entitled "Chief Joseph Montour: The Last King of the Delawares."

123 Speck, *Celestial Bear Comes Down*, 91. Smithsonian Institution, *Manahatta to Manhattan: Native Americans in Lower Manhattan* (New York City: National Museum of the American Indian, 2010), 4.

124 Paul A.W. Wallace, "A Visit to the Six Nations Reserve near Brantford, 8 July 1936," 2, APSL, Wallace Papers.

125 "Indians decide to form League: Grand Council of Many Tribes Convened at Ohsweken," *Brantford Expositor*, 21 Dec. 1918.

126 Big White Owl [Jasper Hill], "My People, the Delaware Indians," *Native Voice*, (July 1951): 2.

127 Michelle A. Hamilton, *Collections and Objections: Aboriginal Material Culture in Southern Ontario, 1791–1914* (Montreal and Kingston: McGill-Queen's University Press, 2010), 112, 114, 132.

128 Paul A.W. Wallace to Edith Joan Lyttleton (she wrote under the pen name, "G.B. Lancaster"), 14 Sept. 1937, Pennsylvania State University, University Park, Pa., Rare Books and Special Collections, the University Libraries, G.B. Lancaster Collection. Edith Lyttleton (1873–1944), a novelist and short-story writer, was New Zealand's widest-read author overseas until the Second World War. See Terry Sturm, *An Unsettled Spirit: The Life & Frontier Fiction of Edith Lyttleton (G.B. Lancaster)* (Auckland, NZ: Auckland University Press, 2003).

129 Paul A.W. Wallace to Chief De ha se, das go wa, c/o Mr William D. Loft, Ohsweken, Ont., dated 14 July 1936, APSL, Wallace Papers.

130 Paul A.W. Wallace to Marius Barbeau, 14 July 1936, ibid.

131 Robert Stacey, Donald Smith, and Bryan Winslow Colwell, introduction in Bernice Loft Winslow, *Iroquois Fires: The Six Nations Lyrics and Lore of Dawendine (Bernice Loft Winslow)*, with introductory and afterword material by George Beaver, Bryan Winslow Colwell, Donald Smith, and Robert Stacey (Ottawa: Penumbra, 1995), 18–19.

132 Interestingly, Paul never knew that his own grandmother, Mary Ann Mulligan (Mrs Edward Wilson) had grown up on a farm at Indiana near Cayuga, Ontario, on land that had originally been part of the Six Nations Territory on the Grand River. I thank David H. Wallace for this information. Indiana became a ghost town after the Grand River Navigation Company collapsed in the 1860s. Barbara Martindale, *Caledonia: Along the Grand River* (Toronto: Natural Heritage / Natural History Inc, 1995), 24.

133 John Murray Gibbon, *Canadian Mosaic: The Making of a Northern Nation* (Toronto: McClelland and Stewart, 1938).

134 Research Committee of the League for Social Reconstruction (Eugene Forsey, J. King Gordon, Leonard Marsh, J.F. Parkinson, F.R. Scott, Graham Spry, F.H. Underhill), *Social Planning for Canada* (Toronto: Thomas Nelson & Sons, 1935).

135 George Wrong, *The Canadians: The Story of a People* (Toronto: Macmillan, 1938), 434.

136 Jenness, "Canada's Indians Yesterday," 95.

137 Richling, *Twilight*, 262–3.

138 The reference to Edward's and Paul's canoe trips appears in Wallace, "The House," 1:10–12. I saw the manuscript at Tony Wallace's, 8 May 1993. He also showed me his father's copy of *The Men of the Last Frontier* (Toronto: Macmillan, 1932) inscribed, "From Edward Wallace," and with the owner's name and date: "Paul A.W. Wallace Lebanon Valley College Annville, Pa. October 31, 1932." Alec Lucas, a specialist on English Canadian literature, wrote of Grey Owl (page 376) in his essay, "Nature Writers and the Animal Story," in the *Literary History of Canada. Canadian Literature in English*, general editor Carl F. Klink (Toronto: University of Toronto Press, 1965): "No other Canadian writer had a greater reputation in the 1930's, both at home and abroad, than Grey Owl."

139 Grey Owl, *The Men of the Last Frontier* (London: Country Life, 1931), 214–15.

140 Harold Innis, "Review of Pilgrims of the Wild by Wa-Sha-Quon-Asin (Grey Owl), *Canadian Historical Review* 16 (June 1935): 199.

141 "Publisher's Note," in Grey Owl, *Men*, vii.

142 Ibid., 209.

143 "Grey Owl's final journey," *Globe and Mail*, 14 Apr. 1938. Full details on Grey Owl's life appear in Donald B. Smith, *From the Land of Shadows: The Making of Grey Owl* (Saskatoon: Western Producer Prairie Books, 1990).

144 Gregory Clark, "Grey Owl really an Englishman, old friends insist," *Toronto Daily Star*, 14 Apr. 1938, almost a full page story with four pictures, p. 1, second section.

145 John Barker, "T.F. McIlwraith and Anthropology at the University of Toronto 1925–63," *Canadian Review of Sociology and Anthropology*, 24/2 (1987): 252–68.

146 For a list of Indigenous delegates, see Donald Smith, "Now We Talk – You Listen: Indian delegates at a conference in 1939 joined together to speak for themselves," *Rotunda: The Magazine of the Royal Ontario Museum*, 23/2 (Fall 1990): 48.

147 E.W. Wallace, "Valedictory Address," in C.T. Loram and T.F. McIlwraith, eds., *The North American Indian Today* (Toronto: University of Toronto Press, 1943), 339–40.

148 T.A. Crerar, "Canada and Her Wards," in *The Indians Speak to Canada* (Ottawa: King's Printer, 1939), 37, quoted in *A Survey of the Contemporary Indians of*

Canada: Economic, Political, Educational Needs and Policies
(the Hawthorn Report), 2 vols. (Ottawa: Indian Affairs Branch, 1966), 1:369.

149 Kristie Sather, Secretary, Commissioner's Office Indian Affairs, to Allan
G. Harper, 1 Sept. 1939, National Archives and Records Administration,
Washington, DC (NARA), RG75, Bureau of Indian Affairs, Entry 178,
Office Files of John Collier, Toronto Seminar, Box 4.

150 John Collier, "Policies and Problems in the United States," in Loram and
McIlwraith, *Indian Today*, 140.

151 C.E.S. Franks, "Indian Policy: Canada and the United States Compared," in
Curtis Cook and Juan D. Lindau, eds., *Aboriginal Rights and Self-Government*
(Montreal and Kingston: McGill-Queen's University Press, 2000), 230–1.

152 J.C. McCaskill, Memorandum for Mr Collier, re: Toronto Conference, 23
Sept. 1939, NARA, RG75, Entry 178, Office Files of John Collier, Toronto
Seminar, Box 4.

153 John Collier, *Indians of the Americas: The Long Hope* (Slightly abridged)
(New York: New American Library, 1947), 176.

154 "Appendix A. Conclusions and Resolutions," in Loram and McIlwraith,
Indian Today, 347.

155 Ibid., 349.

156 The dates of Paul Wallace's visits are taken from his notes in his papers,
APSL, Wallace Papers.

157 Stacey et al., introduction, 19.

158 Interview with Chief William Dewaserageh Loft on the Six Nations Reserve,
Ont., 27, 28, and 29 Dec. 1942, APLS, Wallace Papers.

159 Paul A.W. Wallace to George W. Brown, general editor, *Dictionary of
Canadian Biography*, 27 June 1962, ibid.

160 Paul A. Wallace to Wendy [his wife], dated "Union Hotel, Caledonia,
Sunday night" (late Dec. 1942), ibid.

161 Paul A.W. Wallace to (his wife), dated Caledonia Post Office, 28 Dec. 1942,
ibid. I have been following the spelling of the word in Paul Wallace's
letter of 22 July 1949 to William Fenton, ibid.

162 (Copy) Paul Wallace to "Mrs Winslow," 25 Aug. 1945, ibid.

163 Interview with Chief Loft, Ont., Dec. 1942, ibid. Paul Wallace's note reads:
"Chief Loft permits me to dedicate the book to him but prefers me to use
his private name (not Sharenkhowane, which is an official title that will
be used by other men). Dedicate it to: DEWASERAGEH (William D. Loft),
Ohsweken, Ont."

164 Frank Speck to "Dear Paul," dated Gloucester, Mass., 15 Sept. 1945, APLS,
Wallace Papers.

165 Lyman H. Butterfield, Wilcomb E. Washburn, and William N. Fenton,
bibliography in *American Indian and White Relations to 1830* [1957] (New
York: Russell & Russell, 1971), 119.

166 Paul A.W. Wallace to William N. Fenton, 12 May 1943, APLS, Wallace Papers.

167 Paul A.W. Wallace, *The White Roots of Peace* (Philadelphia: University of Pennsylvania Press, 1946), vii.

168 William N. Fenton, "Simeon Gibson: Iroquois Informant, 1889–1943," *American Anthropologist*, n.s., 46 (1944): 234. The document by John Arthur Gibson and J.N.B. Hewitt, "Deganawi'dah" (1899) is now in the Smithsonian Institution, Washington, DC, National Anthropological Archives, Bureau of American Ethnology, Ms. 1517a. Chief John Arthur Gibson later, in 1912, dictated to the anthropologist A.A Goldenweiser in Onondaga, a longer account of the foundations of the Confederacy. In 1992 a full English translation appeared: Hanni Woodbury, in collaboration with Reg Henry and Harry Webster on the basis of A.A. Goldenweiser's manuscript, *Concerning the League: The Iroquois League, Tradition as Dictated in Onondaga by John Arthur Gibson* (Winnipeg: Algonquian and Iroquoian Linguistics, 1992).

169 Wallace, *White Roots*, viii. He went on to add, "I owe further thanks to Dr Fenton for his kindness and patience in reading my manuscript and offering many valuable criticisms and suggestions."

170 Sample reviews include the following: Elaine Goodale Eastman, *New York Times*, 16 June 1946; Arthur C. Parker, *New York History*, 27 (Oct. 1946): 507–9; C.E. Schaeffer, *Pennsylvania Magazine of History and Biography*, 70 (1946): 441–2. These three and several other reviews appear in the Iroqrafts edition of Paul A.W. Wallace, *The White Roots of Peace* (Philadelphia: University of Pennsylvania Press, 1946; reprinted in 1997 in Ohsweken, Ont., by Iroqrafts), 82–91.

171 Butterfield, Washburn, and Fenton, bibliography in *American Indian and White Relations to 1830*, 105.

172 I thank David H. Wallace for this insight.

173 John Mohawk, epilogue in Paul A.W. Wallace, *The Iroquois Book of Life: The White Roots of Peace* (Sante Fe, NM: Clear Light, 1994), 117.

174 Paul A.W. Wallace, *The White Roots of Peace* (1946); reissued in 1968 in Port Washington, NY, by Ira J. Friedman Inc; in 1986 by the Chauncey Press in Saranac Lake, NY; in 1994 by Clear Light Publishers in Santa Fe, NM; and in 1997 by Iroqrafts in Ohsweken, Ont.

175 William N. Fenton to Paul A.W. Wallace, 20 July 1949, APLS, Wallace Papers. "Annville Writer Is Honoured by Mohawk Indian Tribe," *Lebanon Daily News*, 16 July 1949.

176 Paul A.W. Wallace to John F. Freeman, 6 Nov. 1961, APLS, Wallace Papers. Guy Spittal, editor's epilogue in Wallace, *White Roots* (Iroqrafts, 1997), 93.

177 Robert Bothwell, *Laying the Foundation: A Century of History at University of Toronto* (Toronto: Department of History, University of Toronto, 1991), 87.

178 Violet Elizabeth Parwin, *Authorization of Textbooks for the Schools of Ontario, 1846–1950* (Toronto: University of Toronto Press, 1965), cited in Patricia V. Ofner, "The Indian in Textbooks: A Content Analysis of History Books Authorized for Use in Ontario Schools" (M.A. thesis, Lakehead University, May 1982), 51.

179 Fred Gaffen, *Forgotten Soldiers* (Penticton, BC: Theytus Books, 1985), 24.

180 "Authorized by the Minister of Education for the Public Schools of Ontario," appears on the frontispiece of each printing of Stewart Wallace's *A First Book of Canadian History* (Toronto: Macmillan, 1928) that I was able to consult: 1928. Reprinted annually 1929–37 (twice), 1938, 1940–42 (twice), and 1943–48. The book was removed from the authorization list in 1950–51. Paul's father sent this book to his 5-year-old grandson, with this inscription: "Dear Tony with love from Grandfather F.H.Wallace Oct.1928." Tony Wallace showed me the book when I visited him on 8 May 1993. "Indian Teacher Is Resentful," undated newspaper clipping in LAC, Elliott Moses Papers, MG30 C169, vol. 2, Scrapbook 1936–41; "Professor Wallace to Revise," *Toronto Star*, 6 Apr. 1929, in University of Toronto Archives, Victoria University Archives, Fonds 2187–Wallace Family Fonds, W. Stewart Wallace's file, A73-0020/493(28). Both quotations appear on p. 3 of the text of the 1928 and 1929 printings. My thanks to Shirley Wigmore, Special Collections librarian, Ontario Institute for Studies in Education, Toronto, for her help with information on Stewart Wallace's book. For a biographical sketch of Milton Martin, see Enos T. Montour, *The Feathered U.E.L.'s* (Toronto, Division of Communication, United Church of Canada, 1973), 130–4.

181 Books by Paul A.W. Wallace's include the following: *The Muhlenbergs of Pennsylvania* (1950), *The Travels of John Heckewelder in Frontier America* (1958), *Indians in Pennsylvania* (1961), *Pennsylvania, Seed of a Nation* (1962), and *The Indian Paths of Pennsylvania* (1965).

182 Francis Jennings, *Empire of Fortune: Crowns, Colonies, and Tribes in the Seven Years War in America* (New York: W.W. Norton, 1988), 26n9.

183 C.B. Sissons, *The Memoirs of C.B. Sissons* (Toronto: University of Toronto Press, 1964), 125, 257.

184 Wallace to Brown, general editor, *DCB*, 27 June 1962. Paul A.W. Wallace, "Dekanahwideh," *DCB*, 1, *1000–1700* (1966), 253–55.

185 André Vachon, Le directeur adjoint, *DBC*, dated Quebec City, le 6 octobre 1965, APLS, Wallace Papers.

186 William N. Fenton, "Review: *Dictionary of Canadian Biography*, vol. 1, *1000–1700*," *American Anthropologist*, 69/2 (1967): 270.

187　Frances Halpenny, *"Dictionary of Canadian Biography / Dictionnaire Biographique du Canada,"* in *The Oxford Companion to Canadian Literature,* general editor William Toye (Toronto: Oxford University Press, 1983), 190.

188　Bothwell, *Foundation,* 87. Martin L. Friedland, *The University of Toronto: A History,* 2nd ed. (Toronto: University of Toronto Press, 2013), 306.

189　Jacques Rousseau and George W. Brown, "The Indians of Northeastern North America," *DCB,* 1, *1000 to 1700* (1966), 5.

190　Wallace to Brown, 27 June 1962.

191　George Brown to P.A.W. Wallace, dated Toronto, 18 July 1962, APLS, Wallace Papers.

192　Wallace to Brown, 22 July 1962.

193　Commentary is on the draft article on Membertou, APLS, Wallace Papers. The author of this sketch was the distinguished Jesuit historian Lucien Campeau. See *DCB* 1, *1000–1700* (1966), 500–1.

194　Wallace's commentary is on the draft article on Iroquet, APLS, Wallace Papers.

195　Edward Ahenakew to Paul A.W. Wallace, dated Kinistino, Sask., 28 May 1948, ibid.

196　Paul A.W. Wallace to Edward Ahenakew, dated 31 July 1961, ibid. Unknown to Wallace, his friend had died of a heart attack on 12 July 1961.

197　D.H.K. "Obituary: Paul A.W. Wallace," *Pennsylvania History,* 34 (1967): 208–9.

7. Quebec Viewpoints

1　W.J. Eccles, *Canada under Louis XIV, 1663–1701* (Toronto: McClelland and Stewart, 1964), xi.

2　Patrice Groulx, *Pièges de la mémoire: Dollard des Ormeaux, les Amérindiens et nous* (Hull, Que.: Éditions Vents d'Ouest, 1998), 61.

3　Edward Louis Montizambert, *Canada in the Seventeenth Century: From the French of Pierre Boucher* (Montreal: Printed by George E. Desbarats & Co, 1883), 73. For the original French, see Pierre Boucher, *Histoire véritable et naturelle de moeurs et productions du Pays de la Nouvelle-France vulgairement dite le CANADA* (Boucherville, Que.: La Société Historique de Boucherville, 1964; facsimile copy of the original 1664 volume), for the original French of the passage cited, see 150–1.

4　Catherine Breslin, "The Other Trudeaus: In 1659 a young Frenchman, Etienne Truteau, landed in Quebec to father a long line of hardy farmers that continued right down to Joseph, grandfather of Canada's Prime Minister," *Chatelaine,* (Sept. 1969): 108. The full article appears in the Sept. 1969 issue at 32–3, 108–11, 113, and continues in the Oct. 1969 issue, 42–3, 78–87. Joseph Drouin, avocat et généalogiste, "Le combat du 6 mai,

1662, dans l'est du Montréal. Truteau et Langevin-Lacroix," *La Patrie* (Montreal), 26 Apr. 1936. Thomas J. Laforest, "Etienne Trudeau," in his *Our French Canadian Ancestors* (Palm Harbour, Fla.: LISI Press, 1983), 171–7, 195–6. George Radwanski, *Trudeau* (Toronto: Macmillan, 1978), 43. Radwanski states, "Until recently, when the building to which it was affixed was demolished, a small plaque on the corner of Montreal's La Gauchetiere and St Andre streets recorded one of his [Etienne Trudeau's] adventures: 'Here Truteau, Roulier, and Langevin-Lacroix resisted 50 Iroquois, May 6, 1662.'"

5 Hélène Marotte, "Benjamin Sulte," *Dictionary of Canadian Biography* (*DCB*), vol. 15, *1921–1930* (Toronto: University of Toronto Press, 2005), 985–7.

6 Benjamin Sulte, *Histoire des Canadiens français, 1608–1880* (Montreal: Wilson et cie, 1882–84), 3:57.

7 Marcel Trudel, "New France, 1524–1713," *DCB* 1, *1000–1700* (1966), 31.

8 Claude Gélinas, *Les Autochtones dans le Québec post-Confédéral, 1867–1960* (Sillery, Que.: Éditions du Septentrion, 2007), 20.

9 Joseph-Pierre-Anselme Maurault, *Histoire des Abénakis depuis 1605 jusqu'à nos jours* (Sorel, Que.: L'Atelier typographique de la "Gazette de Sorel," 1866).

10 Thomas Charland, "Joseph-Pierre-Anselme Maurault," *DCB* 9, *1861–1870* (1976), 540–541.

11 Maurault, *Histoire*, 19.

12 Ibid., 17.

13 Thomas-M. Charland, *Histoire des Abénakis d'Odanak (1675–1937)* (Montreal: Les Éditions du Lévrier, 1964), 239.

14 Henry J. Morgan, *Sketches of Celebrated Canadians, and persons connected with Canada* (Quebec: Hunter, Rose & Co, 1862), 678.

15 Raymond Joseph Armand Huel, *Archbishop A.-A. Taché of St Boniface* (Edmonton: University of Alberta Press, 2003), 9.

16 Jean-Guy Nadeau, "Joseph-Charles Taché," *DCB*, vol, 12, *1891–1900* (1990), 1013–14.

17 J.C. Taché, *Les histoires de M. Sulte, protestation* (Montreal: Libraire Saint-Joseph, 1883), 17.

18 Philippe Baby Casgrain, 1 May 1885, Canada, *House of Commons Debates* (1885), 1516.

19 André Siegfried, *The Race Question in Canada* [1907] (Toronto: McClelland and Stewart, 1966; originally published in 1906 in French, in Paris, by A. Colin, as *Le Canada, les deux races; problèmes politiques contemporains*), 95–6.

20 Donald B. Smith, *Le Sauvage: The Native People in Quebec Historical Writing on the Heroic Period (1534–1663) of New France* (Ottawa: National Museums of Canada, 1974), 52, 55–61.

21 Richard A. Preston, *To Save Canada: A History of the Royal Military College since the Second World War* (Ottawa: University of Ottawa Press, 1991), 160.

22 Georges Vattier, *Essai sur la mentalité canadienne-française* (Paris: Champion, 1928), 291.

23 Jean Poirier, "Les toponymes amérindiens encore en usage dans la nomenclature du Québec," *Revue géographique de Montréal*, 21 (1968): 136–7.

24 Lionel Groulx, *La naissance d'une race* (Montreal: Bibliothèque de l'Action française, 1919), 23.

25 Lionel Groulx, *La naissance d'une race*, 2nd ed. (Montreal: Libraire d'Action canadienne-française, 1930), 25.

26 Beverly J. Rasporich, *Made-in-Canada Humour: Literary, Folk and Popular Culture* (Amsterdam: John Benjamins, 2010), 37–9.

27 In 1914 Glasgow, Brook, and Co published three history books by Stephen Leacock: *The Dawn of Canadian History: A Chronicle of Aboriginal Canada and the Coming of the White Man; The Mariner of St Malo: A Chronicle of the Voyages of Jacques Cartier; Adventurers of the Far North: A Chronicle of the Frozen Seas*. For his views of the First Nations, see David A. Nock, "Stephen Leacock: The Not-So-Funny Story of His Evolutionary Ethnology and Canada's First Peoples," *Histories of Anthropology Annual*, 3 (2007): 51–69.

28 Michael R. Marrus, *Mr Sam: The Life and Times of Samuel Bronfman* [1991] (Toronto: Penguin, 1992), 305.

29 Ibid.

30 Ralph L. Curry, *Stephen Leacock: Humorist and Humanist* (Garden City, NY: Doubleday, 1959), 311.

31 Marrus, *Mr Sam*, 304.

32 Stephen Leacock, *Canada: The Foundations of its Future* (Montreal: Privately printed, 1941), 19.

33 The Mnjikaning Fish Weirs are one of the oldest human developments in what is now Canada. See Richard B. Johnston and Kenneth A. Cassavoy, "The Fish Weirs at Atherly Narrows, Ontario," *American Antiquity*, 43, 4 (1978): 697–709.

34 Sherry Simon, *Translating Montreal: Episodes in the Life of a Divided City* (Montreal and Kingston: McGill-Queen's University Press, 2006), 22.

35 Ronald Rudin, *Making History in Twentieth-Century Quebec* (Toronto: University of Toronto Press, 1997), 16.

36 Lionel Groulx, quoted in ibid., 43.

37 Ibid., 78.

38 Giselle Huot, "The Preacher: No English-Canadian Historian Was ever Lionized as Lionel Groulx Was in Quebec," *Horizon Canada*, 7/81 (Sept. 1986): 1943.

39 Rudin, *Making History*, 59.

40 George F.G. Stanley, "Lionel-Adolphe Groulx: Historian and Prophet of French Canada," in Laurier L. LaPierre, ed., *Four O'Clock Lectures: French-Canadian Thinkers of the Nineteenth and Twentieth Centuries* (Montreal: McGill University Press, 1966), 100.

41 Lionel Groulx, *Histoire du Canada français depuis la découverte*, 4 vols. (Montreal: L'Action nationale, 1950–52). Rudin, *Making History*, 98.

42 Juliette Lalonde-Rémillard, "Les souvenirs de Juliette Lalonde-Rémillard," *Les Cahiers d'histoire du XXe siècle*, no. 2 (Summer 1994): 183.

43 Groulx, *Histoire du Canada français*, 1:108.

44 Alan C. Cairns, *Citizens Plus: Aboriginal Peoples and the Canadian State* (Vancouver: UBC Press, 2000), 23.

45 In Stanley's words, "It was virtually ignored." See his "G.F.G. Stanley and the Birth of Western Canada – A Historical Footnote," *Riel Project Bulletin*, no. 5 (Apr. 1981): 5.

46 George F.G. Stanley, preface to the 2nd ed., 1 July 1960, of his *The Birth of Western Canada: A History of the Riel Rebellions* [1936] (Toronto: University of Toronto Press, 1961), x.

47 Bruce G. Trigger,"Alfred G. Bailey – Ethnohistorian," *Acadiensis*, 18/2 (Spring 1989): 3.

48 Alfred G. Bailey, "Retrospective Thoughts of an Ethnohistorian," Canadian Historical Association, *Historical Papers / Communications Historiques*, (1977): 23.

49 Trigger, "Bailey," 11.

50 Alan C. Cairns, "Aboriginal Research in Troubled Times," in Myra Rutherdale, Kerry Abel, and P. Whitney Lackenbauer, eds., *Roots of Entanglement: Essays in the History of Native-Newcomer Relations* (Toronto: University of Toronto Press, 2017), 405.

51 George F.G. Stanley, "Review of *A Canadian Indian Bibliography, 1960–1970*, by Thomas S. Abler, Douglas Sanders, and Sally M. Weaver," *American Indian Quarterly*, 3/1 (Spring 1977): 54–6.

52 Donald G. Creighton, *Dominion of the North: A History of Canada* (Cambridge, Mass.: Houghton Mifflin, 1944), 1–50.

53 Donald Wright, *Donald Creighton: A Life in History* (Toronto: University of Toronto Press, 2015), 159.

54 Arthur R.M. Lower, *Colony to Nation*, [1946] 5th ed. (Toronto: McClelland and Stewart, 1977), xi.

55 Contract to the publication of *Canada: A Political and Social History*, between Edgar McInnis and Farrar and Rinehart, 18 June 1943. Photocopy of the contract given to me by Peggy Nethery, Holt, Rinehart and Winston, Toronto, 4 July 1988. The contract contains the interesting clause: "The author agrees that on or before the end of World War II he

will deliver to the publishers a complete copy of the manuscript of the said work."

56 Robert Fulford, "By the Book," *Saturday Night*, (Apr. 1984): 7.
57 Edgar McInnis, *Canada: A Political and Social History*, 4th ed. (Toronto: Holt, Rinehart and Winston, 1982), 11. At the University of Calgary, this is the textbook we used in the introductory Canadian History survey course in the late 1970s.
58 Rudin, *Making History*, 105–8.
59 Dale Miquelon, "W.J. Eccles: The Young Historian," *Journal of Canadian Studies*, 47/2 (Spring 2013): 268–92. "W.J. Eccles," *The Canadian Encyclopedia*, at https://www.thecanadianencyclopedia.ca/en/article/wj-eccles/.
60 W.J. Eccles, *Essays in New France* (Toronto: Oxford University Press, 1987), 15.
61 Ryerson is described as a "marginal figure in the English-Canadian historical profession," in Donald Wright, *The Professionalization of History in English Canada* (Toronto: University of Toronto Press, 2005), 125.
62 Stanley B. Ryerson, *The Founding of Canada: Beginnings to 1815* [1960] (Toronto: Progress Books, 1963).
63 Ibid., 10.
64 Ibid., 18.
65 Ibid., 88.
66 Robert C.H. Sweeny, "Stanley Bréhaut Ryerson: Prescience, Politics, and the Profession," *Canadian Historical Review*, 80 (Sept. 1999): 464.
67 Gregory S. Kealey, "Stanley Bréhaut Ryerson: Marxist Historian," *Studies in Political Economy: A Socialist Review*, 9 (1982): 149n21.
68 Lionel Groulx, ptre, "Review of *The Founding of Canada: Beginnings to 1815* by Stanley B. Ryerson," *Revue d'histoire de l'Amérique française*, 15 (1961–62): 299. All the translations that follow are my own.
69 Stanley Bréhaut Ryerson, *Les origines du Canada*. Réédition et traduction. (Montreal: VLB éditeur, 1997.
70 "Curriculum Vitae et Bibliographie, Jacques Rousseau," mimeo, 1968, 8. I obtained a copy of this document when I took a reading course with him at Laval, winter 1968–69. A copy is in my file 091.0810, "Jacques Rousseau, CV / Biography to 1966," in the Donald B. Smith Fonds, Acc. 2016.42, Archives and Special Collections, University of Calgary (hereafter, Donald B. Smith Fonds).
71 A good anthropological study of Jacques Rousseau's contributions on the First Nations exists. See Marc-Adélard Tremblay and Josée Thivierge, "The Nature and Scope of Jacques Rousseau's Amerindian Works," in William Cohen, ed., *Actes du 17ème Congrès des Algonquinistes, Proceedings*

of the Seventieth Algonkian Conference (Ottawa: Carleton University Press, 1987), 343–76.

72 Only a short, undocumented biography is currently available. See Pierre Couture and Camille Laverdière, *Jacques Rousseau* (Montreal: XYZ éditeur, 2000).

73 Jean Laporte, *La vieille dame, l'archéologue, et le chanoine: La saga de Dollard des Ormeaux* (Vanier, Ont.: Les Éditions L'Interligne, 1995), 69–70, 89. Jacques Rousseau's correspondence with Chanoine Groulx on this issue (1960–62) has been saved in the Centre de recherche Lionel-Groulx, 257 ave Bloomfield, Outremont, Que., where I examined it, in 1992. I warmly thank the archivist François David.

74 Laporte, *Dame*, 88–9, 102, 133. Jacques Rousseau to Chanoine Lionel Groulx, dated Vanves, France, le 17 mars 1962, Centre de recherche Lionel-Groulx. By the 1980s interest had fallen completely in Dollard, now seen as more of a myth than a hero. See Graham Fraser, "Quebec recovers from 'la fete de Dollard.' Was French hero a saviour or rogue, academics wonder," *Globe and Mail*, 22 May 1984.

75 Three key articles in *Cahiers des Dix* are "Ces Gens qu'on dit sauvages," 23 (1958): 52–90; "Les Sachems délibèrent autour du feu de camp," 24 (1959): 9–49; and "Les Premiers Canadiens," 25 (1960): 9–64.

76 Jacques Rousseau and Madeline Rousseau, "La crainte des Iroquois chez les Mistassins," *Revue d'histoire de l'Amérique française*, 2 (1948–49): 13–26.

77 The Division des archives de l'Université Laval, Fonds Jacques Rousseau, has very rich holdings on Rousseau. During a three-day visit to the Archives in late April 2015, James Lambert and Valérie Lacasse provided invaluable assistance. The Laval Archives has a typed summary of the televised course, "L'Indien et notre Milieu." I thank my good friends in Quebec City, Fernand Harvey and Sophie LaMontagne, and Richard Jones and Lianne Plamandon, for shelter and good company during my Quebec visits!

78 Camille Laverdière and Nicole Carette, *Jacques Rousseau 1905–1970: Curriculum, Anthologie, Témoignages, Bibliographie*, preface by Louis-Edmond Hamelin (Sainte-Foy, Que.: Les Presses de l'Université Laval, 1999).

79 Email to me from Louis-Edmond Hamelin, 3 May 2015.

80 "Curriculum Vitae et Bibliographie, Jacques Rousseau," mimeo, 1968, 1. I am also most grateful for the comments on the family of Jacques Rousseau by his son Jérôme Rousseau, who kindly looked over two drafts of this sketch.

81 Yves Gingras, *Pour L'avancement des sciences: Histoire de l'ACFAS, 1923–1993* (Montreal: Éditions du Boréal, 1994), 37.

82 Laverdière and Carette, *Rousseau*, 133, 137.

83 Jacques Rousseau, "Méfaits des premiers contacts entre Indiens et Blancs," *La Patrie*, 21 Oct. 1951.

84 Pierre Turgeon, "Nos ancêtres, les Indiens," *Perspectives. Le Droit*, 12/21, 23 May 1970, 2–4.

85 Jacques Rousseau, *L'Hérédité et l'homme*, [1945] 2nd ed. (Montreal: Éditions de l'Arbre, 1945.

86 On this topic, see the interesting article by Yves Beauregard, "Mythe ou realité? Les origines amérindiennes des Québécois. Entrevue avec Hubert Charbonneau," *Cap-aux-Diamants*, 34 (Summer1993): 38–42.

87 Half a century later, a new phenomenon has arisen, one that involves white French descendants, using a distant Indigenous ancestor born three to four centuries ago, 10, 11, 12 generations ago, to self-identify as Indigenous. Even twenty years ago this development was inconceivable. Darryl Leroux examines the phenomenon in *Distorted Descent: White Claims to Indigenous Identity* (Winnipeg: University of Manitoba Press, 2019), 1–2, 66. The Indigenous rights lawyer Jean Teillet comments on this issue in *The North-West is Our Mother. The Story of Louis Riel's People: The Metis Nation* (Toronto: HarperCollins Publishers, 2019), 480–4. As Gilles O'Bomaswin, chief of the Conseil des Abénakis d'Odanak, mentioned in a federal government committee meeting in 2003, "There was a day when nobody wanted to be an Indian. Now everybody wants to be an Indian." Leroux, *Descent*, 61.

88 Editors' preface in Denis Vaugeois and Jacques Lacourcière, eds., *Histoire 1534–1968* (Montreal: Éditions du Renouveau Pédagogique, 1968), 6.

89 Paul-Émile Farley and Gustave Lamarche, *Histoire du Canada, Cours supérieur*, [1935] 4th ed. (Montreal: Librarie des Clercs de St-Viateur, 1945), 7.

90 Ibid, 13.

91 Jacques Rousseau, "Du bon sauvage de la littérature à celui de la réalité," *L'Action universitaire*, 20/4 (July 1954): 15–16.

92 Rousseau,"Les Sachems," 15.

93 Jacques Rousseau, *"L'Indien et notre milieu,"* L'Université Laval, Cours télévisé, Jan.–Apr. 1966, mimeo, 16.

94 Laverdière and Carette, *Rousseau*, 145. I also thank Rousseau Heinrich of Edmonton for additional information on his two great-uncles in the Second World War. In memory of the two paratroopers, the *Globe and Mail* published a reference to them, as well as their photo, in the story by Tu Thanh Ha, "Postcards from the Past," 1 June 2019, O5.

95 Jacques Rousseau, "The Northern Quebec Eskimo Problem and the Ottawa-Quebec Struggle," *Anthropological Journal of Canada*, 7/2 (1969): 2.

96 Rousseau, "Du bon sauvage," 13.

97 Marcel Trudel, *Initiation à la Nouvelle-France: Histoire et institutions* (Montreal: Holt, Rinehart, and Winston, 1968), 28.

98 Laverdière and Carette, *Rousseau*, 53–60.

99 Tremblay and Thivierge, "Nature and Scope," 366.

100 Jacques Rousseau, "Persistances païennes chez les Amérindiens de la forêt boréale," *Cahiers des Dix*, 17 (1952): 202.

101 Nicolas N. Smith, *Three Hundred Years in Thirty: Memoir of Transition with the Cree Indians of Lake Mistassini* (Solon, Maine: Polar Bear & Co, Solon Center for Research and Publishing, 2011), 71, 73.

102 Boyce Richardson, *Strangers Devour the Land: The Cree Hunters of the James Bay Area versus Premier Bourassa and the James Bay Development Corporation* (Toronto: Macmillan, 1975), 69.

103 Smith, *Three Hundred Years*, 78–99.

104 Jean-Paul Vinay, "La vie au Mistassini," in *Le Club Musical et Littéraire de Montréal: Huit Conférences, Saison artistique 1947–1948*, vol. A-3 (Montreal: Le Club Musical et Littéraire de Montréal, n.d.).

105 Gélinas, *Les Autochtones*, 111, 94, 96.

106 Ibid., 112.

107 Toby Morantz, *The White Man's Gonna Getcha: The Colonial Challenge to the Crees in Quebec* (Montreal and Kingston: McGill-Queen's University Press, 2002), 220–1.

108 Ibid., 180.

109 The first two chapters of Adrian Tanner, *Bringing Home Animals: Religious Ideology and Mode of Production of the Mistassini Cree Hunters* (St John's, Nfld.: Memorial University of Newfoundland, Institute of Social and Economic Research, 1979), 1–26, proved of great value in writing this introductory sketch of Mistassini.

110 Richardson, *Strangers Devour the Land*, 69. By 1970, the population of Mistassini was estimated at approximately 1,300. Smith, *Three Hundred Years*, 102.

111 Morantz, *Gonna Getcha*, 220. Smith, in *Three Hundred Years*, states the Mistassini territory was about 60,000 square miles, , 73, 98. This would be about the size of Great Britain.

112 Jacques Rousseau, "En Canot avec les Montagnais," *La Patrie*, 28 May 1950.

113 Tremblay and Thivierge, "Nature and Scope," 353.

114 Jacques Rousseau, "Dualisme religieux ou syncretisme chez les Algiques de la forêt boreale," in André Leroi-Gourhan, Pierre Champion, and Monique de Fontanès, eds., *Actes du VIème Congrés International des Sciences anthropologiques et ethnologiques*, tome 2, *Ethnologie*, Paris, 30 July to 6August 1960 (Paris: Musée de l'Homme, 1963), 471.

115 Jacques Rousseau, "Astam Mitchoun! Essai sur la gastronomie amérindienne, *Cahier des Dix*, 22 (1957): 193–213.

116 Tremblay and Thivierge, "Nature and Scope," 359. See also Rousseau, "Les Sachems," 15.

117 Jean-Guy Goulet, "Religious Dualism Among Athabaskan Catholics," *Canadian Journal of Anthropology*, 3/1 (Fall 1982): 5, 3.
118 Rousseau, "L'Indien et notre milieu," 18.
119 Morantz, *Gonna Getcha*, 216.
120 Ibid., 219.
121 Email to me from Andrée Lévesque, 6 Nov. 2017.
122 Sylvie Vincent and Bernard Arcand, *L'Image de l'Amérindien dans les manuels scolaires du Québec, ou Comment les Québécois ne sont pas des sauvages* (Ville La Salle, Que.: Éditions Hurtubise HMH, 1979).
123 Sylvie Vincent and Bernard Arcand, "The Image of the Amerindian in Quebec Textbooks," in *The International Organization for the Elimination of All Forms of Racial Discrimination (EAFORD)* (London, England: EAFORD, June 1983), 4–5.
124 Ibid., 6.
125 Denys Delâge, "La contribution de l'indienne à notre histoire," *Lettres et ecritures, Revue des étudiants de la Faculté des lettres de l'Université Laval*, 2/2 (Dec. 1964): 15.
126 Fernand Ouellet, *Histoire économique et sociale du Québec, 1760–1850* (Montreal: Fides, 1966), 4, 108, 137, 158, 561.
127 Jean Hamelin and Yves Roby, *Histoire économique du Québec, 1851–1896* (Montreal: Fides, 1971), 59.
128 Sylvie Vincent, "Trente-cinq ans de *Recherches amérindiennes au Québec*," *Recherches amérindiennes au Québec*, 36/1 (2006): 3–5.
129 Edouard Privat, an editor in Toulouse, France, commissioned the work for his publishing firm's series, "Univers de la France et des pays francophones." France-Amérique in Montreal brought the book out in Quebec in 1978. The cover indicates that the book sold 14,000 copies in just two years, a most impressive figure for an academic history book. The two chapters on the First Nations are by Serge-André Crête, "Les Amérindiens," 11–28; and Raynald Parent, "L'effritement de la Civilisation amérindienne," 29–58. Laurier Turgeon recognized the volume's milestone inclusion of the First Nations in his essay, "De l'acculturation aux transferts culturels," in Laurier Turgeon, Denys Delâge, Réal Ouellet, eds., *Transferts culturels et métissages Amèrique/Europe XVIe-XXe siècle* (Quebec: Les Presses de l'Université Laval, 1996), 18.
130 Diane Boudreau, *Histoire de la literature amérindienne au Québec: Oralité et écriture* (Montreal: Éditions de l'Hexagone, 1993). See esp. chapters five and six.
131 The Innu are the people known to the French as the Montagnais who lived from present-day Quebec in the seventeenth century throughout northeastern Quebec to Labrador.
132 Boudreau, *Histoire*, 125.

133 An Antane Kapesh, *Je suis une maudite Sauvagesse / Eukuan nin matsshimanitu innu-iskueu* (Montreal: Leméac, 1976), 13. French translation by José Mailhot in collaboration with Anne-Marie André and André Mailhot.

134 Smith, *Three Hundred Years*, 171.

135 Roy MacGregor, *Chief: The Fearless Vision of Billy Diamond* (Markham, Ont.: Penguin, 1989).

136 Dominique Clift, "Bourassa: The politics of power," *Montreal Star*, 5 May 1971, cited in Sylvie Vincent, "Backgrounds and Beginnings," in Sylvie Vincent and Garry Bowers, eds., *Baie James et Nord québécois: Dix ans après / James Bay and Northern Québec: Ten Years After* (Montreal: Recherches amérindiennes au Québec, 1988), 211.

137 Toby Morantz, "Aboriginal Land Claims in Quebec," in Ken Coates, ed., *Aboriginal Land Claims in Canada: A Regional Perspective* (Toronto: Copp Clark Pitman, 1992), 118.

138 Aurélien Gill, quoted in "L'Education et les Initiations," in Bernard Assiniwi, *A l'indienne* (Montreal: Lémeac, 1972), 61.

8. Attitudes on the Pacific Coast

1 George Stocking, Jr, "Franz Boas and the Shaping of Anthropology," *Literary Review of Canada*, (Winter 1999/2000): 7.

2 Wendy Wickwire, *At the Bridge: James Teit and an Anthropology of Belonging* (Vancouver: UBC Press, 2019), 15–16, 120.

3 Douglas Cole, *Franz Boas: The Early Years, 1858–1906* (Vancouver: Douglas & McIntyre, 1999), 16, 61.

4 Ibid.. 3.

5 Douglas Cole, "In the Field" [On Franz Boas], *Horizon Canada*, 10/115 (July 1987): 2758.

6 Douglas Cole, *Captured Heritage: The Scramble for Northwest Coast Artifacts* (Vancouver: Douglas & McIntyre, 1985), 102–9.

7 Cole, *Boas*, 99.

8 William N. Fenton, "Horatio Emmons Hale," *Dictionary of Canadian Biography* (*DCB*), vol. 12, *1891–1900* (Toronto: University of Toronto Press, 1990), 400–2.

9 Cole, "In the Field," 2758.

10 Chief Joseph, quoted in Franz Boas's 1888 diary, entry for 2 June 1888, in *The Ethnography of Franz Boas: Letters and Diaries of Franz Boas written on the Northwest Coast from 1886 to 1931*, compiled and edited by Ronald P. Rohner (Chicago: University of Chicago Press, 1969), 87.

11 Franz Boas to Ernst Boas, dated Fort Rupert, 18 Nov. 1930, ibid., 291.

12 Walter Goldschmidt, introduction in Walter Goldschmidt, ed., *The American Anthropologist: The Anthropology of Franz Boas, Essays on the*

Centennial of this Birth, American Anthropological Association, 61/5, pt. 2, Memoir no. 89 (Oct. 1959).

13 Cole, *Boas*, 3.

14 Jacob W. Grube provides a full biographical review in "Horatio Hale and the Development of American Anthropology," *Proceedings of the American Philosophical Society*, 3/1 (Feb. 1967): 5–37. For the Thoreau connection, see Henry Williams, *Memorials of the Class of 1837 of Harvard University Prepared for the Fiftieth Anniversary of Their Graduation* (Boston: Geo. J. Ellis, 1887), 37–43, 92–8. With great understatement Henry Williams, class secretary, wrote of Thoreau, "His writings as a youth and in early manhood give proof of an elevation and independence of thought not often met in those of his age" (41).

15 Evelyn H.C. Johnson, "Some Visitors at Chiefswood," in "Chiefswood," dictated to and typed by Dorothy Keen, reorganized in 1963 by Martha McKeon. Archives of Ontario (AO), MU4642 Indian Miscellaneous, Manuscripts no. 4, 156.

16 Horatio Hale, "An Iroquois Condoling Council," *Proceedings and Transactions of the Royal Society of Canada* 1895, 2nd series, vol, 1, section II, 1895, 61; reprinted in Horatio Hale, *The Iroquois Book of Rites and Hale on the Iroquois* (Ohsweken, Ont.: Iroqrafts, 1989), 357.

17 Horatio Hale, "The Fall of Hochelaga," *Journal of American Folk-Lore*, 7/24 (1894): 14.

18 David Nock, "Horatio Hale: Forgotten Victorian Author of Positive Aboriginal Representation," in Celia Haig-Brown and David A. Nock, eds., *With Good Intentions: Euro-Canadian and Aboriginal Relations in Colonial Canada* (Vancouver: UBC Press, 2006), 46. Cole, *Boas*, 118.

19 Hale, quoted in Rohner, *Ethnography*, 82.

20 Ibid., 109.

21 Alexander Francis Chamberlain, *The Language of the Mississaga Indians of Skugog: A Contribution to the Linguistics of the Algonkian Tribes of Canada* (Philadelphia: MacCalla & Co, 1892).

22 William A. Koelsch, *Clark University 1887–1987: A Narrative History* (Worcester, Mass.: Clark University Press, 1987), 57.

23 Alexander F. Chamberlain," The Human Side of the Indian," *Popular Science Monthly*, 68 (1906): 506.

24 John Swanton to Franz Boas, 30 Sept. 1900, cited in Aldona Jonaitis, *From the Land of the Totem Poles: The Northwest Coast Indian Art Collection at the American Museum of Natural History* (Vancouver: Douglas & McIntyre, 1988), 198. For an interesting presentation of the Methodist (after 1925 the United Church) side of the story, see R.W. Henderson, *These Hundred Years: The United Church of Canada in the Queen Charlotte Islands 1884–1984* (N.p.p.: Official Board of the Queen Charlotte United Church, 1985).

25 Patricia E. Roy, *Vancouver: An Illustrated History* (Toronto: James Lorimer, 1980), 168.

26 Table 14.1. Population of British Columbia by Racial Origin, 1911–1931, in Joan Brockman, "Exclusionary Tactics: The History of Women and Visible Minorities in the Legal Profession in British Columbia," in Hamar Foster and John McLaren, eds., *Essays in the History of Canadian Law*, vol. 6, *British Columbia and the Yukon* (Toronto: University of Toronto Press, 1995), 519.

27 Keith Thor Carlson, "Rethinking Dialogue and History: The King's Promise and the 1906 Aboriginal Delegation to London," *Native Studies Review*, 16/ 2 (2005): 9–10. Robin Fisher, "Su-a-piu-luck," *DCB* 13, *1901–1910* (1994), 998–9.

28 Chief Simon Baker, *Khot-La-Cha: The Autobiography of Chief Simon Baker*, compiled and edited by Verna J. Kirkness (Vancouver: Douglas & McIntyre, 1994), 7.

29 Hamar Foster, "We Are Not O'Meara's Children: Law, Lawyers, and the First Campaign for Aboriginal Title in British Columbia, 1908–28," in Hamar Foster, Heather Raven, and Jeremy Weber, eds., *Let Right Be Done: Aboriginal Title, the Calder Case, and the Future of Indigenous Rights* (Vancouver: UBC Press, 2007), 65.

30 Brendan F.R. Edwards, "'I Have Lots of Help Behind Me, Lots of Books, To Convince You': Andrew Paull and the Value of Literacy in English," *BC Studies*, no. 164 (Winter 2009–10): 9.

31 Herbert Francis Dunlop, o.m.i., *Andy Paull: As I Knew Him and Understood His Times* (Vancouver: Order of the O.M.I. of St Paul's Province, 1989), 24, 32.

32 E. Palmer Patterson, II, "Andrew Paull and Canadian Indian Resurgence" (Ph.D. dissertation, University of Washington, 1962), 28.

33 Edwards, "Paull," 8–9.

34 Patterson, "Paull," 46.

35 Edwards, "Paull," 8n4. BC only extended the provincial vote to Indians, without obliging them to lose their Indian status, in 1949. The BC Law Society to that date only accepted persons on the provincial voters' list to the Bar. Hence, an Indian registered under the Indian Act could not become a lawyer in BC before 1949.

36 H.B. Hawthorn, C.S. Belshaw, and S.M. Jamieson, *The Indians of British Columbia: A Study of Contemporary Social Adjustment* (Toronto: University of Toronto Press, 1960), 474.

37 For background to early Indian land policy in BC, see Cole Harris, *Making Native Space: Colonialism, Resistance, and Reserves in British Columbia* (Vancouver: UBC Press, 2002), 45–72. Robin Fisher, *Contact and Conflict: Indian-European Relations in British Columbia, 1774–1890* (Vancouver: UBC

Press, 1977), 146–211, esp. 165. In 1866 a European could obtain a grant of 160 acres (65 hectares), as well as the right to purchase an additional up to 480 acres (195 hectares). An Indian family, in contrast, was expected to live on just 10 acres (4 hectares), an insufficient area for their subsistence.

38　Jean Barman, *The West beyond the West: A History of British Columbia*, 3rd ed. (Toronto: University of Toronto Press, 2007), 165.

39　Paul Tennant, *Aboriginal Peoples and Politics: The Indian Land Question in British Columbia, 1849–1989* (Vancouver: UBC Press, 1990), 38.

40　J.R. Miller, *Skyscrapers Hide the Heavens: A History of Native-Newcomer Relations in Canada*, 4th ed. (Toronto: University of Toronto Press, 2018), 161.

41　Tennant, *Aboriginal Peoples*, 52.

42　Arthur J. Ray, "Treaty Eight: A British Columbian Anomaly," *BC Studies*, no. 123 (Autumn 1999): 5–58.

43　John A. Macdonald, 11 Mar. 1881, in Canada, *House of Commons Debates* (1881), vol. 2, 1347. My thanks to Hamar Foster for this information, email to me, 10 Apr. 2019.

44　Gerta Moray, *Unsettling Encounters: First Nations Imagery in the Art of Emily Carr* (Vancouver: UBC Press, 2006), 40.

45　E. Brian Titley, *A Narrow Vision: Duncan Campbell Scott and the Administration of Indian Affairs in Canada* (Vancouver: UBC Press, 1986), 150.

46　Arthur J. Ray, *I Have Lived Here since the World Began* (Toronto: Lester Publishing and Key Porter Books, 1996), 322.

47　Eric Jamieson, *The Native Voice: The Story of How Maisie Hurley and Canada's First Aboriginal Newspaper Changed a Nation* (Halfmoon Bay, BC: Caitlin Press, 2016), 45.

48　Cole Harris, *Making Native Space*, 216–17.

49　Titley, *A Narrow Vision*, 144.

50　On Arthur O'Meara, see Foster, "We Are Not O'Meara's Children," 61–84, 262–9.

51　Wickwire, *Bridge*, 54–8, 123–4.

52　Harris, *Native Space*, 259.

53　Tennant, *Aboriginal Peoples*, 99.

54　Email to me from Hamar Foster, 10 Apr. 2019.

55　Harris, *Native Space*, 248, 250.

56　Morley, *Roar*, 31.

57　Peter Kelly, quoted in ibid., 44, 54.

58　From 1914 to 1934 Coqualeetza had an excellent principal, George Raley. See Paige Raibmon, "'A new Understanding of Things Indian': George Raley's Negotiation of the Residential School Experience," *BC Studies*, no. 110 (Summer 1996): 69–96.

59　Jean Barman, *Stanley Park's Secret: The Forgotten Families of Whoi Whoi, Kanaka Ranch and Brockton Point* (Madeira Park, BC: Harbour Publishing, 2005), 119–21, 137.

60 Morley, *Roar*, 58.
61 Ibid., 60.
62 Ibid., 62, 68.
63 Susan Neylan, *The Heavens Are Changing: Nineteenth-Century Protestant Missions and Tsimshian Christianity* (Montreal and Kingston: McGill-Queen's University Press, 2003), 60, 112, 255, 257. Jan Hare and Jean Barman, *Good Intentions Gone Awry: Emma Crosby and the Methodist Mission on the Northwest Coast* (Vancouver: UBC Press 2006), 143–4, 193. Also see the sketch of Amos Ross by the Canadian historian Hamar Foster in volume 16 of the *Dictionary of Canadian Biography*, http://www .biographi.ca/en/bio/russ_amos_16F.html.
64 Neylan, *Heavens*, 60, 112, 255, 257. Hare and Barman, *Good Intentions*, 143–4, 193.
65 Morley, *Roar*, 75–6.
66 Judy Thompson, *Recording their Story: James Teit and the Tahltan* (Vancouver: Douglas & McIntyre, 2007), 14.
67 Wickwire, *Bridge*, xvi.
68 Ibid., 54.
69 J.A. Teit, "Indian Tribes of the Interior," in A. Shortt and A.G. Doherty, eds., *Canada and Its Provinces*, vol. 21, *The Pacific Province* (Edinburgh: T. & A. Constable, 1914), 283–312.
70 Wickwire, *Bridge*, 21.
71 Ibid., 175, emphasis added.
72 Wendy Wickwire, "'We Shall Drink from the Stream and So Shall You': James A. Teit and Native Resistance in British Columbia, 1908–22," *Canadian Historical Review*, 79 (1998): 200.
73 Wickwire, "Quest," 187, 277.
74 Wickwire, *Bridge*, 218.
75 Ibid., 248–9.
76 Ibid., xiv. The languages were Nlaka'pamux (Thompson), Secwépemc (Shuswap), and Syilx (Okanagan). Franz Boas, "James A. Teit," *Journal of American Folk-Lore*, 36 (1923): 102.
77 Judith J. Banks, "Comparative Biographies of Two British Columbia Anthropologists: Charles Hill-Tout and James A. Teit" (M.A. thesis, University of British Columbia, 1970), 96.
78 Speech given by Peter Kelly, 25 July 1923, at the meeting between Charles Stewart, Minister of the Interior, and the Allied Indian Tribes of BC, LAC, RG10, vol. 3820, file 59-335, pt. 1, quoted in Judy Thompson, *Recording Their Story: James Teit and the Tahlatan* (Vancouver: Douglas & McIntyre, 2007), 171.
79 Gerta Moray, *Unsettling Encounters: First Nations Imagery in the Art of Emily Carr* (Vancouver: UBC Press, 2006), 19.
80 Ibid., 47, 42.

81 Douglas Cole, "The Invented Indian/The Imagined Family," *BC Studies*, no. 125/126 (Spring/Summer 2000): 147.
82 Ibid., 148.
83 Emily Carr, quoted in Paula Blanchard, *The Life of Emily Carr* (Vancouver: Douglas & McIntyre, 1987), 30.
84 Blanchard, *Carr*, 25–6.
85 Ibid., 35.
86 Ira Dilworth, foreword in Emily Carr, *Klee Wyck* (London: Oxford University Press, 1941), viii.
87 Blanchard, *Carr*, 24, 11, 40.
88 Edythe Hembroff-Schleicher, *Emily Carr: The Untold Story* (Saanichton, BC: Hancock House, 1978), 98.
89 John Sutton Lutz, *Makuk: A New History of Aboriginal-White Relations* (Vancouver: UBC Press, 2008), 50–51.
90 Ibid., 88.
91 Ibid., 96–7.
92 Blanchard, *Carr*, 49.
93 Doris Shadbolt, *Emily Carr* (Vancouver: Douglas & McIntyre, 1990), 15.
94 Blanchard, *Carr*, 59.
95 Moray, *Unsettling Encounters*, 77.
96 Shadbolt, *Carr*, 87.
97 Carr, *Klee Wyck*, 10–11.
98 Blanchard, *Carr*, 106.
99 Moray, *Unsettling Encounters*, 33. Maria Tippett, *Emily Carr: A Biography* [1979] (Harmondsworth, Middlesex: Penguin, 1982), 81. Blanchard, *Carr*, 107–8, 149, 224–5, 240, 268.
100 Baker, *Autobiography*, 98.
101 Shadbolt, *Carr*, 89.
102 Emily Carr, *Growing Pains*, in *The Emily Carr Omnibus* (Vancouver: Douglas & McIntyre, 1993), 427.
103 Tippett, *Carr*, 75.
104 Moray, *Unsettling Encounters*, 67.
105 Ibid., 49.
106 Tippett, *Carr*, 107.
107 Ibid., 103, 154. Douglas Cole and Ira Chaikin, *An Iron Hand Upon the People: The Law Against the Potlatch on the North West Coast* (Vancouver: Douglas & McIntyre, 1990), 71–2, and many subsequent references. Halliday helped her again in 1928. See Blanchard, *Carr*, 186.
108 "Paris-trained modern artist," the phrase is Gerta Moray's, in *Unsettling Encounters*, 281.
109 Shadbolt, *Carr*, 97.

110 Moray, *Unsettling Encounters*, 42.

111 Ibid., 42.

112 Moray points out that many of the anti-missionary references in the first edition of *Klee Wyck* (1941) were deleted by the publisher in future editions, ibid., 49.

113 Ibid., 51, 294.

114 Ibid., 113.

115 Marcia Crosby, foreword in Moray, *Unsettling Encounters*, vi. Tippett, *Carr*, 105.

116 Moray, *Unsettling Encounters*, 294–5, 302, 306, 160–1, 289. Five stories in *Klee Wyck* recall Carr's friendship with William and Clara Russ. Four are based on the 1912 journey to Tanoo, Skedans, Cumshewa, and Cha-atl. "Friends" relates to the 1928 visit.

117 Tennant, *Aboriginal Peoples*, 117.

118 Carr, *Klee Wyck*, 107.

119 Kathleen Coburn, foreword to the 1954 edition of Carol Williams Pearson, *Emily as I Knew Her* [1954] (Victoria, BC: TouchWood Editions, 2016), 4. Carol Pearson had known Emily Carr in Victoria from 1920 to 1944, first meeting her when her parents moved to her Victoria neighbourhood. Carol Williams kept in touch with her childhood art teacher after her marriage to William Pearson, and remained a close friend.

120 Shadbolt, *Carr*, 105.

121 Moray, *Unsettling Encounters*, 137.

122 Blanchard, *Carr*, 137.

123 Moray, *Unsettling Encounters*, 138.

124 Emily Carr, quoted in Tibbett, *Carr*, 119.

125 Tippett, *Carr*, 118.

126 Ibid., 190. Blanchard, *Carr*, 155–6, 161.

127 Moray, *Unsettling Encounters*, 276–8, also 366–7n3.

128 Bruce Hutchison, *The Far Side of the Street* (Toronto: Macmillan, 1976), 27.

129 Shadbolt, *Carr*, 117.

130 Tennant, *Aboriginal Peoples*, 104–5.

131 Keith D. Smith, *Liberalism, Surveillance and Resistance: Indigenous Communities in Western Canada, 1877–1927* (Edmonton: AU Press, 2009), 188.

132 Forrest E. LaViolette, *The Struggle for Survival: Indian Cultures and the Protestant Ethic in British Columbia* (Toronto: University of Toronto Press, 1961), 181.

133 Hamar Foster, "Letting Go the Bone: The Idea of Indian Title in British Columbia, 1849–1927," in Foster and McLaren, *Essays in the History of Canadian Law*, vol. 6, 30.

134 Tennant, *Aboriginal Peoples*, 74.

135 Moray, *Unsettling Encounters*, 136.

136 Pierre Duchaussois, *Aux Glaces Polaires: Indiens et Esquimaux* (Lyon: Oeuvre Apostolique de Marie Immaculée, 1921), 22, cited in Achiel Peelman, *Le Christ est amérindien* (Ottawa: Novalis, 1992), 21.

137 Marius Barbeau, "Our Indians – Their Disappearance," *Queen's Quarterly*, 38 (1931): 707.

138 Barnett Richling has written a fine biography of him, *In Twilight and in Dawn: A Biography of Diamond Jenness* (Montreal and Kingston: McGill-Queen's University Press, 2012).

139 Diamond Jenness, *The Indians of Canada*, [1932] 6th ed. (Ottawa: National Museum of Canada, 1967), 264. In the English language Canadian media, William Arthur Deacon, the literary editor of the Toronto *Mail and Empire* (and of the *Globe and Mail* after 1936) endorsed this argument. He wrote (page 133) in his book, *My Vision of Canada* (Toronto: Graphic Press, 1933): "Only one in a hundred of our people claim to be an Indian; and an indefinable proportion of them are already of mixed parentage."

140 Jean Barman, *The West Beyond the West: A History of British Columbia*, 3rd ed. (Vancouver: UBC Press, 2007), 167.

141 T.R.L. MacInnes, "The History and Policies of Indian Administration in Canada," in C.T. Loram and T.F. McIlwraith, eds., *The North American Indian Today: University of Toronto, September 4–16, 1939* (Toronto: University of Toronto Press, 1943), 160.

142 Moray, *Unsettling Encounters*, 333.

143 Ibid., 332–3.

144 Emily Carr, quoted in Tippett, *Carr*, 147.

145 Laurence Nowry, *Man of Mana: Marius Barbeau* (Toronto: NC Press, 1995), 281.

146 Moray, *Unsettling Encounters*, 288.

147 Ibid., 294

148 Marius Barbeau, "The Native Races of Canada," *Royal Society of Canada Proceedings and Transactions*, 3rd series, section 2, vol. 21 (1927), 42–3.

149 Leslie Dawn, *National Visions, National Blindness: Canadian Art and Identities in the 1920s* (Vancouver: UBC Press, 2006), 174.

150 Tibbett, *Carr*, 158.

151 *Department of Indian Affairs Annual Report*, 1912, 396; ibid., 1911, 385; cited in Lutz, *Makuk*, 104, 233.

152 Diamond Jenness, "Canada's Indians Yesterday. What of Today?" *Canadian Journal of Economics and Political Science*, 20 (1954): 97. This paper was presented at the annual meeting of the Canadian Political Science Association in London, Ont., 4 June 1953.

153 Interview with Alan Fry, Whitehorse, Yukon, 27 July 2014. "Sorry for inconvenience, but it's war," *Province* (Vancouver), 14 Oct. 1960, 19.

154 Alan Fry, *How a People Die*, with as introduction and afterword by the author (Madeira Park, BC: Harbour Publishing, 1994; the original edition of the novel was published in 1970 in Toronto by Doubleday), 205.

155 Moray, *Unsettling Encounters*, 310.

156 Shadbolt, *Carr*, 111.

157 Tippett, *Carr*, 188.

158 Emily Carr, quoted in ibid., 229.

159 George Clutesi, quoted in Moray, *Unsettling Encounters*, 343.

160 Maria Tippett, "Emily Carr," *Dictionary of Canadian Biography*, vol. 17, *1941–1950*, at http://www.biographi.ca/en/bio/carr_emily_17E.html.

161 Moray, *Unsettling Encounters*, 344.

162 R. Scott Sheffield, *The Red Man's on the Warpath: The Image of the "Indian" and the Second World War* (Vancouver: UBC Press, 2004), 178.

163 Bruce Hutchison, *The Unknown Country: Canada and Her People* (Toronto: Longmans, Green, 1943; first published in 1942 in New York City by Coward-McCann Inc).

164 Ibid.

165 J.I. Little, *Fashioning the Canadian Landscape: Essays on Travel Writing, Tourism, and National Identity in the Pre-Automobile Era* (Toronto: University of Toronto Press, 2018), 308.

166 Hutchison, *Unknown Country*, 369–73; Little, *Fashioning*, 313.

167 Bruce Hutchison, *Fraser* (Toronto: Clarke, Irwin, 1950).

168 Hutchison, *Far Side*, 316.

169 Ibid., 127, 136–9. Hutchison, *Fraser*, 229–43.

170 Smith, *Liberalism, Surveillance, and Resistance*, 137. He cites Robert Cail, *Land, Man, and the Law: The Disposal of Crown Lands in British Columbia, 1871–1913* (Vancouver: UBC Press, 1974), 14.

171 Joanne Drake-Terry, *The Same as Yesterday: The Lillooet Chronicle the Theft of Their Land and Resources* (Lillooet, BC: Lillooet Tribal Council, 1989), 103.

172 Tennant, *Aboriginal Peoples*, 73.

173 Jamieson, *Maisie Hurley*, 35.

174 Hawthorn et al., *Indians*, 475–6.

175 Cole and Chaikin, *Iron Hand*, 166. Tennant, *Aboriginal Peoples*, 117.

176 Rolf Knight, *Indians at Work: An Informal History of Native Labour in British Columbia 1858–1930* (Vancouver: New Star Books, 1996), 323.

177 Jamieson, *Maisie Hurley*, 49.

178 Ibid., 23.

179 Ibid., 15.

180 Ibid., 27.

181 Ibid., 31–2.

182 Ibid., 25.

183 Maisie Armytage-Moore, publisher of the *Native Voice*, to Hugh Dempsey, dated Vancouver, 7 Feb. 1950; letter in the possession of Hugh Dempsey.

184 "Meet the Editor," *Native Voice*, Dec. 1946.

185 "Our Editor," *Native Voice*, Feb. 1948.

186 Lyn Harrington, "Canadian Woman Editor Guides 'Native Voice' of North American Indian," *Christian Science Monitor*, 25 Mar. 1949. Copy in the University of Toronto, Victoria University Library (VUL), Kathleen Coburn Collection, Box 7, file 2.

187 "Discrimination Against Indians Termed Disgrace," *Native Voice*, Aug. 1949. "Health 'Services' in Lillooet," *Native Voice*, May 1951.

188 Email to me from Hamar Foster, 20 Apr. 2019.

189 Maisie Hurley, "We Don't Accept Treaties as Mere 'Scraps of Paper,'" *Native Voice*, Dec. 1960.

190 Jamieson, *Maisie Hurley*, 222.

191 For background on George Mortimore, see Ron Csilag, "Obituaries. George Mortimore Journalist, 94: Writer was early proponent of native rights. His searing appraisal of aboriginal life in B.C. for Victoria's Daily Colonist won a National Newspaper Award in 1958," *Globe and Mail*, 29 Aug. 2014.

192 George Clutesi, quoted in G.E. Mortimore in the *Daily Colonist*, "Indian Artist Makes Eloquent Plea," *Native Voice*, Dec. 1949, 9. Clutesi outlines in detail the problem of educating First Nations children without an Indigenous cultural base in his introduction to his book, *Son of Raven, Son of Deer* (Sidney, BC: Gray's, 1967), 9–14.

193 Jamieson, *Maisie Hurley*, 151.

194 "The Conference on Native Indian Affairs Successful," *Native Voice*, Apr. 1948, 2–4.

195 George Clutesi, quoted in "The Schools and the Church," *Native Voice*, Apr. 1948, 8. He wanted day schools to be encouraged, but added this comment as well: ""But do not discard the present residential schools. The underprivileged and neglected children have need of them. There are always underprivileged, and some of our people do not look after their children. The residential schools are needed for these children."

196 "The Stone Wall," *Native Voice*, Apr. 1948. In the original article "and only by the logger" is in boldface.

197 "There is Nothing ... There is One," *Native Voice*, Nov. 1947.

198 "Enfranchisement. Dan C. Hill. Moravians of the Thames. Band Number 130," LAC, RG10, vol. 7222, file 8015-25.

199 "Did You Know ... About a Man Called 'Wapi-gok-hos' or Big White Owl," *Tekawennake*, 19 Oct. 1977. This short article based on a text by Jasper Hill, "Some Notes and Sketches on Big White Owl," is included in the collection of Big White Owl's writings collected by Karen Logan, entitled "My People: The Delaware Indians." I thank Darryl Stonefish for bringing this article to my attention.

200 Rev. E.E.M. Joblin, "Big White Owl," *Native Voice*, Nov. 1947.

201 "Big White Owl," *Native Voice*, Aug. 1956, 1, and in the same issue the article, "Tribute to Big White Owl, Our Great Eastern Editor." "Big White Owl Has Done Much for "Voice,'" *Native Voice*, Oct. 1950.

202 The *Native Voice* contains many of Big White Owl's contributions see, e.g., "The Legend of the White Water Lily," Feb. 1947; "A Brief Sketch of Early Native Life," Sept. 1947; "The Creation Myth of the Lenni Lenape," Jan.–Feb. 1949; "In Honour of Brig.-General Tecumseh," Apr. 1954; "A Statue for Tecumseh," Mar. 1960.

203 Anne Merrill, "Indian Life in Canada Presented by New Club," reprinted from the Toronto *Globe and Mail* in *Native Voice*, Feb. 1952. My Ojibwe language teacher, Fred Wheatley, became the program chair in 1954, *Native Voice*, Apr. 1954. Big White Owl, "The Toronto Indian Club of Canada," *Native Voice*, Nov. 1952.

204 Big White Owl, "Don't Integrate the North American Indian," *Native Voice*, Sept. 1962; also reprinted in the issues of Sept. 1964 and Aug. 1966.

205 Ibid.

206 Jasper Hill (Big White Owl) knew about the attempted physical destruction of a people. His Delaware ancestors were those who had settled as refugees at Moraviantown after the American Revolution. The Americans in 1782 had massacred with mallets and hatchets and then scalped some 90 defenceless Christian Delawares and Mahican Indians, including women and children, at the Moravian mission of Gnadenhutten ("tents of grace") in Ohio. See C.A. Weslager, *The Delaware Indian: A History* (New Brunswick, NJ: Rutgers University Press, 1972), 316–17.

207 Joan Harper, *He Moved a Mountain: The Life of Frank Calder and the Nisga'a Land Claims Accord* (Vancouver: Ronsdale, 2013), 22–3, 32.

208 "Coqualeetza Residential School Reunion," *Chilliwack Progress*, 25 Oct. 1972. "Guy Williams Only Indian Senator," *Saskatchewan Indian*, May 1972, 12.

209 Guy E. Williams, foreword in Alan Morley, *Roar of the Breakers: A Biography of Peter Kelly* (Toronto: Ryerson Press, 1966), vi.

210 Carolyn Swayze, *Hard Choices: A Life of Tom Berger* (Vancouver: Douglas & McIntyre, 1987), 26–7.

211 Ibid., 67. In his book, *A Long and Terrible Shadow* (Vancouver: Douglas & McIntye 1981), Thomas Berger writes: "When I had gone to law school in the 1950s the idea of aboriginal rights had never been discussed. Law schools paid no attention to the issue of Indian land or Indian rights [...] No one studied and no one thought about it" (66).

212 Thomas R. Berger, *One Man's Justice: A Life in the Law* (Vancouver: Douglas & McIntyre, 2003), 87, original emphasis.

213 The quote is reprinted in Jamieson, *Maisie Hurley*, 259.

9. Alberta Perspectives

1 For references to Long Lance in Vancouver, see "Freelancing," in Donald B. Smith, *Long Lance: The True Story of an Impostor* (Toronto: Macmillan 1982), 78–89; and "Long Lance, Plains Indian," in *Chief Buffalo Child Long Lance: The Glorious Impostor* (Red Deer, Alta.: Red Deer Press, 1999), 123–35.

2 Summarized by the *Vancouver Sun* in its editor's introduction to Chief Buffalo Child Long Lance, "Vanishing type of Indian is probable," *Vancouver Sun*, 7 May 1922.

3 Francis Paul Prucha, s.j., *American Indian Policy in Crisis: Christian Reformers and the Indian, 1865–1900* (Norman: University of Oklahoma Press, 1976), 276, quoted in Paula Richardson Fleming and Judith Luskey, *The North American Indians in Early Photographs* (New York: Barnes & Noble Books, 1992), 74.

4 Editor's introduction to Long Lance.

5 Editorial, "Sound the War Cry," *Native Voice*, Aug. 1947.

6 Chief Buffalo Child Long Lance, "Kootenays – The mystic tribe of North America," *Vancouver Sun*, 25 June 1922.

7 Walter N. Sage, ed., "Sitting Bull's Own Narrative of the Custer Fight," *Canadian Historical Review*, 16 (1935): 170.

8 "Chief Long Lance tells of Indian history," *Winnipeg Tribune*, 16 Jan. 1923. I thank Ernie Nix for this reference.

9 "How Canada's last frontier outlaw died," *MacLean's*, 1 Jan. 1924, 19–20, 42, 44; "Indian's stand against Mounted Police," *Family Herald and Weekly Star*, 2 Jan. 1924; "When Almighty Voice held the Mounties at bay," *Winnipeg Tribune*, 5 Jan. 1924. The Canadian historian Bill Waiser expertly separates the fact from the fiction in Long Lance's Almighty Voice accounts in his recently published *Almighty Voice: Resistance and Reconciliation* (Markham, Ont.: Fifth House, 2020), 159–71.

10 Chief Buffalo Child Long Lance, "When the Indians owned Manitoba," *Winnipeg Tribune*, 3 Mar. 1923. For background on St Peter's, see Sarah Carter, "St Peter's and the Interpretation of the Agriculture of Manitoba's Aboriginal People," *Manitoba History*, no. 18 (Autumn 1989): 46–52; Richard C. Daniel, "The St Peter's Reserve Claims," in *A History of Native Claims Processes in Canada 1867–1979* (Ottawa: Research Branch, Department of Indian and Northern Affairs, 1980), 105–22.

11 White Owl, quoted in Chief Buffalo Child Long Lance, "The Indian side," *Winnipeg Tribune*, 23 June 1923.

12 Laura Stone, "Saskatchewan First Nation wins $4.5-million from Ottawa: A Saskatchewan group had been awarded treaty payments over a century in the making," *Globe and Mail*, 28 Dec. 2016.

13 Chief Long Lance, "How do the Indians regard the march of civilisation?" *Calgary Herald*, 13 Oct. 1923. Long Lance writes, "On the last afternoon of the recent Indian sports at Banff, I was sitting with Chief White Head outside his tepee."

14 Patricia Parker, *The Feather and the Drum: The History of Banff Indian Days 1889–1978* (Calgary: Consolidated Communications, 1990), 132.

15 Jonathan Clapperton, "Naturalizing Race Relations: Conservation, Colonialism, and Spectacle at the Banff Indian Days," *Canadian Historical Review*, 94 (2013): 352.

16 George McLean, "Life on the Reserve," in section entitled "Indian Narratives Recorded in 1926," in Marius Barbeau, *Indian Days on the Western Prairies*, Bulletin 163, Anthropologial Series 46 (Ottawa: National Museum of Canada, 1960), 213. The date listed is actually incorrect as Barbeau's field notes with the Stoney Nakoda indicate he visited them in September 1923, and not in 1926. My thanks for this correction to Benoît Thériault, Collections Information Specialist–Textual Archives, Canadian Museum of History, Gatineau, Que., for this information. Marius Barbeau, "Stoney Indians, Morley Reserve Alberta, Sept.–Oct. 1923, Books 1–3, Canadian Museum of History Archives, Gatineau, Que., Marius Barbeau Fonds, Box (temp.) 190, files1–3.

17 Marius Barbeau, *Indian Days in the Canadian Rockies* (Toronto: Macmillan, 1923), 10.

18 Hector Crawler, quoted in Chief Buffalo Child Long Lance, "How do the Indians."

19 In Long Lance's article on the Kootenays, *Vancouver Sun*, 25 June 1922, he cites John Maclean's *Canadian Savage Folk: The Native Tribes of Canada* (Toronto: William Briggs, 1896).

20 Maclean, *Canadian Savage Folk*, 29.

21 There are two references to George McLean, one in the *Christian Guardian*, 11 Jan. 1888 (letter from Mr Youmans, principal of McDougall Orphanage) and the other in the *Missionary Outlook*, Apr. 1888 (letter from Mrs Youmans). Also there is a letter from George G. McLean, dated 31 Oct. 1888, McDougall Orphanage, in *Our Forest Children*, 3/4 (July 1889): 31.

22 Grant MacEwan provides a biographical portrait of Walking Buffalo in *Tatanga Mani: Walking Buffalo of the Stonies* (Edmonton: Hurtig, 1969).

23 Typescript of Grant MacEwan's interview with Walking Buffalo, 3 Feb. 1962, University of Calgary Archives, Grant MacEwan Fonds, Acc. 74/74.7, Box 23/02.

24 John McLean, *The Hero of the Saskatchewan: Life among the Ojibway and Cree Indians in Canada*, reprinted from the *Barrie Examiner* (Barrie, Ont.: Barrie

Examiner Printing and Publishing House, 1891), 48. The date of Rev. John Maclean's visit to Morley in the spring of 1884 is confirmed in the article "Morley," *Christian Guardian*, 21 May 1884.

25 MacEwan, *Tatanga Mani*, 84–5.

26 Ibid., 140.

27 Wilfrid Eggleston, "Fastened sleds under canoe in mushing through slush," *Toronto Star Weekly*, 4 May 1929.

28 Smith, *Long Lance*, 137, 141.

29 Paul Radin, "An Indian's Own Story: *Long Lance* by Chief Buffalo Child Long Lance," *New York Herald Tribune*, 14 Oct. 1928.

30 The *New Statesman* is quoted on the back cover of the British paperback edition of *Long Lance* (London: Abacus, 1976).

31 Wilfrid Eggleston, *While I Still Remember: A Personal Record* (Toronto: Ryerson Press, 1968). Wilfred Eggleston, "The Old Homestead: Romance and Reality," in Howard Palmer, ed., *The Settlement of the West* (Calgary: Comprint for the University of Calgary, 1977), 114–29.

32 Wilfrid Eggleston, *Literary Friends* (Ottawa: Borealis Press, 1980), 31.

33 Eggleston, "Fastened sleds."

34 Katherine Govier, *The Three Sisters Bar and Hotel – A Novel* (Toronto: HarperCollins, 2016), 474.

35 Hugh A. Dempsey, "Sylvester Long, Buffalo Child Long Lance," in Margot Liberty, ed., *American Indian Intellectuals* (St Paul, Minn.: West Publishing, 1978), 202.

36 John Laurie, "Dan Wildman Jr, Civil Servant, in 'Stories of Long Ago – Part One,'" Glenbow Archives, John Laurie Fonds.

37 John Laurie, "The Indian Association of Alberta," Glenbow Archives, M656, Completed manuscripts and copies, file 19, 1. Ken Liddell, "Indians helping their own cause," *Calgary Herald*, 27 Feb. 1953.

38 Harry Sanders, "Chart: Population Growth in Calgary, 1891–1991," in *Centennial City: Calgary 1894–1994* (Calgary: University of Calgary Press, 1994), 73.

39 MacEwan, *Tatanga Mani*, 170–1.

40 The question of the Stoneys and the Horseshoe Falls and Kananaskis dam and hydroelectric power plant sites is well covered in Christopher Armstrong and H.V. Nelles, *Wilderness and Waterpower: How Banff National Park Became a Hydroelectric Storage Reservoir* (Calgary: University of Calgary Press, 2013), 15–23, 39–50. Their older essay is still valuable, see Christopher Armstrong and H.V. Nelles, "Competition vs. Convenience: Federal Administration of Bow River Waterpowers, 1906–13," in Henry C. Klassen, ed., *The Canadian West: Social Change and Economic Development* (Calgary: Comprint for the University of Calgary, 1977), 163–80.

41 Laurie, "Indian Association," 2. This must have been in the summer of 1927, as the cairn was unveiled in mid-July, *Crag and Canyon* (Banff), 15 July 1927. I thank Courtney Mason for this reference,

42 "Edgar John Staley," *British Columbia Conference Minutes, 1970*, United Church of Canada Archives, Toronto.

43 I am most grateful to Mrs J.M. Dubauskas, secretary to the Board for assembling his information for me, attached to her letter to me of 8 Aug. 1985. Jan Williams, assistant secretary also helped with this request.

44 Dean H.T. Coutts, "Presentation of John Lee Laurie," *New Trail*, 14/3 (Nov.–Dec. 1956–Jan. 1957): 6.

45 Mrs Marjorie Bond, "Biography of John Laurie. Dictated by him, December, 1958," enclosed in Memorandum from Hugh A. Dempsey to Mr E.L. Harvie, 4 June 1959, Glenbow Archives, John Laurie Fonds.

46 Letters to me from Marion Laurie Corman, 14 Aug. and 11 Oct. 1985, 7 Apr. 1986, 5 Dec. 1986, 9 Oct. 1987, now in Glenbow Archives, John Laurie Fonds. A copy is in my file, Marion Laurie Corman, 121.05, Smith fonds. Please check the Smith fonds, files 120.04 to 122.17 for additional John Laurie items.

47 Laurie Meijer Drees, *The Indian Association of Alberta: A History of Political Action* (Vancouver: UBC Press, 2002), 45–6.

48 Ibid., 46.

49 I thank Roy Wilcox for his genealogical assistance in researching the life of Andrew Bruce Laurie (1867–1950), John Laurie's father, in Feb 2018.

50 Letter from Marion Laurie Corman, 14 Aug. 1985.

51 Ibid.

52 Charles W. Wilson, principal, Galt Collegiate Institute, 2 Dec. 1985, now in Glenbow Archives, John Laurie Fonds.

53 Bishop Strachan, cited in Martin L. Friedland, *The University of Toronto: A History*, 2nd ed. (Toronto: University of Toronto Press, 2013), 277.

54 Letter to me from Argue Martin, dated Hamilton, 24 Oct. 1985, now in Glenbow Archives, John Laurie Fonds.

55 Royal Air Force Certificate of Service of John Lee Laurie, Canadian official Canadian service no. 272012, now in Glenbow Archives, John Laurie Fonds. Photostat copy kindly sent to me by Marion Laurie Corman.

56 Friedland, *University of Toronto*, 278.

57 Gloria Ann Dingwall, *100: A Western Portrait* (Calgary: Author, 2003), 8.

58 Ibid., 14.

59 My telephone interview with Douglas Harkness, 16 Jan. 1986; also the *Crescent Bugle* (1939), 10, 69, and (1940), 10, 74, 118. I thank Cynthia Downe for showing me these school yearbooks.

60 My interview with Aylmer Liesmer, Calgary, 20 Dec. 1985.

61 "Funeral Slated Tuesday for Stoney Band Worker," *Calgary Herald*, 23 Mar. 1970.

62 "Blood Indian Attends Varsity," *Lethbridge Herald*, 29 Sept. 1947.

63 Hugh A. Dempsey, *Tailfeathers: Indian Artist* (Calgary: Glenbow-Alberta Institute, 1970), 14.

64 My interview with Bill McLean, Morley, 28 July 2009.

65 My interview with Gordon Crowchild, Tsuu T'ina Arena, 15 Jan. 1986. Donald B. Smith, "John Laurie: A Good Samaritan," in Max Foran and Sheilagh S. Jameson, eds., *Citymakers: Calgarians After the Frontier* (Calgary: Historical Society of Alberta, Chinook Country Chapter, 1987), 267.

66 "Copy of Minutes, Council Meeting of the Stoney Council Members," 25 Nov. 1947. Enos Hunter, cited in *The Final Report of the Truth and Reconciliation Commission of Canada*, vol. 1, *Canada's Residential Schools: The History, Part 2, 1939 to 2000* (Montreal and Kingston; McGill-Queen's University Press for the Truth and Reconciliation Commission of Canada, 2015), 37.

67 John Laurie, "Chief Enos Hunter, in 'Stories of Long Ago – Part Two,'" Glenbow Archives, John Laurie Fonds. A very short news item in *Crag and Canyon*, 23 July 1921, on p. 1, confirms the outstanding integrity of Enos Hunter. The story, "Munificent Reward," reads: "Enos Hunter, an Indian from the Morley reserve on his way to Banff with a small party to cut teepee poles for Indian day, found a wallet beside the trail. The wallet contained $300.00 and, shortly after picking it up, Enos met a party evidently searching for something. Inquiring if anything had been lost and receiving a descriptive answer, the Indian handed over the money receiving the sum of $1.00 as a reward for his honesty. A contrast between the actions of Red and White men, of which the latter should be ashamed." I thank Courtney Mason for bringing this quote to my attention.

68 Chief John Snow, *These Mountains Are Our Sacred Places* (Toronto: Samuel Stevens, 1977), 92.

69 Ibid.

70 Ruth Gorman, *Behind the Man: John Laurie, Ruth Gorman, and the Indian Vote in Canada*, edited with an introduction by Frits Pannekoek (Calgary: University of Calgary Press, 2007), 54.

71 John Laurie, "Preface to the Sun Dance Legend," in "The Stonies, Rites, Ceremonial and Early Religious Beliefs," Glenbow Archives, John Laurie Fonds.

72 Stan Cuthand, "The Native People of the Prairie Provinces in the 1920's and 1930's," in Ian A.L. Getty and Donald B. Smith, eds., *One Century Later: Western Canadian Reserve Indians Since Treaty 7* (Vancouver: UBC Press, 1978), 41.

73 Meijer Drees, *Association*, xviii, 66.

74 J.L. Laurie, "Indians Consulted for the First Time Regarding Federal Indian Legislation," *The Crescent Clipper, Edited and printed by the students of Crescent Heights High School*, 1/2 (27 Nov. 1953). I thank Ryan Baker and Iris Sadownik for bringing this important article to my attention.

75 Ibid., 70.

76 Laurie, "Indian Association," 94. I thank Jeff Langlois for bringing this quote to my attention.

77 John Laurie, "We Need Bread," *Canadian Cattlemen*, (Apr. 1950): 34.

78 Meijer Drees, *Association*, 44.

79 Laurie Meijer Drees, personal communication with Gordon Crowchild, Sept. 1996, cited in ibid., 52. For background information on Gordon Crowchild, see Dianne Meili, "Chief Gordon Crowchild: Straight-talking Chief Remembered," *Windspeaker*, (June 2015): 22.

80 Leslie, "Development," 101.

81 Hugh Shewell, *"Enough to Keep Them Alive": Indian Welfare in Canada, 1873–1965* (Toronto: University of Toronto Press, 2004), 153.

82 Meijer Drees, *Association*, 152.

83 Snow, *These Mountains*, 90–103.

84 John Laurie, quoted in Fred Kennedy, "City teacher adopted by Indians in tribute to years of guidance," *Calgary Herald*, 2 Feb. 1948.

85 Meijer Drees, *Association*, 43.

86 Laurie, "Indian Association," 45.

87 Meijer Drees, *Association*, 48.

88 Hugh A. Dempsey, *Always an Adventure* (Calgary: University of Calgary Press, 2011), 219.

89 Hugh A. Dempsey, *Gentle Persuader: A Biography of James Dempsey, Indian Senator* (Saskatoon: Western Producer Prairie Books, 1986), 121.

90 Meijer Drees, *Association*, 86. I thank Jeff Langlois for this point.

91 Dempsey, *Gentle Persuader*, 121.

92 The case, *R. v. Wesley*, was decided in the Alberta Court of Appeal in 1932. See Douglas Sanders, "The Queen's Promises," in Louis A. Knafla, ed., *Law and Justice in a New Land: Essays in Western Canadian Legal History* (Toronto: Carswell, 1986), 106.

93 Meijer Drees, *Association*, 132–3.

94 Ibid., 127–8.

95 Ibid., 58.

96 Ibid.

97 Leslie, "Development," 181.

98 Ibid., 176, 184.

99 Diamond Jenness, 1947, included in Keith D. Smith, ed., *Strange Visitors: Documents in Indigenous-Settler Relations in Canada from 1876*

(Toronto: University of Toronto Press, 2014), 233–6. Also see Barnett Richling, *In Twilight and in Dawn: A Biography of Diamond Jenness* (Montreal and Kingston: McGill-Queen's University Press, 2012), 290–3.

100 Diamond Jenness, 25 Mar. 1947, quoted in Leslie, "Development," 134.

101 Richling, *In Twilight*, 301.

102 Leslie, "Development," 134.

103 Alan C. Cairns, *Citizens Plus: Aboriginal Peoples and the Canadian State* (Vancouver: UBC Press, 2000), 161, 54–6.

104 Leslie, "Development," 112, 179.

105 Meijer Drees, *Association*, 148.

106 "Dr John L. Laurie dies at his home," *Calgary Herald*, 8 Apr. 1959.

107 The manuscripts of both the dictionary and the grammar are held with the John Laurie Papers, Glenbow Archives, old reference D970.3.L 378a.

108 Hugh Dempsey, "David Crowchild," in Susie Sparks, ed., *Calgary: A Living Heritage* (Calgary: Junior League of Calgary, 1984), 49.

109 Walking Buffalo, quoted in Elizabeth Motherwell, "Indians mourn beloved friend," *Calgary Albertan*, 10 Apr. 1959.

110 Ibid.

111 The latest title is *Napi: The Trickster* (Victoria: Heritage House, 2018).

112 Dempsey, *Always an Adventure*, vi.

113 Ibid., 3.

114 Ibid., 7, vi, 1, 11–13, 16.

115 Ibid., 74.

116 Dempsey, *Gentle Persuader*, 142.

117 Hugh Dempsey, cited in *"The Way of the Indian,"* an edited transcript of 13 half-hour documentary programs broadcast on CBC Radio in the summer and fall of 1961 (Toronto: CBC Publications, 1963), 5.

118 Hugh A. Dempsey, *The Golden Age of the Canadian Cowboy* (Saskatoon: Fifth House, 1995), acknowledgments.

119 Dempsey, *Always an Adventure*, 80–1. "W. Everard Edmonds (Rev.)," Obituary, *Alberta Historical Review*, 14/4 (1966): 29.

120 "About the Cover," *Alberta Historical Review*, 3/1 (Winter 1955): 42.

121 Patricia Ainslie, *A Lifelong Journey: The Art and Teaching of H.G. Glyde*, with an introduction by Helen Collinson (Calgary: Glenbow Museum, 1987), 72. See also Nancy Townshend, "H.G. Glyde (1906–1998)," in her *A History of Art in Alberta, 1905–1970* (Calgary: Bayeux Arts, 2005), 244–6.

122 Ainslie, *Lifelong Journey*, 54.

123 Walter H. Johns, *A History of the University of Alberta, 1908–1969* (Edmonton: University of Alberta Press, 1981), 231. A photo of the "main reading-room of Rutherford Library" provides a glimpse of the mural, it appears between pp. 306 and 307.

124 H.G. Glyde, "Rutherford Library Mural, May 15th 1951," Glenbow Archives, H.G. Glyde Fonds, M-8900-101, 1.

125 Ibid., 2.

126 "The Mural. Reference Reading Room, Rutherford Library," dated Edmonton, 26 Apr. 1955, ibid., M-8900-160, 1 p.

127 James G. MacGregor, *A History of Alberta* (Edmonton: Hurtig, 1972).

128 Ibid., 12.

129 Dempsey, *Always an Adventure*, 97.

130 Ibid., 382.

131 Ibid., 97.

132 Hugh A. Dempsey, *The Great Blackfoot Treaties* (Victoria, BC: Heritage House, 2015), 175.

133 Dempsey, *Always an Adventure*, 134.

134 Ibid., 290.

135 J.V. Van Tighem, Superintendent of Schools, Calgary Roman Catholic Separate School District, to Hugh A. Dempsey, 5 June 1974, Glenbow Archives, Hugh Dempsey Papers, M8452, Box 3, Correspondence, 1972–76.

136 George Melynk, *The Literary History of Alberta,* vol. 2 (Edmonton: University of Alberta Press, 1999), 113 and 243n13.

137 Dempsey, *Always an Adventure*, 236.

138 F. Laurie Barron, *Walking in Indian Moccassins: The Native Policies of Tommy Douglas and the CCF* (Vancouver: UBC Press, 1997), 10.

139 D. Bruce Sealey and Antoine S. Lussier, *The Métis: Canada's Forgotten People* (Winnipeg: Manitoba Metis Federation Press, 1975), 186.

140 Larry Krotz, in *Photographs by John Paskievish: Urban Indians, the Strangers in Canada's Cities* (Edmonton: Hurtig, 1980), focuses on these three communities.

141 Vol. 1 is dated Oct. l966 and vol. 2, Oct. l967; the Queen's Printer published both volumes.

142 Alan C. Cairns, "Aboriginal Research in Troubled Times," in Myra Rutherdale, Kerry Abel, and P. Whitney Lackenbauer, eds., *Roots of Entanglement: Essays in the History of Native-Newcomer Relations* (Toronto: University of Toronto Press, 2017), 430–1n38.

143 Michael Cassidy, "Treaties and Aboriginal-Government Relations, 1945–2000," in David R. New house, Cora J. Voyageur, and Dan Beavon, eds. *Hidden in Plain Sight: Contibutions of Aboriginal Peoples to Canadian Identity and Culture,* vol. 1 (Toronto: University of Toronto Press, 2005), 53.

144 Cairns, *Citizens Plus*, 52, 54.

145 Leslie, "Development," 269–74.

146 Sally M. Weaver, *Making Canadian Indian Policy: The Hidden Agenda 1968–1970* (Toronto: University of Toronto Press, 1981), 12.

147 Joan Sangster, "Presidential Address. Confronting Our Colonial Past: Reassessing Political Alliances over Canada's Twentieth Century," *Journal of the Canadian Historical Association*, n.s., 28/1 (2017): 20.

148 Weaver, *Making*, 18.

149 Sangster, "Address," 17.

150 James Gray, *Troublemaker! A Personal History* (Halifax, NS: Goodread Biographies, 1983; first published in 1978 in Toronto by Macmillan), 214.

151 Fraser, *Calgary*, 118.

152 Max Foran, *Calgary: An Illustrated History* (Toronto: James Lorimer, 1978), 162. David H. Breen provides a valuable short overview of Calgary's first century in *Calgary: Police Post to Oil Capital*, Canada's Visual History, vol. 47 (Ottawa: National Museum of Man and National Film Board of Canada, 1981), 1–20.

153 MacEwan, *Tatanga Mani*, 49.

154 Hugh A. Dempsey, *Calgary: Spirit of the West* (Saskatoon: Fifth House, 1994), 132.

155 Sanders, "Palliser," 241.

156 John McDougall, *Opening the Great West* [1903], edited by Hugh A. Dempsey, with an introduction by J. Ernest Nix (Calgary: Glenbow-Alberta Institute, 1970).

157 Martin O'Connell, Presidential Address, Indian-Eskimo Association of Canada, Annual Meeting, Palliser Hotel, Calgary, "Talk with Us by the Fires of the Days to Come," 1 Oct. 1967. Copy included in John Leslie Research Papers, PA 1/24-2, held by Public History Inc, Ottawa. I thank Stuart L. Manson for assistance in making John Leslie's notes available to me.

158 Email to me from John Leslie, 17 May 2017.

159 Iris Naish Fleming, "The informal Mr Cardinal," *Globe and Mail*, 3 Sept. 1973.

160 Biographical details of Harold Cardinal appear in a sketch of the author on the back cover of *The Unjust Society* (Edmonton: Hurtig, 1969).

161 Harold Cardinal, "Research Paper of Canadian Indian Youth Council to Company of Young Canadians. In completion of conditions described in contract dated May 1, 1967." Copy included in John Leslie Research Papers, file Indian Associations, Canadian Indian Youth Council 1/24-2-31, vol. 2, 1967–68, held by Public History Inc, Ottawa.

162 Harold Cardinal, "Indian Nations and Constitutional Change," in J. Anthony Long and Menno Boldt in association with Leroy Little Bear, eds., *Governments in Conflict? Provinces and Indian Nations in Canada* (Toronto: University of Toronto Press, 1988), 84.

163 James Maybie, "Indians described as second-class," *Albertan*, 2 Oct. 1967, 11. See also "Annual Meeting and Conference 1967 Indian-Eskimo Association of Canada and Alberta Division, September 30th, October

1st, 1967, Palliser Hotel, Calgary, Alberta," in the University of Manitoba, Archives and Special Collections, Walter Rudnicki Fonds, A2010-038-1, Box 124, folder 5, 14.

164 George Manuel and Michael Posluns, *The Fourth World: An Indian Reality* (Don Mills, Ont.: Collier Macmillan, 1974), xvi.

165 Email to me from John Leslie, 17 May 2017. He died several months later. On John Leslie, see Betsey Baldwin, "John F. Leslie," Canadian Historical Association, *Bulletin*, 43/3 (2017): 23.

166 John Webster Grant, *Moon of Wintertime: Missionaries and the Indians of Canada in Encounter since 1534* (Toronto: University of Toronto Press, 1984), 202. I thank Nathalie Kermoal for bringing this quote to my attention.

Epilogue

1 John F. Leslie, "Assimilation, Integration or Termination? The Development of Canadian Indian Policy, 1943–1963" (Ph.D. dissertation, Department of History, Carleton University, 1999), 7–8.

2 J.R. Miller, *Lethal Legacy: Current Native Controversies in Canada* (Toronto: McClelland and Stewart, 2004), 246.

3 Alan C. Cairns, *Citizens Plus: Aboriginal Peoples and the Canadian State* (Vancouver: UBC Press, 2000), 77.

4 Sally M. Weaver, *Making Canadian Indian Policy: The Hidden Agenda 1968–1970* (Toronto: University of Toronto Press, 1981), 10. This one volume is essential reading for an understanding of the development of and the response to the "White Paper."

5 Ibid., 173.

6 Ibid., 171.

7 National Indian Brotherhood, quoted in Weaver, *Making*, 174.

8 Rolf Knight, *Indians at Work: An Informal History of Native Labour in British Columbia, 1848–1930* (Vancouver: New Star Books, 1996), 365n11.

9 Laurie Meijer Drees, *The Indian Association of Alberta: A History of Political Action* (Vancouver: UBC Press, 2002), 163–4. Cairns, *Citizens Plus*, 67. Leslie, "Development," 414.

10 Armand Garnet Ruffo, "Where the Voice Was Coming From," in Paul De Pasquale, Renate Eigenbrod, and Emma LaRocque, eds., *Across Cultures / Across Borders: Canadian Aboriginal and Native American Literatures* (Peterborough, Ont.: Broadview Press, 2009), 174.

11 Alan R. Velie, "The Rise and Fall of the Red Power Movement," *Native American Studies*, 13/1 (1999): 1–8.

12 H.B. Hawthorn, A *Survey of the Contemporary Indians of Canada: A Report on Economic, Political, Educational Needs and Policies*, 2 vols. (Ottawa: Indian Affairs Branch, 1966), 1: 384.

13 Weaver, *Making*, 187.

14 Edgar J. Dosman, *Indians: The Urban Dilemma* (Toronto: McClelland and Stewart, 1972), 7. Awareness had begun to grow even before the White Paper and the presentation of the Red Paper in 1969/70. For instance, Daniel G. Hill, the director of the Ontario Human Rights Commission, in late November 1968 stated in a public address: "If I were to point to our most serious human rights problem in Canada, it would be in relation to our treatment of native Indians. They are numerically significant and have encountered all forms of discrimination." See Wilfred List, "Provincial rights chief cites U.S. strife," *Globe and Mail*, 22 November 1968. Charles Hendry included this important quote on an entire page in *Beyond Traplines. Does the Church Really Care? Towards an Assessment of the Work of the Anglican Church of Canada with Canada's Native Peoples* (Toronto: Ryerson, 1969), 9. The political scientist Alan Cairns sees the presentation of the Red Paper on 4 June 1970 as one of the great turning points and quotes *The Globe and Mail* journalist Rudy Platiel who was there: "In a scene that deserves to be preserved in oil paints on a giant canvas, Indian leaders stood majestically in feathered headdresses and white deerskin garb and presented the cabinet with an alternative (*Citizen Plus*). It was an affirmation of faith in their Indian identity. After a century of being engulfed by a white tidal wave, they were still here, they were still different, and they were not about to let themselves be pushed into oblivion." Rudy Platiel, "Citizens Plus," *Indian-Eskimo Association of Canada Bulletin*, 11, 5 (1970): 1–2; cited in Cairns, *Citizens Plus*, 67.

15 James S. Frideres, *Indigenous Peoples in the Twenty-First Century*, 3rd ed. (Don Mills, Ont.: Oxford University Press, 2020), 122, 39, 235–7.

16 E. Palmer Patterson II, *The Canadian Indian: A History since 1500* (Don Mills, Ont.: Collier Macmillan, 1972), 11.

17 R. Scott Sheffield, *The Red Man's on the Warpath: The Image of the "Indian" and the Second World War* (Vancouver: UBC Press, 2004), 128, 132, 138.

18 Peter McFarlane, *Brotherhood to Nationhood: George Manuel and the Making of the Modern Indian Movement* (Toronto: Between the Lines, 1993), 69.

19 The historian Olive Dickason notes, "Where Amerindians had represented 1.1 per cent of the population in 1961, 20 years later the proportion had increased to 1.5 per cent. In 1996 the figure was 3.0 per cent; today, it is 4.1 per cent and still growing." Olive Patricia Dickason, *Canada's First Nations: A History of Founding Peoples from Earliest Times*, 3rd ed. (Don Mills, Ont.: Oxford University Press, 2002), 427.

20 Right Rev. Robert Smith, "The United Church of Canada Apology to First Nations Peoples," in *The Missionary Oblates of Mary Immaculate: An Apology to the First Nations of Canada by The Oblate Conference of Canada*, in *"Speaking My Truth," Reflections on Reconciliation & Residential School*,

Selected by Shelagh Rogers, Mike DeGagné, Jonathan Dewar, Glen Lowry (Ottawa: Aboriginal Healing Foundation, 2012), 238.

21 Rev. Doug Crosby, O.M.I., President of the Oblate Conference of Canada, on behalf of the 1,200 Missionary Oblates of Mary Immaculate living and Ministering in Canada, in *The Missionary Oblates of Mary Immaculate*, in *"Speaking My Truth,"* 239.

22 Jane Stewart, Minister of Indian Affairs and Northern Development, "Government of Canada, 'Statement of Reconciliation,'" 7 Jan. 1998, reprinted in Arthur Bear Chief, *My Decade at Old Sun, My Lifetime of Hell* (Edmonton: AU Press, 2016), 162.

23 Frideres, *Indigenous Peoples*, 183.

24 Ibid., 243–5.

25 Greg Poelzer and Ken S. Coates, *From Treaty Peoples to Treaty Nation: A Road Map for All Canadians* (Vancouver: UBC Press, 2015), 138.

26 Tomson Highway, foreword in his *The Dispossessed: Life and Death in Native Canada* (Toronto: Lester & Orpen Dennys, 1989), vii–viii.

27 Blair Stonechild, *The New Buffalo: The Struggle for Aboriginal Post-Secondary Education in Canada* (Winnipeg: University of Manitoba Press, 2006), 49.

28 Ibid., 8, 24–9, 31, 41–3, 45, 63–4. Poelzer and Coates, *From Treaty Peoples*, 139–44.

29 Michael Valpy, "Aboriginal academe, studying for the good of their communities: 'Education is our buffalo,'" *Globe and Mail*, 2 June 2007.

30 An entire issue of *Native Studies Review* 21/2 (2012) is devoted to Olive Dickason and her contribution to our knowledge of Indigenous Canada.

31 Olive Patricia Dickason, *The Myth of the Savage and the Beginnings of French Colonialism in the Americas* (Edmonton: University of Alberta Press. 1984).

32 Ibid., 274.

33 Published by Oxford University Press.

34 *Recovering Canada; The Resurgence of Indigenous Law* (Toronto: University of Toronto Press, 2002).

35 Published by the University of Toronto Press.

36 Rudy Platiel, "Resistance to First Nations as the original owners," *Globe and Mail*, 17 June 1995.

37 Poelzer and Coates, *From Treaty Peoples*, 144.

38 Arthur J. Ray, Jim Miller, and Frank Tough, *Bounty and Benevelence: A History of the Saskatchewan Treaties* (Montreal and Kingston: McGill-Queen's University Press, 2000), 208. John Leslie and Ron Macguire, eds., *The Historical Development of the Indian Act*, 2nd ed. (Ottawa: Treaties and Historical Research Centre, Research Branch, Corporate Policy, Department of Indian and Northern Affairs Canada, 1979). The first edition appeared in 1975, the second in 1979, and the third, edited by John Leslie alone, in 2007.

39 Andrew Nurse, "Narrating Cultural Contact in Northern British Columbia: The Contributions of Gitksan and Tsimshian Oral Traditions to Canadian Historiography," in Cora J. Voyageur, David R. Newhouse, and Dan Beavon, eds., *Hidden in Plain Sight*, vol. 2 (Toronto: University of Toronto Press, 2011), 180.

40 Armand Garnet Ruffo, introduction in Daniel David Moses, Terry Goldie, and Armand Garnet Ruffo, eds., *An Anthology of Canadian Native Literature in English*, 4th ed. (Don Mills, Ont.: Oxford University Press, 2013), xxiii.

41 Harold Cardinal, *The Unjust Society: The Tragedy of Canada's Indians* (Edmonton: Hurtig, 1969).

42 Maria Campbell, *Halfbreed* (Toronto: McClelland and Stewart, 1973). A new edition of this important work has recently been published in 2019 by McClelland and Stewart, updated with a new afterword by the author.

43 Harold Cardinal, *The Unjust Society*, with a new introduction by the author (Vancouver: Douglas & McIntyre, 1999), vii. Cardinal, *The Unjust Society* (1969), 13.

44 Cardinal, *The Unjust Society* (1969), 13.

45 Ruffo, Introduction, xxiii.

46 James Bartleman, *Seasons of Hope: Memoirs of Ontario's First Aboriginal Lieutenant Governor* (Toronto: Dundurn, 2016), 266.

47 Marsha Lederman, "Richard Wagamese writer 61: Ojibway author found salvation in stories," *Globe and Mail*, 25 Mar. 2017.

48 I saw the film *Indian Horse* on National Aboriginal Day, 21 June 2018, at the Oakville Centre for the Performing Arts, which stands on the site of Old Central, the school I attended sixty years earlier (from 1955–59), and mention it in the prologue of this book.

49 Thomas King, *Medicine River* (Toronto: Penguin, 1991).

50 Published by Houghton Miffin Harcourt, 1993.

51 Thomas King, *The Truth about Stories: A Native Narrative* (Toronto: House of Anansi, 2003).

52 Published by HarperCollins in 2014.

53 Published by Doubleday Canada.

54 Ruffo, Introduction, xxix.

55 Ibid., xxx.

56 Published in Winnipeg by the Muses' Company, 2012.

57 Liz Howard and Armand Garnet Ruffo, "Poetry, Place, and Indigenous Identity," *Walrus*, 2 Jan. 2019.

58 Armand Garnet Ruffo, *Norval Morrisseau: Man Changing into Thunderbird* (Madeira Park, BC: Douglas & McIntyre, 2014).

59 Daphne Odjig, through R.M. Vanderburgh and M.E. Southcott, *A Paintbrush in My Hand: Daphne Odjig* (Toronto: Dundurn, 1992).

60 Maria Tippett, *Bill Reid: The Making of an Indian* (Toronto: Random House, 2003).

61 Mary Cummings, "Douglas Joseph Henry Cardinal," in Newhouse et al., *Hidden*, 1:309–11.

62 Randolph Lewis, *Alanis Obomsawin: The Vision of a Native Filmmaker* (Lincoln: University of Nebraska Press, 2006).

63 Frideres, *Indigenous Peoples*, 24.

64 Environics Institute for Survey Research, *Canadian Public Opinion on Aboriginal Peoples* (Toronto: Author, 2016), 1.

65 Ibid.

66 Poltzer and Coates, *From Treaty Peoples*, xv.

67 Fee, *Literary*, 17.

68 Poltzer and Coates, *From Treaty Peoples*, xv.

69 Chief Walter Deiter, president of the Saskatchewan Federation of Indians, Oct. 1968, cited on the inside back cover of Charles E. Hendry, *Beyond Traplines* (Toronto: Ryerson Press, 1969).

70 Christopher Dummit, *Unbuttoned: A History of Mackenzie King's Secret Life* (Montreal and Kingston: McGill-Queen's University Press, 2017), 7.

71 Weaver, *Making*, 183–7.

72 Cairns, *Citizens Plus*, 174–5. Boyce Richardson, *People of Terra Nullius: Betrayal and Rebirth in Aboriginal Canada* (Vancouver: Douglas & McIntyre, 1993), 288–90.

73 Miller, *Skyscrapers*, 278.

74 Email to me from Kathleen Makela, coordinator, Programs and Community Outreach, Wiyasiwewin Mikiwahp Native Law Centre, 26 July 2019.

75 Miller, *Skyscrapers*, 278.

76 Toby Morantz, "Aboriginal Land Claims in Quebec," in Ken Coates, ed., *Aboriginal Land Claims in Canada: A Regional Perspective* (Toronto: Copp Clark Pitman, 1992), 111–16.

77 *Northern Frontier, Northern Homeland: The Report of the Mackenzie Valley Pipeline Inquiry* (Ottawa: Supply and Services Canada, 1977), 1:163.

78 Personal communication with Norman Zlotkin, Saskatoon, 11 July 2019.

79 Brian Titley, "Indian Act," in Gerald Hallowell, ed., *The Oxford Companion to Canadian History* (Don Mills, Ont.: Oxford University Press, 2004), 308. James S. Frideres and René R. Gadacz, *Aboriginal Peoples in Canada*, 9th ed. (Toronto: Pearson, 2012), 45. Frideres, *Indigenous Peoples*, 239.

80 Claude Gélinas, *Les Autochtones dans le Québec post-Confédéral, 1867–1960* (Sillery, Que.: Éditions du Septentrion, 2007), 103.

81 Ghislain Michaud, *Les gardiens des portages: L'histoire des Malécites du Québec* (Sainte-Foy, Que.: Éditions GID, 2003), 286–95. After almost vanishing, the community in 2020 numbers approximately 1,200

individuals. "Government of Canda and the Maliseet of Viger reach agreement of fisheries," seen 8 June 2020 at https://www.newswire.ca /news-releases/government-of-canada-and-the-maliseet-of-viger-first -nation-reach-agreement-on-fisheries-821862022.html.

82 Miller, *Skyscrapers*, 304–6. For a short terse review of the complicated story of the Accord, see Richard Simeon, "Meech Lake Accord," in Hallowell, *Oxford Companion*, 398.

83 Elijah Harper, introduction in Pauline Comeau, *Elijah: No Ordinary Hero* (Vancouver: Douglas & McIntyre, 1993), 3.

84 For an overview of the entire Oka question, see J.R. Miller, "The Oka Controversy and the Federal Land-Claims Process," in Coates, *Aboriginal Land Claims*, 215–42.

85 Miller, *Skyscrapers*, 306–8.

86 Christopher Alcantara, *Negotiating the Deal: Comprehensive Land Claims Agreements in Canada* (Toronto: University of Toronto Press, 2013), 81, 73.

87 Edward J. Hedican, *Ipperwash: The Tragic Failure of Canada's Aboriginal Policy* (Toronto: University of Toronto Press, 2013), 207.

88 "Appendix A: The Terms of Reference," in *Report of the Royal Commission on Aboriginal Peoples*, vol. 1, *Looking Forward, Looking Back* (Ottawa: Canada Communication Group, 1996), 699, cited in John S. Milloy, *A National Crime: The Canadian Government and the Residential School System, 1879 to 1986* (Winnipeg: University of Manitoba Press, 1999), 302–3.

89 *Report for the Royal Commission on Aboriginal Peoples*, vol. 1, *Looking Forward, Looking Back* (Ottawa: Canada Communication Group, 1996), 216, cited in Cairns, *Citizens Plus*, 3.

90 Gloria Galloway, "Moment in Time," *Globe and Mail*, 21 June 2019.

91 For the background and context of the Delgamuukw case, see Dara Culhane, *The Pleasure of the Crown: Anthropology, Law and First Nations* (Burnaby, BC: Talon Books, 1998).

92 Miller, *Skyscrapers*, 315–16.

93 For background, see Tom Molloy, *The World Is Our Witness: The Historic Journey of the Nisga'a into Canada* (Calgary: Fifth House, 2000).

94 Garrett Wilson, *Frontier Farewell: The 1870s and the End of the Old West* (Regina: University of Regina Press, 2007), 442.

95 Ken Coates, *The Marshall Decision and Native Rights* (Montreal and Kingston: McGill-Queen's University Press, 2000), and for a short overview, see his essay "Reclaiming History through the Courts: Aboriginal Rights, the Marshall Decision, and Maritime History," in Myra Rutherdale, Kerry Abel, and P. Whitney Lackenbauer, eds., *Roots of Entanglement: Essays in the History of Native-Newcomer Relations* (Toronto: University of Toronto Press, 2017), 313–34.

96 Shelagh D. Grant, *Polar Imperative: A History of Arctic Sovereignty in North America* (Vancouver: Douglas & McIntyre, 2010), 383–4.

97 Romeo Saganash, "Foreword. The Paix Des Braves: An Attmpt to Renew Relations with the Cree, " in Thibault Martin and Steven M. Hoffman, eds., *Power Struggles: Hydro Development and First Nations in Manitoba and Quebec* (Winnipeg: Unversity of Manitoba Press, 2008), 205–13.

98 Miller, *Skyscrapers*, 324.

99 J.R. Miller, *Residential Schools and Reconciliation: Canada Confronts Its History* (Toronto: University of Toronto Press, 2017), 148.

100 Stephen Harper, 11 June 2008, quoted in Hedican, *Ipperwash*, 60.

101 https://www.thecanadianencyclopedia.ca/en/article/haida-gwaii. Poelzer and Coates, *From Treaty Peoples*, xiv, 284.

102 Ibid,, xiv.

103 Ken Coates, *#IDLENOMORE and the Remaking of Canada* (Regina: University of Regina Press, 2015), 55, 60, 71.

104 Sean Fine, "Historic ruling upholds land rights," *Globe and Mail*, 27 June 2014.

105 Miller, *Skyscrapers*, 341.

106 Erin Anderssen, "Without precedent," *Globe and Mail*, 2 Apr. 2016, F1, 4–5. John Geddes, "Profile. The new nation builder: Jody Wilson-Raybould is pushing to rebuild Canada's relationship with Indigenous people," *Macleans*, Apr. 2018, 24–7.

107 Gloria Galloway, "Missing and Murdered Indigenous Women: Inquiry launches with promise 'to achieve justice and healing,'" *Globe and Mail*, 4 Aug. 2016.

108 *The Final Report of the Truth and Reconciliation Commission of Canada*, vol. l, *Canada's Residential Schools: The History, Part 2, 1939 to 2000* (Montreal and Kingston; McGill-Queen's University Press for the Truth and Reconciliation Commission of Canada, 2015), 277. *Honouring the Truth, Reconciling for the Future: Summary of the Final Report of the Truth and Reconciliation Commission of Canada* (Ottawa: Truth and Reconciliation Commission of Canada, 2015), 147–8. Suzanne Fournier and Ernie Crey, *Stolen from Our Embrace: The Abduction of First Nations Children and the Restoration of Aboriginal Communities* (Vancouver: Douglas & McIntyre, 1997).

109 Kristy Kirkup, "Sixties Scoop survivors say deal offers 'great hope,'" *Globe and Mail*, 7 Oct. 2017. Gloria Galloway, "Sixties Scoop survivor suing over Métis exclusion," *Globe and Mail*, 27 Jan. 2018.

110 Maura Forrest, "Key MMIW report proposal draws flak," *Calgary Herald*, 1 June 2019.

111 Emma Graney, "Oil sands outbreak linked to cases across Canada," *Globe and Mail*, 11 May 2020. James Keller, "Siksika Nation battles virus outbreak," *Globe and Mail*, 3 July 2020, A8.

Selected Bibliography

Primary Sources

American Philosophical Society Library, Philadelphia, Pennsylvania (APSL)
  Paul A.W. Wallace Papers.
Archives de l'université Laval, Quebec, Quebec
  Fonds Jacques Rousseau.
Archives of Ontario (AO), Toronto, Ontario
  MU4642, Indian Miscellaneous.
Bibliothèque et Archives nationales de Québec (BANQ), Quebec, Quebec
  Fonds Famille Picard (P882–P883).
Canadian Museum of History Archives, Gatineau, Quebec
  Marius Barbeau Fonds.
Glenbow Archives, Calgary
  Hugh Dempsey Fonds.
  H.G. Glyde Fonds.
  John Lee Laurie Fonds.
Glenbow Archives, Archives and Special Collections, University of Calgary
  Edgar Dewdney Fonds.
  Gilbert and Luella Goddard Fonds.
  Paul Wallace Fonds.
  Jack F. Dunn Collection.
  Grant MacEwan Fonds.
  McDougall Family Fonds.
  Donald B. Smith, Research Notes for *Seen but Not Seen*, Accession no
    2016.42.
Law Society of Upper Canada Archives, Toronto, Ontario
Library and Archives Canada (LAC), Ottawa, Ontario
  Sir Sandford Fleming Fonds.
  George M. Grant Papers.
  Sir Wilfrid Laurier Fonds.

Sir John A. Macdonald Fonds.
Elliott Moses Papers.
RG10, Indian Affairs.
McGill University Archives, Montreal, Quebec
  Aileen Ross Papers.
Provincial Archives of Alberta, Edmonton, Alberta
  "Memoirs of Rev. Marchmont Ing (1870–1947)."
Provincial Archives of Saskatchewan, Regina, Saskatchewan
  Oral History Collection.
  Interview by Murray Dobbin with Walter Dieter, 22 September, Tape num-
    ber: IH-366, transcript disc 76.
Queen's University Archives, Kingston, Ontario
  George M. Grant Papers.
  Lorne Pierce Papers.
Royal Ontario Museum, Toronto, Ontario
  Ontario newspaper clippings re: "Indians,"compiled by Canadian Press
    Clipping Service, June 1964 to Feb. 1974, sponsored by Dr E.S. Rogers,
    Department of Art and Culture: Indigenous Americas, Royal Ontario
    Museum, Toronto, Ontario (currently in the process of being digitized by
    the ROM Library and Archives).
Smithsonian Institution, Washington, DC
  National Anthropological Archives, Bureau of American Ethnology.
Trent University Archives, Peterborough, Ontario
  Indian-Eskimo Association Papers.
United Church Archives, Toronto, Ontario
  Rev. John McDougall Collection.
  Rev. John McLean Collection.
  Methodist Church of Canada, Board of Missions, Alexander Sutherland
    Letterbooks.
l'Université Laval, Sainte-Foy, Quebec, Division des archives
  Fonds Jacques Rousseau.
University of Calgary Archives, Glenbow Western Heritage Centre Archives,
Calgary, Alberta
  Hugh Dempsey Papers.
  Jack F. Dunn Research Notes on the NWMP
  Edgar Dewdney Papers.
  H.G. Glyde Fonds.
  Gilbert and Luella Goddard Fonds Inventory.
  John Laurie Fonds.
  Grant MacEwan Fonds.
  McDougall Family Papers.
  Donald B. Smith, Research notes, for *Seen but Not Seen*, Accession no. 2016.42.
  Paul A.W. Wallace Papers.

University of Manitoba, Archives and Special Collections, Winnipeg, Manitoba
   Walter Rudnicki Fonds.
University of Toronto Archives, Toronto, Ontario
   Upper Canada College Cumulative List of Pupils.
University of Toronto, Trinity College Archives
   Encounter Club Papers.
University of Toronto, Victoria University, E.J. Pratt Library, Special Collections
   (VUL)
   Wallace Family Fonds, Records of Paul Anthony Wilson Wallace (VUA,
      Wallace Records).
   Kathleen Coburn Collection.
Whyte Museum of the Canadian Rockies, Banff, Alberta
   Alpine Club of Canada Fonds.
Woodland Cultural Centre, Brantford, Ontario
   Milton Martin file

Published Sources and Theses

Abel, Kerry. *Drum Songs: Glimpses of Dene History*. Montreal and Kingston:
   McGill-Queen's University Press, 1993.
Abley, Mark. *Conversations with a Dead Man: The Legacy of Duncan Campbell
   Scott*. Madeira Park, BC: Douglas & McIntyre, 2013.
Aboriginal Healing Foundation. *"Speaking My Truth": Reflections on
   Reconciliation & Residential School*. Selected by Shelagh Rogers, Mike
   DeGagné, Jonathan Dewar, Glen Lowry. Ottawa: Author, 2012.
Ahenakew, Edward. *Voices of the Plains Cree*. Edited by Ruth Buck. Regina:
   Canadian Plains Research Center, University of Regina, 1995.
Ainslie, Patricia. *A Lifelong Journey: The Art and Teaching of H.G. Glyde*.
   Introduction by Helen Collinson. Calgary: Glenbow Museum, 1987.
Alcantara, Christopher. *Negotiating the Deal: Comprehensive Land Claims
   Agreements in Canada*. Toronto: University of Toronto Press, 2013.
Anderson, Mark Cronlund, and Carmen L. Robertson. *Seeing Red: A History
   of Natives in Canadian Newspapers*. Winnipeg: University of Manitoba Press,
   2011.
Antane Kapesh, An. *Je suis une maudite Sauvagesse / Eukuan nin matsshimanitu
   innu-iskueu*. Montreal: Leméac, 1976. Translated by José Mailhot in
   collaboration with Anne-Marie André and André Mailhot.
Antone, Eileen M. "The Educational History of the Onyota'a:ka Nation of the
   Thames." *Ontario History*, 85/4 (Dec. 1993): 307–20.
Ash, Marinell, et al. *Thinking with Both Hands: Sir Daniel Wilson in the Old
   World and the New*. Edited by Elizabeth Hulse. Toronto: University of
   Toronto Press, 1999.
Assiniwi, Bernard. *A l'indienne*. Montreal: Lémeac, 1972.

Assu, Harry, with Joy Inglis. *Assu of Cape Mudge: Recollections of a Coastal Indian Chief.* Vancouver: UBC Press, 1989.

Baker, Chief Simon. *Khot-La-Cha: The Autobiography of Chief Simon Baker.* Compiled and edited by Verna J. Kirkness. Vancouver: Douglas & McIntyre, 1994.

Barman, Jean. *The West beyond the West: A History of British Columbia.* 3rd ed. Vancouver: University of Toronto Press, 2007.

Bartleman, James. *Seasons of Hope: Memoirs of Ontario's First Aboriginal Lieutenant Governor.* Toronto: Dundurn, 2016.

Barton, Peter G. "Sir John Alexander Boyd." In *Dictionary of Canadian Biography,* vol.14, *1911–1920,* 126–8. Toronto: University of Toronto Press, 1998.

Bear Chief, Arthur. *My Decade at Old Sun, My Lifetime of Hell.* Edmonton: AU Press, 2016.

Beaver, Art. "Dancing the Rice: Aboriginal Self-Government Is the Community Reclaiming Traditional Cultural Values / Mnoomini-Gaawin: Nishinaabe Gimaawin na Dani-Daapinaawaa Nishinaabe oodenoo." M.A. thesis, Canadian Heritage and Development Studies, Trent University, 2000.

Bell, D.G. "Was Amerindian Dispossession Lawful? The Response of 19th-Century Maritime Intellectuals." *Dalhousie Law Journal,* 23 (2000): 168–82.

Bella, Leslie. *Parks for Profit.* Montreal: Harvest House, 1987.

Berger, Carl. *Honour and the Search for Influence: A History of the Royal Society of Canada.* Toronto: University of Toronto Press, 1996.

Berger, Thomas R. "John Marshall and the Indians." In *A Long and Terrible Shadow: White Values, Native Rights in the Americas 1492–1992,* 66–84. Vancouver: Douglas & McIntyre, 1991.

– *One Man's Justice: A Life in the Law.* Vancouver: Douglas & McIntyre, 2003.

Berkhofer, Robert F., Jr. *The White Man's Indian: Images of the American Indian from Columbus to the Present.* New York: Vintage Books, 1979.

Betcherman, Lita-Rose. *Ernest Lapointe: Mackenzie King's Great Quebec Lieutenant.* Toronto: University of Toronto Press, 2002.

Blanchard, Paula. *The Life of Emily Carr.* Vancouver: Douglas & McIntyre, 1987.

Bodaker, Heidi. "Anishinaabe Toodaims: Contexts for Politics, Kinship, and Identity in the Eastern Great Lakes." In Carolyn Podruchny and Laura Peers, eds., *Gathering Places: Aboriginal and Fur Trade Histories,* 93–118. Vancouver: UBC Press, 2010.

Boldt, Menno. *Surviving as Indians: The Challenge of Self-Government.* Toronto: University of Toronto Press, 1993.

Bothwell, Robert. *Laying the Foundation: A Century of History at University of Toronto.* Toronto: Department of History, University of Toronto, 1991.

Bouchard, Serge, and Marie-Christine Lévesque. *Le Peuple Rieur: Hommage à mes amis Innus.* Montreal: Lux Éditeur, 2017.

Boudreau, Diane, *Histoire de la literature amérindienne au Québec: Oralité et écriture*. Montreal: Éditions de l'Hexagone, 1993.

Boyd, Walter C. *The Last Chancellor*. Hamilton: McMaster Media Production Services, 1995.

Bracken, Christopher. *The Potlatch Papers: A Colonial Case History*. Chicago: University of Chicago Press, 1997.

Brass, Eleanor. *I Walk in Two Worlds*. Calgary: Glenbow Museum, 1987.

Breslin, Catharine. "The Other Trudeaus. In 1659 a young Frenchman, Etienne Truteau, landed in Quebec to father a long line of hardy farmers that continued right down to Joseph, grandfather of Canada's Prime Minister." *Chatelaine*, (Sept. 1969): 32–3, 108–11, 113; (Oct. 1969): 42–3, 78–87.

Breton, P.E., o.m.i. *Hobbema: Une florissante mission indienne de l'Ouest*. Edmonton: Éditions de l'Ermitage, 1962.

Brown, E.K. "Memoir of Duncan Campbell Scott." In E.K. Brown, ed., *Selected Poems of Duncan Campbell Scott*, xi–xliii. Toronto: Ryerson, 1951. Reprinted as E.K. Brown, ed., "Duncan Campbell Scott: A Memoir," in *Responses and Evaluations: Essays on Canada*, 112–44 (Toronto: McClelland and Stewart, 1977).

Brown, S.H. *An Ethnohistorian in Rupert's Land: Unfinished Conversations*. Edmonton: AU Press, 2017.

Brydges, Charles John. *The Letters of Charles John Brydges, 1879–1882, Hudson's Bay Company Land Commissioner 1878–1882*. Edited by Hartwell Bowsfield. Winnipeg: Hudson's Bay Record Society, 1977.

Cairns, Alan C. *Citizens Plus: Aboriginal Peoples and the Canadian State*. Vancouver: UBC Press, 2000.

– "Aboriginal Research in Troubled Times." In Myra Rutherdale, Kerry Abel, and P. Whitney Lackenbauer, eds., *Roots of Entanglement: Essays in the History of Native-Newcomer Relations*, 403–35. Toronto: University of Toronto Press, 2017.

Calverley, David. *Who Controls the Hunt? First Nations, Treaty Rights, and Wildlife Conservation in Ontario, 1783–1939*. Vancouver: UBC Press, 2018.

Campbell, Maria. *Halfbreed*. 1973. Reprinted with updates and new afterword by the author, Toronto: McClelland and Stewart, 2019.

Cardinal, Harold. *The Unjust Society: The Tragedy of Canada's Indians*. Edmonton: Hurtig, 1969.

– *The Rebirth of Canada's Indians*. Edmonton: Hurtig, 1977.

– *The Unjust Society: The Tragedy of Canada's Indians*. With a new introduction by the author. Vancouver: Douglas &McIntyre, 1999.

Cardinal, H., and W. Hildebrandt. *Treaty Elders of Saskatchewan: Our Dream Is That Our Peoples Will One Day Be Clearly Recognized as Nations*. Calgary: University of Calgary Press, 2000.

Carlson, Keith Thor. "Rethinking Dialogue and History: The King's Promise and the 1906 Aboriginal Delegation to London." *Native Studies Review*, 16/2 (2005): 1–38.

Carroll, Jock. *The Life & Times of Greg Clark: Canada's Favorite Storyteller.* Toronto: Doubleday, 1981.

Carter, Sarah. *Lost Harvest: Prairie Indian Reserve Famers and Government Policy.* Montreal and Kingston: McGill-Queen's University Press, 1990.

– *Capturing Women: The Manipulation of Cultural Imagery in Canada's Prairie West.* Montreal and Kingston: McGill-Queen's University Press, 1997.

– *Aboriginal People and Colonizers of Western Canada to 1900.* Toronto: University of Toronto Press, 1999.

Cassidy, Michael. "Treaties and Aboriginal-Government Relations, 1945–2000." In David R. Newhouse, Cora J. Voyageur, and Dan Beavon, eds., *Hidden in Plain Sight. Contributions of Aboriginal Peoples to Canadian Identity and Culture,* vol. 1, 38–60. Toronto: University of Toronto Press, 2005.

Charland, Thomas-M. *Histoire des Abénakis d'Odanak (1675–1937).* Montreal: Éditions du Lévrier, 1964.

Chiniki Research Team. *Mnotha Wapta Mâkochî: Stoney Place Names.* Morley Alberta: Chiniki Band Council, 1987.

Christensen, Deanna. *Ahtahkakoop: The Epic Account of a Plains Cree Head Chief, His People, and Their Struggle for Survival, 1816–1896.* Shell Lake, Sask.: Ahtahkakoop Publishing, 2000.

Clark, Captain E.D. "In the North-West with 'Sitting Bull.'" *Rose-Belford's Canadian Monthly and National Review,* 5 (1880): 66–73.

Coates, Ken. *The Marshall Decision and Native Rights.* Montreal and Kingston: McGill-Queen's University Press, 2000.

– *#IDLENOMORE and the Remaking of Canada.* Regina: University of Regina Press, 2015.

Coates, Ken, ed. *Aboriginal Land Claims in Canada: A Regional Perspective.* Toronto: Copp Clark Pitman, 1992.

Coburn, Kathleen. *In Pursuit of Coleridge.* Toronto: Clarke, Irwin, 1977.

– Foreword to the 1954 edition of Carol Pearson, *Emily as I Knew Her.* Victoria, BC: TouchWood Editions, 2016.

Cole, Douglas. *Franz Boas: The Early Years, 1858–1906.* Vancouver: Douglas & McIntyre, 1999.

– "The Invented Indian/The Imagined Family." *BC Studies,* no. 125/126 (Spring/summer 2000): 147–62.

Cole, Douglas, and Ira Chaikin. *An Iron Hand upon the People: The Law against the Potlatch on the Northwest Coast.* Vancouver: Douglas &McIntyre, 1990.

Comeau, Pauline. *Elijah: No Ordinary Hero.* Vancouver: Douglas & McIntyre, 1993.

Cottam, S. Barry. "Indian Title as a 'Celestial Institution': David Mills and the St Catherine's Milling Case." In Kerry Abel and Jean Friesen, eds., *Aboriginal Resource Use in Canada: Historical and Legal Aspects,* 247–66. Winnipeg: University of Manitoba Press, 1991.

Coze, Paul. *Wakanda*. Paris: Alexis Redier, Éditeur 1929.

Couture, Pierre, and Camille Laverdière. *Jacques Rousseau*. Montreal: XYZ Éditeur, 2000.

Creighton, Donald G. *Dominion of the North: A History of Canada*. Cambridge, Mass.: Houghton Mifflin, 1944.

Culhane, Dara. *The Pleasure of the Crown: Anthropology, Law and First Nations*. Burnaby, BC: Talon Books, 1998.

Daschuk, James. *Clearing the Plains: Disease, Politics of Starvation, and the Loss of Aboriginal Life*. Regina: University of Regina Press, 2013.

– "Acknowledging Partriarch's Failures Will Help Canada Mature as a Nation," *Canadian Issues*, (Summer 2015): 6–10.

– *Clearing the Plains: Disease, Politics of Starvation, and the Loss of Aboriginal Life*. New edition, introduced by Niigaanwewidam James Sinclair. Regina: University of Regina Press, 2019.

Dawn, Leslie. *National Visions, National Blindness: Canadian Art and Identities in the 1920s*. Vancouver: UBC Press, 2006.

Delâge, Denys. "La contribution de l'indienne à notre histoire." *Lettres et ecritures, Revue des étudiants de la Faculté des lettres de l'Université Laval*, 2/2 (Dec. 1964): 15–18.

– *Le pays renversé: Amérindiens et Européens en Amérique du nord-est, 1600–1664*. Montreal: Boréal, 1985.

Deiter, Patricia Anne. "A Biography of Chief Walter P. Deiter." M.A. thesis, Indian Studies, University of Regina, 1997.

Dempsey, Hugh A. *Crowfoot: Chief of the Blackfeet*. Edmonton: Hurtig, 1972.

– *Red Crow: Warrior Chief*. Saskatoon: Western Producer Prairie Books, 1980.

– *Big Bear: The End of Freedom*. Vancouver: Douglas & McIntyre, 1984.

– "David Crowchild." In Susie Sparks, ed., *Calgary: A Living Heritage*, 49–50. Calgary: Junior League of Calgary, 1984.

– *The Gentle Persuader: A Biography of James Gladstone Indian Senator*. Saskatoon: Western Producer Prairie Books, 1986.

– "The Role of Native Cultures in Western History: An Alberta Focus." In John W. Friesen, ed., *The Cultural Maze: Complex Questions on Native Destiny in Western Canada*, 39–51. Calgary: Detselig, 1991.

– *The Amazing Death of Calf Shirt and Other Blackfoot Stories: Three Hundred Years of Blackfoot History*. Saskatoon: Fifth House, 1994.

– *Maskepetoon: Leader, Warrior, Peacemaker*. Victoria: Heritage House, 2010.

– *Always an Adventure: An Autobiography*. Calgary: University of Calgary Press, 2011.

– *The Great Blackfoot Treaties*. Victoria: Heritage House, 2015.

Denny, Cecil E. *The Law Marches West*. [1939]. Edited and abridged by W.B.Cameron. With foreword by Hon. A.C. Rutherford, first premier of Alberta, 2nd ed. Toronto: J.M. Dent and Sons, 1972.

Dickason, Olive Patricia. *The Myth of the Savage and the Beginnings of French Colonialism in the Americas*. Edmonton: University of Alberta Press, 1984.

– *Canada's First Nations: A History of Founding Peoples from Earliest Times*, 3rd ed. Don Mills, Ont.: Oxford University Press, 2002.

Dion, Joseph F. *My Tribe, the Crees*. Edited and introduction by Hugh A. Dempsey. Calgary: Glenbow Museum, 1979.

Dippie, Brain W. *The Vanishing Indian: White Attitudes and U.S. Indian Policy*. Lawrence: University Press of Kansas, 1982.

Dobbin, Murray. *The One-And-A-Half Men: The Story of Jim Brady and Malcolm Norris*. Metis Patriots of the 20th Century. Introduction by Maria Campbell. Vancouver: New Star Books, 1981.

Dosman, Edgar J. *Indians: The Urban Dilemma*. Toronto: McClelland and Stewart, 1972.

Doucet, Father Léon. *Mon Journal: The Journal and Memoir of Father Leon Doucet o.m.i., 1868 to 1890*. Transcribed and translated by Bronwyn Evans. Edited by Mario Giguère and Bronwyn Evans. Calgary: Historical Society of Alberta, 2018.

Dragland, Stan. *Floating Voice: Duncan Campbell Scott and the Literature of Treaty 9*. Toronto: Anansi, 1994.

Drake-Terry, Joanne. *The Same as Yesterday: The Lillooet Chronicle the Theft of Their Land and Resources*. Lillooet, BC: Lillooet Tribal Council, 1989.

Duff, Wilson. *The Indian History of British Columbia*, vol. 1, *The Impact of the White Man*. 2nd ed. Victoria: British Columbia Provincial Museum, 1969.

Dummit, Christopher. *Unbuttoned: A History of Mackenzie King's Secret Life*. Montreal and Kingston: McGill-Queen's University Press, 2017.

Dunlop, Herbert Francis, o.m.i. *Andy Paull: As I Knew Him and Understood His Times*. Vancouver: Order of the O.M.I. of St Paul's Province, 1989.

Dunn, Jack F. *The North-West Mounted Police, 1873–1885*. Calgary: Author, 2017.

Dutil, Patrice, and Roger Hall, eds. *Macdonald at 200: New Reflections and Legacies*. Toronto: Dundurn, 2014.

Environics Institute for Survey Research. *Canadian Public Opinion on Aboriginal Peoples*. Toronto: Author, 2016.

Erasmus, Peter. *Buffalo Days and Nights, as Told to Henry Thompson*. Calgary: Fifth House, 1999.

Farley, Paul-Emile, and Gustave Lamarche. *Histoire du Canada Cours supérieur*. 4th ed. Montreal: Librarie des Clercs de St-Viateur, 1945.

Fee, Margery. *Literary Land Claims: The "Indian Land Question" from Pontiac's War to Attawapiskat*. Waterloo, Ont.: Wilfrid Laurier University Press, 2015.

Fisher, Robin. *Contact and Conflict: Indian-European Relations in British Columbia, 1774–1890*. Vancouver: UBC, 1977.

Flanagan, Tom. *First Nations? Second Thoughts*. Montreal and Kingston: McGill-Queen's University Press, 2000.

Foran, Timothy P. *Defining Métis: Catholic Missionaries and the Idea of Civilization in Northwestern Saskatchewan, 1845–1898*. Winnipeg: University of Manitoba Press, 2017.

Foster, Hamar. "We Are Not O'Meara's Children: Law, Lawyers, and the First Campaign for Aboriginal Title in British Columbia, 1908–28." In Hamar Foster, Heather Raven, and Jeremy Weber, eds., *Let Right Be Done: Aboriginal Title, the Calder Case, and the Future of Indigenous Rights*, 61–84. Vancouver: UBC Press, 2007.

Fournier, Suzanne and Ernie Crey. *Stolen from Our Embrace: The Abduction of First Nations Children and the Restoration of Aboriginal Communities*. Vancouver: Douglas & McIntyre, 1997.

Francis, Daniel. *The Imaginary Indian: The Image of the Indian in Canadian Culture*. 2nd ed. Vancouver: Arsenal Pulp Press, 2011.

Frideres, James. *Arrows in a Quiver: Indigenous-Canadian Relations from Contact to the Courts*. Regina: University of Regina Press, 2019.

– *Indigenous Peoples in the Twenty-First Century*. 3rd ed. Don Mills, Ont.: Oxford University Press, 2020.

Frideres, James S., and René R. Gadacz. *Aboriginal Peoples in Canada*. 9th ed. Toronto: Pearson, 2012.

Friedland, Martin L. *The University of Toronto: A History*. 2nd ed. Toronto: University of Toronto Press, 2013.

Friesen, Gerald. *The Canadian Prairies: A History*. Toronto: University of Toronto Press, 1984.

Friesen, John W. *Aboriginal Spirituality and Biblical Theology: Closer than You Think*. Calgary: Detselig, 2000.

Fry, Allan. Introduction and an afterword by the author in *How a People Die*, 9–40, 193–207. Madeira Park, BC: Harbour Publishing, 1999. The original edition of the novel was published in 1970 in Toronto by Doubleday.

Gaffen, Fred. *Forgotten Soldiers*. Penticton, B.C.: Theytus Books, 1985

Gélinas, Claude. *Les Autochtones dans le Québec Post-Confédéral 1867–1960*. Sillery, Que.: Éditions du Septentrion, 2007.

Getty, Ian A.L., and Donald B. Smith, eds. *One Century Later: Western Canadian Reserve Indians since Treaty Seven*. Vancouver: UBC Press, 1978.

Gorman, Ruth, ed. *Behind the Man: John Laurie, Ruth Gorman, and the Indian Vote in Canada*. Introduction by Frits Pannekoek. Calgary: University of Calgary Press, 2007.

Graham, Elizabeth, compiler. *The Mush Hole: Life at Two Indian Residential Schools*. Waterloo, Ont.: Heffle, 1997.

Graham, William M. *Treaty Days. Reflections of an Indian Commissioner*. Introduction by James Dempsey. Calgary: Glenbow Museum, 1991.

Grant, George M. *Ocean to Ocean: Sandford Fleming's Expedition through Canada in 1872*. Enlarged and revised edition. Toronto: Belford Brothers, 1877. Facsimile edition was published in 1967 in Rutland, Vt. by Charles E. Tuttle.

Grant, John Webster. *Moon of Wintertime: Missionaries and the Indians of Canada in Encounter since 1534*. Toronto: University of Toronto Press, 1984.

Grant, Shelagh D. *Polar Imperative: A History of Arctic Sovereignty in North America*. Vancouver: Douglas & McIntyre, 2010.

Grant, William Lawson, and Frederick Hamilton. *Principal Grant*. Toronto: Morang & Co, 1904.

Green, Adam J. "Humanitarian, MD: Dr Peter H. Bryce's Contributions to Canadian Federal Native and Immigration Policy, 1904–1921." M.A. thesis, Queen's University, 1999.

Griffiths, Jane. *Words Have a Past: The English Language, Colonialism, and the Newspapers of Indian Boarding Schools*. Toronto: University of Toronto Press, 2019.

Groening, Laura. "Duncan Campbell Scott." In Robert Lecker and Jack David, eds., *The Annotated Bibliography of Canada's Major Authors*, vol. 8, 469–572. Toronto: ECW Press 1994.

Groulx, Lionel. *La naissance d'une race*. [1919]. Montreal: Bibliothèque de l'Action française, 1930.

– *Histoire du Canada français depuis la découverte*. 4 vols. Montreal: L'Action nationale, 1950–52.

– "Review of *The Founding of Canada Beginnings to 1815* by Stanley B. Ryerson." *Revue d'histoire de l'Amérique française*," 15 (1961–62): 297–300.

Grube, Jacob W. "Horatio Hale and the Development of American Anthropology." *Proceedings of the American Philosophical Society*, 3/1 (Feb. 1967): 5–37.

Gwyn, Richard. *John A., the Man Who Made Us: The Life and Times of John A. Macdonald*, vol. 1, *1815–1867*. Toronto: Random House, 2007.

– *Nation Maker, Sir John A Macdonald: His Life, Our Times*, vol. 2, *1867–1891*. Toronto: Random House, 2011.

Gwyn, Sandra. *The Private Capital: Ambition and Love in the Age of Macdonald and Laurier*. Toronto: McClelland and Stewart, 1984.

Hagan, William T. *American Indians*. 3rd ed. Chicago: University of Chicago Press, 1993.

Hale, Horatio. "An Iroquois Condoling Council." *Proceedings and Transactions of the Royal Society of Canada 1895*, 2nd series, vol. 1, section II (1895), 45–65. Reprinted in Horatio Hale, *The Iroquois Book of Rites and Hale on the Iroquois*, 339–61. Ohsweken, Ont.: Iroqrafts, 1989. This is the pagination in the reprinted version of the 1895 article.

Hall, Anthony J. "The St Catherine's Milling and Lumber Company versus the Queen: Indian Land Rights as a Factor in Federal-Provincial Relations in Nineteenth-Century Canada." In Kerry Abel and Jean Friesen, eds., *Aboriginal Resource Use in Canada: Historical and Legal Aspects*, 267–86. Winnipeg: University of Manitoba Press, 1991.

Hall, D.J. *From Treaties to Reserves: The Federal Government and Native Peoples in Territorial Alberta, 1870–1905.* Montreal and Kingston: McGill-Queen's University Press, 2015.

Hallowell, Gerald, ed. *The Oxford Companion to Canadian History.* Don Mills, Ont.: Oxford University Press, 2004.

Hamilton, Michelle A. *Collections and Objections: Aboriginal Material Culture in Southern Ontario, 1791–1914.* Montreal and Kingston: McGill-Queen's University Press, 2010.

Harper, Joan. *He Moved a Mountain: The Life of Frank Calder and the Nisga'a Land Claims Accord.* Vancouver: Ronsdale Press, 2013.

Harring, Sidney L. *White Man's Law: Native People in Nineteenth-Century Canadian Jurisprudence.* Toronto: University of Toronto Press, 1998.

Harris, Cole. *The Resettlement of British Columbia: Essays on Colonialism and Geographic Change.* Vancouver: UBC Press, 1997.

– *Making Native Space: Colonialism, Resistance, and Reserves in British Columbia.* Vancouver: UBC Press, 2002.

– *The Reluctant Land: Society, Space, and Environment in Canada before Confederation.* Vancouver: UBC Press, 2008.

Hawthorn, H.B. A *Survey of the Contemporary Indians of Canada: A Report on Economic, Political, Educational Needs and Policies.* 2 vols. (The Hawthorn Report.) Ottawa: Indian Affairs Branch, 1966.

Hawthorn, H.B., C.S. Belshaw, and S.M. Jamieson. *The Indians of British Columbia: A Study of Contemporary Social Adjustment.* Toronto: University of Toronto Press, 1960.

Hedican, Edward J. *Ipperwash: The Tragic Failure of Canada's Aboriginal Policy.* Toronto: University of Toronto Press, 2013.

Heidenreich, Rosmarin. *Literary Impostors: Canadian Autofiction of the Early Twentieth Century.* Montreal and Kingston: McGill-Queen's University Press, 2018.

Hembroff-Schleicher, Edythe. *Emily Carr: The Untold Story.* Saanichton, BC: Hancock House, 1978.

Hendry, Charles E. *Beyond Traplines: Does the Church Really Care? Towards an Assessment of the Work of the Anglican Church of Canada with Canada's Native Peoples.* Toronto: Ryerson Press, 1969.

Hertzberg, Hazel W. *The Search for an American Indian Identity: Modern Pan-Indian Movements.* Syracuse: Syracuse University Press, 1971.

Hildebrandt, Walter, and Brian Hubner. *The Cypress Hills: An Island by Itself.* Foreword by Sharon Butala. Saskatoon: Purich, 2007.

Hill, Susan M. *The Clay We Are Made Of: Haudenosaunee Land Tenure on the Grand River.* Winnipeg: University of Manitoba Press, 2017.

Horrall, S.W. *The Pictorial History of the Royal Canadian Mounted Police.* Toronto: McGraw-Hill, 1973.

Hoxie, Frederick E. *A Final Promise: The Campaign to Assimilate the Indians, 1880–1920*. Lincoln: University of Nebraska Press, 1984.

Hutchison, Bruce. *The Unknown Country: Canada and Her People*. [1942]. Revised ed. Toronto: McClelland and Stewart, 1965.

– *The Far Side of the Street*. Toronto: Macmillan, 1976.

Jackel, Susan. "Images of the Canadian West, 1872–1911." Ph.D. dissertation, University of Alberta, 1977.

Jamieson, Eric. *The Native Voice: The Story of How Maisie Hurley and Canada's First Aboriginal Newspaper Changed a Nation*. Halfmoon Bay, BC: Caitlin Press, 2016.

Jamieson, Keith, and Michelle A. Hamilton. *Dr Oronhyatekha: Security, Justice, and Equality*. Toronto: Dundurn, 2016.

Jenness, Diamond. *The Indians of Canada*. Ottawa; King's Printer, 1932.

– "Canada's Indians Yesterday. What of Today?" *Canadian Journal of Economics and Political Science*, 20 (1954): 95–100.

Johns, Walter H. *A History of the University of Alberta 1908–1969*. Edmonton: University of Alberta Press, 1981.

Johnston, Basil H. *Indian School Days*. Toronto: Key Porter Books, 1988.

Johnson, J.K., and P.B. Waite, "Sir John Alexander Macdonald." In *Dictionary of Canadian Biography*, vol. 12, *1891–1900*, 591–612. Toronto: University of Toronto Press, 1990.

Jones, Peter. *History of the Ojebway Indians: With Especial Reference to Their Conversion to Christianity*. London: A.W. Bennett, 1861.

Kain, Conrad. *Letters from a Wandering Mountain Guide, 1906–1933*. Edited with an introduction by Zac Robinson. Edmonton: University of Alberta Press, 2014.

Kelm, Mary-Ellen, and Keith D. Smith. *Talking Back to the Indian Act: Critical Readings in Settler Colonial Histories*. Toronto: University of Toronto Press, 2018.

King, Thomas. *The Inconvenient Indian: A Curious Account of Native People in North America*. N.p.p.: Doubleday, 2012.

Knight, Rolf. *Indians at Work: An Informal History of Native Labour in British Columbia 1858–1930*. Vancouver: New Star Books, 1996,

Krasowski, Sheldon. *No Surrender: The Land Remains Indigenous*. Regina: University of Regina Press, 2019.

Krotz, Larry. *Urban Indians: The Strangers in Canada's Cities*. Photographs by John Paskevich. Edmonton: Hurtig, 1980.

LaDow, Beth. *The Medicine Line: Life and Death on a North American Borderland*. New York: Routledge. 2001.

Laporte, Jean. *La Vieille Dame L'Archéologue et le Chanoine: La Saga de Dollard des Ormeaux*. Vanier, Ont.: Éditions l'Interligne, 1995.

LaRocque, Emma. *When the Other Is Me: Native Resistance Discourses, 1850–1990*. Winnipeg: University of Manitoba Press, 2010.

Laurier, L. LaPierre, ed. *Four O'clock Lectures: French-Canadian Thinkers of the Nineteenth and Twentieth Centuries*. Montreal: McGill University Press, 1966.

Laverdière, Camille, and Nicole Carette. *Jacques Rousseau 1905–1970: Bio-Bibliographie*. Preface by Louis-Edmond Hamelin. Sainte-Foy, Que.: Presses de l'Université Laval, 1999.

LaViolette, Forrest E. *The Struggle for Survival: Indian Cultures and the Protestant Ethic in British Columbia*. Toronto: University of Toronto Press, 1961.

Leacock, Stephen. *Canada: The Foundations of Its Future*. Montreal: Privately printed, 1941.

Leroux, Darryl. *Distorted Descent: White Claims to Indigenous Identity*. Winnipeg: University of Manitoba Press, 2019.

Leslie, John F. "Assimilation, Integration or Termination? The Development of Canadian Indian Policy, 1943–1963." Ph.D. dissertation, Department of History, Carleton University, 1999.

– "The Indian Act: An Historical Perspective." *Canadian Parliamentary Review*, (Summer 2002): 23–7.

Leslie, John F. Updated and edited by Ron Maguire. *Volume I. The Historical Development of the Indian Act from Colonial Days to 1951*. 3rd ed. Ottawa: Claims and Historical Research Centre, Special Claims, Specific Claims Branch, Department of Indian and Northern Affairs Canada, 2007. 1st edition, 1975, written by Kahn-Tineta Hiller and George Lerchs, ed. John F. Leslie and Ronald C. Maguire; 2nd ed. 1978, researched by Robert G. Moore, ed. John Leslie and Ron Maguire.

Lewis, Randolph. *Alanis Obomsawin: The Vision of a Native Filmmaker*. Lincoln: University of Nebraska Press, 2006.

Little, J.I., "Courting the First Nations Vote: Ontario's Grand River Reserve and the *Electoral Franchise Act* of 1885." *Journal of Canadian Studies*, 52/2 (Spring 2018): 538–69.

– *Fashioning the Canadian Landscape: Essays on Travel Writing, Tourism, and National Identity in the Pre-Automobile Era*. Toronto: University of Toronto Press, 2018.

Long, John S. *Treaty No. 9: Making the Agreement to Share the Land in Far Northern Ontario in 1905*. Montreal and Kingston: McGill-Queen's University Press, 2010.

Loram, C.T., and T.F. McIlwraith, eds. *The North American Indian Today*. Toronto: University of Toronto Press, 1943.

Lovesey, Dorothy May. *To Be a Pilgrim: A Biography of Silas Tertius Rand, 1810–1889, Nineteenth-Century Protestant Missionary to the Micmac*. Hantsport, NS: Lancelot Press, 1992.

Lower, Arthur R.M. *Colony to Nation*. 5th ed. Toronto: McClelland and Stewart, 1977.

Lutz, John Sutton. *Makuk: A New History of Aboriginal-White Relations*. Vancouver: UBC Press, 2008.

Lux, Maureen K. *Medicine That Walks: Disease, Medicine, and Canadian Plains Native People, 1880–1940.* Toronto: University of Toronto Press, 2001.

MacDonald, David B. *The Sleeping Giant Awakens: Genocide, Indian Residential Schools, and the Challenge of Conciliation.* Toronto: University of Toronto Press, 2019.

Macdonald, John A. *Affectionately Yours: The Letters of Sir John A. Macdonald and His Family.* Edited and with an introduction by J.K. Johnson. Toronto: Macmillan, 1969.

Macfarlane, Heather and Armand Garnet Ruffo, eds. *Introduction to Indigenous Literary Criticism in Canada.* Peterborough, Ont.: Broadview Press, 2016.

McCardle, Bennett H. "Walter Deiter," *The Canadian Encyclopedia,* 2nd ed., volume 1 (Edmonton: Hurtig Publications, 1988), 581.

McDougall, John. *In the Days of the Red River Rebellion.* Introduction by Susan Jackel. [1903]. Edmonton: University of Alberta Press, 1983.

– *Opening the Great West: Experiences of a Missionary in 1875–76.* Introduction by J. Ernest Nix. Calgary: Glenbow-Alberta Institute, 1970.

McFarlane, Peter. *Brotherhood to Nationhood: George Manuel and the Making of the Modern Indian Movement.* Toronto: Between the Lines, 1993.

MacGregor, Roy. Chief. *The Fearless Vision of Billy Diamond.* Markham, Ont.: Viking, 1989.

– *Canadians: A Portrait of a Country and Its People.* Toronto: Viking, 2007.

McInnis, Edgar. *Canada: A Political and Social History.* 4th ed. Toronto: Holt, Rinehart and Winston, 1982.

Mack, Donald Barry. "George Monro Grant: Evangelical Prophet." Ph.D. dissertation, Queen's University, 1992.

McLachlin, Beverley. *Truth Be Told: My Journey Through Life and the Law.* Toronto: Simon & Schuster, 2019.

McLean [Maclean], John. "The Blackfoot Indian Confederacy." Ph.D. dissertation, Illinois Wesleyan University, Bloomington, Illinois, 1888. Record Group 13-3/2: Non-Resident Theses. Tate Archives & Special Collections, The Ames Library, Illinois Wesleyan University Bloomington, Illinois.

Maclean, John. *McDougall of Alberta: A Life of Rev. John McDougall, D.D., Pathfinder of Empire and Prophet of the Plains.* Toronto: Ryerson Press, 1927.

Macleod, Rod. *Sam Steele: A Biography.* Edmonton: University of Alberta Press, 2018.

McNeil, Kent. *Flawed Precedent. The St Catherine's Case and Aboriginal Title.* Vancouver: UBC Press, 2019.

Manuel, George, and Michael Posluns. *The Fourth World: An Indian Reality.* Don Mills, Ont.: Collier Macmillan, 1974.

Marrus, Michael R. *Mr Sam: The Life and Times of Samuel Bronfman.* [1991]. Toronto: Penguin, 1992.

Martin, Ged. *Favourite Son? John A. Macdonald and the Voters of Kingston, 1841–1891*. Kingston: Kingston Historical Society, 2010.

Maurault, Joseph-Pierre-Anselme. *Histoire des Abénakis depuis 1605 jusqu'à nos jours*. Sorel, Que.: L'Atelier typographique de la "Gazette de Sorel," 1866.

Meijer Drees, Laurie. *The Indian Association of Alberta: A History of Political Action*. Vancouver: UBC Press, 2002.

– "White Paper/Red Paper: Aboriginal Contributions to Canadian Politics and Government." In Cora J. Voyageur, David R. Newhouse, and Dan Beavon, eds., *Hidden in Plain Sight*, 282–99. Toronto: University of Toronto Press, 2011.

Meili, Dianne. *Those Who Know: Profiles of Alberta's Native Elders*. Edmonton: NeWest Press, 1991.

Michaud, Ghislain. *Les gardiens des portages: L'histoire des Malécites du Québec*. Sainte-Foy, Que.: Éditions GID, 2003.

Miller, David. "Edward Ahenakew's Tutelage by Paul Wallace: Reluctant Scholarship, Inadvertent Preservation." In Carolyn Podruchny and Laura Peers, eds., *Gathering Places: Aboriginal and Fur Trade Histories*, 249–73. Vancouver: UBC Press, 2010.

Miller, J.R. *Shingwauk's Vision: A History of Native Residential Schools*. Toronto: University of Toronto Press, 1996.

– *Lethal Legacy: Current Native Controversies in Canada*. Toronto: McClelland and Stewart, 2004.

– *Compact, Contract, Convenant: Aboriginal Treaty-Making in Canada*. Toronto: University of Toronto Press, 2007.

– *Residential Schools and Reconciliation: Canada Confronts Its History*. Toronto: University of Toronto Press, 2017.

– *Skyscrapers Hide the Heavens: A History of Native-Newcomer Relations in Canada*. 4th ed. Toronto: University of Toronto Press, 2018.

– "Research and Outcomes at the Truth and Reconciliation Commission," *Canadian Historical Review*, 100/2 (June 2019): 163–81.

Milloy, John S. "The Early Indian Acts: Developmental Strategy and Constitutional Change." In Ian A.L. Getty and Antoine S. Lussier, eds., *As Long as the Sun Shines and Water Flows: A Reader in Canadian Native Studies*, 56–64. Vancouver: UBC Press, 1983.

– *A National Crime: The Canadian Government and the Residential School System, 1879 to 1986*. Winnipeg: University of Manitoba Press, 1999.

Molloy, Tom. *The World Is Our Witness: The Historic Journey of the Nisga'a into Canada*. Calgary: Fifth House, 2000.

Moore, Kermot A. *Kipawa: Portrait of a People*. Cobalt, Ont.: Highway Book Shop, 1982.

Morantz, Toby. *The White Man's Gonna Getcha: The Colonial Challenge to the Crees in Quebec*. Montreal and Kingston: McGill-Queen's University Press, 2002.

Moray, Greta. *Unsettling Encounters: First Nations Imagery in the Art of Emily Carr*. Vancouver: UBC Press, 2006.

Morley, Alan. *Roar of the Breakers: A Biography of Peter Kelly*. Toronto: Ryerson Press, 1967.

Moses, Daniel David, Terry Goldie, and Armand Garnet Ruffo, eds. *An Anthology of Canadian Native Literature in English*. 4th ed. Don Mills, Ont.: Oxford University Press, 2013.

Neylan, Susan. *The Heavens Are Changing: Nineteenth-Century Protestant Missions and Tsimshian Christianity*. Montreal and Kingston: McGill-Queen's University Press, 2003.

Niezen, Ronald. *Truth and Indignation: Canada's Truth and Reconciliation Commission on Residential Schools*. 2nd ed. Toronto: University of Toronto Press, 2017.

– Foreword in Brieg Capitaine and Karine Vanthuyne, eds., *Power through Testimony: Reframing Residential Schools in the Age of Reconciliation*, vii–xi. Vancouver, BC: UBC Press, 2017.

Nix, James Ernest. *Mission among the Buffalo: The Labours of the Reverends George M. and John C. McDougall in the Canadian Northwest, 1860–1876*. Toronto: Ryerson Press, 1960.

Nowry, Laurence. *Man of Mana: Marius Barbeau*. Toronto: NC Press, 1995.

Nurse, Andrew. "'But Now Things Have Changed': Marius Barbeau and he Politics of Amerindian Identity." *Ethnohistory*, 48/3 (2001): 433–72.

– "Narrating Cultural Contact in Northern British Columbia: Contributions of Gitksan and Tsimshian Oral Traditions to Canadian Historiography." In Cora J. Voyageur, David R. Newhouse, and Dan Beavon, eds., *Hidden in Plain Sight: Contributions of Aboriginal Peoples to Canadian Identity and Culture*, vol. 2, 181–93. Toronto: University of Toronto Press, 2011.

Manuel, George, and Michael Posluns. *The Fourth World: An Indian Reality*. Don Mills, Ont.: Collier Macmillian, 1974.

Oliver, Frank. "The Blackfeet Indian Treaty." *MacLean's*, 15 March, 8–9, 28, 32, 56.

Page, Robert. "The Railway Analogy." In Martin O'Malley, ed., *The Past and Future Land: An Account of the Berger Inquiry into the Mackenzie Valley pipeline*, 55–68. Toronto: Peter Martin, 1976.

Patterson, E. Palmer II. *The Canadian Indian: A History since 1500*. Don Mills, Ont.: Collier Macmillan, 1972.

Paul, Daniel N. *We Were Not the Savages: A Micmac Perspective on the Collision of European and Aboriginal Civilization*. Halifax, NS: Nimbus, 1993.

Peace, Thomas, and Kathryn Magee Labelle, eds. *From Huronia to Wendakes: Adversity, Migrations, and Resilience, 1650–1900*. Norman: University of Oklahoma Press, 2016.

Pettipas, Katherine. *Severing the Ties That Bind: Government Repression of Indigenous Religious Ceremonies on the Prairies*. Winnipeg: University of Manitoba Press, 1994.

Platiel, Rudy, "Report Card. Resistance to First Nations as the original owners," *Globe and Mail*, 17 June 1995.

Poelzer, Greg, and Ken S. Coates. *From Treaty Peoples to Treaty Nation: A Road Map for all Canadians*. Vancouver: UBC Press, 2015.

Ponting, J. Rick, and Roger Gibbins. *Out of Irrelevance*. Toronto: Butterworths, 1980.

Price, Richard T., ed. *The Spirit of the Alberta Indian Treaties*. 3rd ed. Edmonton: University of Alberta Press, 1999.

Prucha, Francis Paul. *The Indians in American Society: From the Revolutionary War to the Present*. Berkeley: University of California Press, 1985.

Putnam, William L., Glen W. Bowes, and Roger W. Laurilla. *Place Names in the Canadian Rockies*. Revelstoke, BC: Footprint Publishing, 1990.

Raibmon, Paige. *Authentic Indians: Episodes of Encounter from the Late-Nineteenth-Century Northwest Coast*. Durham: Duke University Press, 2005.

Ray, Arthur J. *Telling It to the Judge: Taking Native History to Court*. Introduction by Peter W. Hutchins. Montreal and Kingston: McGill-Queen's University Press, 2011.

Ray, Arthur J., Jim Miller, and Frank J. Tough. *Bounty and Benevolence: A History of Saskatchewan Treaties*. Montreal and Kingston: McGill-Queen's University Press, 2000.

Reid, Gerald F. "'To Renew Our Fire': Political Activism, Nationalism, and Identity in Three Rotinonhsionni Communities." In Brian Hosmer and Larry Nesper, eds., *Tribal Worlds: Critical Studies in American Indian Nations Building*, 37–64. Albany, NY: State University of New York Press, 2013.

Richardson, Boyce. *People of Terra Nullius: Betrayal and Rebirth in Aboriginal Canada*. Vancouver: Douglas & McIntyre, 1993.

Richling, Barnett. *In Twilight and in Dawn: A Biography of Diamond Jenness*. Montreal and Kingston: McGill-Queen's University Press, 2012.

Robinson, Zac. "Storming the Heights: Canadian Frontier Nationalism and the Making of Manhood in the Conquest of Mount Robson, 1906–1913." *International Journal of the History of Sport*, 22/3 (May 2005): 425–33.

Rogers, Edward S., and Donald B. Smith, eds. *Aboriginal Ontario: Historical Perspectives on the First Nations*. Toronto: Dundurn, 1994.

Rohner, Ronald P., comp. and ed. *The Ethnography of Franz Boas: Letters and Diaries of Franz Boas Written on the Northwest Coast from 1886 to 1931*. Chicago: University of Chicago Press, 1969.

Rousseau, Jacques. *L'Hérédité et l'homme*. Montreal: Éditions de l'Arbre, 1945.

– "Persistances païennes chez les Amérindiens de la forêt boréale." *Cahiers des Dix*, 17 (1952): 183–202.

– "Du bon sauvage de la littérature à celui de la réalité." *L'Action universitaire*, 20/4 (1954): 12–23.

- "Astam Mitchoun! Essai sur la gastronomie amérindienne." *Cahiers des Dix*, 22 (1957): 193–213.
- "Ces Gens qu'on dit sauvages." *Cahiers des Dix*, 23 (1958): 52–90.
- "Les Sachems délibèrent autour du feu de camp." *Cahiers des Dix*, 24 (1959): 9–49.
- "Les Premiers Canadiens." *Cahiers des Dix*, 25 (1960): 9–64.
- "Dualisme religieux ou syncretisme chez les Algiques de la forêt boreale." *Actes du VIème Congrés International des Sciences anthropologiques et ethnologiques* (Paris), 2 (1960): 471–3.
- "*L'Indien et notre milieu*." Université Laval, Cours télévisé, Jan.–Apr. 1966, mimeographed.
- "The Northern Québec Eskimo Problem and the Ottawa-Quebec Struggle." *Anthropological Journal of Canada*, 7/2 (1969): 2–15.
Rousseau, Jacques, and Madeline Rousseau. "La crainte des Iroquois chez les Mistassins." *Revue d'histoire de l'Amérique française*, 2 (1948–49): 13–26.
Rudin, Ronald. *Making History in Twentieth-Century Quebec*. Toronto: University of Toronto Press, 1997.
Ruffo, Armand Garnet. *Norval Morrisseau: Man Changing into Thunderbird*. Madeira Park, BC: Douglas & McIntyre, 2014.
Russell, Peter H. *Canada's Odyssey: A Country Based on Incomplete Conquests*. Toronto: University of Toronto Press, 2017.
Ryerson, Stanley B. *The Founding of Canada: Beginnings to 1815*. [1960]. Toronto: Progress Books, 1963.
Saganash, Romeo. "Foreword, "*The Paix Des Braves*: An attempt to Renew Relations with the Cree." In Thibault Martin and Steven M. Hoffman, eds., *Power Struggles: Hydro Development and First Nations in Manitoba and Quebec*, 205–13. Winnipeg: University of Manitoba Press, 2008.
Saul, John Ralston. *The Comeback*. Toronto: Viking Canada, 2014.
Sealey, D. Bruce, and Antoine S. Lussier. *The Métis: Canada's Forgotten People*. Winnipeg: Manitoba Metis Federation Press, 1975.
Sewid, James. *Guests Never Leave Hungry: The Autobiography of James Sewid, a Kwakiutl Indian*. Edited by James P. Spradley. Montreal and London: McGill-Queen's University Press, 1972.
Shadbolt, Doris. *Emily Carr*. Vancouver: Douglas & McIntyre, 1990.
Sheffield, R. Scott. *The Red Man's on the Warpath: The Image of the "Indian" and the Second World War*. Vancouver: UBC Press, 2004.
Sherwin, Allan. *Bridging Two Peoples: Chief Peter E. Jones, 1843–1909*. Waterloo, Ont.: Wilfrid Laurier University Press, 2012.
Shewell, Hugh. *"Enough to Keep Them Alive": Indian Welfare Canada, 1873–1965*. Toronto: University of Toronto Press, 2004.
Shields, Norman E. "Anishinabek Political Alliance in the Post-Confederation Period: The Grand General Indian Council of Ontario, 1870–1936." M.A. thesis, Queen's University, 2001.

Sluman, Norma, and Jean Goodwill. *John Tootoosis: A Biography of a Political Leader*. Ottawa: Golden Dog Press, 1982.

Smith, Donald B. "French Canadian Historians' Images of the Indian in the 'Heroic Period' of New France, 1534–1663." M.A. thesis, Laval University, 1969.

– *Le Sauvage: The Native People in Quebec Historical Writing on the Heroic Period (1534–1663) of New France*. Ottawa: National Museums of Canada, 1974.

– *Chief Buffalo Child Long Lance, the Glorious Impostor*. Red Deer, Alberta: Red Deer Press, 1999. 2nd ed. of *Long Lance: The True Story of an Impostor* (Toronto: Macmillan, 1982).

– *Sacred Feathers: The Reverend Peter Jones (Kahkewaquonaby) and the Mississauga Indians*. Toronto: University of Toronto Press, 1987.

– "The Great Wars in the Rockies: Towering Monuments." *Beaver*, 70/1 (Feb.–Mar. 1990): 46–9.

– *From the Land of Shadows: The Making of Grey Owl*. Saskatoon: Western Producer Prairie Books, 1990.

– "Elizabeth Barrett." *Alberta History* 46/4 (1998): 19–27.

– "Deskaheh (Levi General)." In *Dictionary of Canadian Biography*, vol. 15, *1921–1930*, 278–80. Toronto: University of Toronto Press, 2005, and at http://www.biographi.ca/en/bio/deskaheh_15E.html.

– *Honoré Jaxon: Prairie Visionary*. Regina: Coteau Books, 2007.

– *Mississauga Portraits: Ojibwe Voices from Nineteenth-Century Canada*. Toronto: University of Toronto Press, 2013.

– "Hugh Dempsey: Dean of Alberta Historians – and Bridge between Worlds." *Alberta Views*, (Jan.–Feb. 2016): 42–6.

– "Worlds Apart: A Flurry of Visits to Central Canada in 1886 Gave Plains First Nations Chiefs a Disturbing Glimpse into their Future." *Canada's History*, 97/5 (2017): 30–7. The full version of the annotated article is available at CanadasHistory/Worlds Apart. http://www.canadashistory.ca/Explore/First-Nations,-Inuit-Metis/Chiefs-Journey.

– "Rev. John McDougall and the Duke of Connaught." *Alberta History*, 65/1 (Winter 2017): 2–12.

– "Lord Bury and the First Nations: A Year in the Canadas." In Myra Rutherdale, Kerry Abel and P. Whitney Lackenbauer, eds., *Roots of Entanglement: Essays in the History of Native-Newcomer Relations*, 49–93. Toronto: University of Toronto Press, 2017.

Smith, Keith D. *Liberalism, Surveillance, and Resistance: Indigenous Communities in Western Canada, 1877–1927*. Edmonton: AU Press, 2009.

Smith, Nicolas N. *Three Hundred Years in Thirty: Memoir of Transition with the Cree Indians of Lake Mistassini*. Solon, Maine: Polar Bear & Co, Solon Center for Research and Publishing, 2011.

Snow, Chief John. *These Mountains Are Our Sacred Places: The Story of the Stoney People*. Toronto: Samuel-Stevens Publishers, 1977.

Sproule-Jones, Megan. "Crusading for the Forgotten: Dr Peter Bryce, Public Health, and Prairie Native Residential Schools." *Canadian Bulletin of Medical Health*, 13 (1966): 199–224.

Stanley, George F.G. "New Brunswick and Nova Scotia and the North-West Rebellion, 1885." In John E. Foster, ed., *The Developing West: Essays on Canadian History in Honor of Lewis H. Thomas*, 73–99. Edmonton: University of Alberta Press, 1983.

Steele, Col. S.B., *Forty Years in Canada: Reminiscences of the Great North-West with Some Account of his Service in South Africa*. New York: Dodd, Mead & Co, 1915.

Steinhauer, Melvin D. *Shawahnekizhek–Henry Bird Steinhauer: Child of Two Cultures*. Edmonton: Priority Printing, 2015.

Stevenson, Allyson D. *Intimate Integration: A History of the Sixties Scoop and the Colonization of Indigenous Kinship*. Toronto: University of Toronto Press, in press.

Stonechild, Blair. *The New Buffalo: The Struggle for Aboriginal Post-Secondary Education in Canada*. Winnipeg: University of Manitoba Press. 2006.

Stonechild, Blair, and Bill Waiser. *Loyal till Death: Indians and the North-West Rebellion*. Calgary: Fifth House, 1997.

Swayze, Carolyn. *Hard Choices: A Life of Tom Berger*. Vancouver: Douglas & McIntyre, 1987.

Swayze, Nanci. *The Man Hunters, Canadian Portraits: Diamond Jenness, Marius Barbeau, William J Wintenberg*. Toronto: Clarke, Irwin, 1960.

Swenson, Sally. *"Who Is Abigail? An Adopted Woman's Late Discovery of Her Rich Heritage Illuminated by the Life of Abigail Steinhauer McDougall, 1848–1871*. Ottawa: n.p., 1996.

Symons, Thomas H.B. "John A. Macdonald: A Founder and a Builder," *Canadian Issues*, (Summer 2015): 6–10.

Taekema, Sarah. "Sir John A. Macdonald's influence on the development of Canadian Indigenous Policy, 1844–1876." M.A. thesis, University of Victoria, 2020.

Talbot, Robert J. *Negotiating the Numbered Treaties: An Intellectual and Political Biography of Alexander Morris*. Saskatoon: Purich, 2009.

Taylor, John Leonard. *Canadian Indian Policy during the Inter-War Years, 1918–1939*. Ottawa: Indian and Northern Affairs Canada, 1984.

Teillet, Jean. *The North-West is Our Mother. The Story of Louis Riel's People. The Métis Nation*. Toronto: Harper Collins Publishers, 2019.

Thompson, Judy. *Treaty Six (1876)*. Treaty Research Report. Ottawa: Treaties and Historical Research Centre, Indian and Northern Affairs Canada, 1985.

– *Recording Their Story: James Teit and the Tahltan*. Vancouver: Douglas & McIntyre, 2007.

Teit, J.A. "Indian Tribes of the Interior." In A. Shortt and A.G. Doherty, eds., *Canada and Its Provinces*, vol. 21, *The Pacific Province*, 283–312. Glasgow: Brook & Co, 1914.

Tennant, Paul. *Aboriginal Peoples and Politics: The Indian Land Question in British Columbia, 1849–1989*. Vancouver: UBC Press, 1990.

Thomas, Clara, and John Lennox, *William Arthur Deacon. A Canadian Literary Life*. Toronto: University of Toronto Press, 1982.

Tippett, Maria. *Emily Carr: A Biography*. Hammondsworth, Middlesex: Penguin, 1982. First published in 1979 by Oxford University Press.

– *Bill Reid: The Making of an Indian*. Toronto: Random House, 2003.

Titley, E. Brian. *A Narrow Vision: Duncan Campbell Scott and the Administration of Indian Affairs in Canada*. Vancouver: UBC Press, 1986.

Tobias, John L. "Canada's Subjugation of the Plains Cree, 1879–1885." *Canadian Historical Review*, 64 (1983): 333–49.

Townshend, Nancy. *A History of Art in Alberta 1905–1970*. Calgary: Bayeux Arts, 2005.

Treaty 7 Elders and Tribal Council, with Walter Hildebrandt, Dorothy First Rider, and Sarah Carter. *The True Spirit and Original Intent of Treaty 7*. Montreal and Kingston: McGill-Queen's University Press, 1996.

Tremblay, Marc-Adélard, and Josée Thivierge. "La nature et la portée de l'oeuvre amérindienne de Jacques Rousseau." *Anthropologie et Sociétés*, 10/2 (1986): 163–82.

Trevithick, Scott. "Conflicting Outlooks: The Background to the 1924 Deposing of the Six Nations Hereditary Council." M.A. thesis, University of Calgary, 1998.

Trudel, Marcel. *The Beginning of New France, 1524–1663*. Translated by Patricia Claxton. Toronto: McClelland and Stewart, 1973.

Truth and Reconciliation Commission of Canada. *Honouring the Truth, Reconciling for the Future: Summary of the Final Report of the Truth and Reconciliation Commission of Canada*. Ottawa: Truth and Reconciliation Commission of Canada, 2015.

– *The Final Report of the Truth and Reconciliation Commission*, vol. 1, *Canada's Residential Schools: The History, Part 1, Origins to 1939*. . Montreal and Kingston: Published for the Truth and Reconciliation Commission by McGill-Queen's University Press, 2015.

– *The Final Report of the Truth and Reconciliation Commission*, vol. 1, *Canada's Residential Schools: The History, Part 2, 1939 to 2000*. Montreal and Kingston: Published for the Truth and Reconciliation Commission by McGill-Queen's University Press, 2015.

Vincent, Sylvie, and Bernard Arcand. *L'Image de l'Amérindien dans les manuels scolaires du Québec, ou Comment les Québécois ne sont pas des sauvages*. Ville La Salle, Que.: Éditions Hurtubise HMH, 1979.

Vowel, Chelsea. *Indigenous Writes: A Guide to First Nations, Métis & Inuit Issues in Canada*. Winnipeg: HighWater Press, 2016.

Waiser, Bill. *A World We Have Lost: Saskatchewan before 1905*. Markham, Ont.: Fifth House, 2016.

– *Almighty Voice. Resistance and Reconciliation*. Markham, Ont.: Fifth House, 2020.

Wallace, Paul A.W. *The White Roots of Peace*. [1946]. Ohsweken, Ont.: Iroqrafts, 1997.

– *Indian Paths of Pennsylvania*. Harrisburg, Pennsylvania: The Pennsylvania Historical and Museum Commission, 1965.

Weaver, Sally M. "The Iroquois: The Grand River Reserve in the Late Nineteenth and Early Twentieth Centuries, 1875–1945." In *Aboriginal Ontario: Historical Perspectives on the First Nations*, 213–57. Toronto: Dundurn, 1994.

– *Making Canadian Indian Policy: The Hidden Agenda 1968–1970*. Toronto: University of Toronto Press, 1981.

Weslager, C.A. *The Delaware Indian: A History*. New Brunswick, NJ: Rutgers University Press, 1972.

Wheeler, Winona. "Cree Intellectual Traditions in History." In Alvin Finkel, Sarah Carter, and Peter Fortna, eds., *The West and Beyond: New Perspectives on an Imagined Region*, 47–61. Edmonton: AU Press, 2010.

Whetung-Derrick, Mae. "Oshkigmong; The Curve in the Lake – A History of the Mississauga Community of Curve Lake: Origins of the Curve Lake Anishnabek (2015)." Occasional Paper published by the Peterborough Historical Society, Mar. 2015.

White, Pamela. "Restructuring the Domestic Sphere – Prairie Women on Reserves: Image, Ideology and State Policy 1880–1930." Ph.D. dissertation, McGill University, 1987.

Wickwire, Wendy. *At the Bridge: James Teit and an Anthropology of Belonging*. Vancouver: UBC Press, 2019.

Williams, Doug. *(Godigaa Migizi). Michi Saagig Nishnaabeg: This Is Our Territory*. Winnipeg: ARP Books, 2018.

Wilson, Garrett. *Frontier Farewell: The 1870s and the End of the Old West*. [2007]. Regina: University of Regina Press, 2014.

Winegard, Timothy C. *For King and Kanata: Canadian Indians and the First World War*. Winnipeg: University of Manitoba Press, 2012,

Williams, Glen. *Blood Must Tell: Debating Race and Identity in the Canadian House of Commons 1880–1925*. Ottawa: willowBXPress, 2014.

Winslow, Bernice Loft. *Iroquois Fires: The Six Nations Lyrics and Lore of Dawendine (Bernice Loft Winslow)*. With introductory and afterword material by George Beaver, Bryan Winslow Colwell, Donald Smith, and Robert Stacey. Ottawa: Penumbra Press, 1995.

Wood, Patricia K. "Pressured from All Sides: The February 1913 Surrender of the Northeast Corner of the Tsuu T'ina Nation." *Journal of Historical Geography*, 30 (2004): 112–29.

Wuttunee, William I. C. *Ruffled Feathers. Indians in Canadian Society*. Calgary: Bell Books Ltd., 1971.

Wybenga, Darin P. *A Celebration of Versatility: Mississaugas of the New Credit Historical Council House*. Brantford: Paramount Printers, 2015.

York, Geoffrey. *The Dispossessed: Life and Death in Native Canada*. Foreword by Tomson Highway. Toronto: McArthur, 2007.

Younging, Gregory. *Elements of Indigenous Style: A Guide for Writing By and About Indigenous Peoples*. Edmonton: Brush Education, 2018.

Zaslow, Morris. *The Opening of the Canadian North, 1870–1914*. Toronto: McClelland and Stewart, 1971.

– *The Northward Expansion of Canada, 1914–1967*. Toronto: McClelland and Stewart, 1988.

Index

Loyal Chiefs tours, 25–9, *26*, 27; Loyal
Methodist Chiefs tour, 59; North-West
Mounted Police (NWMP), 15, 17, 118,
293n97; Ontario-Manitoba border, 102,
104; Plains First Nations, 17–19, 21;
racism, 36–8, 302n220; Riel and 1885
troubles, 23–4, 31; D.C. Scott's first
government job, 118
– quotes: on assimilation, 15, 31, 34, 37;
on J. Brant, 25; on enfranchisement,
33, 36; on friendship, 88; on the Indian
Act, 17; on Indigenous religious
ceremonies, 85–6; as "original owners
of the soil," 18; on Treaties, 12, 13; on
troubles of 1885, 23, 55
MacDowell, Laurel Sefton (historian), 112
MacEwan, Grant (historian): *Tatanga
Mani: Walking Buffalo of the Stonies*, 260
MacGregor, James G. (Historical Society
of Alberta): *History of Alberta*, 255
MacGregor, Roy (biographer), 197–8
Mack, Barry (historian), 73
Mackenzie, Alexander (prime minister),
16–17
MacKenzie, John (Ian) (Anglican
minister), xviii–xix, *xix*
Mackenzie King, William Lyon (prime
minister): enfranchisement, 141; Indian
Affairs demotion, 114
Mackenzie Valley Pipeline Inquiry or
Berger Commission, 276
Maclean, John (Methodist missionary),
44, 49, 78; Long Lance and, 233;
Canadian Savage Folk, 236
Macleod, R.C. (historian), 49
Malecite or Maliseet (Wolasioqiyik or
Wustukwiuck), 276–7, 401–2n81
Manitoba: Indian Affairs spending, 19;
Indian land sales, 64; Indigenous
decline commentary, 81; lieutenant
governor, 17–18; Ontario-Manitoba
border dispute, 101–4, *103* (*see also*
St Catharines Milling and Lumber
Company case); Treaties, 14
Manitoba Indian Brotherhood, xxii
Manitoulin First Nations: Treaty, 13
Manitou Stone, place of worship, 79–80,
322nn86–7
Manouane, Attikamek community,
Quebec, 190

Maracle, Floretta (Florence) (first
Indigenous woman Indian Affairs
clerk), 20, 122–3, 295n123
Marie-Victorin, Brother (pioneer of
botany, Quebec), 188
Maritimes: map, *71*; Mi'kmaq history,
70–3; Treaties, 71
marriage: Bill C-31, 254; Indian status, 14,
210, 254, 276–7, 292n78; of Indigenous
to missionaries, 9, 46–7; intermarriage
and assimilation, 8–10, 46–7, 95, 124;
J.A. Macdonald on intermarriage,
9, 37; Quebec Amerindian ancestry
(*métissage*), 178, 190, 374n87
Marshall, John (US chief justice), 105
Marshall decision (fishing rights), 278
Martin, Milton (Mohawk; teacher), 136,
172, 367n180
Maskepetoon (Broken Arm), Chief
(Cree), 57, 78
Massey Commission, 386n195
Maurault, Joseph-Pierre-Anselme
(Catholic missionary): *Histoire des
Abénakis*, 176–7
McCaskill, J.C. (US Indian Affairs): *The
Indians of the Americas*, 167
McDougall, George (Methodist minister):
biography, 77–8; death, 82, 241; G.
Grant and expedition to the Pacific, 77,
79–80; Manitou Stone, place of worship,
79–80, 322nn86–7; smallpox, 78–9
McDougall, John Chantler (Methodist
missionary): early life and family, 44–5,
46–8, *49*, 260, 308n92; as boastful, 51–3,
310n131; education, 52; Indigenous
religion, 65; languages, 39, 44–5, 304n5,
304n9, 306n47; opinion of First Nations,
45–6, 66; racism experienced, 49–50;
role in settler's world, 42–3; smallpox,
79; "wilderness" experience, 53
– government and church work: advice
to government about reservations,
40–1, 42; assimilation beliefs, 62–7;
disagreements with colleagues, 53,
311n136; district responsibilities,
60; Duke of Connaught and, 66, *67*;
Glyde mural, 255, *256*; government
commissions, 43; Indian Act and, 54–5,
82–3; Indian Affairs and, 54, 62–5,
311n143; Indian commissioner, 62–5,